The Metaphysical Quest

Historical Sources
and
Contemporary Challenges

Edited by

Paul Gaffney
Arthur F. Gianelli
Kevin Kennedy

St. John's University

KENDALL/HUNT PUBLISHING COMPANY
4050 Westmark Drive   Dubuque, Iowa 52002

This book is dedicated

to

the students of

St. John's University

Contents

Part II: Contemporary Challenges

Section A: The Challenge of Modern Science to the God Question

Introduction

This book intends to introduce the undergraduate to the study of metaphysics. Our discipline is at once the most characteristically philosophical of all the divisions of philosophy, and yet, paradoxically, the one most often threatened with extinction or curtailment by its practitioners. This statement requires some explanation. Let us say that, generally speaking, the labor of philosophy is to search for the ultimate structures and justifications that underlie our more proximate explanations and convictions. Philosophical ethics, for example, reflects critically on values such as 'good' and 'right' and attempts to present a systematic integration of such notions that makes optimal sense of current practices; the philosophy of art inquires into the meaning of the 'beautiful' often, if not usually, in terms of structural integrity, symbolic meaning, and aesthetic pleasure; the philosopher of nature is concerned to explain, within the broad categories of space and time, the ever-changing phenomena of the physical universe. In each of these specific inquiries the philosopher seeks not merely to provide a fuller explanation of the conventional wisdom but also, and perhaps especially, to probe that wisdom, thereby indicating the way for future discoveries and practical developments. One need only recall the drama of Socrates' life in Athens to remember that this enterprise is neither solely apologetic nor solely critical in its intention.

The metaphysical quest, one might say, represents the logical culmination of this intellectual pursuit. For here the philosopher turns his attention to the most fundamental questions conceivable by the human mind: What is real? Is the world ultimately intelligible to the human mind? Does an adequate explanation of the world necessarily point to the existence of some otherworldly principle, as a source of its design, its motion, or its being? What, in other words, are the ultimate structures according to which one is able to conceptualize being and knowing? These questions are obviously quite removed from the practical concerns of everyday life; nevertheless, the answers we are able to give them fundamentally condition the manner in which we approach the concerns of everyday life, through the proximate implications in the realms of politics, art, science, and theology. In short, every intellectual inquiry epitomizes and ultimately grounds itself upon a metaphysical investigation. As ethics might be said to study the being of the good and the right, art the being of beautiful constructions, and natural philosophy the being of physical actualities, the metaphysician undertakes to study systematically what Aristotle calls being *qua* being. In this sense, it could be said that the metaphysician is the philosopher's philosopher, or, less contentiously, that all true philosophy, so far as it poses its questions in the context of ultimacy, is metaphysical in character.

But despite the apparent centrality of the metaphysician's concern, his lofty ambitions are continually called into question, even ridiculed, by fellow philosophers. In fact, many metaphysical controversies have been thought by later philosophers to be fundamentally misguided disputes, unnecessary for and even detrimental to the advancement of the human condition. Often this sort of criticism presents itself as a sober reassessment of our epistemological capability: we must estimate more realistically, it is suggested, what kind of question the human intellect is designed to consider. For example, Scottish philosopher David Hume (1711–1776), one of the most important of the skeptical voices, offers this advice in the opening pages of *An Enquiry Concerning Human Understanding:*

> *The only method of freeing learning, at once, from these abstruse questions, is to enquire seriously into the nature of human understanding, and show, from an exact analysis of its powers and capacity, that it is by no means fitted for such remote and abstruse questions. We must submit to this fatigue, in order to live at ease ever after.*

It is probably fair to say that the doubts expressed here by Hume have grown in the two centuries since his death, even as in many respects they have become more sophisticated and diversified in their articulation.

This anthology outlines three basic ways in which the traditional questions of metaphysics are today, if not directly challenged to defend their legitimacy, at the very least reformulated in light of these ever-sharpening criticisms and shifting concerns. The discussions in the second part of the book will aquaint the student with some of the most influential and suggestive contributions to the current debates. It is both desirable and necessary that our discussions be so informed, so that we may treat metaphysical questions as live issues. For example, no one contemplating the ultimate questions today can afford to ignore the astonishing theoretical and technological success of modern science, nor its disturbing challenges to traditional theodicy; nor can one attempting to present ultimate explanations fail to consider the gravity and the well-springs of post-modernism's concern with cultural and linguistic contexts; finally, the contemporary student of metaphysics must appreciate fully the growing tendency to value practice over theory, which brings with it a pervasive distrust of systematic claims.

At the same time, no serious student of metaphysics can hope to comprehend the discipline's central questions, in any depth, without a thorough knowledge of the history of the discussion in which these questions arise and are given their classic formulation. Contemporary thinkers (including ourselves) who address themselves to the fundamental questions do so in the shadow of giants; we must familiarize ourselves with these giants, for however much we might depart from them in the course of the argument, we do so in their debt. The first part of the book, therefore, presents some of the classic statements of the issues and arguments that constitute the present inquiry.

The animating principle of this book is that metaphysics is indeed a legitimate and indispensable intellectual inquiry. It is best simply to let that inquiry unfold according to its own logic and direction, and so characterize itself as it articulates its central concerns. No attempt, therefore, will be made here to state in any detail what metaphysics is primarily about; nor can we present any uncontroversial criterion of what constitutes successful argumentation. But we can, perhaps, help-

fully shape our discussion by offering two basic characteristics that seem to condition the metaphysical inquiry. First, the metaphysician must address himself to the *totality* of things. Whatever is, simply because it *is*, comes within the purview of the metaphysician's study. Second, as was alluded to above, the metaphysician wants to provide an account of the totality of things that is *ultimate*. Precisely what constitutes the totality of things, as well as what counts as an ultimate account, are themselves fundamental questions within the discipline. But any inquiry that did not strive to provide answers that are both final and all-inclusive would not seem to qualify as metaphysical.

Paul Gaffney

Part I

Historical Sources

1 R.E. Allen
Pre-Socratic Cosmology

The Milesians

Philosophy begins in Miletus, an Ionian city on the Mediterranean shore of what is now Turkey. A great port with a large carrying trade, Miletus served not only Greece but also Egypt and Babylonia, then at the height of their culture. The thought of the Milesian philosophers, Thales, Anaximander, and Anaximenes, shows traces of this influence. If Thales predicted a solar eclipse that occurred in 585 B.C., he must have been born toward the latter part of the seventh century. Anaximander appears to have been his slightly younger contemporary; Anaximenes, a younger contemporary of both.

Thales

Every history of philosophy begins with Thales, and records with proper solemnity his opinion that the source of all things is water. And every beginning student is shocked. Not until he reaches Plato and Aristotle does he find himself in a world recognizably his own, a world whose science, law, and logic are a type his own experience has made familiar.

The pronouncements of philosophers are usually answers to questions, whether or not the questions are explicitly put. If Thales claimed that the source of all things is water, his questions must presumably have been, What is the source of all things?

This seems but little progress: we appear to have passed from a naive answer to a naive question. In fact, the question is one of great importance. Questions do not express propositions; they are neither true nor false; but every question assumes that certain propositions are true. Questions arise in a context of beliefs and attitudes, and they turn upon their source, transforming their own assumptions.

Thales' question, understood through its answer, assumes that at least two things are true: that all things have a source, and that the source of all things is one thing. The universe is bound to a single principle, the primordial water, by a single relation, that of derivation. Nature is one whole, with unchanging ways of its own, to be accounted for in terms of a unitary principle of explanation: there is an order in nature, which the mind can comprehend.

The details of Thales' world view are not known with any accuracy. He seems to have supposed that the earth floats on a vast body of water, a clot in a sea of liquid. The liquid itself he must have thought to be "unbounded"—not infinite, since the concept of the infinite had not yet been invented, but rather of indefinite extent. This conception of unbounded, primordial water is not Greek; it is found in the myths of the great river-civilizations of Egypt and Babylonia, and in *Genesis.* The world itself was probably thought by Thales to have grown from this liquid, perhaps, Aristotle suggested, as an animal grows from the moist seed.

Thales thought the primordial water alive, and its life the source of motion: to be

---

alive is to be capable of spontaneous movement. This may have been the reason Thales chose water as his primordial stuff, for water is an ancient symbol of life. Thales, no doubt, thought that it *is* life, thought that, in the living liquid, there was no distinction between its life and its liquidity.

Anaximander

In his account of Anaximander, Aristotle preserves a genuine and important objection to Thales—the first recorded criticism of one philosopher by another. Thales had conceived the primordial element as both unbounded and as water. But, Aristotle remarks:

> *There are some (i.e. Anaximander) who make this the Unbounded, and not air or water; in order that the other things may not be destroyed by their unboundness. They are in opposition to one another— air is cold, water is moist, and fire hot— and therefore, if any one of them were unbounded, the rest would have ceased to be by this time. Accordingly, they say that what is unbounded is something other than the elements, and from it the elements arise.*
>
> **(Physics 204b 24).**
>
> *Burnet's translation, slightly altered.*

Anaximander's objection evidently was that the hot, the cold, the wet, and the dry, and the things which embody them, stand to each other in a relation of opposition; therefore, if one of them were made primary and unbounded, the others could not continue to exist. So far as we can now tell, Thales could have had no answer to this objection. Anaximander supposed the answer to lie in ridding the primordial principle of its association with any single sensible opposite and

making it simply the Unbounded. This is a great leap of the creative imagination, an abstraction of very high order: Anaximander posited as explanatory of the world of sense experience a principle that had no characteristic found in the world of sense experience.

The Unbounded could not merely have been unbounded in extent, for water was unbounded in that sense. It must have been unbounded in that it was internally undifferentiated. This was in fact Aristotle's view, who supposed Anaximander's Boundless to be a mixture of all opposites: the opposites fuse in it as water and wine fuse in watered wine, and it is "boundless" because it is itself of no determinate sort, a thing which is no kind because it is all kinds.

The elements of the world, then, its opposites, separate out or separate off from this primitive mixture, and, once separated, they war upon one another. The one remaining fragment of Anaximander, the oldest remaining fragment of philosophy, bears directly on this point: "The source of coming to be for existent things is that into which destruction, too, happens, 'according to necessity; for they pay penalty and retribution to each other for their injustice according to the assessment of Time.'"

The warring opposites, then, commit injustice upon each other. The concrete case that Anaximander probably had in mind is the perpetual war between winter (the moist and cold) and summer (the hot and dry); the cycle of the seasons, and perhaps the lesser cycle of day and night, prompt this view, as they prompt the predominance in primitive thought of these particular opposites rather than others. Anaximander's view is that one opposite encroaches on the domain of the other, a case of "injustice," and "a reaction takes place through the infliction of punishment by the restoration of equality—of more than equality, since the wrong-doer is deprived of part of his original substance too. This is given to the victim in addition to what was his own, and in turn leads (it might be inferred) to *koros*, surfeit, on the part of the former victim, who now commits injustice on the former aggressor." (Kirk and Raven, p. 119) The cycle of recurring injustice is held in balance by the assessment of Time, which functions as a judge. The world, like a pendulum, maintains equilibrium through the alternation of its extremes.

Anaximenes

Anaximander had presented a question to Thales: How is the qualitative diversity of the world to be reconciled with the primordial unity of its source? Anaximenes undertook to answer that question in a way very different from that of Anaximander, a way of which Thales himself might have approved.

Anaximenes' answer, very simply, was that the primordial unity is to be treated as a stuff, a matter out of which things are made. The diverse elements of the world are to be attributed to changes in this primitive matter, changes that are quantitative. Qualitative differences, that is, are to be accounted for by the thickening and thinning, condensation and rarefaction, of a primordial stuff. This answer has about it an air of distinct modernity. Anaximenes here anticipated Democritus, as well as every modern philosopher who undertakes to derive the colors, sights, and sounds of the world from the arrangement in space of a matter which is qualitatively homogenous.

This primordial stuff Anaximenes believed to be air (or mist, or breath), which when rarefied became fire and when condensed, wind, then cloud, then water, then earth, then stone. Associated with these substances were appropriate qualities, especially the hot and the cold. Condensation is a source of cold, while rarefaction is a source of heat. Anaximenes adduced an empirical argument for this conclusion: breath blown through compressed lips is cold, but with the mouth open, it is warm—a curious observation, but something of a historical landmark.

As in Thales, so in Anaximenes, the primordial stuff is alive or ensouled, and the motion in the world is traced to the living character of its origin. As water is an ancient symbol of life, so is air or breath.

Anaximander and Anaximenes

In the *Physics* (187a 11) Aristotle divides the natural philosophers into two schools: those who hold that there is an underlying body from which other things are generated by thickening and thinning, and those who "separate out" the opposites from a mixture. Anaximander belongs to the latter school, Anaximenes to the former, and the contrast is important.

The principles by which Anaximander interprets the universe are closely linked to that psychology of the tragic passions by which Aeschylus interprets human life. The order of nature is essentially a dramatic order: the agonists are the warring opposites, alternately triumphing in the cycle of days and seasons—a cycle of Hubris and Nemesis, of Excess and Retribution. Separated off from the Unbounded and grown wanton, the opposites pay penalty to each other and lapse once more into their source, "according to the assessment of Time." Seasons return, and in their return we find evidence for a type of causality which is, in the peculiar sense, moral: balance or harmony is a principle of nature, and the equilibrium of the world process is its product. Because harmony is a basic principle of explanation, and because harmony is the harmony of opposites, the opposites themselves are in this scheme irreducible; they are "separated off" from their primitive togetherness, not generated by a combination of prior causes. Implicitly, then, understanding of the universe, for Anaximander, is qualitative and moral: the seeds of the teleological pattern of explanation which was to bulk so large in Plato and Aristotle are already in his thought.

With Anaximenes it is different. The universe is not to be explained by the dramatic tension of qualities and their balance; those qualities are themselves generated by the thickening and thinning of a matter which is qualitatively homogenous. Quantity is prior to quality; causality is implicitly mechanical, not moral. Though Anaximenes' Air is alive, and its life the source of natural motion, there is no hint in this of teleology. The development of speculation in the Ionian tradition will progressively drain the mythical elements from Anaximenes' world view: the primitive life of the world's source will be abandoned, leaving only its physical residue, a spontaneous and uninitiated swirl of atoms, postulated as the origin of motion and change in the world. But Anaximenes' fundamental conception will be kept: the notion that the world consists in matter and its arrangement, that the ultimate explanation of it must be quantitative and mechanical. Anaximenes stands in a direct line with

Democritus, where this ultimate reduction is made; and Democritus is perhaps the one Greek who foreshadowed most clearly the scientific world view which has dominated thought from the time of Newton to the present.

In the dawn of philosophy, the outlines of figures are dim. We shall never know as much as we should like to know of Thales, Anaximander, and Anaximenes. But in the distance, their figures seem very much of a size—all men of extraordinary genius, each of whom made a unique contribution to thought. A division of Greek—and modern—philosophy, the division between mechanists and teleologists, is already to be found, in embryo, in their thought. That division arose within a common context of ideas, provided by Thales: the world is a natural whole, with unchanging ways of its own, and it issues from a primitive and unitary source. The result of this claim was revolution, the passage from myth to philosophy. That revolution Thales' pupils carried forward, each in his own way. The magnitude of their achievement may be measured by its fruit.

Pythagoras and Pythagoreanism

Pythagoras was born on the island of Samos, before the middle of the sixth century. As a young man he migrated to Italy, where he founded the society which bore his name.

Contrast to Milesian Speculation

Religion. Pythagoras founded, in effect, a cult society with religious taboos. Philosophy, or inquiry into the nature of things, was understood as a way of life whose aim was salvation—the purification of the soul and its release from the prison of the body. There was nothing of this in the Milesians, who were motivated by simple curiosity, not desire for salvation, and whose work is distinguished by its uncompromising naturalism.

The Soul. The religious impulse in Pythagoreanism led to the doctrine that the soul is immortal, that it undergoes reincarnation in various forms of animal life, and that, therefore, all life is akin—a claim that found practical expression in abstention from meat. Salvation, release from the wheel of rebirth, was to be attained by coming to understand the beauty and order of the cosmos, especially as shown in the circles of the heavens, and by reproducing that order in one's own soul. Philosophy, then, is purification or catharsis, a regimen designed to free the soul from the burden of sense and the corruption of the physical, prominent sources of disorder. Once again, there was nothing of this in the Milesians, for whom soul, or life, though of fundamental importance as an attribute of the primordial stuff, had no ethical or religious implications.

Form and Mathematics. Broadly speaking, the Ionian tradition was materialistic: it sought explanation in such sensible opposites as the hot, the cold, the wet, and the dry—characters proper to perception. The Pythagoreans, on the contrary, sought explanation in terms of structure or form, a form in essence numerical. They assumed that the world is a *harmonia,* an orderly and proportionate adjustment of parts within a complex whole: they assumed that the book of nature—to borrow a metaphor from one of Pythagoras' intellectual heirs, Galileo—is written in the language of mathematics.

Doctrine

Difficulties of Interpretation. Attempts to reconstruct the history of early Pythagoreanism are made difficult by the absence of early documents, a difficulty already encountered by Aristotle and Theophrastus. The Pythagoreans published little, partly because the school was so tightly knit that oral teaching was sufficient, partly because of its character as a cult society, with an emphasis on secrecy. As one ancient testimonium remarks, "their silence was of no ordinary kind." Also, the tradition of the school attributed all discoveries to the founder, which often makes it difficult to decide what is a primitive feature of their thought and what is not. Still, some things may be ascribed to Pythagoras himself with a high degree of probability.

Things are Numbers. It was universally attested by the ancients that Pythagoras was the author of the doctrine that numbers are the real nature of things. The meaning of this dark saying was obscure even to Aristotle, and scholars have reached no agreement on its interpretation. The doctrine appears to have been suggested by a discovery in music. Pythagoras, experimenting perhaps with a monochord and a movable bridge, found that the perfect consonances which form the basis of musical scales, the fourth, the fifth, and the octave, could be expressed as ratios of the least whole numbers: the octave is 2:1, the fifth 3:2, the fourth 4:3. The welter and chaos of sound, then, is reduced to the beauty and order of music by the introduction of arithmetical proportion. Pythagoras, "recognizing the universal in the clearly known particular," to use Aristotle's description of induction, extended this account to the order of the universe at large. His intuition was very like that of an artist, grasping through significant detail the form of the whole. This is the source of the Pythagorean doctrine, as stated by Aristotle, that "the whole heaven or visible universe is a musical scale or number."

The Tetractys of the Decad. For the Pythagoreans, 10 was (according to Aristotle) "the whole nature of number," presumably because it formed the base of Pythagorean (as well as our own) arithmetic. It is also the sum of 1, 2, 3, and 4—the numbers which occur in the ratios of the perfect consonances: according to Aristotle, ten "contains all the consonances." The tetractys of the decad was a symbol of great significance, and like other such symbols, capable of many interpretations. The symbol is as follows:

a

a a

a a a

a a a a

Notice that it contains ten units, ranked in four rows, with the rows (from whatever angle approached) containing, progressively, one, two, three, and four units. Also, the symbol is an equilateral triangle, the simplest plane figure; it contains both points and lines; and seen from above, it is a pyramid, the simplest solid figure.

Mathematical Discoveries. The Pythagorean school, in a period of two hundred years, helped to lay the foundations of mathematics as we known it today, inaugurating a tradition that ranks with the poetry of Aeschylus and the philosophy of Plato as among the greatest intellectual contributions of Greece to civilization. Pythagoras found geometry a system of land measurement used in Egypt, not unlike the practical rules of thumb used by carpenters today. He transformed it by making it abstract. He was probably the first man in history to establish theorems by demonstration and to undertake the systematic development of geometry as a science. The ideals of science he founded—ideals of simplicity, economy, and rigor—were to influence every facet of Greek art and Greek thought. It may be that he himself discovered and demonstrated the so-called "Pythagorean Theorem," at least for the isosceles right triangle: that the square of the hypotenuse of a right triangle is equal to the sum of the squares of its sides, and its corollary, the incommensurability of the diagonal with its sides. To discover that corollary was to discover the existence of incommensurability and irrational ratios, a triumph of mathematical imagination. In addition, Pythagoras probably refined current arithmetical symbolism, and invented the *gnomon* representation of numbers. The *gnomon,* literally, was the carpenter's square. By application of successive *gnomons,* with 1 as base, one could generate all odd numbers; with 2 as base, all even numbers. As follows:

The Table of Opposites. The table of opposites described by Aristotle should perhaps be ascribed to Pythagoras himself. It is as follows:

```
a   a   a   a           a   a   a   a   a
┌───────────┐           ┌───────────────┐
│a   a   a │a           │a   a   a   a │a
│   ┌───────┤           │       ┌───────┤
│a   a │a │a            │a   a   a │a │a
│   ┌───┤  │            │       ┌───┤  │
│a │a │a │a             │a   a │a │a │a
```

3   5   7 etc.   4   6   8 etc.

The Table of Opposites, the table of opposites described by Aristole should perhaps be ascribed to Pythagoras himself. It is as follows:

Limit	Unlimited
Odd	*Even*
One	*Many*
Right	*Left*
Male	*Female*
Rest	*Motion*
Straight	*Curved*
Light	*Dark*
Good	*Bad*
Square	*Oblong*

There are ten opposites, whose relations are best understood through the *gnomon* representation of numbers. One generates Odd. Two is Many, and generates Even. The *gnomon* shapes of odd numbers are Square, of even numbers, Oblong. Since the ratio of side to side in odd numbers is always 1:1, the odd is Limited; the ratio of side to side in even numbers is continually different—2:3, 3:4, 4:5, and so on—so that the Even is Unlimited. Since the ratio in odd numbers is always the same, Odd is correlated with Rest; since in even numbers it is always different, Even is correlated with Motion; the same consideration explains Straight and Curved. Good/Bad, Right/Left, Male/Female, and Light/Dark are evaluative terms, respectively associated with Limit and Unlimited. The table of opposites, then, is a unity. It provides the categories in terms of which the Pythagoreans understood the world.

Cosmology. Aristotle's testimony tends to indicate that Pythagoreanism was dualistic, containing as primitive principles both Limit and Unlimited. If true, this is in sharp contrast to the Milesians, who were monists.

Heraclitus

Heraclitus was born in Ephesus after the middle of the sixth century, a younger contemporary of Pythagoras and an elder contemporary of Parmenides. The riddling, gnomic character of his writings won him the name of "the dark one" in later antiquity.

His view of the universe turns on his concept of *logos*—an untranslatable word which in fact means "word," but which has connotations of proportion, measure, and perhaps even here pattern. The *logos* is the first principle of knowledge: understanding of the world involves understanding of the structure or pattern of the world, a pattern concealed from the eyes of ordinary men. The *logos* is also the first principle of existence, that unity of the world process which sustains it as a process. This unity lies beneath the surface, for it is a unity of diverse and conflicting opposites, in whose strife the *logos* maintains a continuing balance: the world, in being drawn asunder, is drawn together—a backstretched connection, as in the bow and the lyre. The *logos* itself is an ever-living fire, kindling and dying out in measures. As it dies, it produces sea and earth, which in turn kindle into fire, measure answering to measure. The world process is a circle, in which the way up and the way down are continually balanced, and thus, in some sense, the same.

Heraclitus' thought differs from the Milesians in its concern for ethics and the soul; on these topics, and in the prominence he gives to the *logos*, a structural principle, he in some ways resembles the Pythagoreans. Yet the *logos* is identified with a perceptible element, fire, and its function in Heraclitus' world view is very like that of Time in Anaximander. Like Time, the *logos* is a principle of isonomy, maintaining proportion in the world process. But whereas Anaximander's Time produces equilibrium in a cyclical alteration of excess, the *logos* maintains equilibrium in the universe at every moment. The reason for this is that, though the opposites continually war on one another, as they did in Anaximander, they are maintained constantly in equal measures, and are even, perhaps, fundamentally one and the same.

Both Plato and Aristotle ascribed to Heraclitus the doctrine of perpetual flux: "all things change, and nothing remains at rest." It is to be remembered, however, that the *logos* is itself stable, the measured pattern of flow.

Heraclitus' vision of the universe—a universe in which enemies sustain each other in and through their enmity, in which war and contention are inseparable elements of unity and peace, in which identity is identity in difference, and difference, difference in identity—has never ceased to grip the imaginations of his successors.

The Eleatics

The Eleatics, with their claim for priority of reason over the senses and their radical skepticism of common sense, sharply altered the course of future philosophy. The great pluralistic systems of the fifth century, and even the work of Plato and Aristotle in the fourth, are largely concerned to answer questions they first raised. The most prominent members of the school were Parmenides, its founder, and Zeno, his pupil.

Parmenides

Parmenides was born about 515 B.C. in Elea, a Greek city on the coast of Italy. He was associated in his youth with the Pythagoreans, against whom he later reacted. Most of the first section of his poem in hexameter verse, the *Way of Truth*, has been preserved.

The *Way of Truth* is the first philosophical demonstration in history. It is modeled upon, and means to exhibit the cogency of, geometry. The demonstration rests upon a disjunction which, reduced to its lowest terms, is simply "It is, or It is not." No antecedent for "It" is supplied and none is intended. The first disjunct is the true way of inquiry. The second disjunct is to be wholly rejected: it is unthinkable, unknowable, not to be uttered, for the same thing exists for thinking and for being. The second way of inquiry, in brief, is not really a way at all.

In the proem of the *Way of Truth* (Fr. 1), the goddess who grants Parmenides his deductive revelation promises to reveal to him, not only "the unshaken heart of well-rounded Truth," that is, reality itself, but also "the opinions of mortals in which is no true belief at all," and to teach him "how, passing right through all things, one should judge the things that seem to be." After the disjunction of the two ways is laid down, this promise is fulfilled. To "It is" and "It is not" we are to add what appears to be another way, "It is and is not." (Fr. 6) This is the way of mortal opinion, which supposes real the world of nature, whose contents come to be and cease to be. This way has often been supposed distinct, a third way derived from the combination of the first two. The text, however, forbids that view: it is explicitly stated that there are two, and *only* two, ways (Fr. 2), and later, after their combination has been discussed, the original disjunction is again recalled and treated as exhaustive. (Fr. 8) There are not, then, three ways; the third way is merely as aspect of the second. "It is and is not" reduces to "It is not."

The primary object of Parmenides' poem is to demonstrate that the common-sense belief in the reality of the physical world, a world of plurality and change, is mistaken, and to set in its place a One Being, unchanging, ungenerated, indestructible, shaped as a sphere. The characteristics with which Parmenides qualifies the One resemble the Limited side of the Pythagorean table of opposites. It is perhaps worth noting that the One is not qualified by both of any pair of opposites.

Parmenides' distinction between appearance and reality and between opinion and knowledge laid the foundation for Platonism; his objections to change and plurality helped to inspire, in Aristotle's thought, the identification of matter and potentiality, and in Plato, the doctrine that the sensible world is lower in degree of reality than the world apprehended by intelligence. But despite the stimulus he lent his successors, it has become the fashion to locate the springs of his argument in a simple logical fallacy, the confusion between existential and predicative statements. Kirk and Raven put the view as follows:

Parmenides is attacking those who believe, as all men always had believed, that it is possible to make a significant negative prediction; but he is enabled to attack them only because of his own confusion between a negative predication and a negative existential judgement. The gist of this difficult and important fragment (Fr. 2) is therefore this: Either it is right only to think or say of a thing, "it is ... " (i.e., "it is so-and-so, e.g. white"), or else it is right to think and say only "it is not . . . " (i.e., "it is not something else, e.g., black"). This latter is to be firmly rejected on the ground (a mistaken one, owing to the confusion between existential and predicative) that it is impossible to conceive of Not-being, the non-existent. Any propositions about Not-being are necessarily meaningless; the only significant thoughts or statements concern Being.

This interpretation ascribes two assumptions to Parmenides. The first is that negative predicative statements, of the form "a is not F," imply negative existential statements, of the form "a does not exist." The second is that negative existential statements are meaningless, or otherwise logically absurd.

The first claim is false. It may be dismissed on the textual ground that Parmenides qualifies his One with negative predicates—it is *un*generated, *in*destructible, *un*changing—and further, that he would surely have agreed that it therefore is *not* changing, *not* generated, *not* destructible. Beyond this, the claim falls on the common-sense ground that a man who habitually inferred from "Jones is not bald" to "Jones does not exist" would not be a philosopher, but either a lunatic or a sophist. Parmenides was presumably neither.

The second claim is true, logically independent of the first, and the key to the problem. Parmenides' position appears to be this: To think (but when do we really think, if ever?) is to think of what is, and what is is intelligible. Suppose, then, that we think of some individual, *a*, which has come to be and will pass away; it follows that we can think of *a* that it is not. But we cannot think this, since to think is to think of what is; therefore *a* is not an object of thought, for the thought of it is self-contradictory; and since what exists can be thought of, *a* does not exist. This argument assumes (i) that existence is attributable to individuals, (ii) that thought or discourse has for its object what exists.

Zeno

Zeno was born in approximately 490 B.C. and became a pupil of Parmenides while still a young man. His philosophical activity was primarily negative, devoted to refutation rather than construction; his pattern of argument, to the *reductio ad absurdum,* he borrowed from the geometers.

Aristotle, and the doxographical tradition that followed him, supposed that Zeno's arguments were directed, in the interests of Eleatic Monism, against the existence of any sort of plurality and motion, however conceived—directed, not only against other philosophers, but against common-sense belief in the reality of the empirical world.

The Pluralists

Parmenides posed a simple problem to his successors, that of reconciling the sensible world with criteria of reality it cannot satisfy. To be real is to be intelligible and therefore free from generation or destruc-

tion; since the sensible world does not fulfill these conditions, it cannot be real. But an unreal world is a philosophical embarrassment, especially when it happens to be a world in which we live; such a world must in *some* sense exist, even to be illusion.

The Pluralists—Empedocles, Anaxagoras, and the Atomists, Leucippus and Democritus—all undertook to solve this difficulty, undertook to justify the reality of motion and the existence of the sensible world. In broad outline, their solution was in each case the same, resting on a distinction between elements, which satisfy the Parmenidean requirements, and compounds of those elements, which do not. Anaxagoras (Fr. 17) summed up the point admirably: "No object comes-to-be or passes away, but is mixed or separated from existing objects." Parmenides' denial of generation and destruction is accepted; his denial of plurality is itself denied.

Empedocles

Empedocles was born in Acragas, a Greek city in Sicily, in the early years of the fifth century. His philosophy may be read as an attempt to restate the world view of Anaximander and Heraclitus, while yet taking account of the criticism of Parmenides. From Parmenides he takes his insistence that coming to be and passing away are alike impossible; from Parmenides too he takes the Sphere of Being, everywhere full. But the Sphere is now full of four sensible opposites, the hot, the cold, the wet, and the dry, which change places in the sphere, combine and separate in varying proportions, under the impulse of the cosmic forces of Love and Strife. The various complex substances of the world—its men and tables, horses and trees—come to be and pass away; but that is because they are mere arrangements of elements that do not.

By distinguishing between simple elements and their compounds, Empedocles justified the world of coming to be and passing away which Parmenides' strictures had threatened to destroy. Like Anaximander and Heraclitus, his world view makes qualities primitive in the explanation of nature, and in the balanced alternation of his cosmic forces we have an echo of Heraclitus' *logos* and Anaximander's Time. The peculiar way in which this alternation is exhibited—the rearrangement of qualities in space—perhaps owes something to Anaximenes.

Anaxagoras

Anaxagoras was born in Clazomenae, in Asia Minor, at the beginning of the fifth century. As a young man he came to Athens, where he taught for many years. A friend of Pericles, he played an important role in the intellectual life of the city in its golden age. He was exiled from Athens in middle life, and retired to Lampsacus, a colony of Miletus, where he founded a school.

Like Empedocles, Anaxagoras denied that things come to be and pass away. He held that generation and destruction are really mixture and separation of ingenerable and indestructible elements. His account of mixture and separation, however, is difficult to interpret. It involves two principles. The first is homoeomereity: a natural substance, such as gold or bone, consists solely of parts which are like the whole. Divide gold however finely, and the remnants are still gold. The second principle, that there is a portion

of everything in everything, appears to mean that a piece of gold, or of any other natural substance, contains portions of everything else.

These two principles, as stated, are inconsistent with each other, and it is unclear how their inconsistency is to be resolved. One suggestion is that Anaxagoras, however little he would have put it in these terms, means for us to distinguish between physical division and analysis. If one *divides* a natural substance, one is left with parts which are identical in kind to the whole: a piece of gold is still gold. But if one *analyzes* a natural substance, one will find in it portions, or shares, which are also to be found in every other natural substance.

What are these portions, portions of? Not of other natural substances, presumably, for that leads to a vicious cycle. The answer must be, portions of opposites, portions of hot, cold, wet, dry, light, dark, and so on. These are not physically separable from things, but are discriminable elements in things.

If this interpretation is correct, Anaxagoras anticipated Plato. He certainly anticipated him, and Aristotle too, in the crucial place he gives to Mind as cause of motion.

The Atomists: Leucippus and Democritus

Very little is known of Leucippus. His writings have mainly been lost, and his very birthplace is uncertain, though there is a tradition connecting him with Elea and Parmenides. He has survived in and through the work of his follower, Democritus, whose elder contemporary he was. Democritus was born about 460 B.C., and founded a school at Abdera in Thrace.

Parmenides had denied the existence of empty space, or void, on the ground that since Being is, void could only be where Being is not, and therefore cannot be. Leucippus and Democritus accepted the argument but denied the conclusion, maintaining that "Not-being exists as much as being." The remark may seem self-contradictory, but in fact is not. Parmenides' concept of Being contained the latent confusion of existence with material existence—a confusion Plato was the first to detect. The Atomists' claim, stated as a paradox, amounts to this: material bodies are not the only things that exist, since space exists as well.

The universe of Leucippus and Democritus consists of atoms, physically indivisible material particles that differ in size and shape and move about at random in empty space. The characteristics of these particles are geometrical, not perceptual; the colors and sounds and tastes of the world are secondary qualities, which arise in virtue of the interaction of certain kinds of physical objects (such as eyes and ears) with others (such as tables and chairs).

The atoms move, but no cause of motion, nothing analogous to the Love and Strife of Empedocles or the Mind of Anaxagoras, impels them. This theory called forth severe criticism from Aristotle, who supposed, with most Greeks, that rest is the natural state of things and that motion must always be explained by prior causes. In fact, the atomists' treatment of motion closely anticipated the modern account of inertia.

In their atomism, their theory of motion, their distinction between primary and sec-

ondary qualities, and most of all, in their insistence that explanation of natural processes shall be mechanical, the atomists anticipated much in the world view of modern science, and many historians have hailed them as far in advance of their time. It is well to remember, however, that their doctrines were not the result of empirical inquiry: they were posited a priori, to meet the difficulty Parmenides had first put, that out of nothing nothing comes and that generation or destruction is impossible. That same difficulty, it may be added, was to prompt in Aristotle a very different solution, that matter is potentiality.

The Sophists

The sophists were the wandering teachers of Greece in the latter part of the fifth century, traveling from city to city to lecture for a fee. They taught a variety of subjects—literary criticism, for example, especially of the poets, and grammar—but their chief aim was to provide training in rhetoric, the techniques and devices of winning over opinion in courts of law and public assemblies. There was need for their services. The decay of aristocratic institutions in Greece toward the end of the sixth century and the subsequent rise of democracy—direct, not representative, democracy—made skill in rhetoric important not only to those ambitious for political advancement, but to ordinary citizens concerned to safeguard before the law their property, their citizenship, and their lives.

Sophism was not a doctrine, hardly even an attitude of mind, but a social movement, which could contain men of genuine intellectual eminence such as Protagoras and

Gorgias and contain also Euthydemus and his brother Dionysodorus, a pair of elderly ex-athletes who took to lecturing when they found it hard to stay in shape. But the movement was tinged from the beginning with a certain skepticism which increasingly brought it into disrepute. Much prejudice arose from the very task which sophistry performed. Rhetoric aims at persuasion, not truth, and the popular charge that the sophists undertook to make the weak argument stronger and the strong argument weak was quite correct.

An important trait of sophism was its skepticism of the intellect, in large measure prompted, paradoxically enough, by Parmenides. Parmenides had divorced the world of thought from the world of fact, had put claims of logic in sharp opposition to the claims of experience. Faced with a choice, Parmenides rejected experience. The sophists, facing the same choice, rejected logic. Protagoras offered a subjective theory of truth and claimed that man is the measure of all things; he meant, or so Plato thought, that what seems true to each man is true, that nothing is true or false but thinking makes it so. Mathematics, which provides truths independent of anyone's opinions, Protagoras dealt with by denying its relevance to the world of fact; there are, after all, no examples in nature of the geometer's lengthless points and breadthless lines. Gorgias, again, reacting to Parmenides' claim that what exists must be one and unchanging, concluded that nothing exists; that if anything did exist, it would be unknowable; and that if it were knowable, it would be incommunicable.

Skepticism of the intellect was coupled with moral skepticism: many sophists challenged the objective validity of the attitudes and beliefs of Greek moral and political life. This challenge took the form of a contrast between *phusis* and *nomos,* "nature," and "convention" or "law." By nature, men are selfish and self-seeking: their appetites are directed toward pleasure, power, and self-aggrandisement and are exercised without regard to, or at the expense of, their neighbors. If men do not behave in society solely as their appetites direct, the reason is that they are checked and inhibited by convention and law. The sole sanction for law is compulsion; where no compulsion is present, men are bound by no obligation.

This thesis to some degree was prompted by anthropology. It is perhaps no accident that most of the sophists came from the periphery of the Greek world—Protagoras from Abdera in Thrace, Prodicus from Ceos in the Aegean, Gorgias from Leontini in Sicily—from cities in constant contact with foreign culture. As Aristotle once remarked, fire burns both here and in Persia; but if fire is constant, morals are not, and the sophists inferred, as many modern anthropologists have done, that the basis of morality lies solely in custom and law. This is the thesis of cultural relativity, a thesis which has two parts. The first is that what is regarded as right or morally good in one culture may be regarded as wrong or morally bad in another. The second is that there are no "absolute" standards by which to judge whether anything is right or wrong in itself, apart from the attitude a given society takes to it. The first claim is empirical, a matter of fact; the second is a claim in moral philosophy, and indeed metaphysics, a claim in no way implied by the fact.

Cultural relativity, if taken not simply as a theory, but as a working basis for political and private conduct, is a heady doctrine. For if moral standards are subjective in that they are relative to culture, it is an easy inference that they are subjective in that they are further relative to the individual—that nothing is either right or wrong but thinking makes it so. Many sophists and their pupils drew this conclusion, which Socrates was to make it the main purpose of his life to challenge.

2   Parmenides
Being is One

The Way of Truth. The steeds that carry me took me as far as my heart could desire, when once they had brought me and set me on the renowned way of the goddess, which leads the man who knows through every town. On that way I was conveyed; for on it did the wise steeds convey me, drawing my chariot, and maidens led the way. And the axle glowing in the socket—for it was urged round by well-turned wheels at each end—was making the holes of the naves sing, while the daughters of the Sun, hastening to convey me into the light, threw back the veils from off their faces and left the abode of night. There are the gates of Night and Day, fitted above with a lintel and below with a threshold of stone. They themselves, high in the air, are closed by mighty doors, and avenging Justice controls the double bolts. Her did the maidens entreat with gentle words and cunningly persuade to unfasten without demur the bolted bar from the gates. Then, when the doors are thrown back, they disclosed a wide opening, when their brazen posts fitted with rivets and nails swung in turn on their hinges. Straight through them, on the broad way, did the maidens guide the horses and the car. And the goddess greeted me kindly, and took my right hand in hers, and spoke to me these words: "Welcome, O youth, that comest to my abode on the car that bears thee, tended by immortal charioteers. It is no ill chance, but right and justice, that has sent thee forth to travel on this way. Far indeed does it lie from the beaten track of men. Meet it is that thou shouldst learn all things, as well and unshaken heart of well-rounded truth, as the opinions of mortals in which is no true belief at all. Yet none the less shalt thou learn these things also—how, passing right through all things, one should judge the things that seem to be. (Fr. 1)

Come now, and I will tell thee—and do thou hearken and carry my word away—the only ways of enquiry that exist for thinking: the one way, that it is and cannot not-be, is the path of Persuasion, for it attends upon Truth; the other, that it is-not and needs must not-be, that I tell thee is a path altogether unthinkable. For thou couldst not know that which is-not (that is impossible) nor utter it; for the same thing exists for thinking and for being. (Fr. 2)

That which can be spoken and thought needs must be; for it is possible for it, but not for nothing, to be; that is what I bid thee

---

Excerpts of "The Way of Truth" are from *The Pre-Socratic Philosophers,* translated & edited by Kirk and Raven. Copyright© 1957 Cambridge University Press. Reprinted with the permission of Cambridge University Press.

ponder. This is the first way of enquiry from which I hold thee back, and then from that way also on which mortals wander knowing nothing, two-headed; for helplessness guides the wandering thought in their breasts; they are carried along, deaf and blind at once, altogether dazed—hordes devoid of judgement, who are persuaded that to be and to be-not are the same, yet not the same, and that of all things the path is backward-turning. (Fr. 6)

For never shall this be proved, that things that are not are; but do thou hold back thy thought from this way of enquiry, nor let custom, born of much experience, force thee to let wander along this road thy aimless eye, thy echoing ear or thy tongue; but do thou judge by reason the strife-encompassed proof that I have spoken.

One way only is left to be spoken of, that it is; and on this way are full many signs that what is is uncreated and imperishable, for it is entire, immovable and without end. It was not in the past, nor shall it be, since it is now, all at once, one, continuous; for what creation wilt thou seek for it? How and whence did it grow? Nor shall I allow thee to say or to think, "from that which is not"; for it is not to be said or thought that it is not. And what need would have driven it on to grow, starting from nothing, at a later time rather than an earlier? Thus it must either completely be or be not. Nor will the force of true belief allow that, beside what is, there could also arise anything from what is not; wherefore Justice looseth not her fetters to allow it to come into being or perish, but holdeth it fast; and the decision on these matters rests here; it is or it is not. But it has surely been decided, as it must be, to leave alone the one way as unthinkable and name-less (for it is no true way), and that the other is real and true. How could what is thereafter perish? And how could it come into being? For if it came into being, it is not, nor if it is going to be in the future. So coming into being is extinguished and perishing unimaginable. Nor is it divisible, since it is all alike; nor is there more here or less there, which would prevent it from cleaving together, but it is all full of what is. So it is all continuous; for what is clings close to what is. But motionless within the limits of mighty bonds, it is without beginning or end, since coming into being and perishing have been driven far away, cast out by true belief. Abiding the same in the same place it rests by itself, and so abides firm where it is; for strong Necessity holds it firm within the bonds of the limit that keeps it back on every side, because it is not lawful that what is should be unlimited; for it is not in need—if it were, it would need all. But since there is a furthest limit, it is bounded on every side, like the bulk of a well-rounded sphere, from the center equally balanced in every direction; for it needs must not be somewhat more here or somewhat less there. For neither is there that which is not, which might stop it from meeting its like, nor can what is be more here and less there than what is, since it is all inviolate; for being equal to itself on every side, it rests uniformly within its limits. What can be thought is only the thought that it is. For you will not find thought without what is, in relation to which it is uttered; for there is not, nor shall be, anything else besides what is, since Fate fettered it to be entire and immovable. Wherefore all these are mere names which mortals laid down believing them to be true—coming into being and perishing, being and not being, change of place and variation of bright color. (Fr. 8. Lines 42–49 and 34–41 transposed.)

3

Plato
Dialectic and Scientific Explanation

'Now your problem may be summed up like this: you require it to be proved that our souls are indestructible and immortal, if the confidence shown by a philosopher at the point of death, who believes that he will be far better off in the other world than if he had lived a different sort of life, is not to be an irrational, foolish confidence. To show that the soul is something strong and godlike, and that it existed even before we were born as men—all that, you urge, may well be a revelation not of its immortality, but of its being longlasting, of its having existed somewhere for ever so long, knowing much and doing much; but that leaves it as far as ever from being immortal, and indeed its very entry into a human body was the beginning of a sickness which would end in its destruction; its life here is a life of distress, and it finally perishes in what men call death. And in respect of our individual fears it makes no difference, you argue, whether it enters a body once or many times; anyone who is not

a fool will naturally be afraid if he doesn't know, and cannot give a ground for believing, that it is immortal.

'That, I think, Cebes, is more or less what you maintain: and I am deliberately going over it again and again in order that no point may escape us, and that you may add or subtract anything that you wish.'

To this Cebes replied, 'There is nothing that I want to subtract or add at the moment; my contention is what you have said.'

At this point Socrates paused for a long time in meditation; finally he resumed: 'The problem you raise, Cebes, is no light one: we have got to have a thorough inquiry into the general question of the cause of coming into being and perishing. I will therefore, if you like, narrate my own experiences bearing on the matter; and then, if anything I have to say should appear to you helpful, you can make use of it to settle the points you have been raising.'

'Why of course,' said Cebes, 'I should like that.'

'Then listen and I will tell you. When I was young, Cebes, I had a remarkable enthusiasm for the kind of wisdom known as natural science; it seemed to me magnificent to know the causes of everything, why a thing comes into being, why it perishes, why it exists. Often I used to shift backwards and forwards trying to answer questions like this, to start with: Is it when the conjunction of the hot and the cold results in putrefaction that living creatures develop? Is it blood that we think with, or air or fire? Or is thought due to something else, namely the brain's providing our senses of hearing, sight and smell, which give rise to memory and judgement, and ultimately, when memory and judgement have acquired stability, to knowledge?

'Next I tried to investigate how things perish, and what went on in the heavens and on the earth, until in the end I decided that I had simply no gift whatever for this sort of investigation. To show how right I was about that, I may tell you that, whereas there were some things which up till then I had, as I thought myself and other people thought too, definitely understood, I was now smitten with such complete blindness as the result of my investigations that I unlearnt even what I previously thought I knew, including more particularly the cause of a human being's growth. I had supposed that to be obvious to anybody: he grew because he ate and drank; on taking food flesh was added to flesh, bone to bone, and similarly the appropriate matter was added to each part of a man, until in the end his small bulk had become a large one, and so the little child had become a big man. That was what I used to believe: reasonably enough, wouldn't you say?'

'I would,' said Cebes.

'Now see what you think about this. I used to find it perfectly satisfactory when a tall man standing beside a short one appeared to be taller just by a head; similarly with two horses. And to take an even plainer case, I thought that ten was more than eight because of the addition of two, and that an object two yards long was greater than one only one yard long because the one extended by half its own length beyond the other.'

'And what do you think about it all now?'

'I assure you I am very far from supposing that I know the cause of any of these things; why, I am dubious even about saying that, when we add one to one, either the one to which the addition is made becomes two, or that the one and the other together become two by reason of the addition of this to that. What puzzles me is that when the units were apart from each other each was one, and there was as yet no two, whereas as soon as they had approached each other there was the cause of the coming into being of two, namely the union in which they are put next to each other. Nor again can I any longer persuade myself that if we divide one it is the division this time that causes two to come into being; for then the cause of two would be the opposite of that just suggested: a moment ago it was because the units were brought into close proximity each to each, and now it is because they are kept away and separated each from each. And for that matter I no longer feel sure that by adhering to the old method I can understand how a unit comes into being or perishes or exists: that method has lost all attraction for me, and in its place I am gaily substituting a new sort of hotch-potch of my own.

'One day, however, I heard someone reading an extract from what he said was a book by Anaxagoras, to the effect that it is Mind that arranges all things in order and causes all things; now there was a cause that delighted me, for I felt that in a way it was good that Mind should be the cause of everything; and I decided that if this were true Mind must do all its ordering and arranging in the fashion that is best for each individual thing. Hence if one wanted to discover the cause for anything coming into being or perishing or existing, the question to ask was how it was best for that thing to exist or to act or be acted upon. On this principle then the only thing that a man had to think about, whether in regard to himself or anything else, was what is best, what is the highest good; though of course he would also have to know what is bad, since knowledge of good involves knowledge of bad. With these reflexions I was delighted to think I had found in Anaxagoras an instructor about the cause of things after my own heart; I expected him to tell me in the first place whether the earth is flat or round, and then go on to explain the cause why it must be the one or the other, using the term "better", and showing how it was better for it to be as it is; and then if he said the earth is in the centre of the universe, he would proceed to explain how it was better for it to be there. If he could make all these things plain to me, I was ready to abandon the quest of any other sort of cause. Indeed I was ready to go further, applying the same principle of inquiry to sun, moon and stars, their relative velocities and turnings and so forth: I would ask which is the better way for these bodies to act or be acted upon. For I never supposed that when Anaxagoras had said that they were ordered by Mind he would bring in some other cause for them, and not be content with showing that it is best for them to be as they are; I imagined that in assigning the cause of particular things and of things in general he would proceed to explain what was the individual best and the general good; and I wouldn't have sold my hopes for a fortune. I made all haste to get hold of the books, and read them as soon as ever I could, in order to discover without delay what was best and what was worst.

'And then, my friend, from my marvellous height of hope I came hurtling down; for as I went on with my reading I found the man making no use of Mind, not crediting it with any causality for setting things in order, but finding causes in things like air and aether and water and a host of other absurdities. It seemed to me that his position was like that of a man who said that all the actions of Socrates are due to his mind, and then attempted to give the causes of my several actions by saying that the reason why I am now sitting here is that my body is composed of bones and sinews, and the bones are hard and separated by joints, with the sinews, which can be tightened or relaxed, envelop the bones along with the flesh and skin which hold them together; so that when the bones move about in their sockets, the sinews, by lessening or increasing the tension, make it possible for me at this moment to bend my limbs, and that is the cause of my sitting here in this bent position. Analogous causes might also be given of my conversing with you, sounds, air-currents, streams of hearing and so on and so forth, to the neglect of the true causes, to wit that, inasmuch as the Athenians have thought it better to condemn me, I too in my turn think it better to sit here, and more right and proper to stay where I am and submit to such punishment as they enjoin. For, by Jingo, I fancy these same sinews and bones would long since have been somewhere in Megara or Boeotia, impelled by their notion of what was best, if I had not thought it right and proper to submit to the penalty appointed by the State rather than take to my heels and run away.

'No: to call things like that causes is quite absurd; it would be true to say that if I did not possess things like that—bones and sinews and so on—I shouldn't be able to do what I had resolved upon; but to say that I do what I do because of them—and that too when I am acting with my mind—and not because of my choice of what is best, would be to use extremely careless language. Fancy not being able to distinguish between the cause of a thing and that without which the cause would not be a cause! It is evidently this latter that most people, groping in the dark, call by the name of cause, a name which doesn't belong to it. Hence we find one man making the earth be kept in position by the heavens, encompassing it with a rotatory movement; and another treating it as a flat lid supported on a base of air; but the power thanks to which heaven and earth are now in the position that it was the best possible position for them to be set in, *that* they never look for, and have no notion of its amazing strength; instead they expect to discover one day a stronger and more immortal Atlas, better able to hold things together; for they don't believe in any good, binding force which literally binds things together and holds them fast.

'Well, I for my part should be most happy to be instructed by anybody about a cause of this sort; but I was baulked of it: I failed to discover it for myself, and I couldn't learn of it from others; and so I have had recourse to a second-best method to help my quest of a cause; would you like me to give a formal account of it, Cebes?'

'Yes, indeed; I should like that immensely.'

'Well, at that point, when I had wearied of my investigations, I felt that I must be careful not to meet the fate which befalls those who observe and investigate an eclipse of the sun; sometimes, I believe, they ruin their eyesight, unless they look at its image

in water or some other medium. I had the same sort of idea; I was afraid I might be completely blinded in my mind if I looked at things with my eyes and attempted to apprehend them with one or other of my senses; so I decided I must take refuge in propositions, and study the truth of things in them. Perhaps, however, my comparison in one aspect does not hold good: for I don't altogether admit that studying things in propositions is more of an image-study than studying them in external objects. Anyhow, it was on this path I set out: on each occasion I assume the proposition which I judge to be the soundest, and I put down as true whatever seems to me to be in agreement with this, whether the question is about causes or anything else; what does not seem to be in agreement I put down as false. But I should like to make my meaning clearer to you; I fancy you don't as yet understand.'

'Indeed no,' said Cebes, 'not very well.'

'Well, here is what I mean; it is nothing new, but what I have constantly spoken of both in the talk we have been having and at other times too. I am going to attempt a formal account of the sort of cause that I have been concerned with and I shall go back to my well-worn theme and make it my starting point; that is, I shall assume the existence of a beautiful that is in and by itself, and a good, and a great, and so on with the rest of them; and if you grant me them and admit their existence, I hope they will make it possible for me to discover and expound to you the cause of the soul's immortality.'

'Why of course I grant you that,' said Cebes: 'so pray lose no time in finishing your story.'

'Now consider whether you think as I do about the next point. I appears to me that if anything else is beautiful besides the beautiful itself the sole reason for its being so is that it participates in that beautiful; and I assert that the same principle applies in all cases. Do you assent to a cause of that sort?'

'Yes, I do.'

'It follows that I can no longer understand nor recognize those other learned causes which they speak of; if anyone tells me that the reason why such-and-such a thing is beautiful is that it has a bright colour or a certain shape or something of that kind, I take no notice of it all, for I find in all confusing, save for one fact, which in my simple, naive and maybe foolish fashion I hug close: namely that what makes a thing beautiful is nothing other than the presence or communion of that beautiful itself—if indeed these are the right terms to express how it comes to be there; for I won't go so far as to dogmatize about that, but merely affirm that all beautiful things are beautiful because of the beautiful itself. That seems to me the safest answer for me to give whether to myself or to another; if I hold fast to that I feel I am not likely to come to grief; yes, the safe course is to tell myself or anybody else that beautiful things are beautiful because of the beautiful itself. Do you not agree?'

'I do.'

'Similarly big things are big, and bigger things are bigger, because of bigness, while smaller things are smaller because of smallness.'

'Yes.'

'Then you would reject, as I do, the assertion that one man is bigger than another by, or because of, his head, and that the latter is smaller by, or because of, that same thing;

you would protest that the only thing you could say is that anything bigger than another thing is so solely because of bigness, that bigness is the reason for its being bigger; and again that a smaller thing is smaller because of smallness, and smallness is the reason for its being smaller. You would, I fancy, be afraid that if you said that someone was bigger or smaller "by a head", you would be met with the objection that in the first place it would be by the same thing that the bigger is bigger and the smaller smaller, and in the second place that the head by which the bigger man is bigger is itself small; and that, it would be objected, is monstrous, for a big man to be big by, or because of, something small. Or wouldn't you be afraid of that?'

'Yes, I should,' replied Cebes with a laugh.

'Then would you be afraid to say that ten is more than eight by two, and that two is the cause of the excess, instead of saying by quantity and because of quantity? Or the length of two yards is greater than a length of one yard by half its own length, rather than by greatness? Surely you should have the same qualms as before.'

'Quite so.'

'Or again, wouldn't you hesitate to say that when one is added to one the addition is the cause of there coming to be two, or that when one is divided the division is the cause? Would you not loudly protest that the only way you know of, by which anything comes to be, is by its participating in the special being in which it does participate; and that in the case just mentioned you know of no other cause of there coming to be two save coming to participate in duality, in which everything that is to be two must participate, just as anything that is to be one must participate in unity; all these divisions and additions and suchlike subtleties you would have nothing to do with; you would leave questions about them to be answered by wiser folks; conscious of your inexperience you would shy, as the phrase goes, at your own shadow, cling to the safety of your hypothesis, and answer accordingly. And if anyone were to fasten upon the hypothesis itself, you would disregard him, and refuse to answer until you could consider the consequences of it, and see whether they agree or disagree with each other. But when the time came for you to establish the hypothesis itself, you would pursue the same method; you would assume some more ultimate hypothesis, the best you could find, and continue until you reached something satisfactory. But you wouldn't muddle matters as contentious people do, by simultaneously discussing premiss and consequences, that is if you wanted to discover a truth. Such discovery is perhaps a matter of complete unconcern to the contentious, whose wisdom enables them to jumble everything up together, and nevertheless to be well pleased with themselves. But you, I fancy, if you are a philosopher, will do as I have said.'

'What you say,' replied Simmias and Cebes together, 'is perfectly true.'

ECHECRATES. Upon my word, Phaedo, they had good reason to say so. As I see it, Socrates make matters wonderfully clear even to a feeble intelligence.

PHAEDO. Just so, Echecrates; that is what everyone there thought.

ECHECRATES. As do we who were not there, your present audience. But how did the conversation proceed?

PHAEDO. It was like this, I think. When Socrates had gained their assent, and it was agreed that every Form was a real existent, and that other things bore their names by virtue of participating in those Forms, he then put this question:

'If,' he said, 'that is your view, then when you say that Simmias is taller than Socrates and shorter than Phaedo, are you not saying that both tallness and shortness are in Simmias?'

'Yes, I am.'

'But of course you admit that the words "Simmias overtops Socrates" do not express the truth of the matter. For surely it isn't part of the nature of Simmias to overtop him: he doesn't do so by being Simmias, but by tallness which he happens to possess. Again, you will admit that he doesn't overtop Socrates because Socrates is Socrates, but because Socrates possesses shortness over against Simmias's tallness.'

'True.'

'Once again, Simmias is not overtopped by Phaedo because Phaedo is Phaedo, but because Phaedo has tallness over against Simmias's shortness.'

'Yes.'

'So that is how Simmias comes to be spoken of as both short and tall, being as he is between the two others; he offers his shortness to the tallness of Phaedo to be overtopped, and presents his tallness to Socrates to overtop the shortness of Socrates.'

Socrates smiled as he said this, and added: 'That sounds as if I were going to talk like a book; however, what I have said surely is true.' Simmias agreed, and Socrates continued: 'My purpose in saying this is to get you to share my view: which is this, that not only will tallness itself never consent to be simultaneously tall and short, but the tallness in us can never admit shortness, and never consent to be overtopped; instead, one of these two things must happen: it must either retreat and withdraw when its opposite, shortness, advances, or it must perish at that advance; what it won't consent to is to endure and admit shortness, and so to be something other than it was. For example, I have admitted and endured shortness, and am short without ceasing to be what I am; but the Form that is tall can never bring itself to be short; and similarly shortness, even the shortness in us, can never consent to be or become tall; nor can any other opposite, while still being what it was, simultaneously become or be its own opposite; when that threatens, it either takes its departure or perishes.'

'I agree entirely,' said Cebes.

On hearing this one of the company (I am not sure who it was) intervened: 'Look here,' he said, 'did we not agree a while ago to the exact opposite of what is now asserted? Didn't we say that the greater comes into being from the smaller, and the smaller from the greater? Was not the coming-to-be of an opposite agreed to be just this coming out of its opposite? Whereas now apparently it is maintained that that can never happen.'

Socrates inclined his head towards the speaker, and having listened to him remarked: 'A courageous reminder; but you don't realise the difference between what we said then and what we say now. Then we said that of two opposite *things* the one comes into being from the other; now we say that an opposite *itself* can never become its own opposite, whether the opposite in question be in us or in the world of true being. Previously, my friend, we were speaking of things that *have* opposites, and calling them by the names of those opposites which they possessed; but now we are speaking of the opposites themselves from whose imma-

nence the things called after them derive their names: these opposites themselves, we maintain, could never consent to originate from one another.'

With these words he glanced at Cebes, and added: 'Can it be, Cebes, that you too were disturbed by anything our friend here said?'

'No,' said Cebes, 'I don't feel like that on this occasion; yet I won't deny that many matters do disturb me.'

'We agree then, without reserve, on this point, that no opposite will ever be its own opposite.'

'Absolutely.'

'Now please consider whether you will agree to my next point. Do you speak of "hot" and "cold"?'

'I do.'

'Meaning by them the same as "snow" and "fire"?'

'Why no, of course not.'

'That is to say, the hot is different from fire, and the cold from snow.'

'Yes.'

'But I think you would agree that what starts as snow cannot ever, as we were saying just now, admit the hot and still be what it was: still be snow and also hot; on the approach of the hot it will either withdraw or perish.'

'Quite so.'

'Again fire, when the cold approaches it, will either get out of its way or perish; it will never bring itself to admit coldness and still be what it was, still be fire and also cold.'

'That is true.'

'Then in some of these cases we find that it is not only the form itself that is entitled to its own name for all time, but something else too which, though not being that form, yet always bears that form's character, whenever it exists. Here's an example which will perhaps make my meaning clearer: the odd, I presume, must ways have this name which we now give it, mustn't it?'

'Of course.'

'But will it be the only thing in the world to have it—that is what I am asking—or is there something else which, though not identical with the odd, nevertheless must be called by the name "odd" as well as by its own name, owing to the fact that its nature is such that it can never be apart from the odd? What I mean may be illustrated by the case of the number three, to take one of many instances. Consider the number three: wouldn't you say that it must always be designated both by its own name and also by the name "odd", though it is not identical with the odd? Not identical: nevertheless such is the nature of three and five and half the entire number-series that every one of these numbers is odd. Correspondingly two and four and the whole of the other column of numbers are not identical with the even, but nevertheless each of them is for ever even. Do you agree?'

'Certainly.'

'Then mark what I want to show; it is this, that not only do we find the opposites that we spoke of refusing to admit each other, but all things which, while not being mutually opposed, always possess opposites, themselves likewise appear not to admit the character which is opposite to that contained in themselves; when that character advances upon them they either perish or withdraw. Thus shall we not affirm that three will sooner perish, sooner allow anything to happen to it, than endure,

while still being three, to become even?'

'Indeed we shall,' said Cebes.

['And similarly shall we not affirm that two will sooner perish, sooner allow anything to happen to it than endure, while still being two, to become odd?'

'Indeed we shall.']

'Nevertheless two is not the opposite of three.'

'No, it is not.'

'Hence it is not only two opposite forms that won't endure an onset by one on the other: there are others also that won't endure the onset of opposites.'

'Very true.'

'Then would you like us, if we can, to specify what sort of forms these are?'

'Certainly.'

'Must they not be those which compel the object which they come to occupy to have not only its own character, but also the character of a certain opposite, which it will never lose?'

'How do you mean?'

'Remember what we said just now. You know presumably that anything occupied by the character of three must be not only three but also odd.'

'Certainly.'

'Well, what we maintain is that such a thing can never be visited by the character that is opposite to the form which brings that about.'

'No.'

'And what brought it about was the form of odd?'

'Yes.'

'Whose opposite is the form of even?'

'Yes.'

'Then the character of even will never visit three.'

'No, it will not.'

'That is to say, three has nothing to do with even.'

'Nothing.'

'In fact three is non-even.'

'Yes.'

'Now I was saying that we must specify what sort of things they are which, while not the opposite of a given thing, nevertheless will not admit that thing; our example just now was the refusal of the number three to admit the even, despite its not being the opposite of even; the reason being that three always brings up the opposite of even, just as two brings up the opposite of odd, fire the opposite of cold, and so on and so forth. Well, I wonder if you would specify them in this way: it is not only two opposites that refuse to admit each other, but if any form brings up one of two opposites into that which it itself enters, that form itself will never admit the character opposite to the one brought up. Let me refresh your memory; it does no harm to hear a thing more than once; five will not admit the character of even, nor ten, its double, the character of odd. Of course the double is also in itself opposite to something else: nevertheless ten will not admit the character of odd. Again the fraction 3/2 and all the other members of the series of halves will not admit the character of wholeness, and the same is true of 1/3 and all the terms of that series. I hope you go along with me here and share my view.'

'I do so most emphatically.'

'Well now, go back to the beginning, will you? And please don't meet my questions with that safe answer we spoke of, but copy my example. I say that because the course of our argument has led me to discern a different kind of safety from that which I mentioned originally. Thus, if you were to ask me what must come to be present in a thing's body to make it hot, I should not give you that safe, stupid answer "heat", but a cleverer one now at my disposal, namely "fire". Again, if you ask what must come to be present in a body to make it sick, I shall not say "sickness" but "fever". Similarly, what must be present in a number for it to be odd? Not oddness, but a unit; and so on. I wonder if you see clearly by now what I want?'

'Oh yes, quite clearly.'

'Then tell me, what must come to be present in a body for it to be alive?'

'Soul.'

'Does that hold good always?'

'Certainly.'

'Then soul always brings life along with it to anything that it occupies?'

'Yes indeed.'

'And is there an opposite to life, or is there none?'

'There is.'

'What?'

'Death.'

'Now soul will assuredly never admit the opposite of what it introduces: that has been agreed already, hasn't it?'

'Emphatically so.'

'Well now: what name did we give just now to the thing that won't admit the character of even?'

'Non-even.'

'And to that which won't admit "just" or "musical"?'

'"Unjust" and "unmusical".'

'All right: then what name shall we give to that which won't admit death?'

'Deathless.'

'And isn't it soul that won't admit death?'

'Yes.'

'Then soul is deathless.'

'Very well; may we say that that has been proved? Or how do you feel about it?'

'Yes, and very adequately proved, Socrates.'

'Now a further point, Cebes: if the non-even were necessarily imperishable, presumably three would be imperishable.'

'Undoubtedly.'

'Or again, if the non-hot were necessarily imperishable, then when you confront snow with something hot, the snow would retreat out of its way, intact and unmelted; for it couldn't perish, nor could it endure to admit heat.'

'That is true.'

'Similarly, I suppose, if the non-coolable were imperishable, then when a cold object approached fire, the fire could never be extinguished, or perish, but would take itself off intact.'

'It would have to do so.'

'Then must we not apply the same principle in the case of what is deathless? That is to say, if the deathless is also imperishable, it is impossible for a soul to perish when death approaches it, for it follows from what we have said that the soul will not admit death, will never be dead, any more than three, and of course oddness, will ever be even, or fire, and of course the heat in fire, ever be cold. But it may be objected, "Granting that the odd cannot become even when the even approaches, what is to prevent it perishing, and an even taking its place?" In reply, we could not contend that the odd cannot perish, for the non-even is not imperishable. Of course, if that had been admitted to be so, we could easily now contend that on the approach of the even oddness and three take their departure; and we could have maintained the same thing about fire and the hot, and the rest of them, couldn't we?'

'Yes indeed.'

'Then similarly in our present instance of the deathless, if that is admitted to be also imperishable, soul would be imperishable in addition to being deathless; but if that is not admitted, we shall need a further argument.'

'Oh but, so far as that goes, we need nothing further: for if the deathless, which lasts for ever, is to admit destruction, it is hardly likely that anything else will escape destruction.'

'Yes, and I suppose it would be agreed by everyone that God, and the Form of life itself, and any other deathless entity there may be, can never perish.'

'Why yes, to be sure: agreed by every human being; and the gods, I expect, would be even more inclined to agree.'

'Then inasmuch as the deathless is also indestructible, I presume that soul, if it really is deathless, must be indestructible too.'

'There can be no question of that.'

'So when death approaches a man his mortal part, it seems, dies, but his immortal part gets out of the way of death and takes its departure intact and indestructible.'

'Evidently.'

'Beyond all doubt then, Cebes, soul is deathless and imperishable, and our souls will in truth exist in Hades.'

'I for my part, Socrates,' replied Cebes, cannot dispute that, nor can I feel any doubt about our arguments. But if Simmias here or anyone else has anything to say, it is desirable that he should not suppress it; any further discussion of these matters that may be desired can hardly, I think, be put off for a later occasion.'

4

Plato
The Ascent to the Beautiful Itself

Into these things of love, Socrates, perhaps even you may be initiated; but I do not know whether you can be initiated into the rites and revelations for the sake of which these actually exist if one pursues them correctly. Well, I will speak of them and spare no effort, she said; try to follow if you can.

It is necessary, she said, for him who proceeds rightly to this thing to begin while still young by going to beautiful bodies; and first, if his guide guides rightly, to love one single body and beget there beautiful discourses; next, to recognize that the beauty in any body whatever is akin to that in any other body, and if it is necessary to pursue the beautiful as it attaches to form, it is quite unreasonable to believe that the beauty in all bodies is not one and the same. Realizing this, he is constituted a lover of all beautiful bodies and relaxes this vehemence for one, looking down on it and believing it of small importance.

After this he must come to believe that beauty in souls is more to be valued than that in body, so that even if someone good of soul has but a slight bloom, it suffices for him, and he loves and cares and begets and seeks those sorts of discourses which will make the young better, in order that he may be constrained in turn to contemplate what is beautiful in practices and laws and to see that it is in itself all akin to itself, in order that he may believe bodily beauty a small thing.

After practices, he must lead him to the various branches of knowledge, in order that he may in turn see their beauty too, and, looking now to the beautiful in its multitude, no longer delight like a slave, a worthless petty-minded servant, in the beauty of one single thing, whether beauty of a young child or man or of one practice; but rather, having been turned toward the multitudinous ocean of the beautiful and contemplating it, he begets many beautiful and imposing discourses and thoughts in ungrudging love of wisdom, until, having at this point grown and waxed strong, he beholds a certain kind of knowledge which is one, and such that it is the following kind of beauty. Try, she said, to pay me the closest attention possible.

He who has been educated in the things of love up to this point, beholding beautiful things rightly and in due order, will then, suddenly, in an instant, proceeding at that point to the end of the things of love, see something marvelous, beautiful in nature: it is *that,* Socrates, for the sake of which in fact all his previous labors existed.

First, it ever is and neither comes to be nor perishes, nor has it growth nor diminution.

Again, it is not in one respect beautiful but in another ugly, nor beautiful at one time but not at another, nor beautiful relative to this but ugly relative to that, nor beautiful here but ugly there, as being beautiful to some but ugly to others.

Nor on the other hand will it appear beautiful to him as a face does, or hands, or anything else of which body partakes, nor as any discourse or any knowledge does, nor as what is somewhere in something else, as in an animal, or in earth, or in heaven, or in anything else; but it exists in itself alone by itself, single in nature forever, while all other things are beautiful by sharing in *that* in such manner that though the rest come to be and perish, *that* comes to be neither in greater degree nor less and is not at all affected.

But when someone, ascending from things here through the right love of boys, begins clearly to see *that*, the Beautiful, he would pretty well touch the end. For this is the right way to proceed in matters of love, or to be led by another—beginning from these beautiful things here, to ascend ever upward for the sake of *that*, the Beautiful, as though using the steps of a ladder, from one to two, and from two to all beautiful bodies, and from beautiful bodies to beautiful practices, and from practices to beautiful studies, and from studies one arrives in the end at *that* study which is nothing other than the study of *that*, the Beautiful itself, and one knows in the end, by itself, what it is to be beautiful. It is there, if anywhere, dear Socrates, said the Mantinaean Stranger, that human life is to be lived: in contemplating the Beautiful itself. If ever you see it, it will not seem to you as gold or raiment or beautiful boys and youths, which now you look upon dumbstruck; you and many another are ready to gaze on those you love and dwell with them forever, if somehow it were possible, not to eat nor drink but only to watch and be with them.

What then do we suppose it would be like, she said, if it were possible for someone to see the Beautiful itself, pure, unalloyed, unmixed, not full of human flesh and colors, and the many other kinds of nonsense which attach to mortality, but if he could behold the divine Beauty itself, single in nature? Do you think it a worthless life, she said, for a man to look *there* and contemplate *that* with that by which one must contemplate it, and to be with it? Or are you not convinced, she said, that there alone it will befall him, in seeing the Beautiful with that by which it is visible, to beget, not images of virtue, because he does not touch an image, but true virtue, because he touches the truth? But in begetting true virtue and nurturing it, it is given to him to become dear to god, and if any other among men is immortal, he is too.

These then, Phaedrus and you others, are the things Diotima said, and I am persuaded. Being persuaded, I try also to persuade others that one would not easily get a better partner for our human nature in acquiring this possession than Eros. Therefore I say that every man should honor Eros, and I myself honor and surpassingly devote myself to the things of love and summon others to do so; now and always, I praise the power and courage of Eros so far as I am able.

5

Plato
Knowledge as Recollection and Definition
(selections from *Meno*)

MENO. Can you tell me Socrates—is virtue something that can be taught? Or does it come by practice? Or is it neither teaching nor practice that gives it to a man but natural aptitude or something else?

SOCRATES. Well Meno, in the old days the Thessalians had a great reputation among the Greeks for their wealth and their horsemanship. Now it seems they are philosophers as well—especially the men of Larissa, where your friend Aristippus comes from. It is Gorgias who has done it. He went to that city and captured the hearts of the foremost of the Aleuadae for his wisdom (among them your own admirer Aristippus), not to speak of other leading Thessalians. In particular he got you into the habit of answering any question you might be asked, with the confidence and dignity appropriate to those who know the answers, just as he himself invites questions of every kind from anyone in the Greek world who wishes to ask, and never fails to answer them. But here at Athens, my dear Meno, it is just the reverse. There is a dearth of wisdom, and it looks as if it had migrated from our part of the country to yours. At any rate if you put your question to any of our people, they will all alike laugh and say: 'You must think I am singularly fortunate, to know whether virtue can be taught or how it is acquired. The fact is that far from knowing whether it can be taught, I have no idea what virtue itself is.'

That is my own case. I share the poverty of my fellow-countrymen in this respect, and confess to my shame that I have no knowledge about virtue at all. And how can I know a property of something when I don't even know what it is? Do you suppose that somebody entirely ignorant who Meno is could say whether he is handsome and rich and well-born or the reverse? Is that possible, do you think?

MENO. No. But is this true about yourself, Socrates, that you don't even know

what virtue is? Is this the report that we are to take home about you?

SOCRATES. Not only that; you may say also that, to the best of my belief, I have never yet met anyone who did know.

MENO. What! Didn't you meet Gorgias when he was here?

SOCRATES. Yes.

MENO. And you still didn't think he knew?

SOCRATES. I'm a forgetful sort of person, and I can't say just now what I thought at the time. Probably he did know, and I expect you know what he used to say about it. So remind me what it was, or tell me yourself if you will. No doubt you agree with him.

MENO. Yes I do.

SOCRATES. Then let's leave him out of it, since after all he isn't here. What do you yourself say virtue is? I do ask you in all earnestness not to refuse me, but to speak out. I shall be only too happy to be proved wrong if you and Gorgias turn out to know this, although I said I had never met anyone who did.

MENO. But there is no difficulty about it. First of all, if it is manly virtue you are after, it is easy to see that the virtue of a man consists of managing the city's affairs capably, and so that he will help his friends and injure his foes while taking care to come to no harm himself. Or if you want a woman's virtue, that is easily described. She must be a good housewife, careful with her stores and obedient to her husband. Then there is another virtue for a child, male or female, and another for an old man, free or slave as you like; and a great many more kinds of virtue, so that no one need to be at a loss to say what it is. For every act and every time of life, with reference to each separate function, there is a virtue for each one of us, and similarly, I should say, a vice.

SOCRATES. I seem to be in luck. I wanted one virtue and I find that you have a whole swarm of virtues to offer. But seriously, to carry on this metaphor of the swarm, suppose I asked you what a bee is, what is its essential nature, and you replied that bees were of many different kinds, what would you say if I went on to ask: 'And is it in being bees that they are many and various and different from one another? Or would you agree that it is not in this respect that they differ, but in something else, some other quality like size or beauty?'

MENO. I should say that in so far as they are bees, they don't differ from one another at all.

SOCRATES. Suppose I then continued: 'Well, this is just what I want you to tell me. What is that character in respect of which they don't differ at all, but are all the same?' I presume you would have something to say?

MENO. I should.

SOCRATES. Then do the same with the virtues. Even if they are many and various, yet at least they all have some common character which makes them virtues. That is what ought to be kept in view by anyone who answers the question: 'What is virtue?' Do you follow me?

MENO. I think I do, but I don't yet really grasp the question as I should wish.

SOCRATES. Well, does this apply in your mind only to virtue, that there is a different one for a man and a woman and the rest? Is it the same with health and size and strength, or has health the same character everywhere, if it is health, whether it be in a man or any other creature?

MENO. I agree that health is the same in a man or in a woman.

SOCRATES. And what about size and strength? If a woman is strong, will it be the same thing, the same strength, that makes her strong? My meaning is that in its character as strength, it is no different, whether it be in a man or in a woman. Or do you think it is?

MENO. No.

SOCRATES. And will virtue differ, in its character as virtue, whether it be in a child or an old man, a woman or man?

MENO. I somehow feel that this is not on the same level as the other cases.

SOCRATES. Well then, didn't you say that a man's virtue lay in directing the city well, and a woman's in directing her household well?

MENO. Yes.

SOCRATES. And is it possible to direct anything well—city or household or anything else—if not temperately and justly?

MENO. Certainly not.

SOCRATES. And that means with temperance and justice?

MENO. Of course.

SOCRATES. Then both man and woman need the same qualities, justice and temperance, if they are going to be good.

MENO. It looks like it.

SOCRATES. And what about your child and old man? Could they be good if they were incontinent and unjust?

MENO. Of course not.

SOCRATES. They must be temperate and just?

MENO. Yes.

SOCRATES. So everyone is good in the same way, since they become good by possessing the same qualities.

MENO. So it seems.

SOCRATES. And if they did not share the same virtue, they would not be good in the same way.

MENO. No.

SOCRATES. Seeing then that they all have the same virtue, try to remember and tell me what Gorgias, and you who share his opinion, say it is.

MENO. It must be simply the capacity to govern men, if you are looking for one quality to cover all the instances.

SOCRATES. Indeed I am. But does this virtue apply to a child or a slave? Should a slave be capable of governing his master, and if he does, is he still a slave?

MENO. I hardly think so.

SOCRATES. It certainly doesn't sound likely. And here is another point. You speak of 'capacity to govern'. Shall we not add 'justly but not otherwise'?

MENO. I think we should, for justice is virtue.

SOCRATES. Virtue, do you say, or *a* virtue?

MENO. What do you mean?

SOCRATES. Something quite general. Take roundness, for instance. I should say that it is a shape, not simply that it is shape, my reason being that there are other shapes as well.

MENO. I see your point, and I agree that there are other virtues besides justice.

SOCRATES. Tell me what they are. Just as I could name other shapes if you told me to, in the same way mention some other virtues.

MENO. In my opinion then courage is a virtue and temperance and wisdom and dignity and many other things.

SOCRATES. This puts us back where we were. In a different way we have discovered a number of virtues when we were looking for one only. This single virtue, which permeates each of them, we cannot find.

MENO. No, I cannot yet grasp it as you want, a single virtue covering them all, as I do in other instances.

SOCRATES. I'm not surprised, but I shall do my best to get us a bit further if I can. You understand, I expect, that the question applies to everything. If someone took the example I mentioned just now, and asked you: 'What is shape?' and you replied that roundness is shape, and he then asked you as I did, 'Do you mean it is shape or *a* shape?' you would reply of course that it is *a* shape.

MENO. Certainly.

SOCRATES. Your reason being that there are other shapes as well.

MENO. Yes.

SOCRATES. And if he went on to ask you what they were, you would tell him.

MENO. Yes.

SOCRATES. And the same with colour—if he asked you what it is, and on your replying 'White", took you up with: 'Is white colour or *a* colour?' you would say it is *a* colour, because there are other colours as well.

MENO. I should.

SOCRATES. And if he asked you to, you would mention other colours which are just as much colours as white is.

MENO. Yes.

SOCRATES. Suppose then he pursued the question as I did, and objected: 'We always arrive at a plurality, but that is not the kind of answer I want. Seeing that you call these many particulars by one and the same name, and say that every one of them is a shape, even though they are the contrary of each other, tell me what this is which embraces round as well as straight, and what you mean by shape when you say that straightness is a shape as much as roundness. You do say that?'

MENO. Yes.

SOCRATES. 'And in saying it, do you mean that roundness is no more round than straight, and straightness no more straight than round?'

MENO. Of course not.

SOCRATES. 'Yet you do say that roundness is no more a shape than straightness, and the other way about.'

MENO. Quite true.

SOCRATES. 'Then what is this thing which is called "shape"? Try to tell me.' If when asked this question either about shape or colour you said: 'But I don't understand what you want, or what you mean,' your questioner would perhaps be surprised and say: 'Don't you see that I am looking for what is the same in all of them?' Would you even so be unable to reply, if the question was: 'What is it that is common to roundness and straightness and the other things which you call shapes?' Do your best to answer, as practice for the question about virtue.

MENO. No, you do it, Socrates.

SOCRATES. Do you want me to give in to you?

MENO. Yes.

SOCRATES. And will you in your turn give me an answer about virtue?

MENO. I will.

SOCRATES. In that case I must do my best. It's in a good cause.

MENO. Certainly.

SOCRATES. Well now, let's try to tell you what shape is. See if you accept this

definition. Let us define it as the only thing which always accompanies colour. Does this satisfy you, or do you want it in some other way? I should be content if your definition of virtue were on similar lines.

MENO. But that's a naive sort of definition, Socrates.

SOCRATES. How?

MENO. Shape, if I understand what you say, is what always accompanies colour. Well and good—but if somebody says that he doesn't know what colour is, but is no better off with it than he is with shape, what sort of answer have you given him, do you think?

SOCRATES. A true one: and if my questioner were one of the clever, disputatious and quarrelsome kind, I should say to him: 'You have heard my answer. If it is wrong, it is for you to take up the argument and refute it.' However, when friendly people, like you and me, want to converse with each other, one's reply must be milder and more conducive to discussion. By that I mean that it must not only be true, but must employ terms with which the questioner admits he is familiar. So I will try to answer you like that. Tell me therefore, whether you recognize the term 'end'; I mean limit or boundary—all these words I use in the same sense. Prodicus might perhaps quarrel with us, but I assume you speak of something being bounded or coming to an end. That is all I mean, nothing subtle.

MENO. I admit the notion, and believe I understand your meaning.

SOCRATES. And again, you recognize 'surface' and 'solid', as they are used in geometry?

MENO. Yes.

SOCRATES. Then with these you

should by this time understand my definition of shape. To cover all its instances, I say that shape is that in which a solid terminates, or more briefly, it is the limit of a solid.

MENO. And how do you define colour?

SOCRATES. What a shameless fellow you are, Meno . . .

SOCRATES. It isn't that, knowing the answers myself, I perplex other people. The truth is rather that I infect them also with the perplexity I feel myself. So with virtue now, I don't know what it is. You may have known before you came into contact with me, but now you look as if you don't. Nevertheless I am ready to carry out, together with you, a joint investigation and inquiry into what it is.

MENO. But how will you look for something when you don't in the least know what it is? How on earth are you going to set up something you don't know as the object of your search? To put it another way, even if you come right up against it, how will you know that what you have found is the thing you didn't know?

SOCRATES. I know what you mean. Do you realize that what you are bringing up is the trick argument that a man cannot try to discover either what he knows or what he does not know? He would not seek what he knows, for since he knows it there is no need of the inquiry, nor what he does not know, for in that case he does not even know what he is to look for.

MENO. Well, do you think it a good argument?

SOCRATES. No.

MENO. Can you explain how it fails?

SOCRATES. I can. I have heard from men and women who understand the truths of religion—

(Here he presumably pauses to emphasize the solemn change of tone which the dialogue undergoes at this point.)

MENO. What did they say?

SOCRATES. Something true, I thought, and fine.

MENO. What was it, and who were they?

SOCRATES. Those who tell it are priests and priestesses of the sort who make it their business to be able to account for the functions which they perform. Pindar speaks of it too, and many another of the poets who are divinely inspired. What they say is this—see whether you think they are speaking the truth. They say that the soul of man is immortal: at one time it comes to an end—that which is called death—and at another is born again, but is never finally exterminated. On these grounds a man must live all his days as righteously as possible. For those from whom

Persephone receives requital for ancient doom,
In the ninth year she restores again
Their souls to the sun above.
From whom rise noble kings
And the swift in strength and greatest in wisdom;
And for the rest of time
They are called heroes and sanctified by men.

Thus the soul, since it is immortal and has been born many times, and has seen all things both here and in the other world, has learned everything that is. So we need not be surprised if it can recall the knowledge of virtue or anything else which, as we see, it once possessed. All nature is akin, and the soul has learned everything, so that when a man has recalled a single piece of knowledge—*learned* it, in ordinary language—

there is no reason why he should not find out all the rest, if he keeps a stout heart and does not grow weary of the search; for seeking and learning are in fact nothing but recollection.

We ought not then to be led astray by the contentious argument you quoted. It would make us lazy, and is music in the ears of weaklings. The other doctrine produces energetic seekers after knowledge; and being convinced of its truth, I am ready, with your help, to inquire into the nature of virtue.

MENO. I see, Socrates. But what do you mean when you say that we don't learn anything, but that what we call learning is recollection? Can you teach me that it is so?

SOCRATES. I have just said that you're a rascal, and now you ask me if I can teach you, when I say there is no such thing as teaching, only recollection. Evidently you want to catch me contradicting myself straight away.

MENO. No, honestly, Socrates, I wasn't thinking of that. It was just habit. If you can in any way make clear to me that what you say is true, please do.

SOCRATES. It isn't an easy thing, but still I should like to do what I can since you ask me. I see you have a large number of retainers here. Call one of them, anyone you like, and I will use him to demonstrate it to you.

MENO. Certainly. *(To a slave-boy.)* Come here.

SOCRATES. He is a Greek and speaks our language?

MENO. Indeed yes—born and bred in the house.

SOCRATES. Listen carefully then, and see whether it seems to you that he is learning from me or simply being reminded.

MENO. I will.

SOCRATES. Now boy, you know that a square is a figure like this?

BOY. That is so, Socrates.

What follows is a geometrical demonstration in which, simply by asking questions, Socrates leads the boy to the correct conclusion.

SOCRATES. What do you think, Meno? Has he answered with any opinions that were not his own?

MENO. No, they were all his.

SOCRATES. Yet he did not know, as we agreed a few minutes ago.

MENO. True.

SOCRATES. But these opinions were somewhere in him, were they not?

MENO. Yes.

SOCRATES. So a man who does not know has in himself true opinions on a subject without having knowledge.

MENO. It would appear so.

SOCRATES. At present these opinions, being newly aroused, have a dream-like quality. But if the same questions are put to him on many occasions and in different ways, you can see that in the end he will have a knowledge on the subject as accurate as anybody's.

MENO. Probably.

SOCRATES. This knowledge will not come from teaching but from questioning. He will recover it for himself.

MENO. Yes.

SOCRATES. And the spontaneous recovery of knowledge that is in him is recollection, isn't it?

MENO. Yes.

SOCRATES. Either then he has at some time acquired the knowledge which he now has, or he has always possessed it. If he always possessed it, he must always have known; if on the other hand he acquired it at some previous time, it cannot have been in this life, unless somebody has taught him geometry. He will behave in the same way with all geometrical knowledge, and every other subject. Has anyone taught him all these? You ought to know, especially as he has been brought up in your household.

MENO. Yes, I know that no one ever taught him.

SOCRATES. And has he these opinions, or hasn't he?

MENO. It seems we can't deny it.

SOCRATES. Then if he did not acquire them in this life, isn't it immediately clear that he possessed and had learned them during some other period?

MENO. It seems so.

SOCRATES. When he was not in human shape?

MENO. Yes.

SOCRATES. If then there are going to exist in him, both while he is and while he is not a man, true opinions which can be aroused by questioning and turned into knowledge, may we say that his soul has been forever in a state of knowledge? Clearly he always either is or is not a man.

MENO. Clearly.

SOCRATES. And if the truth about reality is always in our soul, the soul must be immortal, and one must take courage and try to discover—that is, to recollect—what one doesn't happen to know, or (more correctly) remember, at the moment.

MENO. Somehow or other I believe you are right.

SOCRATES. I think I am. I shouldn't like to take my oath on the whole story, but one thing I am ready to fight for as long as I can, in word and act: that is, that we shall be better, braver and more active men if we believe it right to look for what we don't know than if we believe there is no point in looking because what we don't know we can never discover.

6

Plato
Nature of the Philosopher
(from *Republic*)

Now, I continued, if we are to elude those assailants you have described, we must, I think, define for them whom we mean by these lovers of wisdom who, we have dared to assert, ought to be our rulers. Once we have a clear view of their character, we shall be able to defend our position by pointing to some who are naturally fitted to combine philosophic study with political leadership, while the rest of the world should accept their guidance and let philosophy alone.

Yes, this is the moment for a definition.

Here, then, is a line of thought which may lead to a satisfactory explanation. Need I remind you that a man will deserve to be called a lover of this or that, only if it is clear that he loves that thing as a whole, not merely in parts?

You must remind me, it seems; for I do not see what you mean.

That answer would have come better from someone less susceptible to love than yourself, Glaucon. You ought not to have forgotten that any boy in the bloom of youth will arouse some sting of passion in a man of your amorous temperament and seem worthy of his attentions. Is not this your way with your favourites? You will praise a snub nose as piquant and a hooked one as giving a regal air, while you call a straight nose perfectly proportioned; the swarthy, you say, have a manly look, the fair are children of the gods; and what do you think is that word 'honey-pale', if not the euphemism of some lover who had no fault to find with sallowness on the cheek of youth? In a word, you will carry pretence and extravagance to any length sooner than reject a single one that is in the flower of his prime.

If you insist on taking me as an example of how lovers behave, I will agree for the sake of argument.

Again, do you not see the same behaviour in people with a passion for wine? They are glad of any excuse to drink wine of any sort. And there are the men who convet honour, who, if they cannot lead an army, will command a company, and if they cannot win the respect of important people, are glad to be looked up to by nobodies, because they must have someone to esteem them.

Quite true.

Do you agree, then, that when we speak of a man as having a passion for a certain kind of thing, we mean that he has an appetite for everything of that kind without discrimination?

Yes.

So the philosopher, with his passion for wisdom, will be one who desires all wisdom, not only some part of it. If a student is particular about his studies, especially while he is too young to know which are useful and which are not, we shall say he is no lover of learning or of wisdom; just as, if he were dainty about his food, we should say he was not hungry or fond of eating, but had a poor appetite. Only the man who has a taste for every sort of knowledge and throws himself into acquiring it with an insatiable curiosity will deserve to be called a philosopher. Am I not right?

That description, Glaucon replied, would include a large and ill-assorted company. It is curiosity, I suppose, and a delight in fresh experience that gives some people a passion for all that is to be seen and heard at theatrical and musical performances. But they are a queer set to reckon among philosophers, considering that they would never go near anything like a philosophical discussion, though they run round at all the Dionysiac festivals in town or country as if they were under contract to listen to every company of performers without fail. Will curiosity entitle all these enthusiasts, not to mention amateurs of the minor arts, to be called philosophers?

Certainly not; though they have a certain counterfeit resemblance.

And whom do you mean by the genuine philosophers?

Those whose passion it is to see the truth.

That must be so; but will you explain?

It would not be easy to explain to everyone; but you, I believe, will grant my premiss.

Which is —?

That since beauty and ugliness are opposite, they are two things; and consequently each of them is one. The same holds of justice and injustice, good and bad, and all the essential Forms: each in itself is one; but they manifest themselves in a great variety of combinations, with actions, with material things, and with one another, and so each seems to be many.

That is true.

On the strength of this premiss, then, I can distinguish your amateurs of the arts and men of action from the philosophers we are concerned with, who are alone worthy of the name.

What is your distinction?

Your lovers of sights and sounds delight in beautiful tones and colours and shapes and in all the works of art into which these enter; but they have not the power of thought to behold and to take delight in the nature of Beauty itself. That power to approach Beauty and behold it as it is in itself, is rare indeed.

Quite true.

Now if a man believes in the existence of beautiful things, but not of Beauty itself, and cannot follow a guide who would lead him to a knowledge of it, is he not living in a dream? Consider: does not dreaming, whether one is awake or asleep, consist in mistaking a semblance for the reality it resembles?

I should certainly call that dreaming.

Contrast with him the man who holds that there is such a thing as Beauty itself and can discern that essence as well as the things that partake of its character, without ever confusing the one with the other—is he a dreamer or living in a waking state?

He is very much awake.

So may we say that he knows, while the other has only a belief in appearances; and might call their states of mind knowledge and belief?

Certainly.

But this person who, we say, has only belief without knowledge may be aggrieved and challenge our statement. Is there any means of soothing his resentment and con-

verting him gently, without telling him plainly that he is not in his right mind?

We surely ought to try.

Come then, consider what we are to say to him. Or shall we ask him a question, assuring him that, far from grudging him any knowledge he may have, we shall be only too glad to find that there is something he knows? But, we shall say, tell us this: When a man knows, must there not be something that he knows? Will you answer for him, Glaucon?

My answer will be, that there must.

Something real or unreal?

Something real; how could a thing that is unreal ever be known?

Are we satisfied, then, on this point, from however many points of view we might examine it: that the perfectly real is perfectly knowable, and the utterly unreal is entirely unknowable?

Quite satisfied.

Good. Now if there is something so constituted that it both *is* and *is not,* will it not lie between the purely real and the utterly unreal?

It will.

Well then, as knowledge corresponds to the real, and absence of knowledge necessarily to the unreal, so, to correspond to this intermediate thing, we must look for something between ignorance and knowledge, if such a thing there be.

Certainly.

Is there not a thing we call belief?

Surely.

A different power from knowledge, or the same?

Different.

Knowledge and belief, then, must have different objects, answering to their respective powers.

Yes.

And knowledge has for its natural object the real—to know the truth about reality. However, before going further, I think we need a definition. Shall we distinguish under the general name of 'faculties' those powers which enable us—or anything else—to do what we can do? Sight and hearing, for instance, are what I call faculties, if that will help you to see the class of things I have in mind.

Yes, I understand.

Then let me tell you what view I take of them. In a faculty I cannot find any of those qualities, such as colour or shape, which, in the case of many other things, enable me to distinguish one thing from another. I can only look to its field of objects and the state of mind it produces, and regard these as sufficient to identify it and to distinguish it from faculties which have different fields and produce different states. Is that how you would to go work?

Yes.

Let us go back, then, to knowledge. Would you class that as a faculty?

Yes; and I should call it the most powerful of all.

And is belief also a faculty?

It can be nothing else, since it is what gives us the power of believing.

But a little while ago you agreed that knowledge and belief are not the same thing.

Yes; there could be no sense in identifying the infallible with the fallible.

Good. So we are quite clear that knowledge and belief are different things?

They are.

If so, each of them, having a different power, must have a different field of objects.

Necessarily.

The field of knowledge being the real; and its power, the power of knowing the real as it is.

Yes.

Whereas belief, we say, is the power of believing. Is its object the same as that which knowledge knows? Can the same things be possible objects of knowledge and of belief?

Not if we hold to the principles we agreed upon. If it is of the nature of a different faculty to have a different field, and if both knowledge and belief are faculties and, as we assert, different ones, it follows that the same things cannot be possible objects of both.

So if the real is the object of knowledge, the object of belief must be something other than the real.

Yes.

Can it be the unreal? Or is that an impossible object even for belief? Consider: if a man has a belief, there must be something before his mind; he cannot be believing nothing, can he?

No.

He is believing something, then; whereas the unreal could only be called nothing at all.

Certainly.

Now we said that ignorance must correspond to the unreal, knowledge to the real. So what he is believing cannot be real nor yet unreal.

True.

Belief, then, cannot be either ignorance or knowledge.

It appears not.

Then does it lie outside and beyond these two? It is either more clear and certain than knowledge or less clear and certain than ignorance?

No, it is neither.

It rather seems to you to be something more obscure than knowledge, but not so dark as ignorance, and so to lie between the two extremes?

Quite so.

Well, we said earlier that if some object could be found such that it both *is* and at the same time *is not*, that object would lie between the perfectly real and the utterly unreal; and that the corresponding faculty would be neither knowledge nor ignorance, but a faculty to be found situated between the two.

Yes.

And now what we have found between the two is the faculty we call belief.

True.

It seems, then, that what remains to be discovered is that object which can be said both to be and not to be and cannot properly be called either purely real or purely unreal. If that can be found, we may justly call it the object of belief, and so give the intermediate faculty the intermediate object, while the two extreme objects will fall to the extreme faculties.

Yes.

On these assumptions, then, I shall call for an answer from our friend who denies the existence of Beauty itself or of anything that can be called an essential Form of Beauty remaining unchangeably in the same state for ever, though he does recognize the existence of beautiful things as a plurality—that lover of things seen who will not listen to anyone who says that Beauty is one, Justice is one, and so on. I shall say to him, Be so good as to tell us: of all these many beautiful things is there one which will not appear ugly? Or of these many just or righteous actions, is there one that will not appear unjust or unrighteous?

No, replied Glaucon, they must inevitably appear to be in some way both beautiful and ugly; and so with all the other terms your question refers to.

And again the many things which are doubles are just as much halves as they are doubles. And the things we call large or heavy have just as much right to be called small or light.

Yes; any such thing will always have a claim to both opposite designations.

Then, whatever any one of these many things may be said to be, can you say that it absolutely *is* that, any more than that it *is not* that?

They remind me of those punning riddles people ask at dinner parties, or the child's puzzle about what the eunuch threw at the bat and what the bat was perched on. These things have the same ambiguous character, and one cannot form any stable conception of them either as being or as not being, or as both being and not being, or as neither.

Can you think of any better way of disposing of them than by placing them between reality and unreality? For I suppose they will not appear more obscure and so less real than unreality, or clearer and so more real than reality.

Quite true.

It seems, then, we have discovered that the many conventional notions of the mass of mankind about what is beautiful or honourable or just and so on are adrift in a sort of twilight between pure reality and pure unreality.

We have.

And we agreed earlier that, if any such object were discovered, it should be called the object of belief and not of knowledge.

Fluctuating in that half-way region, it would be seized upon by the intermediate faculty.

Yes.

So when people have an eye for the multitude of beautiful things or of just actions or whatever it may be, but can neither behold Beauty or Justice itself nor follow a guide who would lead them to it, we shall say that all they have is belief, without any real knowledge of the objects of their belief.

That follows.

But what of those who contemplate the realities themselves as they are for ever in the same unchanging state? Shall we not say that they have, not mere belief, but knowledge?

That too follows.

And, further, that their affection goes out to the object of knowledge, whereas the others set their affections on the objects of belief; for it was they, you remember, who had a passion for the spectacle of beautiful colours and sounds, but would not hear of Beauty itself being a real thing.

I remember.

So we may fairly call them lovers of belief rather than of wisdom—not philosophical, in fact, but philodoxical. Will they be seriously annoyed by that description?

Not if they will listen to my advice. No one ought to take offence at the truth.

The name of philosopher, then, will be reserved for those whose affections are set, in every case, on the reality.

By all means.

7
Plato
Allegories of Learning: The Line and the Cave (from *Republic*)

Conceive, then, that there are these two powers I speak of, the Good reigning over the domain of all that is intelligible, the Sun over the visible world—or the heaven as I might call it; only you would think I was showing off my skill in etymology. At any rate you have these two orders of things clearly before your mind: the visible and the intelligible?

I have.

Now take a line divided into two unequal parts, one to represent the visible order, the other the intelligible; and divide each part again in the same proportion, symbolizing degrees of comparative clearness or obscurity. Then (A) one of the two sections in the visible world will stand for images. By images I mean first shadows, and then reflections in water or in close-grained, polished surfaces, and everything of that kind, if you understand.

Yes, I understand.

Let the second section (B) stand for the actual things of which the first are likenesses, the living creatures about us and all the works of nature or of human hands.

So be it.

Will you also take the proportion in which the visible world has been divided as corresponding to degrees of reality and truth, so that the likeness shall stand to the original in the same ratio as the sphere of appearances and belief to the sphere of knowledge?

Certainly.

Now consider how we are to divide the part which stands for the intelligible world. There are two sections. In the first (C) the mind uses as images those actual things which themselves had images in the visible world; and it is compelled to pursue its inquiry by starting from assumptions and travelling, not up to a principle, but down to a conclusion. In the second (D) the mind moves in the other direction, from an assumption up towards a principle which is not hypothetical; and it makes no use of the images employed in the other section, but only Forms, and conducts its inquiry solely by their means.

I don't quite understand what you mean.

Then we will try again; what I have just said will help you to understand. (C) You know, of course, how students of subjects like geometry and arithmetic begin by postulating odd and even numbers, or the various figures and the three kinds of angle, and other such data in each subject. These data they take as known; and, having adopted them as assumptions, they do not feel called upon to give any account of them to themselves or to anyone else, but treat them as self-evident. Then, starting from these assumptions, they go on until they arrive, by a series of consistent steps, at all the conclusions they set out to investigate.

Yes, I know that.

You also know how they make use of visible figures and discourse about them, though what they really have in mind is the originals of which these figures are images: they are not reasoning, for instance, about this particular square and diagonal which they have drawn, but about *the* Square and *the* Diagonal; and so in all cases. The diagrams they draw and the models they make

are actual things, which may have their shadows or images in water; but now they serve in their turn as images, while the student is seeking to behold those realities which only thought can apprehend.

True.

This, then, is the class of things that I spoke of as intelligible, but with two qualifications: first, that the mind, in studying them, is compelled to employ assumptions, and, because it cannot rise above these, does not travel upwards to a first principle; and second, that it uses as images those actual things which have images of their own in the section below them and which, in comparison with those shadows and reflections, are reputed to be more palpable and valued accordingly.

I understand: you mean the procedure of geometry and of the kindred arts.

(D) Then by the second section of the intelligible world you may understand me to mean all that unaided reasoning apprehends by the power of dialectic, when it treats its assumptions, not as first principles, but as *hypotheses* in the literal sense, things 'laid down' like a flight of steps up which it may mount all the way to something that is not hypothetical, the first principle of all; and having grasped this, may turn back and, holding on to the consequences which depend upon it, descend at last to a conclusion, never making use of any sensible object, but only of Forms, moving through Forms from one to another, and ending with Forms.

I understand, he said, though not perfectly; for the procedure you describe sounds like an enormous undertaking. But I see that you mean to distinguish the field of intelligible reality studied by dialectic as having a greater certainty and truth than the subject-matter of the 'arts', as they are called, which treat their assumptions as first principles. The students of these arts are, it is true, compelled to exercise thought in contemplating objects which the senses cannot perceive; but because they start from assumptions without going back to a first principle, you do not regard them as gaining true understanding about those objects, although the objects themselves, when connected with a first principle, are intelligible. And I think you would call the state of mind of the students of geometry and other such arts, not intelligence, but thinking, as being something between intelligence and mere acceptance of appearances.

You have understood me quite well enough, I replied. And now you may take, as corresponding to the four sections, these four states of mind: *intelligence* for the highest, *thinking* for the second, *belief* for the third, and for the last *imagining*. These you may arrange as the terms in a proportion, assigning to each a degree of clearness and certainty corresponding to the measure in which their objects possess truth and reality.

I understand and agree with you. I will arrange them as you say.

The Allegory of the Cave

Next, said I, here is a parable to illustrate the degrees in which our nature may be enlightened or unenlightened. Imagine the condition of men living in a sort of cavernous chamber underground, with an entrance open to the light and a long passage all down the cave. Here they have been from childhood, chained by the leg and also by the neck, so that they cannot move and can see only what is in front of them, because the chains will not let them turn their heads. At some distance higher up is the light of a fire burning behind them; and between the prisoners and the fire is a track with a parapet built along it, like the screen at a puppet-show, which hides the performers while they show their puppets over the top.

I see, said he.

Now behind this parapet imagine persons carrying along various artificial objects, including figures of men and animals in wood or stone or other materials, which project above the parapet. Naturally, some of these persons will be talking, others silent.

It is a strange picture, he said, and a strange sort of prisoners.

Like ourselves, I replied; for in the first place prisoners so confined would have seen nothing of themselves or of one another, except the shadows thrown by the fire-light on the wall of the Cave facing them, would they?

Not if all their lives they had been prevented from moving their heads.

And they would have seen as little of the objects carried past.

Of course.

Now, if they could talk to one another, would they not suppose that their words referred only to those passing shadows which they saw?

Necessarily.

And suppose their prison had an echo from the wall facing them? When one of the people crossing behind them spoke, they could only suppose that the sound came from the shadow passing before their eyes.

No doubt.

In every way, then, such prisoners would recognize as reality nothing but the shadows of those artificial objects.

Inevitably.

Now consider what would happen if their release from the chains and the healing of their unwisdom should come about in this way. Suppose one of them set free and forced suddenly to stand up, turn his head, and walk with eyes lifted to the light; all these movements would be painful, and he would be too dazzled to make out the objects whose shadows he had been used to see. What do you think he would say, if someone told him that what he had formerly seen was meaningless illusion, but now, being somewhat nearer to reality and turned towards more real objects, he was getting a truer view? Suppose further that he were shown the various objects being carried by and were made to say, in reply to questions, what each of them was. Would he not be perplexed and believe the objects now shown him to be not so real as what he formerly saw?

Yes, not nearly so real.

And if he were forced to look at the fire-light itself, would not his eyes ache, so that he would try to escape and turn back to the things which he could see distinctly, convinced that they really were clearer than these other objects now being shown to him?

Yes.

And suppose someone were to drag him away forcibly up the steep and rugged ascent and not let him go until he had hauled him out into the sunlight, would he not suffer pain and vexation at such treatment, and, when he had come out into the light, find his eyes so full of its radiance that he could not see a single one of the things that he was now told were real?

Certainly he would not see them all at once.

He would need, then, to grow accustomed before he could see things in that upper world. At first it would be easiest to make out shadows, and then the images of men and things reflected in water, and later on the things themselves. After that, it would be easier to watch the heavenly bodies and the sky itself by night, looking at the light of the moon and stars rather than the Sun and the Sun's light in the day-time.

Yes, surely.

Last of all, he would be able to look at the Sun and contemplate its nature, not as it appears when reflected in water or any alien medium, but as it is in itself in its own domain.

No doubt.

And now he would begin to draw the conclusion that it is the Sun that produces the seasons and the course of the year and controls everything in the visible world, and moreover is in a way the cause of all that he and his companions used to see.

Clearly he would come at last to that conclusion.

Then if he called to mind his fellow prisoners and what passed for wisdom in his former dwelling-place, he would surely think himself happy in the change and be sorry for them. They may have had a practice of honouring and commending one another, with prizes for the man who had the keenest eye for the passing shadows and the best memory for the order in which they followed or accompanied one another, so that he could make a good guess as to which was going to come next. Would our released prisoner be likely to covet those prizes or to envy the men exalted to honour and power in the Cave? Would he not feel like Homer's Achilles, that he would far sooner 'be on earth as a hired servant in the house of a landless man' or endure anything rather than go back to his old beliefs and live in the old way?

Yes, he would prefer any fate to such a life.

Now imagine what would happen if he went down again to take his former seat in the Cave. Coming suddenly out of the sunlight, his eyes would be filled with darkness. He might be required once more to deliver his opinion on these shadows, in competition with the prisoners who had never been released, while his eyesight was still dim and unsteady; and it might take some time to become used to the darkness. They would laugh at him and say that he had gone up only to come back with his sight ruined; it was worth no one's while even to attempt the ascent. If they could lay hands on the man who was trying to set them free and lead them up, they would kill him.

Yes, they would.

Every feature in this parable, my dear Glaucon, is meant to fit our earlier analysis. The prison dwelling corresponds to the region revealed to us through the sense of sight, and the fire-light within it to the power of the Sun. The ascent to see the things in the upper world you may take as standing for the upward journey of the soul into the region of the intelligible; then you will be in possession of what I surmise, since that is what you wish to be told. Heaven knows whether it is true; but that, at any rate, is how it appears to me. In the world of knowledge, the last thing to be perceived and only with great difficulty is the essential Form of Goodness. Once it is perceived, the conclusion must follow that, for all things, this is the cause of whatever is right and good; in the visible world it gives birth to light and to the lord of light, while it is itself sovereign in the intelligible world and the parent of intelligence and truth. Without having had a vision of this Form no one can act with wisdom, either in his own life or in matters of state.

So far as I can understand, I share your belief.

Then you may also agree that it is no wonder if those who have reached this height are reluctant to manage the affairs of men. Their souls long to spend all their time in that upper world—naturally enough, if here once more our parable holds true. Nor, again, is it at all strange that one who comes from the contemplation of divine things to the miseries of human life should appear awkward and ridiculous when, with eyes still dazed and not yet accustomed to the darkness, he is compelled, in a law-court or elsewhere, to dispute about the shadows of justice or the images that cast those shadows, and to wrangle over the notions of what is right in the minds of men who have never beheld Justice itself.

It is not at all strange.

No; a sensible man will remember that the eyes may be confused in two ways—by a change from light to darkness or from darkness to light; and he will recognize that the same thing happens to the soul. When he sees it troubled and unable to discern anything clearly, instead of laughing thoughtlessly, he will ask whether, coming from a brighter existence, its unaccustomed vision is obscured by the darkness, in which case he will think its condition enviable and its life a happy one; or whether, emerging from the depths of ignorance, it is dazzled by excess of light. If so, he will rather feel sorry for it; or, if he were inclined to laugh, that would be less ridiculous than to laugh at the soul which has come down from the light.

That is a fair statement.

If this is true, then, we must conclude that education is not what it is said to be by some, who profess to put knowledge into a soul which does not possess it, as if they could put sight into blind eyes. On the contrary, our own account signifies that the soul of every man does possess the power of learning the truth and the organ to see it with; and that, just as one might have to turn the whole body round in order that the eye should see light instead of darkness, so the entire soul must be turned away from this changing world, until its eye can bear to contemplate reality and that supreme splendour which we have called the Good. Hence there may well be an art whose aim would be to effect this very thing, the conversion of the soul, in the readiest way; not to put the power of sight into the soul's eye, which already has it, but to ensure that, instead of looking in the wrong direction, it is turned the way it ought to be.

Yes it may well be so.

It looks then, as though wisdom were different from those ordinary virtues, as they are called, which are not far removed from bodily qualities, in that they can be produced by habituation and exercise in a soul which has not possessed them from the first. Wisdom, it seems, is certainly the virtue of some diviner faculty, which never loses its power, though its use for good or harm depends on the direction towards which it is turned. You must have noticed in dishonest men with a reputation for sagacity the shrewd glance of a narrow intelligence piercing the objects to which it is directed. There is nothing wrong with their power of vision, but it has been forced into the service of evil, so that the keener its sight, the more harm it works.

Quite true.

And yet if the growth of a nature like this had been pruned from earliest childhood, cleared of those clinging overgrowths which come of gluttony and all luxurious pleasure and, like leaden weights charged with affinity to this mortal world, hang upon the soul, bending its vision downwards; if, freed from these, the soul were turned round towards true reality, then this same power in these very men would see the truth as keenly as the objects it is turned to now.

Yes, very likely.

Is it not also likely, or indeed certain after what has been said, that a state can never be properly governed either by the uneducated who know nothing of truth or by men who are allowed to spend all their days in the pursuit of culture? The ignorant have no single mark before their eyes at which they must aim in all the conduct of their own lives and of affairs of state; and the others will not engage in action if they can help it, dreaming that, while still alive, they have been translated to the Islands of the Blest.

Quite true.

It is for us, then, as founders of a commonwealth, to bring compulsion to bear on the noblest natures. They must be made to climb the ascent to the vision of Goodness, which we called the highest object of knowledge; and, when they have looked upon it long enough, they must not be allowed, as they now are, to remain on the heights, refusing to come down again to the prisoners or to take any part in their labours and rewards, however much or little these may be worth.

Shall we not be doing them an injustice,

if we force on them a worse life than they might have?

You have forgotten again, my friend, that the law is not concerned to make any one class specially happy, but to ensure the welfare of the commonwealth as a whole. By persuasion or constraint it will unite the citizens in harmony, making them share whatever benefits each class can contribute to the common good; and its purpose in forming men of that spirit was not that each should be left to go his own way, but that they should be instrumental in binding the community into one.

True, I had forgotten.

You will see, then, Glaucon, that there will be no real injustice in compelling our philosophers to watch over and care for the other citizens. We can fairly tell them that their compeers in other states may quite reasonably refuse to collaborate: there they have sprung up, like a self-sown plant, in despite of their country's institutions; no one has fostered their growth, and they cannot be expected to show gratitude for a care they have never received. 'But', we shall say, 'it is not so with you. We have brought you into existence for your country's sake as well as for your own, to be like leaders and king-bees in a hive; you have been better and more thoroughly educated than those others and hence you are more capable of playing your part both as men of thought and as men of action. You must go down, then, each in his turn, to live with the rest and let your eyes grow accustomed to the darkness. You will then see a thousand times better than those who live there always; you will recognize every image for what it is and know what it represents, because you have seen justice, beauty, and goodness in their reality; and so you and we shall find life in our commonwealth no mere dream, as it is in most existing states, where men live fighting one another about shadows and quarrelling for power, as if that were a great prize; whereas in truth government can be at its best and free from dissension only where the destined rulers are least desirous of holding office.'

8 Aristotle Grammar and the Categories of Being (From *Categories*)

Chapter I

Things are said equivocally which have only a name in common, but the definition of being answering to the name is different; for example, both man and picture of animal. For of these name alone is common, but the definition of being answering to the name is different. For should one give what it is for each of the two to be animal, one will render an account peculiar to each of them.

Things are said univocally which have the name in common and the definition of being answering to the name is the same; for example, man and ox are animal. For man and ox are called by a common name, animal, and the definition of being is the same. For if one renders an account of what it is for each of the two of them to be animal, one will render the same account.

Things are said paronymously which are named after something else, with difference in ending; for example, the grammarian after grammar, the courageous after courage.

Chapter II

Of things said, some are said in combination, some without combination. Things said in combination: man runs, man wins. Things said without combination: man, ox, runs, wins.

Of things which are, some are said of a substrate but not present in a substrate; for example, man is said of a substrate, but present in no substrate. Some are present in a substrate, but said of no substrate (by in a substrate I mean what is in something, not as a part, and cannot exist separately from what it is in); for example, a given knowledge of grammar is in the soul as substrate, but said of no substrate, and a given white is in the body as substrate (for all color is in body), but said of no substrate. Some things are both said of some substrate and present in a substrate; for example, knowledge is in the soul as substrate, but said of grammar as a substrate. Some things are neither present in a substrate nor said of some substrate; for example, a given man, a given horse. For nothing of this sort is either present in a substrate or said of a substrate. Things indivisible and one in number are not said simply of any substrate, but nothing prevents some of them from being present in a substrate: for a given knowledge of grammar is present in a substrate.

Chapter III

When one thing is predicated of another as of a substrate, everything said of what is predicated will also be said of the substrate; for example, man is predicated of a given man, but animal of man, so animal will also be predicated of a given man. For a given man and man are both animal.

Of genera different and not subordinate to each other, differentiae are different in kind; for example, animal and knowledge. Footed, two-footed, winged, aquatic are differentiae of animal, but not of knowledge. For knowledge does not differ from knowledge in being two footed.

Of genera subordinate to each other, nothing prevents the same differentiae: for the superior are predicated of the genera below them, so that there will be as many differentiae of substrate as there are of what is predicated.

Chapter IV

Of things said without combination, each indicates either substance or quantity or quality or relation or place or time or position or possession or action or being acted on. To speak in outline: *Substance* is for example man, horse. *Quantity:* two cubits, three cubits. *Quality:* white, grammatical. *Relation:* double, half, greater than. *Place:* in the Lyceum, in the Agora. *Time:* Yesterday, a year ago. *Position:* sits, lies. *Possession:* has shoes on, has armor on. *Action,* to cut, to burn. *Being acted on:* to be cut, to be burned.

None among things said is said alone by itself in any affirmation; affirmation and denial occur by combination of them relative to each other. For it seems that all affirmation and denial is either true or false. But things said without combination are neither true nor false; for example, man, white, runs, wins.

Chapter V

Substance, in the most determinative and primary and strict sense of the term, is neither said of a substrate nor present in a substrate; for example, this given man, this given horse. But secondary substances, both the species which substances in the primary sense are in and the genera of those species, are said of a substrate; for example, this particular man is in the species man, and animal is the genus of the species. These substances then are said to be secondary; for example, man and animal.

It is evident from what has been said that of things said of a substrate, both the name and the definition are necessarily predicated of the substrate; for example, man is said of a substrate, a given man, and the name is predicated. For you will predicate man of a given man. And the definition of man will be predicated of the individual man; for a man and man are both animal. So that both the name and the definition will be predicated of the substrate.

But of things present in a substrate, for the most part neither the name nor the definition will be predicated of the substrate. In some cases nothing prevents the name from being predicated of the substrate, but it is impossible to predicate the definition; for example, white, being present in a substrate, is predicted of the substrate (for a body is called white), but the definition of white will never be predicated of body.

All other things are said of primary substances as substrates or are present in them as substrates. This is evident from grasping particular instances. For example, animal is predicated of man; so animal will also be predicated of this particular man; for if of no particular man, then not of man generally. Again, color is in body, therefore also in some given body; for if not in a given body, then not in body generally. So that all other things are either said of primary substances or in them as substrates. If there were no primary substances, then, it would be impossible for anything else to be.

Of secondary substances, the species or form is more substance than the genus: for it is closer to the primary substance. For if someone should render an account of what the primary substance is, he will render it more intelligibly and more properly in giving the species rather than the genus; for example, he would render an account of the individual man more intelligibly by giving man rather than animal—for the one is more proper to this individual man, the other more common. And he will give what a particular tree is by giving tree rather than plant.

Again, primary substances are said especially to be substances because they are substrates for all other things; all other things are predicated of them or present in them, because they underlie all other things, and all other things are predicated of them or present in them. But as primary substances are to other things, so also is species to genus. For species is substrate to genus. For the genus is predicated of species, but species not in turn of genera. So that from this too, the species is more substance then the genus.

Of species themselves, as many as are not genera, none is more substance than another: for one will not give man as more proper to this particular man than horse to this particular horse. In like manner, one primary substance is not more substance than another: for a given man is not more substance than a given ox.

After primary substances, species and genera alone are reasonably said to be secondary substances. For it is clear that they alone are predicated of primary substance. For if someone renders what a particular man is, he will properly render the species or the genus, and he will make it more intelligible by rendering man or animal. For example, white or runs or anything of that sort will have been rendered as more alien. So that only these among the rest are reasonably said to be substances.

Again, primary substances are said to be substances in the most determinative sense. But as primary substances are to all other things, so the species and genera of primary substances are to all the rest; for all the rest are predicated of them. For you will say that a given man is grammatical; therefore you will also say that man and animal are grammatical. And so similarly for the rest.

It is common to all substance not to be present in a substrate. For primary substance is neither said of a substrate nor present in a substrate. But it is evident of secondary substances as well that they are not present in a substrate. For man is said of a substrate, this particular man, but is not present in a substrate. For man is not present in a given man. In like manner, animal is said of a substrate, a given man, but animal is not present in a given man.

Again, of things present in a substrate, nothing prevents the name being sometimes predicated of the substance, but it is impos-

sible for the definition. But of secondary substances, both the definition and the name are predicated of the substrate. For you will predicate the definition of man of this particular man, and that of animal; so that substance would not be present in a subject.

This is not peculiar to substances; differentia also is not present in a substrate. For footed or two-footed is said of a substrate, the man, but not present in a substrate—for neither two-footed nor footed is present in man—and the definition of the differentia is predicated of that of which the differentia is said; for example, if footed is said of man, the definition of footed is also predicated of man, for man is footed.

Let us not be worried that the parts of substances are in wholes as in substrates, lest we ever be compelled to say they are not substances. For it was said of things present in a substrate that they are not in something as a part.

All things said of substances and of their differentiae are said univocally. For all predication of them are either of individuals or of species. For of primary substances, none is predicate, for said of no substrate; but of secondary substances, the species and form is predicated of the individual, and the genus of both the species and of the individual. In like manner also, differentiae are predicated of species and of individuals. And primary substances admit the definition of the species and genera, and species of the genus: for everything said of what is predicated will also be said of the substrate. In like manner, species and individuals admit the definition of their differentiae. But things are univocal of which the name is common and the definition the same, so that all things said from substances and from differentiae are said univocally.

Every substance seems to signify a this. Now in respect to primary substances, it is indisputably true that they signify a this: for what is made evident is individual and one in number. But in respect to secondary substances, though it likewise appears that they signify a this by the form of statement when one says man or animal, this is not really true. Rather, it signifies something of a certain sort; for the substrate is not one as the primary substance is, but man is said of many things, as is animal. But it does not signify something of a certain quality simply, as white does; for white signifies nothing other than a certain quality. But the species and genus mark off a certain quality with respect to substance; for they signify some sort of substance. But more is marked off by the genus than the species; for saying animal encompasses more things that saying man.

Substances have no opposite. For what would be opposite to primary substance? For example, nothing is opposite to a given man; again, nothing is opposite to man, or animal. This is not peculiar to substance, but to many other things too; for example, quantity. For nothing is opposite to two cubits or three cubits or ten or anything of that sort, unless one says more is opposite to fewer, or large to small. But of determinate quantities, none is opposite to any other.

It seems substance does not admit the more and less. I do not mean that a substance is not more substance than a substance, and less substance (for it has been said this is possible), but rather that each substance is not said to be more or less that which it is. For example, if this substance is a man, it will not be more and less man, either compared to itself or to another. For one man is not more man than another, as one white is more and less white then another, and one beautiful thing said to be more and less beautiful than another. The same thing is said to be more and less than itself; for example the white body is said to be more white now than before, and being warm is said to be more warm and less. But substance is not said to be more and less; for a man is not said to be more man now than before, nor anything else in so far as it is substance. So that substance does not admit the more and less, admit of degree.

It seems especially peculiar to substance that, being one and the same in number, it is able to accept opposites. One could not put forward anything else which, being one in number, can accept opposites; for example, color, which is one and the same in number, will not be white and black; the same action, also one in number, will not be good and bad, and so in like manner for as many things as are not substances. But substance, being one and the same in number, is able to accept opposites; for example, a given man, being one and the same, sometimes becomes pale and sometimes dark, and hot and cold, good and bad.

With respect to nothing else does this sort of thing appear, unless one were to object by claiming that statement and opinion are of this sort: for the same statement seems to be both true and false. For example, if the statement that someone is sitting is true, this same statement will be false when he stands up, and so in like manner with opinion. For if one has the opinion that someone is sitting, the same opinion about him will be false when he stands up.

But even if one accepts this, there is difference in manner. Substances are able to admit opposites by changing: what becomes cold after being hot changes, for it changes quality; and dark after pale, good after bad, and so in like manner of each of the others, substance is able to accept opposites by admitting change. But statement and opinion remain unmoved in any and every way; but when the thing changes, the opposite becomes true of it. For the statement that someone is sitting remains the same, but the thing is changed when it becomes true and when it becomes false. So in like manner with opinion. The result is that it would be peculiar to substance to be able in a manner to accept opposites by changing.

Suppose then one should decide that statement and opinion are able to receive opposites: this is not true. For statement and opinion are not said to be able to admit opposites because they can themselves admit something, but because something different has been affected. For the statement is said to be true or false because of the fact being or not being, not because it itself is able to admit opposites. For neither statement nor opinion is changed by anything *simpliciter*, so that they could not admit opposites by anything coming to be in them. But substance itself admits opposites, by reason of which it is said to be able to receive opposite affections; it admits disease and health, paleness and darkness, and, receiving each of such things as these, it is said to be able to admit opposites. So that it would be peculiar to substance that, being the same and one in number, it can admit opposites. Let so much be said, then about substance.

Chapter VI

Of quantity, some is discrete, some continuous; some composed of parts having position relative to each other, others not composed of parts having position.

Number and language are discrete; line, plane, and body are continuous, as are time and place. For the parts of number have no common boundary at which they touch; for example, if five is part of ten, five and five do not touch at a common boundary but are discrete; and three and seven do not touch at any common boundary. In general, you cannot have a common boundary of the part of any number; they are always discrete, so number is discrete quantity.

So is language a discrete quantity. That language is a quantity is evident: syllables are measured long and short—I mean spoken language. For its parts do not touch at any common boundary. There is no common boundary at which syllables touch; each is discrete, alone by itself.

But the line is continuous. For you have a common boundary at which its parts touch, a point, and for a surface, a line; for the parts of a plane also touch at a common boundary. In like manner you have a common boundary for a body—line or surface—at which the parts of the body touch. Time and place are of this sort. Present time, the now, touches past and future. Place again is continuous, for the parts of the body contain some place which touches at some common boundary. So also the parts of place which each of the parts of the body contain touch the same boundary the parts of the body touch. So place is continuous, for its parts touch at one common boundary.

9

Aristotle
The Four Causes
(from *Physics,* Bk. II)

1

Of things that exist, some exist by nature, some from other causes.

'By nature' the animals and their parts exist, [*10*] and the plants and the simple bodies (earth, fire, air, water)—for we say that these and the like exist 'by nature'.

All the things mentioned present a feature in which they differ from things which are *not* constituted by nature. Each of them has *within itself* a principle of motion and of stationariness [*15*] (in respect of place, or of growth and decrease, or by way of alteration). On the other hand, a bed and a coat and anything else of that sort, *qua* receiving these designations—i.e. in so far as they are products of art—have no innate impulse to change. But in so far as they happen to be composed of stone or of [*20*] earth or of a mixture of the two, they *do* have such an impulse, and just to that extent—which seems to indicate that *nature is a source or cause of being moved and of being at rest in that to which it belongs primarily,* in virtue of itself and not in virtue of a concomitant attribute.

I say 'not in virtue of a concomitant attribute', because (for instance) a man who is a doctor might cure himself. Nevertheless it is not in so far as he is a patient that he possesses [*25*] the art of medicine: it merely has happened that the same man is doctor and patient—and that is why these attributes are not always found together. So it is with all other artificial products. None of them has in itself the source of its own production. But while in some cases (for instance houses and the other products of manual labor) that principle is in something else external to the thing, in others [*30*]—those which may cause a change in themselves in virtue of a concomitant attribute—it lies in the things themselves (but not in virtue of what they are).

'Nature' then is what has been stated. Things 'have a nature' which have a principle of this kind. Each of them is a substance; for it is a subject, and nature always implies a subject in which it inheres.

[*35*] The term 'according to nature' is applied to all these things and also to the attributes which belong to them in virtue of what they are, for instance the property of fire to be carried upwards—which is not a 'nature' or 'has a nature' but is 'by nature' or 'according to nature'.

193^a *What* nature is, then, and the meaning of the terms 'by nature' and 'according to nature', has been stated. *That* nature exists, it would be absurd to try to prove; for it is obvious that there are many things of this kind, [*5*] and to prove what is obvious by what is not is the mark of a man who is unable to distinguish what is self-evident from what is not. (This state of mind is clearly possible. A man blind from birth might reason about colours. Presumably therefore such persons must be talking about words without any thought to correspond.)

Some identify the nature or substance of a [*10*] natural object with that immediate constituent of it which taken by itself is without arrangement, e.g. the wood is the 'nature' of the bed, and the bronze the 'nature' of the statue.

As an indication of this Antiphon points out that if you planted a bed and the rotting wood acquired the power of sending up a shoot, it would not be a bed that would come up, but *wood*—which shows that the arrangement in [*15*] accordance with the rules of the art is merely an incidental attribute, whereas the real nature is the other, which, further, persists continuously through the process of making.

But if the material of each of these objects has itself the same relation to something else, [*20*] say bronze (or gold) to water, bones (or wood) to earth and so on, *that* (they say) would be their nature and essence. Consequently some assert earth, others fire or air or water or some or all of these, to be the nature of the things that are. For whatever any one of them supposed to have this character—whether one thing or more than one thing—[*25*] this or these he declared to be the whole of substance, all else being its affections, states, or dispositions. Every such thing they held to be eternal (for it could not pass into anything else), but other things to come into being and cease to be times without number.

This then is one account of 'nature', namely that it is the immediate material substratum of things which have in themselves a principle of motion or change.

[*30*] Another account is that 'nature' is the shape or form which is specified in the definition of the thing.

For the word 'nature' is applied to what is according to nature and the natural in the same way as 'art' is applied to what is artistic or a work of art. We should not say in the latter case that there is anything artistic about a thing; if it is a bed only potentially, not yet having the form of a bed; nor should we call

[*35*] it a work of art. The same is true of natural compounds. What is potentially flesh or bone has not yet its own 'nature', and does not exist 'by nature', until it receives the form specified 193[b] in the definition, which we name in defining what flesh or bone is. Thus in the second sense of 'nature' it would be the shape or form (not separable except in statement) of [*5*] things which have in themselves a source of motion. (The combination of the two, e.g. man, is not 'nature' but 'by nature' or 'natural'.)

The form indeed is 'nature' rather than the matter; for a thing is more properly said to be what it is when it has attained to fulfillment than when it exists potentially. Again man is born from man, but not bed from bed. That is why people say that the figure is not the nature [*10*] of a bed, but the wood is—if the bed sprouted not a bed but wood would come up. But even if the figure *is* art, then on the same principle the shape of man is his nature. For man is born from man.

We also speak of a thing's nature as being exhibited in the process of growth by which its nature is attained. The 'nature' in this sense is not like 'doctoring', which leads not to the [*15*] art of doctoring but to health. Doctoring must start from the art, not lead to it. But it is not in this way that nature (in the one sense) is related to nature (in the other). What grows *qua* growing grows from something into something. Into what then does it grow? Not into that from which it arose but into that to which it tends. The shape then is nature.

'Shape' and 'nature', it should be added, are [*20*] used in two senses. For the privation too is in a way form. But whether in unqualified coming to be there is privation, i.e. a contrary to what comes to be, we must consider later.

2

We have distinguished, then, the different ways in which the term 'nature' is used.

The next point to consider is how the mathematician differs from the physicist. Obviously physical bodies contain surfaces and volumes, lines and points, and these are the subject-matter of mathematics.

[25] Further, is astronomy different from physics or a department of it? It seems absurd that the physicist should be supposed to know the nature of sun or moon, but not to know any of their essential attributes, particularly as the writers on physics obviously do discuss [30] their shape also and whether the earth and the world are spherical or not.

Now the mathematician, though he too treats of these things, nevertheless does not treat of them as the limits of a physical body; nor does he consider the attributes indicated as the attributes of such bodies. That is why he separates them; for in thought they are separable from motion, and it makes no difference, nor does any falsity result, if they are [35] separated. The holders of the theory of Forms do the same, though they are not aware of it; for they separate the objects of physics, which are less separable than those of 194ª mathematics. This becomes plain if one tries to state in each of the two cases the definitions of the things and of their attributes. 'Odd' and 'even', 'straight' and 'curved', and likewise 'number', 'line', and 'figure', do not involve [5] motion; not so 'flesh' and 'bone' and 'man'—*these* are defined like 'snub nose', not like 'curved'.

Similar evidence is supplied by the more physical of the branches of mathematics, such as optics, harmonics, and astronomy. These are in a way the converse of geometry. While geometry investigates physical lines but not [10] *qua* physical, optics investigates mathematical lines, but *qua* physical, not *qua* mathematical.

Since 'nature' has two senses, the form and the matter, we must investigate its objects as we would the essence of snubness. That is, such things are neither independent of matter nor can be defined in terms of matter only. Here [15] too indeed one might raise a difficulty. Since there are two natures, with which is the physicist concerned? Or should he investigate the combination of the two? But if the combination of the two, then also each severally. Does it belong then to the same or to different sciences to know each severally?

If we look at the ancients, physics would [20] seem to be concerned with the *matter*. (It was only very slightly that Empedocles and Democritus touched on the forms and the essence.)

But if on the other hand art imitates nature, and it is the part of the same discipline to know the form and the matter up to a point (e.g. the doctor has a knowledge of health and also of bile and phlegm, in which health is realized, and the builder both of the form of the house [25] and of the matter, namely that it is bricks and beams, and so forth): if this is so, it would be the part of physics also to know nature in both its senses.

Again, 'that for the sake of which', or the end, belongs to the same department of knowledge as the means. But the nature is the end or 'that for the sake of which'. For if a thing undergoes a continuous change and there is a stage which is last, this stage is the end or [30] 'that for the sake of which'. (That is why the poet was carried away into making an absurd statement when he said 'he has the end for the sake of which he was born'. For not every stage that is last claims to be an end, but only that which is best.)

For the arts make their material (some simply 'make' it, others make it serviceable), and we use everything as if it was there for our [35] sake. (We also are in a sense an end. 'That for the sake of which' has two senses: the distinction is made in our work *On Philosophy*.) The arts, therefore, which govern 194ᵇ the matter and have knowledge are two, namely the art which uses the product and the art which directs the production of it. That is why the using art also is in a sense directive; but it differs in that it knows the form, whereas the art which is directive as being concerned with production knows the matter. For the [5] helmsman knows and prescribes what sort of form a helm should have, the other from what wood it should be made and by means of what operations. In the products of art, however, we make the material with a view to the function, whereas in the products of nature the matter is there all along.

Again, matter is a relative term: to each form there corresponds a special matter. How far then must the physicist know the form or [10] essence? Up to a point, perhaps, as the doctor must know sinew or the smith bronze (i.e. until he understands the purpose of each): and the physicist is concerned only with things whose forms are separable indeed, but do not exist apart from matter. Man is begotten by man and by the sun as well. The mode of existence and essence of the separable it is [15] the business of the primary type of philosophy to define.

3

Now that we have established these distinctions, we must proceed to consider causes, their character and number. Knowledge is the object of our inquiry, and men do not think they know a thing till they have grasped the 'why' of it [20] (which is to grasp its primary cause). So clearly we too must do this as regards both coming to be and passing away and every kind of physical change, in order that, knowing their principles, we may try to refer to these principles each of our problems.

In one sense, then (1) that out of which a thing comes to be and which persists, is called 'cause', e.g. the bronze of the statue, the silver [25] of the bowl, and the genera of which the bronze and the silver are species.

In another sense (2) the form or the archetype, i.e. the statement of the essence, and its genera, are called 'causes' (e.g. of the octave the relation of 2 : I, and generally number), and the parts in the definition.

Again (3) the primary source of the change [30] or coming to rest; e.g. the man who gave advice is a cause, the father is cause of the child, and generally what makes of what is made and what causes change of what is changed.

Again (4) in the sense of end or 'that for the sake of which' a thing is done, e.g. health is the cause of walking about. ('Why is he walking about?' we say. 'To be healthy', and, having said that, we think we have assigned [35] the cause.) The same is true also of all the intermediate steps which are brought about through the action of something else as means towards the end, e.g., reduction of flesh, purging, drugs, or surgical instruments are means 195[a] towards health. All these things are 'for the sake of' the end, though they differ from one another in that some are activities, others instruments.

This then perhaps exhausts the number of ways in which the term 'cause' is used.

As the word has several senses, it follows that there are several causes of the same thing (not merely in virtue of a concomitant attribute [5]), e.g. both the art of the sculptor and the bronze are causes of the statue. These are causes of the statue *qua* statue, not in virtue of anything else that it may be— only not in the same way, the one being the material cause, the other the cause whence the motion comes. Some things cause each other reciprocally, [10] e.g. hard work causes fitness and *vice versa,* but again not in the same way, but the one as end, the other as the origin of change. Further the same thing is the cause of contrary results. For that which by its presence brings about one result is sometimes blamed for bringing about the contrary by its absence. Thus we ascribe the wreck of a ship to the absence of the pilot whose presence was the cause of its safety.

[15] All the causes now mentioned fall into four familiar divisions. The letters are the causes of syllables, and material of artificial products, fire, &c., of bodies, the parts of the whole, and the premisses of the conclusion, in the sense of 'that from which'. Of these pairs [20] the one set are causes in the sense of substratum, e.g. the parts, the other set in the sense of essence—the whole and the combination and the form. But the seed and the doctor and the adviser, and generally the maker, are all sources whence the change or stationariness originates, while the others are causes in the sense of the end or the good of the rest; for 'that for the sake of which' means what is best [25] and the end of the things that lead up to it. (Whether we say the 'good itself' or the 'apparent good' makes no difference.)

Such then is the number and nature of the kinds of cause.

10 Aristotle The Nature of Wisdom (from *Metaphysics,* Bk. 1)

1. All men naturally desire knowledge. An indication of this is our esteem for the senses: for apart from their use we esteem them for their own sake, and most of all the sense of sight. Not only with a view to action, but even when no action is contemplated, we prefer sight, generally speaking, to all the other senses. The reason of this is that of all the senses sight best helps us to know things, and reveals many distinctions.

Now animals are by nature born with the power of sensation, and from this some acquire the faculty of memory, whereas others do not. Accordingly the former are more intelligent and capable of learning than those which cannot remember. Such as cannot hear sounds (as the bee, and any other similar type of creature) are intelligent, but cannot learn; those only are capable of learning

Reprinted by permission of the publishers and Loeb Classical Library from Aristotle's *Metaphysics,* translated by Hugh Tredennick, Cambridge, Mass.: Harvard University Press.

which possess this sense in addition to the faculty of memory.

Thus the other animals live by impressions and memories, and have but a small share of experience; but the human race lives also by art and reasoning. It is from memory that men acquire experience, because the numerous memories of the same thing eventually produce the effect of a single experience. Experience seems very similar to science and art, but actually it is through experience that men acquire science and art; for as Polus rightly says, "experience produces art, but inexperience chance." Art is produced when from many notions of experience a single universal judgment is formed with regard to like objects. To have a judgment that when Callias was suffering from this or that disease this or that benefitted him, and similarly with Socrates and various other individuals, is a matter of experience, but to judge that it benefits all persons of a certain type, considered as a class, who suffer from this or that disease (e.g. the phlegmatic or bilious when suffering from burning fever) is a matter of art.

It would seem that for practical purposes experience is in no way inferior to art: indeed we see men of experience succeeding more than those who have theory without experience. The reason of this is that experience is knowledge of particulars, but art of universals; and action and the effects produced are all concerned with the particular. For it is not man that the physician cures, except incidentally, but Callias or Socrates or some other person similarly named, who is incidentally a man as well. So if a man has theory without experience, and knows the universal, but does not know the particular contained in it, he will often fail in his treatment; for it is the particular that must be treated. Nevertheless we consider that knowledge and proficiency belong to art rather than to experience, and we assume that artists are wiser than men of mere experience (which implies that in all cases wisdom depends rather upon knowledge); and this is because the former know the cause whereas the latter do not. For the experienced know the fact, but not the wherefore; but the artists know the wherefore and the cause. For the same reason we consider that the master craftsmen in every profession are more estimable and know more and are wiser than the artisans, because they know the reasons of the things which are done; but we think the artisans, like certain inanimate objects, do things, but without knowing what they are doing (as, for instance, fire burns); only whereas inanimate objects perform all their actions in virtue of a certain natural quality, artisans perform theirs through habit. Thus the master craftsmen are superior in wisdom, not because they can do things, but because they possess a theory and know the causes.

In general the sign of knowledge or ignorance is the ability to teach, and for this reason we hold that art rather than experience is scientific knowledge; for the artists can teach, but the others cannot. Further, we do not consider any of the senses to be Wisdom. They are indeed our chief sources of knowledge about particulars, but they do not tell us the reason for anything, as for example why fire is hot, but only that it is hot.

It is therefore probable that at first the inventor of any art which went further than the ordinary sensations was admired by his fellowmen, not merely because some of his inventions were useful, but as being a wise and superior person. And as more and more arts were discovered, some relating to the necessities and some to the pastimes of life, the inventors of the latter were always considered wiser than those of the former, because their branches of knowledge did not aim at utility. Hence when all the discoveries of this kind were fully developed, the sciences which relate neither to pleasure nor yet to the necessities of life were invented, and first in those places where men had leisure. Thus the mathematical sciences originated in the neighborhood of Egypt, because there the priestly class was allowed leisure.

The difference between art and science and the other kindred mental activities has been stated in the *Ethics*. The reason for our present discussion is that it is generally assumed that what is called Wisdom is concerned with the primary causes and principles, so that, as has been already stated, the man of experience is held to be wiser than the mere possessors of any power of sensation, the artist than the man of experience, the master craftsman than the artisan; and the speculative sciences to be more learned that the productive. Thus it is clear that Wisdom is knowledge of certain principles and causes.

II. Since we are investigating this kind of knowledge, we must consider what these causes and principles are whose knowledge is Wisdom. Perhaps it will be clearer if we take the opinions which we hold about the wise man. We consider first, then, that the wise man knows all things, so far as it is possible, without having knowledge of every one of them individually; next, that the wise man is he who can comprehend diffi-

cult things, such as are not easy for human comprehension (for sense-perception, being common to all, is easy, and has nothing to do with Wisdom); and further that in every branch of knowledge a man is wiser in proportion as he is more accurately informed and better able to expound the causes. Again among the sciences we consider that that science which is desirable in itself and for the sake of knowledge is more nearly Wisdom than that which is desirable for its results, and that the superior is more nearly Wisdom than the subsidiary; for the wise man should give orders, not receive them, nor should he obey others, but the less wise should obey him.

Such in kind and in number are the opinions which we hold with regard to Wisdom and the wise. Of the qualities there described the knowledge of everything must necessarily belong to him who in the highest degree possesses knowledge of the universal, because he knows in a sense all the particulars which it comprises. These things, viz, the most universal, are perhaps the hardest for man to grasp, because they are furthest removed from the senses. Again, the most exact of the sciences are those which are most concerned with the first principles; for those which are based on fewer principles are more exact than those which include additional principles; *e.g.,* arithmetic is more exact than geometry. Moreover, the science which investigates causes is more instructive than one which does not, for it is those who tell us the causes of any particular thing who instruct us. Moreover, knowledge and understanding which are desirable for their own sake are most attainable or are generated for the sake of it. So it follows that in a sense they both assert and deny that the Good is a cause; for they treat it as such not absolutely, but incidentally. It appears, then, that all these thinkers too (being unable to arrive at any other cause) testify that we have classified the causes rightly, as regards both number and nature. Further, it is clear that all the principles must be sought either along these lines or in some similar way . . .

11

Aristotle
The Order of Being
and the Order
of Knowing
(from *Metaphysics*, Bk. II)

I. The study of Truth is in one sense difficult, in another easy. This is shown by the fact that whereas no one person can obtain an adequate grasp of it, we cannot *all* fail in the attempt; each thinker makes some statement about the natural world, and as an individual contributes little or nothing to the inquiry; but a combination of all conjectures results in something considerable. Thus in so far as it seems that Truth is like the proverbial door which no one can miss, in this sense our study will be easy; but the fact that we cannot, although having some grasp of the whole, grasp a particular part, shows its difficulty. However, since difficulty also can be accounted for in two ways, its cause may exist not in the objects of our study but in ourselves; just as it is with bats' eyes in respect of daylight, so it is with our mental intelligence in respect of those which are by nature most obvious.

It is only fair to be grateful not only to those whose views we can share but also to those who have expressed rather superficial opinions. They too have contributed something; by their preliminary work they have formed our mental experience. If there had been no Timotheus, we should not possess much of our music, and if there had been no Phrynis, there would have been no Timotheus. It is just the same in the case of those who have theorized about reality: we have derived certain views from some of them, and they in turn were indebted to others.

Moreover, philosophy is rightly called a knowledge of Truth. The object of theoretical knowledge is truth, while that of practical knowledge is action; for even when they are investigating *how* a thing is so, practical men study not the eternal principle but the relative and immediate application. But we cannot know the truth apart from the cause. Now every thing through which a common quality is communicated to other things is itself of all those things in the highest degree possessed of that quality (*e.g.* fire is hottest, because it is the cause of heat in everything else); hence that also is most true which causes all subsequent things to be true. Therefore in every case the first principles of things must necessarily be true above everything else—since they are not merely *sometimes* true, nor is anything the cause of their existence, but they are the cause of the existence of other things,—and so as each thing is in respect of existence, so it is in respect of truth.

II. Moreover, it is obvious that there is some first principle, and that the causes of things are not infinitely many either in a direct sequence or in kind. For the material generation of one thing from another cannot go on in an infinite progression (e.g. flesh from earth, earth from air, air from fire, and so on without a stop); nor can the source of motion (e.g. man be moved by air, air by the sun, the sun by Strife, with no limit to the series). In the same way neither can the Final Cause recede to infinity—walking having health for its object, and health happiness, and happiness something else: one thing always being done for the sake of another. And it is just the same with the Formal Cause. For in the case of all intermediate terms of a series which are contained between a first and last term, the prior term is necessarily the cause of those which follow it; because if we had to say which of the three is the cause, we should say "the first." At any rate it is not the last term, because what comes at the end is not the cause of anything. Neither, again, is the intermediate term, which is only the cause of one (and it makes no difference whether there is one intermediate term or several, nor whether they are infinite or limited in number). But of series which are infinite in this way, and in general of the infinite, all the parts are equally intermediate, down to the present moment. Thus if there is no first term, there is no cause at all.

On the other hand there can be no infinite progression downward (where there is a beginning in the upper direction) such that from fire comes water, and from water earth, and in this way some other kind of thing is always being produced. There are two senses in which one thing "comes from" another—apart from that in which one thing is said to come *after* another, e.g. the Olym-

pian "from" the Isthmian games—either as a man comes from a child as it develops, or as air comes from water. Now we say that a man "comes from" a child in the sense that that which *has* become something comes from that which *is* becoming: i.e. the perfect from the imperfect. (For just as "becoming" is always intermediate between being and not-being, so is that which is becoming between what is and what is not. The learner is becoming informed, and that is the meaning of the statement that the informed person "comes from" the learner). On the other hand A comes from B in the sense that water comes from air by the destruction of B. Hence the former class of process is not reversible (e.g. a child cannot come from a man, for the result of the process of becoming is not the thing which is becoming, but that which exists after the process is complete. So day comes from early dawn, because it is after dawn; and hence dawn does not come from day). But the other class is reversible. In both cases progression to infinity is impossible, for in the former the intermediate terms must have an end, and in the second the process is reversible, for the destruction of one member of a pair is the generation of the other. At the same time the first cause, being eternal, cannot be destroyed; because, since the process of generation is not infinite in the upper direction, that cause which first, on its destruction, becomes something else, cannot possibly be eternal.

Further, the Final cause of a thing is an *end,* and is such that it does not happen for the sake of something else, but all other things happen for its sake. So if there is to be a last term of this kind, the series will not be infinite; and if there is no such term, there will be no Final cause. Those who introduce infinity do not realize that they are abolishing the nature of the Good (although no one would attempt to do anything if he were not likely to reach some limit); nor would there be any intelligence in the world, because the man who has intelligence always acts for the sake of something, and this is a limit, because the *end* is a limit.

Nor again can the Formal cause be referred back to another fuller definition; for the prior definition is always closer, and the posterior is not; and where the original definition does not apply, neither does the subsequent one. Further, those who hold such a view do away with scientific knowledge, for on this view it is impossible to know anything until one comes to terms which cannot be analyzed. Understanding, too, is impossible; for how can one conceive of things which are infinite in this way? It is different in the case of the line, which, although in respect of divisibility it never stops, yet cannot be conceived of unless we make a stop (which is why, in examining an infinite line, one cannot count the sections). Even matter has to be conceived under the form of something which changes, and there can be nothing which is infinite. In any case the concept of infinity is not infinite.

Again, if the kinds of causes were infinite in *number* it would still be impossible to acquire knowledge, for it is only when we have become acquainted with the causes that we assume that we know a thing; and we cannot, in a finite time, go completely through what is additively infinite.

III. The effect of a lecture depends upon the habits of the listener; because we expect the language to which we are accustomed, and anything beyond this seems not to be on the same level, but somewhat strange and unintelligible on account of its unfamiliarity; for it is the familiar that is intelligible. The powerful effect of familiarity is clearly shown by the laws, in which the fanciful and puerile survivals prevail, through force of habit, against our recognition of them. Thus some people will not accept the statements of a speaker unless he gives a mathematical proof; others will not unless he makes use of illustrations; others expect to have a poet adduced as witness. Again, some require exactness in everything, while others are annoyed by it, either because they cannot follow the reasoning or because of its pettiness, for there is something about exactness which seems to some people to be mean, no less in an argument than in a business transaction.

Hence one must have been already trained how to take each kind of argument, because it is absurd to seek simultaneously for knowledge and for the method of obtaining it; and neither is easy to acquire. Mathematical accuracy is not to be demanded in everything, but only in things which do not contain matter. Hence this method is not that of natural science, because presumably all nature is concerned with matter. Hence we should first inquire what nature is, for in this way it will become clear what the objects of natural science are (and whether it belongs to one science or more than one to study the causes and principles of things).

12
Aristotle
The Law of Thought and Being
(from *Metaphysics,* Bk.IV)

I. There is a science which studies Being *qua* Being, and the properties inherent in it in virtue of its own nature. This science is not the same as any of the so-called particular sciences, for none of the others contemplates Being generally *qua* Being; they divide off some portion of it and study the attribute of this portion, as do for example the mathematical sciences. But since it is for the first principles and the most ultimate causes that we are searching, clearly they must belong to something in virtue of its own nature. Hence if these principles were investigated by those also who investigated the elements of existing things, the elements must be elements of Being not incidentally, but *qua* Being. Therefore it is of Being *qua* Being that we too must grasp the first causes.

II. The term "being" is used in various senses, but with reference to one central idea and one definite characteristic, and not as merely a common epithet. Thus as the term "healthy" always relates to health (either as preserving it or as producing it or as indicating it or as receptive of it), and as "medical" relates to the art of medicine (either as possessing it or as naturally adapted for it or as being a function of medicine)—and we shall find other terms used similarly to these—so "being" is used in various senses, but always with reference to one principle. For some things are said to "be" because they are substances; others because they are modifications of substance; other because they are a process towards substance, or destructions

or privations or qualities of substance, or productive or generative of substance or of terms relating to substance, or negations of certain of these terms or of substance. (Hence we even say that not-being *is* not-being.) And so, just as there is one science of all healthy things, so it is true of everything else. For it is not only in the case of terms which express one common notion that the investigation belongs to one science, but also in the case of terms which relate to one particular characteristic, for the latter too, in a sense, express one common notion. Clearly then the study of things which *are, qua* being, also belongs to one science. Now in every case knowledge is principally concerned with that which is primary, *i.e.* that upon which all other things depend, and from which they get their names. If, then, substance is this primary thing, it is of substances that the philosopher must grasp the first principles and causes.

Now of every single class of things, as there is one perception, so there is one science: *e.g.,* grammar, which is one science, studies all articulate sounds. Hence the study of all the species of Being *qua* Being belongs to a science which is generically one, and the study of the several species of Being belongs to the specific parts of that science.

Now if Being and Unity are the same, *i.e.* a single nature, in the sense that they are associated as principle and cause are, and not as being denoted by the same definition (although it makes no difference but rather helps our argument if we understand them in the same sense), since "one man" and "man" and "existent man" and "man" are the same thing, *i.e.* the duplication in the statement "he is a man and an *existent* man" gives no fresh meaning (clearly the concepts of humanity and existence are not dissociated in respect of either coming to be or ceasing to be), and similarly in the case of the term "one," so that obviously the additional term in these phrases has the same significance, and Unity is nothing distinct from Being; and further if the substance of each thing is one in no accidental sense, and similarly is of its very nature something which *is*—then there are just as many species of Being as of Unity. And to study the essence of these species (I mean, *e.g.* the study of Same and Other and all the other similar concepts—roughly speaking all the "contraries" are reducible to this first principle; but we may consider that they have been sufficiently studied in the "Selection of Contraries") is the province of a science which is generally one.

And there are just as many divisions of philosophy as there are kinds of substance, so that there must be among them a First Philosophy and one which follows upon it. For Being and Unity at once entail genera, and so the sciences will correspond to these genera. The term "philosopher" is like the term "mathematician" in its uses; for mathematics too has divisions,—there is a primary and a secondary science, and others successively, in the realm of mathematics.

Now since it is the province of one science to study opposites, and the opposite of unity is plurality, and it is the province of one science to study the negation and privation of Unity, because in both cases we are studying Unity, to which the negation (or privation) refers, stated either in the simple form that Unity is not present, or in the form that it is not present in a particular class; in the latter case Unity is modified by the differentia, apart from the content of the negation (for the negation of Unity is its absence); but in privation there is a substrate of which the privation is predicated.—The opposite of Unity then, is Plurality; and so the opposites of the above-mentioned concepts—Otherness, Dissimilarity, Inequality and everything else which is derived from these or from Plurality or Unity—fall under the cognizance of the aforesaid science. And one of them is Oppositeness; for this is a form of difference, and Difference is a form of Otherness. Hence since the term "one" is used in various senses, so too will these terms be used; yet it pertains to one science to take cognizance of them all. For terms fall under different sciences, not if they are used in various senses, but if their definitions are neither identical nor referable to a common notion. And since everything is referred to that which is primary, *e.g.* all things which are called "one" are referred to the primary "One," we must admit that this is also true of Identity and Otherness and the Contraries. Thus we must first distinguish all the senses in which each term is used, and then attribute them to the primary in the case of each predicate, and see how they are related to it; for some will derive their name from possessing and others from producing it, and others for similar reasons.

Thus clearly it pertains to one science to give an account both of these concepts and of substance (this was one of the questions raised in the "Difficulties"), and it is the function of the philosopher to be able to study all subjects. If this is not so, who is it who will investigate whether "Socrates" and "Socrates seated" are the same thing; or whether one thing has one contrary, or what the contrary is, or how many meanings it has? and similarly with all other such questions. Thus since these are the essential modifications of Unity *qua* Unity and of Being *qua* Being, and not *qua* numbers or lines or fire, clearly it pertains to that science to discover both the essence and the attributes of these concepts. And those who investigate them err, not in being unphilosophical, but because the sub- stance, of which they have no real knowledge, is prior. For just as number *qua* number has its peculiar modification, *e.g.* oddness and evenness, commensurable and equality, excess and defect, and these things are inherent in numbers both considered independently and in relation to other numbers; and as similarly other peculiar modifications are inherent in the solid and the immovable and the moving and the weightless and that which has weight; so Being *qua* Being has certain peculiar modifications, and it is about these that it is the philosopher's function to discover the truth. And here is evidence of this fact. Dialecticians and sophists wear the same appearance as the philosopher, for sophistry is Wisdom in appearance only, and dialecticians discuss all subjects, and Being is a subject common to them all; but clearly they discuss these concepts because they appertain to philosophy. For sophistry and dialectic are concerned with the same class as subjects as philosophy, but philosophy differs from the former in the nature of its capability and from the latter in its outlook on life. Dialectic treats as an exercise what philosophy tries to understand, and sophistry seems to be philosophy, but is not.

Further, the second column of contraries is privative, and everything is reducible to Being and Not-being, and Unity and Plurality; *e.g.*Rest falls under Unity and Motion under Plurality. And nearly every-

one agrees that substance and existing things are composed of contraries; at any rate all speak of the first principles as contraries— some as Odd and Even, some as Hot and Cold, some as Limit and Unlimited, some as Love and Strife. And it is apparent that all other things also are reducible to Unity and Plurality (we may assume this reduction); and the principles adduced by other thinkers fall entirely under these as genera. It is clear, then, from these considerations also, that it pertains to a single science to study Being *qua* Being; for all things are either contraries or derived from contraries, and the first principles of the contraries are Unity and Plurality. And these belong to one science, whether they have reference to one common notion or not. Probably the truth is that they have not; but nevertheless even if the term "one" is used in various senses, the others will be related to the primary sense (and similarly with the contraries)—even if Being or Unity is not a universal and the same in all cases, or is not separable from particulars (as it presumably is not; the unity is in some cases one of reference and in others one of succession). For this very reason it is not the function of the geometrician to inquire what is Contrariety or Completeness or Being or Unity or Identity or Otherness, but to proceed from the assumption of them.

Clearly, then, it pertains to one science to study Being *qua* Being, and the attributes inherent in it *qua* Being, and the same science investigates, besides the concepts mentioned above, Priority and Posteriority, Genus and Species, Whole and Part, and all other such concepts.

III. We must pronounce whether it pertains to the same science to study both the so-called axioms in mathematics and substance, or in different sciences. It is obvious that the investigation of these axioms too pertains to one science, namely the science of the philosopher; for they apply to all existing things, and not to a particular class separate and distinct from the rest. Moreover all thinkers employ them—because they are axioms of Being *qua* Being, and every genus possesses Being—but employ them only in so far as their purposes require, *i.e.*, so far as the genus extends about which they are carrying out their proofs. Hence since the axioms apply to all things *qua* Being (for this is what is common to them), it is the function of him who studies Being *qua* Being to investigate them as well. For this reason no one who is pursuing a particular inquiry— neither a geometrician nor an arithmetician—attempts to state whether they are true or false; but some of the physicists did so, quite naturally, for they alone professed to investigate nature as a whole, and Being. But inasmuch as there is a more ultimate type of thinker than the natural philosopher (for nature is only a genus of Being), the investigation of these axioms too will belong to the universal thinker who studies the primary reality. Natural philosophy is a kind of Wisdom, but not the primary kind. As for the attempts of some of those who discuss how the truth should be received, they are due to lack of training in logic; for they should understand these things before they approach their task, and not investigate while they are still learning. Clearly then it is the function of the philosopher, *i.e.* the student of the whole of reality in its essential nature, to investigate also the principles of syllogistic reasoning. And it is proper for him who best understands each class of subject to be able to state

the most certain principles of that subject; so that he who understands the modes of Being *qua* Being should be able to state the most certain principles of all things. Now this person is the philosopher, and the most certain principle of all is that about which one cannot be mistaken; for such a principle must be both the most familiar (for it is about the unfamiliar that errors are always made), and not based on hypotheses. For the principle which the student of any form of Being must grasp is no hypothesis; and that which a man must know if he knows anything he must bring with him to this task.

Clearly, then, it is a principle of this kind that is the most certain of all principles. Let us next state *what* this principle is. "It is impossible for the same attribute at once to belong and not to belong to the same thing and in the same relation"; and we must add any further qualifications that may be necessary to meet logical objections. This is the most certain of all principles, since it possesses the required definition; for it is impossible for anyone to suppose that the same thing is and is not, as some imagine that Heraclitus says—for what a man says does not necessarily represent what he believes. And if it is impossible for contrary attributes to belong at the same time to the same subject (the usual qualifications must be added to this premise also), and an opinion which contradicts another is contrary to it, then clearly it is impossible for the same men to suppose at the same time that the same thing is and is not; for the man who made this error would entertain two contrary opinions at the same time. Hence all men who are demonstrating anything refer back to this as an ultimate belief; for it is by nature the starting-point of all the other axioms as well.

IV. There are some, however, as we have said, who both state themselves that the same thing can be and not be, and say that it is possible to hold this view. Many even of the physicists adopt this theory. But we have just assumed that it is impossible at once to be and not to be, and by this means we have proved that this is the most certain of all principles. Some, indeed, demand to have the law proved, but this is because they lack education; for it shows lack of education not to know of what we should require proof, and of what we should not. For it is quite impossible that everything should have a proof: the process would go on to infinity, so that even so there would be no proof. If on the other hand there are some things of which no proof need be sought, they cannot say what principle they think to be more self-evident. Even in the case of this law, however, we can demonstrate the impossibility by refutation, if only our opponent makes some statement. If he makes none, it is absurd to seek for an argument against one who has no arguments of his own about any thing, in so far as he has none; for such a person, in so far as he is such, is really no better than a vegetable. And I say that proof by refutation differs from simple proof in that he who attempts to prove might seem to beg the fundamental question, whereas if the discussion is provoked thus by someone else, refutation and not proof will result. The starting-point for all such discussions is not the claim that he should state that something is or is not so (because this might be supposed to be a begging of the question), but that he should say something significant both to himself and to another (this is essential if any argument is to follow; for otherwise such a person cannot reason either with himself or with another); and if this is granted, demon-stration will be possible, for there will be something already defined. But the person responsible is not he who demonstrates but he who acquiesces; for though he disowns reason he acquiesces to reason. Moreover, he who makes such an admission as this has admitted the truth of something apart from demonstration (so that not everything will be "so and that so").

Thus in the first place it is obvious that this at any rate is true: that the term "to be" or "not to be" has a definite meaning; so that not everything can be "so and not so." Again, if "man" has one meaning, let this be "two-footed animal." By "has one meaning" I mean this: if X means "man," then if any-thing is a man, its humanity will consist in being X. And it makes no difference even if it be said that "man" has several meanings, provided that they are limited in number; for one could assign a different name to each formula. For instance, it might be said that "man" has not one meaning but several, one of which has the formula "two-footed ani-mal," and there might be many other formu-lae as well, if they were limited in number; for a particular name could be assigned to each formula. If on the other hand it be said that "man" has an infinite number of mean-ings, obviously there can be no discourse, for not to have one meaning is to have no meaning, and if words have no meaning there is an end of discourse with others, and even, strictly speaking, with oneself; be-cause it is impossible to think of anything if we do not think of one thing, and even if this were possible, one name might be assigned to that of which we think.

13 Aristotle The Absolute Priority of Actuality (from *Metaphysics*, Bk. VII

I. The term "being" has several senses, which we have classified in our discussion of the number of senses in which terms are used. It denotes first the *"what"* of a thing, *i.e.* the individuality; and then the quality or quantity or any other such category. Now of all these senses which "being" has, the primary sense is clearly the "what," which denotes the *substance* (because when we describe the quality of a particular thing we say that it is "good" or "bad," and not "five feet high" or " a man", but when we describe *what* it is, we say not that it is "white" or "hot" or "five feet high," but that it is "a man" or "a god"), and all other things are said to "be" because they are either quantities or qualities or affections or some other such thing.

Hence one might raise the question whether the terms "to walk" and "to be well" and "to sit" signify each of these things as "being," or not; and similarly in the case of any other such terms, for not one of them by nature has an independent existence or can be separated from its substance. Rather, if anything it is the *thing* which walks or sits or is well that is existent. The reason why these things are more truly existent is because their subject is something definite, *i.e.* the substance and the individual, which is clearly implied in a designation of this kind, since apart from it we cannot speak of "the good" or "the sitting". Clearly then it is by reason of the substance that each of the things

referred to exists. Hence that which *is* primarily, not in a qualified sense but absolutely, will be substance.

Now "primary" has several meanings; but nevertheless substance is primary in all senses, both in definition and in knowledge and in time. For none of the other categories can exist separately, but substance alone; and it is primary also in definition, because in the formula of each thing the formula of substance must be inherent; and we assume that we know each particular thing most truly when we know *what* "man" or "fire" is— rather than its quality or quantity or position; because we know each of these points too when we know *what* the quantity or quality is. Indeed, the question which was raised long ago, is still and always will be, and which always baffles us—"What is Being?"—is in other words "What is substance?" Some say that it is one; others, more than one; some, finite; others infinite. And so for us too our chief and primary and practically our only concern is to investigate the nature of "being" in the sense of substance.

VI. Since we have now dealt with the kind of potency which is related to motion, let us now discuss actuality; what it is, and what its qualities are. For as we continue our analysis it will also become clear with regard to the potential that we apply the name not only to that whose nature it is to move or be moved by something else, either without qualification or in some definite way, but also in other senses; and it is on this account that in the course of our inquiry we have discussed these as well.

"Actuality" means the presence of the thing, not in the sense which we mean by "potentially." We say that a thing is present potentially as Hermes is present in the wood, or the half-line in the whole, because it can be separated from it; and as we call even a man who is not studying "a scholar" if he is capable of studying. That which is present in the opposite sense to this is present actually. What we mean can be plainly seen in the particular cases in induction; we need not seek a definition for every term, but must comprehend the analogy; that as that which is actually building is to that which is capable of building, so is that which is awake to that which is asleep; and that which is seeing to that which has the eyes shut, but has the power of sight; and that which is differentiated out of matter to the matter; and the finished article to the raw material. Let actuality be defined by one member of this antithesis, and the potential by the other.

But things are not all said to exist actually in the same sense, but only by analogy—as A is in B or to B, so is C in or to D; for the relation is either that of motion to potentiality, or that of substance to some particular matter.

Infinity and void and other concepts of this kind are said to "be" potentially or actually in a different sense from the majority of existing things, *e.g.* that which sees, or walks, or is seen. For in these latter cases the predication may sometimes be truly made without qualification, since "that which is seen" is so called sometimes because it is seen and sometimes because it is capable of being seen; but the Infinite does not exist potentially in the sense that it will ever exist separately in actuality; it is separable only in knowledge. For the fact that the process of division never ceases makes this actuality exist potentially, but not separately.

Since no action which has a limit is an end, but only a means to the end, as *e.g.*, the process of thinning, and since the parts of the body themselves, when one is thinning them, are in motion in the sense that they are not already that which it is the object of the motion to make them, this process is not an action, or at least not a complete one, since it is not an end; it is the process which includes the end that is an action. *E.g.* at the same time we see and have seen, understand and have understood, think and have thought; but we cannot at the same time learn and have learnt, or become healthy and be healthy. We are living well and have lived well, we are happy and have been happy, at the same time; otherwise the process would have to cease at some time, like the thinning-process; but it has not ceased at the present moment; we both are living and have lived.

Now of these processes we should call the one type motions, and the other actualizations. Every motion is incomplete—the process of thinning, learning, walking, building—these are motions, and incomplete at that. For it is not the same thing which at the same time is walking and has walked, or is building and has built, or is becoming and has become, or is being moved and has been moved, but two different things: and that which is causing motion is different from that which has caused motion. But the same thing at the same time is seeing and has seen, is thinking and has thought. The latter kind of process, then, is what I mean by actualization, and the former what I mean by motion.

What the actual is, then, and what it is like, may be regarded as demonstrated from these and similar consideration.

VII. We must, however, distinguish when a particular thing exists potentially, and when it does not; for it does not so exist at any and every time. *E.g.*, is earth potentially a man? No, but rather when it has already become semen, and perhaps not even then; just as not *everything* can be healed by medicine, or even by chance, but there is some definite kind of thing which is capable of it, and this is that which is potentially healthy.

The definition of that which as a result of thought comes, from existing potentially, to exist actually, is that, when it has been willed, if no external influence hinders it, it comes to pass; and the condition in the case of the patient, *i.e.* in the person who is being healed, is that nothing in him should hinder the process. Similarly a house exists potentially if there is nothing in X, the matter, to prevent it from becoming a house, *i.e.* if there is nothing which must be added or removed or changed; then X is potentially a house; and similarly in all other cases where the generative principle is contained in the thing itself, one thing is potentially another when, if nothing external hinders, it will of itself become the other. *E.g.* the semen is not yet potentially a man; for it must further undergo a change in some other medium. But when, by its own generative principle, it has already come to have the necessary attributes, in this state it is now potentially a man, whereas in the former state it has need of another principle; just as earth is not yet potentially a statue, because it must undergo a change before it becomes bronze.

It seems that what we are describing is not a particular thing, but a definite material; *e.g.,* a box is not wood, but wooden material, and wood is not earth, but earthen material; and earth also is an illustration of our point if it is similarly not some other thing, but a definite material—it is always the latter term in this series which is, in the fullest sense, potentially something else. *E.g.,* a box is not earth, nor earthen, but wooden; for it is this that is potentially a box, and this is the matter of the box—that is, wooden material in general is the matter of "box" in general, whereas the matter of a particular box is a particular piece of wood.

If there is some primary stuff, which is not further called the material of some other thing, this is primary matter. *E.g.,* if earth is "made of air," and air is not fire, but "made of fire," then fire is primary matter, not being an individual thing. For the subject or substratum is distinguishable into two kinds by either being or not being an individual thing. Take for example as the subject of the attributes "man," or "body" or "soul," and as an attribute "cultured" or "white." Now the subject, when culture is induced in it, is called not "culture" but "cultured," and the man is called not whiteness but white; nor is he called "ambulation" or "motion," but "walking" or "moving"; just as we said that things are of a definite material. Thus where "subject" has this sense, the ultimate substratum is substance; but where it has not this sense, and the predicate is a form or individuality, the ultimate substratum is matter or material substance. It is quite proper that both matter and attributes should be described by a derivative predicate, since they are both indefinite.

Thus it has now been stated when a thing should be said to exist potentially, and when it should not.

VIII. Now since we have distinguished the several senses of priority, it is obvious that actuality is prior to potentiality. By potentiality I mean not that which we have defined as a principle of change which is in something other than the thing changed, or in that same thing *qua* other," but in general any principle of motion or of rest; for nature also is in the same genus as potentiality, because it is a principle of motion, although not in some other thing, but in the thing itself *qua* itself. To every potentiality of this kind actuality is prior, both in formula and in substance; in time it is sometimes prior and sometimes not.

That actuality is prior in formula is evident; for it is because it can be actualized that the potential, in the primary sense, is potential. I mean, *e.g.*, that the potentially constructive is that which can construct, the potentially seeing that which can see, and the potentially visible that which can be seen. The same principle holds in all other cases too, so that the formula and knowledge of the actual must precede the knowledge of the potential.

In time it is prior in this sense; the actual is prior to the potential with which it is formally identical, but not to that with which it is identical numerically. What I mean is this: that the matter and the seed and the thing which is capable of seeing, which are potentially a man and corn and seeing, but are not yet so actually, are prior in time to the individual man and corn and seeing subject which already exist in actuality. But prior in time to these potential entities are other actual entities from which the former are generated; for the actually existent is always generated from the potentially existent *by* something which is actually existen—*e.g.*, man by man, cultured by cultured—there is always some prime mover; and that which initiates motion exists already in actuality.

We have said in our discussion of sub-stance that everything which is generated is generated from something and by something; and by something formally identical with itself. Hence it seems impossible that a man can be a builder if he has never built, or a harpist if he has never played a harp; because he who learns to play the harp learns by playing it, and similarly in all other cases. This was the origin of the sophists' quibble that a man who does not know a given science will be doing that which is the object of that science, because the learner does not know the science. But since something of that which is being generated is already generated, and something of that which is being moved as a whole is already moved (this is demonstrated in our discussion on Motion), presumably the learner too must possess something of the science. At any rate from this argument it is clear that actuality is prior to potentiality in this sense too, *i.e.* in respect of generation and time.

But it is also prior in substantiality; (a) because things which are posterior in generation are prior in form and substantiality; *e.g.* adult is prior to child, and man to semen, because the one already possesses the form, but the other does not, and (b) because everything which is generated moves toward a principle, *i.e.* its *end*. For the object of a thing is its principle; and generation has as its object the *end*. And the actuality is the end, and it is for the sake of this that the potentiality is acquired; for animals do not see in order that they may have sight, but have sight in order that they may see. Similarly men possess the art of building in order that they may build, and the power of speculation that they may speculate; they do not speculate in order that they may have the power of speculation—except those who are learning by practice; and they do not really speculate, but only in a limited sense, or about a subject about which they have no desire to speculate.

Further, matter exists potentially, because it may attain to the form; but when it exists actually, it is then *in* the form. The same applies in all other cases, including those where the end is motion. Hence just as teachers think that they have achieved their end when they have exhibited their pupil performing, so it is with nature. For if this is not so, it will be another case of "Pauson's Hermes"; it will be impossible to say whether the knowledge is *in* the pupil or outside him, as in the case of the Hermes. For the activity is the end, and the actuality is the activity; hence the term "actuality" is derived from "activity," and tends to have the meaning of "complete reality."

Now whereas in some cases the ultimate thing is the use of the faculty, as *e.g.,* in the case of sight seeing is the ultimate thing, and sight produces nothing else besides this; but in other cases something is produced, *e.g.* the art of building produces not only the act of building but a house; nevertheless in the one case the use of the faculty is the end, and in the other it is more truly the end than is the potentiality. For the act of building resides in the thing built; *i.e.,* it comes to be and exists simultaneously with the house.

Thus in all cases where the result is something other than the exercise of the faculty, the actuality resides in the thing produced; *e.g.* the act of building in the thing built, the act of weaving in the thing woven, and so on; and in general the motion resides in the thing moved. But where there is no other result besides the actualization, the actualization resides in the subject; *e.g.* see-

ing in the seer, and speculation in the speculator, and life in the soul (and hence also happiness, since happiness is a particular kind of life). Evidently, therefore, substance or form is actuality. Thus it is obvious by this argument that actuality is prior in substantiality to potentiality; and that in point of time, as we have said, one actuality presupposes another right back to that of the prime mover in each case.

It is also prior in a deeper sense; because that which is eternal is prior in substantiality to that which is perishable, and nothing eternal is potential. The argument is as follows: Every potentiality is at the same time a potentiality for the opposite. For whereas that which is incapable of happening cannot happen to anything, everything which is capable may fail to be actualized. Therefore that which is capable of being may both be and not be. Therefore the same thing is capable both of being and of not being. But that which is capable of not being may possibly not be; and that which may possibly not be is perishable; either absolutely, or in the particular sense in which it is said that it may possibly not be; that is, in respect either of place or of quantity or of quality. "Absolutely" means in respect of substance. Hence nothing which is absolutely imperishable is absolutely potential (although there is no reason why it should not be potential in some particular respect; *e.g.* of quality or place); therefore all imperishable things are actual. Nor can anything which is of necessity be potential; and yet these things are primary, for if they did not exist, nothing would exist. Nor can motion be potential, if there is any eternal motion. Nor, if there is anything eternally in motion, is it potentially in motion (except in respect of some starting-point or destination), and there is no reason why the matter of such a thing should not exist. Hence the sun and stars and whole visible heaven are always active, and there is no fear that they will ever stop—a fear which the writers on physics entertain. Nor do the heavenly bodies tire in their activity; for motion does not imply for them, as it does for perishable things, the potentiality for the opposite, which makes the continuity of the motion distressing; this results when the substance is matter and potentiality, not actuality.

Imperishable things are resembled in this respect by things which are always undergoing transformation, such as earth and fire; for latter too are always active, since they have their motion independently and in themselves. Other potentialities, according to the distinctions already made, all admit of the opposite result; for that which is capable of causing motion in a certain way can also cause it not in that way; that is if it acts rationally. The same irrational potentialities can only produce opposite results by their presence or absence.

Thus if there are any entities or substances such as the dialecticians describe the Ideas to be, there must be something which has much more knowledge than absolute knowledge, and much more mobility than motion; for these will be in a truer sense actualities, whereas knowledge and motion will be their potentialities. Thus it is obvious that actuality is prior both to potentiality and to every principle of change.

IX. That a good actuality is both better and more estimable than a good potentiality will be obvious from the following argu- ment. Everything of which we speak as capable is alike capable of contrary results; *e.g.,* that which we call capable of being well is alike capable of being ill, and has both potentialities at once; for the same potentiality admits of health and disease, or of rest and motion, or of building and of pulling down, or of being built and of falling down. Thus the capacity for two contraries can belong to a thing at the same time, but the contraries cannot belong at the same time, *i.e.,* the actualities, *e.g.* health and disease, cannot belong to a thing at the same time. Therefore one of them must be the good; but the potentiality may equally well be both or neither. Therefore the actuality is better.

14 Anselm
The Ontological
Argument
(from *Proslogium*)

Chapter 1

Teach me to seek thee, and reveal thyself to me, when I seek thee, for I cannot seek thee, expect thou teach me, nor find thee, except thou reveal thyself. Let me seek thee in longing, let me long for thee in seeking; let me find thee in love, and love thee in finding. Lord, I acknowledge and I thank thee that thou hast created me in this thine image, in

Proslogium, Chapters I through V, reprinted from *St. Anselm: Basic Writings,* translated by S.N. Deane, 2nd Ed., by permission of Open Court Publishing Company, LaSalle, Illinois.

order that I may be mindful of thee, may conceive of thee, and love thee; but that image has been so consumed and wasted away by vices, and obscured by the smoke of wrong-doing, that it cannot achieve that for which it was made, except thou renew it, and create it anew. I do not endeavor, O Lord, to penetrate thy sublimity, for in no wise do I compare my understanding with that; but I long to understand in some degree thy truth, which my heart believes and loves. For I do not seek to understand that I may believe, but I believe in order to understand. For this also I believe,—that unless I believed, I should not understand.

Chapter II

Truly there is a God, although the fool hath said in his heart, There is no God.

And so, Lord, do thou, who dost give understanding to faith, give me, so far as thou knowest it to be profitable, to understand that thou art as we believe; and that thou art that which we believe. And, indeed, we believe that thou art a being than which nothing greater can be conceived. Or is there no such nature, since the fool hath said in his heart, there is no God? (Psalms xiv.1). But, at any rate, this very fool, when he hears of this being of which I speak—a being than which nothing greater can be conceived—understands what he hears, and what he understands is in his understanding; although he does not understand it to exist.

For, it is one thing for an object to be in the understanding, and another to understand that the object exists. When a painter first conceives of what he will afterwards perform, he has it in his understanding, but he does not yet understand it to be, because he has not yet performed it. But after he has made the painting, he both has it in his understanding, and he understands that it exists, because he has made it.

Hence, even the fool is convinced that something exists in the understanding, at least, than which nothing greater can be conceived. For, when he hears of this, he understands it. And whatever is understood, exists in the understanding. And assuredly that, than which nothing greater can be conceived, cannot exist in the understanding alone. For, suppose it exists in the understanding alone: then it can be conceived to exist in reality; which is greater.

Therefore, if that, than which nothing greater can be conceived, exists in the understanding alone, the very being, than which nothing greater can be conceived, is one, than which a greater can be conceived. But obviously this is impossible. Hence, there is no doubt that there exists a being, than which nothing greater can be conceived, and it exists both in the understanding and in reality.

Chapter II

God cannot be conceived not to exist.— God is that, than which nothing greater can be conceived.—That which can be conceived not to exist is not God.

And it assuredly exists so truly, that it cannot be conceived not to exist. For, it is possible to conceive of a being which cannot be conceived not to exist; and this is greater than one which can be conceived not to exist. Hence, if that, than which nothing greater can be conceived, can be conceived not to exist, it is not that, than which nothing greater can be conceived. But this is an irreconcilable contradiction. There is, then, so truly a being than which nothing greater can be conceived to exist, that it cannot even be conceived not to exist; and this being thou art, O Lord, our God.

So truly, therefore, dost thou exist, O Lord, my God, that thou canst not be conceived not to exist; and rightly. For, if a mind could conceive of a being better than thee, the creature would rise above the Creator; and this is most absurd. And, indeed, whatever else there is, except thee alone, can be conceived not to exist. To thee alone, therefore, it belongs to exist more truly than all other beings, and hence in a higher degree than all others. For, whatever else exists does not exist so truly, and hence in a less degree it belongs to it to exist. Why, then, has the fool said in his heart, there is no God (Psalms xiv.1), since it is so evident, to a rational mind, that thou dost exist in the highest degree of all? Why, except that he is dull and a fool?

Chapter IV.

How the fool has said in his heart what cannot be conceived.—A thing may be conceived in two ways: (1) when the word signifying it is conceived; (2) when the thing itself is understood. As far as the word goes, God can be conceived not to exist; in reality he cannot.

But how has the fool said in his heart what he could not conceive; or how is it that he could not conceive what he said in his heart? since it is the same to say in the heart, and to conceive.

But, if really, nay, since really, he both conceived, because he said in his heart; and did not say in his heart, because he could not conceive; there is more than one way in which a thing is said in the heart or conceived. For, in one sense, an object is conceived, when the word signifying it is conceived; and in another, when the very entity, which the object is, is understood.

In the former sense, then, God can be conceived not to exist; but in the latter, not at all. For no one who understands what fire and water are can conceive fire to be water, in accordance with the nature of the facts themselves, although this is possible according to the words. So, then, no one who understands what God is can conceive that God does not exist; although he says these words in his heart, either without any, or with some foreign, signification. For, God is that than which a greater cannot be conceived. And he who thoroughly understands this, assuredly understands that this being so truly exists, that not even in concept can it be non-existent. Therefore, he who understands that God so exists, cannot conceive that he does not exist.

I thank thee, gracious Lord, I thank thee; because what I formerly believed by thy bounty, I now so understand by thine illumination, that if I were unwilling to believe that thou does exist, I should not be able not to understand this to be true.

Chapter V.

God is whatever it is better to be than not to be; and he, as the only self-existent being, creates all things from nothing.

What art thou, then, Lord God, than whom nothing greater can be conceived? But what art thou, except that which, as the highest of all beings, alone exists through itself, and creates all other things from nothing? For, whatever is not this is less than a thing which can be conceived of. But this cannot be conceived of thee. What good, therefore, does the supreme Good lack, through which every good is? Therefore, thou art just, truthful, blessed, and whatever it is better to be than not to be. For it is better to be just than not just; better to be blessed than not blessed.

15 Thomas Aquinas
The Objects
of Speculation

It must be said that the theoretical or speculative intellect is distinguished properly from the operative or practical intellect in this: the speculative intellect has for its end the truth which it considers, whereas the practical intellect orders the truth reflected upon to an operation as to its end. For this reason the Philosopher says in the third book of *The Soul* that the speculative and the practical intellect differ from each other in

their end, and in the second book of the *Metaphysics* it is said that the end of speculative science is truth, whereas the end of operative science is action. Naturally the subject-matter must be congruent with the end; consequently the subject-matter of the practical sciences must be those things which can be made or done by our work, so that knowledge of them can be ordered to operation as to an end. But the subject-matter of the speculative sciences must be things that are not made by our own work. Therefore the contemplation of such things cannot be ordered to operation as to an end. And it is according to differentiations found within this order of things that the speculative sciences have to be distinguished.

There are certain objects of speculative knowledge which depend upon matter existentially because they cannot exist except in matter. These are distinguished as follows. Some of them depend upon matter both for their being and their being known, such as things in whose definition sensible matter is included, so that they cannot be understood without such matter. In the definition of man, for example, it is necessary to include flesh and bones. It is of such things that physics or natural science treats. But certain other things, although dependent upon matter for their existence, do not so depend for their being known, because in definitions of them sensible matter is not included. Such is the case with lines and number. And of such things mathematics treats. There are still other objects of speculative knowledge, however, which do not depend on matter for existence because they can exist without matter: either they are never found in matter, as God and the angels, or they are in some cases in matter and in other cases not, as substance, quality, being, potency, act, one and many, and things of this sort. The science that treats of all such things is (natural) theology, that is, divine science, its pre-eminent object being God. By another name this science is called metaphysics, that is to say, trans-physics, because it is properly to be learned by us after physics (or natural philosophy), for it is from sensible things that we must take our point of departure in order to arrive at the knowledge of non-sensible things. This science is also called first philosophy, inasmuch as all the other sciences, receiving their principles from it, follow after it. Now, it is impossible that there should be things which depend upon matter for their being known but not for their existence. For the intellect, considered in itself, is immaterial. Consequently there is no fourth generic division of philosophy in addition to the aforenamed three.

16   Thomas Aquinas
The Order of the Sciences

Although divine science is the first of all sciences, nevertheless for us other sciences are naturally prior. For, as Avicenna says in the beginning of his *Metaphysics,* the position of this science is such that it is learned after the natural sciences, in which many things are established which this divine sci-

ence makes use of: generation, for example, corruption, motion, and the like. So, too, it is learned after mathematics. Thus, for theology to acquire knowledge of separated substances, number and the order of the celestial bodies must be known, and knowledge of these things is not possible without astrology, a science to which, in turn, the whole of mathematics is prerequisite. Indeed other sciences—music and ethics, for example—contribute to the full development of divine science. Nor, because the same science (natural theology or metaphysics) which supposes those things that are proved in other sciences is the very science that proves the latter's principles, is there a vicious circle here. For the principles which another science, namely, natural philosophy, receives from first philosophy do not prove those things which the first philosopher appropriates from the natural philosopher. On the contrary, such things are proved by different, self-evident, principles. It is because the first philosopher does not prove the principles which he passes on to the natural philosopher by principles he receives from the latter, but by other self-evident principles, that there is no vicious circle in the first philosopher's definitions. Moreover, the sensible effects from which demonstrations in natural science or philosophy proceed are more known to us at first. But when through them we have arrived at a knowledge of first causes, from these latter there will be evident to us the essential explanatory cause *(propter quid)* of those effects, proceeding from which, by way of demonstration of the fact *(demonstratio quia)*, the existence of the first causes was established. In this way natural science contributes something to divine science, and yet it is through divine science that the principles of natural science are made known. And for this reason does Boethius place divine science last: it is the ultimate science in the order of human knowing.

17 Thomas Aquinas The Excellence of Metaphysics

As the Philosopher teaches in the *Politics,* when a number of things are ordered to a single thing, one of that number must be regulative or directive, and the others regulated or directed. This indeed is evident in the case of the union of the soul and the body, for the soul naturally commands and the body obeys. So too, within the powers of the soul, the irascible and the concupiscible, by a natural ordering, are governed by the reason. Indeed, all sciences and arts are ordained to one thing, namely, the perfection of man, which is his beatitude. Hence, among them that one must be the mistress of all others which rightly lays claim to the title of wisdom. For it is the office of the wise to order others.

What this science is and what it treats of can be ascertained if one carefully considers how a person is qualified to rule. Now, as the Philosopher says in the work alluded to, just as men powerful in intellect are naturally the rulers and masters of others—whereas men physically robust yet deficient in intellect are naturally servile—, so, that science is by right naturally mistress of the others which is in the highest degree intellectual. This science, however, is the one that treats of the most intelligible things.

The latter we can regard in three ways: firstly, from the standpoint of the order of knowing, for those things that are the source of the intellect's attainment of certitude seem to be the more intelligible ones. Thus, since it is from causes that the intellect achieves the certitude of science, the cognition of causes apparently is in the highest degree intellectual. Consequently that science which considers first causes evidently is regulative of the other sciences.

Secondly, the supremely intelligible objects can be considered from the point of view of the intellect's relation to sense knowledge. For, although the latter is the cognition of particulars, intellect seems to differ from it in this, that intellect comprehends universals. Thus, the science which is maximally intellectual is the one which treats of those things (or principles) that follow upon being, as one and many, potency and act. Such principles, however, ought not to remain completely indeterminate, since without them full cognition of things proper to a given genus or species cannot be had. Moreover, since each genus of beings needs these principles for the very knowledge of itself, they would with equal justification be treated in any particular science at all. It follows that principles of this kind are not to be dealt with in any one *particular* science. Therefore the task of dealing with such principles devolves upon that single common science which, being in the highest degree intellectual, is regulative of the other sciences.

Thirdly, the supremely intelligible objects of which we speak can be considered from the standpoint of the intellect's own cognition. Thus, since every thing has intellective power in consequence of its freedom from matter, those things must be pre-eminently intelligible which exist in complete separation from matter. The intelligible object and the intellect must be proportioned to each other, and must be of one genus, since the intellect and the intelligible are in act one. Now, those things are in the highest degree separated from matter which abstract not only from signate matter, "as do natural forms taken universally, of which natural science treats," but which abstract altogether from sensible matter—and not only according to reason, as mathematical objects do, but also in respect to actual existence, as with God and the intelligences. Evidently, therefore, the science that considers these things is supremely intellectual and the chief or mistress of the others.

Therefore, in accordance with the aforesaid three things from which the perfection of this science is derived, it receives three names: "divine science" or "theology" inasmuch as it considers the substances in question, "metaphysics" inasmuch as it considers being and the things that follow upon it— for these transphysical principles are discovered in the process of resolution as the more common after the less common—; and "first philosophy" inasmuch as it considers the first causes of things. It is evident, then, what the subject of this science is, and how it is related to other sciences, and how it is named.

18

Thomas Aquinas
The Science of Being *qua* Being

On Being as Being

Because a science ought to investigate not only its proper subject but also the latter's essential attributes, Aristotle says that there exists a science which takes as its subject being precisely as such, and "those things which belong to being in virtue of its own nature," namely, being's essential attributes.

Aristotle here uses the expression "being in so far as it is being" because the other sciences, which treat of particular beings do indeed consider being, for all the subjects of sciences are beings, yet they do not consider being as being, but as this sort of being; for example, number, line, fire, or something of the kind.

Aristotle employs the phrase "and those things belonging to being in virtue of its own nature" not simply "those things which appertain to or exist in being," in order to point out that it is not the office of a science to consider those things that exist in its subject accidentally but only those that are present in it essentially. Thus, geometry is not concerned with the question whether a triangle is made of copper or of wood, but only with its absolute nature, according to which it has three equal angles. It does not, therefore, appertain to the science whose subject is being to consider all that exists in it accidentally, since it would then be taking into account accidents which are investigated in all sciences. For although all accidents exist in some being, not all accidents exist in a being inasmuch as it is being. Thus essential accidents of an inferior or a subordinate thing are accidental accidents in relation to the superior; for example, accidents essential to man are not essential to animal.

The necessity of this science of metaphysics, which contemplates being and its essential attributes, is manifest; such things ought not to remain unknown because it is upon them that knowledge of other things depends, for on the knowledge of common or universal things hinges the knowledge of proper or individual things.

That this science is not a particular science, Aristotle shows by the following argument. No particular science considers universal being as such, but only some part of being cut off from its other parts, and of this separated part it examines the essential attribute. The mathematical sciences, for instance, investigate a particular kind of being, namely, the quantitative, whereas the common science, metaphysics, considers universal being as being. Therefore it is not to be identified with any particular science.

No particular science treats of being as being, that is, being-in-common, nor does any particular science treat of any particular being, simply as being. For instance, arithmetic does not consider number as being, but as number. It is the office of the metaphysician, however, to consider any and every being, precisely as being.

And because it pertains to the same science to consider being as being, "and, concerning being, what it is," namely, its essence (for every thing has actual existence through its essence), so it is that the particular sciences . . . are not concerned with the problem of determining what being is—its quiddity or essence and its definition, which signifies the essence. Rather, from the essence such sciences proceed to other matters, using the presupposed essence, as if it were an already demonstrated principle, in order to prove other things.

Just as no particular science determines the essence of its subject, so none of them says regarding its subject, that it is or is not. And understandably so; for it belongs to one and the same science to settle the problem of existence and to discover the essence. . . It is proper to the philosopher, to him who studies being as being, to consider both problems. But every particular science presupposes concerning its own subject both that it is and what it is, as Aristotle states in the first book of the *Posterior Analytics*. And this shows that no particular science treats of being as such, nor of any being precisely as being.

The Meaning of Being (*ens*)

In Relation to the Act of Existing (*esse*)

That which first falls under the intellect's grasp is being (*ens*). Thus the intellect necessarily attributes being to everything it apprehends. *Being* means that-which-is, or exists (*esse habens*).

The verb *is consignifies* composition, because it does not signify this principally but secondarily. *Is* signifies primarily that which the intellect apprehends as being absolutely actual, for in the absolute sense *is* means to be in act, and thus its mode of signification is that of a verb. But, since the actuality which *is* principally signifies is universally the actuality of every form, whether substantial or accidental, when we wish to signify that any form or any act whatever actually exists in a subject, we express that fact by this verb *is*.

The word *being (ens)* is imposed from the very act of existing, as Avicenna remarks, whereas the word *thing (res)* is imposed from the essence or quiddity. *Being* properly signifies: something-existing-in-act. *Being* means that-which-has-existence-in-act. Now, this is substance, which subsists.

The act of existing *(esse)* is that by which substance is given the name of being *(ens)*. This act is the actuality of every form or nature.

What I call *esse* is among all principles the most perfect; which is evident from the fact that act is always more perfect than potentiality. Now, any designated form is understood to exist actually only in virtue of the fact that it is held to *be*. Thus, humanity or fire can be considered as existing in the potentiality of matter, or as existing in the active power of an agent, or also as existing in an intellect. But that which has *esse* is made actually existent. It is evident, therefore, that what I call *esse* is the actuality of all acts, and for this reason it is the perfection of all perfections. Nor is it to be thought that something is added to what I call *esse* which is more formal that *esse* itself, thus determining it as an act determines a potentiality. For the *esse* I speak of is essentially other than that to which it is added as a certain determining principle.

Now, nothing can be added to *esse* that is extraneous to it, since nothing is extraneous to it except nothing *(non ens)* . . . *Esse*, then, is not determined by another as a potentiality is determined by an act, but *esse* is determined as an act by a potentiality . . . And in this way is one *esse* distinguished from another *esse*, namely, according as it is the *esse* of this nature, or essence, or of that.

Esse is what is innermost in each and every thing, and what is deepest in them all, for it is formal in respect of all that is in a thing.

Esse itself is act in relation to both composite and simple natures. Composite natures are not made specifically what they are by this act, but rather by the form in them, for specification concerns a thing's essence whereas *esse* evidently pertains to the question whether a thing is. Nor are angelic substances so specified. Rather, their differentiation into species is based on those simple subsisting forms which they themselves are, and which differ specifically according to their own grade of perfection.

Taken absolutely, as including in itself every perfection of being, *esse* is superior to life and to all other subsequent perfections. . . . Yet if *esse* is considered as it is participated in any thing whatever which does not possess the total perfection of being, but has imperfect being—and this is the case with all creatures—, then clearly *esse* in union with the superadded perfection is higher. Accordingly Dionysius says that living things are better than merely existing things, and intelligent things than merely living things.

Esse, as such, is nobler than everything that follows upon it. Thus, considered absolutely and in itself, this act is nobler than the act of understanding. . . Indeed, that which excels in being(in esse) is purely and simply nobler than any thing which excels in any perfection consequent upon being. . .

In Relation to Essence

Being *(ens)* understood as signifying the entity of a thing *(entitas rei)*, is divided into the ten categories, and thus taken, being *(ens)* is convertible with thing *(res)*.

The name *essence* is taken from being expressed in the first mode (namely, as it is divided into the ten categories), not from being expressed in the second mode (namely, as it signifies the truth of propositions). For, as is clear in the case of privations, in the latter mode we call some things beings which do not have an essence . . . Because *being* said in the first mode is divided into the ten categories, *essence* must signify something common to all natures, through which diverse beings are placed in diverse genera and species. For instance, humanity is the essence of man, and so with other things.

Moreover, since that by which a thing is constituted in its proper genus and species is what is signified by the definition indicating what the thing is, philosophers have taken to using the name quiddity for the name essence. The Philosopher frequently calls this the *quod quid erat esse* that by which a thing is a *what*. It is also called form inasmuch as form signifies the complete essential determination of each thing. . . . Also, it is called nature . . . according as nature is said to be that which can be grasped by the intellect in any way; for a thing is intelligible only by its definition and essence . . .But "nature" also seems to signify the essence of the thing as ordered to its proper operation, for nothing is without its proper operation. The name quiddity, on the other hand, is derived from that which is signified by the definition, whereas essence means that through which and in which a thing has its act of existing.

19 Thomas Aquinas
The Division of Being by Potency and Act

The primary simple principles cannot be defined, for in definitions there can be no infinite regress. *Act* is such a principle. Therefore it cannot be defined. Yet, through the proportion of two things to each other, it can be seen what act is. So if we take the relation of the builder to the buildable, and of one who is awake to one asleep, and of that which sees to that which has its eyes closed while having the power of sight . . ., proportionally, from such particular examples, we can arrive at a knowledge of what act and potency are.

Now in any two things whatever, if one of them completes the other, then the relation between them is that of act to potentiality; for nothing is brought to completion, fulfilled, except by its own act. . .But it is the act of existing itself which completes, fulfills, the existing substance; each and every being is in act as a result of having the act of existing. It follows that in every one of the aforesaid substances there is a composition of act and potentiality.

Moreover, in a thing that which is derived from an agent must be act; for an agent's office is to make something actual. But it was proved earlier that all substances except the first have existence from it. In every case it is because they receive their existence from something else that caused substances themselves *are*. This very existence, then, is present in caused substances as their act. That in which an act is present is a potentiality. Indeed act as such is referred to potentiality. Hence, in every created substance there is potentiality and act.

Again. Whatever participates in something is related to that which is participated as potentiality to act. For, through that which is participated (received) the participator is actualized in such and such a manner. But it was shown previously that God alone is being in virtue of His own essence, while all other things participate in the act of existing. Every created substance, therefore, is related to its own existence as potentiality to act.

Further. It is through an act that a thing becomes like its efficient cause, for an agent produces its like so far as it is in act. But every created substance attains likeness to God through the very act of existing (*ipsum esse*), as was proved earlier. Therefore, existence itself *(ipsum esse)* has this status with respect to all created substances: it is their act. Thus, in every created substance there is composition of act and potentiality.

In every composite being there must be act and potentiality. Indeed no plurality can become one in an absolute sense unless in it something be act and something else potentiality. (Complete) entities actually existing do not form a unit, except, as it were, by way of conjunction or aggregation; and thus united they are not one in an absolute sense. But even in such wholes, the parts themselves are potential with respect to their unification, since they are unified actually after having been unified potentially. . . . Moreover, every composite, precisely as compos-

ite, is potentially dissolved, although in certain things something is present that resists dissolution. But what is dissoluble is in potentiality with respect to non-existence.

Every thing other than God has being participatively; so that in it substance (or essence), sharing the act of existence, is other than this act itself which is shared. But every participator is related to that which is participated in it as potentiality to act. Hence, the substance of every created thing whatever is to its own existence as potentiality to act. So it is that every created substance is composed of potentiality and act, or, as Boethius says, of what-it-is (*quod est*) and act of existing (*esse*).

20 Thomas Aquinas
The Real Distinction of Essence and the Act of Existence

It is clear from what has been said already that in every created thing essence is *distinct* from existence and is compared to the latter as potentiality to act. Every created being participates in the act of existing, God alone is His act of existing. The act of existing of every finite thing is participated, because no thing outside God is its own act of existing.

Whatever is participated is related to the participator as its act. . . . But participated act of existing is limited by the (receptive) capacity of the participator. Hence God alone, who is His own act of existing, is pure and infinite act. In intellectual substances, indeed, there is a composition of act and potentiality; not, however, of matter and form, but of form and participated act of existing.

Now, act of existing, as such, cannot be diverse; yet it can be diversified by something extrinsic to itself; for instance, a stone's act of existing is other than that of a man.

God's act of existing is distinguished and set apart from every other act of existing by the fact that it is self-subsistent, and does not come to a nature (or an essence) other than itself. Every other act of existing, being non-subsisting, must be individuated by the nature and substance which subsists in the act of existing. And regarding these things (namely all creatures) it is true to say that the act of existing of this one is other than the act of existing of that one, inasmuch as it belongs to another nature. So, if there were one color existing in itself, without matter, or without a subject by this very fact it would be distinguished from every other color; since colors existing in subjects are distinguished only through those subjects.

Because the quiddity of an intelligence is that very intelligence itself, its quiddity or essence is that which it itself is, and its existence, received from God, is that by which it subsists in the nature of things. Some therefore have said that substances of this kind are composed of that-by-which-they-are (the *quo est*) and that-which-they-are (the *quod est*), or of that-by-which-they-are and essence. . .

Whatever does not belong to the concept of essence or quiddity comes from without and enters into composition with the essence, for no essence can be understood without its essential parts. But every essence or quiddity can be understood without any-

thing being known of its actual existence. For example, I can understand what a man or a phoenix is and yet be ignorant whether either one exists in reality. It is evident, then, that the act of existing is other than essence or quiddity—unless, perhaps, there exists a reality whose quiddity is its very act of existing. And there can be only one such reality: the First Being. . . . In every other being, act of existing is other than quiddity, nature, or form.

The act of existing belongs to the first agent, God, through His own nature; for God's act of existing is His substance. . . . But that which belongs to something according to its own nature, appertains to other things only by participation. . . . Thus the act of existing is possessed by other things, from the First Agent, through a certain participation. But that which a thing has by participation is not its very own substance. Therefore it is impossible that the substance of anything except the first agent should be the act of existing itself.

Now, the composition of matter and form is not of the same nature as the composition of substance and act of existing, though both compositions are of potentiality and act. This is so, first of all, because matter is not the very substance of a thing. If it were, then all forms would be accidents, as the ancient Naturalists thought. Rather, matter is a part of the substance. Secondly, this is so because the act of existing itself is not the proper act of the matter, but of the whole substance. For *esse* is the act of that whereof we can say: it *is*; *esse* is not said of the matter, but of the whole. Matter, therefore, cannot be termed that-which-is. On the contrary, the substance itself is that-which-is. Thirdly, the aforesaid compositions are diverse, because the form is not the act of existing, though between the two there exists a certain order. Form is compared to the act of existing as light to the act of illuminating, for instance, or as whiteness to the act of being white. Finally, there is this consideration: existence is act even in relation to the form itself. For in things composed of matter and form, the form is said to be a principle of existing because it is what completes the substance, whose act is *esse* itself; just as the air's transparency is the principle of illumination because it makes the air a proper subject (or receiver) of light.

It is evident, therefore, that the composition of act and potentiality is more comprehensive than that of form and matter; matter and form divide natural substance, potentiality and act divide universal being. Accordingly, whatever follows upon potentiality and act, as such, is common to both material and immaterial created substances, as *to receive* and *to be received, to perfect* and *to be perfected.* Yet, all that is proper to matter and form, as such, as *to be generated* and *corrupted,* and the like, appertain to material substances only, and in no way belong to immaterial created substances.

21 Thomas Aquinas
Analogy of Being

Some Primary Considerations

As the Philosopher says, the term *being,* or *that-which-is,* is used in various senses. It must be borne in mind that a term is predicated of diverse things in several different ways. 1) In some cases the term is predicated according to a concept altogether identical, and then it is said to be predicated univocally, as *animal,* said of the horse and the cow.) In other instances the term is predicated according to concepts altogether diverse in meaning, and then it is said to be predicated of things equivocally, as *dog,* said of the animal of that name and of a certain heavenly body.) In still other cases the term is predicated according to concepts diverse in some respect and in some respect not— diverse inasmuch as they entail diverse relations, but one in that these diverse relations are all referred to some one term. A thing is then said to be "predicated analogically," that is, proportionally, each member of the analogy being predicated according to its relation to that one term.

It happens in two ways that a term is predicated of a number of things according to different concepts. In one way, according to concepts completely diverse, having no relationship to one (common meaning). And such things are said to be equivocal by chance, because it is only fortuitously that a man applies one name to one thing and another name to something else, as is particularly evident in the case of different men who are called by the same name. In another way, one name is predicated of a number of things according to concepts not totally other but agreeing in some one thing—sometimes, indeed, in the fact that they are referred to one principle. Thus a thing is called *military* either because it is a military man's instrument—a sword, perhaps—or because it is his clothing, such as a cuirass, or because it is his vehicle, for example, a horse. But sometimes those concepts agree in being all referred to one end, as medicine is called *healthy* because it produces health, diet because it conserves health, urine because it indicates health. In other instances, however, terms agree according to different proportions to the same subject, as a quality is called a *being* because it is a disposition of per se being, namely, of substance, quantity because it is a measure of substance, and so forth. Finally, the terms may agree according to one proportion to diverse subjects. Thus sight is in relation to the body what intellect is in relation to the soul, so that just as sight is a power of a bodily organ, so intellect is a power of the soul in which the body does not participate. Aristotle therefore says that *good* is predicated of many things, not through concepts completely different, as with things equivocal purely by chance, but rather by way of analogy, that is, by the same proportion, seeing that all goods depend upon one first principle, of goodness, or are all ordered to one end. For Aristotle did not mean that that separated Good was the idea and intelligible form (*ratio*) of all goods, but their principle and end. Or, again, all things are said to be good according to analogy or the same proportion in this way, that just as sight, for example, is a good of the body, so intellect is a good of

the soul. Indeed Aristotle prefers this third mode of analogy because it is based upon the goodness inhering in things. In the first two modes, involving as they do predication in respect to the *separated* good, a thing is not so properly denominated *good* as it is in the third one.

Applications: The Problem of the Analogical Community between Creatures and God

It must be said that nothing can be predicated univocally of the creature and God; for in all univocals the intelligible nature signified by the name (*ratio nominis*) is common to each of the things of which that name is univocally predicated. Thus, with respect to that nature, univocals are equal, although in its actual existence one can be prior or posterior to another. For example, so far as the concept of number itself is concerned, all numbers are on a par, yet in fact one number may be prior to another. Now, however much it may imitate God, no creature can ever attain to this, that anything the same in its very intelligible essence should be common to it and to God. For, those things which, as regards the same intelligible essence, are present to diverse subjects, are common to them in point of substance (second substance) or of quiddity, but are distinct in point of existence (*esse*). But whatever is in God *is* His own proper act of existing; for just as essence in Him is the same as act of existing, so science (*scientia*), for example, is the same in Him as His actual scientific knowing (*scientem esse*). Consequently, since the act of existing proper to one thing cannot be communicated to another, it is impossible that the creature should have anything in common with God quidditatively, even as it cannot possibly acquire the same act of existing as His. Similarly in our case: if for instance in Peter, man and the act of being a man did not differ, it would be impossible to predicate *man* univocally of Peter and Paul, whose very existences are diverse. Yet it cannot be asserted that whatever is predicated of God and creature is predicated in a purely equivocal sense, because if there existed no real likeness of creature to God, God's essence would not be the likeness of created things, and thus in knowing His own essence, He would not know creatures. Likewise, in that case we would be unable to attain to any knowledge of God from creatures. Nor, then, among names befitting creatures would any one of them be predicable of Him in preference to any other; for in regard to terms purely equivocal it matters not what name be used, seeing that there is no likeness in reality between them. Therefore it must be said that the name *science* is said of God's science, and of ours neither in an altogether univocal sense, nor purely equivocally, but by way of analogy; which simply means according to a proportion.

Now proportional likeness can be twofold, giving rise to a double community of analogy. 1) There exists a certain conformity among things proportioned to each other because of a mutual determinate distance or some other (determinate) relation between them, as two is proportioned to one by being the double of one. 2) Sometimes we find a mutual conformity of two things between which there is no (determinate) proportions, but rather a mutual likeness of two proportions; *e.g.,* six is "like" four in this,

that just as six is the double of three, so four is the double of two. The first kind of conformity is thus one of proportion, the second, of proportionality. So, in accordance with that first kind of conformity we find something predicated analogically of two things one of which is related to the other; as being (*ens*) is said of substance and of accident through the relation that substance and accident have to each other, and as *healthy* is predicated of urine and of animal because urine has a certain likeness to the health of the animal. But sometimes a term is predicated analogically according to the second kind of conformity (proportionality), as the name *vision* is said of corporeal vision and of intellectual vision by reason of the fact that just as sight is in the eye, so intellect is in the soul. (As was said), in things predicated analogically in the first way (according to proportion) there must be some determinate relation between the entities to which a term is common by analogy. It is therefore impossible for anything to be said of God and creature by this mode of analogy. For no creature has a relation to God such that, through it, the divine perfection could be determined. But in the second mode of analogy no determinate relation exists between those things to which something is common by analogy. Therefore nothing prevents some name from being predicated analogically of God and creature according to this mode of analogy.

There are, however, two modes of predication by way of proportionality. 1) Sometimes the name to be predicated implies in its primary meaning something respecting which no likeness can obtain between God and creature. . . . Such is the case in all things predicated of God symbolically, as when words like *lion* or *sun* are said of Him. For in the definition of such terms is included matter—which cannot be attributed to God. 2) Sometimes the name predicated of God and creature involves in its principal signification nothing that could prevent the aforesaid mode of community (proportionality) from existing between the creature and God. Such is the case with all names whose definition entails no imperfection, nor any actual dependence upon matter. This (absence of limitation) we find in the terms being, good, and the like.

The Basis of Metaphysical Analogy: Diversity in Act of Existing

. . . two principles are to be considered in a thing, namely, its nature or quiddity and its act of existing. Now in all univocals there must be community according to nature and not according to act of existing, because one act of existing only is present in each thing. Thus human nature does not exist in two men according to the same act of existing. So it is that when the form signified by a name is the act of existing itself (*ipsum esse*), it cannot appertain to things univocally; neither therefore is being (*ens*) predicated univocally.

The act of existing of each and every being is proper to it and is distinct from the act of existing of every other being.

Diversity with respect to act of existing prevents the univocal predication of being (*ens*) . . . A diverse way of existing (*diversus modus existendi*) bars such predication.

22 Thomas Aquinas
Doctrine of Transcendentals

For the first object envisaged by the intellect is being, without which nothing can be apprehended by it, just as the first object of intellectual conviction is first principles, and especially this one: that contradictories are not simultaneously true. Thus all the other [divine names] are somehow included in being, unitedly and indistinctly, as in their source. And for this reason, too, it is fitting that *being* should be the most proper of the divine names. However, the other names we mentioned—*good, true* and *one*—do add "something" to being, not indeed any essence or nature at all, but only a certain intelligible aspect. Thus, *one* introduces the aspect of indivision; and it is because it adds to being only a negation that it is the closest [transcendental] to being. *True* and *good,* on the other hand, add to being a certain relation: good, a relation to an end; true, a relation to an exemplar form. For anything whatever is said to be true in virtue of the fact that it imitates the divine exemplar or is in a relationship [of conformity] to a cognitive power; e.g., we speak of gold as being "true" because it has the form of gold which it manifests, and accordingly a true judgement is made about it. But if the transcendental properties of being [especially the good and the true] are considered under the aspect of causality, then the good is prior, because goodness has the nature of a final cause . . . and the final cause is the first cause in the order of causality.

Now beauty and goodness are the same in subject . . . and differ only in reason. . . . Whereas goodness has the character of a final cause, beauty properly pertains to the order of formal causality.

23   Thomas Aquinas
One

One does not add any reality to being, but is only the negation of division; for *one* simply means undivided being. It is clear from this very fact that *one* is convertible with *being*. For every being is either simple or composite. But what is simple is undivided both actually and potentially; whereas the composite has no being as such so long as its parts remain separately existent but only after they come together to make up and compose it. Manifestly, therefore, the actual being *(esse)* of everything that is consists in indivision. And so it is that everything guards its unity as it guards its very existence *(esse)*.

It can be shown from three sources that God is one. First, from His simplicity. For it is manifest that the reason why any singular thing is this particular thing is because it cannot be communicated to many. Thus, although that whereby Socrates is a man can be communicated to many, what makes him this particular man is communicable to one being only. Therefore, if Socrates were a man in virtue of what makes him to be this particular man, as there cannot be many Socrateses, so there could not in that way be many men. Now this belongs to God alone; for God Himself is His own nature, as was shown above. Therefore in identically the same way God is God and this God. So it is impossible that there should be many gods.

Secondly, this is proved from the infinity of God's perfection. For it was shown above that God comprehends in Himself the whole perfection of being *(totam perfectionem essendi)*. Hence, if many gods existed, they would necessarily differ from each other, so that something would belong to one which did not belong to another. In this case, a perfection would be lacking in one of them, and the thing deprived of this perfection then would not be absolutely perfect. It is therefore impossible for many gods to exist. And thus when the ancient philosophers, compelled as it were by the truth, asserted an infinite principle, they asserted likewise that there was only one such principle.

Thirdly, this is shown from the unity of the world. For all things that exist are seen to be ordered to each other since some serve others. But things mutually diverse do not come together in the same order unless they be ordered thereto by some single being. For many are reduced into one order by one thing better than by many: because what is one is the essential cause of what is one, while the many are the cause of the one only accidentally, i.e., so far as they themselves are in some way one. Since, then, what is first is most perfect, and is so essentially and not accidentally, it must be that the first which reduces all into one order is only one. And this is God.

24 Thomas Aquinas
True

All knowledge is brought about by the assimilation of the knower to the thing known, so that the assimilation is said to be the cause of the knowledge. Thus sight knows color through the fact that it is disposed to the species of color. Therefore, the primary relation of being to intellect consists in the one's corresponding to the other; which correspondence is called the adequation of the thing and the intellect. And in this the notion of truth is realized formally. It is this, then, that truth adds to being: conformity or adequation of thing and intellect; and upon this conformity, as was said, knowledge of the thing follows. Thus the entity of the thing precedes truth formally so called; but knowledge is a certain effect of truth.

A natural thing, then, set up between two intellects, is said to be true by an adequation to both; for, according to the divine intellect, it is said to be true so far as it fulfills that to which it is ordered by the divine intellect, as is made evident by Anselm in his book *On Truth,* by Augustine in *The True Religion,* and by Avicenna in the definition previously quoted, namely, "The truth of each thing is a property of the being which has been given to it." On the other hand, as regards adequation to the human intellect, a natural thing is said to be *true* so far as it is naturally constituted to produce a true estimation of itself, just as, on the contrary, things are said to be *false* which are by nature apt to seem what they are not or as they are not, as is said in the fifth book of the *Meta-physics.* The notion of truth, however, is by priority realized in the thing by the first relation [that of the thing to the divine intellect] rather than by the second one [that of the thing to the human intellect], because the relation to the divine intellect is prior to the human, so that even if the human intellect did not exist, things would still be said to be true in their relation to the divine intellect. But if both intellects were understood to be removed, which is impossible, the principle of truth would in no wise remain.

25 Thomas Aquinas
Good

Since the essence of goodness consists in this, that something be perfective of another in the manner of an end, every thing having the nature of an end, has also the nature of goodness. Two things, however, pertain to the nature of an end: 1) that it be sought after or desired by those things which have not yet attained it, and 2) that it be loved by, and as it were lovable to, those things which share in its possession; for it pertains to the same nature to tend toward its end, and in some way to rest in it, just as it is by one and the same nature that the stone is moved toward the center and rests there. Now these two things [tendency and rest] belong to the very act of existing *(ipsum esse).* For those things which do not yet have this act, tend toward it by certain natural appetite. Thus matter, as the Philosopher says, desires form. All things that presently have existence, however, naturally love that existence, and preserve it with all their power. So, in the third book of *The Consolation of Philosophy,* Boethius says: "The divine providence gave to the things created by Him this special reason for remaining in existence, that to the extent of their capacity they would naturally desire to preserve their being. Wherefore you can in no way doubt this fact, that all things naturally desire the continuance of their existence and naturally shun their own destruction." The very act of existing *(ipsum esse)* thus has the character of goodness. Hence, just as it is impossible that there be any being which does not have this act, so it is necessary that every being be good precisely because it has this act; although in certain entities many aspects of goodness are superadded to the act of being whereby they subsist.

Now, since goodness includes the notion of being, as is clear from what has been said already, there could be no good which is not a being. It remains, therefore, that good and being are convertible.

Are All Things Good By God's Goodness?

In things which entail relation, there is no reason why a thing cannot be denominated from something extrinsic to it. Thus a thing is denominated *placed* from place, and *measured* from measure. But as regards things that are called absolute, opinions differ. Plato held the separate existence of the essence of all things, and that individuals were denominated by them as participating in the separate essences; for instance, that

Socrates is called man according to the separate Idea (or Form) of man. Now, just as he laid down separate Ideas of man and horse, which he called absolute [*per se*] man and absolute horse, so likewise he posited separate Ideas of *being* and of *one*, which he called absolute being and absolute oneness; and by participation in these everything was called being or one. What was thus absolute being and absolute unity, he said was the highest good. And because *good* is convertible with *being*, as is also *one*, he called the absolute good God, from whom all things are called good by way of participation.

Although this opinion appears to be unreasonable in maintaining that there are separate forms of natural things subsisting of themselves—as Aristotle argues in many nays—nevertheless it is absolutely true that there is something first which is being and good in virtue of its own essence, namely, He whom we call God, as is clear from what was proved above. . . .

Everything is therefore called good from God's goodness, as from the first exemplar, efficient, and final principle of all goodness. Nevertheless, everything is called good by reason of the likeness of God's goodness inhering in it, which likeness is its own goodness whereby it is denominated good. And so of all things there is one Goodness, and yet many goodnesses.

26   Thomas Aquinas
Beautiful

Nothing exists which does not participate in beauty and goodness, since each thing is beautiful and good according to its proper form. . . . Created beauty is nothing other than a likeness of the divine beauty participated in things.

Now beauty and goodness are the same in subject because they are based upon the same reality, the form. And for this reason goodness is praised as beautiful. Yet they differ in reason. For the good properly regards the appetite (the good being what all desire), and thus it has the character of an end, seeing that appetite is a certain motion toward a thing. Beauty, on the other hand, regards the cognitive power, because those things are said to be beautiful which please when seen. Beauty accordingly consists in due proportion, for sense delights in things rightly proportioned, as in things like unto itself; indeed sense itself is a kind of reason, as every cognitive power is. And because cognition is effected through assimilation, and assimilation concerns the form, beauty properly pertains to the nature of a formal cause.

For beauty three things are required: a) integrity or perfection, b) right proportion or consonance, c) splendor of form.

On Beauty and the Divine Beauty

God, Who is "supersubstantially beautiful, is called Beauty," as Dionysius says, because He confers beauty upon all created beings according to the peculiar nature of each one. . . . God bestows beauty inasmuch as He is "the cause of harmony *(consonantia)* and splendor of form *(claritas)* in all things." For we say a man is beautiful by reason of the seemly proportion, in quantity and position, of his members, and therefore we declare that he has a distinguished and splendid appearance. This notion, then, is to be applied analogously *(proportionaliter)* in all other contexts, so that everything will be called "beautiful" according to its own kind of luminousness *(claritas)*, whether spiritual or corporeal, and according as it is disposed in due proportion *(debita proportione)*.

Now Dionysius shows how God is the cause of splendor of form, saying that He transmits to all creatures with a certain lightning-like brightness, a ray of His own brilliant light, which is the source of all illumination. And these lightning-like communications of the divine ray of light are to be understood according to analogical participation; and as Dionysius says, they are "beautifying," that is, productive of beauty in things.

Regarding the other point made by Dionysius, namely, that God if the cause of harmony *(consonantia*—order and proportion) in things, we must note that this harmony is twofold. First, there is the harmony that consists in the ordination of creatures to God. And here Dionysius says God is the cause of harmony "as summoning all things to Himself" in that He converts all things to Himself as their end. . . . And of this reason beauty in Greek is καλὸs, a word derived from the act of calling [καλέω]. The second harmony in things, however, lies in their ordination to each other. And this Dionysius refers to when he says that God unites all with all in relation to the same. Superiors, indeed, as the Platonists held, are in inferiors by participation, whereas inferiors are in superiors by a certain excellence, or transcendence; so that all things *are* in all things. And from the fact that all are in all in a certain order, it follows that all are ordered to the same end.

Now, just as a thing is said to be "more white" because it is less mixed with black, so a thing is said to be "more beautiful" in proportion to its immunity from any defect of beauty. But in creatures there is a twofold defect of beauty. *One* consists in the fact that some things exist whose beauty is variable, as is evidently the case with corruptible things. This defect Dionysius excludes from God first of all, saying that God is beautiful always, in the same respect and the same mode, any alteration of beauty being foreign to Him. Moreover, there is in God neither generation nor corruption of beauty, nor any change, either of increase or diminution, as is manifestly true of corporeal things. Now *the second defect of beauty* lies in this: all creatures have beauty that is in some way particularized, just as they have a particularized nature. This defect Dionysius excludes from God as regards every mode of particularity. God, he says, is not in one part beautiful and in another ugly, as happens sometimes in particular things; nor is God beautiful at one time and at another not, as are things whose beauty is subject to time; nor is He beautiful in one relation and not in another, as with all things ordained to one determinate use or end (for, were they directed to something else, harmony would not be served, and hence neither would beauty); nor, again, is God in one place beautiful and in another not, as some things are because they seem beautiful to certain

persons and to others not. On the contrary, God is absolutely and in every way beautiful. And Dionysius gives the explanation of all this by saying God is beautiful "according to Himself." For this phrase eliminates any possibility that He is beautiful in one respect only, or in a certain time only, or in a certain place only, because what belongs to a being "according to itself," or in virtue of its own being, and does so primarily, belongs to it totally and everlastingly and ubiquitously. Further, God is beautiful in Himself, not in respect to something determinate, or limited; so that it cannot be said He is beautiful in one regard and in another, not. . . . Finally, God is always and uniformly beautiful; and thus is excluded from Him the first defect of beauty, namely, variability.

The Causality of Beauty

Dionysius points out from this divine Beauty, existence *(esse)* comes to all existing beings. Now, as was said, splendor of form *(claritas)* pertains to the consideration of beauty. But every form, through which a thing has actual existence, is a certain participation of the divine intelligible Splendor *(divina claritas)*. And so Dionysius adds: "singular things are beautiful according to their proper intelligible essence *(ratio)*"; and this means, according to their proper form. It is therefore evident that the act of existing *(esse)* of all things stems from the divine Beauty. It was noted, moreover, that harmony *(consonantia)* is intrinsic to the essence of beauty. Hence all things which in any way appertain to harmony [and thus to order and proportion] proceed from the divine Beauty. Dionysius thus states that it is because of the divine Beauty that there are "harmonious relationships" (*concordiae*), as regards understanding, among all rational creatures (for those are in accord with each other whose thought is one), and "friendships" (*amicitiae*), as regards affection, and "fellowships" (*communiones*), as regards action, or something extrinsic; and universally, all creatures, whatsoever unity they may have among themselves, possess that unity in virtue of the beautiful.

Dionysius goes on to say, in the first place, that "the beautiful is the principle of all things as their effective cause," bestowing being upon them, and as their "moving cause," and as the containing (that is, conserving) cause of all things." Now these three offices seem to pertain to the efficient cause, namely, to give existence (*esse*), to move, and to conserve. But there is a certain kind of efficient cause that acts out of desire for an end, and such action is proper to an imperfect agent, one which does not yet possess what it desires, or tends toward. On the contrary, it pertains to the perfect agent to act out of love of that which it possesses. And for this reason, Dionysius adds that the Beauty which is God is the effective, motive, and containing Cause "through love of His own beauty." For since God possesses beauty, He wishes to multiply it so far as that is possible, namely, by communication of its likeness. Secondly, Dionysius says that the Beauty which is God is "the end of all things, as final cause" of all things. For it is in order to imitate, in whatsoever manner, the divine Beauty that all things are made. Thirdly, the divine Beauty is the exemplar cause, since it is by reference to the divine Beauty that all things are distinguished, and the sign of this is that no one cares to portray or represent anything except in accordance with his idea of beauty (*nisi ad pulchrum*).

Finally, when Dionysius avers, "On this account, too, the beautiful is the same as the good," he draws a certain corollary from what he had said, remarking that because the beautiful is the cause of all things in all these ways, it follows that the good and the beautiful are the same. For indeed all things desire the beautiful and the good in all these modes, and there is nothing that does not participate in beauty and goodness, since each thing is beautiful and good according to its proper form. Moreover, we can even declare boldly with Dionysius that "the non-existent," that is to say, prime matter, "participates in beauty and goodness," inasmuch as this non-actual primal "being" has a certain likeness to the divine beauty and goodness. For beauty and goodness in God are extolled through the exclusion of all imperfections or limitations. In the case of prime matter it is indeed a question of exclusion by way of defect; in God, of exclusion by way of excess, seeing that God exists supersubstantially.

However, although beauty and goodness are the same in reality—for both splendor of form (*claritas*) and harmony (*consonantia*) are contained in the notion of goodness—nevertheless, they differ in reason, because beauty adds to goodness ordination to cognitive power.

Now Dionysius explains that although goodness and beauty are one in their very being (*unum esse*), they are the "cause of all goods and beauties"—which are many. . . . He points out that beauty is the cause of the substantial essences of things. For every essence is either a simple form, or has its substantial completion through its substantial form. But a form is a certain irradiation from the Primary Splendor of Form. And, as was said, splendor of form pertains to the essence of beauty.

Again in speaking of "unities and distinctions," Dionysius notes the things that pertain to the concept of unity. And what we must consider here is that *one* adds to the notion of being, indivision; for *one* means undivided being. Thus, opposed to unity is distinction or division. Now the cause of the "unities and distinctions" of things, Dionysius declares, is the divine Beauty. Let us recall that oneness in substance is the cause of identity; distinctness in substance, the cause of diversity . . . , while similarity is caused by oneness in quality. . . . It is an evident fact, moreover, that dissimilar entities agree in something (e.g., contraries agree in genus and in matter, or subject), and that things united accidentally remain distinct as parts in their whole. (Respecting the first of these Dionysius uses the expression "communions of contraries," and for the second "intermixtures of units.") Now the point is this: all these things are reduced to the causality of the beautiful, because they appertain to harmony (*consonantia*—order, proportion), which in turn is of the essence of beauty, as was said above.

Further, speaking of the "providence of superiors," Dionysius enumerates that which pertains to the order of things. And first he considers this problem from the standpoint of action—according as superiors provide for inferiors (he touches upon this in referring to "the reciprocal relations of coordinate things," that is, of equals), and also according as inferiors are ordained to the reception from superiors of perfection and governance. . . .

Secondly, he notes what pertains to the existence of things in themselves, declaring that the perdurances whereby certain things (that is, things-in-themselves) are kept in being have their principle in the beautiful. For a thing is kept in existence by the fact that it remains within the limits of its nature, since if it so to speak poured itself out altogether, it would perish. And Dionysius adds the phrase: "And dissimilar collocations," that is, foundations. For, just as a thing is conserved in being by remaining in itself, so it is intransmutable by having something intrinsically solid upon which it is founded.

Thirdly, Dionysius cites the things that pertain to the abiding presence of one thing in another. It must be borne in mind, he points out, that when something is to be constructed from a number of other things, the *prime requisite* is that the parts be in conformity. For instance, the stones of which a house is built are by nature conformed to each other. Similarly, all the parts of the universe come together and form a unity in virtue of their common act of existing. Dionysius therefore says that not only the abiding presence of things in themselves has its source in the beautiful, but also the "communions of all things in all things according to the proper nature of each." For it is not in one mode that all things are in all things; rather, superiors are in inferiors by participation; inferiors in superiors excellently. Yet all share something in common with all.

Moreover, for something to be constituted by a number of things, it is necessary, *secondly*, that they be adaptable to one another even as regards that in which they are diverse. Thus a house would not be made of cement and stone unless these things were fitted to exist together. Likewise the parts of the universe are adapted to each other inasmuch as they can fall under one order.

The *third requirement* is that the one part be served by the other. Thus the walls and the roof of a building are supported by the foundation, and the roof completely covers the walls and the foundation. So, too, in the universe higher things give perfection to lower things, and in the lower thing a higher power is manifested. Hence Dionysius' phrase: "and friendships not disordered"; for relations of mutual service among things are not prejudicial to their distinctness.

A *fourth requirement* is due proportion in the parts. The foundation, for example, must be proportioned to the other parts. Therefore Dionysius adds: "and the harmony of the whole," that is, of all the parts of the universe. Thus harmony is caused in sounds by the right proportion of numbers. Therefore, the parts having been thus disposed, their unification in the whole follows, so that from all the parts of the universe one totality (*universitas*) of things is constituted.
. . .

This "concretion" of parts in the universe is attained in two ways. First, by means of that "local" containment whereby superiors in some fashion are in things in place of inferiors, whether spiritual or corporeal. Hence Dionysius' phrase: "indissoluble containments of existing things"; that is to say, superiors contain inferiors in an indissoluble order. Secondly, this concretion of parts in the universal whole is attained as regards the succession of time, so far as generable and corruptible things (wherein the posterior succeed the prior) are concerned. Consequently, Dionysius appends this expression: "the unfailing successions of the things that are made." The successions of things indeed

are said to be "unfailing," not because genera endure forever, but because some succeed others without interruption as long as this world process (*cursus mundi*) lasts. Now all these things, as Dionysius says, are caused by beauty, because they pertain to the nature of harmony (*consonantia*), which in turn is of the essence of beauty.

Further, Dionysius says that "all rests and motions," inasmuch as they import some relation of one thing to another, belong to the notion of harmony and beauty. . . . Indeed he declares that all rests and motions, whether of souls or of bodies, are caused by the divine Beauty. And he says this because . . . that which is above all rest and motion is the cause of both rest and motion in all things, inasmuch as it establishes each thing in its proper nature, wherein the thing has its resting place [so to speak], and inasmuch as it moves all things in relation to the divine motion. For the motions of all things are ordered to the motion whereby they are moved toward God, as the motions relative to secondary ends are ordered to the motion which is directed to the ultimate end. Now the form upon which the proper nature of a thing depends, pertains to intelligible splendor (*claritas*), and order to the end [finality] pertains to harmony (*consonantia*). Therefore motion and rest are reduced to the causality of the beautiful.

27 Thomas Aquinas
The Existence of God (from *Summa Theologiae* I, 2, 1–3)

Whether the Existence of God Is Self-Evident?

We Proceed Thus to the First Article:—

Objection 1. It seems that the existence of God is self-evident. For those things are said to be self-evident to us the knowledge of which exists naturally in us, as we can see in regard to first principles. But as Damascene says, "the knowledge of God is naturally implanted in all." Therefore the existence of God is self-evident.

Objection 2. Further, those things are said to be self-evident which are known as soon as the terms are known, which the Philosopher [Aristotle] says is true of the first principles of demonstration. Thus, when the nature of a whole and of a part is known, it is at once recognized that every whole is greater than its part. But as soon as the signification of the name *God* is understood, it is at once seen that God exists. For by this name is signified that thing than which nothing greater can be conceived. But that which exists actually and mentally is greater than that which exists only mentally. Therefore, since as soon as the name *God* is understood it exists mentally, it also follows that is exists actually. Therefore the proposition *God exists* is self-evident.

Objection 3. Further, the existence of truth is self-evident. For whoever denies the existence of truth grants that truth does not exist: and, if truth does not exist, then the proposition *Truth does not exist* is true: and if there is anything true, there must be truth. But God is truth itself: "I am the way, the truth, and the life" (John, 14:6). Therefore *God exists* is self-evident.

On the contrary, No one can mentally admit the opposite of what is self-evident, as the Philosopher states concerning the first principles of demonstration. But the opposite of the proposition *God is* can be mentally admitted: "The fool said in his heart, There is no God" (Ps. 52:1). Therefore, that God exists is not self-evident.

I answer that, A thing can be self-evident in either of two ways: on the one hand, self-evident in itself, though not to us; on the other, self-evident in itself, and to us. A proposition is self-evident because the predicate is included in the essence of the subject: e.g., *Man is an animal*, for animal is contained in the essence of man. If, therefore, the essence of the predicate and subject be known to all, the proposition will be self-evident to all; as is clear with regard to the first principles of demonstration, the terms of which are certain common notions that no one is ignorant of, such as being and non-being, whole and part, and the like. If, however, there are some to whom the essence of the predicate and subject is unknown, the proposition will be self-evident in itself, but not to those who do not know the meaning of then predicate and subject of the proposition. Therefore, it happens, as Boethius says, that there are some notions of the mind which are common and self-evident only to the learned, as that incorporeal substances are not in space. Therefore I say that this proposition, *God exists,* of itself is self-evident, for the predicate is the same as the subject, because God is His own existence as will be hereafter shown. Now because we do not know the essence of God, the proposition is not self-evident to us, but needs to be demonstrated by things that are more known to us, though less known in their nature—namely, by His effects.

Reply Objection 1. To know that God exists in a general and confused way is implanted in us by nature, inasmuch as God is man's beatitude. For man naturally desires happiness, and what is naturally desired by man is naturally known by him. This, however, is not to know absolutely that God exists; just as to know that someone is approaching is not the same as to know that Peter is approaching, even though it is Peter who is approaching for there are many who imagine that man's perfect good, which is happiness, consists in riches, and others in pleasures, and others in something else.

Reply Objection 2. Perhaps not everyone who hears this name *God* understands it to signify something than which nothing greater can be thought, seeing that some have believed God to be a body. Yet, granted that everyone understands that by the name *God* is signified something than which nothing greater can be thought, nevertheless, it does not therefore follow that he understands that what the name signifies exists actually, but only that it exists mentally. Nor can it be argued that it actually exists, unless it be admitted that there actually exists something than which nothing

greater can be thought; and this precisely is not admitted by those who hold that God does not exist.

Reply Objection 3. The existence of truth in general is self-evident, but the existence of a Primal Truth is not self-evident to us.

Whether It Can Be Demonstrated That God Exists?

We Proceed thus to the Second Article:—

Objection 1. It seems that the existence of God cannot demonstrated. For it is an article of faith that God exists. But what is of faith cannot be demonstrated, because a demonstration produces scientific knowledge, whereas faith is of the unseen, as is clear from Apostle (Heb. 11:1), Therefore it cannot de demonstrated that God exists.

Objection 2. Further, essence is the middle term of demonstration. But we cannot know in what God's essence consists, but solely in which it does not consist, as Damascene says. Therefore we cannot demonstrate that God exists.

Objection 3. Further, if the existence of God were demonstrated, this could only be from His effects. But His effects are not proportioned to Him, since He is infinite and His effects are finite, and between the finite and infinite there is no proportion. Therefore, since a cause cannot be demonstrated by an effect not proportioned to it, it seems that the existence of God cannot be demonstrated.

On the contrary, The Apostle says: "The invisible things of Him are clearly seen, being understood by the things that are made" (Rom. 1:20). But this would not be unless the existence of God could be demonstrated through the things that are made; for the first thing we must know of anything is whether it exists.

I answer that, Demonstration can be made in two ways: One is through the cause, and is called *propter quid*, and this is to argue from what is prior absolutely. The other is through the effect, and is called a demonstration *quia*; this is to argue from what is prior relatively only to us. When an effect is better known to us than its cause, from the effect we proceed to the knowledge of the cause. And from every effect the existence of its proper cause can be demonstrated, so long as its effects are better known to us; because, since every effect depends upon its cause, if the effect exists, the cause must preexist. Hence the existence of God, insofar as it is not self-evident to us, can be demonstrated from those of His effects which are known to us.

Reply Objection 1. The existence of God and other like truths about God, which can be known by natural reason, are not articles of faith, but are preambles to the articles; for faith presupposes natural knowledge, even as grace presupposes nature and perfection the perfectible. Nevertheless, there is nothing to prevent a man, who cannot grasp a proof, from accepting, as a matter of faith, something which in itself is capable of being scientifically known and demonstrated.

Reply Objection 2. When the existence of a cause is demonstrated from an effect, this effect takes the place of the definition of the cause in proving the cause's existence. This is especially the case in regard to God, because, in order to prove the existence of anything, it is necessary to ac-

cept as a middle term the meaning of the name, and not its essence, for the question of its essence follows on the question of its existence. Now the names given to God are derived from His effects, as will be later shown. Consequently, in demonstrating the existence of God from His effects, we may take for the middle term the meaning of the name *God.*

Reply Objection 3. From effects not proportioned to the cause no perfect knowledge of that cause can be obtained. Yet from every effect the existence of the cause can be clearly demonstrated, and so we can demonstrate the existence of God from His effects; though from them we cannot know God perfectly as He is in His essence.

Whether God Exists?

We proceed thus to the Third Article:—

Objection 1. It seems that God does not exist; because if one of two contraries be infinite, the other would be altogether destroyed. But the name *God* means that He is infinite goodness. If, therefore, God existed, there would be no evil discoverable; but there is evil in the world. Therefore God does not exist.

Objective 2. Further, it is superfluous to suppose that what can be accounted for by a few principles has been produced by many. But it seems that everything we see in the world can be accounted for by other principles, supposing God did not exists. For all natural things can be reduced to one principle, which nature; and all voluntary things can be reduced to one principle, which is human reason, or will. Therefore there is no need to suppose God's existence.

On the contrary, it is said in the person of God: "I am Who am" (Exod. 3:14).

I answer that, The existence of God can be proved in five ways.

The first and more manifest way is the argument from motion. It is certain, and evident to our senses, that in the world some things are in motion. Now whatever is moved is moved by another, for nothing can be moved except it is potentiality to that towards which it is moved; whereas a thing moves inasmuch as it is in act. For motion is nothing else than the reduction of something from potentiality to actuality. But nothing can be reduced from potentiality to actuality, except by something in a state of actuality. Thus what is actually hot, as fire, makes wood, which is potentially hot, to be actually hot, and thereby moves and changes it, Now it is not possible that the same thing should be at once in actuality and potentiality in the same respect, but only in different respects. For what is actually hot cannot simultaneously be potentially hot; but it is simultaneously potentially cold. It is therefore impossible that in the same respect and in the same way a thing should be both mover and moved, i.e., that it should move itself. Therefore, whatever is moved must be moved by another. If that by which it is moved be itself moved, then this also must be moved by another, and that by another again. But this cannot go on to infinity, because then there would be no first mover, and, consequently, no other moved, seeing that subsequent movers move only in as much as they moved by the first mover; as the staff moves only because it is moved by the hand. Therefore it is necessary to arrive at a first mover,

moved by no other and this everyone understands to be God.

The second way is from the nature of efficient cause. In the world of sensible things we find there is an order of efficient causes. There is no case known (neither is it, indeed, possible) in which a thing is found to be the efficient cause of itself; for so it would be prior to itself, which is impossible. Now in efficient causes it is not possible to go to infinity, because in all efficient causes following in order, the first is the cause of the intermediate cause, and the intermediate is the cause of the ultimate cause, whether the intermediate cause be several, or one only. Now to take away the cause is to take away the effect. Therefore, if there be no first cause among efficient causes, there will be no ultimate, nor any intermediate, cause. But if in efficient causes it is possible to go on to infinity, there will be no first efficient cause, neither will there be an ultimate effect, nor any intermediate efficient causes; all of which is plainly false. Therefore it is necessary to admit a first efficient cause, to which everyone gives the name of God.

The third way is taken from possibility and necessity, and runs thus. We find in nature things are possible to be and not to be, since they are found to be generated, and to be corrupted, and consequently, it is possible for them to be and not to be. But it is impossible for these always to exist, for that which can not-be at some time is not.

Therefore, if everything can not-be, then at one time there was nothing in existence. Now if this were true, even now there would be nothing in existence, because that which does not exist begins to exist only through something already existing. Therefore, if at one time nothing was in existence, it would have been impossible for anything to have begun to exist; and thus even now nothing would be in existence—which is absurd. Therefore, not all things are merely possible, but there must exist something the existence of which is necessary. But every necessary thing either has its necessity caused by another, or not. Now it is impossible to go on to infinity in necessary things which have their necessity caused by another, as has been already proved in regard to efficient causes. Therefore we cannot but admit the existence of some being having of itself its own necessity, and not receiving it from another, but rather causing in others their necessity. This all men speak of as God.

The fourth way is taken from the gradation to be found in things. Among beings there are some more and some less good, true, noble, and the like. But *more* and *less* are predicated of different things according as they resemble in their different ways something which is the maximum, as a thing is said to be hotter according as it more nearly resembles that which is hottest; so that there is something which is truest, something best, something noblest, and, consequently, something which is most being, for those things that are greatest in truth are greatest in being, as it is written in *Metaphysics II*. Now the maximum in any genus is the cause of all in that genus, as fire, which is the maximum of heat, is the cause of all hot things, as is said in the same book. Therefore there must also be something which is to all beings the cause of their being, goodness, and every other perfection; and this we call God.

The fifth way is taken from the governance of the world. We see that things which lack knowledge, such as natural bodies, act for an end, and this is evident from their acting always, or nearly always, in the same way, so as to obtain the best result. Hence it is plain that they achieve their end, not fortuitously, but designedly. Now whatever lacks knowledge cannot move towards an end, unless it be directed by some being endowed with knowledge and intelligence; as the arrow is directed by the archer. Therefore some intelligent being exists by whom all natural things are directed to their end; and this being we call God.

Reply Objection 1. As Augustine says: "Since God is the highest good, He would not allow an evil to exist in His works, unless His omnipotence and goodness were such as to bring good even out of evil" (*Enchiridion,* XI). This is part of the infinite goodness of God, that He should allow evil to exist, and out of it produce good.

Reply Objection 2. Since nature works for a determinate end under the direction of a higher agent, whatever is done must be traced back to God as to its first cause. So likewise whatever is done voluntarily must be traced back to some higher cause other than human reason and will, since these can change and fail; for all things that are changeable and capable of defect must be traced back to an immovable and self-necessary first principle, as has been shown.

28

Rene Descartes (from *Meditations on First Philosophy*)

Meditation I

Of the things which may be brought within the sphere of the doubtful.

It is now some years since I detected how many were the false beliefs that I had from my earliest youth admitted as true, and how doubtful was everything I had since constructed on this basis; and from that time I was convinced that I must once for all seriously undertake to rid myself of all the opinions which I had formerly accepted, and commence to build anew from the foundation, if I wanted to establish any firm and permanent structure in the sciences. But as this enterprise appeared to be a very great one, I waited until I had attained an age so mature that I could not hope that at any later date I should be better fitted to execute my design. This reason caused me to delay so long that I should feel that I was doing wrong were I to occupy in deliberation the time that yet remains to me for action. To-day, then, since very opportunely for the plan I have in view I have delivered my mind from every care [and am happily agitated by no passions] and since I have procured for myself an assured leisure in a peaceable retirement, I shall at last seriously and freely address myself to the general upheaval of all my former opinions.

Now for this object it is not necessary that I should show that all of these are false—I shall perhaps never arrive at this end. But inasmuch as reason already persuades me that I ought no less carefully to withhold my assent from matters which are not entirely certain and indubitable than from those which appear to me manifestly to be false, if I am able to find in each one some reason to doubt, this will suffice to justify my rejecting the whole. And for that end it will not be requisite that I should examine each in particular, which would be an endless undertaking; for owing to the fact that the destruction of the foundations of necessity brings with it the downfall of the rest of the edifice, I shall only in the first place attack those principles upon which all my former opinions rested.

All that up to the present time I have accepted as most true and certain I have learned either from the senses or through the senses; but it is sometimes proved to me that these senses are deceptive, and it is wiser not to trust entirely to anything by which we have once been deceived.

But it may be that although the senses sometimes deceive us concerning things which are hardly perceptible, or very far away, there are yet many others to be met with as to which we cannot reasonably have any doubt, although we recognize them by their means. For example, there is the fact that I am here, seated by the fire, attired in a dressing gown, having this paper in my hands and other similar matters. And how could I deny that these hands and this body are mine, were it not perhaps that I compare myself to certain persons, devoid of sense, whose cerebella are so troubled and clouded by the violent vapours of black bile, that they constantly assure us that they think they are kings when they are really quite poor, or that they are clothed in purple when they are really without covering, or who imagine that they have an earthenware head or are nothing but pumpkins or are made of glass. But they are mad, and I should not be any the less insane were I to follow examples so extravagant.

At the same time I must remember that I am a man, and that consequently I am in the habit of sleeping, and in my dreams representing to myself the same things or sometimes even less probable things, than do those who are insane in their waking moments. How often has it happened to me that in the night I dreamt that I found myself in this particular place, that I was dressed and seated near the fire, whilst in reality I was lying undressed in bed! At this moment it does indeed seem to me that it is with eyes awake that I am looking at this paper; that this head which I move is not asleep, that it is deliberately and of set purpose that I extend my hand and perceive it; what happens in sleep does not appear so clear nor so distinct as does all this. But in thinking over this I remind myself that on many occasions I have in sleep been deceived by similar illusions, and in dwelling carefully on this reflection I see so manifestly that there are no certain indications by which we may clearly distinguish wakefulness from sleep that I am lost in astonishment. And my astonishment is such that it is almost capable of persuading me that I now dream.

Now let us assume that we are asleep and that all these particulars, e.g. that we open our eyes, shake our head, extend our hands, and so on, are but false delusions; and let us reflect that possibly neither our hands nor our whole body are such as they appear to us to be. At the same time we must at least confess that the things which are represented to us in sleep are like painted representations which can only have been formed as the counterparts of something real and true, and that in this way those general things at least, i.e. eyes, a head, hands, and a whole body, are not imaginary things, but things really existent. For, as a matter of fact, painters, even when they study with the greatest skill to represent sirens and satyrs by forms the most strange and extraordinary, cannot give them natures which are entirely new, but merely make a certain medley of the members of different animals; or if their imagination is extravagant enough to invent something so novel that nothing similar has ever before been seen, and that then their work represents a thing purely fictitious and absolutely false, it is certain all the same that the colours of which this is composed are necessarily real. And for the same reason, although these general things, to wit, [a body], eyes, a head, hands, and such like, may be imaginary, we are bound at the same time to confess that there are at least some other objects yet more simple and more universal, which are real and true; and of these just in the same way as with certain real colours, all these images of things which dwell in our thoughts, whether true and real or false and fantastic are formed.

To such a class of things pertains corporeal nature in general, and its extension, the figure of extended things, their quantity or magnitude and number, as also the place in which they are, the time which measures their duration, and so on.

That is possibly why our reasoning is not unjust when we conclude from this that Physics, Astronomy, Medicine and all other sciences which have as their end the consideration of composite things, are very dubious and uncertain; but that Arithmetic, Geometry and other sciences of that kind which only treat of things that are very simple and very general, without taking great trouble to ascertain whether they are actually existent or not, contain some measure of certainty and an element of the indubitable. For whether I am awake or asleep, two and three together always form five, and the square can never have more than four equal sides, and it does not seem possible that truths so clear and apparent can be suspected of any falsity [or uncertainty].

Nevertheless I have long had fixed in my mind the belief that an all-powerful God existed by whom I have been created such as I am. But how do I know that He has not brought it to pass that there is no earth, no heaven, no extended body, no magnitude, no place, and that nevertheless [I possess the perceptions of all these things and that] they seem to me to exist just exactly as I now see them? And, besides, as I sometimes imagine that others deceive themselves in the things which they think they know best, how do I know that I am not deceived every time I add two and three, or count the sides of a square, or judge of things yet simpler, if anything simpler can be imagined? But possibly God has not desired that I should be thus deceived, for He is said to be supremely good. If, however, it is contrary to His goodness to have made me such that I constantly deceive myself, it would also appear to be contrary to His goodness to permit me to be sometimes deceived, and nevertheless I cannot doubt that He does permit this.

There may indeed be those who would prefer to deny the existence of a God so powerful, rather than believe that all other things are uncertain. But let us not oppose them for the present, and grant that all that is here said of a God is a fable; nevertheless in whatever way they suppose that I have arrived at the state of being that I have reached—whether they attribute it to fate or to accident, or make out that it is by a continual succession of antecedents, or by some other method—since to err and deceive oneself is a defect, it is clear that the greater will be the probability of my being so imperfect as to deceive myself ever, as is the Author to whom they assign my origin the less powerful. To these reasons I have certainly nothing to reply, but at the end I feel constrained to confess that there is nothing in all that I formerly believed to be true, of which I cannot in some measure doubt, and that not merely through want of thought or through levity, but for reasons which are very powerful and maturely considered; so that henceforth I ought not the less carefully to refrain from giving credence to these opinions than to that which is manifestly false, if I desire to arrive at any certainty [in the sciences].

But it is not sufficient to have made these remarks, we must also be careful to keep them in mind. For these ancient and commonly held opinions still revert frequently to my mind, long and familiar custom having given them the right to occupy my mind against my inclination and rendered them almost masters of my belief; nor will I ever lose the habit of deferring to them or of placing my confidence in them, so long as I consider them as they really are, i.e. opinions in some measure doubtful, as I have just shown, and at the same time highly probable, so that there is much more reason to believe in than to deny them. That is why I consider that I shall not be acting amiss, if, taking of set purpose a contrary belief, I allow myself to be deceived, and for a certain time pretend that all these opinions are entirely false and imaginary, until at last, having thus balanced my former prejudices with my latter [so that they cannot divert my opinions more to one side than to the other], my judgement will no longer be dominated by bad usage or turned away from the right knowledge of the truth. For I am assured that there can be neither peril nor error in this course, and that I cannot at present yield too much to distrust, since I am not considering the question of action, but only of knowledge.

I shall then suppose, not that God who is supremely good and the fountain of truth, but some evil genius not less powerful than deceitful, has employed his whole energies in deceiving me; I shall consider that the heavens, the earth, colours, figures, sound, and all other external things are nought but the illusions and dreams of which this genius has availed himself in order to lay traps for my credulity; I shall consider myself as having no hands, no eyes, no flesh, no blood, nor any senses, yet falsely believing myself to possess all these things; I shall remain obstinately attached to this idea, and if by this means it is not in my power to arrive at the knowledge of any truth, I may at least do what is in my power [i.e. suspend my judgement], and with firm purpose avoid giving credence to any false thing, or being imposed upon by this arch deceiver, however

powerful and deceptive he may be. But this task is a laborious one, and insensibly a certain lassitude leads me into the course of my ordinary life. And just as a captive who in sleep enjoys an imaginary liberty, when he begins to suspect that his liberty is but a dream, fears to awaken, and conspires with these agreeable illusions that the deception may be prolonged, so insensibly of my own accord I fall back into my former opinions, and I dread awakening from this slumber, lest the laborious wakefulness which would follow the tranquility of this repose should have to be spent not in daylight, but in the excessive darkness of the difficulties which have just been discussed.

Meditation II

Of the Nature of the Human Mind; and that it is more easily known than the Body.

The Meditation of yesterday filled my mind with so many doubts that it is no longer in my power to forget them. And yet I do not see in what manner I can resolve them; and, just as if I had all of a sudden fallen into very deep water, I am so disconcerted that I can neither make certain of setting my feet on the bottom, nor can I swim and so support myself on the surface. I shall nevertheless make an effort and follow anew the same path as that on which I yesterday entered, i.e. I shall proceed by setting aside all that in which the least doubt could be supposed to exist, just as if I had discovered that it was absolutely false; and I shall ever follow in this road until I have met with something which is certain, or at least, if I can do nothing else, until I have learned for certain that there is nothing in the world that is certain. Archimedes, in order that he might draw the terrestrial globe out of its place, and transport it elsewhere, demanded only that one point should be fixed and immovable; in the same way I shall have the right to conceive high hopes if I am happy enough to discover one thing only which is certain and indubitable.

I suppose, then, that all the things that I see are false; I persuade myself that nothing has ever existed of all that my fallacious memory represents to me. I consider that I possess no senses; I imagine that body, figure, extension, movement and place are but the fictions of my mind. What, then, can be esteemed as true? Perhaps nothing at all, unless that there is nothing in the world that is certain.

But how can I know there is not something different from those things that I have just considered, of which one cannot have the slightest doubt? Is there not some God, or some other being by whatever name we call it, who puts these reflections into my mind? That is not necessary, for is it not possible that I am capable of producing them myself? I myself, am I not at least something? But I have already denied that I had senses and body. Yet I hesitate, for what follows from that? Am I so dependent on body and senses that I cannot exist without these? But I was persuaded that there was nothing in all the world, that there was no heaven, no earth, that there were no minds, nor any bodies: was I not then likewise persuaded that I did not exist? Not at all; of a surety I myself did exist since I persuaded myself of something [or merely because I thought of something]. But there is some deceiver or other, very powerful and very cunning, who ever employs his ingenuity in deceiving me. Then without doubt I exist also if he deceives me, and let him deceive me as much as he will, he can never cause me to be nothing so long as I think that I am something. So that after having reflected well and carefully examined all things, we must come to the definite conclusion that this proposition: I am, I exist, is necessarily true each time that I pronounce it, or that I mentally conceive it.

But I do not yet know clearly enough what I am, I who am certain that I am; and hence I must be careful to see that I do not imprudently take some other object in place of myself, and thus that I do not go astray in respect of this knowledge that I hold to be the most certain and most evident of all that I have formerly learned. That is why I shall now consider anew what I believed myself to be before I embarked upon these last reflections; and of my former opinions I shall withdraw all that might even in a small degree be invalidated by the reasons which I have just brought forward, in order that there may be nothing at all left beyond what is absolutely certain and indubitable.

What then did I formerly believe myself to be? Undoubtedly I believed myself to be a man. But what is a man? Shall I say a reasonable animal? Certainly not; for then I should have to inquire what an animal is, and what is reasonable; and thus from a single question I should insensibly fall into an infinitude of others more difficult; and I should not wish to waste the little time and leisure remaining to me in trying to unravel subtleties like these. But I shall rather stop here to consider the thoughts which of themselves spring up in my mind, and which were not inspired by anything beyond my own nature alone when I applied myself to the consideration of my being. In the first place, then, I considered myself as having a face, hands, arms, and all that system of members composed of bones and flesh as seen in a corpse which I designated by the name of body. In addition to this I considered that I was nourished, that I walked, that I felt, and that I thought, and I referred all these actions to the soul: but I did not stop to consider what the soul was, or if I did stop, I imagined that it was something extremely rare and subtle like a wind, a flame, or an ether, which was spread throughout my grosser parts. As to body I had no manner of doubt about its nature, but thought I had a very clear knowledge of it; and if I had desired to explain it according to the notions that I had then formed of it, I should have described it thus: By the body I understand all that which can be defined by a certain figure: something which can be confined in a certain place, and which can fill a given space in such a way that every other body will be excluded from it; which can be perceived either by touch, or by sight, or by hearing, or by taste, or by smell: which can be moved in many ways not, in truth, by itself, but by something which is foreign to it, by which it is touched [and from which it receives impressions] : for to have the power of self-movement as also of feeling or of thinking, I did not consider to appertain to the nature of body : on the contrary, I was rather astonished to find that faculties similar to them existed in some bodies.

But what am I, now that I suppose that there is a certain genius which is extremely powerful, and, if I may say so, malicious, who employs all his powers in deceiving me? Can I affirm that I possess the least of all those things which I have just said pertain to the nature of body? I pause to consider, I revolve all these things in my mind, and I find none of which I can say that it pertains to me. It would be tedious to stop to enumerate them. Let us pass to the attributes of soul and see if there is any one which is in me? What of nutrition or walking [the first mentioned]? But if it is so that I have no body it is also true that I can neither walk nor take nourishment. Another attribute is sensation. But one cannot feel without body, and besides I have thought I perceived many things during sleep that I recognized in my waking moments as not having been experienced at all. What of thinking? I find here that thought is an attribute that belongs to me; it alone cannot be separated from me. I am, I exist, that is certain. But how often? Just when I think; for it might possibly be the case if I ceased entirely to think, that I should likewise cease altogether to exist. I do not now admit anything which is not necessarily true: to speak accurately I am not more than a thing which thinks, that is to say a mind or a soul, or an understanding, or a reason, which are terms whose significance was formerly unknown to me. I am, however, a real thing and really exist; but what thing? I have answered: a thing which thinks.

And what more? I shall exercise my imagination [in order to see if I am not something more]. I am not a collection of members which we call the human body: I am not a subtle air distributed through these members, I am not a wind, a fire, a vapour, a breath, nor anything at all which I can imagine or conceive; because I have assumed that all these were nothing . Without changing that supposition I find that I only leave myself certain of the fact that I am somewhat. But perhaps it is true that these same things which I supposed were nonexistent because they are unknown to me, are really not different from the self which I know. I am not sure about this, I shall not dispute about it now; I can only give judgement on things that are known to me. I know that I exist, and I inquire what I am, I whom I know to exist. But it is very certain that the knowledge of my existence taken in its precise significance does not depend on things whose existence is not yet known to me; consequently it does not depend on those which I can feign in imagination. And indeed the very term *feign* in imagination proves to me my error, for I really do this if I image myself a something, since to imagine is nothing else than to contemplate the figure or image of a corporeal thing. But I already know for certain that I am, and that it may be that all these images, and, speaking generally, all things that relate to the nature of body are nothing but dreams [and chimeras]. For this reason I see clearly that I have as little reason to say, 'I shall stimulate my imagination in order to know more distinctly what I am,' than if I were to say, 'I am now awake, and I perceive somewhat that is real and true: but because I do not yet perceive it distinctly enough, I shall go to sleep of express purpose, so that my dreams may represent the perception with greatest truth and evidence.' And, thus, I know for certain that nothing of all that I can understand by means of my imagination belongs to this knowledge which I have of myself, and that it is necessary to recall the mind from this mode of thought with the utmost diligence in order that it may be able to know its own nature with perfect distinctness.

But what then am I? A thing which thinks. What is a thing which thinks? It is a thing which doubts, understands, [conceives], affirms, denies, wills, refuses, which also imagines and feels.

Certainly it is no small matter if all these things pertain to my nature. But why should they not so pertain? Am I not that being who now doubts nearly everything, who nevertheless understands certain things, who affirms that one only is true, who denies all the others, who desires to know more, is averse from being deceived, who imagines many things, sometimes indeed despite his will, and who perceives many likewise, as by the intervention of the bodily organs? Is there nothing in all this which is as true as it is certain that I exist, even though I should always sleep and though he who has given me being employed all his ingenuity in deceiving me? Is there likewise any one of these attributes which can be distinguished from my thought, or which might be said to be separated from myself? For it is so evident of itself that it is I who doubts, who understands, and who desires, that there is no reason here to add anything to explain it. And I have certainly the power of imagining likewise; for although it may happen (as I formerly supposed) that none of the things which I imagine are true, nevertheless this power of imagining does not cease to be really in use, and it forms part of my thought. Finally, I am the same who feels, that is to say, who perceives certain things, as by the organs of sense, since in truth I see light, I hear noise, I feel heat. But it will be said that these phenomena are false and that I am dreaming. Let it be so; still it is at least quite certain that it seems to me that I see light, that I hear noise and that I feel heat. That cannot be false; properly speaking it is what is in me called feeling; and used in this precise sense that is no other thing than thinking.

From this time I begin to know what I am with a little more clearness and distinction than before; but nevertheless it still seems to me, and I cannot prevent myself from thinking, that corporeal things, whose images are framed by thought, which are tested by the senses, are much more distinctly known than that obscure part of me which does not come under the imagination. Although really it is very strange to say that I know and understand more distinctly these things whose existence seems to me dubious, which are unknown to me, and which do not belong to me, than others of the truth of which I am convinced, which are known to me and which pertain to my real nature, in a word, than myself. But I see clearly how the case stands: my mind loves to wander, and cannot yet suffer itself to be retained within the just limits of truth. Very good, let us once more give it the freest rein, so that, when afterwards we seize the proper occasion for pulling up, it may the more easily be regulated and controlled.

Let us begin by considering the commonest matters, those which we believe to be the most distinctly comprehended, to wit, the bodies which we touch and see; not indeed bodies in general, for these general ideas are usually a little more confused, but let us consider one body in particular. Let us take, for example, this piece of wax: it has been taken quite freshly from the hive, and it has not yet lost the sweetness of the honey which it contains; it still retains somewhat of the odor of the flowers from which it has been culled; its colour, its figure, its size are apparent; it is hard, cold, easily handled, and if you strike it with the finger, it will emit a sound. Finally all the things which are requi-

site to cause us distinctly to recognize a body, are met with in it. But notice that while I speak and approach the fire what remained of the taste is exhaled, the smell evaporates, the colour alters, the figure is destroyed, the size increases, it becomes liquid, it heats, scarcely can one handle it, and when one strikes it, no sound is emitted. Does the same wax remain after this change? We must confess that it remains; none would judge otherwise. What then did I know so distinctly in this piece of wax? It could certainly be nothing of all that the senses brought to my notice, since all these things which fall under taste, smell, sight, touch, and hearing, are found to be changed, and yet the same wax remains.

Perhaps it was what I now think, viz. that this wax was not that sweetness of honey, nor that agreeable scent of flowers, nor that particular whiteness, nor that figure, nor that sound, but simply a body which a little while before appeared to me as perceptible under these forms, and which is now perceptible under others. But what, precisely, is it that I imagine when I form such conceptions? Let us attentively consider this, and, abstracting from all that does not belong to the wax, let us see what remains. Certainly nothing remains excepting a certain extended thing which is flexible and movable. But what is the meaning of flexible and movable? Is it not that I imagine that this piece of wax being round is capable of becoming square and of passing from a square to a triangular figure? No, certainly it is not that, since I imagine it admits of an infinitude of similar changes, and I nevertheless do not know how to compass the infinitude by my imagination, and consequently this conception which I have of the wax is not brought about by the faculty of imagination. What now is this extension? Is it not also unknown? For it becomes greater when the wax is melted, greater when it is boiled, and greater still when the heat increases; and I should not conceive [clearly] according to truth what wax is, if I did not think that even this piece that we are considering is capable of receiving more variations in extension than I have ever imagined. We must then grant that I could not even understand through the imagination what this piece of wax is, and that it is my mind alone which perceives it. I say this piece of wax in particular, for as to wax in general it is yet clearer. But what is this piece of wax which cannot be understood excepting by the [understanding or] mind? It is certainly the same that I see, touch, imagine, and finally it is the same which I have always believed it to be from the beginning. But what must particularly be observed is that its perception is neither an act of vision, nor of touch, nor of imagination, and has never been such although it may have appeared formerly to be so, but only an institution of the mind, which may be imperfect and confused as it was formerly, or clear and distinct as it is at present, according as my attention is more or less directed to the elements which are found in it, and of which it is composed.

Yet in the meantime I am greatly astonished when I consider [the great feebleness of mind] and its proneness to fall [insensibly] into error; for although without giving expression to my thoughts I consider all this in my own mind, words often impede me and I am almost deceived by the terms of ordinary language. For we say that we see the same wax, if it is present, and not that we simply judge that it is the same from its having the same colour and figure. From this I should conclude that I knew the wax by means of vision and not simply by the intuition of the mind; unless by chance I remember that, when looking from a window and saying I see men who pass in the street, I really do not see them, but infer that what I see is men, just as I say that I see wax. And yet what do I see from the window but hats and coats which may cover automatic machines? Yet I judge these to be men. And similarly solely by the faculty of judgement which rests in my mind, I comprehend that which I believed I saw with my eyes.

A man who makes it his aim to raise his knowledge above the common should be ashamed to derive the occasion for doubting from the forms of speech invented by the vulgar; I prefer to pass on and consider whether I had a more evident and perfect conception of what the wax was when I first perceived it, and when I believed I knew it by means of the external senses or at least by the common sense as it is called, that is to say by the imaginative faculty, or whether my present conception is clearer now that I have most carefully examined what it is, and in what way it can be known. It would certainly be absurd to doubt as to this. For what was there in this first perception which was distinct? What was there which might not as well have been perceived by any of the animals? But when I distinguish the wax from its external forms, and when, just as if I had taken from it its vestments, I consider it quite naked, it is certain that although some error may still be found in my judgement, I can nevertheless not perceive it thus without a human mind.

But finally what shall I say of this mind, that is, of myself, for up to this point I do not admit in myself anything but mind? What then, I who seem to perceive this piece of wax so distinctly, do I not know myself, not only with much more truth and certainty, but also with much more distinctness and clearness? For if I judge that the wax is or exists from the fact that I see it, it certainly follows much more clearly that I am or that I exist myself from the fact that I see it. For it may be that what I see is not really wax, it may also be that I do not possess eyes with which to see anything; but it cannot be that when I see, or (for I no longer take account of the distinction) when I think I see, that I myself who think am nought. So if I judge that the wax exists from the fact that I touch it, the same thing will follow, to wit, that I am; and if I judge that my imagination, or some other cause, whatever it is, persuades me that the wax exists, I shall still conclude the same. And what I have here remarked of wax may be applied to all other things which are external to me [and which are met with outside of me]. And further, if the [notion or] perception of wax has seemed to me clearer and more distinct, not only after the sight or the touch, but also after many other causes have rendered it quite manifest to me, with how much more [evidence] and distinctness must it be said that I now know myself, since all the reasons which contribute to the knowledge of wax, or any other body whatever, are yet better proofs of the nature of my mind! And there are so many other things in the mind itself which may contribute to the elucidation of its nature, that those which depend on body such as these just mentioned, hardly merit being taken into account.

But finally here I am, having insensibly reverted to the point I desired, for, since it is now manifest to me that even bodies are not properly speaking known by the senses or by the faculty of imagination, but by the understanding only, and since they are not known from the fact that they are seen or touched, but only because they are understood, I see clearly that there is nothing which is easier for me to know than my mind. But because it is difficult to rid oneself so promptly of an opinion to which one was accustomed for so long, it will be well that I should halt a little at this point, so that by the length of my meditation I may more deeply imprint on my memory this new knowledge.

Meditation III

Of God: that He exists

I shall now close my eyes, I shall stop my ears, I shall call away all my senses, I shall efface even from my thoughts all the images of corporeal things, or at least (for that is hardly possible) I shall esteem them as vain and false; and thus holding converse only with myself and considering my own nature, I shall try little by little to reach a better knowledge of and a more familiar acquaintanceship with myself. I am a thing that thinks, that is to say, that doubts, affirms, denies, that knows a few things, that is ignorant of many [that loves, that hates], that wills, that desires, that also imagines and perceives; for as I remarked before, although the things which I perceive and imagine are perhaps nothing at all apart from me and in themselves, I am nevertheless assured that these modes of thought that I call perceptions and imaginations, inasmuch only as they are modes of thought, certainly reside [and are met with] in me.

And in the little that I have just said, I think I have summed up all that I really know, or at least all that hitherto I was aware that I knew. In order to try to extend my knowledge further, I shall now look around more carefully and see whether I cannot still discover in myself some other things which I have not hitherto perceived. I am certain that I am a thing which thinks; but do I not then likewise know what is requisite to render me certain of a truth? Certainly in this first knowledge there is nothing that assures me of its truth, excepting the clear and distinct perception of that which I state, which would not indeed suffice to assure me that what I say is true, if it could ever happen that a thing which I conceived so clearly and distinctly could be false; and accordingly it seems to me that already I can establish as a general rule that all things which I perceive very clearly and very distinctly are true.

At the same time I have before received and admitted many things to be very certain and manifest, which yet I afterwards recognized as being dubious. What then were these things? They were the earth, sky, stars and all other objects which I apprehended by means of the senses. But what did I clearly [and distinctly] perceive in them? Nothing more than that the ideas or thoughts of these things were presented to my mind. And not even now do I deny that these ideas are met with in me. But there was yet another thing which I affirmed, and which, owing to the habit which I had formed of believing it, I thought I perceived very clearly, although in truth I did not perceive it at all, to wit, that there were objects outside of me from which these ideas proceeded, and to which they were entirely similar. And it was in this that I erred, or, if perchance my judgement was correct, this was not due to any knowledge arising from my perception.

But when I took anything very simple and easy in the sphere of arithmetic or geometry into consideration, e.g. that two and three together made five, and other things of the sort, were not these present to my mind so clearly as to enable me to affirm that they were true? Certainly if I judged that since such matters could be doubted, this would not have been so for any other reason than that it came into my mind that perhaps a God might have endowed me with such a nature that I may have been deceived even concerning things which seemed to me most manifest. But every time that this preconceived opinion of the sovereign power of a God presents itself to my thought, I am constrained to confess that it is easy to Him, if He wishes it, to cause me to err, even in matters in which I believe myself to have the best evidence. And, on the other hand, always when I direct my attention to things which I believe myself to perceive very clearly, I am so persuaded of their truth that I let myself break out into words such as these: Let who will deceive me, He can never cause me to be nothing while I think that I am, or some day cause it to be true to say that I have never been, it being true now to say that I am, or that two and three make more or less than five, or any such thing in which I see a manifest contradiction. And, certainly, since I have no reason to believe that there is a God who is a deceiver, and as I have not yet satisfied myself that there is a God at all, the reason for doubt which depends on this opinion alone is very slight, and so to speak metaphysical. But in order to be able altogether to remove it, I must inquire whether there is a God as soon as the occasion presents itself; and if I find that there is a God, I must also inquire whether He may be a deceiver; for without a knowledge of these two truths I do not see that I can ever be certain of anything.

And in order that I may have an opportunity of inquiring into this in an orderly way [without interrupting the order of meditation which I have proposed to myself, and which is little by little to pass from the notions which I find first of all in my mind to those which I shall later on discover in it] it is requisite that I should here divide my thoughts into certain kinds, and that I should consider in which of these kinds there is, properly speaking, truth or error to be found. Of my thoughts some are, so to speak, images of the things, and to these alone is the title 'idea' properly applied; examples are my thought of a man or of a chimera, of heaven, of an angel, or [even] of God. But other thoughts possess other forms as well. For example in willing, fearing, approving, denying, though I always perceive something as the subject of the action of my mind, yet by this action I always add something else to the idea which I have of that thing; and of the thoughts of this kind some are called volitions or affections, and others judgements.

Now as to what concerns ideas, if we consider them only in themselves and do not relate them to anything else beyond themselves, they cannot properly speaking be false; for whether I imagine a goat or a chimera, it is not less true that I imagine the one than the other. We must not fear likewise that falsity can enter into will and into affections, for although I may desire evil things, or even things that never existed, it is not the less true that I desire them. Thus there remains no more than the judgements which

we make, in which I must take the greatest care not to deceive myself. But the principal error and the commonest which we may meet with in them, consists in my judging that the ideas which are in me are similar or conformable to the things which are outside me; for without doubt if I considered the ideas only as certain modes of my thoughts, without trying to relate them to anything beyond, they could scarcely give me material for error.

But among these ideas, some appear to me to be innate, some adventitious, and others to be formed [or invented] by myself; for, as I have the power of understanding what is called a thing, or a truth, or a thought, it appears to me that I hold this power from no other source than my own nature. But if I now hear some sound, if I see the sun, or feel heat, I have hitherto judged that these sensations proceeded from certain things that exist outside of me; and finally it appears to me that sirens, hippogryphs, and the like, are formed out of my own mind. But again I may possibly persuade myself that all these ideas are of the nature of those which I term adventitious, or else that they are all innate, or all fictitious: for I have not yet clearly discovered their true origin.

And my principal task in this place is to consider, in respect to those ideas which appear to me to proceed from certain objects that are outside me, what are the reasons which cause me to think them similar to these objects. It seems indeed in the first place that I am taught this lesson by nature; and, secondly, I experience in myself that these ideas do not depend on my will nor therefore on myself—for they often present themselves to my mind in spite of my will. Just now, for instance, whether I will or whether I do not will, I feel heat, and thus I persuade myself that this feeling, or at least this idea of heat, is produced in me by something which is different from me, i.e. by the heat of the fire near which I sit. And nothing seems to me more obvious than to judge that this object imprints its likeness rather than anything else upon me.

Now I must discover whether these proofs are sufficiently strong and convincing. When I say that I am so instructed by nature, I merely mean a certain spontaneous inclination which impels me to believe in this connection, and not a natural light which makes me recognize that it is true. But these two things are very different; for I cannot doubt that which the natural light causes me to believe to be true, as, for example, it has shown me that I am from the fact that I doubt, or other facts of the same kind. And I possess no other faculty whereby to distinguish truth from falsehood, which can teach me that what this light shows me to be true is not really true, and no other faculty that is equally trustworthy. But as far as [apparently] natural impulses are concerned, I have frequently remarked, when I had to make active choice between virtue and vice, that they often enough led me to the part that was worse; and this is why I do not see any reason for following them in what regards truth and error.

And as to the other reason, which is that these ideas must proceed from objects outside me, since they do not depend on my will, I do not find it any the more convincing. For just as these impulses of which I have spoken are found in me, notwithstanding that they do not always concur with my will, so perhaps there is in me some faculty fitted to produce these ideas without the assistance of any external things, even though it is not yet known by me; just as, apparently, they have hitherto always been found in me during sleep without the aid of any external objects.

And finally, though they did proceed from objects different from myself, it is not a necessary consequence that they should resemble these. On the contrary, I have noticed that in many cases there was a great difference between the object and its idea. I find, for example, two completely diverse ideas of the sun in my mind; the one derives its origin from the senses, and should be placed in the category of adventitious ideas; according to this idea the sun seems to be extremely small; but the other is derived from astronomical reasonings, i.e. is elicited from certain notions that are innate in me, or else it is formed by me in some other manner; in accordance with it the sun appears to be several times greater than the earth. These two ideas cannot, indeed, both resemble same sun, and reason makes me believe that the one which seems to have originated directly from the sun itself, is the one which is most dissimilar to it.

All this causes me to believe that until the present time it has not been by a judgement that was certain [or premeditated], but only by a sort of blind impulse that I believed that things existed outside of, and different from me, which, by the organs of my senses, or by some other method whatever it might be, conveyed these ideas or images to me [and imprinted on me their similitudes].

But there is yet another method of inquiring whether any of the objects of which I have ideas within me exist outside of me. If ideas are only taken as certain modes of thought, I recognize amongst them no difference or inequality, and all appear to proceed from me in the same manner; but when we consider them as images, one representing one thing and the other another, it is clear that they are very different one from the other. There is no doubt that those which represent to me substances are something more, and contain so to speak more objective reality within them [that is to say, by representation participate in a higher degree of being or perfection] than those that simply represent modes or accidents; and that idea again by which I understand a supreme God, eternal, infinite, [immutable], omniscient, omnipotent, and Creator of all things which are outside of Himself, has certainly more objective reality in itself than those ideas by which finite substances are represented.

Now it is manifest by the natural light that there must at least be as much reality in the efficient and total cause as in its effect. For, pray, whence can the effect derive its reality, if not from its cause? And in what way can this cause communicate this reality to it, unless it possessed it in itself? And from this it follows, not only that something cannot proceed from nothing, but likewise that what is more perfect—that is to say, which has more reality within itself—cannot proceed from the less perfect. And this is not only evidently true of those effects which possess actual or formal reality, but also of the ideas in which we consider merely what is termed objective reality. To take an example, the stone which has not yet existed not only cannot now commence to be unless it has been produced by something which possesses within itself, either formally or eminently, all that enters into the composition of the stone [i.e. it must possess the same

things or other more excellent things than those which exist in the stone] and heat can only be produced in a subject in which it did not previously exist by a cause that is of an order [degree or kind] at least as perfect as heat, and so in all other cases. But further, the idea of heat, or of a stone, cannot exist in me unless it has been placed within me by some cause which possesses within it at least as much reality as that which I conceive to exist in the heat or the stone. For although this cause does not transmit anything of its actual or formal reality to my idea, we must not for that reason imagine that it is necessarily a less real cause; we must remember that [since every idea is a work of the mind] its nature is such that it demands of itself no other formal reality than that which it borrows from my thought, of which it is only a mode [i.e. a manner or way of thinking]. But in order that an idea should contain some one certain objective reality rather than another, it must without doubt derive it from some cause in which there is at least as much formal reality as this idea contains of objective reality. For if we imagine that something is found in an idea which is not found in the cause, it must then have been derived from nought; but however imperfect may be this mode of being by which a thing is objectively [or by representation] in the understanding by its idea, we cannot certainly say that this mode of being is nothing, nor, consequently, that the idea derives its origin from nothing.

Nor must I imagine that, since the reality that I consider in these ideas is only objective, it is not essential that this reality should be formally in the causes of my ideas, but that it is sufficient that it should be found objectively. For just as this mode of objective existence pertains to ideas by their proper nature, so does the mode of formal existence pertain to the causes of those ideas (this is at least true of the first and principal) by the nature peculiar to them. And although it may be the case that one idea gives birth to another idea, that cannot continue to be so indefinitely; for in the end we must reach an idea whose cause shall be so to speak an archetype, in which the whole reality [or perfection] which is so to speak objectively [or by representation] in these ideas is contained formally [and really]. Thus the light of nature causes me to know clearly that the ideas in me are like [pictures or] images which can, in truth, easily fall short of the perfection of the objects from which they have been derived, but which can never contain anything greater or more perfect.

And the longer and the more carefully that I investigate these matters, the more clearly and distinctly do I recognize their truth. But what am I to conclude from it all in the end? It is this, that if the objective reality of any one of my ideas is of such a nature as clearly to make me recognize that it is not in me either formally or eminently, and that consequently I cannot myself be the cause of it, it follows of necessity that I am not alone in the world, but that there is another being which exists, or which is the cause of this idea. On the other hand, had no such an idea existed in me, I should have had no sufficient argument to convince me of the existence of any being beyond myself; for I have made very careful investigation everywhere and up to the present time have been able to find no other ground.

But of my ideas, beyond that which represents me to myself, as to which there can here be no difficulty, there is another

which represents a God, and there are others representing corporeal and inanimate things, others angels, others animals, and others again which represent to me men similar to myself.

As regards the ideas which represent to me other men or animals, or angels, I can however easily conceive that they might be formed by an admixture of the other ideas which I have of myself, of corporeal things, and of God, even although there were apart from me neither men nor animals, nor angels, in all the world.

And in regard to the ideas of corporeal objects, I do not recognize in them anything so great or so excellent that they might not have possibly proceeded from myself; for if I consider them more closely, and examine them individually, as I yesterday examined the idea of wax, I find that there is very little in them which I perceive clearly and distinctly. Magnitude or extension in length, breadth, or depth, I do so perceive; also figure which results from a termination of this extension, the situation which bodies of different figure preserve in relation to one another, and movement or change of situation; to which we may also add substance, duration and number. As to other things such as light, colours, sounds, scents, tastes, heat, cold and the other tactile qualities, they are thought by me with so much obscurity and confusion that I do not even know if they are true or false, i.e. whether the ideas which I form of these qualities are actually the ideas of real objects or not [or whether they only represent chimeras which cannot exist in fact]. For although I have before remarked that it is only in judgements that falsity, properly speaking, or formal falsity, can be met with, a certain material falsity may nevertheless be found in ideas, i.e. when these ideas represent what is nothing as though it were something. For example, the ideas which I have of cold and heat are so far from clear and distinct that by their means I cannot tell whether cold is merely a privation of heat, or heat a privation of cold, or whether both are real qualities, or are not such. And inasmuch as [since ideas resemble images] there cannot be any ideas which do not appear to represent some things, if it is correct to say that cold is merely a privation of heat, the idea which represents it to me as something real and positive will not be improperly termed false, the same holds good of other similar ideas.

To these it is certainly not necessary that I should attribute any author other than myself. For if they are false, i.e. if they represent things which do not exist, the light of nature shows me that they issue from nought, that is to say, that they are only in me in so far as something is lacking to the perfection of my nature. But if they are true, nevertheless because they exhibit so little reality to me that I cannot even clearly distinguish the thing represented from non-being, I do not see any reason why they should not be produced by myself.

As to the clear and distinct idea which I have of corporeal things, some of them seem as though I might have derived them from the idea which I possess of myself, as those which I have of substance, duration, number, and such like. For [even] when I think that a stone is a substance, or at least a thing capable of existing of itself, and that I am a substance also, although I conceive that I am a thing that thinks and not one that is extended, and that the stone on the other hand is an extended thing which does not think,

and that thus there is a notable difference between the two conceptions—they seem, nevertheless, to agree in this, that both represent substances. In the same way, when I perceive that I now exist and further recollect that I have in former times existed, and when I remember that I have various thoughts of which I can recognize the number, I acquire ideas of duration and number which I can afterwards transfer to any object that I please. But as to all the other qualities of which the ideas of corporeal things are composed, to wit, extension, figure, situation and motion, it is true that they are not formally in me, since I am only a thing that thinks; but because they are merely certain modes of substance [and so to speak the vestments under which corporeal substance appears to us] and because I myself am also a substance, it would seem that they might be contained in me eminently.

Hence there remains only the idea of God, concerning which we must consider whether it is something which cannot have proceeded from me myself. By the name God I understand a substance that is infinite [eternal, immutable], independent, all-knowing, all-powerful, and by which I myself and everything else, if anything else does exist, have been created. Now all these characteristics are such that the more diligently I attend to them, the less do they appear capable of proceeding from me alone; hence, from what has been already said, we must conclude that God necessarily exists.

For although the idea of substance is within me owing to the fact that I am substance, nevertheless I should not have the idea of an infinite substance—since I am finite—if it had not proceeded from some substance which was veritably infinite.

Nor should I imagine that I do not perceive the infinite by a true idea, but only by the negation of the finite, just as I perceive repose and darkness by the negation of movement and of light; for, on the contrary, I see that there is manifestly more reality in infinite substance than in finite, and therefore that in some way I have in me the notion of the infinite earlier than the finite—to wit, the notion of God before that of myself. For how would it be possible that I should know that I doubt and desire, that is to say, that something is lacking to me, and that I am not quite perfect, unless I had within me some idea of a Being more perfect than myself, in comparison with which I should recognize the deficiencies of my nature?

And we cannot say that this idea of God is perhaps materially false and that consequently I can derive it from nought [i.e. that possibly it exists in me because I am imperfect], as I have just said is the case with ideas of heat, cold and other such things; for on the contrary, as this idea is very clear and distinct and contains within it more objective reality than any other, there can be none which is of itself more true, nor any in which there can be less suspicion of falsehood. The idea, I say, of this Being who is absolutely perfect and infinite, is entirely true; for although, perhaps, we can imagine that such a Being does not exist, we cannot nevertheless imagine that His idea represents nothing real to me, as I have said of the idea of cold. This idea is also very clear and distinct; since all that I conceive clearly and distinctly of the real and the true, and of what conveys some perfection, is in its entirety contained in this idea. And this does not cease to be true although I do not comprehend the infinite, or though in God there is an infinitude of things

which I cannot comprehend, nor possibly even reach in any way by thought; for it is the nature of the infinite that my nature, which is finite and limited, should not comprehend it; and it is sufficient that I should understand this, and that I should judge that all things which I clearly perceive and in which I know that there is some perfection, and possibly likewise an infinitude of properties of which I am ignorant, are in God formally or eminently, so that the idea which I have of Him may become the most true, most clear, and most distinct of all the ideas that are in my mind.

But possibly I am something more than I suppose myself to be, and perhaps all those perfections which I attribute to God are in some way potentially in me, although they do not yet disclose themselves, or issue in action. As a matter of fact I am already sensible that my knowledge increases [and perfects itself] little by little, and I see nothing which can prevent it from increasing more and more into infinitude; nor do I see, after it has thus been increased [or perfected], anything to prevent my being able to acquire by its means all the other perfections of the Divine nature; nor finally why the power I have of acquiring these perfections, if it really exists in me, shall not suffice to produce the ideas of them.

At the same time I recognize that this cannot be. For, in the first place, although it were true that every day my knowledge acquired new degrees of perfection, and that there were in my nature many things potentially which are not yet there actually, nevertheless these excellences do not pertain to [or make the smallest approach to] the idea which I have of God in whom there is nothing merely potential [but in whom all is present really and actually]; for it is an infallible token of imperfection in my knowledge that it increases little by little. And further, although my knowledge grows more and more, nevertheless I do not for that reason believe that it can never reach a point so high that it will be unable to attain to any greater increase. But I understand God to be actually infinite, so that He can add nothing to His supreme perfection. And finally I perceive that the objective being of an idea cannot be produced by a being that exists potentially only, which properly speaking is nothing, but only by a being which is formal or actual.

To speak the truth, I see nothing in all that I have just said which by the light of nature is not manifest to anyone who desires to think attentively on the subject; but when I slightly relax my attention, my mind, finding its vision somewhat obscured and so to speak blinded by the images of sensible objects, I do not easily recollect the reason why the idea that I possess of a being more perfect than I, must necessarily have been placed in me by a being which is really more perfect; and this is why I wish here to go on to inquire whether I, who have this idea, can exist if no such being exists.

And I ask, from whom do I then derive my existence? Perhaps from myself or from my parents, or from some other source less perfect than God; for we can imagine nothing more perfect than God; or even as perfect as He is.

But [were I independent of every other and] were I myself the author of my being, I should doubt nothing and I should desire nothing, and finally no perfection would be lacking to me; for I should have bestowed on myself every perfection of which I pos-

sessed any idea and should thus be God. And it must not be imagined that those things that are lacking to me are perhaps more difficult of attainment than those which I already possess; for, on the contrary, it is quite evident that it was a matter of much greater difficulty to bring to pass that I, that is to say, a thing or a substance that thinks, should emerge out of nothing, than it would be to attain to the knowledge of many things of which I am ignorant, and which are only the accidents of this thinking substance. But it is clear that if I had of myself possessed this greater perfection of which I have just spoken [that is to say, if I had been the author of my own existence], I should not at least have denied myself the things which are the more easy to acquire [to wit, many branches of knowledge of which my nature is destitute]; nor should I have deprived myself of any of the things contained in the idea which I form of God, because there are none of them which seem to me specially difficult to acquire: and if there were any that were more difficult to acquire, they would certainly appear to me to be such (supposing I myself were the origin of the other things which I possess) since I should discover in them that my powers were limited.

But though I assume that perhaps I have already existed just as I am at present, neither can I escape the force of this reasoning, and imagine that the conclusion to be drawn from this is, that I need not seek for any author of my existence. For all the course of my life may be divided into an infinite number of parts, none of which is in any way dependent on the other; and thus from the fact that I was in existence a short time ago it does not follow that I must be in existence now, unless some cause at this instant, so to speak, produces me anew, that is to say, conserves me. It is as a matter of fact perfectly clear and evident to all those who consider with attention the nature of time, that, in order to be conserved in each moment in which it endures, a substance has need of the same power and action as would be necessary to produce and create it anew, supposing it did not yet exist, so that the light of nature shows us clearly that the distinction between creation and conservation is solely a distinction of the reason.

All that I thus require here is that I should interrogate myself, if I wish to know whether I possess a power which is capable of bringing it to pass that I who now am shall still be in the future; for since I am nothing but a thinking thing, or at least since thus far it is only this portion of myself which is precisely in question at present, if such a power did reside in me, I should certainly be conscious of it. But I am conscious of nothing of the kind, and by this I know clearly that I depend on some being different from myself.

Possibly, however, this being on which I depend is not that which I call God, and I am created either by my parents or by some other cause less perfect than God. This cannot be, because, as I have just said, it is perfectly evident that there must be at least as much reality in the cause as in the effect; and thus since I am a thinking thing, and possess an idea of God within me, whatever in the end be the cause assigned to my existence, it must be allowed that it is likewise a thinking thing and that it possesses in itself the idea of all the perfections which I attribute to God. We may again inquire whether this cause derives its origin from itself or from some other thing. For if from

itself, it follows by the reasons before brought forward, that this cause must itself be God; for since it possesses the virtue of self-existence, it must also without doubt have the power of actually possessing all the perfections of which it has the idea, that is, all those which I conceive as existing in God. But if it derives its existence from some other cause than itself, we shall again ask, for the same reason, whether this second cause exists by itself or through another, until from one step to another, we finally arrive at an ultimate cause, which will be God.

And it is perfectly manifest that in this there can be no regression into infinity, since what is in question is not so much the cause which formerly created me, as that which conserves me at the present time.

Nor can we suppose that several causes may have concurred in my production, and that from one I have received the idea of one of the perfections which I attribute to God, and from another the idea of some other, so that all these perfections indeed exist somewhere in the universe, but not as complete in one unity which is God. On the contrary, the unity, the simplicity or the inseparability of all things which are in God is one of the principal perfections which I conceive to be in him. And certainly the idea of this unity of all Divine perfections cannot have been placed in me by any cause from which I have not likewise received the ideas of all the other perfections; for this cause could not make me able to comprehend them as joined together in an inseparable unity without having at the same time caused me in some measure to know what they are [and in some way to recognize each of them].

Finally, so far as my parents [from whom

it appears I have sprung] are concerned, although all that I have ever been able to believe of them were true, that does not make it follow that it is they who conserve me, nor are they even the authors of my being in any sense, in so far as I am a thinking being; since what they did was merely to implant certain dispositions in that matter in which the self—i.e. the mind, which alone I at present identify with myself—is by me deemed to exist. And thus there can be no difficulty in their regard, but we must of necessity conclude from the fact alone that I exist, or that the idea of a Being supremely perfect—that is of God—is in me, that the proof of God's existence is grounded on the highest evidence.

It only remains to me to examine into the manner in which I have acquired this idea from God; for I have not received it through the senses, and it is never presented to me unexpectedly, as is usual with the ideas of sensible things when these things present themselves, or seem to present themselves, to the external organs of my senses; nor is it likewise a fiction of my mind, for it is not in my power to take form or to add anything to it; and consequently the only alternative is that it is innate in me, just as the idea of myself is innate in me.

And one certainly ought not to find it strange that God, in creating me, placed this idea within me to be like the mark of the workman imprinted on his work; and it is likewise not essential that the mark shall be something different from the work itself. For from the sole fact that God created me it is most probable that in some way he has placed his image and similitude upon me, and that I perceive this similitude (in which the idea of God is contained) by means of the

same faculty by which I perceive myself—that is to say, when I reflect on myself I not only know that I am something [imperfect], incomplete and dependent on another, which incessantly aspires after something which is better and greater than myself, but I also know that He on whom I depend possesses in Himself all the great things towards which I aspire [and the ideas of which I find within myself], and that not indefinitely or potentially alone, but really, actually and infinitely; and that thus He is God. And the whole strength of the argument which I have here made use of to prove the existence of God consists in this, that I recognize that it is not possible that my nature should be what it is, and indeed that I should have in myself the idea of a God, if God did not veritably exist—a God, I say, whose idea is in me, i.e. who possesses all those supreme perfections of which our mind may indeed have some idea but without understanding them all, who is liable to errors or defect [and who has none of all those marks which denote imperfection]. From this it is manifest that He cannot be a deceiver, since the light of nature teaches us that fraud and deception necessarily proceed from some defect.

But before I examine this matter with more care, and pass on to the consideration of other truths which may be derived from it, it seems to me right to pause for a while in order to contemplate God Himself, to ponder at leisure His marvelous attributes, to consider, and admire, and adore, the beauty of this light so resplendent, at least as far as the strength of my mind, which is in some measure dazzled by the sight, will allow me to do so. For just as faith teaches us that the supreme felicity of the other life consists only in this contemplation of the Divine

Majesty, so we continue to learn by experience that a similar meditation, though incomparably less perfect, causes us to enjoy the greatest satisfaction of which we are capable in this life.

Meditation IV

Of the True and the False

I have been well accustomed these past days to detach my mind from my senses, and I have accurately observed that there are very few things that one knows with certainty respecting corporeal objects, that there are many more which are known to us respecting the human mind, and yet more still regarding God himself; so that I shall now without any difficulty abstract my thoughts from the consideration of [sensible or] imaginable objects, and carry them to those which, being withdrawn from all contact with matter, are purely intelligible. And certainly the idea which I possess of the human mind inasmuch as it is a thinking thing, and not extended in length, width and depth, not participating in anything pertaining to body, is incomparably more distinct than is the idea of any corporeal thing. And when I consider that I doubt, that is to say, that I am an incomplete and dependent being, the idea of a being that is complete and independent, that is of God, presents itself to deliberate; or simply by His engraving deeply in my memory the resolution never to form a judgement on anything without having a clear and distinct understanding of it, so that I could never forget it. And it is easy for me to understand that, in so far as I consider myself alone, and as if there were only myself in the world, I should have been much more

perfect than I am, if God had created me so that I could never err. Nevertheless I cannot deny that in some sense it is a greater perfection in the whole universe that certain parts should not be exempt from error as others are than that all parts should be exactly similar. And I have no right to complain if God, having placed me in the world, has not called upon me to play a part that excels all others in distinction and perfection.

And further I have reason to be glad on the ground that if He has not given me the power of never going astray by the first means pointed out above, which depends on a clear and evident knowledge of all the things regarding which I can deliberate, He has at least left within my power the other means, which is firmly to adhere to the resolution never to give judgement on matters whose truth is not clearly known to me; for although I notice a certain weakness in my nature in that I cannot continually concentrate my mind on one single thought, I can yet, by attentive and frequently repeated meditation, impress it so forcibly on my memory that I shall never fail to recollect it whenever I have need of it, and thus acquire the habit of never going astray.

And inasmuch as it is in this that the greatest and principal perfection of man consists, it seems to me that I have not gained little by this day's Meditation, since I have discovered the source of falsity and error. And certainly there can be no other source than that which I have explained; for as often as I so restrain my will within the limits of my knowledge that it forms no judgement except on matters which are clearly and distinctly represented to it by the understanding, I can never be deceived; for every clear and distinct conception is without doubt something, and hence cannot derive its origin from what is nought, but must of necessity have God as its author—God, I say, who being supremely perfect, cannot be the cause of any error; and consequently we must conclude that such a conception [or such a judgement] is true. Nor have I only learned to-day what I should avoid in order that I may not err, but also how I should act in order to arrive at a knowledge of the truth; for without doubt I shall arrive at this end if I devote my attention sufficiently to those things which I perfectly understand; and if I separate from these that which I only understand confusedly and with obscurity. To these I shall henceforth diligently give heed.

Meditation V

Of the essence of material things, and, again, of God, that He exists.

Many other matters respecting the attributes of God and my own nature or mind remain for consideration; but I shall possibly on another occasion resume the investigation of these. Now (after first noting what must be done or avoided, in order to arrive at a knowledge of the truth) my principal task is to endeavor to emerge from the state of doubt into which I have these last days fallen, and to see whether nothing certain can be known regarding material things.

But before examining whether any such objects as I conceive exist outside of me, I must consider the ideas of them in so far as they are in my thought, and see which of them are distinct and which confused.

In the first place, I am able distinctly to imagine that quantity which philosophers commonly call continuous, or the extension in length, breadth, or depth, that is this quantity, or rather in the object to which it is attributed. Further, I can number in it many different parts, and attribute to each of its parts many sorts of size, figure, situation and local movement, and, finally, I can assign to each of these movements all degrees of duration.

And not only do I know these things with distinctness when I consider them in general, but, likewise [however little I apply my attention to the matter], I discover an infinitude of particulars respecting numbers, figures, movements, and other such things, whose truth is so manifest, and so well accords with my nature, that when I begin to discover them, it seems to me that I learn nothing new, or recollect what I formerly knew—that is to say, that I for the first time perceive things which were already present to my mind, although I had not as yet applied my mind to them.

And what I here find to be most important is that I discover in myself an infinitude of ideas of certain things which cannot be esteemed as pure negations, although they may possibly have no existence outside of my thought, and which are not framed by me, although it is within my power either to think or not to think them, but which possess natures which are true and immutable. For example, when I imagine a triangle, although there may nowhere in the world be such a figure outside my thought, or ever have been, there is nevertheless in this figure a certain determinate nature, form, or essence, which is immutable and eternal, which I have not invented, and which in no wise depends on my mind, as appears from the fact that diverse properties of that triangle can be demonstrated, viz. that its three angles are equal to two right angles, that the greatest side is subtended by the greatest angle, and the like, which now, whether I wish it or do not wish it, I recognize very clearly as pertaining to it, although I never thought of the matter at all when I imagined a triangle for the first time, and which therefore cannot be said to have been invented by me.

Nor does the objection hold good that possibly this idea of a triangle has reached my mind through the medium of my senses, since I have sometimes seen bodies triangular in shape; because I can form in my mind an infinitude of other figures regarding which we cannot have the least conception of their ever having been objects of sense, and I can nevertheless demonstrate various properties pertaining to their nature as well as to that of the triangle, and these must certainly all be true since I conceive them clearly. Hence they are something, and not pure negation; for it is perfectly clear that all that is true is something, and I have already fully demonstrated that all that I know clearly is true. And even although I had not demonstrated this, the nature of my mind is such that I could not prevent myself from holding them to be true so long as I conceive them clearly; and I recollect that even when I was still strongly attached to the objects of sense, I counted as the most certain those truths which I conceived clearly as regards figures, numbers, and the other matters which pertain to arithmetic and geometry, and, in general, to pure and abstract mathematics.

But now, if just because I can draw the idea of something from my thought, it follows that all which I know clearly and distinctly as pertaining to this object does really belong to it, may I not derive from this an argument demonstrating the existence of God? It is certain that I no less find the idea of God, that is to say, the idea of a supremely perfect Being, in me, than that of any figure or number whatever it is; and I do not know any less clearly and distinctly that an [actual and] eternal existence pertains to this nature than I know that all that which I am able to demonstrate of some figure or number truly pertains to the nature of this figure or number, and therefore, although all that I concluded in the preceding Meditations were found to be false, the existence of God would pass with me as at least as certain as I have ever held the truths of mathematics (which concern only numbers and figures) to be.

This indeed is not at first manifest, since it would seem to present some appearance of being a sophism. For being accustomed in all other things to make a distinction between existence and essence, I easily persuade myself that the existence can be separated from the essence of God, and that we can thus conceive God as not actually existing. But, nevertheless, when I think of it with more attention, I clearly see that existence can no more be separated from the essence of God than can its having its three angles equal to two right angles be separated from the essence of a [rectilinear] triangle, or the idea of a mountain from the idea of a valley; and so there is not any less repugnance to our conceiving a God (that is, a Being supremely perfect) to whom existence is lacking (that is to say, to whom a certain perfection is lacking), than to conceive of a mountain which has no valley.

But although I cannot really conceive of a God without existence any more than a mountain without a valley, still from the fact that I conceive of a mountain with a valley, it does not follow that there is such a mountain in the world; similarly although I conceive of God as possessing existence, it would seem that it does not follow that there is a God which exists; for my thought does not impose any necessity upon things, and just as I may imagine a winged horse, although no horse with wings exists, so I could perhaps attribute existence to God, although no God existed.

But a sophism is concealed in this objection; for from the fact that I cannot conceive a mountain without a valley, it does not follow that there is any mountain or any valley in existence, but only that the mountain and the valley, whether they exist or do not exist, cannot in any way be separated one from the other. While from the fact that I cannot conceive God without existence, it follows that existence is inseparable from Him, and hence that He really exists; not that my thought can bring this to pass, or impose any necessity on things, but, on the contrary, because the necessity which lies in the thing itself, i.e. the necessity of the existence of God determines me to think this way. For it is not within my power to think of God without existence (that is of a supremely perfect Being devoid of a supreme perfection) though it is in my power to imagine a horse either with wings or without wings.

And we must not here object that it is in truth necessary for me to assert that God exists after having presupposed that He possesses every sort of perfection, since existence is one of these, but that as a matter of fact my original supposition was not necessary, just as it is not necessary to consider that all quadrilateral figures can be inscribed in the circle; for supposing I thought this, I should be constrained to admit that the rhombus might be inscribed in the circle since it is

a quadrilateral figure, which, however, is manifestly false. [We must not, I say, make any such allegations because] although it is not necessary that I should at any time entertain the notion of God, nevertheless whenever it happens that I think of a first and a sovereign Being, and, so to speak, derive the idea of Him from the storehouse of my mind, it is necessary that I should attribute to Him every sort of perfection, although I do not get so far as to enumerate them all, or to apply my mind to each one in particular. And this necessity suffices to make me conclude (after having recognized that existence is a perfection) that this first and sovereign Being really exists; just as though it is not necessary for me ever to imagine any triangle, yet, whenever I wish to consider a rectilinear figure composed only of three angles, it is absolutely essential that I should attribute to it all those properties which serve to bring about the conclusion that its three angles are not greater than two right angles, even though I may not then be considering this point in particular. But when I consider which figures are capable of being inscribed in the circle, it is in no wise necessary that I should think that all quadrilateral figures are of this number; on the contrary, I cannot even pretend that this is the case, so long as I do not desire to accept anything which I cannot conceive clearly and distinctly. And in consequence there is a great difference between the false suppositions such as this, and the true ideas born within me, the first and principal of which is that of God. For really I discern in many ways that this idea is not something factitious, and depending solely on my thought, but that it is the image of a true and immutable nature; first of all, because I cannot conceive anything but God himself to whose essence existence [necessarily] pertains; in the second place because it is not possible for me to conceive two or more Gods in this same position; and, granted that there is one such God who now exists, I see clearly that it is necessary that He should have existed from all eternity, and that He must exist eternally; and finally, because I know an infinitude of other properties in God, none of which I can either diminish or change.

For the rest, whatever proof or argument I avail myself of, we must always return to the point that it is only those things which we conceive clearly and distinctly that have the power of persuading me entirely. And although amongst the matters which I conceive of in this way, some indeed are manifestly obvious to all, while others only manifest themselves to those who consider them closely and examine them attentively; still, after they have once been discovered, the latter are not esteemed as any less certain than the former. For example, in the case of every right-angled triangle, although it does not so manifestly appear that the square of the base is equal to the squares of the two other sides as that this base is opposite to the greatest angle; still, when this has once been apprehended, we are just as certain of its truth as of the truth of the other. And as regards God, if my mind were not preoccupied with prejudices, and if my thought did not find itself on all hands diverted by the continual pressure of sensible things, there would be nothing which I could know more immediately and more easily than Him. For is there anything more manifest than that there is a God, that is to say, a Supreme Being, to whose essence alone existence pertains?

And although for a firm grasp of this truth I have need of a strenuous application of mind, at present I not only feel myself to be as assured of it as of all that I hold as most certain, but I also remark the certainty of all other things depends on it so absolutely, that without this knowledge it is impossible ever to know anything perfectly.

For although I am of such a nature that as long as I understand anything very clearly and distinctly, I am naturally impelled to believe it to be true, yet because I am also of such a nature that I cannot have my mind constantly fixed on the same object in order to perceive it clearly, and as I often recollect having formed a past judgement without at the same time properly recollecting the reasons that led me to make it, it may happen meanwhile that other reasons present themselves to me, which would easily cause me to change my opinion, if I were ignorant of the facts of the existence of God, and thus I should have no true and certain knowledge, but only vague and vacillating opinions. Thus, for example, when I consider the nature of a [rectilinear] triangle, I who have some little knowledge of the principles of geometry recognize quite clearly that the three angles are equal to two right angles, and it is not possible for me not to believe this so long as I apply my mind to its demonstration; but so soon as I abstain from attending to the proof, although I still recollect having clearly comprehended it, it may easily occur that I come to doubt its truth, if I am ignorant of there being a God. For I can persuade myself of having been so constituted by nature that I can easily deceive myself even in those matters which I believe to apprehend with the greatest evidence and certainty, especially when I recollect that I have frequently judged matters to be true and certain which other reasons have afterwards impelled me to judge to be altogether false.

But after I have recognized that there is a God—because at the same time I have also recognized that all things depend upon Him, and that He is not a deceiver, and from that have inferred that what I perceive clearly and distinctly cannot fail to be true—although I no longer pay attention to the reasons for which I have judged this to be true, provided that I recollect having clearly and distinctly perceived it no contrary reason can be brought forward which could ever cause me to doubt of its truth; and thus I have a true and certain knowledge of it. And this same knowledge extends likewise to all other things which I recollect having formerly demonstrated, such as the truths of geometry and the like; for what can be alleged against them to cause me to place them in doubt? Will it be said that my nature is such as to cause me to be frequently deceived? But I already know that I cannot be deceived in the judgement whose grounds I know clearly. Will it be said that I formerly held many things to be true and certain which I have afterwards recognized to be false? But I had not had any clear and distinct knowledge of these things, and not as yet knowing the rule whereby I assure myself of the truth, I had been impelled to give my assent from reasons which I have since recognized to be less strong than I had at the time imagined them to be. What further objection can then be raised? That possibly I am dreaming (an objection I myself made a little while ago), or that all the thoughts which I now have are no more true than the phantasies of my dreams? But even though I slept the case would be the same, for all that is clearly present to my mind is absolutely true.

And so I very clearly recognize that the certainty and truth of all knowledge depends alone on the knowledge of the true God, in so much that, before I knew Him, I could not have a perfect knowledge of any other thing. And now that I know Him I have the means of acquiring a perfect knowledge of an infinitude of things, not only of those which relate to God Himself and other intellectual matters, but also of those which pertain to corporeal nature in so far as it is the object of pure mathematics [which have no concern with whether it exists or not].

29 David Hume
(from *An Enquiry Concerning Human Understanding*)

Section II—*Of the Origin of Ideas*

Every one will readily allow, that there is a *considerable difference* between *the perceptions of the mind*, when a man feels the pain of excessive heat, or the pleasure of moderate warmth, and when he afterwards recalls to his memory this sensation, or anticipates it by his imagination. These faculties may *mimic or copy* the perceptions of the senses; but they never can entirely reach the *force and vivacity* of the original sentiment. The utmost we say of them, even when they operate with greatest vigour, is, that they represent their object in so lively a manner, that we could *almost* say we feel or see it: But, except the mind be disordered by disease or madness, they never can arrive at such a pitch of vivacity, as to render these perceptions altogether undistinguishable. All the colours of poetry, however splendid, can never paint natural objects in such a manner as to make the description be taken for a real landskip. *The most lively thought is still inferior to the dullest sensation.*

We may observe a like distinction to run through all the other perceptions of the mind. A man in a fit of anger, is actuated in a very different manner from one who only thinks of that emotion. If you tell me, that any person is in love, I easily understand your meaning, and form a just conception of his situation; but *never can mistake that conception for the real disorders and agitations of the passion.* When we reflect on our past sentiments and affections, our thought is a faithful mirror, and copies its objects truly; but the colours which it employs are faint and dull, in comparison of those in which our original perceptions were clothed. It requires no nice discernment or metaphysical head to mark the distinction between them.

Here therefore we may divide all the perceptions of the mind into two classes or species, which are distinguished by their different degrees of force and vivacity. The less forcible and lively are commonly denominated THOUGHTS or IDEAS. The other species want a name in our language, and in most others; I suppose, because it was not requisite for any, but philosophical purposes, to rank them under a general term or appellation. Let us, therefore, use a little freedom, and call them IMPRESSIONS; employing that word in a sense somewhat different from the usual.

By the term *impression*, then, I mean all our more lively perceptions, when we hear, or see, or feel, or love, or hate, or desire, or will. And impressions are distinguished from ideas, which are the less lively perceptions, of which we are conscious, when we reflect on any of those sensations or movements above mentioned.

Nothing, at first view, may seem more unbounded than the thought of man, which not only escapes all human power and authority, but is not even restrained within the limits of nature and reality. To form monsters, and join incongruous shapes and appearances, costs the imagination no more trouble than to conceive the most natural and familiar objects. And while the body is confined to one planet, along which it creeps with pain and difficulty; the thought can in an instant transport us into the most distant regions of the universe; or even beyond the universe, into the unbounded chaos, where nature is supposed to lie in total confusion. What never was seen, or heard of, may yet be conceived; nor is anything beyond the power of thought, except what implies an absolute contradiction.

But though our thought seems to possess this unbounded liberty, we shall find, upon a nearer examination, that it is really confined within *very narrow limits*, and that all this creative power of the mind amounts to no more than the faculty of compounding, transposing, augmenting, or diminishing the materials afforded us by the senses and experience. When we think of a golden mountain, we only join two consistent ideas, *gold*, and *mountain*, with which we were formerly acquainted. A virtuous horse we can conceive; because, from our own feeling, we can conceive virtue; and this we may unite to the figure and shape of a horse, which is an animal familiar to us. *In short, all the materials of thinking are derived either from our outward or inward sentiment:* The mixture and composition of these belongs alone to the mind and will. Or, to express myself *in philosophical language, all our ideas or more feeble perceptions are copies of our impressions or more lively ones.*

To prove this, the *two following arguments* will, I hope, be sufficient. *First*, when we analyse our *thoughts or ideas,* however compounded or sublime, we always find, that they *resolve themselves into such simple ideas as were copied from a precedent feeling or sentiment.* Even those ideas, which, at first view, seem the most wide of this origin, are found, upon a nearer scrutiny, to be derived from it. The idea of God, as meaning an infinitely intelligent, wise, and good Being, arises from reflecting on the operations of our own mind, and augmenting, without limit, those qualities of goodness and wisdom. We may prosecute this enquiry to what length we please; where we shall always find, that every idea which we examine is copied from a similar impression. Those who would assert, that this position is not universally true nor without exception, have only one, and that an easy method of refuting it; by producing that idea, which, in their opinion, is not derived from this source. It

will then be incumbent on us, if we would maintain our doctrine, to produce the impression or lively perception, which corresponds to it.

Secondly. If it happen, from a defect of the organ, that *a man is not susceptible of any species of sensation*, we always find, that *he is as little susceptible of the correspondent ideas.* A blind man can form no idea of colours; a deaf man of sounds. Restore either of them that sense, in which he is deficient; by opening this new inlet for his sensations, you also open an inlet for the ideas; and he finds no difficulty in conceiving these objects. The case is the same, if the object, proper for exciting any sensation, has never been applied to the organ. A LAPLANDER or NEGRO has no notion of the relish of wine. And though there are few or no instances of a like deficiency in the mind, where a person has never felt or is wholly incapable of a sentiment or passion, that belongs to his species; yet we find the same observation to take place in a less degree. A man of mild manners can form no idea of inveterate revenge or cruelty; nor can a selfish heart easily conceive the heights of friendship and generosity. It is readily allowed, that other beings may possess many senses of which we can have no conception; because the ideas of them have never been introduced to us, in *the only manner, by which an idea can have access to the mind, to wit, by the actual feeling and sensation.*

There is, however, one contradictory phenomenon, which may prove, that it is not absolutely impossible for ideas to arise, independent of their correspondent impressions. I believe it will readily be allowed, that the several distinct ideas of colour, which enter by the eye, or those of sound, which are conveyed by the ear, are really different from each other; though, at the same time, resembling. Now if this be true of different colours, it must be no less so of the different shades of the same colour; and each shade produces a distinct idea, independent of the rest. For if this should be denied, it is possible, by the continual gradation of shades, to run a colour insensibly into what is most remote from it; and if you will not allow any of the means to be different, you cannot, without absurdity, deny the extremes to be the same. Suppose, therefore, a person to have enjoyed his sight for thirty years, and to have become perfectly acquainted with colours of all kinds, except one particular shade of blue, for instance, which it never has been his fortune to meet with. Let all the different shades of that colour, except that single one, be placed before him, descending gradually from the deepest to the lightest; it is plain, that he will perceive a blank, where that shade is wanting, and will be sensible, that there is a greater distance in that place between the contiguous colours than in any other. Now I ask, whether it be possible for him, from his own imagination, to supply this deficiency, and raise up to himself the idea of that particular shade, though it had never been conveyed to him by his senses? I believe there are few but will be of opinion that he can: And this may serve as a proof, that the simple ideas are not always, in every instance, derived from the correspondent impressions; though this instance is so singular, that it is scarcely worth our observing, and does not merit, that for it alone we should alter our general maxim.

Here, therefore, is a proposition, which not only seems, in itself, simple and intelli-

gible; but, if a proper use were made of it, might render every dispute equally intelligible, and banish all that jargon, which has so long taken possession of metaphysical reasonings, and drawn disgrace upon them. All ideas, especially abstract ones, are naturally faint and obscure: The mind has but a slendor hold of them: They are apt to be confounded with other resembling ideas; and when we have often employed any term, though without a distinct meaning, we are apt to imagine it has a determinate idea, annexed to it. On the contrary, all impressions, that is, all sensations, either outward or inward, are strong and vivid: The limits between them are more exactly determined: Nor is it easy to fall into any error or mistake with regard to them. When we entertain, therefore, any suspicion, that a philosophical term is employed without any meaning or idea (as is but too frequent), we need but enquire, *from what impression is that supposed idea derived?* And if it be impossible to assign any, this will serve to confirm our suspicion. By bringing ideas into so clear a light, we may reasonably hope to remove all dispute, which may arise, concerning their nature and reality.

Section III—*Of the Association of Ideas*

It is evident, that there is *a principal of connexion* between the different thoughts or ideas of the mind, and that, in their appearance to the memory or imagination, they introduce each other with a certain degree of method and regularity. In our more serious thinking or discourse, this is so observable, that any particular thought, which breaks in upon the regular tract or chain of ideas, is immediately remarked and rejected. And even in our wildest and most wandering reveries, nay in our very dreams, we shall find, if we reflect, that the imagination ran not altogether at adventures, but that there was still a connexion upheld among the different ideas, which succeeded each other. Were the loosest and freest conversation to be transcribed, there would immediately be observed something, which connected it in all its transitions. Or where this is wanting, the person, who broke the thread of discourse, might still inform you, that there had secretly revolved in his mind a succession of thought, which had gradually led him from the subject of conversation. Among different languages, even where we cannot suspect the least connexion or communication, it is found, that the words, expressive of ideas, the most compounded, do yet nearly correspond to each other: A certain proof, that the *simple ideas, comprehended in the compound ones, were bound together by some universal principle,* which had an equal influence on all mankind.

Though it be too obvious to escape observation, that different ideas are connected together; I do not find, that any philosopher has attempted to *enumerate or class all the principles of association*; a subject, however, that seems worthy of curiosity. To me, there appear to be only three principles of connexion among ideas, namely, *Resemblance, Contiguity in time or place, and Cause or Effect.*

That these principles serve to connect ideas will not, I believe, be much doubted. A picture naturally leads our thoughts to the original: The mention of one apartment in a building naturally introduces an enquiry or discourse concerning the others: And if we think of a wound, we can scarcely forbear reflecting on the pain which follows it. But that this enumeration is complete, and that there are no other principles of association, except these, may be difficult to prove to the satisfaction of the reader, or even to a man's own satisfaction. All we can do, in such cases, is to run over several instances, and examine carefully the principle, which binds the different thoughts to each other, never stopping till we render the principle as general as possible. The more instances we examine, and the more care we employ, the more assurance shall we acquire, that the enumeration, which we form from the whole, is complete and entire.

Section IV—*Sceptical Doubts Concerning the Operations of the Understanding*

Part I

All the objects of human reason or enquiry may naturally be divided into two kinds, to wit, *Relations of Ideas,* and *Matters of Fact.* Of the first kind are the sciences of Geometry, Algebra, and Arithmetic; and in short, every affirmation, which is either intuitively or demonstratively certain. *That the square of the hypothenuse is equal to the square of the two sides,* is a proposition, which expresses a relation between these figures. *That three times five is equal to the half of thirty,* expresses a relation between these numbers. Propositions of this kind are discoverable by the *mere operation of thought,* without dependence on what is any where existent in the universe. Though there never were a circle or triangle in nature, the truths, demonstrated by EUCLID, would for ever retain their certainty and evidence.

Matters of fact, which are the second objects of human reason, are not ascertained in the same manner; nor is our *evidence* of their truth, however great, of a like nature with the foregoing. The *contrary of every matter of fact is still possible;* because it can never imply a contradiction, and is conceived by the mind with the same facility and distinctness, as if ever so conformable to reality. *That the sun will not rise to-morrow is no less intelligible a proposition, and implies no more contradiction*, than the affirmation, *that it will rise*. We should in vain, therefore, attempt to demonstrate its falsehood. Were it demonstratively false, it would imply a contradiction, and could never be distinctly conceived by the mind.

It may, therefore, be a subject worthy of curiosity, to enquire what is *the nature of that evidence, which assures us of any real existence and matter of fact, beyond the present testimony of our senses, or the records of our memory.* This part of philosophy, it is observable, has been little cultivated, either by the ancients or moderns; and therefore our doubts and errors, in the prosecution of so important an enquiry, may be the more excusable; while we march through such difficult paths, without any guide or direction. They may even prove useful, by exciting curiosity, and destroying that implicit faith and security, which is the bane of all reasoning and free enquiry. The discovery of defects in the common philosophy, if any such there be, will not, I presume, be a discouragement, but rather an incitement, as is usual, to attempt something more full and satisfactory, than has yet been proposed to the public.

All reasonings concerning matter of fact seem to be founded on the relation of *Cause and Effect.* By means of that relation alone we can go beyond the evidence of our memory and senses. If you were to ask a man, why he believes any matter of fact, which is absent; for instance, that his friend is in the country, or in FRANCE; he would give you a reason; and this reason would be some other fact; as a letter received from him, or the knowledge of his former resolutions and promises. A man, finding a watch or any other machine in a desert island, would conclude, that there had once been men in that island. All our reasonings concerning fact are of the same nature. And here it is constantly supposed, that there is a connexion between the present fact and that which is inferred from it. Were there nothing to bind them together, the inference would be entirely precarious. The hearing of an articulate voice and rational discourse in the dark assures us of the presence of some person: Why? because these are the effects of the human make and fabric, and closely connected with it. If we *anatomize* all the other reasonings of this nature, we shall find, that they are founded on the relation of cause and effect, and that this relation is either *near or remote, direct or collateral.* Heat and light are collateral effects of fire, and the one effect may justly be inferred from the other.

If we would satisfy ourselves, therefore, *concerning the nature of that evidence,* which assures us of matters of fact, we must enquire how we arrive at the *knowledge of cause and effect.*

I shall venture to affirm, as a general proposition, which admits of no exception, that the knowledge of this relation is not, in any instance, attained by reasonings *a priori*; but arises entirely from experience, when we find, that any particular objects are constantly conjoined with each other. Let an object be presented to a man of ever so strong natural reason and abilities; if that object be entirely new to him, he will not be able, by the most accurate examination of its sensible qualities, to discover any of its causes or effects. ADAM, though his rational faculties be supposed, at the very first, entirely perfect, could not have inferred from the fluidity, and transparency of water, that it would suffocate him, or from the light and warmth of fire, that it would consume him. No object ever discovers, by the qualities which appear to the senses, either the causes which produced it, or the effects which will arise from it; *nor can our reason, unassisted by experience, ever draw any inference concerning real existence and matter of fact.*

This proposition, *that causes and effects are discoverable, not by reason, but by experience,* will readily be admitted with regard to such objects, as we remember to have once been altogether unknown to us; since we must be conscious of the utter inability, which we then lay under, of foretelling, what would arise from them. Present two smooth pieces of marble to a man, who has no tincture of natural philosophy; he will never discover, that they will adhere together, in such a manner as to require great force to separate them in a direct line, while they make so small a resistance to a lateral pressure. Such events, as bear little analogy to the common course of nature, are also readily confessed to be known only by experience; nor does any man imagine that the explosion of gunpowder, or the attraction of a loadstone, could ever be discovered by argu-

ments *a priori.* In like manner, when an effect is supposed to depend upon an intricate machinery or secret structure of parts, we make no difficulty in attributing all our knowledge of it to experience. Who will assert, that he can give the ultimate reason, why milk or bread is proper nourishment for a man, not for a lion or a tiger?

But the same truth may not appear, at first sight, to have the same evidence with regard to events, which have become familiar to us from our first appearance in the world, which bear a close analogy to the whole course of nature, and which are supposed to depend on the *simple qualities* of objects, without any *secret structure of parts.* We are apt to imagine, that we could discover these effects by the mere operation of our reason, without experience. We fancy, that were we brought, on a sudden, into this world, we could at first have inferred, that one Billiard-ball would communicate motion to another upon impulse; and that we needed not to have waited for the event, in order to pronounce with certainty concerning it. Such is the influence of custom, that, where it is strongest, it not only covers our natural ignorance, but even conceals itself, and seems not to take place, merely because it is found in the highest degree.

But to convince us, that *all the laws of nature, and all the operations of bodies without exception, are known only by experience,* the following reflections may, perhaps, suffice. Were any object presented to us, and were we required to pronounce concerning the effect, which will result from it, without consulting past observation; after what manner, I beseech you, must the mind proceed in this operation? It must invent or imagine some event, which it ascribes to the object as its effect; and it is plain that this invention must be entirely arbitrary. The mind can never possibly find the effect in the supposed cause, by the most accurate scrutiny and examination. For the effect is totally different from the cause, and consequently can never be discovered in it. Motion in the second Billiard-ball is a *quite distinct event* from motion in the first; nor is there any thing in the one to suggest the smallest hint of the other. A stone or piece of metal raised into the air, and left without any support, immediately falls: But to consider the matter *a priori,* is there anything we discover in this situation, which can beget the idea of a downward, rather than an upward, or any other motion, in the stone or metal?

And as the first imagination or invention of a particular effect, in all natural operations, is arbitrary, where we consult not experience; so must we also esteem the supposed tie or connexion between the cause and effect, which binds them together, and renders it impossible, that any other *defect* could result from the operation of that cause. When I see, for instance, a Billiard-ball moving in a straight line towards another; even suppose motion in the second ball should by accident be suggested to me, as the result of their contact or impulse; may I not conceive, that a hundred different events might as well follow from that cause? May not both these balls remain at absolute rest? May not the first ball return in a straight line, or leap off from the second in any line or direction? All these suppositions are consistent and conceivable. Why then should we give the preference to one which is no more consistent or conceivable than the rest? All our reasonings *a priori* will never be able to show us any foundation for this preference.

In a word, then, *every effect is a distinct event from its cause.* It could not, therefore, be discovered in the cause, and the first invention or conception of it, *a priori,* must be entirely arbitrary. And even after it is suggested, the conjunction of it with the cause must appear equally arbitrary; since there are always many other effects, which, to reason, must seem fully as consistent and natural. *In vain, therefore, should we pretend to determine any single event, or infer any cause or effect, without the assistance of observation and experience.*

Hence we may discover the reason, why no philosopher, who is rational and modest, has ever pretended to assign the ultimate cause of any natural operation, or to show distinctly the action of that power, which produces any single effect in the universe. It is confessed, that the utmost effort of human reason is, to reduce the principles, productive of natural phenomena, to a greater simplicity, and to resolve the many particular effects into a few general causes, by means of reasonings from analogy, experience, and observation. But as to *the causes of these general causes,* we should in vain attempt their discovery; nor shall we ever be able to satisfy ourselves, by any particular explication of them. These ultimate springs and principles are totally shut up from human curiosity and enquiry. *Elasticity, gravity, cohesion of parts,* communication of motion by impulse; these are probably the ultimate causes and principles which we shall ever discover in nature; and we may esteem ourselves sufficiently happy, if, by accurate enquiry and reasoning, we can trace up the particular phenomena to, or near to, these general principles. The most perfect philosophy of the natural kind only staves off our ignorance a little longer: as perhaps the most perfect philosophy of the moral or meta-physical kind serves only to discover larger portions of it. Thus the observation of human blindness and weakness is the result of all philosophy, and meets us, at every turn, in spite of our endeavors to elude or avoid it.

Section V

Nor need we fear, that this philosophy, while it endeavors to limit our enquiries to common life, should ever undermine the reasonings of common life, and carry its doubts so far as to destroy all action, as well as speculation. Nature will always maintain her rights, and prevail in the end over any abstract reasoning whatsoever. Though we should conclude, for instance, as in the fore-going section, that, in all reasonings from experience, there is a step taken by the mind, which is not supported by any argument or process of the understanding; there is no danger, that these reasonings, on which almost all knowledge depends, will ever be affected by such a discovery. If the mind be not engaged by argument to make this step, it must be induced by some other principle of equal weight and authority; and that principle will preserve its influence as long as human nature remains the same. What that principle is, may well be worth the pains of enquiry.

Suppose a person, though endowed with the strongest faculties of reason and reflection, to be brought on a sudden into this world; he would, indeed, immediately observe a continual succession of objects, and one event following another; but he would not be able to discover any thing farther. He would not, at first, by any reasoning, be able to reach the idea of cause and effect; since

the particular powers, by which all natural operations are performed, never appear to the senses; nor is it reasonable to conclude, merely because one event, in one instance, precedes another, that therefore the one is the cause, the other the effect. Their conjunction may be arbitrary and casual. There may be no reason to infer the existence of one from the appearance of the other. And in a word, such a person, without more experience, could never employ his conjecture or reasoning concerning any matter of fact, or be assured of any thing beyond what was immediately present to his memory and senses.

Suppose again that he has acquired more experience, and has lived so long in the world as to have observed similar objects or events to be constantly conjoined together; what is the consequence of this experience? He immediately infers the existence of one object from the appearance of the other. Yet he has not, by all his experience, acquired any idea or knowledge of the *secret power,* by which the one object produces the other; nor is it, by any process of reasoning, he is engaged to draw this inference. But still he finds himself determined to draw it: And though he should be convinced, that his understanding has no part in the operation, he would nevertheless continue in the same course of thinking. There is some other principle, which determines him to form such a conclusion.

This principle is CUSTOM or HABIT. For wherever the repetition of any particular act or operation produces a propensity to renew the same act or operation, without being impelled by any reasoning or process of the understanding; we always say, that this propensity is the effect of *Custom.* By employing that word, we pretend not to have given the ultimate reason of such a propensity. We only point out a principle of human nature, which is universally acknowledged, and which is well known by its effects. Perhaps, we can push our enquiries no farther, or pretend to give the cause of this cause; but must rest contented with it as the ultimate principle, which we can assign, of all our conclusions from experience. It is sufficient satisfaction, that we can go so far; without repining at the narrowness of our faculties, because they will carry us no farther. And it is certain we here advance a very intelligible proposition at least, if not a true one, when we assert, that, after the constant conjunction of two objects, heat and flame, for instance, weight and solidity, we are determined by custom alone to expect the one from the appearance of the other. This hypothesis seems even the only one, which explains the difficulty, why we draw, from a thousand instances, an inference, which we are not able to draw from one instance, that is, in no respect, different from them. Reason is incapable of any such variation. The conclusions, which it draws from considering one circle, are the same which it would form upon surveying all the circles in the universe. But no man, having seen only one body move after being impelled by another, could infer, that every other body will move after a like impulse. *All inferences from experience, therefore, are effects of custom, not of reasoning.*

Custom, then, is the great guide of human life. It is that principle alone, which renders our experience useful to us, and makes us expect, for the future, a similar train of events, with those which have appeared in the past. *Without the influence of custom, we should be entirely ignorant of every matter of fact, be-yond what is immediately present to the memory and senses.* We should never know how to adjust means to ends, or to employ our natural powers in the production of any effect. There would be an end at once of all action, as well as of the chief part of speculation.

Section VI—*Of Probability*

Though there be no such thing as *Chance* in the world; our ignorance of the real cause of any event has the same influence on the understanding, and begets a like species of belief or opinion.

There is certainly a *probability*; which arises from a superiority of chances on any side; and according as this superiority increases, and surpasses the opposite chances, the probability receives a proportionable increase, and begets still *a higher degree of belief or assent* to that side, in which we discover the superiority. If a die were marked with one figure or number of spots on four sides, and with another figure or number of spots on the two remaining sides, it would be more probable, that the former would turn up than the latter; though, if it had a thousand sides marked in the same manner, and only one side different, the probability would be much higher, and our belief or expectation of the event more steady and secure. This process of the thought or reasoning may seem trivial and obvious; but to those who consider it more narrowly, it may, perhaps, afford matter for curious speculation.

It seems evident, that, when the mind looks forward to discover the event, which may result from the throw of such a die, it considers the turning up of each particular side as alike probable; and this is the very nature of chance, to render all the particular events, comprehended in it, entirely equal. But finding a greater number of sides concur in the one event than in the other, the mind is carried more frequently to that event, and meets it oftener, in revolving the various possibilities or chances, on which the ultimate result depends. This concurrence of several views in one particular event begets immediately, by an inexplicable contrivance of nature, the sentiment of belief, and gives that event the advantage over its antagonist, which is supported by a smaller number of views, and recurs less frequently to the mind. If we allow, that belief is nothing but a firmer and stronger conception of an object than what attends the mere fictions of the imagination, this operation may, perhaps, in some measure, be accounted for. The concurrence of these several views or glimpses imprints the idea more strongly on the imagination; gives it superior force and vigour; renders its influence on the passions and affections more sensible; and in a word, begets that reliance or security, which constitutes the nature of belief and opinion.

The case is the same with the probability of causes, as with that of chance. There are some causes, which are entirely uniform and constant in producing a particular effect; and no instance has ever yet been found of any failure or irregularity in their operation. Fire has always burned, and water suffocated every human creature: The production of motion by impulse and gravity is an universal law, which has hitherto admitted of no exception. But there are other causes, which have been found more irregular and uncertain; nor has rhubarb always proved a purge, or opium a soporific to every one, who has taken these medicines. It is true, when any cause fails of producing its usual effect, philosophers as-

cribe not this to any *irregularity in nature*; but suppose, that *some secret causes*, in the particular structure of parts, have prevented the operation. Our reasonings, however, and conclusions concerning the event are the same as if this principle had no place. Being determined by custom to transfer the past to the future, in all our inferences; where the past has been entirely regular and uniform, we expect the event with the greatest assurance, and leave no room for any contrary supposition. But where different effects have been found to follow from causes, which are to *appearance* exactly similar, all these various effects must occur to the mind in transferring the past to the future, and enter into our consideration, when we determine the probability of the event. Though we give the preference to that which has been found most usual, and believe that this effect will exist, we must not overlook the other effects, but must assign to each of them a particular weight and authority, in proportion as we have found it to be more or less frequent. It is more probable, in almost every country of EUROPE, there will be frost sometime in JANUARY, than that the weather will continue open throughout that whole month; though this probability varies according to the different climates, and approaches to a certainty in the more northern kingdoms. Here then it seems evident, that, when we transfer the past to the future, in order to determine the effect, which will result from any cause, we transfer all the different events, in the same proportion as they have appeared in the past, and conceive one to have existed a hundred times, for instance, another ten times, and another once. *As a great number of views do here concur in one event, they fortify and confirm it to the imagination, beget that sentiment which we call belief, and give its object the preference above the contrary event, which is not supported by an equal number of experiments,* and recurs not so frequently to the thought in transferring the past to the future. Let any one try to account for this operation of the mind upon any of the received systems of philosophy, and he will be sensible of the difficulty. For my part, I shall think it sufficient, if the present hints excite the curiosity of philosophers, and make them sensible how defective all common theories are in treating of such curious and such sublime subjects.

30   David Hume
(from Dialogues Concerning Natural Religion)

Part V

But to show you still more inconveniences, continued Philo, in your anthropomorphism, please to take a new survey of your principles. *Like effects prove like causes.* This is the experimental argument; and this, you say too, is the sole theological argument. Now it is certain that the liker the effects are which are seen and the liker the causes which are inferred, the stronger is the argument. Every departure on either side diminishes the probability and renders the experiment less conclusive. You cannot doubt of the principle; neither ought you to reject its consequences.

All the new discoveries in astronomy which prove the immense grandeur and magnificence of the works of nature are so many additional arguments for a Diety, according to the true system of theism; but, according to your hypothesis of experimental theism, they become so many objections, by removing the effect still farther from all resemblance to the effects of human art and contrivance. For if Lucretius, even following the old system of the world, could exclaim:

> *Who can rule the sum, who hold in his hand with controlling force the strong reins, of the immeasurable deep?*

> *Who can at once make all the different heavens to roll and warm with ethereal fires all the fruitful earths, or be present in all places at all times?*

If Tully [Cicero] esteemed this reasoning so natural as to put it into the mouth of his Epicurean:

> *For with what eyes could your Plato see the construction of so vast a work which, according to him, God was putting together and building?*

> *What materials, what tools, what bars, what machines, what servants were employed in such gigantic work?*

> *How could the air, fire, water, and earth pay obedience and submit to the will of the architect?*

If this argument, I say, had any force in former ages, how much greater must it have at present when the bounds of Nature are so infinitely enlarged and such a magnificent scene is opened to us? It is still more unreasonable to form our idea of so unlimited a cause from our experience of the narrow productions of human design and invention.

The discoveries by microscopes, as they open a new universe in miniature, are still objections, according to you, arguments, according to me. The further we push our researches of this kind, we are still led to infer the universal cause of all to be vastly different from mankind, or from any object of human experience and observation.

And what say you to the discoveries in anatomy, chemistry, botany? . . . These surely are no objections, replied Cleanthes; they only discover new instances of art and contrivance. It is still the image of mind reflected on us from innumerable objects. Add a mind *like the human*, said Philo. I know of no other, replied Cleanthes. And the liker, the better, insisted Philo. To be sure, said Cleanthes.

Now, Cleanthes, said Philo, with an air of alacrity and triumph, mark the consequences. *First,* by this method of reasoning you renounce all claim to infinity in any of the attributes of the Deity. For, as the cause ought only to be proportioned to the effect, and the effect, so far as it falls under our cognizance, is not infinite, what pretensions have we, upon your suppositions, to ascribe that attribute to the Divine Being? You will still insist that, by removing him so much from all similarity to human creatures, we give in to the most arbitrary hypothesis, and at the same time weaken all proofs of his existence.

Secondly, you have no reason, on your theory, for ascribing perfection to the Deity, even in his finite capacity, or for supposing him free from every error, mistake, or incoherence, in his undertakings. There are many inexplicable difficulties in the works of nature which, if we allow a perfect author to be proved *a priori*, are easily solved, and become only seeming difficulties from the narrow capacity of man, who cannot trace infinite relations. But according to your method of reasoning, these difficulties become all real, and, perhaps, will be insisted on as new instances of likeness to human art and contrivance. At least, you must acknowledge that it is impossible for us to tell, from our limited views, whether this system contains any great faults or deserves any considerable praise if compared to other possible and even real systems. Could a peasant, if the *Æneid* were read to him, pronounce that poem to be absolutely faultless, or even assign to it its proper rank among the productions of human wit, he who had never seen any other production?

But were this world ever so perfect a production, it must still remain uncertain whether all the excellences of the work can justly be ascribed to the workman. If we survey a ship, what an exalted idea must we form of the ingenuity of the carpenter who framed so complicated, useful, and beautiful a machine? And what surprise must we feel when we find him a stupid mechanic who imitated others, and copied an art which, through a long succession of ages, after multiplied trials, mistakes, corrections, deliberations, and controversies, had been gradually improving? Many worlds might have been botched and bungled, throughout an eternity, ere this system was struck out;

much labour lost, many fruitless trials made, and a slow but continued improvement carried on during infinite ages in the art of world-making. In such subjects, who can determine where the truth, nay, who can conjecture where the probability lies, amidst a great number of hypotheses which may be proposed, and a still greater which may be imagined?

And what shadow of an argument, continued Philo, can you produce from your hypothesis to prove the unity of the Deity? A great number of men join in building a house or ship, in rearing a city, in framing a commonwealth; why may not several deities combine in contriving and framing a world? This is only so much greater similarity to human affairs. By the work among several, we may further limit the attributes of each, and get rid of that extensive power and knowledge which must be supposed in one deity, and which, according to you, can only serve to weaken the proof of his existence. *And if such foolish, such vicious creatures as man can yet often unite in framing and executing one plan, how much more those deities or demons, whom we may suppose several degrees more perfect!*

To multiply causes without necessity is indeed contrary to true philosophy, but this principle applies not to the present case. Were one deity antecedently proved by your theory who were possessed of every attribute requisite to the production of the universe, it would be needless, I own, (though not absurd) to suppose any other deity existent. But while it is still a question whether all these attributes are united in one subject or dispersed among several independent beings, by what phenomena in nature can we pretend to decide the controversy? Where

we see a body raised in a scale, we are sure that there is in the opposite scale, however concealed from sight, some counterpoising weight equal to it; but it is still allowed to doubt whether that weight be an aggregate of several distinct bodies or one uniform united mass. And if the weight requisite very much exceeds anything which we have ever seen conjoined in any single body, the former supposition becomes still more probable and natural. An intelligent being of such vast power and capacity as is necessary to produce the universe, or, to speak in the language of ancient philosophy, so prodigious an animal exceeds all analogy and even comprehension.

But further, Cleanthes: Men are mortal, and renew their species by generation; and this is common to all living creatures. The two great sexes of male and female, says Milton, animate the world. Why must this circumstance, so universal, so essential, be excluded from those numerous and limited deities? Behold, then, the theogeny of ancient times brought back upon us.

And why not become a perfect anthropomorphite? Why not assert the deity or deities to be corporeal, and to have eyes, a nose, mouth, ears, etc.? Epicurus maintained that no man had ever seen reason but in a human figure; therefore, the gods must have a human figure. And this argument, which is deservedly so much ridiculed by Cicero, becomes, according to you, solid and philosophical.

In a word, Cleanthes, a man who follows your hypothesis is able, perhaps, to assert or conjecture that the universe sometime arose from something like design; but beyond that position he cannot ascertain one single circumstance, and is left afterwards to fix every point of his theology by the utmost license of fancy and hypothesis. This world, for aught he knows, is very faulty and imperfect, compared to a superior standard, and was only the first rude essay of some infant deity who afterwards abandoned it, ashamed of his lame performance; it is the work only of some dependent, inferior deity, and is the object of derision to his superiors; it is the production of old age and dotage in some superannuated deity, and ever since his death has run on at adventures, from the first impulse and active force which it received from him. You justly give signs of horror, Demea, at these strange suppositions; but these, and a thousand more of the same kind, are Cleanthes' suppositions, not mine. From the moment the attributes of the Deity are supposed finite, all these have place. And I cannot, for my part, think that so wild and unsettled a system of theology is, in any respect, preferable to none at all.

These suppositions I absolutely disown, cried Cleanthes: they strike me, however, with no horror, especially when proposed in that rambling way in which they drop from you. On the contrary, they give me pleasure when I see that, by the utmost indulgence of your imagination, you never get rid of the hypothesis of design in the universe, but are obliged at every turn to have recourse to it. To this concession I adhere steadily; and this I regard as a sufficient foundation for religion.

Part VIII

What you ascribe to the fertility of my invention, replied Philo, is entirely owing to the nature of the subject. In subjects adapted to the narrow compass of human reason there is commonly but one determination which carries probability or conviction with it; and to a man of sound judgment all other suppositions but that one appear entirely absurd and chimerical. But in such questions as the present, a hundred contradictory views may preserve a kind of imperfect analogy, and invention has here full scope to exert itself. Without any great effort of thought, I believe that I could, in an instant, propose other systems of cosmogony which would have some faint appearance of truth, though it is a thousand, a million to one if either yours or any one of mine be the true system.

For instance, what if I should revive the old Epicurean hypothesis? This is commonly, and I believe justly, esteemed the most absurd system that has yet been proposed; yet I know not whether, with a few alterations, it might not be brought to bear a faint appearance of probability. Instead of supposing matter infinite, as Epicurus did, let us suppose it finite. A finite number of particles is only susceptible of finite transpositions; and it must happen, in an eternal duration, that every possible order or position must be tried an infinite number of times. This world, therefore, with all its events, even the most minute, has before been produced and destroyed, and will again be produced and destroyed, without any bounds and limitations. No one who has a conception of the powers of infinite, in comparison of finite, will ever scruple this determination.

But this supposes, said Demea, that matter can acquire motion without any voluntary agent or first mover.

And where is the difficulty, replied Philo, of that supposition? Every event, before experience, is equally difficult and incomprehensible; and every event, after experience, is equally easy and intelligible. Motion, in many instances, from gravity, from elasticity, from electricity, begins in matter, without any known voluntary agent; and to suppose always, in these cases, an unknown voluntary agent is mere hypothesis and hypothesis attended with no advantages. The beginning of motion in matter itself is as conceivable *a priori* as its communication from mind and intelligence.

Besides, why may not motion have been propagated by impulse through all eternity, and the same stock of it, or nearly the same, be still upheld in the universe? As much is lost by the composition of motion, as much is gained by its resolution. And whatever the causes are, the fact is certain that matter is and always has been in continual agitation, as far as human experience or tradition reaches. There is not probably, at present, in the whole universe, one particle of matter at absolute rest.

And this very consideration, too, continued Philo, which we have stumbled on in the course of the argument suggests a new hypothesis of cosmogony that is not absolutely absurd and improbable. Is there a system, an order, an economy of things, by which matter can preserve that perpetual agitation which seems essential to it, and yet maintain a constancy in the forms which it produces? There certainly is such an economy, for this is actually the case with the present world. The continual motion of matter, therefore, in less than infinite transpositions, must produce this economy or order, and, by its very nature, that order, when once established, supports itself for many ages if not to eternity. But wherever matter is so poised, arranged, and adjusted, as to continue in perpetual motion, and yet preserve a constancy in the forms, its situation must, of necessity, have all the same appearance of art and contrivance which we observe at present. All the parts of each form must have a relation to each other and to the whole; and the whole itself must have a relation to the other parts of the universe, to the element in which the form subsists, to the materials with which it repairs its waste and decay, and to every other form which is hostile or friendly. A defect in any of these particulars destroys the form, and the matter of which it is composed is again set loose, and is thrown into irregular motions and fermentations till it unite itself to some other regular form. If no such form be prepared to receive it, and if there be a great quantity of this corrupted matter in the universe, the universe itself is entirely disordered, whether it be the feeble embryo of a world in its first beginnings that is thus destroyed or the rotten carcase of one languishing in old age and infirmity. In either case, a chaos ensues till finite though innumerable revolutions produce, at last, some forms whose parts and organs are so adjusted as to support the forms amidst a continued succession of matter.

Suppose (for we shall endeavour to vary the expression) that matter were thrown into any position by a blind, unguided force; it is evident that this first position must, in all probability, be the most confused and most disorderly imaginable, without any resemblance to those works of human contrivance which, along with a symmetry of parts, discover an adjustment of means to ends and a tendency to self-preservation. If the actuating force cease after this operation, matter must remain for ever in disorder and continue an immense chaos, without any proportion or activity. But suppose that the actuating force, whatever it be, still continues in matter, this first position will immediately give place to a second which will likewise, in all probability, be as disorderly as the first, and so on through many successions of changes and revolutions. No particular order or position ever continues a moment unaltered. The original force, still remaining in activity, gives a perpetual restlessness to matter. Every possible situation is produced, and instantly destroyed. If a glimpse or dawn of order appears for a moment, it is instantly hurried away and confounded by that never-ceasing force which actuates every part of matter.

Thus the universe goes on for many ages in a continued succession of chaos and disorder. But is it not possible that it may settle at last, so as not to lose its motion and active force (for that we have supposed inherent in it), yet so as to preserve an uniformity of appearance, amidst the continual motion and fluctuation of its parts? This we find to be the case with the universe at present. Every individual is perpetually changing, and every part of every individual; and yet the whole remains, in appearance, the same. May we not hope for such a position or rather be assured of it from the external revolutions of unguided matter; and may not this account for all the appearing wisdom and contrivance which is in the universe? Let us contemplate the subject a little, and we shall find that this adjustment if attained by matter of a seeming stability in the forms, with a real and perpetual revolution or motion of parts, affords a plausible, if not a true, solution of the difficulty.

Part X

It is my opinion, I own, replied Demea, that each man feels, in a manner, the truth of religion within his own breast, and, from a consciousness of his imbecility and misery rather than from any reasoning, is led to seek protection from that Being on whom he and all nature is dependent. So anxious or so tedious are even the best scenes of life that futurity is still the object of all our hopes and fears. We incessantly look forward and endeavour, by prayers, adoration, and sacrifice, to appease those unknown powers whom we find, by experience, so able to afflict and oppress us. Wretched creatures that we are! What resource for us amidst the innumerable ills of life did not religion suggest some methods of atonement, and appease those terrors with which we are incessantly agitated and tormented?

I am indeed persuaded, said Philo, that the best and indeed the only method of bringing everyone to a due sense of religion is by just representations of the misery and wickedness of men. And for that purpose a talent of eloquence and strong imagery is more requisite than that of reasoning and argument. For it is necessary to prove what everyone feels within himself? It is only necessary to make us feel it, if possible, more intimately and sensibly.

The people, indeed, replied Demea, are sufficiently convinced of this great and melancholy truth. The miseries of life, the unhappiness of man, the general corruptions of our nature, the unsatisfactory enjoyment of pleasures, riches, honours—these phrases have become almost proverbial in all languages. And who can doubt of what all men declare from their own immediate feeling and experience?

In this point, said Philo, the learned are perfectly agreed with the vulgar; and in all letters, *sacred* and *profane*, the topic of human misery has been insisted on with the most pathetic eloquence that sorrow and melancholy could inspire. The poets, who speak from sentiment, without a system, and whose testimony has therefore the more authority, abound in images of this nature. From Homer down to Dr. Young, the whole inspired tribe have ever been sensible that no other representation of things would suit the feeling and observation of each individual.

As to authorities, replied Demea, you need not seek them. Look round this library of Cleanthes. I shall venture to affirm that, except authors of particular sciences, such as chemistry or botany, who have no occasion to treat of human life, there is scarce one of those innumerable writers from whom the sense of human misery has not, in some passage or other, extorted a complaint and confession of it. At least, the chance is entirely on that side; and no one author has ever, so far as I can recollect, been so extravagant as to deny it.

There you must excuse me, said Philo: Leibniz has denied it, and is perhaps the first who ventured upon so bold and paradoxical an opinion; at least, the first who made it essential to his philosophical system.

And by being the first, replied Demea, might he not have been sensible of his error? For is this a subject in which philosophers can propose to make discoveries especially in so late an age? And can any man hope by a simple denial (for the subject scarcely admits of reasoning) to bear down the united testimony of mankind, founded on sense and consciousness?

And why should man, added he, pretend to an exemption from the lot of all other animals? The whole earth, believe me, Philo, is cursed and polluted. A perpetual war is kindled amongst all living creatures. Necessity, hunger, want stimulate the strong and courageous; fear, anxiety, terror agitate the weak and infirm. The first entrance into life gives anguish to the new-born infant and to its wretched parent; weakness, impotence, distress attend each stage of that life, and it is, at last, finished in agony and horror.

Observe, too, says Philo, the curious artifices of nature in order to embitter the life of every living being. The stronger prey upon the weaker and keep them in perpetual terror and anxiety. The weaker, too, in their turn, often prey upon the stronger, and vex and molest them without relaxation. Consider that innumerable race of insects, which either are bred on the body of each animal or, flying about, infix their stings in him. These insects have others still less than themselves which torment them. And thus on each hand, before and behind, above and below, every animal is surrounded with enemies which incessantly seek his misery and destruction.

Man alone, said Demea, seems to be, in part, an exception to this rule. For by combination in society he can easily master lions, tigers, and bears, whose greater strength and agility naturally enable them to prey upon him.

On the contrary, it is here chiefly, cried Philo, that the uniform and equal maxims of nature are most apparent. Man, it is true, can, by combination, surmount all his *real* enemies and become master of the whole animal creation; but does he not immediately raise up to himself *imaginary* enemies, the demons of his fancy, who haunt him with superstitious terrors and blast every enjoyment of life? His pleasure, as he imagines, becomes in their eyes a crime; his food and repose give them umbrage and offence; his very sleep and dreams furnish new materials to anxious fear; and even death, his refuge from every other ill, presents only the dread of endless and innumerable woes. Nor does the wolf molest more the timid flock than superstition does the anxious breast of wretched mortals.

Besides, consider, Demea: This very society by which we surmount those wild beasts, our natural enemies, what new enemies does it not raise to us? What woe and misery does it not occasion? Man is the greatest enemy of man. Oppression, injustice, contempt, contumely, violence, sedition, war, calumny, treachery, fraud—by these they mutually torment each other, and they would soon dissolve that society which they had formed were it not for the dread of still greater ills which must attend their separation.

But though these external insults, said Demea, from animals, from men, from all the elements, which assault us form a frightful catalogue of woes, they are nothing in comparison of those which arise within ourselves, from the distempered condition of our mind and body. How many lie under the lingering torment of diseases? Hear the pathetic enumeration of the great poet.

Intestine stone and ulcer, colic-pangs,

Demoniac frenzy, moping melancholy,

And moon-struck madness, pining atrophy,

Marasmus, and wide-wasting pestilence.

Dire was the tossing, deep the groans: *De-*

spair

Tended the sick, busiest from couch to couch.

And over them triumphant *Death* his dart

Shook: but delay'd to strike, though oft invok'd

With vows, as their chief good and final hope.

The disorders of the mind, continued Demea, though more secret, are not perhaps less dismal and vexatious. Remorse, shame, anguish, rage, disappointment, anxiety, fear, dejection, despair—who has ever passed through life without cruel inroads from these tormentors? How many have scarcely ever felt any better sensations? Labour and poverty, so abhorred by everyone, are the certain lot of the far greater number; and those few privileged persons who enjoy ease and opulence never reach contentment or true felicity. All the goods of life united would not make a very happy man, but all the ills united would make a wretch indeed; and any one of them almost (and who can be free from every one?), nay, often the absence of one good (and who can possess all?) is sufficient to render life ineligible.

Were a stranger to drop on a sudden into this world, I would show him, as a specimen of its ills, an hospital full of diseases, a prison crowded with malefactors and debtors, a field of battle strewed with carcases, a fleet foundering in the ocean, a nation languishing under tyranny, famine, or pestilence. To turn the gay side of life to him and give him a notion of its pleasures—whether should I conduct him? To a ball, to an opera, to court? He might justly think that I was only showing him a diversity of distress and sorrow.

There is no evading such striking instances, said Philo, but by apologies which still further aggravate the charge. Why have all men, I ask, in all ages, complained incessantly of the miseries of life? . . . They have no just reason, says one: these complaints proceed only from their discontented, repining, anxious disposition . . . And can there possibly, I reply, be a more certain foundation of misery than such a wretched temper?

But if they were really as unhappy as they pretend, says my antagonist, why do they remain in life? . . .

Not satisfied with life, afraid of death—this is the secret chain, say I, that holds us. We are terrified, not bribed to the continuance of our existence.

It is only a false delicacy, he may insist, which a few refined spirits indulge, and which has spread these complaints among the whole race of mankind . . . And what is this delicacy, I ask, which you blame? Is it anything but a greater sensibility to all the pleasures and pains of life? And if the man of a delicate, refined temper, by being so much more alive than the the the world, is only so much more unhappy, what judgement must we form in general of human life?

Let men remain at rest, says our adversary, and they will be easy. They are willing artificers of their own misery. . . . No! reply I: an anxious languor follows their repose; disappointment, vexation, trouble, their activity and ambition.

I can observe something like what you mention in some others, replied Cleanthes, but I confess I feel little or nothing of it in myself, and hope that it is not so common as you represent it.

If you feel not human misery yourself, cried Demea, I congratulate you on so happy a singularity. Others, seemingly the most

prosperous, have not been ashamed to vent their complaints in the most melancholy strains. Let us attend to the great, the fortunate emperor, Charles V, when, tired with human grandeur, he resigned all his extensive dominions into the hands of his son. In the last harangue which he made on that memorable occasion, he publicly avowed *that the greatest prosperities which he had ever enjoyed had been mixed with so many adversities he might truly say he had never enjoyed any satisfaction or contentment.* But did the retired life in which he sought for shelter afford him any greater happiness? If we may credit his son's account, his repentance commenced the very day of his resignation.

Cicero's fortune, from small beginnings, rose to the greatest lustre and renown; yet what pathetic complaints of the ills of life do his familiar letters, as well as philosophical discourses, contain? And suitably to his own experience, he introduces Cato, the great, the fortunate Cato protesting in his old age that had he a new life in his offer he would reject the present.

Ask yourself, ask any of your acquaintance, whether they would live over again the last ten or twenty years of their life. No! but the next twenty, they say, will be better:

And from the dregs of life, hope to receive

What the first sprightly running could not give.

Thus, at last, they find (such is the greatness of human misery, it reconciles even contradictions) that they complain at once of the shortness of life and of its vanity and sorrow.

And it is possible, Cleanthes, said Philo, that after all these reflections, and infinitely more which might be suggested, you can still persevere in your anthropomorphism, and assert the moral attributes of the Deity, his justice, benevolence, mercy, and rectitude, to be of the same nature with these virtues in human creatures? His power, we allow, is infinite; whatever he wills is executed; but neither man nor any other animal is happy; therefore, he does not will their happiness. His wisdom is infinite; he is never mistaken in choosing the means to any end; but the course of nature tends not to human or animal felicity; therefore, it is not established for that purpose. Through the whole compass of human knowledge there are no inferences more certain and infallible than these. In what respect, then, do his benevolence and mercy resemble the benevolence and mercy of men?

Epicurus' old questions are yet unanswered.

Is he willing to prevent evil, but not able? then is he impotent. Is he able, but not willing? then is he malevolent. Is he both able and willing? whence then is evil?

You ascribe, Cleanthes, (and I believe justly) a purpose and intention to nature. But what, I beseech you, is the object of that curious artifice and machinery which she has displayed in all animals—the preservation alone of individuals, and propagation of the species? It seems enough for her purpose, if such a rank be barely upheld in the universe, without any care or concern for the happiness of the members that compose it. No resource for this purpose: no machinery in order merely to give pleasure or ease; no fund of pure joy and contentment; no indulgence without some want or necessity accompanying it. At least, the few phenomena of this nature are overbalanced by opposite phenomena of still greater importance.

Our sense of music, harmony, and indeed beauty of all kinds, gives satisfaction, without being absolutely necessary to the preservation and propagation of the species. But what racking pains, on the other hand, arise from gouts, gravels, megrims, toothaches, rheumatisms, where the injury to the animal machinery is either small or incurable? Mirth, laughter, play, frolic seem gratuitous satisfactions which have no further tendency; spleen, melancholy, discontent, superstition are pains of the same nature. How then does the Divine benevolence display itself, in the sense of you anthropomorphites? None but we mystics, as you were pleased to call us, can account for this strange mixture of phenomena, by deriving it from attributes infinitely perfect but incomprehensible.

And have you, at last, said Cleanthes smiling, betrayed your intentions, Philo? Your long agreement with Demea did indeed a little surprise me, but I find you were all the while erecting a concealed battery against me. And I must confess that you have now fallen upon a subject worthy of your noble spirit of opposition and controversy. If you can make out the present point, and prove mankind to be unhappy or corrupted, there is an end at once of all religion. For to what purpose establish the natural attributes of the Deity, while the moral are still doubtful and uncertain?

You take umbrage very easily, replied Demea, at opinions the most innocent and the most generally received, even amongst the religious and devout themselves; and nothing can be more surprising than to find a topic like this—concerning the wickedness and misery of man—charged with no less than atheism and profaneness. Have not all pious divines and preachers who have indulged their rhetoric on so fertile a subject, have they not easily, I say, given a solution of any difficulties which may attend it? This world is but a point in comparison of the universe; this life but a moment in comparison of eternity. The present evil phenomena, therefore, are rectified in other regions, and in some future period of existence. And the eyes of men, being then opened to larger views of things, see the whole connection of general laws, and trace, with adoration, the benevolence and rectitude of the Deity through all the mazes and intricacies of his providence.

No! replied Cleanthes, no! These arbitrary suppositions can never be admitted, contrary to matter of fact, visible and uncontroverted. Whence can any cause be known but from its known effects? Whence can any hypothesis be proved but from the apparent phenomena? To establish one hypothesis upon another is building entirely in the air; and the utmost we ever attain by these conjectures and fictions is to ascertain the bare possibility of our opinion, but never can we, upon such terms, establish its reality.

The only method of supporting Divine benevolence—and it is what I willingly embrace—is to deny absolutely the misery and wickedness of man. Your representations are exaggerated; your melancholy views mostly fictitious; your inferences contrary to fact and experience. Health is more common than sickness; pleasure than pain; happiness than misery. And for one vexation which we meet with, we attain, upon computation, a hundred enjoyments.

Admitting your position, replied Philo, which yet is extremely doubtful, you must at the same time allow that, if pain be less frequent than pleasure, it is infinitely more violent and durable. One hour of it is often able to outweigh a day, a week, a month of our common insipid enjoyments; and how many days, weeks, and months are passed by several in the most acute torments? Pleasure, scarcely in one instance, is ever able to reach ecstasy and rapture; and in no one instance can it continue for any time at its highest pitch and altitude. The spirits evaporate, the nerves relax, the fabric is disordered, and the enjoyment quickly degenerates into fatigue and uneasiness. But pain often, good God, how often! rises to torture and agony; and the longer it continues, it becomes still more genuine agony and torture. Patience is exhausted, courage languishes, melancholy seizes us, and nothing terminates our misery but the removal of its cause or another event which is the sole cure of all evil, but which, from our natural folly, we regard with still greater horror and consternation.

But not to insist upon these topics, continued Philo, though most obvious, certain, and important, I must use the freedom to admonish you, Cleanthes, that you have put the controversy upon a most dangerous issue, and are unawares introducing a total scepticism into the most essential articles of natural and revealed theology. What! no method of fixing a just foundation for religion unless we allow the happiness of human life, and maintain a continued existence even in this world, with all our present pains, infirmities, vexations, and follies, to be eligible and desirable! But this is contrary to everyone's feeling and experience; it is contrary to an authority so established as nothing can subvert. No decisive proofs can ever be produced against this authority; nor is it possible for you to compute, estimate, and compare all the pains and all the pleasures in the lives of all men and of all animals; and thus, by your resting the whole system of religion on a point which, from its very nature, must for ever be uncertain, you tacitly confess that that system is equally uncertain.

But allowing you what never will be believed, at least, what you never possibly can prove, that animal or, at least, human happiness in this life exceeds its misery, you have yet done nothing; for this is not, by any means, what we expect from infinite power, infinite wisdom, and infinite goodness. Why is there any misery at all in the world? Not by chance, surely. From some cause then. Is it from the intention of the Deity? But he is perfectly benevolent. Is it contrary to his intention? But he is almighty. Nothing can shake the solidity of this reasoning, so short, so clear, so decisive, except we assert that these subjects exceed all human capacity, and that our common measures of truth and falsehood are not applicable to them—a topic which I have all along insisted on, but which you have, from the beginning, rejected with scorn and indignation.

31   Isaac Newton
General Scholium

The hypothesis of vortices is pressed with many difficulties. That every planet by a radius drawn to the sun may describe areas proportional to the times of description, the periodic times of the several parts of the vortices should observe the square of their distances from the sun; but that the periodic times of the planets may obtain the 3/2th power of their distances from the sun, the periodic times of the parts of the vortex ought to be as the 3/2th power of their distances. That the smaller vortices may maintain their lesser revolutions about Saturn, Jupiter, and other planets, and swim quietly and undisturbed in the greater vortex of the sun, the periodic times of the parts of the sun's vortex should be equal; but the rotation of the sun and planets about their axes, which ought to correspond with the motions of their vortices, recede far from all these proportions. The motions of the comets are exceedingly regular, are governed by the same laws with the motions of the planets, and can by no means be accounted for by the hypothesis of vortices; for comets are carried with very eccentric motions through all parts of the heavens indifferently, with a freedom that is incompatible with the notion of a vortex.

Bodies projected in our air suffer no resistance but from the air. Withdraw the air, as is done in Mr. Boyle's vacuum, and the resistance ceases; for in this void a bit of fine down and a piece of solid gold descend with equal velocity. And the same argument must apply to the celestial spaces above the earth's atmosphere; in these spaces, where there is no air to resist their motions, all bodies will move with the greatest freedom; and the planets and comets will constantly pursue their revolutions in orbits given in kind and position, according to the laws above explained; but though these bodies may, indeed, continue in their orbits by the mere laws of gravity, yet they could by no means have at first derived the regular position of the orbits themselves from those laws.

The six primary planets are revolved about the sun in circles concentric with the sun, and with motions directed towards the same parts, and almost in the same plane. Ten moons are revolved about the earth, Jupiter, and Saturn, in circles concentric with them, with the same direction of motion, and nearly in the planes of the orbits of those planets; but it is not to be conceived that mere mechanical causes could give birth to so many regular motions, since the comets range over all parts of the heavens in very eccentric orbits; for by that kind of motion they pass easily through the orbs of the planets, and with great rapidity; and in their aphelions, where they move the slowest, and are detained the longest, they recede to the greatest distances from each other, and hence suffer the least disturbance from their mutual attractions. This most beautiful system of the sun, planets, and comets, could only proceed from the counsel and dominion of an intelligent and powerful Being. And if the fixed stars are the centres of other like systems, these, being formed by the like wise counsel, must be all subject to the dominion of One; especially since the light of the fixed stars is of the same nature with the light of the sun, and from every system light passes into all the other systems: and lest the systems of the fixed stars should, by their gravity, fall on each other, he hath placed those systems at immense distances from one another.

This Being governs all things, not as the soul of the world, but as Lord over all; and on account of his dominion he is wont to be called *Lord God* παντοκρατωρ, or *Universal Ruler;* for *God* is a relative word ,

and has a respect to servants; and *Deity* is the dominion of God not over his own body, as those imagine who fancy God to be the soul of the world, but over servants. The Supreme God is a Being eternal, infinite, absolutely perfect; but a being, however perfect, without dominion, cannot be said to be Lord God; for we say, my God, your God, the God of Israel, the God of Gods, and Lord of Lords; but we do not say, my Eternal, your Eternal, the Eternal of Israel, the Eternal of Gods; we do not say, my Infinite, or my Perfect: these are titles which have no respect to servants. The word *God* usually signifies *Lord*; but every lord is not a God. It is the dominion of a spiritual being which constitutes a God; a true, supreme, or imaginary dominion makes a true, supreme, or imaginary God. And from his true dominion it follows that the true God is a living, intelligent, and powerful Being; and, from his other perfections, that he is supreme, or most perfect. He is eternal and infinite, omnipotent and omniscient; that is, his duration reaches from eternity to eternity; his presence from infinity to infinity; he governs all things, and knows all things that are or can be done. He is not eternity and infinity, but eternal and infinite; he is not duration or space, but he endures and is present. He endures forever, and is everywhere present; and, by existing always and everywhere, he constitutes duration and space. Since every particle of space is *always*, and every indivisible moment of duration is *everywhere*, certainly the Maker and Lord of all things cannot be *never* and *nowhere*. Every soul that has perception is, though in different times and in different organs of sense and motion, still the same indivisible person.

There are given successive parts in duration, coexistent parts in space, but neither the one nor the other in the person of a man, or his thinking principle; and much less can they be found in the thinking substance of God. Every man, so far as he is a thing that has perception, is one and the same man during his whole life, in all and each of his organs of sense. God is the same God, always and everywhere. He is omnipresent not *virtually* only, but also *substantially;* for virtue cannot subsist without substance. In him are all things contained and moved; yet neither affects the other: God suffers nothing from the motion of bodies; bodies find no resistance from the omnipresence of God. It is allowed by all that the Supreme God exists necessarily; and by the same necessity he exists *always* and *everywhere.* Whence also he is all similar, all eye, all ear, all brain, all arm, all power to perceive, to understand, and to act; but in a manner not at all human, in a manner not at all corporeal, in a manner utterly unknown to us. As a blind man has no idea of colors, so have we no idea of the manner by which the all-wise God perceives and understands all things. He is utterly void of all body and bodily figure, and can therefore neither be seen, nor heard, nor touched; nor ought he to be worshiped under the representation of any corporeal thing. We have ideas of his attributes, but what the real substance of anything is we know not. In bodies, we see only their figures and colors, we hear only the sounds, we touch only their outward surfaces, we smell only the smells, and taste the savors; but their inward substances are not to be known either by our senses, or by any reflex act of our minds: much less, than, have we any idea of the substance of God. We know him only by his most wise and excellent contrivances of things, and final causes; we admire him for his perfections; but we reverence and adore him on account of his dominion: for we adore him as his servants; and a god without domination, providence, and final causes, is nothing else but Fate and Nature. Blind metaphysical necessity, which is certainly the same always and everywhere, could produce no variety of things. All that diversity of natural things which we find suited to different times and places could arise from nothing but the ideas and will of a Being necessarily existing. But, by way of allegory, God is said to see, to speak, to laugh, to love, to hate, to desire, to give, to receive, to rejoice, to be angry, to fight, to frame, to work, to build; for all our notions of God are taken from the ways of mankind by a certain similitude, which, though not perfect, has some likeness, however. And thus much concerning God; to discourse of whom from the appearances of things, does certainly belong to natural philosophy.

Hitherto we have explained the phenomena of the heavens and of our sea by the power of gravity, but have not yet assigned the cause of this power. This is certain, that it must proceed from a cause that penetrates to the very centres of the sun and planets, without suffering the least diminution of its force; that operates not according to the quantity of the surfaces of the particles upon which it acts (as mechanical causes used to do), but according to the quantity of the solid matter which they contain, and propagates its virtue on all sides to immense distances, decreasing always as the inverse square of the distances. Gravitation towards the sun is made up out of the gravitations towards the several particles of which the body of the sun is composed; and in receding from the sun decreases accurately as the inverse square of the distances as far as the orbit of Saturn, as evidently appears from the quiescence of the aphelion of the planets; nay, and even to the remotest aphelion of the comets, if those aphelions are also quiescent. But hitherto I have not been able to discover the cause of those properties of gravity from phenomena, and I frame no hypothesis; for whatever is not deduced from the phenomena is to be called an hypothesis; and hypothe, whether metaphysical or physical, whether of occult qualities or mechanical, have no place in experimental philosophy. In this philosophy particular propositions are inferred from the phenomena, and afterwards rendered general by induction. Thus it was that the impenetrability, the mobility, and the impulsive force of bodies, and the laws of motion and gravitation, were discovered. And to us it is enough that gravity does really exist, and act according to the laws which we have explained, and abundantly serves to account for all the motions of the celestial bodies, and of our sea.

And now we might add something concerning a certain most subtle spirit which pervades and lies hid in all gross bodies; by the force and action of which spirit the particles of bodies attract one another at near distances, and cohere, if contiguous; and electric bodies operate to greater distances, as well repelling as attracting the neighboring corpuscles; and light is emitted, reflected, refracted, inflected, and heats bodies; and all sensation is excited, and the members of animal bodies move at the command of the will, namely, by the vibrations of this spirit, mutually propagated along the solid filaments of the nerves, from the outward organs of sense to the brain, and from the brain into the muscles. But these are things that cannot be explained in few words, nor are we furnished with that sufficiency of experiments which is required to an accurate determination and demonstration of the laws by which this electric and elastic spirit operates.

32   Gottfried Leibniz
from *New Essays Concerning Human Understanding*

I call every simple quality which is positive and absolute, or expresses whatever it expresses without any limits, a *perfection*.

But a quality of this sort, because it is simple, is therefore irresolvable or indefinable, for otherwise, either it will not be a simple quality but an aggregate of many, or, if it is one, it will be circumscribed by limits and so be known through negations of further progress contrary to the hypothesis, for a purely positive quality was assumed.

From these considerations it is not difficult to show that *all perfections are compatible with each other* or can exist in the same subject.

For let the proposition be of this kind:

A and B are incompatible

(for understanding by A and B two simple forms of this kind of perfections, and it is the same if more are assumed like them), it is evident that it cannot be demonstrated without the resolution of the terms A and B, of each or both; for otherwise their nature would not enter into the ratiocination and the incompatibility could be demonstrated as well from any others as from themselves. But now (by hypothesis) they are irresolvable. Therefore this proposition cannot be demonstrated from these forms.

But it might certainly be demonstrated by these if it were true, because it is not true *per se*, for all propositions necessarily true are either demonstrable or known *per se*. Therefore, this proposition is not necessarily true. Or if it is not necessary that A and B exist in the same subject they cannot therefore exist in the same subject, and since the reasoning is the same as regards any other assumed qualities of this kind, therefore all perfections are compatible.

It is granted, therefore, that either a subject of all perfections or the most perfect being can be known.

Whence it is evident that it also exists, since existence is contained in the number of the perfections.

I showed this reasoning to D. Spinoza when I was in The Hague, who thought it solid; for when at first he opposed it, I put it in writing and read this paper before him.

Schol

The reasoning of Descartes concerning the existence of the most perfect being assumed that the most perfect being can be known, or is possible. For this being assumed because a notion of this kind is granted, it immediately follows that that being exists, since we framed the notion in such a way that it immediately contains existence. But the question is asked whether it is within our power to conceive such a being, or whether such a notion exists on the side of the thing, and can be clearly and distinctly known without contradiction. For the opponents will say that such a notion of the most perfect being or of a being existing through his essence is a chimera. Nor is it sufficient for Descartes to appeal to experience and to allege that he perceives the same in such a manner in himself clearly and distinctly, for this is to break off, not to complete the demonstration, unless he shows the method through which others also can attain the same experience; for as often as we bring experiences into the midst of the demonstration, we ought to show others also the method of producing the same experience, unless we wish to convince them by our authority alone.

33   William Paley
The
Design Argument

In crossing a heath, suppose I pitched my foot against a *stone*, and were asked how the stone came to be there, I might possibly answer, that, for anything I knew to the contrary, it had lain there for ever; nor would it, perhaps, be very easy to show the absurdity of this answer. But suppose I found a *watch* upon the ground, and it should be inquired how the watch happened to be in that place, I should hardly think of the answer which I had before given—that, for anything I knew, the watch might have always been there. Yet why should not this answer serve for the watch as well as for the stone? why is it not as admissible in the second case as in the first? For this reason, and for no other, viz., that, when we come to inspect the watch, we perceive (what we could not discover in the stone) that its several parts are framed and put together for a purpose, e.g. that they are so formed and adjusted as to produce motion, and that motion so regulated as to point out the hour of the day; that, if the different parts had been differently shaped from what they are, if a different size from what they are, or placed after any other manner, or in any other order than that in which they are placed, either no motion at all would have been carried on in the machine, or none which would have answered the use that is now served by it. To reckon up a few of the plainest of these parts, and of their offices, all tending to one result:—We see a cylindrical box containing a coiled elastic spring, which, by its endeavor to relax itself, turns round the box. We next observe a flexible chain (artificially wrought for the sake of flexure) communicating the action of the spring from the box to the fusee. We then find a series of wheels, the teeth of which catch in, and apply to, each other, conducting the motion from the fusee to the balance, and from the balance to the pointer, and, at the same time, by the size and shape of those wheels, so regulating that motion as to terminate in causing an index, by an equable and measured progression, to pass over a given space in a given time. We take notice that the wheels are made of brass, in order to keep them from rust; the springs of steel, no other metal being so elastic; that over the face of the watch there is placed a glass, a material employed in no other part of the work, but in the room of which, if there had been any other than a transparent substance, the hour could not be seen without opening the case. This mechanism being observed, (it requires indeed an examination of the instrument, and perhaps some previous knowledge of the subject, to perceive and understand it; but being once, as we have said, observed and understood,) the inference, we think, is inevitable, that the watch must have had a maker; that there must have existed, at some time, and at some place or other, an artificer or artificers who formed it for the purpose which we find it actually to answer; who comprehended its construction, and designed its use.

I.   Nor would it, I apprehend, weaken the conclusion, that we had never seen a watch made; that we had never known an artist capable of making one; that we were altogether incapable of executing such a piece of workmanship ourselves, or of understanding in what manner it was performed; all this being no more than what is true of some exquisite remains of ancient art, of some lost arts, and, to the generality of mankind, of the more curious productions of modern manufacture. Does one man in a million know how oval frames are turned? Ignorance of this kind exalts our opinion of the unseen and unknown artist's skill, if he be unseen and unknown, but raises no doubt in our minds of the existence and agency of such an artist, at some former time, and in some place or other. Nor can I perceive that it varies at all the inference, whether the question arise concerning a human agent, or concerning an agent of a different species, or an agent possessing, in some respect, a different nature.

II.   Neither, secondly, would it invalidate our conclusion, that the watch sometimes went wrong, or that it seldom went exactly right. The purpose of the machinery, the design, and the designer, might be evident, and, in the case supposed, would be evident, in whatever way we accounted for the irregularity of the movement, or whether we could account for it or not. It is not necessary that a machine be perfect, in order to show with what design it was made; still less necessary, where the only question is, whether it were made with any design at all.

III.   Nor, thirdly, would it bring any uncertainty into the argument, if there were a few parts of the watch, concerning which we could not discover, or had not yet discovered, in what manner they conduced to the general effect; or even some parts, concerning which we could not ascertain whether they conduced to that effect in any manner whatever. For, as to the first branch of the case, if by the loss, or disorder, or decay of the parts in question, the movement of the watch were found in fact to be stopped, or disturbed, or retarded, no doubt would remain in our minds as to the utility or intention of these parts, although we should be unable to investigate the manner according to which, or the connection by which, the ultimate effect depended upon their action or assistance; and the more complex is the machine, the more likely is this obscurity to arise. Then, as to the second thing supposed, namely, that there were parts which might be spared without prejudice to the movement of the watch, and that he had proved this by experiment, these superfluous parts, even if we were completely assured that they were such, would not vacate the reasoning which we had instituted concerning other parts. The indication of contrivance remained, with respect to them, nearly as it was before.

IV.   Nor, fourthly, would any man in his senses think the existence of the watch, with its various machinery, accounted for, by being told that it was one out of possible combinations of material forms; that whatever he had found in the place where he found the watch, must have contained some internal configuration or other; and that this configuration might be the structure now exhibited, viz., of the works of a watch, as well as a different structure.

V.   Nor, fifthly, would it yield his inquiry more satisfaction, to be answered, that there existed in things a principle of order, which had disposed the parts of the watch into their present form and situation. He never knew a watch made by the principle of order; nor can he even form to himself an idea of what is meant by a principle of order, distinct from the intelligence of the watch-maker.

VI.   Sixthly, he would be surprised to hear that the mechanism of the watch was not proof of contrivance, only a motive to induce the mind to think so:

VII.   And not less surprised to be informed, that the watch in his hand was nothing more than the result of the laws of *metallic* nature. It is a perversion of language to assign any law as the efficient, operative cause of anything. A law presupposes an agent; for it is only the mode according to which an agent proceeds; it implies a power; for it is the order according to which the power acts. Without this agent, without this power, which are both distinct from itself, the *law* does nothing, is nothing. The expression, "the law of metallic nature," may sound strange and harsh to a philosophic ear; but it seems quite as justifiable as some others which are more familiar to him such as "the law of vegetable nature," "the law of animal nature," or, indeed, as "the law of nature" in general, when assigned as the cause of phenomena in exclusion of agency and power, or when it is substituted into the place of these.

VIII.   Neither, lastly, would our observer be driven out of his conclusion, or from his confidence in its truth, by being told that he knew nothing at all about the matter. He knows enough for his argument: he knows the utility of the end: he knows the subserviency and adaptation of the means to the end. These points being known, his ignorance of other points, his doubts concerning other points, affect not the certainty of his reasoning. The consciousness of knowing little need not beget a distrust of that which he does not know. . . .

Application of the Argument

Every indication of contrivance, every manifestation of design, which existed in the watch, exists in the works of nature; with the difference, on the side of nature, of being greater and more, and that in a degree which exceeds all computation. I mean that the contrivances of nature surpass the contrivances of art, in the complexity, subtilty, and curiosity of the mechanism; and still more, if possible, do they go beyond them in number and variety; yet in a multitude of cases, are not less evidently mechanical, not less evidently contrivances, not less evidently accommodated to their end, or suited to their office, than are the most perfect productions of human ingenuity. . . .

34   Immanuel Kant
Critique of Pure Reason

Metaphysics is a completely isolated speculative science of reason, which soars far above the teachings of experience, and in which reason is indeed meant to be its own pupil. Metaphysics rests on concepts alone—not, like mathematics, on their application to intuition. But though it is older than all other sciences, and would survive even if all the rest were swallowed up in the abyss of an all-destroying barbarism, it has not yet had the good fortune to enter upon the secure path of a science. For in it reason is perpetually being brought to a stand, even when the laws into which it is seeking to have, as it professes, an *a priori* insight are those that are confirmed by our most common experiences. Ever and again we have to retrace our steps, as not leading us in the direction in which we desire to go. So far, too, are the students of metaphysics from exhibiting any kind of unanimity in their contentions, that metaphysics has rather to be regarded as a battle-ground quite peculiarly suited for those who desire to exercise themselves in mock combats, and in which no participant has ever yet succeeded in gaining even so much as an inch of territory, not at least in such manner as to secure him in its permanent possession. This shows, beyond all questioning, that the procedure of metaphysics has hitherto been a merely random groping, and, what is worst of all, a groping among mere concepts.

What, then, is the reason why, in this field, the sure road to science has not hitherto been found? Is it, perhaps, impossible of discovery? Why, in that case, should nature have visited our reason with the restless endeavor whereby it is ever searching for such a path, as if this were one of its most important concerns? Nay, more, how little cause have we to place trust in our reason, if, in one of the most important domains of which we would fain have knowledge, it does not merely fail us, but lures us on by deceitful promises, and in the end betrays us! Or if it be only that we have thus far failed to find the true path, are there any indications to justify the hope that by renewed efforts we may have better fortune than has fallen to our predecessors?

The examples of mathematics and natural science, which by a single and sudden revolution have become what they now are, seem to me sufficiently remarkable to suggest our considering what may have been the essential features in the changed point of view by which they have so greatly benefited. Their success should incline us, at least by way of experiment, to imitate their procedure, so far as the analogy which, as species of rational knowledge, they bear to metaphysics may permit. Hitherto it has been assumed that all our knowledge must conform to objects. But all attempts to extend our knowledge of objects by establishing something in regard to them *a priori,* by means of concepts, have, on this assumption, ended in failure. We must therefore make trial whether we may not have more success in the tasks of metaphysics, if we suppose that objects must conform to our knowledge. This would agree better with what is desired, namely, that it should be possible to have knowledge of objects *a priori*, determining something in regard to them prior to their being given. We should then be proceeding precisely on the lines of Copernicus' primary hypothesis. Failing of satisfactory progress in explaining the movements of the heavenly bodies on the supposition that they all revolved round the spectator, he tried whether he might not have better success if he made the spectator to revolve and the stars to remain at rest. A similar experiment can be tried in metaphysics, as regards the *intuition* of objects. If intuition must conform to the constitution of the objects, I do not see how we could know anything of the latter *a priori*; but if the object (as object of the senses) must conform to the constitution of our faculty of intuition, I have no difficulty in conceiving such a possibility. Since I cannot rest in these intuitions if they are to become known, but must relate them as representations to something as their object and determine this latter through them, either I must assume the *concepts*, by means of which I obtain this determination, conform to the object, or else I assume that the objects, or what is the same thing, that the *experience* in which alone, as given objects, they can be known, conform to the concepts. In the former case, I am again in the same perplexity as to how I can know anything *a priori* in regard to the objects. In the latter case the outlook is more hopeful. For experience is itself a species of knowledge which involves understanding; and understanding has rules which I must presuppose as being in me prior to objects being given to me, and therefore as being *a priori*. They find expression in *a priori* concepts to which all objects of experience necessarily conform, and with which they must agree. As regards objects which are thought solely through reason, and indeed as necessary, but which can never—at least not in the manner in which reason thinks them—be given in experience, the attempts at thinking them (for they must admit of being thought) will furnish an excellent touchstone of what we are adopting as our new method of thought, namely, that we can know *a priori* of things only what we ourselves put into them.

This experiment succeeds as well as could be desired, and promises to metaphysics, in its first part—the part that is occupied with those concepts *a priori* to which the corresponding objects, commensurate with them, can be given in experience—the secure path of a science. For the new point of view enables us to explain how there can be knowledge *a priori*; and, in addition, to furnish satisfactory proofs of the laws which form the *a priori* basis of nature, regarded as the sum of the objects of experience—neither achievement being possible on the procedure hitherto followed. But this deduction of our power of knowing *a priori*, in the first part of metaphysics, has a consequence which is startling, and which has the appearance of being highly prejudicial to the whole purpose of metaphysics, as dealt with in the second part. For we are brought to the conclusion that we can never transcend the limits of possible experience, though that is precisely what this science is concerned, above all else, to achieve. This situation yields, however, just the very experiment by which, indirectly, we are enabled to prove the truth of this first estimate of our *a priori* knowledge of reason, namely, that such knowledge has to do only with appearances, and must leave the thing in itself as indeed real *per se*, but as not known by us. For what necessarily forces us to transcend the limits of experience and of all appearances is the *unconditioned*, which reason, by necessity and by right, demands in things in themselves, as required to complete the series of conditions. If, then, on the supposition that our empirical knowledge conforms to objects as things in themselves, we find that the unconditioned *cannot be thought without contradiction*, and that when, on the other hand, we suppose that our representation of things, as they are given to us, does not conform to these things as they are in themselves, but that these objects, as appearances, conform to our mode of representation, *the contradiction vanishes*; and if, therefore, we thus find that the unconditioned is not to be met with in things, so far as we know them, that is, so far as they are given to us, but only so far as we do not know them, that is, so far as they are things in themselves, we are justified in concluding that what we at first assumed for the purposes of experiment is now definitely confirmed. But when all progress in the field of the supersensible has thus been denied to speculative reason, it is still open to us to enquire whether, in the practical knowledge of reason, data may not be found sufficient to determine reason's transcendent concept of the unconditioned, and so to enable us, in accordance with the wish of metaphysics, and by means of knowledge that is possible *a priori*, though only from a practical point of view, to pass beyond the limits of all possible experience. Speculative reason has thus at least made room for such an extension; and if it must at the same time leave it empty, yet none the less we are at liberty, indeed we are summoned, to take occupation of it, if we can, by practical data of reason.

The Distinction Between Pure and Empirical Knowledge

There can be no doubt that all our knowledge begins with experience. For how should our faculty of knowledge be awakened into action did not objects affecting our senses partly of themselves produce representations, partly arouse the activity of our understanding to compare these representations, and, by combining or separating them, work up the raw material of the sensible impressions into that knowledge of objects which is entitled experience? In the order of time, therefore, we have no knowledge anteced-

ent to experience, and with experience all our knowledge begins.

But though all our knowledge begins with experience, it does not follow that it all arises out of experience. For it may well be that even our empirical knowledge is made up of what we receive through impressions and of what our own faculty of knowledge (sensible impressions serving merely as the occasion) supplies from itself. If our faculty of knowledge makes any such addition, it may be that we are not in a position to distinguish it from the raw material, until with long practice of attention we have become skilled in separating it.

This, then, is a question which at least calls for closer examination, and does not allow of any off-hand answer:—whether there is any knowledge that is thus independent of experience and even of all impressions of the senses. Such knowledge is entitled *a priori*, and distinguished from the *empirical*, which has its sources *a posteriori*, that is, in experience.

The expression '*a priori*' does not, however, indicate with sufficient precision the full meaning of our question. For it has been customary to say, even of much knowledge that is derived from empirical sources, that we have it or are capable of having it *a priori*, meaning thereby that we do not derive it immediately from experience, but from a universal rule—a rule which is itself, however, borrowed by us from experience. Thus we would say of a man who undermined the foundations of his house, that he might have known *a priori* that it would fall, that is, that he need not have waited for the experience of its actual falling. But still he could not know this completely *a priori*. For he had first to learn through experience that bodies are heavy, and therefore fall when their supports are withdrawn.

In what follows, therefore, we shall understand by *a priori* knowledge, not knowledge independent of this or that experience, but knowledge absolutely independent of all experience. Opposed to it is empirical knowledge, which is knowledge possible only *a posteriori*, that is, through experience. *A priori* modes of knowledge are entitled pure when there is no admixture of anything empirical. Thus, for instance, the proposition, 'every alteration has its cause', while an *a priori* proposition, is not a pure proposition, because alteration is a concept which can be derived only from experience.

We are in Possession of Certain Modes of *A Priori* Knowledge, and Even the Common Understanding is Never Without Them

What we here require is a criterion by which to distinguish with certainty between pure and empirical knowledge. Experience teaches us that a thing is so and so, but not that it cannot be otherwise. First, then, if we have a proposition which in being thought is thought as *necessary*, it is an *a priori* judgment; and if, besides, it is not derived from any proposition except one which also has the validity of a necessary judgment, it is an absolutely *a priori* judgment. Secondly, experience never confers on its judgments true or strict, but only assumed and comparative *universality*, through induction. We can properly only say, therefore, that, so far as we have hitherto observed, there is no exception to this or that

rule. If, then, a judgment is thought with strict universality, that is, in such manner that no exception is allowed as possible, it is not derived from experience, but is valid absolutely *a priori*. Empirical universality is only an arbitrary extension of a validity holding in most cases to one which holds in all, for instance, in the proposition, 'all bodies are heavy'. When on the other hand, strict universality is essential to a judgment, this indicates a special source of knowledge, namely, a faculty of *a priori* knowledge. Necessity and strict universality are thus sure criteria of *a priori* knowledge, and are inseparable from one another. But since in the employment of these criteria the contingency of judgments is sometimes more easily shown than their empirical limitation, or, as sometimes also happens, their unlimited universality can be more convincingly proved than their necessity, it is advisable to use the two criteria separately, each by itself being infallible.

Now it is easy to show that there actually are in human knowledge judgments which are necessarily and in the strictest sense universal, and which are therefore pure *a priori* judgments. If an example from the sciences be desired, we have only to look to any of the propositions of mathematics; if we seek an example from the understanding in its quite ordinary employment, the proposition, 'every alteration must have a cause', will serve our purpose. In the latter case, indeed, the very concept of a cause so manifestly contains the concept of a necessity of connection with an effect and of the strict universality of the rule, that the concept would be altogether lost if we attempted to derive it, as Hume has done, from a repeated association of that which happens with that which precedes, and from a custom of connecting representations, a custom originating in this repeated association, and constituting therefore a merely subjective necessity. Even without appealing to such examples, it is possible to show that pure *a priori* principles are indispensable for the possibility of experience, and so to prove their existence *a priori*. For whence could experience derive its certainty, if all the rules, according to which it proceeds, were always themselves empirical, and therefore contingent? Such rules could hardly be regarded as first principles. At present, however we may be content to have established the fact that our faculty of knowledge does have a pure employment, and to have shown what are the criteria of such an employment.

Such *a priori* origin is manifest in certain concepts, no less than in judgments. If we remove from our empirical concept of a body, one by one, every feature in it which is [merely] empirical, the colour, the hardness or softness, the weight, even the impenetrability, there still remains the space which the body (now entirely vanished) occupied, and this cannot be removed. Again, if we remove from our empirical concept of any object, corporeal or incorporeal, all properties which experience has taught us, we yet cannot take away that property through which the object is thought as substance or as inhering in a substance (although this concept of substance is more determinate than that of an object in general). Owing, therefore, to the necessity with which this concept of substance forces itself upon us, we have no option save to admit that it has its seat in our faculty of *a priori* knowledge.

Philosophy Stands in Need of a Science Which Shall Determine the Possibility, the Principles, and the Extent of all *A Priori* Knowledge

But what is still more extraordinary than all the preceding is this, that certain modes of knowledge leave the field of all possible experiences and have the appearance of extending the scope of our judgments beyond all limits of experience, and this by means of concepts to which no corresponding object can ever be given in experience.

It is precisely by means of the latter modes of knowledge, in a realm beyond the world of the senses, where experience can yield neither guidance nor correction, that our reason carries on those enquiries which owing to their importance we consider to be far more excellent, and in their purpose far more lofty, than all that the understanding can learn in the field of appearances. Indeed we prefer to run every risk of error rather than desist from such urgent enquiries, on the ground of their dubious character, or from disdain and indifference. These unavoidable problems set by pure reason itself are *God*, *freedom*, and *immortality*. The science which, with all its preparations, is in its final intention directed solely to their solution is metaphysics; and its procedure is at first dogmatic, that is, it confidently sets itself to this task without any previous examination of the capacity or incapacity of reason for so great an undertaking.

Now it does indeed seem natural that, as soon as we have left the ground of experience, we should, through careful enquiries, assure ourselves as to the foundations of any building that we propose to erect, not making use of any knowledge that we possess without first determining whence it has come, and not trusting to principles without knowing their origin. It is natural, that is to say, that the question should first be considered, how the understanding can arrive at all this knowledge *a priori*, and what extent, validity, and worth it may have. Nothing, indeed, could be more natural, if by the term 'natural' we signify what fittingly and reasonably ought to happen. But if we mean by 'natural' what ordinarily happens, then on the contrary nothing is more natural and more intelligible than the fact that this enquiry has been so long neglected. For one part of this knowledge, the mathematical, has long been of established reliability, and so gives rise to a favourable presumption as regards the other part, which may yet be of quite different nature. Besides, once we are outside the circle of experience, we can be sure of not being *contradicted* by experience. The charm of extending our knowledge is so great that nothing short of encountering a direct contradiction can suffice to arrest us in our course; and this can be avoided, if we are careful in our fabrications—which none the less will still remain fabrications. Mathematics gives us a shining example of how far, independently of experience, we can progress in *a priori* knowledge. It does, indeed, occupy itself with objects and with knowledge solely in so far as they allow of being exhibited in intuition. But this circumstance is easily overlooked, since this intuition can itself be given *a priori*, and is therefore hardly to be distinguished from a bare and pure concept. Misled by such a

proof of the power of reason, the demand for the extension of knowledge recognizes no limits. The light dove, cleaving the air in her free flight, and feeling its resistance, might imagine that its flight would be still easier in empty space. It was thus that Plato left the world of the senses, as setting too narrow limits to the understanding, and ventured out beyond it on the wings of the ideas, in the empty space of the pure understanding. He did not observe that with all his efforts he made no advance—meeting no resistance that might, as it were, serve as a support upon which he could take a stand, to which he could apply his powers, and so set his understanding in motion. It is, indeed, the common fate of human reason to complete its speculative structures as speedily as may be, and only afterwards to enquire whether the foundations are reliable. All sorts of excuses will then be appealed to, in order to reassure us of their solidity, or rather indeed to enable us to dispense altogether with so late and so dangerous an enquiry. But what keeps us, during the actual building, free from all apprehension and suspicion, and flatters us with a seeming thoroughness, is this other circumstance, namely, that a great, perhaps the greatest, part of the business of our reason consists in analysis of the concepts which we already have of objects. This analysis supplies us with a considerable body of knowledge, which, while nothing but explanation or elucidation of what has already been thought in our concepts, though in a confused manner, is yet prized as being, at least as regards its form, new insight. But as far as the matter or content is concerned, there has been no extension of our previously possessed concepts, but only an analysis of them. Since this procedure yields real knowledge *a priori*, which progresses in an assured and useful fashion, reason is so far misled as surreptitiously to introduce, without itself being aware of so doing, assertions of an entirely different order, in which it attaches to given concepts others completely foreign to them, and moreover attaches them *a priori*. And yet it is not known how reason can be in position to do this. Such a question is never so much as thought of. I shall therefore at once proceed to deal with the difference between these two kinds of knowledge.

The Distinction Between Analytic and Synthetic Judgements

In all judgments in which the relation of a subject to the predicate is thought (I take into consideration affirmative judgments only, the subsequent application to negative judgments being easily made), this relation is possible in two different ways. Either the predicate B belongs to the subject A, as something which is (covertly) contained in this concept A; or B lies outside the concept A, although it does indeed stand in connection with it. In the one case I entitle the judgment analytic, in the other synthetic. Analytic judgments (affirmative) are therefore those in which the connection of the predicate with the subject is thought through identity; those in which this connection is thought without identity should be entitled synthetic. The former, as adding nothing through the predicate to the concept of the subject, but merely breaking it up into those constituent concepts that have

all along been thought in it, although confusedly, can also be entitled explicative. The latter, on the other hand, add to the concept of the subject a predicate which has not been in any wise thought in it, and which no analysis could possibly extract from it; and they may therefore be entitled ampliative. If I say, for instance, 'All bodies are extended', this is an analytic judgment. For I do not require to go beyond the concept which I connect with 'body' in order to find extension as bound up with it. To meet with this predicate, I have merely to analyze the concept, that is, to become conscious to myself of the manifold which I always think in that concept. The judgment is therefore analytic. But when I say, 'All bodies are heavy', the predicate is something quite different from anything that I think in the mere concept of body in general; and the addition of such a predicate therefore yields a synthetic judgment.

Judgments of experience, as such, are one and all synthetic. For it would be absurd to found an analytic judgment on experience. Since, in framing the judgment, I must not go outside my concept, there is no need to appeal to the testimony of experience in its support . That a body is extended is a proposition that holds *a priori* and is not empirical. For, before appealing to experience, I have already in the concept of body all the conditions required for my judgment. I have only to extract from it, in accordance with the principle of contradiction, the required predicate, and in so doing can at the same time become conscious of the necessity of the judgment—and that is what experience could never have taught me. On the other hand, though I do not include in the concept of a body in general the predicate 'weight', none the less this concept indicates an object of experience through one of its parts, and I can add to that part other parts of this same experience, as in this way belonging together with the concept. From the start I can apprehend the concept of body analytically through the characters of extension, impenetrability, figure, etc., all of which are thought in the concept. Now, however, looking back on the experience from which I have derived this concept of body, and finding weight to be invariably connected with the above characters, I attach it as a predicate to the concept; and in doing so I attach it synthetically, and am therefore extending my knowledge. The possibility of the synthesis of the predicate 'weight' with the concept of 'body' thus rests upon experience. While the one concept is not contained in the other, they yet belong to one another, though only contingently, as parts of a whole, namely, of an experience which is itself a synthetic combination of intuitions.

But in *a priori* synthetic judgments this is entirely lacking: [I do not here have the advantage of looking around in the field of experience.] Upon what, then, am I to rely, when I seek to go beyond the concept A, and to know that another concept B is connected with it? Through what is the synthesis made possible? Let us take the proposition, 'Everything which happens has its cause'. In the concept of 'something which happens'. I do indeed think an existence which is preceded by a time, etc., and from this concept analytic judgments may be obtained. But the concept of a 'cause' lies entirely outside the other concept, and signifies something different from 'that

which happens', and is not therefore in any way contained in this latter representation. How come I then to predicate of that which happens something quite different, and to apprehend that the concept of cause, though not contained in it, yet belongs, and indeed necessarily belongs, to it? What is here the unknown = X which gives support to the understanding when it believes that it can discover outside the concept A a predicate B foreign to this concept, which it yet at the same time considers to be connected with it? It cannot be experience, because the suggested principle has connected the second representation with the first, not only with greater universality, but also with the character of necessity, and therefore completely *a priori* and on the basis of mere concepts. Upon such synthetic, that is, ampliative principles, all our *a priori* speculative knowledge must ultimately rest; analytic judgments are very important, and indeed necessary, but only for obtaining that clearness in the concepts which is requisite for such a sure and wide synthesis as will lead to a genuinely new addition to all previous knowledge.

In All Theoretical Sciences of Reason Synthetic *A Priori* Judgements are Contained as Principles

1. *All mathematical judgments, without exception, are synthetic.* This fact, though incontestably certain and in its consequences very important, has hitherto escaped the notice of those who are engaged in the analysis of human reason, and is, indeed, directly opposed to all their conjec-

tures. For as it was found that all mathematical inferences proceed in accordance with the principle of contradiction (which the nature of all apodeictic certainty requires), it was supposed that the fundamental propositions of the science can themselves be known to be true through that principle. This is an erroneous view. For though a synthetic proposition can indeed be discerned in accordance with the principle of contradiction, this can only be if another synthetic proposition is presupposed, and if it can then be apprehended as following from this other proposition; it can never be so discerned in and by itself.

First of all, it has to be noted that mathematical propositions, strictly so called, are always judgments *a priori,* not empirical; because they carry with them necessity, which cannot be derived from experience. If this be demurred to, I am willing to limit my statement to *pure* mathematics, the very concept of which implies that it does not contain empirical, but only pure *a priori* knowledge.

We might, indeed, at first suppose that the proposition $7 + 5 = 12$ is a merely analytic proposition, and follows by the principle of contradiction from the concept of a sum of 7 and 5. But if we look more closely we find that the concept of the sum 7 and 5 contains nothing save the union of the two numbers into one, and in this no thought is being taken as to what that single number may be which combines both. The concept of 12 is by no means already thought in merely thinking this union of 7 and 5; and I may analyze my concept of such a possible sum as long as I please, still I shall never find the 12 in it. We have to go outside these concepts,

and call in the aid of the intuition which corresponds to one of them, our five fingers, for instance, or, as Segner does in his *Arithmetic*, five points, adding to the concept of 7, unit by unit, the five given in intuition. For starting with the number 7, and for the concept of 5 calling in the aid of the fingers of my hand as intuition, I now add one by one to the number 7 the units which I previously took together to form the number 5, and with the aid of that figure [the hand] see the number 12 come into being. That 5 should be added to 7, I have indeed already thought in the concept of a sum $= 7+5$, but not that this sum is equivalent to the number 12. Arithmetical propositions are therefore always synthetic. This is still more evident if we take larger numbers. For it is then obvious that, however we might turn and twist our concepts, we could never, by the mere analysis of them, and without the aid of intuition, discover what [the number is that] is the sum.

Just as little is any fundamental proposition of pure geometry analytic. That the straight line between two points is the shortest, is a synthetic proposition. For my concept of *straight* contains nothing of quantity, but only of quality. The concept of the shortest is wholly an addition, and cannot be derived, through any process of analysis, from the concept of the straight line. Intuition, therefore, must here be called in; only by its aid is the synthesis possible. What here causes us commonly to believe that the predicate of such apodeictic judgments is already contained in our concept, and that the judgment is therefore analytic, is merely the ambiguous character of the terms used. We are required to join in thought a certain predicate to a given concept, and this necessity is inherent in the concepts themselves. But the question is not what we *ought* to join in thought to the given concept, but what we *actually* think in it, even if only obscurely; and it is then manifest that, while the predicate is indeed attached necessarily to the concept, it is so in virtue of an intuition which must be added to the concept, not as thought in the concept itself.

Some few fundamental propositions, presupposed by the geometrician, are, indeed, really analytic, and rest on the principle of contradiction. But, as identical propositions, they serve only as links in the chain of method and not as principles; for instance, *a=a*; the whole is equal to itself; or (a+b)>a, that is, the whole is greater than its part. And even these propositions though they are valid according to pure concepts, are only admitted in mathematics because they can be exhibited in intuition.

2. *Natural science (physics) contains* a priori *synthetic judgments as principles.* I need cite only two such judgments: that in all changes of the material world the quantity of matter remains unchanged; and that in all communication of motion, action and reaction must always be equal. Both propositions, it is evident, are not only necessary, and therefore in their origin a *priori,* but also synthetic. For in the concept of matter I do not think its permanence, but only its presence in the space which it occupies. I go outside and beyond the concept of matter, joining to it *a priori* in thought something which I have not thought *in* it. The proposition is not, therefore, analytic, but synthetic, and yet is thought *a priori*; and so likewise are the other propositions of the pure part of natural science.

3. *Metaphysics*, even if we look upon it as having hitherto failed in all its endeavours, is yet, owing to the nature of human reason, a quite indispensable science, and *ought to contain* a priori *synthetic knowledge*. For its business is not merely to analyze concepts which we make for ourselves *a priori* of things, and thereby to clarify them analytically, but to extend our *a priori* knowledge. And for this purpose we must employ principles which add to the given concept something that was not contained in it, and through *a priori* synthetic judgments venture out so far that experience is quite unable to follow us, as, for instance, in the proposition, that the world must have a first beginning, and such like. Thus metaphysics consists, at least *in intention*, entirely of *a priori* synthetic propositions.

The General Problem of Pure Reason

Much is already gained if we can bring a number of investigations under the formula of a single problem. For we not only lighten our own task, by defining it accurately, but make it easier for others, who would test our results, to judge whether or not we have succeeded in what we set out to do. Now the proper problem of pure reason is contained in the question: How are *a priori* synthetic judgments possible?

That metaphysics has hitherto remained in so vacillating a state of uncertainty and contradiction, is entirely due to the fact that this problem, and perhaps even the distinction between analytic and synthetic judgments, has never previously been considered. Upon the solution of this problem, or upon a sufficient proof that the possibility which it desires to have explained does in fact not exist at all, depends the success or failure of metaphysics. Among philosophers, David Hume came nearest to envisaging this problem, but still was very far from conceiving it with sufficient definiteness and universality. He occupied himself exclusively with the synthetic proposition regarding the connection of an effect with its cause *(principium causalitatis),* and he believed himself to have shown that such an *a priori* proposition is entirely impossible. If we accept his conclusions, then all that we call metaphysics is a mere delusion whereby we fancy ourselves to have rational insight into what, in actual fact, is borrowed solely from experience, and under the influence of custom has taken the illusory semblance of necessity. If he had envisaged our problem in all its universality, he would never have been guilty of this statement, so destructive of all pure philosophy. For he would then have recognized that, according to his own argument, pure mathematics, as certainly containing *a priori* synthetic propositions, would also not be possible; and from such an assertion his good sense would have saved him.

In the solution of the above problem, we are at the same time deciding as to the possibility of the employment of pure reason in establishing and developing all those sciences which contain a theoretical *a priori* knowledge of objects, and have therefore to answer the questions:

How is pure mathematics possible?

How is pure science of nature possible?

Since these sciences actually exist, it is quite proper to ask how they are possible; for that they must be possible is proved by the fact that they exist.[a] But the poor progress which has hitherto been made in metaphysics, and the fact that no system yet propounded can, in view of the essential purpose of metaphysics, be said really to exist, leaves everyone sufficient ground for doubting as to its possibility.

Yet, in a certain sense, this *kind of knowledge* is to be looked upon as given; that is to say, metaphysics actually exists, if not as a science, yet still as natural disposition *(metaphysica naturalis).* For human reason, without being moved merely by the idle desire for extent and variety of knowledge, proceeds impetuously, driven on by an inward need, to questions such as cannot be answered by any empirical employment of reason, or by principles thence derived. Thus in all men, as soon as their reason has become ripe for speculation, there has always existed and will always continue to exist some kind of metaphysics. And so we have the question:

How is metaphysics, as natural disposition, possible? That is, how from the nature of universal human reason do those questions arise which pure reason propounds to itself, and which it is impelled by its own need to answer as best it can?

But since all attempts which have hith-

---

a. Many may still have doubts as regards pure natural science. We have only, however, to consider the various propositions that are to be found at the beginning of (empirical) physics, properly so called, those, for instance, relating to the permanence in the quantity of matter, to inertia, to the equality of action and reaction, etc., in order to be soon convinced that they constitute a *physica pura,* or *rationalis,* which well deserves, as an independent science, to be separately dealt with in its whole extent, be that narrow or wide.

erto been made to answer these natural questions—for instance, whether the world has a beginning or is from eternity—have always met with unavoidable contradictions, we cannot rest satisfied with the mere natural disposition to metaphysics, that is, with the pure faculty of reason itself, from which, indeed, some sort of metaphysics (be it what it may) always arises. It must be possible for reason to attain to certainty whether we know or do not know the objects of metaphysics, that is, to come to a decision either in regard to the objects of its enquiries or in regard to the capacity or incapacity of reason to pass any judgment upon them, so that we may either with confidence extend our pure reason or set to it sure and determinate limits. This last question, which arises out of the previous general problem, may, rightly stated, take the form:

How is metaphysics, as science, possible?   Thus the critique of reason, in the end, necessarily leads to scientific knowledge; while its dogmatic employment, on the other hand, lands us in dogmatic assertions to which other assertions, equally specious, can always be opposed—that is, in *scepticism*.

This science cannot be of any very formidable prolixity, since it has to deal not with the objects of reason, the variety of which is inexhaustible, but only with itself and the problems which arise entirely from within itself, and which are imposed upon it by its own nature, not by the nature of things which are distinct from it. When once reason has learnt completely to understand its own power in respect of objects which can be presented to it in experience, it should easily be able to determine, with completeness and certainty, the extent and the limits of its attempted employment beyond the bounds of all experience.

We may, then, and indeed we must, regard as abortive all attempts, hitherto made, to establish a metaphysic *dogmatically*. For the analytic part in any such attempted system, namely, the mere analysis of the concepts that inhere in our reason *a priori,* is by no means the aim of, but only a preparation for, metaphysics proper, that is, the extension of its *a priori* synthetic knowledge. For such a purpose, the analysis of concepts is useless, since it merely shows what is contained in these concepts, not how we arrive at them *a priori*. A solution of this latter problem is required, that we may be able to determine the valid employment of such concepts in regard to the objects of all knowledge in general. Nor is much self-denial needed to give up these claims, seeing that the undeniable, and in the dogmatic procedure of reason also unavoidable, contradictions of reason with itself have long since undermined the authority of every metaphysical system yet propounded. Greater firmness will be required if we are not to be deterred by inward difficulties and outward opposition from endeavouring, though application of a method entirely different from any hitherto employed, at last to bring to a prosperous and fruitful growth a science indispensable to human reason—a science whose every branch may be cut away but whose root cannot be destroyed.

The Idea and Division of a Special Science, Under the Title "Critique of Pure Reason"

In view of all these considerations, we arrive at the idea of a special science which can be entitled the Critique of Pure Reason. For reason is the faculty which supplies the principles of *a priori* knowledge. Pure reason is, therefore, that which contains the principles whereby we know anything absolutely *a priori*. An organon of pure reason would be the sum-total of those principles according to which all modes of pure *a priori* knowledge can be acquired and actually brought into being. The exhaustive application of such an organon would give rise to a system of pure reason. But as this would be asking rather much, and as it is still doubtful whether, and in what cases, any extension of our knowledge be here possible, we can regard a science of the mere examination of pure reason, of its sources and limits, as the *propaedeutic* to the system of pure reason. As such, it should be called a critique, not a doctrine, of pure reason. Its utility, in speculation, ought properly to be only negative, not to extend, but only to clarify our reason, and keep it free from errors—which is already a very great gain. I entitle *transcendental* all knowledge which is occupied not so much with objects as with the mode of our knowledge of objects in so far as this mode of knowledge is to be possible *a priori*. A system of such concepts might be entitled transcendental philosophy. But that is still, at this stage, too large an undertaking. For since such a science must contain, with completeness, both kinds of *a priori* knowledge, the analytic no less than the synthetic,

it is, so far as our present purpose is concerned, much too comprehensive. We have to carry the analysis so far only as is indispensably necessary in order to comprehend, in their whole extent, the principles of *a priori* synthesis, with which alone we are called upon to deal. It is upon this enquiry, which should be entitled not a doctrine, but only a transcendental critique, that we are now engaged. Its purpose is not to extend knowledge, but only to correct it, and to supply a touchstone of the value, or lack of value, of all *a priori* knowledge. Such a critique is therefore a preparation, so far as may be possible, for an organon; and should this turn out not to be possible, then at least for a canon, according to which, in due course, the complete system of the philosophy of pure reason—be it in extension or merely in limitation of its knowledge—may be carried into execution, analytically as well as synthetically. That such a system is possible, and indeed that it may not be of such great extent as to cut us off from the hope of entirely completing it, may already be gathered from the fact that what here constitutes our subject-matter is not the nature of things, which is inexhaustible, but the understanding which passes judgment upon the nature of things; and this understanding, again, only in respect of its *a priori* knowledge. These *a priori* possessions of the understanding, since they have not to be sought for without, cannot remain hidden from us, and in all probability are sufficiently small in extent to allow of our apprehending them in their completeness, of judging as to their value or lack of value, and so of rightly appraising them. Still less may the reader here expect a critique of books and systems of pure reason; we are concerned only with the critique of the faculty of pure reason itself. Only in so far as we build upon this foundation do we have a reliable touchstone for estimating the philosophical value of old and new works in this field. Otherwise the unqualified historian or critic is passing judgments upon the groundless assertions of others by means of his own, which are equally groundless.

Transcendental philosophy is only the idea of a science, for which the critique of pure reason has to lay down the complete architectonic plan. That is to say, it has to guarantee, as following from principles, the completeness and certainty of the structure in all its parts. It is the system of all principles of pure reason. And if this critique is not itself to be entitled a transcendental philosophy, it is solely because, to be a complete system, it would also have to contain an exhaustive analysis of the whole of *a priori* human knowledge. Our critique must, indeed, supply a complete enumeration of all the fundamental concepts that go to constitute such pure knowledge. But it is not required to give an exhaustive analysis of these concepts, nor a complete review of those that can be derived from them. Such a demand would be unreasonable, partly because this analysis would not be appropriate to our main purpose, inasmuch as there is no such uncertainty in regard to analysis as we encounter in the case of synthesis, for the sake of which alone our whole critique is undertaken; and partly because it would be inconsistent with the unity of our plan to assume responsibility for the completeness of such an analysis and derivation, when in view of our purpose we can be excused from doing so. The analysis of these *a priori* concepts, which later we shall have to

enumerate, and the derivation of other concepts from them, can easily, however, be made complete when once they have been established as exhausting the principles of synthesis, and if in this essential respect nothing be lacking in them.

The critique of pure reason therefore will contain all that is essential in transcendental philosophy. While it is the complete idea of transcendental philosophy, it is not equivalent to that latter science; for it carries the analysis only so far as is requisite for the complete examination of knowledge which is *a priori* and synthetic.

What has chiefly to be kept in view in the division of such a science, is that no concepts be allowed to enter which contain themselves anything empirical, or, in other words, that it consist in knowledge wholly *a priori*. Accordingly, although the highest principles and fundamental concepts of morality are *a priori* knowledge, they have no place in transcendental philosophy, because, although they do not lay at the foundation of their precepts the concepts of pleasure and pain, of the desires and inclinations, etc., all of which are of empirical origin, yet in the construction of a system of pure morality these empirical concepts must necessarily be brought into the concept of duty, as representing either a hindrance, which we have to overcome, or an allurement, which must not be made into a motive. Transcendental philosophy is therefore a philosophy of pure and merely speculative reason. All that is practical, so far as it contains motives, relates to feelings, and these belong to the empirical sources of knowledge.

If we are to make a systematic division of the science which we are engaged in presenting, it must have first a *doctrine of the elements*, and secondly, a *doctrine of the method* of pure reason. Each of these chief divisions will have its subdivisions, but the grounds of these we are not yet in a position to explain. By way of introduction or anticipation we need only say that there are two stems of human knowledge, namely, *sensibility* and *understanding,* which perhaps spring from a common, but to us unknown, root. Through the former, objects are given to us; through the latter, they are thought. Now in so far as sensibility may be found to contain *a priori* representations constituting the condition under which objections are given to us, it will belong to transcendental philosophy. And since the conditions under which alone the objects of human knowledge are given must precede those under which they are thought, the transcendental doctrine of sensibility will constitute the first part of the science of the elements.

35 Immanuel Kant
The Impossibility of an Ontological Proof

It is evident, from what has been said, that the concept of an absolutely necessary being is a concept of pure reason, that is, a mere idea the objective reality of which is very far from being proved by the fact that reason requires it. For the idea instructs us only in regard to a certain unattainable completeness, and so serves rather to limit the understanding than to extend it to new

objects. But we are here faced by what is indeed strange and perplexing, namely, that while the inference from a given existence in general to some absolutely necessary being seems to be both imperative and legitimate, all those conditions under which alone the understanding can form a concept of such a necessity are so many obstacles in the way of our doing so.

In all ages men have spoken of an *absolutely necessary* being, and in so doing have endeavoured, not so much to understand whether and how a thing of this kind allows even of being thought, but rather to prove its existence. There is, of course, no difficulty in giving a verbal definition of the concept, namely, that it is something the non-existence of which is impossible. But this yields no insight into the conditions which make it necessary to regard the non-existence of a thing as absolutely unthinkable. It is precisely these conditions that we desire to know, in order that we may determine whether or not, in resorting to this concept, we are thinking anything at all. The expedient of removing all those conditions which the understanding indispensably requires in order to regard something as necessary, simply through the introduction of the word *unconditioned,* is very far from sufficing to show whether I am still thinking anything in the concept of the unconditionally necessary, or perhaps rather nothing at all.

Nay more, this concept, at first ventured upon blindly, and now become so completely familiar, has been supposed to have its meaning exhibited in a number of examples; and on this account all further inquiry into its intelligibility has seemed to be quite needless. Thus the fact that every geometrical proposition, as, for instance, that a triangle has three angles, is absolutely necessary, has been taken as justifying us in speaking of an object which lies entirely outside the sphere of our understanding as if we understood perfectly what it is that we intend to convey by the concept of that object.

All the alleged examples are, without exception, taken from *judgments,* not from *things* and their existence. But the unconditioned necessity of judgments is not the same as an absolute necessity of things. The absolute necessity of the judgment is only a conditioned necessity of the thing, or of the predicate in the judgment. The above proposition does not declare that three angles are absolutely necessary, but that, under the condition that there is a triangle (that is, that a triangle is given), three angles will necessarily be found in it. So great, indeed, is the deluding influence exercised by this logical necessity that, by the simple device of forming an a *priori* concept of a thing in such a manner as to include existence within the scope of its meaning, we have supposed ourselves to have justified the conclusion that because existence necessarily belongs to the object of this concept—always under the condition that we posit the thing as given (as existing)—we are also of necessity, in accordance with the law of identity, required to posit the existence of its object, and that this being is therefore itself absolutely necessary—and this, to repeat, for the reason that the existence of this being has already been thought in a concept which is assumed arbitrarily and on condition that we posit its object.

If, in an identical preposition, I reject the predicate while retaining the subject, contradiction results; and I therefore say that the former belongs necessarily to the latter. But if we reject subject and predicate alike, there is no contradiction; for nothing is then left that can be contradicted. To posit a triangle, and yet to reject its three angles, is self-contradictory; but there is no contradiction in rejecting the triangle together with its three angles. The same holds true of the concept of an absolutely necessary being. If its existence is rejected, we reject the thing itself with all its predicates; and no question of contradiction can then arise. There is nothing outside it that would then be contradicted, since the necessity of the thing is not supposed to be derived from anything external; nor is there anything internal that would be contradicted, since in rejecting the thing itself we have at the same time rejected all its internal properties. 'God is omnipotent' is a necessary judgment. The omnipotence cannot be rejected if we posit a Deity, that is, an infinite being; for the two concepts are identical. But if we say, 'There is no God', neither the omnipotence nor any other of its predicates is given; they are one and all rejected together with the subject, and there is therefore not the least contradiction in such a judgment.

We have thus seen that if the predicate of a judgment is rejected together with the subject, no internal contradiction can result, and that this holds no matter what the predicate may be. The only way of evading this conclusion is to argue that there are subjects which cannot be removed, and must always remain. That, however, would only be another way of saying that there are absolutely necessary subjects;

and this is the very assumption which I have called in question, and the possibility of which the above argument professes to establish. For I cannot form the least concept of a thing which, should it be rejected with all its predicates, leaves behind a contradiction; and in the absence of contradiction I have, through pure *a priori* concepts alone, no criterion of impossibility.

Notwithstanding all these general considerations, in which every one must concur, we may be challenged with a case which is brought forward as proof that in actual fact the contrary holds, namely, that there is one concept, and indeed only one, in reference to which the not-being or rejection of its object is in itself contradictory, namely, the concept of the *ens realissimum*. It is declared that it possesses all reality, and that we are justified in assuming that such a being is possible (the fact that a concept does not contradict itself by no means proves the possibility of its object: but the contrary assertion I am for the moment willing to allow).[a] Now (the argument proceeds) 'all reality' includes existence; existence is therefore contained in the concept of a thing that is possible. If, then, this thing is rejected, the internal possibility of the thing is rejected—which is self-contradictory.

My answer is as follows. There is already a contradiction in introducing the concept of existence—no matter under what title it may be disguised—into the concept of a thing which we profess to be thinking solely in reference to its possibility. If that be allowed as legitimate, a seeming victory has been won; but in actual fact nothing at all is said: the assertion is a mere tautology. We must ask: Is the proposition that *this or that thing* (which, whatever it may be, is allowed as possible) *exists,* an analytic or a synthetic proposition? If it is analytic, the assertion of the existence of the thing adds nothing to the thought of the thing; but in that case either the thought, which is in us, is the thing itself, or we have presupposed an existence as belonging to the realm of the possible, and have then, on that pretext, inferred its existence from its internal possibility—which is nothing but a miserable tautology. The word 'reality', which in the concept of the thing sounds other than the word 'existence' in the concept of the predicate, is of no avail in meeting this objection. For if all positing (no matter what it may be that is posited) is entitled reality, the thing with all its predicates is already posited in the concept of the subject, and is assumed as actual; and in the predicate this is merely repeated. But if, on the other hand, we admit, as every reasonable person must, that all existential propositions are synthetic, how can we profess to maintain that the predicate of existence cannot be rejected without contradiction? This is a feature which is found only in analytic propositions, and is indeed precisely what consti-

---

a. A concept is always possible if it is not self-contradictory. This is the logical criterion of possibility, and by it the object of the concept is distinguishable from the *nihil negativum.* But it may none the less be an empty concept, unless the objective reality of the synthesis through which the concept is generated has been specifically proved; and such proof, as we have shown above, rests on principles of possible experience, and not on the principle of analysis (the law of contradiction). This is a warning against arguing directly from the logical possibility of concepts to the real possibility of things.

tutes their analytic character.

I should have hoped to put an end to these idle and fruitless disputations in a direct manner, by an accurate determination of the concept of existence, had I not found that the illusion which is caused by the confusion of a logical with a real predicate (that is, with a predicate which determines a thing) is almost beyond correction. Anything we please can be made to serve as a logical predicate; the subject can even be predicated of itself; for logic abstracts from all content. But a *determining* predicate is a predicate which is added to the concept of the subject and enlarges it. Consequently, it must not be already contained in the concept.

'*Being*' is obviously not a real predicate, that is, it is not a concept of something which could be added to the concept of a thing. It is merely the positing of a thing, or of certain determinations, as existing in themselves. Logically, it is merely the copula of a judgment. The proposition, 'God is omnipotent', contains two concepts, each of which has its object—God and omnipotence. The small word 'is' adds no new predicate, but only serves to posit the predicate *in its relation to* the subject. If, now, we take the subject (God) with all its predicates (among which is omnipotence), and say 'God is', or 'There is a God', we attach no new predicate to the concept of God, but only posit the subject in itself with all its predicates, and indeed posit it as being an *object* that stands in relation to my *concept*. The content of both must be one and the same; nothing can have been added to the concept, which expresses merely what is possible, by my thinking its object (through the expression 'it is') as given absolutely. Otherwise stated, the real contains no more

than the merely possible. A hundred real thalers do not contain the least coin more than a hundred possible thalers. For as the latter signify the concept, and the former the object and the positing of the object, should the former contain more than the latter, my concept would not, in that case, express the whole object, and would not therefore be an adequate concept of it. My financial position is, however, affected very differently by a hundred real thalers than it is by the mere concept of them (that is, of their possibility). For the object, as it actually exists, is not analytically contained in my concept, but is added to my concept (which is a determination of my state) synthetically; and yet the conceived hundred thalers are not themselves in the least increased through thus acquiring existence outside my concept.

By whatever and by however many predicates we may think a thing—even if we completely determine it—we do not make the least addition to the thing when we further declare that this thing *is*. Otherwise, it would not be exactly the same thing that exists, but something more than we had thought in the concept; and we could not, therefore, say that the exact object of my concept exists. If we think in a thing every feature of reality except one, the missing reality is not added by my saying that this defective thing exists. On the contrary, it exists with the same defect with which I have thought it, since otherwise what exists would be something different from what I thought. When, therefore, I think a being as a supreme reality, without any defect, the question still remains whether it exists or not. For though, in my concept, nothing may be lacking of the possible real content of a thing in general, something is still lacking in its relation to my whole state of thought, namely, (in so far as I am unable to assert) that knowledge of this object is also possible *a posteriori*. And here we find the source of our present difficulty. Were we dealing with an object of the senses, we could not confound the existence of the thing with the mere concept of it. For through the concept the object is thought only as conforming to the *universal conditions* of possible empirical knowledge in general, whereas through its existence it is thought as belonging to the context of experience as a whole. In being thus connected with the *content* of experience as a whole, the concept of the object is not, however, in the least enlarged; all that has happened is that our thought has thereby obtained an additional possible perception. It is not, therefore, surprising that, if we attempt to think existence through the pure category alone, we cannot specify a single mark distinguishing it from mere possibility.

Whatever, therefore, and however much, our concept of an object may contain, we must go outside it, if we are to ascribe existence to the object. In the case of objects of the senses, this takes place through their connection with some one of our perceptions, in accordance with empirical laws. But in dealing with objects of pure thought, we have no means whatsoever of knowing their existence, since it would have to be known in a completely *a priori* manner. Our consciousness of all existence (whether immediately through perception, or mediately through inferences which connect something with perception) belongs exclusively to the unity of experience; any (alleged) existence outside this field, while not indeed such as we can declare to be absolutely impossible, is of the nature of an assumption which we can never be in a position to justify.

The concept of a supreme being is in many respects a very useful idea; but just because it is a mere idea, it is altogether incapable, by itself alone, of enlarging our knowledge in regard to what exists. It is not even competent to enlighten us as to the *possibility* of any existence beyond that which is known in and through experience. The analytic criterion of possibility, as consisting in the principle that bare positives (realities) give rise to no contradiction, cannot be denied to it. But since the realities are not given to us in their specific characters; since even if they were, we should still not be in a position to pass judgment; since the criterion of the possibility of synthetic knowledge is never to be looked for save in experience, to which the object of an idea cannot belong, the connection of all real properties in a thing is a synthesis, the possibility of which we are unable to determine *a priori*. And thus the celebrated Leibniz is far from having succeeded in what he plumed himself on achieving—the comprehension *a priori* of the possibility of this sublime ideal being.

The attempt to establish the existence of a supreme being by means of the famous ontological argument of Descartes is therefore merely so much labour and effort lost; we can no more extend our stock of (theoretical) insight by mere ideas, than a merchant can better his position by adding a few noughts to his cash account.

36 Immanuel Kant
God as a Postulate of Pure Practical Reason

In the foregoing analysis the moral law led to a practical problem which is prescribed by pure reason alone, without the aid of any sensible motives, namely, that of the necessary completeness of the first and principal element of the *summum bonum,* viz. Morality; and as this can be perfectly solved only in eternity, to the postulate of *immortality.* The same law must also lead us to affirm the possibility of the second element of *summum bonum,* viz. Happiness proportioned to that morality, and this on grounds as disinterested as before, and solely from impartial reason; that is, it must lead to the supposition of the existence of a cause adequate to this effect; in other words, it must postulate the *existence of God* as the necessary condition of the possibility of the *summum bonum* (an object of the will which is necessarily connected with the moral legislation of pure reason). We proceed to exhibit this connexion in a convincing manner.

Happiness is the condition of a rational being in the world with whom *everything goes according to his wish and will;* it rests, therefore, on the harmony of physical nature with his whole end, and likewise with the essential determining principle of his will. Now the moral law as a law of freedom commands by determining principles, which ought to be quite independent on nature and on its harmony with our faculty of desire (as springs). But the acting rational being in the world is not the cause of the world and of nature itself. There is not the least ground, therefore, in the moral law for a necessary connexion between morality and proportionate happiness in a being that belongs to the world as part of it, and therefore dependent on it, and which for that reason cannot by his will be a cause of this nature, nor by his own power make it thoroughly harmonize, as far as his happiness is concerned, with his practical principles. Nevertheless, in the practical problem of pure reason, *i.e.* the necessary pursuit of the *summum bonum,* such a connexion is postulated as necessary: we ought to endeavour to promote the *summum bonum,* which, therefore, must be possible. Accordingly, the existence of a cause of all nature, distinct from nature itself and containing the principle of this connexion, namely, of the exact harmony of happiness with morality, is also *postulated.* Now, this supreme cause must contain the principle of the harmony of nature, not merely with a law of the will of rational beings, but with the conception of this law, in so far as they make it the *supreme determining principle of the will,* and consequently not merely with the form of morals, but with their morality as their motive, that is, with their moral character. Therefore, the *summum bonum* is possible in the world only on the supposition of a supreme Being having a causality corresponding to moral character. Now a being that is capable of acting on the conception of laws is an *intelligence* (a rational being), and the causality of such a being according to this conception of laws is his *will*; therefore the supreme cause of nature, which must be presupposed as a condition of the *summum bonum, is* a being which is the cause of nature by *intelligence* and *will,* consequently its author, that is God. It follows that the postulate of the possibility of the *highest derived good* (the best world) is likewise the postulate of the reality of a *highest original good,* that is to say, of the existence of God. Now it was seen to be a duty for us to promote the *summum bonum;* consequently it is not merely allowable, but it is a necessity connected with duty as a requisite, that we should presuppose the possibility of this *summum bonum;* and as this is possible only on condition of the existence of God, it inseparably connects the supposition of this with duty; that is, it is morally necessary to assume the existence of God.

It must be remarked here that this moral necessity is *subjective,* that is, it is a want, and not *objective,* that is, itself a duty, for there cannot be a duty to suppose the existence of anything (since this concerns only the theoretical employment of reason). Moreover it is not meant by this that it is necessary to suppose the existence of God *as a basis of all obligation in general* (for this rests, as has been sufficiently proved, simply on the autonomy of reason itself). What belongs to duty here is only the endeavour to realize and promote the *summum bonum* in the world, the possibility of which can therefore be postulated; and as our reason finds it not conceivable except on the supposition of a supreme intelligence, the admission of this existence is therefore connected with the consciousness of our duty, although the admission itself belongs to the domain of speculative reason. Considered in respect of this alone, as a principle of explanation, it may be called a *hypothesis,* but in reference to the intelligibility of an object given us by the moral law (the *summum bonum),* and consequently of a requirement for practical purposes, it may be called *faith,* that is to say a pure *rational faith,* since pure reason (both in its theoretical and its practical use) is the

sole source from which it springs.

From this *deduction* it is now intelligible why the *Greek* schools could never attain the solution of their problem of the practical possibility of the *summum bonum,* because they made the rule of the use which the will of man makes of his freedom the sole and sufficient ground of this possibility, thinking that they had no need for that purpose of the existence of God. No doubt they were so far right that they established the principle of morals of itself independently on this postulate, from the relation of reason only to the will, and consequently made it the *supreme* practical condition of the *summum bonum;* but it was not therefore the whole condition of its possibility. The *Epicureans* had indeed assumed as the supreme principle of morality a wholly false one, namely that of happiness, and had substituted for a law a maxim of arbitrary choice according to every man's inclination; they proceeded, however, *consistently* enough in this, that they degraded their *summum bonum* likewise just in proportion to the meanness of their fundamental principle, and looked for no greater happiness than can be attained by human prudence (including temperance and moderation of the inclinations), and this as we know would be scanty enough and would be very different according to circumstances; not to mention the exceptions that their maxims must perpetually admit and which make them incapable of being laws. The *Stoics,* on the contrary, had chosen their supreme practical principle quite rightly, making virtue the condition of the *summum bonum;* but when they represented the degree of virtue required by its pure law as fully attainable in this life, they not only strained the moral powers of the *man* whom they called *the wise* beyond all the limits of his nature, and assumed a thing that contradicts all our knowledge of men, but also and principally they would not allow the second *element* of the *summum bonum*, namely, happiness, to be properly a special object of human desire, but made their *wise man,* like a divinity in his consciousness of the excellence of his person, wholly independent on nature (as regards his own contentment); they exposed him indeed to the evils of life, but made him not subject to them (at the same time representing him also as free from moral evil). They thus in fact left out the second element of the *summum bonum,* namely, personal happiness, placing it solely in action and satisfaction with one's own personal worth, thus including it in the consciousness of being morally minded, in which they might have been sufficiently refuted by the voice of their own nature.

The doctrine of Christianity, even if we do not yet consider it as a religious doctrine, gives, touching this point, a conception of the *summum bonum* (the kingdom of God), which alone satisfies the strictest demand of practical reason. The moral law is holy (unyielding) and demands holiness of morals, although all the moral perfection to which man can attain is still only virtue, that is, a rightful disposition arising from *respect* for the law, implying consciousness of a constant propensity to transgression, or at least a want of purity, that is, a mixture of many spurious (not moral) motives of obedience to the law, consequently a self-esteem combined with humility. In respect then of the holiness which the Christian law requires, this leaves the creature nothing but a progress *in infinitum,* but for that very reason it justifies him in hoping for an endless duration of his existence. The *worth* of a character *perfectly* accordant with the moral law is infinite, since the only restriction on all possible happiness in the judgment of a wise and all-powerful distributor of it is the absence of conformity of rational beings to their duty. But the moral law of itself does not *promise* any happiness, for according to our conceptions of an order of nature in general, this is not necessarily connected with obedience to the law. Now Christian morality supplies this defect (of the second indispensable element of the *summum bonum)* by representing the world, in which rational beings devote themselves with all their soul to the moral law, as a *kingdom of God,* in which nature and morality are brought into a harmony foreign to each of itself, by a holy Author who makes the derived *summum bonum* possible. *Holiness* of life is prescribed to them as a rule even in this life, while the welfare proportioned to it, namely, *bliss* is represented as attainable only in an eternity; because the *former* must always be the pattern of their conduct in every state, and progress towards it is already possible and necessary in this life; while the *latter,* under the name of happiness, cannot be attained at all in this world (so far as our own power is concerned), and therefore is made simply an object of hope. Nevertheless, the Christian principle of *morality* itself is not theological (so as to be heteronomy) but is autonomy of pure practical reason, since it does not make the knowledge of God and his will the foundation of these laws, but only of the attainment of the *summum bonum,* on condition of following these laws, and it does not even place the proper *spring* of this obedience in the desired results, but solely in the conception of duty, as that of which the faithful observance alone constitutes the worthiness to obtain those happy consequences.

In this manner the moral laws lead through the conception of the *summum bonum* as the object and final end of pure practical reason to *religion,* that is, to the *recognition of all duties as divine commands, not as sanction, that is to say, arbitrary ordinances of a foreign will and contingent in themselves ,* but as essential *laws* of every free will in itself, which, nevertheless, must be regarded as commands of the Supreme Being, because it is only from a morally perfect (holy and good) and at the same time all-powerful will, and consequently only through harmony with this will that we can hope to attain the *summum bonum* which the moral law makes it our duty to take as the object of our endeavours. Here again, then, all remains disinterested and founded merely on duty; neither fear nor hope being made the fundamental springs, which if taken as principles would destroy the whole moral worth of actions. The moral law commands me to make the highest possible good in a world the ultimate object of all my conduct. But I cannot hope to effect this otherwise than by the harmony of my will with that of a holy and good Author of the world; and although the conception of the *summun bonum* as a whole, in which the greatest happiness is conceived as combined in the most exact proportion with the highest degree of moral perfection (possible in creatures), includes *my own happiness,* yet it is not this that is the determining principle of the will which is enjoined to promote the *summum bonum,* but the moral law, which on the contrary limits by strict conditions my unbounded desire of happiness.

Hence also morality is not properly the doctrine how we should *make* ourselves happy, but how we should become *worthy* of happiness. It is only when religion is added that there also comes in the hope of participating some day in happiness in proportion as we have endeavoured to be not unworthy of it.

A man is *worthy* to possess a thing or a state when his possession of it is in harmony with the *summum bonum.* We can now easily see that all worthiness depends on moral conduct, since in the conception of the *summum bonum* this constitutes the condition of the rest (which belongs to one's state), namely, the participation of happiness. Now it follows from this that *morality* should never be treated as a *doctrine of happiness,* that is, an instruction how to become happy; for it has to do simply with the rational condition *(conditio sine qua non)* of happiness, not with the means of attaining it. But when morality has been completely expounded (which merely imposes duties instead of providing rules for selfish desires), then, first, after the moral desire to promote the *summum bonum* (to bring the kingdom of God to us) has been awakened, a desire founded on a law, and which could not previously arise in any selfish mind, and when for the behoof of this desire the step to religion has been taken, then this ethical doctrine may be also called a doctrine of happiness, because the *hope* of happiness first begins with religion only.

We can also see from this that, when we ask what is *God's ultimate end* in creating the world, we must not name the *happiness* of the rational beings in it, but the *summum bonum,* which adds a further condition to that wish of such beings, namely, the condition of being worthy of happiness, that is, the *morality* of these same rational beings, a condition which alone contains the rule by which only they can hope to share in the former at the hand of a *wise* Author. For as *wisdom* theoretically considered signifies *the knowledge of the summum bonum,* and practically *the accordance of the will with the summum bonum,* we cannot contribute to a supreme independent wisdom an end based merely on *goodness.* For we cannot conceive the action of this goodness (in respect of the happiness of rational beings) as suitable to the highest original good, except under the restrictive conditions of harmony with the holiness of his will. Therefore those who placed the end of creation in the glory of God (provided that this is not conceived anthropomorphically as a desire to be praised) have perhaps hit upon the best expression. For nothing glorifies God more than that which is the most estimable thing in the world, respect for His command, the observance of the holy duty that His law imposes on us, when there is added thereto His glorious plan of crowning such a beautiful order of things with corresponding happiness. If the latter (to speak humanly) makes Him worthy of love, by the *former* He is an object of adoration. Even men can never acquire respect by benevolence alone, though they may gain love, so that the greatest beneficence only procures them honour when it is regulated by worthiness.

That in the order of ends, man (and with him every rational being) is *an end in himself,* that is, that he can never be used merely

as a means by any (not even by God) without being at the same time an end also himself, that therefore *humanity* in our person must be *holy* ourselves, this follows now of itself because he is the *subject of the moral law,* in other words of that which is holy in itself, and on account of which and in agreement with which alone can anything be termed holy. For this moral law is founded on the autonomy of his will, as a free will which by its universal laws must necessarily be able to agree with that to which it is to submit itself.

37   Georg Wilhelm Friedrich Hegel
from
Phenomenology of Spirit

It is a natural assumption that in philosophy, before we start to deal with its proper subject-matter, viz. the actual cognition of what truly is, one must first of all come to an understanding about cognition, which is regarded either as the instrument to get hold of the Absolute, or as the medium through which one discovers it. A certain uneasiness seems justified, partly because there are different types of cognition, and one of them might be more appropriate than another for the attainment of this goal, so that we could make a bad choice of means; and partly because cognition is a faculty of a definite

Reprinted from *Hegel's Phenomenology of Spirit,* translated by A.V. Miller (1977) by permission of Oxford University Press.

kind and scope, and thus, without a more precise definition of its nature and limits, we might grasp clouds of error instead of the heaven of truth. This feeling of uneasiness is surely bound to be transformed into the conviction that the whole project of securing for consciousness through cognition what exists in itself is absurd, and that there is a boundary between cognition and the Absolute that completely separates them. For, if cognition is the instrument for getting hold of absolute being, it is obvious that the use of an instrument on a thing certainly does not let it be what it is for itself, but rather sets out to reshape and alter it. If on the other hand, cognition is not an instrument of our activity but a more or less passive medium through which the light of truth reaches us, then again we do not receive the truth as it is in itself, but only as it exists through and in this medium. Either way we employ a means which immediately brings about the opposite of its own end; or rather, what is really absurd is that we should make use of a means at all.

It would seem, to be sure, that this evil could be remedied through an acquaintance with the way in which the *instrument* works; for this would enable us to eliminate from the representation of the Absolute which we have gained through it whatever is due to the instrument, and thus get the truth in its purity. But this 'improvement' would in fact only bring us back to where we were before. If we remove from a reshaped thing what the instrument has done to it, then the thing— here the Absolute—becomes for us exactly what it was before this (accordingly) super-fluous effort. On the other hand, if the Absolute is supposed merely to be brought nearer to us through this instrument, without any-thing in it being altered, like a bird caught by a lime-twig, it would surely laugh our little ruse to scorn, if it were not with us, in and for itself, all along, and of its own volition. For a ruse is just what cognition would be in such a case, since it would, with its manifold exertions, be giving itself the air of doing something quite different from creating a merely immediate and therefore effortless relationship. Or, if by testing cognition, which we conceive of as a *medium* we get to know the law of its refraction, it is again useless to subtract this from the end result. For it is not the refraction of the ray, but the ray itself whereby truth reaches us, that is cognition; and if this were removed, all that would be indicated would be a pure direction or a blank space.

Meanwhile, if the fear of falling into error sets up a mistrust of Science, which in the absence of such scruples gets on with the work itself, and actually cognizes some-thing, it is hard to see why we should not turn round and mistrust this very mistrust. Should we not be concerned as to whether this fear of error is not just the error itself? Indeed, this fear takes something—a great deal in fact—for granted as truth, supporting its scruples and inferences on what is itself in need of prior scrutiny to see if it is true. To be specific, it takes for granted certain ideas about cognition as an *instrument* and as a *medium,* and assumes that there is a *differ-ence between ourselves and this cognition.* Above all, it presupposes that the Absolute stands on one side and cognition on the other, independent and separated from it, and yet is something real; or in other words, it presupposes that cognition which, since it is excluded from the Absolute, is surely outside of the truth as well, is nevertheless true, an assumption whereby what calls itself fear of error reveals itself rather as fear of the truth.

This conclusion stems from the fact that the Absolute alone is true, or the truth alone is absolute. One may set this aside on the grounds that there is a type of cognition which, though it does not recognize the Absolute as Science aims to, is still true, and that cognition in general, though it be incapable of grasping the Absolute, is still capable of grasping other kinds of truth. But we gradually come to see that this kind of talk which goes back and forth only leads to a hazy distinction between an absolute truth and some other kind of truth, and that words like 'absolute', 'cognition', etc. presuppose a meaning which has yet to be ascertained.

Instead of troubling ourselves with such useless ideas and locutions about cognition as 'an instrument for getting hold of the Absolute', or as 'a medium through which we view the truth' (relationships which surely, in the end, are what all these ideas of a cognition cut off from the Absolute, and an Absolute separated from cognition, amount to); instead of putting up with excuses which create the incapacity of Science by assuming relationships of this kind in order to be exempt from the hard work of Science, while at the same time giving the impression of working seriously and zealously; instead of bothering to refute all these ideas, we could reject them out of hand as adventitious and arbitrary, and the words associated with them like 'absolute', 'cognition', and 'subjective', and countless others whose meaning is assumed to be generally familiar, could even be regarded as so much deception. For to give the impression that their meaning is generally well known, or that

their Notion is comprehended, looks more like an attempt to avoid the main problem, which is precisely to provide this Notion. We could, with better justification, simply spare ourselves the trouble of paying any attention to ward off Science itself, and constitute merely an empty appearance of knowing, which vanishes immediately as soon as Science comes on the scene. But Science, just because it comes on the scene, is itself an appearance: in coming on the scene it is not yet Science in its developed and unfolded truth. In this connection it makes no difference whether we think of Science as the appearance because it comes on the scene alongside another mode of knowledge, or whether we call that other untrue knowledge its manifestation. In any case Science must liberate itself from this semblance, and it can do so only by turning against it. For, when confronted with a knowledge that is without truth, Science can neither merely reject it as an ordinary way of looking at things, while assuring us that its Science is a quite different sort of cognition for which that ordinary knowledge is of no account whatever; nor can it appeal to the vulgar view for the intimations it gives us of something better to come. By the former *assurance,* Science would be declaring its power to lie simply in its *being;* but the untrue knowledge likewise appeals to the fact that *it is,* and *assures* us that for it Science is of no account. *One* bare assurance is worth just as much as another. Still less can Science appeal to whatever intimations of something better it may detect in the cognition that is without truth, to the signs which point in the direction of Science. For one thing, it would only be appealing again to what merely *is*; and for another, it would only be appealing to itself, and to itself in the mode in which it exists in the cognition that is without truth. In other words, it would be appealing to an inferior form of its being, to the way it appears, rather than to what it is in and for itself. It is for this reason that an exposition of how knowledge makes its appearance will here be undertaken.

Now, because it has only phenomenal knowledge for its object, this exposition seems not to be Science, free and self-moving in its own peculiar shape; yet from this standpoint it can be regarded as the path of the natural consciousness which presses forward to true knowledge; or as the way of the Soul which journeys through the series of its own configurations as though they were the stations appointed for it by its own nature, so that it may purify itself for the life of the Spirit, and achieve finally, through a completed experience of itself, the awareness of what it really is in itself.

Natural consciousness will show itself to be only the Notion of knowledge, or in other words, not to be real knowledge. But since it directly takes itself to be real knowledge, this path has a negative significance for it, and what is in fact the realization of the Notion, counts for it rather as the loss of its own self; for it does lose its truth on this path. The road can therefore be regarded as the pathway of *doubt,* or more precisely as the way of despair. For what happens on it is not what is ordinarily understood when the word 'doubt' is used; shilly-shallying about this or that presumed truth, followed by a return to that truth again, after the doubt has been appropriately dispensed—so that at the end of the process the matter is taken to be what it was in the first place. On the contrary, this path is the conscious insight into the untruth

of phenomenal knowledge, for which the supreme reality is what is in truth only the unrealized Notion. Therefore this thoroughgoing skepticism is also not the skepticism with which an earnest zeal for truth and Science fancies it has prepared and equipped itself in their service; the *resolve*, in Science, not to give oneself over to the thoughts of others, upon mere authority, but to examine everything for oneself and follow only one's own conviction, or better still, to produce everything oneself, and accept only one's own deed as what is true.

The series of configurations which consciousness goes through along this road is, in reality, the detailed history of the *education* of consciousness itself to the standpoint of Science. That zealous resolve represents this education simplistically as something directly over and done with in the making of the resolution; but the way of the Soul is the actual fulfillment of the resolution, in contrast to the untruth of that view. Now, following one's own conviction is, of course, more than giving oneself over to authority, but changing an opinion accepted on authority into an opinion held out of personal conviction, does not necessarily alter the content of the opinion, or replace error with truth. The only difference between being caught up in a system of opinions and prejudices based on personal conviction, and being caught up in one based on the authority of others, lies in the added conceit that is innate in the former position. The skepticism that is directed against the whole range of phenomenal consciousness, on the other hand, renders the Spirit for the first time competent to examine what truth is. For it brings about a state of despair about all the so-called natural ideas, thoughts, and opinions, regardless of whether they are called one's own or someone else's ideas with which the consciousness that sets about the examination (of truth) *straight away* still filled and hampered, so that it is, in fact, incapable of carrying out what it wants to undertake.

The necessary progression and interconnection of the forms of the unreal consciousness will by itself bring to pass the *completion* of the series. To make this more intelligible, it may be remarked, in a preliminary and general way, that the exposition of the untrue consciousness in its untruth is not a merely *negative* procedure. The natural consciousness itself normally takes this one-sided view of it; and a knowledge which makes this one-sidedness its very essence is itself one of the patterns of incomplete consciousness which occurs on the road itself, and will manifest itself in due course. This is just the skepticism which only ever sees pure nothingness in its result, and abstracts from the fact that this nothingness is specifically the nothingness of that *from which it results.* For it is only when it is taken as the result of that from which it emerges, that it is, in fact, the true result; in that case it is itself a *determinate* nothingness, one which has a *content.* The skepticism that ends up with the bare abstraction of nothingness or emptiness cannot get any further from there, but must wait to see whether something new comes along and what it is, in order to throw it too into the same empty abyss. But when, on the other hand, the result is conceived as it is in truth, namely, as a *determinate* negation, a new form has thereby immediately arisen, and in the negation the transition is made through which the progress through the complete series of forms comes about of itself.

But the *goal* is as necessarily fixed for knowledge as the serial progression; it is the point where knowledge no longer needs to go beyond itself, where knowledge finds itself, where Notion corresponds to object and object to Notion. Hence the progress towards this goal is also unhalting, and short of it no satisfaction is to be found at any of the stations on the way. Whatever is confined within the limits of a natural life cannot by its own efforts go beyond its immediate existence; but it is driven beyond it by something else, and this uprooting entails its death. Consciousness, however, is explicitly the *Notion* of itself. Hence it is something that goes beyond limits, and since these limits are its own, it is something that goes beyond itself. With the positing of a single particular the beyond is also established for consciousness, even if it is only *alongside* the limited object as in the case of spatial intuition. Thus consciousness suffers this violence at its own hands: it spoils its own limited satisfaction. When consciousness feels this violence, its anxiety may well make it retreat from the truth, and strive to hold on to what it is in danger of losing. But it can find no peace. If it wishes to remain in a state of unthinking inertia, then thought troubles its thoughtlessness, and its own unrest disturbs its inertia. Or, if it entrenches itself in sentimentality, which assures us that it finds everything to be *good in its kind,* then this assurance likewise suffers violence at the hands of Reason, for, precisely in so far as something is merely a kind, Reason finds it *not* to be good. Or again, its fear of the truth may lead consciousness to hide, from itself and others, being the pretension that its burning zeal for truth makes it difficult or even impossible to find any other truth but the unique truth of vanity—that of being at any rate cleverer than any thoughts that one gets by oneself or from others. This conceit which understands how to belittle every truth, in order to turn back into itself and gloat over its own understanding, which knows how to dissolve every thought and always find the same barren Ego instead of any content—this is a satisfaction which we must leave to itself, for it flees from the universal, and seeks only to be for itself.

In addition to these preliminary general remarks about the manner and the necessity of the progression, it may be useful to say something about the method of carrying out the inquiry. If this exposition is viewed as a way of *relating Science* to *phenomenal* knowledge, and as an investigation and *examination of the reality of cognition,* it would seem that it cannot take place without some presupposition which can serve as its underlying *criterion.* For an examination consists in applying an accepted standard, and in determining whether something is right or wrong on the basis of the resulting agreement or disagreement of the thing examined; thus the standard as such (and Science likewise if it were the criterion), is accepted as the *essence* or as the *in-itself.* But here, where Science has just begun to come on the scene, neither Science nor anything else has yet justified itself as the essence or the in-itself; and without something of the sort it seems that no examination can take place.

This contradiction and its removal will become more definite if we call to mind the abstract determinations of truth and knowledge as they occur in consciousness. Consciousness simultaneously *distinguishes* itself from something, and at the same time

relates itself to it, or, as it is said, this something exists *for* consciousness: and the determinate aspect of this *relating,* or of the *being* of something for a consciousness, is *knowing.* But we distinguish this being-for-another from *being-in-itself;* whatever is related to knowledge for knowing is also distinguished from it, and posited as existing outside of this relationship; this *being-in-itself* is called *truth.* Just what might be involved in these determinations is of no further concern to us here. Since our object is phenomenal knowledge, its determinations too will at first be taken directly as they present themselves; and they do present themselves very much as we have already apprehended them.

Now, if we inquire into the truth of knowledge, it seems that we are asking what knowledge is *in itself.* Yet in this inquiry knowledge is *our* object, something that exists *for us;* and the *in-itself* that would supposedly result from it would rather be the being of knowledge *for us.* What we asserted to be its essence would be not so much its truth but rather just our knowledge of it. The essence or criterion would lie within ourselves, and that which was to be compared with it and about which a decision would be reached through this comparison would not necessarily have to recognize the validity of such a standard.

But the dissociation, or this semblance of dissociation and presupposition, is overcome by the nature of the object we are investigating. Consciousness provides its own criterion from within itself, so that the investigation becomes a comparison of consciousness with itself; for the distinction made above falls within it. In consciousness one thing exists *for* another, *i.e.* consciousness regularly contains the determinateness of the moment of knowledge; at the same time, this other is to consciousness not merely *for it*, but is also outside of this relationship, or exists *in itself*: the moment of truth. Thus in what consciousness affirms from within itself as *being-in-itself* or the *True* we have the standard which consciousness itself sets up by which to measure what it knows. If we designate *knowledge* as the Notion, but the essence or the *True* as what exists, or the *object*, then the examination consists in seeing whether the Notion corresponds to the object. But if we call the *essence* or in-itself of the *object* the *Notion,* and on the other hand understand by the *object* the Notion itself as *object,* viz, as it exists *for an other,* then the examination consists in seeing whether the object corresponds to its Notion. It is evident, of course, that the two procedures are the same. But the essential point to bear in mind throughout the whole investigation is that these two moments, 'Notion' and 'object', 'being-for-another' and 'being-in-itself', both fall *within* that knowledge which we are investigating. Consequently, we do not need to import criteria, or to make use of our own bright ideas and thoughts during the course of the inquiry; it is precisely when we leave these aside that we succeed in contemplating the matter in hand as it is *in and for itself.*

But not only is a contribution by us superfluous, since Notion and object, the criterion and what is to be tested, are present in consciousness itself, but we are also spared the trouble of comparing the two and really *testing* them, so that, since what consciousness examines is its own self, all that is left for us to do is simply to look on. For consciousness is, on the one hand, conscious-

ness of the object, and on the other, consciousness of itself; consciousness of what for it is the True, and consciousness of its knowledge of the truth. Since both are *for* the same consciousness, this consciousness is itself their comparison; it is for this same consciousness to know whether its knowledge of the object corresponds to the object or not. The object, it is true, seems only to be for consciousness in the way that consciousness knows it; it seems that consciousness cannot, as it were, get behind the object as it exists for consciousness so as to examine what the object is *in itself,* and hence, too, cannot test its own knowledge by that standard. But the distinction between the in-itself and knowledge is already present in the very fact that consciousness knows an object at all. Something is *for it* the *in-itself*; and knowledge, or the being of the object for consciousness, is for it, another moment. Upon this distinction, which is present as a fact, the examination rests. If the comparison shows that these two moments do not correspond to one another, it would seem that consciousness must alter its knowledge to make it conform to the object. But, in fact, in the alteration of the knowledge, the object itself alters for it too, for the knowledge that was present was essentially a knowledge of the object: as the knowledge changes, so too does the object, for it essentially belonged to this knowledge. Hence it comes to pass for consciousness that what it previously took to be the *in-itself* is not an *in-itself,* or that it was only an in-itself *for consciousness.* Since consciousness thus finds that its knowledge does not correspond to its object, the object itself does not stand the test; in other words; the criterion for testing is altered when that for which it was to have been the criterion fails to pass the test; and the testing is not only a testing of what we know, but also a testing of the criterion of what knowing is.

Inasmuch as the new true object issues from it, this *dialectical* movement which consciousness exercises on itself and which affects both its knowledge and its object, is precisely what is called *experience* (*Erfahrung*). In this connection there is a moment in the process just mentioned which must be brought out more clearly, for through it a new light will be thrown on the exposition which follows. Consciousness knows *something;* this object is the essence or the *in-itself*; but it is also for consciousness the in-itself. This is where the ambiguity of this truth enters. We see that consciousness now has two objects; one is the first *in-itself,* the second is the *being-for-consciousness of this in-itself.* The latter appears at first sight to be merely the reflection of consciousness into itself, *i.e.* what consciousness has in mind is not an object, but only its knowledge of that first object. But, as was shown previously, the first object, in being known, is altered for consciousness; it ceases to be the in-itself, and becomes something that is the *in-itself* only for consciousness. And this then is the True; and being-for-consciousness of this in-itself. Or, in other words, this is the *essence,* or the *object* of consciousness. This new object contains the nothingness of the first, it is what experience has made of it.

This exposition of the course of experience contains a moment in virtue of which it does not seem to agree with what is ordinarily understood by experience. This is the moment of transition from the first object and the knowledge of it, to the other object, which experience is said to be about. Our account implied that our knowledge of the first object, or the being-*for*-consciousness of the first in-itself, itself becomes the second object. It usually seems to be the case, on the contrary, that our experience of the untruth of our first notion comes by way of a second object which we come upon by chance and externally, so that our part in all this is simply the pure *apprehension* of what is in and for itself. From the present viewpoint, however, the new object shows itself to have come about through a *reversal of consciousness itself.* This way of looking at the matter is something contributed by *us,* by means of which the succession of experiences through which consciousness passes is raised into a scientific progression—but it is not known to the consciousness that we are observing. But, as a matter of fact, we have here the same situation as the one discussed in regard to the relation between our exposition and skepticism, viz. that in every case the result of an untrue mode of knowledge must not be allowed to run away into an empty nothing, but must necessarily be grasped as the nothing *of that from which it results*—a result which contains what was true in the preceding knowledge. It shows up here like this: since what first appeared as the object sinks for consciousness to the level of its way of knowing it, and since the in-itself becomes a *being-for-consciousness* of the in-itself, the latter is now the new object. Herewith a new pattern of consciousness comes on the scene as well, for which the essence is something different from what it was at the preceding stage. It is this fact that guides the entire series of the patterns of consciousness in their necessary sequence. But it is just this necessity itself, or the *origination* of the new object, that presents itself to consciousness without its understanding how this happens, which proceeds for us, as it were, behind the back of consciousness. Thus in the movement of consciousness there occurs a moment of *being-in-itself* or *being-for-us* which is not present to the consciousness comprehended in the experience itself. The *content,* however, of what presents itself to us does exist *for it;* we comprehend only the formal aspect of that content, or its pure origination. *For it,* what has thus arisen exists only as an object, *for us,* it appears at the same time as movement and a process of becoming.

Because of this necessity, the way to Science is itself already *Science,* and hence, in virtue of its content, is the Science of the *experience of consciousness.*

The experience of itself which consciousness goes through can, in accordance with its Notion, comprehend nothing less than the entire system of consciousness, or the entire realm of the truth of Spirit. For this reason, the moments of this truth are exhibited in their own proper determinateness, viz. as being not abstract moments, but as they are for consciousness, or as consciousness itself stands forth in its relation to them. Thus the moments of the whole are *patterns of consciousness.* In pressing forward to its true existence, consciousness will arrive at a point at which it gets rid of its semblance of being burdened with something alien, with what is only for it, and some sort of 'other', at a point where appearance becomes identical with essence, so that its exposition will coincide at just this point with the authentic Science of Spirit. And finally, when consciousness itself grasps this its own essence, it will signify the nature of absolute knowledge itself.

Part II

Contemporary Challenges

Section A

The Challenge of Modern Science to the God Question

As I see philosophy, it never ought to be, and indeed never can be, divorced from the sciences.

Karl Popper

38 Harry Prosch
The Copernican Revolution

Medieval notions about the nature of the cosmos—the totality of the existing universe—strike us as fairy tales; and yet, like fairy tales, there is something naturally charming and satisfying about them, if we endeavor to "feel" our way back into them. All the world then seemed familiar and personal, much as, perhaps, it appeared to us in childhood. Of this time I suppose we could all say with Wordsworth:

The earth, and every common sight,
To me did seem
apparelled in celestial light.

We might also want to go on and say what he then finds necessary to add:

"It is not now as it hath been of yore." It is clear that it certainly is not—either for us as adults or for us as modern men. That, as Wordsworth went on to say, "there hath passed away a glory from the earth" seems only too true when we compare our cold, hard views of things with those of medieval man and come to understand something of that "glory" which shone upon his world.

When we pick up our story, at the turn of the sixteenth century, in the days of Leonardo da Vinci, Michelangelo, and Luther, man still felt a sort of animated, personal kinship with all other things in his world. This feeling of personal kinship was partly a carry-over from the frank animism of the ancients, both on the Grecian side of the European family and on the Norse side. For them the Sun had really ridden his flaming chariot across the sky. The North Wind had really blown. These pagan personifications, indeed deifications, of the natural "elements" and of the forces of nature in general were only partly erased by Christianity. They lingered yet as vague, superstitious beliefs in the personalities of these elements, on the part of the most ignorant, and in an imaginative, poetic personalization of them, on the part of the more sophisticated. These latter did not actually believe the "elements" were persons or gods, yet they found a beauty and poetic truth in such an imaginative grasp of things, since the attitudes toward nature which coincided with a poetic personification of nature were thought to be the true or appropriate attitudes, inasmuch as they seemed to follow from a belief in what we now call "fundamentalist" Christianity, together with commitments to certain ancient secular ideas concerning the nature of things.

The analysis of natural things in terms of natural ends or "purposes" which they "pursued" had been inherited remotely from Aristotle, and had been merged by St. Thomas Aquinas with Christian theology by the middle of the thirteenth century in such a way that, although the educated man did not usually suppose these natural things to be "persons", nor their "pursuit" of their own natural ends to be necessarily a conscious one, nevertheless they acquired something like personal relations to him, since, like himself, they all did, somehow, pursue purposes. Nothing in nature, therefore, was totally dead, inert, or meaningless. Every-

From *20th Century Philosophy* by Harry Prosch. New York: Thomas Y. Crowell Co. Copyright© 1964 Harry Prosch.

thing, at least potentially, became either man's personal friend or his personal enemy. Yet he was also able to believe, in poetic and contemplative moments, that the over-all purpose of everything was really good. Even though some purposes pursued by some things sometimes ran afoul of his own temporal aims, man could conceive that these "natural enemies" of his served his own long-run purposes—if only as just punishment for his sins. For his Christian religion told him that everything ultimately served God's purposes, and that man was the highest purpose of God's creation—not man as he existed on this base earth, but man in the fulfillment of his ultimate potentiality, his ultimate happiness in the company of God. Thus, although all creation served God's purposes, not man's mundane ones, in a deeper and deliciously mysterious sense all creation served *man's* purpose, since man fulfilled himself in making his purpose one with God's. Man was realized in God, and—what was not often said, as bordering upon the irreverence of sinful pride—God was realized in man. Man, although he was supposed to humble himself before God, was really proud therefore, and in truth regarded himself as the lord of creation. Wasn't it true that even the sun served him daily like a faithful servant? For what other reason could it have been created?

Naturally, then, the habitat of man, the earth, was assumed to be the center of the universe. This was not to say that the earth was thought to be the best thing in the universe. The natural science of the day seemed to imply, in fact, that it necessarily was the worst, since it was the natural abode of everything that by its own nature was so gross and crude as to tend downward. Such

notions as these may be somewhat natural to "natural" man, but they too can be traced back to Aristotle, and strangely enough they actually tended to reinforce the notion that the earth was the true center of all things.

Aristotle had divided natural substances according to weight into (1) things that moved downward (e.g., stones) and (2) things that moved upward (e.g., flames) and (3) things that *stayed* up (e.g., stars) and (4) things that *stayed* down e.g. the earth). Thus the more lively, spirited, and immaterial things were associated with "upness", and the more inert, dead, gross, and dirty things were associated with "downness."

Therefore, on these grounds also, Aristotle found the earth to be the center of the cosmos. Earth was the epitome of downness-of inertness. It was the "unmoving" *par excellence,* and so it had to be the fixed point around which everything else circled. These views of Aristotle were the remoter basis for the "Ptolemaic" system of astronomy which the famous Ptolemy of Alexandria developed in the second century A.D. and which was generally accepted as scientific fact until Copernicus. Christian thought found nothing out of the way in such views as these, of course. These ideas fitted in beautifully with the Christian notion that heaven was up and hell was down, for these views implied that at the center of the earth and thus at the *true* center of the cosmos—the ultimate "down"—was hell, the final resting place of those evil souls condemned to "eternal death." Things got progressively purer as one went "up" (i.e., away from the center of the earth), until one came to the outermost "heaven" of all—heaven, the special abode of God and the saints.

Any suspicion of absurdity in the idea of

the whole universe revolving about the most ignoble of all things was prevented from developing because, as we have seen, Christian theology held that man was actually the center of attention in creation. The notion that the earth was the fixed point in the center of the universe seemed then to the men of those days to be beyond question, both on philosophic and on theological grounds. But, of course, this notion agreed perfectly with raw perception as well. All the heavenly bodies visibly rose in the east and set in the west every day, and, too, the fixed stars (the outermost visible "heaven") made a visible yearly revolution about the earth. The sun and the moon made similar journeys about the earth, and the planets did also, although they did do some peculiar wandering about on their journeys, now moving in one direction in the sky and now moving in the opposite direction. But explanations, as we shall soon see, were forthcoming for this seemingly erratic behavior. Thus the basic feature of the whole theory—the central fixed position of the earth—did not even appear to need the backing of any theories. It was simply tacitly considered to be a self-evident or *observed* fact; it is most natural to view and to measure things from where one is. It would have been incredible, as a matter of fact, for man to have assumed at the start of his inquiries that he was anywhere but at the hub of the universe. A small child naturally assumes, with open mouth and complete, unthinking confidence, that the center of all things is his own town, or street, or house—or even his own bed (in a chronological sequence the opposite of this order, no doubt) until he is finally *taught* differently by experience. Some people, in fact, seem never really to have learned differ-

ently, and still, as adults, consider, emotionally at least, that their own nation, or "way of life." or their own section of their nation is somehow the unique vantage point from which everything else can be objectively viewed and measured.

What I am trying to point out is that, however quaint and curious these medieval views seem to us, they possessed one very great advantage: they fitted in perfectly with the natural tendency of man to view things from the point of view of *man*, and somehow or other to consider that those standards of reason, beauty, and goodness most natural and convincing to him are the true standards in terms of which all things are to be viewed, measured, and valued.

To medieval man the "scientific" problem in astronomy came to be that of making sense of the observed motions of the heavenly bodies. For the motions observed by raw perception were understood to be the *true* motions of these bodies, since the point of their observation, the earth, was thought to be fixed—that is, not moving. These motions, it was assumed almost without thought, were not random, nor describable only in terms of unrelated mathematical formulas. It was axiomatic that, being the creation of God, the system of heavenly bodies was a work of supreme art and craftsmanship, structured by harmonic ratios and adding up to a perfect whole. Thus all things had meaning and purpose, and the heavens were familiar to man, at the same time as they truly declared the glory of God. Even the mechanisms by which the heavenly bodies were conceived to operate so nobly were also noble. Each of the heavenly bodies was thought to be attached to a pure, transparent sphere (the sphere being the "perfect" figure) that moved about according to the laws of its own being. The size of each sphere, however, was also thought to be related to the distances between it and the other spheres and to the motions of all the other spheres in such a way that the most exquisite harmonic ratio was achieved. This was the "music" of the spheres—the divine music or harmony most worthy of the region nearest God—the idea of which gave to man the notion of a universe that was thoroughly and throughout <u>his</u>, for its highest and best principles, i.e., its most fundamental structural features, were the same as those elements recognized by his own being as the highest or best principles: reason, beauty, and goodness. In other words, man belonged to his universe and found there nothing foreign to his highest aspirations.

Even Johannes Kepler, whom, as we shall see, we remember in our day as having contributed one essential step in the destruction of all this wonderful "music," had dif-

ferent ideas from us and considered his foremost achievement to have been the reduction of the ratios of the orbits of the planets to a harmony he could translate into ordinary musical notation. He considered he had discovered the genuine "music of the spheres."

Before Kepler's day the actual reduction of all this to a superb harmony was rendered somewhat difficult by the necessity for various odd numbers of epicycles—circles, upon circles or, better, spheres upon spheres—in order to describe the observed motions of the planets in our sky and thus to make prediction possible.

Prediction was achieved by means of these epicycles, of course, within the limits of error of the measuring devices of those days. Although the perfect harmony of these spheres proved to be an elusive will-o'-the-wisp, it was nevertheless believed to be present. Thus Kepler, weaned on such views, might well congratulate himself upon having found what had been sought for so long,

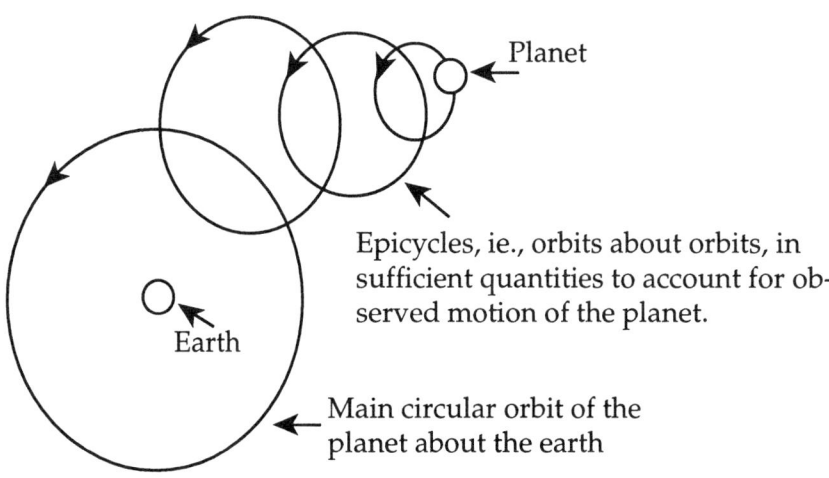

Planet

Epicycles, ie., orbits about orbits, in sufficient quantities to account for observed motion of the planet.

Earth

Main circular orbit of the planet about the earth

Figure 1

and so regard this discovery of his as the true fruit and proof of the correctness of his new description of the orbits of the planets.

But whether or not the true music of the spheres could be found or solved, the universe or cosmos could be pictured, prior to Copernicus, in a straightforward manner which at once agreed with the literal remarks in Scripture, with the secular authority of such worthy ancient thinkers as Aristotle and Ptolemy, and with forthright common sense based on the immediate appearances of things. A whole empirical physics was, in fact, entwined with this view of the cosmos, and although it has been customary to treat it with the snobbery we of the modern world reserve for any views held in earlier times, it does not deserve our disdain. It was a very careful, comprehensive, and intricate scientific theory that was, like all scientific theories, gradually modified in accord with new and closer observations. It served quite admirably for accurate predictions of celestial phenomena, and by all known tests was as "scientific" a theory as any theories have ever been. It became outmoded in a manner which we are about to relate and, like all outmoded "scientific" theories, it is now as dead as a dodo. However, this recognition that it is now dead should not induce in us a lack of respect for it. It was one of mankind's great ideas and a truly monumental milestone on the road to human knowledge.

There might have been, of course, some difficulty in seeing exactly what the reason was for having a system so intricate that seventy or eighty spheres, or epicycles, had to revolve on each other in order that a planet should move; but to assume that there really *was* a reason in the eternal wisdom of the Almighty was not difficult. In other respects,

the whole view of the world and of man in it was so complete and satisfying and so capable of measurement that the necessity for all these epicycles could easily be swallowed.

Any unsolved problems in this system, therefore, were recognized as ones of mere detail, while about the broad picture there was a serenity of outlook and a confidence so secure it really required no thought. The import of this confidence and of these views was that the cosmos, in its true character, was displayed before man's eyes for his free contemplation and for the realization of his kinship to God, and all the forces of evil and good in the world were felt to be battling for possession of his immortal soul. All events were therefore intriguing and fraught with deep, mysterious, spiritual meaning. It would not be exactly correct to say that man enjoyed his importance in those days. He rather took his importance for granted, the way children take their parents for granted before it dawns upon them that they might lose them. The assumption of his own importance, one might say, was one of the *conditions* for his enjoyment—but one he was then blissfully unaware of.

The man initially responsible for breaking up this pretty picture—for the "Copernican revolution" was not a revolutionary. Nicolaus Copernicus was a quiet, retiring, dignified public administrator, as well as an "economist", theologian, mathematician, astronomer, and—most important to his own immediate community in Poland perhaps— a physician. It seems likely he was also something of a poet and an artist. He lived in a day (1473–1543) when it was expected that any man of talents should turn to many things, so this diversification was not un-

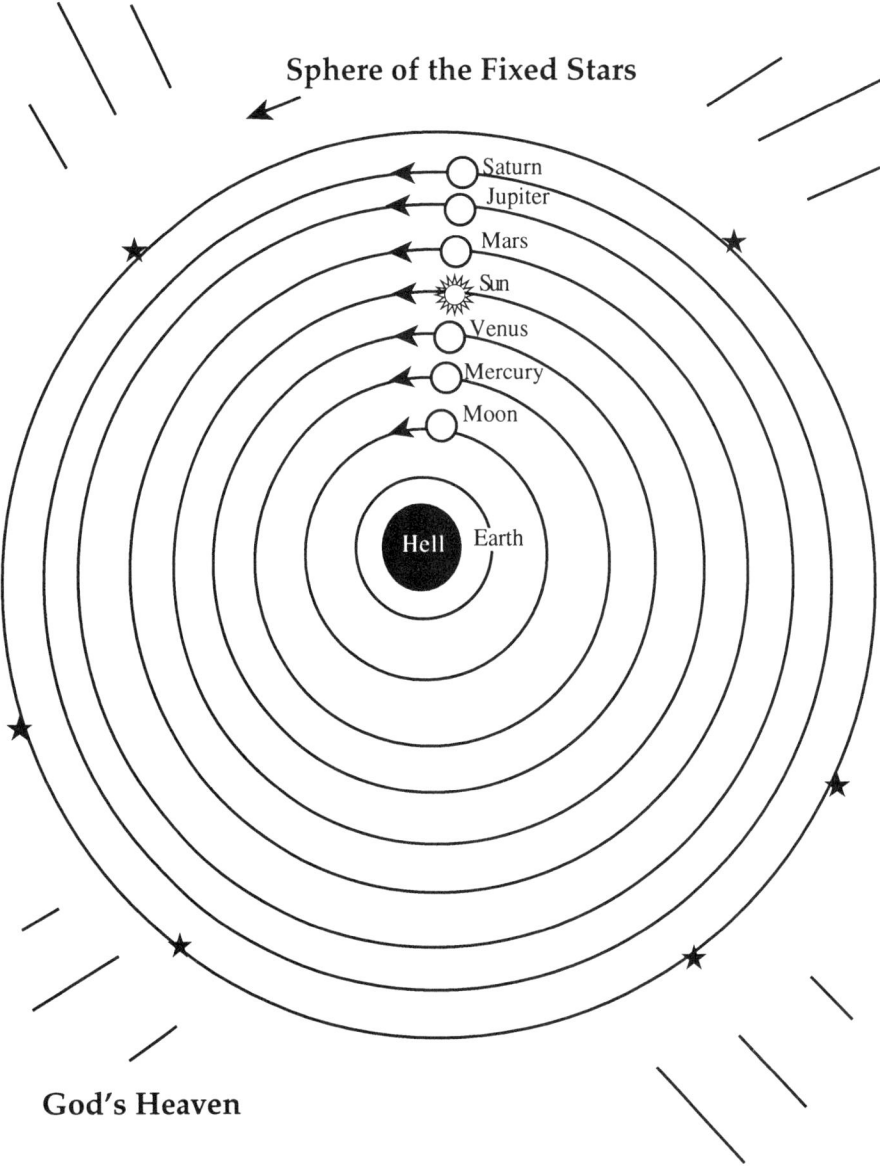

Figure 2   Rough Diagram of the Medieval Notion of the System of the World.

heard of. His "revolutionary" theory developed out of the combination of two interests—a theoretical and a practical—that in themselves seemed quite innocent. Owing to small errors in the computation of the length of the year, the old calendar established by Julius Caesar had fallen very obviously behind by Copernicus' day. A reform of the calendar was a necessity and Copernicus was interested in bringing it about. However, he declined the invitation of Pope Leo X to work on the project, saying that the motions of the sun and moon had to be worked out more exactly first and that he was busy trying to solve this prior problem. Doubtless he was interested anyway in the motions of the sun and moon as a theoretic problem in itself. In so far as there were any additional ulterior motives, they seemed quite ordinary and practical, not at all involving a revolution in thought.

And at first not many people seemed to consider his new system of the heavens a revolution. Most of the serene professors continued in their serenity and largely ignored or laughed at it. The Church did not really get excited about it for seventy years after its publication, which meant about a hundred years after the gist of Copernicus' views became generally known. The Church of Rome in the sixteenth century was having other troubles. Ironically, however, some of the Protestant divines with whom the Church was disputing in this Reformation period were among the first to condemn Copernicus' views. Luther denounced them before they were even published, perhaps sensing ;more acutely than the Romans the loss of the cosmological serenity implied in them; because Luther, driven from the Church, had, as he once said, only "the sky" under which

he could take shelter. Copernicus may have seemed to him to be dissolving this "sky."

In itself the new idea was simple, and is now quite commonplace to us; the sun, not the earth, is the center of things. The planets, of which the earth is one, revolve about the sun, and the moon revolves about the earth.

Nothing about this idea astonishes people today or makes them feel the dissolution of anything. Nevertheless this idea was quite aptly called a revolution. For it meant much more than simply assigning the earth a position some few millions of miles over in space from where it was heretofore considered to be. It meant removing it from the physical center of things and sending it flying about in space—and men with it. If this view were accepted it would mean that man must always correct the obvious deliverances of his senses—that things, even in the heavens, are not as they seem to man's perceptions.

The implications of all this for man's conception of himself and of his problems are many (and this book will concern itself largely with the job of witnessing the unfolding of them), but one of the most upsetting and far-reaching of these implications was the pall of improbability which it threw upon the notion that things had been designed especially for men. For the state of affairs which this theory supposed meant that men were not naturally in a favorable position to view things as they really were, that they had to strain themselves in an unnatural way and compute the positions of other bodies in the universe by making allowances for their *own* motion—a motion they were totally unaware of in any natural manner and only knew, as a matter of fact, because of the greater logical simplicity and

Region of the Fixed Stars

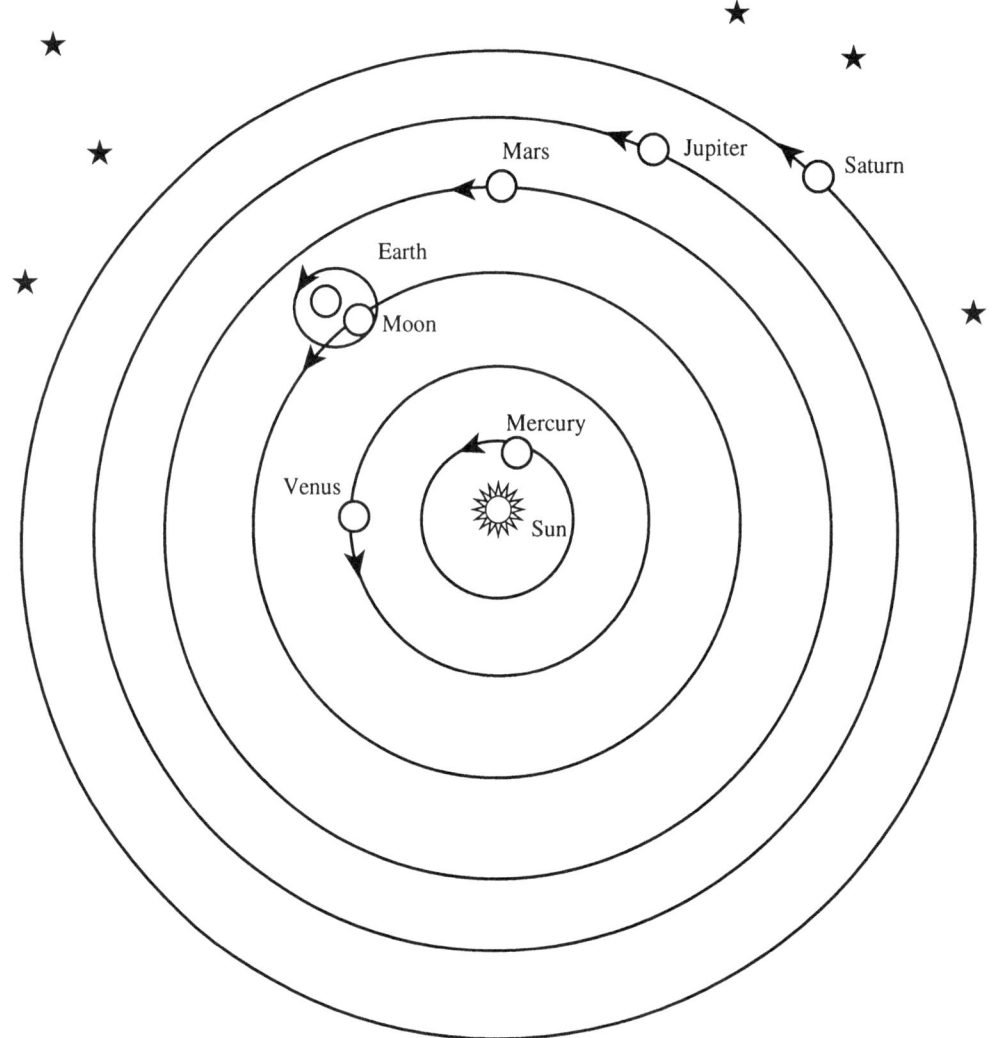

Figure 3. The World System of Copernicus

workability of their computations when made from this assumption. For this was all that Copernicus could offer as "proof," of course. Everything seemed so beautifully explicable his way, however, and so simple when compared with the clumsiness and arbitrariness of the epicycles, that his view of things struck people, especially mathematicians, with great force, regardless of the "strained" manner in which it was achieved.

This view of the cosmos, however, made it seem that what *man* might tend to think of things was of no concern to their Creator. For God had been exceedingly careless about the physical position He had assigned to man. Man, then, with the acceptance of this new idea as truly descriptive of the real state of affairs, necessarily lost his conception of his own lordship and became simply one creature among many creatures. And perhaps it was the theologians' dim suspicion that such was the essential meaning of the Copernican theory that lay behind their dislike for it.

There were other more immediate difficulties, of course. In terms of this theory no one could tell up from down—literally. Where now was heaven—and hell? Hell especially suffered from this arrangement, since it was also whirling around the sun for no apparently good reason—if it remained in the center of the earth, i.e., what man knew as "down." But this was now only "down" relative to the earth. Actually hell should now be in the center of the sun, *true* "down" being the center of the universe—but this was "up" relative to the earth and to man. And anyhow, how could such a noble, shining, luminous, "pure" body as the sun be the location of hell" Or, in the first place, how could this "pure" sun possibly occupy so

degraded a place in the universe, the true "down", the center?

Heaven also became somewhat unlocalized, since there was now not a definite sphere of fixed stars beyond which was heaven. Fixed stars were scattered "out there" somewhere in space, and heaven might still be conceived to be beyond them, wherever *that* was (apparently Copernicus still seemed to think of it this way) but it was all now hazy, indefinite, and slipshod—somehow unworthy of God.

The music of the spheres seemed also to be stilled. Instead of the delightful mystery and magic of a perfect order hidden in all things, everything on this view threatened to slip away into random, haphazard motion, *appearing* ordered from the earth perhaps, but actually, if truly ordered, ordered entirely irrelevant to earth and thus to man. Man for the first time could begin to feel strange and left out in the whole scheme of things.

I am not saying that this was all understood, much less expressed, by those who opposed the views of Copernicus. The churchmen (Catholics and Protestants) and the scholars who opposed his views did so on the basis of passages in the Scriptures, the authority of ancient and honored scholars, and the force of the Inquisition, when possible. Perhaps the sensation of the rug being pulled out from under them and their fairytale universe was what disturbed them most when they tried to think of the earth spinning and moving through space. The feeling of giddiness this engendered and the accompanying sense of loss of support had to be opposed. Whether or not it is true that the opponents of the moving earth sensed all this, they should have sensed it, if they were sufficiently perceptive and imaginative. For it is quite clear to us now that all this and more *was* truly involved in the idea of the moving earth, and that men have in fact felt this estrangement from their universe and this loss of support, not for their physical selves— they have grown used to riding on their merry-go-round—but for their highest values, hopes, and aspirations. It is a loss they cannot help feeling when they dare to contemplate the vast and seemingly inhuman, impersonal, and purposeless world of independent, teeming "things," and the frighteningly large and possibly infinite cosmos that Copernicus first—inadvertently, I am sure— opened to view. Man is lost—literally lost— swallowed up in space. For no finite part can count for anything in an infinity of parts.

This gnawing sense of loss was not the only difficulty that man inherited from the intellectual upheaval begun in Copernicus' day; perhaps it was not even the principal difficulty. At the same time as man lost his central position in the universe, in physical and honorific terms, he also lost the secure place from which to observe and measure all things. But this did not make him any less the measure of all things. In fact he now found himself even more the measure of all things. Now the very position from which he ought to measure became something for him to "measure." i.e., to determine, inasmuch as his natural position in space was no longer understood by him to be fixed, but in motion itself. From what point now could true or absolute motion be measured" And by what sort of measurement could the location of this truly fixed point be determined" Man

must now regard this point from which to measure all things as also a problem of measurement for him, since he could no longer suppose naively that he was *at* it.

It was this problem that made man's task so disastrously messy . . .

39 R. F. Tennant
The Contemporary Teleological Argument

The forcibleness of Nature's suggestion that she is the outcome of intelligent design lies not in particular cases of adaptedness in the world, nor even in the multiplicity of them. It is conceivable that every such instance may individually admit of explanation in terms of proximate causes or, in the first instance, of explanation other than in terms of cosmic or "external" teleology. And if it also admits of teleological interpretation, that fact will not of itself constitute a rigorous certification of external design. The forcibleness of the world's appeal consists rather in the conspiration of innumerable causes to produce, by their united and reciprocal action, and to maintain, a general order of Nature. Narrower kinds of teleological argument, bases on surveys of restricted spheres of fact, are much more precarious then that for which the name of "the wider teleology" may be appropriated in that the comprehensive design argument is the outcome of synopsis or conspection of the knowable world.

The knowable world, however, is not identical with the universe as to which, as a whole, we have no knowledge. It may be objected, therefore, that to use the phrase "the world" to denote both of these things seems to beg a vital question. Of course, if trustworthy evidence of design in the limited portion of the universe that we know were forthcoming, a world-designer would be "proved," and our ignorance as to other parts would be irrelevant. But it is a graver objection - perhaps the gravest that the teleologist has to encounter - that rich suggestions of design in the known world yield no proof of design in the universe, since our ordered fragment may be but a temporary and casual episode in the history of the universe, an oasis in a desert of "chaos," a chance product of mindless agency in a universe which has had opportunity to produce all sorts of local and ephemeral worlds within A World. To this objection it may be replied that teleology does not profess to base itself on the principle of "the inconceivability of the opposite," while interpretations of the known cannot be refuted, even if they can be made to appear more precarious, by considerations as to possibilities within the unknowable. Certainly a mechanical theory of the universe must not be tacitly assumed to which ore known world gives the lie. More specifically it may be said that the ordered oasis is not an isolable fragment. It and the supposes desert or "chaos" are interdependent. It is because the desert is what it is that the oasis is what it is; and the one has orderedness only by permission, so to say, of the other. The force of the objection, indeed, seems to be derived from the assumption that our ordered world is due to some evolutionary process within the whole universe analogous to that secured within organic Nature by natural selection out of random variations. This is but conjecture or appeal to the unknown, and confronted with the second law of thermodynamics, is overwhelmingly improbable. And if it includes the supposition that even unlimited reshufflings of matter by mechanical forces can produce minds and personalities in a corner of the universe, it conflicts with knowledge. Further, if the nerve of the teleological argument be that design issues in the realization of ethical values, the spatio-temporal immensities of the universe become less significant than the petty oasis. Teleology, after all, is a value-concept; and magnitude and worth are incommensurable.

Nevertheless the inquiry that is here first to be undertaken, whether the knowable world, or Nature, has been devised by intelligence, is to be distinguished, though it cannot be separated, form the further inquiry, what the ultimate purpose or goal of the world-process is. The latter question may admit of no complete answer by man: reasonable belief as to the former involves but the application of mother-wit to forthcoming facts. A machine can evince intelligent contrivance or design to a man ignorant of engineering and unable to tell precisely what the machine is for. Once more, by way of making relevant distinctions, a teleological interpretation of Nature does not require that every detail in Nature was purposed or fore-ordained. Processes may inevitable produce by-products which, as such, were not purposed, but are the necessary outcome of processes but which a purpose is fulfilled.

The main field of fact in which adaptation is conspicuous, and which have severally afforded data for particular arguments of the teleological kind and of restricted scope, are those of the knowability or intelligibility of the world (or the adaptation of thought of things), the internal adaptedness of organic beings, the fitness of the inorganic to minister to life, the aesthetic value of Nature, the world's instrumentality in the realization of moral ends, and the progressiveness in the evolutionary process culminating in the emergence of man with his rational and moral status. A brief examination of these fields in turn will not only enable us to estimate the respective strengths of the more or less independent arguments derived from them severally, but also to appreciate the interconnections within the world, and the comprehensive teleology which such interconnectedness suggests.

I. We may begin with the mutual adaptation of thought and things, Nature and Knowledge. The correspondence between human thought and the external world, rendering science possible, has evoked what may be called epistemological arguments for the being of God. Descartes accounted for the marvel, as it seemed to him, of this correspondence by invoking, as its necessary cause, the veracious Deity, whose existence he sought to prove—almost superfluously, on his own presuppositions—by other lines of reasoning. If a subject's "ideas" were as disparate from percepts and from external Objects as Descartes supposes, each class forming a closed system independent of the other, there might be something to be said for the invocation of divine agency to explain the elaborate correspondence between the two systems. But if our primary ideas of objects are but images of such

objects defecated to pure transparency, or are but elements of the objective matter of perceptual experience isolated for thought by selective and restricted attention, then that they apply to the objects from which they have but been abstracted is no wonder to be supernaturally accounted for. And if, as in science, general ideas and the constituents of developed thought are determined and controlled by things external to thought, and so enjoy validity, there is no cause for amazement even at the productiveness of theoretical physics. The mysterious element in knowledge does not lie where Descartes would place it: it lies deeper. Similarly, Shelley's apostrophe,

O thou immortal Deity
Whose throne is in the depths of human
thought,

supposing it to have any relevance to the present context, errs as to the location of the "throne." It is in the world, as allowing itself to be thought about, rather than in our thinking, if anywhere, that considerations as to the penetrability of things by thought may lead teleology to enthrone its Deity. Reason might soliloquize: world or no world, I must think thus and thus, in order to think at all. Pure reason may have power to decree how thoughts must be linked in order to yield Thought, and certainly can without limit form ideas—as in the pure sciences—to which there is no knowable counterpart in Actuality; but it is powerless to prescribe to things what they shall be, and that they shall satisfy the demands of any pure science. The world might answer: you must think me thus and thus, as to my "what," and not otherwise, if you would know me. Nature will open to the right pass-word; but she has chosen it, not we. To revert to plain speech: the primary epistemological contribution to teleological reasoning consists in the fact that the world is more or less intelligible, in that it happens to be more or less a cosmos, when conceivable it might have been a self-subsistent and determinate "chaos" in which similar events never occurred, none recurred, universals had no place, relations no fixity, things no nexus of determination, and "real" categories no foothold. But whether such logico-mathematical order as had been found to obtain in our world bespeaks "chance" in self-subsistent entities, or purposiveness in a designer or a creator, there is of course no logical method of deciding: the probability-calculus can gain no purchase. We know that similar ordering is sometimes due to human design; that it always is due to design we have no means of knowing. Again, the amenability of things to the more interpretative kind of knowledge, constituted by the "real" or the anthropic categories, shews that things, or their ontal counterparts, have so mush of affinity with us as to be assimilable and to be understood, or alogically interpreted, as well as to be ordered by number, etc.: it does not of itself testify that the adaptedness is teleological . . .

II. The adaptiveness that is so abundantly evinced in the organic world had already been discussed from the point of view of science and proximate causation. We have seen that if the behavior of matter be regarded as completely describable in terms of least action, shortest path, dissipation of kinetic energy, and so forth, matter must be regarded also as unable, of itself, to fall into such systems as organisms. There is indeed some tendency to-day in scientific circles to seek an organic conception of the

physical atom, etc., rather than a mechanical conception of the organism. But as for the organic at the molar and phenomenal level of description, its formative principle, irreducible to rigid mechanism, is provided by mentality wherever we have reason to infer psychic behavior; there we can account for the facts of function and structure, heredity and progressive adaptation. Where, as in plants, there is no macroscopic evidence of psychic behavior, the formative principle, as yet mysterious to science, is further to seek. It may be that only in metaphysics such as spiritualistic monadism, or hylozoism of the microscopic order, is a natural explanation to be found. But in proportion as psychological or other explanation is forthcoming in the organic realm as a whole, resort to external or cosmic teleology in order to account for adaptations within the organism, becomes superfluous for the special sciences. So long as organisms were believed to have originated, in their present forms and with all their specialized organs "ready made," the argument that adaptation of part to whole, of whole to environment, and of organ to function implied design, was forcible. But its premiss became untenable when Darwin shewed that every organic structure had come to be what it now is through a long series of successive and gradual modifications. Gradualness of construction is in itself no proof of the absence of external design: it is not at this point that Darwinism delivered its alleged death-blow to teleology. The sting of Darwinism rather lay in the suggestion that proximate and "mechanical" causes were sufficient to produce the adaptations from which the teleology of the eighteenth century had argued to God. Assignable proximate causes, whether mechanical or not, are sufficient to dispose of the particular kind of teleological proof supplied by Paley. But the fact of organic evolution, even when the maximum of instrumentality is accredited to what is figuratively called natural selection, is not incompatible with teleology on a grander scale; as exponents of Darwinism were perhaps the first to recognize and to proclaim. Subversive of Paley's argument, it does not invalidate his theistic conclusion, nor even his view that every organism and organ is an end as well as a means. Indeed the science of evolution was the primary source of the wider teleology current for the last half century, as well as the main incentive to the recovery of the closely connected doctrine of divine immanence. This kind of teleology does not set out from the particular adaptations in individual organisms or species so much as from considerations as to the progressiveness of the evolutionary process and as to the organic realm as a whole; but its connection with the former class of facts belongs to the subject-matter of the present section.

The survival of the fittest presupposes the arrival of the fit, and throws no light thereupon. Darwin did not account for the origin of variations; their forthcomingness was simply a datum for him. It is of no great significance for the wider teleology that variations are not in all cases so indefinite or random, nor so infinitesimal and gradual, as was generally assumed in The *Origin of Species*. But it may be observed that, in the absence either of a mechanical or of an "internal" explanation of variation, room is left for the possibility that variation is externally predetermined or guided, so that not only the general trend of the organic process, but also its every detail, may be pre-ordained

or divinely controlled. Even this observation is pointless save for those who regard a nexus of traceable proxmate causes and a theistic interpretation as incompatibilities. Theism such as has over-emphasized the idea of God's immanence denies proximate causes as distinct from acts of God; and advocates of antitheistic mechanism sometimes appear to think that the traceability of proximate causes bespeaks the superfluity, to philosophy as well as to science, of the idea of God. Thus, in connection with the topic now before us, Weismann wrote: "It is certainly the absence of a theoretical definition of variability which leaves open the door for smuggling in a teleological power. A mechanical explanation of variability must form the basis of this side of natural selection." But theism, such as is sufficiently leavened with deism to distinguish itself from pantheism, and the world from a deified mechanism, is indifferent to the banishment of the Paleyan type of teleology which relied on particular organic adaptations, any one of which was deemed sufficient to prove a divine artificer; and at the same time it has no need of going to the extreme of asserting that God is "either everywhere or nowhere," or that He is nothing if not all. The discovery of organic evolution has caused the teleologist to shift his ground from special design in the products to directivity in the process, and plan in the primary collocations. It has also served to suggest that the organic realm supplies no better basis for teleological argument of the narrower type than does inorganic Nature. Indeed it suggests that, since the adaptiveness of an organism is non-teleological, the adaptiveness of the whole world may perhaps similarly be *Zwechmassigkeit ohne Zweck* [adaptation without a purpose]. But this suggestion calls for examination later.

III. Although teleologists in the past have generally set out from adaptations in organisms, it has occurred now and again to a theistic apologist, e.g. to Aquinas, that adaptation in inorganic Nature, where there cannot be a formative principle such as non-intelligent organisms evince, should more unequivocally bespeak external design. The teleologist of to-day, however, would rather call attention to the continuity of apparent purposiveness between the two realms, or to the dependence of adaptation in the one on adaptiveness in the other. Since Darwin, we have realized that organisms can only be understood in connection with their environment. And more recently it has been argued, as by Mr. Henderson, that the inorganic environment is as plainly adapted to life as living creatures are to their environment. The vast complexity of the physico-chemical conditions of life on the earth suggests to common sense that the inorganic world may retrospectively receive a biocentric explanation, which, if "unconscious purpose" do but restate the facts rather than account for them, and ungrounded coincidence be as humanly incredible as it is logically unassailable, becomes a teleological explanation. Waiving, as here irrelevant, the metaphysical possibility that what we call inorganic matter is an appearance of relatively unorganized spirit, we may say that if science is to be trusted when it regards the organic realm as later in time than the inorganic world, and when it asserts that the processes, which made the emergence and persistence of life possible, would have been precisely the same had life not emerged at all, then there would seem to be a develop-

ment of this fitness for life, involving convergence of innumerable events towards a result, as if that result were an end to which the inorganic processes were means. The fitness of our world to be the home of living beings depends upon certain primary conditions, astronomical, thermal, chemical, etc., and on the coincidence of qualities apparently not causally connected with one another, the number of which would doubtless surprise anyone wholly unlearned in the sciences; and these primary conditions, in their turn, involve many of secondary order. Unique assemblages of unique properties on so vast a scale being thus essential to the maintenance of life, their forthcomingness makes the inorganic world seem in some respects comparable with an organism. It is suggestive of a formative principle. But, if there be such a principle, it is not conceivable after analogy with the life and mind of organisms, and cannot be said to be intrinsic or internal; because the inorganic—at the molar and phenomenal level of explanation—is devoid of life, and—at any level of explanation—is devoid of intelligence and foresight. Unless cosmic teleology is invoked, the intricate adaptations that have been mentioned must be referred by the dualist to a mechanically controlled concourse of atoms, and by the pluralistic spiritualist to conative monads that are no more capable of conspiration than are inert particles.

Such is the teleological appeal of this field of facts to commonsense reasonableness, or mother-wit, which regards the "probability," that the apparent preparedness of the world to be a theatre of life is due to "chance," as infinitesimally small. It remains to ask whether either science or logic is able to abate the forcibleness of this appeal.

Science does not seem to lessen the convincingness of the argument now before us when it suggests that (as if organic chemistry were irrelevant), had the conditions upon which life, as we know it, depends been wholly or partly different, other forms of organism might equally well have emerged, adapted to the altered environment: silicon perhaps replacing carbon in another kind of protoplasm, and iron replacing calcium phosphate in skeletons. For the point is that, for the existence of any forms of life that we may conceive, the necessary environment, whatever its nature, must be complex and dependent on a multiplicity of coincident conditions, such as are not reasonable attributable to blind forces or to pure mechanism. Nor, again, can science explain the adaptation of the inorganic environment to life after the manner in which Darwinism, its sufficiency being assumed, explains progressive adaptations in organisms without resort to design. Of a struggle for existence between rival worlds, out of which ours has survived as the fittest, we have no knowledge upon which to draw. Natural selection cannot here be invoked; and if the term "evolution" be applicable at all to the whole world-process, it must have a different meaning from that which it bears in Darwinian biology. Presumably the world is comparable with a single throw of dice. And common sense is not foolish in suspecting the dice to have been loaded.

But here the logician intervenes. He will first point out that the remarkableness, or surprisingness, of manifold coincidences, evoking our teleological explanation of them, is but a fact pertaining to human phychology, unless "remarkable" means what he calls antecedently improbable. He will then remind us that a remarkable world might result from "one throw" in spite of there being indefinitely large chances against it, just as double sixes may be cast in one's first toss of two unloaded dice, although the adverse odds are 35 to 1. But his most harmful observation will be that, if the world be the sole instance of its kind, or be analogous to a single throw, there can be no talk of chances or of antecedent probability in connection with our question. Sound as this caution is, it does not affect the teleologist; for, when he calls coincidence on the vast scale improbable, he has in mind not mathematical probability, or a logical relation, but the alogical probability which is the guide of life and which has been found to be the ultimate bases of all scientific induction. If teleology here strays from the path of logical rectitude into one marked by logicians with a warning-post, it does so in the light-hearted company of common sense and inductive science. Science has been so continuously successful in its venturesomeness that the wisehead,logic, now lets it pass without remonstrance; but theology, though arm in arm with science, receives a reprimand. The teleologist is told that there is no antecedent probability, as to the existence of the intelligent Being invoked to explain adaptation suggestive of intelligent activity, after observation of the facts in question, unless there was an appreciable probability, before observation of them, that such a Being exists. Robinson Crusoe can be said to have inferred Friday from footprints legitimately, because he already knew that men existed and that they could reach his island; but the teleologist does not know beforehand that any superhuman being exist, and therefore cannot legitimately reason from what apparently are Mind-prints to their divine causation. But some favoritism would seem to be shewn to science in this illustration; for when we inquire how Crusoe originally got his knowledge as to the existence of fellow-men who can not only make footprints but also supply service and friendship, we find that it seems to have been mediated in much the same way as is the teleologist's belief in God.

It is true that in the former case there is a psychologically stronger compulsion, a nearer analogy, and a more immediate and constantly reiterated verification-process than in the latter; but the origination of our belief in fellow-subjects, like remarkableness of coincidences, is ultimately an affair of human psychology and life, of teleology and not of logic or of direct apprehension of soul-substance. Moreover, though we have no "knowledge" of a spirit above man in the hierarchy of spirits that we "know," neither have we knowledge that there is no such being. Knowledge leaves room for the faith which teleology involves; and the faith-venture is similar in kind to that on which all scientific knowledge relies. Previously to verification of his faith the teleologist need ask of science no further recognition than this. He would but insist that, in so far as relations with logic are concerned, it is not true that science rests on reason while, in a corresponding sense, teleology rests on unreason.

IV. Besides possessing a structure that happens to render it habitable by living creatures and intelligible to some of them, the world is a bearer of values, thus evincing affinity with beings such as can appreciate as well as understand. The beauty and sublimity of Nature have been made the basis of a special teleological argument; and if, as standing by itself, this argument falls short of cogency, the facts from which it sets out may be said to form a link in the chain of evidence which comprehensive teleology presents. The few considerations that lend themselves to either of these uses do not call for lengthy or subtle disputation; and fortunately it is not necessary to enter the scientifically trackless domain of aesthetics in order to ascertain their bearing on theism. Whether the adaptation to out faculties, involved in aesthetic estimation, be, as Kant thought, formal and the same for all, though subjective; whether it be subjectively constituted and not the same for all; whether beauty be wholly Objective and literally intrinsic to Nature: these controversial questions are here immaterial. For the doctrine that aesthetic value is constituted by feeling does not imply that the feeling is not objectively evoked, as if we could see beauty when and where we chose. It has a parallel in the phenomenalist theory of knowledge: that is to say, beauty is not created by minds out of nothing, but is subjectively made out of *rapport* with the ontal. Thus diverse theories as to the constitution of beauty may be said to have in common the implication that the ontal world is ultimately responsible for the evocation of aesthetic thrills and sentiments, though the value-judgments evoked by the same "perceptual" Objects are different in different percipients. Theories differ but as to what exactly is intrinsic, whether that is intrinsic to Nature as ontal or as phenomenal, and how much is subjectively contributed. And whatever be out proportioning of the shares of the human mind and external

Reality in constituting aesthetic value, the dependence or non-dependence of beauty on design will not be affected by it. There is a point in Toby Veck's remark as to the chimes: "If I hear 'em, what does it matter whether they speak it or not?" Yet "We receive but what we give," in this connection, is a partial truth because it suppresses the fact that our giving is solicited by a prior and different gift to us. If we minimise phenomenal Nature's gift by denying that her beauty is intrinsic, as is form or color, we must allow to ontal Nature an intrinsic constitution such that minds can make beauty as well as nomic order out of it. And the more we magnify man's part in this making, phenomenalizing, and appreciating, the more motivation have we to believe that Nature is meaningless and valueless without God behind it and man in front; and that is what teleology in its comprehensiveness, and the aesthetic argument in its particularity, endeavor to establish.

The latter argument, and least in its more popular forms, treats the beauty of Nature as Paley treated organic adaptations. That it discusses the beauty of the world, as we now contemplate it, as if it were a "special creation" with no past history or development, may not signify. The weak spot in what purports to be a special proof of theism lies rather in the assumption that,since in human art a beautiful or sublime production is the outcome of human design, similar effects must everywhere be due to design. This generalization is all too precarious; it can hardly be maintained that arrangements of matter, accounted beautiful, humanly caused but not contrived or selectively constructed with a view to exciting aesthetic admiration, *never* occur. Prescience or purpose is involved in art; but art is not necessarily the sole source of beauty. We may deem some of Kant's criticisms of the teleological explanation of the beautiful and the sublime to be captious, and such explanation to be natural and reasonable; but it is hardly necessitated by the considerations on which this would-be coercive arguments relies.

The aesthetic argument for theism becomes more persuasive when it renounces all claim to proof and appeals to alogical probability. And it becomes stronger when it takes as the most significant fact not the forthcomingness of beautiful phenomena but what may be called, with almost negligible need of qualification, the saturation of Nature with beauty. On the telescopic and on the microscopic scale, from the starry heaven to the siliceous skeleton of the diatom, in her inward parts (if scientific imagination be veridical) as well as on the surface, in flowers that "blush unseen" and gems that the "unfathomed caves of ocean bear," Nature is sublime or beautiful, and the exceptions do but prove the rule. However various be the taste for beauty, and however diverse the levels of its education or the degree of its refinement, Nature elicits aesthetic sentiment from men severally and collectively; and the more fastidious becomes this taste, the more poignantly and the more lavishly does she gratify it. Indeed, from contemplation of Nature, whose "every prospect pleases," the atheist might be led to conclude that processes only need *not* to be fraught with aesthetic design in order to excite, almost without fail, aesthetic admiration. But his generalization would become untenable as soon as he bethought himself of similar causal nexa into which human agency, seeding any end save beauty, enters. In general, man's productions (other than professed works of art), and almost only they, are aesthetically vile. An automobile, with its noises, stench, etc., can disgust all our senses simultaneously, and is not wholly untypical; while human output of larger scale is often not only unsightly and otherwise offensive in itself, but mars the fair face of Nature. Here, then, are two kinds of agency, *ex hypothesi* proceeding with indifference to the realization of aesthetic values: we might almost say the one never achieves, while the other never misses, the beautiful. And the same contrast subsists between their processes as between their products. Compare, e. g., "the rattling looms and the hammering noise of human workshops" with Nature's silent or musical constructiveness; or the devastating stinks of chemical works with Natures's fragrant distillations. "In the very act of laboring as a machine [Nature] also sleeps as a picture."

If "God made the country" whereas man made the town—and the black country—we have a possible explanation of these things; but if the theism contained in this saying be rejected, explanation does not seem to be forthcoming. The universality of Nature's beauty,—to speak as if beauty were the same for all and were intrinsic—is a generalization roughly comparable with the uniformity of natural law. That natural Objects evoke aesthetic sentiment is as much a fact about them as that they obey the laws of motion or that they have such and such chemical composition. And this potency is not coextensive with "mechanicalness," or absence of aesthetic design, as man's utilitarian productions shew. Nor can Nature's mechanism be regarded as a sufficient cause of the adaptiveness to our subjectivity in

which beauty consists; for we may still ask why *Nature's* mechanism affects us in such wise that we deem her sublime and beautiful, since mere mechanism, as such, is under no universal necessity to do so, and what we may call human mechanisms usually fail to do so. Yet this potency, describable as the Objective factor in beauty, belongs to Nature's very texture. And our scientific knowledge that the world-elements are ordered by number brings us no nearer to understanding why Nature in comparable with elaborately polyphonic music, or a harmony of many combined melodies.

It may further be observed that, in so far as the mechanical stability and the analytic intelligibility of the inorganic world are concerned, beauty is a superfluity . Also that in the organic world aesthetic pleasingness of color, etc., seems to possess survival-value on but a limited scale, and then is not to be identified with the complex and intellectualized aesthetic sentiments of humanity, which apparently have no survival-value. From the point of view of science, beauty proper is, in both its subjective and its objective factors, but a by-product, an epiphenomenon, a biologically superfluous accompaniment of the cosmic process. Once more then lucky accidents and coincidences bewilderingly accumulate until the idea of purposiveness, already lying to hand as indispensable within the sphere of human conduct, is applied to effect the substitution of reasonable, if alogical, probability for groundless contingency. If we do apply this category of design to the whole time-process, the beauty of Nature may not only be assigned a cause but also a meaning, or a revelational function. It may then be regarded as no mere by-product, like physical evil, in a teleologically ordered world whose *raison d' etre* is the realization of other values—the moral and the religious. Indeed Nature's potency to evoke aesthetic sentiment, however otiose in the cosmic process studied by science, is efficient in the world's *rapport* with man. From its very origination religious experience seems to have been conditioned by the impressiveness or the awesomeness of natural phenomena, suggestive of an invisible and mysterious presence. Aesthetic values are closely associated, and often are inextricable interwoven, with ethico-religious values. God reveals Himself, to such as have differentiated these valuations, in many ways; and some men enter His Temple by the Gate Beautiful. Values alone can provide guidance as to the world's meaning, structure being unable to suggest more than intelligent power. And beauty may well be a meaning. That is the element of sense contained in the romanticist's paradox, beauty is truth, or truth is beauty.

It may be remarked by the way that if sensuous beauty be accounted a world-meaning, so far will the anthropocentric factor in interpretation of the world become accentuated. For as to the ontal counterpart to sensory beauty, or what Nature's beauty is for the Creator Himself, we cannot speculate. If Nature's beauty embody a purpose *of* God, it would seem to be a purpose *for* man, and to bespeak that God is "mindful of him." Theistically regarded, Nature's beauty is of a piece with the world's intelligibility and with its being a theatre for moral life; and thus far the case for theism is strengthened by aesthetic considerations.

Notes

1. Vol. II, chapter IV, "Cosmic Teleology,"pp. 79-93 (Cambridge: The University Press, and New York: The Cambridge University Press, 1930).

2. By "chance" is here meant absence of a sufficient ground. The word, as commonly used, carries several meanings; and which of them is to the fore in any context where the term subsequently appears will perhaps not need to be stated. Among its senses the following may be mentioned. It may signify an event not as yet included by known law, or one which, in that it is unique, is absolutely non-subsumable under a general law; or one that is determined by causes as to which we have but imperfect, or perhaps no relevant, knowledge. It may even suggest the supposed indeterminateness, which can never actually subsist, e.g. of a configuration.

3.   . . . We receive but what we give,
   And in our life alone does Nature live:
   Ours is her wedding-garment, ours her shroud!

   —S. T. Coleridge,
   "Dejection: An Ode."

4. J. B. Mozley, *University Sermons*, 6th ed., p. 123.

40

H.J. McCloskey
God and Evil

Evil is a problem for the theist in that a contradiction is involved in the fact of evil on the one hand, and the belief in the omnipotence and perfection of God on the other. God cannot be both all-powerful and perfectly good if evil is real. This contradiction is well set out in its detail by Mackie in his discussion of the problem. In his discussion Mackie seeks to show that this contradiction cannot be resolved in terms of man's free will. In arguing in this way Mackie neglects a large number of important points, and concedes far too much to the theist. He implicitly allows that while physical evil creates a problem, this problem is reducible to the problem of moral evil and that therefore the satisfactoriness of solutions of the problem of evil turns on the compatibility of free will and absolute goodness. In fact physical evils create a number of distinct problems which are not reducible to the problem of moral evil. Further, the proposed solution of the problem of moral evil in terms of free will renders the attempt to account for physical evil in terms of moral good, and the attempt thereby to reduce the problem of evil to the problem of moral evil, completely untenable. Moreover, the account of moral evil in terms of free will breaks down on more obvious and less disputable grounds than those indicated by Mackie. Moral evil can be shown to remain a problem whether or not free will is compatible with absolute goodness. I therefore propose in this paper to reopen the discussion of "the problem of evil," by approaching it from a more general standpoint, examining a wider variety of solutions than those considered by Mackie and his critics.

The fact of evil creates a problem for the theist; but there are a number of simple solutions available to a theist who is content seriously to modify his theism. He can either admit a limit to God's power, or he can deny God's moral perfection. He can assert either (1) that God is not powerful enough to make a world that does not contain evil, or (2) that God created only the good in the universe and that some other power created the evil, or (3) that God is all-powerful but morally imperfect, and chose to create an imperfect universe. Few Christians accept these solutions, and this is no doubt partly because such "solutions" ignore the real inspiration of religious beliefs, and partly because they introduce embarrassing complications for the theist in his attempts to deal with other serious problems. However, if any one of these "solutions" is accepted, then the problem of evil is avoided, and a weakened version of theism is made secure from attacks based upon the fact of the occurrence of evil.

For more orthodox theism, according to which God is both omnipotent and perfectly good, evil creates a real problem; and this problem is well stated by the Jesuit, Father G. H. Joyce writes:

> *The existence of evil in the world must at all times be the greatest of all problems which the mind encounters when it reflects on God and His relation to the world. If He is, indeed, all-good and all-powerful, how has evil any place in the*

world which He has made? Whence came it? Why is it here? If He is all-good why did He allow it to arise? If all-powerful why does He not deliver us from the burden? Alike in the physical and moral order creation seems so grievously marred that we find it hard to understand how it can derive in its entirety from God.

The facts which give rise to the problem are of two general kinds, and give rise to two distinct types of problem. These two general kinds of evil are usually referred to as "physical" and as "moral" evil. These terms are by no means apt—suffering for instance is not strictly physical evil—and they conceal significant differences. However, this terminology is too widely accepted, and too convenient to be dispensed with here, the more especially as the various kinds of evil, while important as distinct kinds, need not for our purposes be designated by separate names.

Physical evil and moral evil then are the two general forms of evil which independently and jointly constitute conclusive grounds for denying the existence of God in the sense defined, namely as an all-powerful, perfect Being. The acuteness of these two general problems is evident when we consider the nature and extent of the evils of which account must be given. To take physical evils, looking first at the less important of these.

Physical evils.   Physical evils are involved in the very constitution of the earth and animal kingdom. There are deserts and icebound areas; there are dangerous animals of prey, as well as creatures such as scorpions and snakes. There are also pests such as flies and fleas and the hosts of other insect pests, as well as the multitude of lower parasites such as tapeworms, hookworms and the like. Secondly, there are the various natural calamities and the immense human suffering that follows in their wake—fires, floods, tempests, tidal waves, volcanoes, earthquakes, droughts and famines. Thirdly, there are the vast numbers of diseases that torment and ravage man. Diseases such as leprosy, cancer, poliomyelitis, appear prima facie not to be creations which are to be expected of a benevolent Creator. Fourthly, there are the evils with which so many are born—the various physical deformities and defects such as misshapen limbs, blindness, deafness, dumbness, mental deficiency and insanity. Most of these evils contribute towards increasing human pain and suffering; but not all physical evils are reducible simply to pain. Many of these evils are evils whether or not they result in pain. This is important, for it means that, unless there is one solution to such diverse evils, it is both inaccurate and positively misleading to speak of *the* problem of physical evil. Shortly I shall be arguing that no one "solution" covers not one problem but a number of distinct problems for the theist.

The nature of the various difficulties referred to by the theist as the problem of physical evil is indicated by Joyce in a way not untypical among the more honest, philosophical theists, as follows:

The actual amount of suffering which the human race endures is immense. Disease has store and to spare of torments for the body: and disease and death are the lot to which we must all look forward. At all times, too, great numbers of the race are pinched by want. Nor is the world ever free for very long from the terrible sufferings which follow in the track of war. If we concentrate our attention on human woes, to the exclusion of the joys of life, we gain an appalling picture of the ills to which the flesh is heir. So too if we fasten our attention on the sterner side of nature, on the pains which men endure from natural forces—on the storms which wreck their ships, the cold which freezes them to death, the fire which consumes them—if we contemplate this aspect of nature alone we may be led to wonder how God came to deal so harshly with His Creatures as to provide them with such a home.

Many such statements of the problem proceed by suggesting, if not by stating, that the problem arises at least in part by concentrating one's attention too exclusively on one aspect of the world. This is quite contrary to the facts. The problem is not one that results from looking at only one aspect of the universe. It may be the case that over-all pleasure predominates over pain, and that physical goods in general predominate over physical evils, but the opposite may equally well be the case. It is both practically impossible and logically impossible for this question to be resolved. However, it is not an unreasonable presumption, with the large bulk of mankind inadequately fed and housed and without adequate medical and health services, to suppose that physical evils at present predominate over physical goods. In the light of the facts at our disposal, this would seem to be a much more reasonable conclusion than the conclusion hinted at by Joyce and openly advanced by less cautious theists, namely, that physical goods in fact outweigh physical evils in the world.

However, the question is not "Which predominates, physical good or physical evil?" The problem of physical evil remains a problem whether the balance in the universe is one the side of physical good or not, because the problem is that of accounting for the fact that physical evil occurs at all.

Moral evil. Physical evils create one of the groups of problems referred to by the theist as "the problem of evil." Moral evil creates quite a distinct problem. Moral evil is simply immorality—evils such as selfishness, envy, greed, deceit, cruelty, callousness, cowardice and the larger scale evils such as wars and the atrocities they involve.

Moral evil is commonly regarded as constituting an even more serious problem than physical evil. Joyce so regards it, observing:

The man who sins thereby offends God . . . We are called on to explain how God came to create an order of things in which rebellion and even final rejection have such a place. Since a choice from among an infinite number of possible worlds lay open to God, how came He to choose one in which these occur? Is not such a choice in flagrant opposition to the Divine Goodness?

Some theists seek a solution by denying the reality of evil or by describing it as a "privation" or absence of good. They hope thereby to explain it away as not needing a solution. This, in the case of most of the evils which require explanation, seems to amount to little more than an attempt to sidestep the problem simply by changing the name of that which has to be explained. It can be exposed for what it is simply by describing some of the evils which have to be explained. That is why a survey of the data to be accounted for is a most important part of the discussion of the problem of evil.

In *The Brothers Karamazov,* Dostoevski introduces a discussion of the problem of evil by reference to some then recently committed atrocities. Ivan states the problem:

"By the way, a Bulgarian I met lately in

Moscow," Ivan went on..."told me about the crimes committed by Turks in all parts of Bulgaria through fear of a general rising of the Slavs. They burn villages, murder, outrage women and children, and nail their prisoners by the ears to the fences, leave them till morning, and in the morning hang them—all sorts of things you can't imagine. People talk sometimes of bestial cruelty, but that's a great injustice and insult to the beasts; a beast can never be so cruel as a man, so artistically cruel. The tiger only tears and gnaws and that's all he can do. He would never think of nailing people by the ears, even if he were able to do it. These Turks took a pleasure in torturing children too; cutting the unborn child from the mother's womb, and tossing babies up in the air and catching them on the points of their bayonets before their mothers' eyes. Doing it before the mother's eyes was what gave zest to the amusement. Here is another scene that I thought very interesting. Imagine a trembling mother with her baby in her arms, a circle of invading Turks around her. They've planned a diversion: they pet the baby to make it laugh. They succeed; the baby laughs. At that moment, a Turk points a pistol four inches from the baby's face. They baby laughs with glee, holds out its little hands to the pistol, and he pulls the trigger in the baby's face and blows out its brains. Artistic, wasn't it?"

Ivan's statement of the problem was based on historical events. Such happenings did not cease in the nineteenth century. *The Scourge of the Swastika* by Lord Russell of Liverpool contains little else than descriptions of such atrocities; and it is simply one of a host of writings giving documented lists of instances of evils, both physical and moral.

Thus the problem of evil is both real and acute. There is a clear prima facie case that evil and God are incompatible—both cannot

exist. Most theists admit this, and that the onus in on them to show that the conflict is not fatal to theism; but a consequence is that a host of proposed solutions are advanced.

The mere fact of such a multiplicity of proposed solutions, and the widespread repudiation of each other's solutions by theists, in itself suggests that the fact of evil is an insuperable obstacle to theism as defined here. It also makes it impossible to treat of all proposed solutions, and all that can be attempted here is an examination of those proposed solutions which are most commonly invoked and most generally thought to be important by theists.

Some theists admit the reality of the problem of evil, and then seek to sidestep it, declaring it to be a great mystery which we poor humans cannot hope to comprehend. Other theists adopt a rational approach and advance rational arguments to show that evil, properly understood, is compatible with, and even a consequence of God's goodness. The arguments to be advanced in this paper are directed against the arguments of the latter theists; but in so far as these arguments are successful against the rational theists, to that extent they are also effective in showing that the nonrational approach in terms of great mysteries is positively irrational.

Proposed Solutions to the Problem of Physical Evil

Of the large variety of arguments advanced by theists as solutions to the problem of physical evil, five popularly used and philosophically significant solutions will be examined. They are, in brief: (1) Physical good (pleasure) requires physical evil (pain) to exist at all; (2) Physical evil is God's punishment of sinners; (3) Physical evil is God's warning and reminder to man; (4) Physical evil is the result of the natural laws, the operations of which are on the whole good; (5) Physical evil increases the total good.

Physical Good Is Impossible without Physical Evil. Pleasure is possible only by way of contrast with pain. Here the analogy of color is used. If everything were blue we should, it is argued, understand neither what color is nor what blue is. So with pleasure and pain.

The most obvious defect of such an argument commonly invoked by those who think of physical evil as creating only one problem, namely the problem of human pain. However, the problems of physical evils are not reducible to the one problem, the problem of pain; hence the argument is simply irrelevant to much physical evil. Disease and insanity are evils, but health and sanity are possible in the total absence of disease and insanity. Further, if the argument were in any way valid even in respect of pain, it would imply the existence of only a speck of pain, and not the immense amount of pain in the universe. A speck of yellow is all that is needed for an appreciation of blueness and of color generally. The argument is therefore seen to be seriously defective on two counts even if its underlying principle is left unquestioned. If its underlying principle is questioned, the argument is seen to be essentially invalid. Can it seriously be maintained that if an individual were born crippled and deformed and never in his life experienced pleasure, that he could not experience pain, not even if he were severely injured? It is clear that pain is possible in the absence of pleasure. It is true that it might not be distinguished by a special name and called "pain,"

but the state we now describe as a painful state would nonetheless be possible in the total absence of pleasure. So too the converse would seem to apply. Plato brings this out very clearly in Book 9 of the *Republic* in respect of the pleasures of taste and smell. These pleasures seem not to depend for their existence on any prior experience of pain. Thus the argument is unsound in respect of its main contention; and in being unsound in this respect, it is at the same time ascribing a serious limitation to God's power. It maintains that God cannot create pleasure without creating pain, although as we have seen, pleasure and pain are not correlatives.

Physical Evil Is God's Punishment for Sin; This kind of explanation was advanced to explain the terrible Lisbon earthquake in the eighteenth century, in which 40,000 (people were killed. There are many replies to this argument, for instance Voltaire's. Volraire asked: "Did God in this earthquake select the 40,000) least virtuous of the Portuguese citizens?" The distribution of disease and pain is in no obvious way related to the virtue of the persons afflicted, and popular saying has it that the distribution is slanted in the opposite direction. The only way of meeting the fact that evils are not distributed proportionately to the evil of the sufferer is by suggesting that all human beings, including children, are such miserable sinners, that our offences are of such enormity, that God would be justified in punishing all of us as severely as it is possible for humans to be punished; but even then, God's apparent caprice in the selection of His victims requires explanation. In any case it is by no means clear that young children who very often suffer severely are guilty of sin of such an enormity as would be necessary to justify their sufferings as punishment.

Further, many physical evils are simultaneous with birth—insanity, mental defectiveness, blindness, deformities, as well as much disease. No crime or sin of the *child* can explain and justify these physical evils as punishment; and, for a parent's sin to be punished in the child is injustice or evil of another kind.

Similarly, the sufferings of animals cannot be accounted for as punishment. For these various reasons, therefore, this argument must be rejected. In fact it has dropped out of favor in philosophical and theological circles, but it continues to be invoked at the popular level.

Physical Evil Is God's Warning to Men.

It is argued, for instance of physical calamities, that "they serve a moral end which compensates the physical evil which they cause. The awful nature of these phenomena, the overwhelming power of the forces at work, and man's utter helplessness before them, rouse him from the religious indifference to which he is so prone. They inspire a reverential awe of the Creator who made them, and controls them, and a salutary fear of violating the laws which He has imposed" (Joyce). this is where immortality is often alluded to as justifying evil.

This argument proceeds from a proposition that is plainly false; and that the proposition from which is proceeds is false is conceded implicitly by most theologians. Natural calamities do not necessarily turn people to God, but rather present the problem of evil in an acute from and the problem . . . from religion than any other cause. Thus if God's object in bringing about natural calamities is to inspire reverence and awe, He is a bungler. There are many more reliable methods of achieving this end. Equally important, the use of physical evil to achieve this object is hardly the course one would expect a benevolent God to adopt when other, more effective, less evil methods are available to Him, for example, miracles, special revelation, etc.

Evils Are the Results of the Operation of Laws of Nature;

This fourth argument related to most physical evil, but is more usually used to account for animal suffering and physical calamities. These evils are said to result from the operation of the natural laws which govern these objects, the relevant natural laws being the various causal laws, the law of pleasure-pain as a law governing sentient beings, etc. The theist argues that the nonoccurrence of these evils would involve either the constant intervention by God in a miraculous way, and contrary to his won natural laws, or else the construction of a universe with different components subject to different laws of nature; for God, in creating a certain kind of being, must create it subject to its appropriate law; He cannot create it and subject it to any law of His own choosing. Hence He creates a world which has components and laws good in their total effect, although calamitous in some particular effects.

Against this argument three objections are to be urged. First, it does not cover all physical evil. Clearly not all disease can be accounted for along these lines. Secondly, it is not to give a reason against God's miraculous intervention simply to assert that it would be unreasonable for Him constantly to intervene in the operation of His own laws. Yet this is the only reason that theists seem to offer here. If, by intervening in respect to the operation of His laws, God could thereby eliminate an evil, it would seem to be unreasonable and evil of Him not to do so. Some theists seek a way out of this difficulty by denying that God has the power miraculously to intervene; but this is to ascribe a severe limitation to His power. It amounts to asserting that when His Creation has been effected, God can do nothing else except contemplate it. The third objection is related to this, and is to the effect that it is already to ascribe a serious limitation to God's omnipotence to suggest that He could not make sentient beings which did not experience pain, nor sentient beings without deformities and deficiencies, nor natural phenomena with different laws of nature governing them. There is no reason why better laws of nature governing the existing objects are not produce calamities and pain. To maintain this is not to suggest that an omnipotent God should be capable of achieving what is logically impossible. All that has been indicated here is logically possible, and therefore not beyond the powers of a being Who is really omnipotent.

This fourth argument seeks to exonerate God by explaining that He created a universe sound on the whole, but such that He had no direct control over the laws governing His creations, and had control only in His selection of His creations. The previous two arguments attribute the detailed results of the operations of these laws directly to God's will. Theists commonly use all three arguments. It is not without significance that they betray such uncertainty as to whether God is to be *commended or exonerated.*

The Universe Is Better With Evil in It.   This is the important argument. One version of it runs:

> *Just as the human artist has in view the beauty of his composition as a whole, not making it his aim to give to each several part the highest degree of brilliancy, but that measure of adornment which most contributes to the combined effect, so it is with God (Joyce).*

Another version of this general type of argument explains evil not so much as a *component* of a good whole, seen out of its context as a mere component, but rather as a *means* to a greater good. Different as these versions are, they may be treated here as one general type of argument, for the same criticisms are fatal to both versions.

This kind of argument if valid simply shows that some evil may enrich the Universe; it tells us nothing about how *much evil* will enrich this particular universe, and how much will be too much. So, even if valid in principle—and shortly I shall argue that it is not valid—such an argument does not in itself provide a justification for the evil in the universe. It shows simply that the evil which occurs might have a justification. In view of the immense amount of evil the probabilities are against it.

This is the main point made by Wisdom in his discussion of this argument. Wisdom sums up his criticism as follows:

> *It remains to add that, unless there are independent arguments in favor of this world's being the best logically possible world, it is probable that some of the evils in it are not logically necessary to a compensating good; it is probable because there are so many evils.*

Wisdom's reply brings out that the person who relies upon this argument as a conclusive and complete argument is seriously mistaken. The arguments, if valid, justifies only some evil. A belief that it justifies all the evil that occurs in the world is mistaken, for a second argument, by way of a supplement to it, is needed. This supplementary argument would take the form of a proof that all the evil that occurs is *in fact* valuable and necessary as a means to greater good. Such a supplementary proof is in principle impossible; so, at best, this fifth argument can be taken to show only that some evil *may be* necessary for the production of good, and that the evil in the world may perhaps have a justification on this account. This is not to justify a physical evil, but simply to suggest that physical evil might nonetheless have a justification, although we may never come to know this justification.

Thus the argument even if it is valid as a general form of reasoning is unsatisfactory because inconclusive. It is, however, also unsatisfactory in that it follows on the principle of the argument that, just as it is possible that evil in the total context contributes to increasing the total ultimate good, so equally, it will hold that good in the total context may increase the ultimate evil. Thus if the principle of the argument were sound, we could never know whether evil is really evil, or good really good. (Aesthetic analogies may be used to illustrate this point.) By implication it follows that it would be dangerous to eliminate evil because we may thereby introduce a discordant element into the divine symphony of the universe; and, conversely, it may be wrong to condemn the elimination of what is good, because the latter may result in the production of more, higher goods.

So it follows that, even if the general principle of the argument is not questioned, it is still seen to be a defective argument. On the one hand, it proves too little—it justifies only some evil and not necessarily all the evil in the universe; on the other hand it proves too much because it creates doubts about the goodness of apparent goods. These criticisms in themselves are fatal to the argument as a solution to the problem of physical evil. However, because this is one of the most popular and plausible accounts of physical evil, it is worthwhile considering whether it can properly be claimed to establish even the very weak conclusion indicated above.

Why, and in what way, is it supposed that physical evils such as pain and misery, disease and deformity, will heighten the total effect and add to the value of the moral whole? The answer given is that physical evil enriches the whole by giving rise to moral goodness. Disease, insanity, physical suffering and the like are said to bring into being the noble moral virtues—courage, endurance, benevolence, sympathy and the like. This is what the talk about the enriched whole comes to. W. D. Niven makes this explicit in his version of the arguments:

> *Physical evil has been the goad which has impelled men to most of those achievements which make the history of man so wonderful. Hardship is a stern but fecund parent of invention. Where life is easy because physical ills are at a minimum we find man degenerating in body, mind, and character.*

And Niven concludes by asking:
"Which is preferable—a grim fight with the possibility of splendid triumph; or no battle at all?"

The argument is: Physical evil brings moral good into being, and in fact is an essential precondition for the existence of some moral goods. Further, it is sometimes argued in this context that those moral goods which are possible in the total absence of physical evils are more valuable in themselves if they are achieved as a result of a struggle. Hence physical evil is said to be justified on the grounds that moral good plus physical evil is better than the absence of physical evil.

A common reply, and an obvious one, is that urged by Mackie. Mackie argues that whilst it is true that moral good plus physical evil together are better than physical good alone, the issue is not as simple as that, for physical evil also gives rise to and makes possible many moral evils that would not or could not occur in the absence of physical evil. It is then urged that it is not clear that physical evils (for example, disease and pain) plus some moral goods (for example, courage) plus some moral evil (for example, brutality) are better than physical good and those moral goods which are possible and which would occur in the absence of physical evil.

This sort of reply, however, is not completely satisfactory. The objection it raises is a sound one, but it proceeds by conceding too much to the theist, and by overlooking two more basic defects of the argument. It allows implicitly that the problem of physical evil may be reduced to the problem of moral evil; and it neglects the two objections which show that the problem of physical evil cannot be so reduced.

The theist therefore happily accepts this kind of reply, and argues that, if he can give a satisfactory account of moral evil he will then have accounted for both physical and moral evil. He then goes on to account for moral evil in terms of the value of free will and /or its goods. This general argument is deceptively plausible. It breaks down for the two reasons indicated here, but it breaks down at another point as well. If free will alone is used to justify moral evil, then even if no moral good occurred, moral evil would still be said to be justified; but physical evil would have no justification. Physical evil is not essential to free will; it is only justified if moral good actually occurs, and if the moral good which results from physical evils outweighs the moral evils. This means that the argument from free will cannot alone justify physical evil along these lines; and it means that the argument from free will and its goods does not justify physical evil, because such an argument is incomplete, and necessarily incomplete. It needs to be supplemented by factual evidence that it is logically and practically impossible to obtain.

The correct reply, therefore, is first that the argument is irrelevant to many instances of physical evil, and secondly that it is not true that physical evil plus the moral good it produces is better than physical good and its moral goods. Much pain and suffering, in fact much physical evil generally, for example in children who die in infancy, animals and the insane passes unnoticed; it therefore has no morally uplifting effects upon others, and cannot by virtue of the examples chosen have such effects on the sufferers. Further, there are physical evils such as insanity and much disease to which the argument is inapplicable. So there is a large group of significant cases not covered by the argument. And where the argument is relevant, its premise is plainly false. It can be shown to be false by exposing its implications in the following way:

We either have obligations to lessen physical evil or we have not. If we have obligations to lessen physical evil then we are thereby reducing the total good in the universe. If, on the other hand, our obligation is to increase the total good in the universe it is our duty to prevent the reduction of physical evil and possibly even to increase the total amount of physical evil. Theists usually hold that we are obliged to reduce the physical evil in the universe; but in maintaining this, the theist is, in terms of this account of physical evil, maintaining that it is his duty to reduce the total amount of real good in the universe, and thereby to make the universe worse, then that amount of evil which he eliminates was unnecessary and in need of justification. It is relevant to notice here that evil is not always eliminated for morally praiseworthy reason. Some discoveries have been due to no higher a motive than a scientist's desire to earn a reasonable living wage.

This reply to the theist's argument brings out its untenability. The theist's argument is seen to imply that war plus courage plus the many other moral virtues war brings into play are better than peace and its virtues; that famine and its moral virtues are better than plenty; that disease and its moral virtues are better than health. Some Christians in the past, in consistency with this mode of reasoning, opposed the use of anesthetics to leave scope for the virtues of endurance and courage, and they opposed state aid to the sick and needy to leave scope for the virtues of charity and sympathy. Some have even contended that war is a good in disguise, again in consistency with this argument. Similarly the theist should, in terms of this fifth argument, in his heart, if not aloud, regret the discovery of the Salk polio vaccine because Dr. Salk has in one blow destroyed infinite possibilities of moral good.

There are three important points that need to be made concerning this kind of account of physical evil. (a) We are told, as by Niven, Joyce and others, that pain is a goad to action and that part of its justification lies in this fact. This claim is empirically false as a generalization about all people and all pain. Much pain frustrates action and wrecks people and personalities. On the other hand many men work and work well without being goaded by pain or discomfort. Further, to assert that men need goading is to ascribe another evil to God, for it is to claim that God made men naturally industrious; the one is no more incompatible with free will than the other. Thus the argument from physical evil being a goad to man breaks down on three distinct counts. Pain often frustrates human endeavor, pain is not essential as a goad with many men, and where pain is a goad to higher endeavors, it is clear that less evil means to this same end are available to an omnipotent God. (b) The real fallacy in the argument is in the assumption that all or the highest moral excellence results from physical evil. As we have already seen, this assumption is completely false. Neither all moral goodness nor the highest moral goodness is triumph in the face of adversity or benevolence towards others in suffering. Christ Himself stressed this when He observed that the two great commandments were commandments to love. Love does not depend for its possibility on the existence and conquest of evil. (c) The "negative" moral virtues which are brought into play by the various evils—courage, endurance, charity, sympathy and the like—besides not representing the highest forms of moral virtue, are in fact commonly supposed by the theist and atheist alike not to have the value this fifth argument ascribes to them.

We—theists and atheists alike—reveal our comparative valuations of these virtues and of physical evil when we insist on state aid for the needy; when we strive for peace, for plenty, and for harmony within the state.

In brief, the good man, the morally admirable man, is he who loves what is good knowing that it is good and preferring it because it is good. He does not need to be torn by suffering or by the spectacle of another's sufferings to be morally admirable. Fortitude in his own sufferings, and sympathetic kindness in others' may reveal to us his goodness; but his goodness is not necessarily increased by such things.

Five arguments concerning physical evil have now been examined. We have seen that the problem of physical evil is a problem in its own right, and one that cannot be reduced to the problem of moral evil; and further, we have seen that physical evil creates not one but a number of problems to which no one nor any combination of the arguments examined offers a solution.

Proposed Solutions to the Problem of Moral Evil

The problem of moral evil is commonly regarded as being the greater of the problems concerning evil. As we shall see, it does create what appears to be insuperable difficulties of the theist; but so too, apparently, do physical evils.

For the theist moral evil must be interpreted as a breach of God's law and as a rejection of God Himself. It may involve the eternal damnation of the sinner, and in many of its forms it involves the infliction of suffering on other persons. Thus it aggravates the problem of physical evil, but its own peculiar character consists in the fact of sin. How could a morally perfect, all-powerful God create a universe in which occur such moral evils as cruelty, cowardice and hatred, the more especially as these evils constitute a rejection of God Himself by His creations, and as such involve them in eternal damnation?

The two main solutions advanced relate to free will and to the fact that moral evil is a consequence of free will. There is a third kind of solution more often invoked implicitly than as an explicit and serious argument, which need not be examined here as its weaknesses are plainly evident. This third solution is to the effect that moral evils and even the most brutal atrocities have their justification in the moral goodness they make possible or bring into being.

Free will alone provides a justification for moral evil. This is perhaps the more popular of the serious attempts to explain moral evil. The argument in brief runs: men have free will; moral evil is a consequence of free will; a universe in which men exercise free will even with lapses into moral evil is better than a universe in which men become *automata* doing good always because predestined to do so. Thus on this argument it is the mere fact of the supreme value of free will itself that is taken to provide a justification for its corollary moral evil.

The goods made possible by free will provide a basis for accounting for moral evil. According to this second argument, it is not the mere fact of free will that is claimed to be of such value as to provide a justification of moral evil, but the fact that free will makes certain goods possible. Some indicate the various moral virtues as the goods that free will makes possible, whilst others point to beatitude, and others again to beatitude achieved by man's own efforts or the virtues achieved as a result of one's own efforts. What all these have in common is the claim that the good consequences of free will provide a justification of the bad consequences of free will, namely moral evil.

Each of these two proposed solutions encounters two specific criticisms, which are fatal to their claims to be real solutions.

1. To consider first the difficulties to which the former proposed solution is exposed. (a) A difficulty for the first argument—that it is free will alone that provides a justification for moral evil—lies in the fact that the theist who argues in this way has to allow that it is logically possible on the free will hypothesis that all men should always will what is evil, and that even so, a universe of completely evil men possessing free will is better than one in which men are predestined to virtuous living. It has to be contended that the value of free will itself is so immense that it more than outweighs the total moral evil, the eternal punishment of the wicked, and the sufferings inflicted on others by the sinners in their evilness. It is this paradox that leads to the formulation of the second argument; and it is to be noted that the explanation of moral evil switches to the second argument or to a combination of the first and second argument, immediately the theist refuses to face the logical possibility of complete wickedness, and insists instead that in fact men do not always choose what is evil.

(b) The second difficulty encountered by the first argument relates to the possibility that free will is compatible with less evil, and even with no evil, that is, with absolute goodness. If it could be shown that free will is compatible with absolute goodness, or even with less moral evil than actually occurs, then all or at least some evil will be left unexplained by free will alone.

Mackie, in his recent paper, and Joyce, in his discussion of this argument, both contend that free will is compatible with absolute goodness. Mackie argues that if it is not possible for God to confer free will on men and at the same time ensure that no moral evil is committed, He cannot really be omnipotent. Joyce directs his argument rather to fellow theists, and it is more of an *ad hominem* argument addressed to them. He writes:

> *Free will need not (as is often assumed) involve the power to choose wrong. Our ability to misuse the gift is due to the conditions under which it is exercised here. In our present state we are able to reject what is truly good, and exercise our power of preference in favor of some baser attraction. Yet, it is not necessary that it should be so. And all who accept Christian revelation admit that those who attain their final beatitude exercise freedom of will, and yet cannot choose aught but what is truly good. They possess the knowledge of Essential Goodness; and to it, not simply to good in general, they refer every choice. Moreover, even in our present condition it is open to omnipotence so to order our circumstances and to confer on the will such instinctive impulses that we should in every election adopt the right course and not the wrong one.*

To this objection, that free will is compatible with absolute goodness and that therefore a benevolent, omnipotent God would have given man free will and ensured his absolute virtue, it is replied that God is being required to perform what is logically impossible. It is logically impossible, so it is argued, for free will and absolute goodness to be combined, and hence, if God lacks omnipotence only in this respect, He cannot be claimed to lack omnipotence in any sense in which serious theists have ascribed it to Him.

Quite clearly, if free will and absolute goodness are logically incompatible, then God, in not being able to confer both on man, does not lack omnipotence in any important sense of the term. However, it is not clear that free will and absolute goodness are logically opposed; and Joyce does point to considerations which suggest that they are not logical incompatibles. For my own part I am uncertain on this point; but my uncertainty is not a factual one but one concerning a point of usage. It is clear that an omnipotent God could create rational agents predestined always to make virtuous "decisions"; what is not clear is whether we should describe such agents as having free will. The considerations to which Joyce points have something of the status of test cases, and they would suggest that we should describe such agents as having free will. However, no matter how we resolve the linguistic point, the question remains—Which is more desirable, free will and moral evil and the physical evil to which free will gives rise, or this special free will or pseudo-free will which goes with absolute goodness? I suggest that the latter is clearly preferable. Later I shall endeavor to defend this conclusion; for the moment I am content to indicate the nature of the value judgment on which the question turns at this point.

The second objection to the proposed solution of the problem of moral evil in terms of free will alone, is related to the contention that free will is compatible with less moral evil than occurs, and possibly with no moral evil. We have seen what is involved in the latter contention. We may now consider what is involved in the former. It may be argued that free will is compatible with less moral evil than in fact occurs on various grounds. (i) God, if He were all-powerful, could miraculously intervene to prevent some or perhaps all moral evil; and He is said to do so on occasions in answer to prayers (for example, to prevent wars) or of His own initiative (for instance, by producing calamities which serve as warnings, or by working miracles, etc.).

(ii) God has made man with a certain nature. This nature is often interpreted by theologians as having a bias to evil. Clearly God could have created man with a strong bias to good, whilst still leaving scope for a decision to act evilly. Such a bias to good would be compatible with freedom of the will. (iii) An omnipotent God could so have ordered the world that it was less conducive to the practice of evil.

These are all considerations advanced by Joyce, and separately and jointly, they establish that God could have conferred free will upon us, and at least very considerably *reduced* the amount of moral evil that would have resulted from the exercise of free will. This is sufficient to show that *not all* the moral evil that exists can be justified by reference to free will alone. This conclusion is fatal to the account of moral evil in terms of free will alone. The more extreme conclusion that Mackie seeks to establish—that absolute goodness is compatible with free will—is not essential as a basis for refuting the free will argument. The difficulty is as fatal to the claims of theism whether all moral evil or only some moral evil is unaccountable. However, whether Mackie's contentions are sound is still a matter of logical interest, although not of any real moment in the context of the case against theism, once the fact that less moral evil is compatible with free will has been established.

2. The second free will argument arises out of an attempt to circumvent these objections. It is not free will, but the value of the goods achieved through free will that is said to be so great as to provide a justification for moral evil.

(a) This second argument meets a difficulty in that it is now necessary for it to be supplemented by a proof that the number of people who practice moral virtue or who attain beatitude and/or virtue after a struggle is sufficient to outweigh the evilness of moral evil, the evilness of their eternal damnation and the physical evil they cause to others. This is a serious defect in the argument, because it means that the argument can at best show that moral evil *may have a* justification, and not that it has a justification. It is both logically and practically impossible to supplement and complete the argument. It is necessarily incomplete and inconclusive even if its general principle is sound.

(b) This second argument is designed also to avoid the other difficulty of the first argument—that free will may be compatible with no evil and certainly with less evil. It is argued that even if free will is compatible with absolute goodness it is still better that virtue and beatitude be attained after a genuine personal struggle; and this, it is said, would not occur if God in conferring free will nonetheless prevented moral evil or

reduced the risk of it. Joyce argues in this way:

> *To receive our final beatitude as the fruit of out labors, and as the recompense of a hard-won victory, is an incomparably higher destiny than to receive it without any effort on out part. And since God in His wisdom has seen fit to give us such a lot as this, it was inevitable that man should have the power to choose wrong. We could not be called to merit the reward due to victory without being exposed to the possibility of defeat.*

There are various objections which may be urged here. First, this argument implies that the more intense the struggle, the greater is the triumph and resultant good, and the better the world; hence we should apparently, on this argument, court temptation and moral struggles to attain greater virtue and to be more worthy of our reward. Secondly, it may be urged that God is being said to be demanding too high a price for the goods produced. He is omniscient. He knows that many will sin and not attain the goods or the Good free will is said to make possible. He creates men with free will, with the natures men have, in the world as it is constituted, knowing that in His doing so He is committing many to moral evil and eternal damnation. He could avoid all this evil by creating men with rational wills predestined to virtue, or He could eliminate much of it by making men's natures and the conditions in the world more conducive to the practice of virtue. He is said not to choose to do this. Instead, at the cost of the sacrifice of the many, He is said to have ordered things so as to allow fewer men to attain this higher virtue and higher beatitude that result from the more intense struggle.

In attributing such behavior to God, and

in attempting to account for moral evil along these lines, theists are, I suggest, attributing to God immoral behavior of a serious kind —of a kind we should all unhesitatingly condemn in a fellow human being.

We do not commend people for putting temptation in the way of others. On the contrary, anyone who today advocated, or even allowed where he could prevent it, the occurrence of evil and the sacrifice of the many— even as a result of their own freely chosen actions—for the sake of the higher virtue of the few, would be blatant immorality; and it would be immoral whether or not those who yielded to the temptation possessed free will. This point can be brought out by considering how a conscientious moral agent would answer the question: Which should I choose for other people, a world in which there are intense moral struggles and the possibility of magnificent triumphs and the certainty of many defeats, or a world in which there are less intense struggles, less magnificent triumphs but more triumphs and fewer defeats, or a world in which there are no struggles, no triumphs and no defeats? We are constantly answering less easy questions than this in a way that conflicts with the theist's contentions. If by modifying our own behavior we can save someone else from an intense moral struggle and almost certain moral evil, for example if by refraining from gambling or excessive drinking ourselves we can help a weaker person not to become a confirmed gambler or an alcoholic, or if by locking our car and not leaving it unlocked and with the key in it we can prevent people yielding to the temptation to become car thieves, we feel obliged to act accordingly, even though the persons concerned would freely choose the evil course of conduct. How much clearer is

the decision with which God is said to be faced —the choice between the higher virtue of some and the evil of others, or the higher but less high virtue of many more, and the evil of many fewer. Neither alternative denies free will to men.

These various difficulties dispose of each of the main arguments relating to moral evil. There are in addition to these difficulties two other objections that might be urged.

If it could be shown that man has not free will both arguments collapse; and even if it could be shown that God's omniscience is incompatible with free will they would still break down. The issues raised here are too great to be pursued in this paper; and they can simply be noted as possible additional grounds from which criticisms of the main proposed solutions of the problem of moral evil may be advanced.

The other general objection is by way of a follow-up to points made in objections (b) to both arguments (1) and (2). It concerns the relative value of free will and its goods and evils and the value of the best of the alternatives to free will and its goods. Are free will and its goods so much more valuable than the next best alternatives that their superior value can really justify the immense amount of evil that is introduced into the world by free will?

Theologians who discuss this issue ask, Which is better—men with free will striving to work out their own destinies, or automata-machinelike creatures, who never make mistakes because they never make decisions? When put in this form we naturally doubt whether free will plus moral evil plus the possibility of the eternal damnation of the many and the physical evil of untold billions are quite so unjustified after all; but the fact of the matter is that the question has not been fairly put. The real alternative is, on the one hand, rational agents with free wills making many bad and some good decisions on rational and nonrational grounds, and "rational" agents predestined always "to choose" the right things for the right reasons—that is, if the language of automata must be used, rational automata. Predestination does not imply the absence of rationality in all senses of that term. God, were He omnipotent, could preordain the decisions and the reasons upon which they were based; and such a mode of existence would seem to be in itself a worthy mode of existence, and one preferable to an existence with free will, irrationality and evil.

Conclusion

In this paper it has been maintained that God, were He all-powerful and perfectly good, would have created a world in which there was no unnecessary evil. It has not been argued that God ought to have created a perfect world, nor that He should have made one that is in any way logically impossible. It has simply been argued that a benevolent God could, and would, have created a world devoid of superfluous evil. It has been contended that there is evil in this world—unnecessary evil—and that the more popular and philosophically more significant of the many attempts to explain this evil are completely unsatisfactory. Hence we must conclude from the existence of evil that there cannot be an omnipotent, benevolent God.

41 Arthur A. Gianelli
Scientific Realism in the Post-Modern Age

"Someone once remarked that the two great errors in...philosophy are the belief that we know the truth and the belief that there is no truth to be known. Only people who have had the benefit of a higher education seem inclined to fall into so false a choice. Ordinary people do not make that mistake."

James Q. Wilson
The Moral Sense

Introduction

In light of post-modern challenges to universalism and objectivity, the intellectual pillars of both ancient and Enlightenment philosophy, is it still possible to talk meaningfully about the realism of scientific explanations?[1] Put differently, do scientific explanations illuminate, in any demonstrable sense, the workings of the physical world, or does science, Western science in this case, simply represent the collective efforts of the members of an historically contingent culture to impose their conceptual frameworks on the chaos and confusion of nature?

Generally speaking, philosophers fall into one of two camps regarding these questions.[2] Traditional realist philosophers maintain an unyielding and abiding faith in the capacity of the human intellect, with effort, to engage and understand nature. For these philosophers, science is nothing less than *the* paradigmatic intellectual activity, and the history of science provides clear evidence of unrivaled theoretical and technological progress. Post-modern philosophers challenge the optimism of their traditional counterparts. Inspired by the collapse of past attempts to secure a philosophical basis from which to establish the truth of descriptions and explanations in the various sciences, post-modern philosophers question the idea that scientific theories accurately represent, depict, or explain the processes operative in the physical world. To be sure, these philosophers do not ignore the technological breakthroughs spurred by scientific inquiry. What they dispute, instead, is the notion that developments in our capacity to control or cope with nature are linked, necessarily, to advancements in our understanding of how, precisely, nature works.

Among post-modern critics of scientific realism, perhaps the most prominent, and arguably the most devastating is Richard Rorty. Drawing from holistic analyses of language and revisionist accounts of the history of science, Rorty reasons that *all* attempts to underwrite the accomplishments of science are destined to fail because philosophers cannot produce an unassailable epistemology within which to ground not simply scientific claims, but, in fact, any claim to knowledge. Given the insuperable limits of language, philosophers do not have at their disposal the means by which to connect the descriptions and explanations of science with the actual objects and processes predominate in the physical world. With the link between scientific theories and physical phenomena severed and future pretenses to establish this link jettisoned, Rorty concludes that the traditional aspirations of

realist philosophers are misguided. Genuine scientific knowledge is not "out there" awaiting disclosure; scientific truth is not a matter of correspondence with nature. Instead, "truth" is simply a title bestowed, almost honorifically, upon those descriptions and explanations with which the community of scientists concur, given the standards, methods, and evidence available to them today. For Rorty, the quest for anything deeper, the very quest which has animated Western philosophy since the time of the pre-Socratics, invites inevitable failure and should without hesitation be abandoned.

Typically, the response from philosophical defenders of the realism of science is to highlight the internal inconsistencies and the self-refuting assumptions made, not just by Rorty, but in fact by all who renounce the project of securing an epistemic framework within which all scientific conversations, disputes, inquiries, and evidence can be translated and appropriately assessed.[3] To be honest, this line of argument is tired and, in my opinion, too dismissive of some of the important inroads made by Rorty and other post-modern thinkers. Therefore, what I propose to do in this paper is construct a defense of scientific realism which takes seriously the post-modern critique of epistemic foundationalism. With Rorty's work representing the most important exposition of this critique, I will develop my argument as follows. First, I will lay out the historical context within which both the post-modern problematic and contemporary scientific practices can be understood. I shall suggest the evolution of an important paradox: even as doubts were cast on the ability of philosophers to determine the truth of scientific theories, scientists themselves grew increasingly confident in the role predictions should play in the appraisal of their explanations of natural phenomena. Then, I will examine in more detail arguments presented by Karl Popper and Richard Rorty, two philosophers who recognized, despite their divergent orientations, the failures of the foundationalist project. I shall show that Popper failed to realize the implications of his thesis. If all observations are theory-laden, and all theories are conjectural, then how can philosophers establish the realism of explanations in the physical sciences? Assuming their realism or relying on an unproblematic observation language will not do. I shall then suggest that while Rorty correctly recognizes these implications, he goes much farther than the evidence warrants. The inability of philosophers to determine the truth of theories developed in the sciences *does not necessarily imply* that these same theories fail to tell us *anything* about the objects and processes predominate in nature. In the end, I will argue that, under the appropriate conditions, the capacity of the most powerful theories in the sciences, particularly those in the natural sciences, to predict previously unforeseen and unobserved events *at a rate better than random,* cannot be made philosophically consistent with a *complete* rejection of scientific realism. To be certain, this is not to argue that the predictive prowess of scientific theories establishes their truth; it is to argue that the ability of select scientific theories both to anticipate discoveries not yet made and to foresee occurrences not yet witnessed indicates that these theories cannot simply be mere conceptual impositions on nature. However partial and imperfect, these theories do indeed offer us an undeniable glimpse into "what's really out there."

Background

The quest for the means by which to discover and articulate the truth about nature dates back to the time of the ancients. Against his mentor, Plato, who argued that only contemplation revealed the reality which lay behind the flux and flow of processes in the universe, Aristotle elaborated a philosophical schema in which he asserted that the human mind possessed the capacity, through simple observation, to know the physical world. He maintained that all phenomena in nature had within them essences, dispositions or proclivities to seek predetermined ends or goals—in short, to become certain types of things and not something else. Through an abstractive process, our intellects could isolate and ascertain these essences, and, in so doing, come to know these phenomena as they really were. Aristotle adopted a common-sense approach to knowledge: the world was as it appeared to be, and the mind was always adequate to knowing. This approach secured the realism of scientific observations and explanations because nothing occluded intellectual access to nature; our understanding of the physical world was transparent, untainted by conceptual or empirical distortion. Aristotle's theories of nature and knowledge pervailed for nearly 1800 years. As Europe emerged from its dark age, however, his views gradually encountered challenge from two fronts: the scientists and the philosophers.

Since Aristotle, scientists had presumed that the earth rested at the center of the universe. This presumption fit common sense; heavenly bodies appeared to revolve around the earth, and heavy objects fell to the surface of the earth when unrestrained. Yet as time progressed, scientists ran into difficulty using Aristotle's cosmology to account for and predict planetary motion. In 1543, Copernicus argued against Aristotle's geocentric view, insisting instead that the earth was one among several satellites which revolved around the sun. In opposition to common sense and simple observations, Copernicus endorsed the heliocentrism of the solar system because the assumption that the sun was the focus of heavenly motion simplified the calculation of planetary trajectories. Still, in spite of the elegance of the Copernican model, scientists lacked concrete evidence in its favor; empirical support continued to reside with Aristotle. However, in 1610, Galileo supplied the requisite corroborative evidence. Images seen through his telescope confirmed that the planets looked very much like the earth. Now, not only did this evidence support a heliocentric cosmology, but it also called into question the common-sense approach to knowledge advocated by Aristotle. As Galileo's telescopic discoveries demonstrated so well, the senses can deceive, particularly when unaided by sophisticated instrumentation.

These discoveries shook the confidence of the scientific community. Aristotle's cosmology, the dominant paradigm for so long, no longer held under the weight of mounting disconfirmatory evidence. Yet the breech was soon filled, and confidence restored. In 1688, Isaac Newton argued that, despite the failure of Aristotelian essentialism, scientists could still apprehend·nature through a general set of mathematically expressed axioms. These axioms, developed as the three laws of motion and the universal law of gravitation, enabled Newton to render predictions concerning the orbits of the planets, the tides, and, in fact, nearly all observable movement of objects through space. Because the scope of Newton's physics was so broad and his predictions so accurate, scientists were convinced that the Newtonian world-view was correct. In fact, some scientists, Laplace among the most prominent, were so enamored with Newton's achievements to suggest that, if the initial background conditions were known, Newton's laws would permit them to make precise predictions about how motion would unfold in the universe until the end of time. So, in spite of the collapse of the Aristotelian explanatory framework, scientific confidence endured because of Newton's mathematically simple yet predictively powerful laws of motion and gravity.

While scientists emerged from the Enlightenment emboldened by the predictive successes of Newtonian physics, philosophers were not nearly so sanguine. They too had been questioning the viability of Aristotelian essentialism, but their conclusions were decidedly less optimistic regarding the revival of a variant of scientific realism. Their philosophical challenge to Aristotelian essentialism began most piercingly with Descartes. He disputed Aristotle's most fundamental assertion, that observations and perceptions accurately represent and reflect what exists in nature. He circumvented doubt in his own observations, however, by grounding his impressions in an ontological proof for the existence of God. Divine beneficence, claimed Descartes, guarded our concepts against distortion, provided they were developed clearly and distinctly. Yet this defense was tenuous at best, as Hume later noticed.

Rejecting metaphysical justifications for our ideas regarding nature, Hume revived the skepticism implicit in the premises of the Cartesian philosophical project. Interestingly, Hume resuscitated Cartesian-inspired skepticism at the very height of scientific reverence for the predictive successes of Newtonian physics. As scientists basked in their ability to subsume motion in nature under the rubric of Newton's axioms, Hume cast a spectre of philosophical doubt on the correspondence of their explanatory claims to the actual processes operative in the physical world. His attack was two-pronged. First, Hume questioned the inferences scientists typically made regarding causality in nature. Second, he condemned inductive inferences as logically indefensible, arguing that no amount of confirmatory evidence was sufficient to justify scientific generalizations, even Newton's generalizations about motion and gravity. For Hume, the notions of causation and induction, notions upon which scientists relied to explain physical phenomena, were derived, not from reason, not from secured epistemic foundations, but from the experience of past events coupled with acculturated expectations about the regularity of the future. Habit and custom, not reason, provided "skeptical" support for the pragmatic viability, if not the representative accuracy, of our scientific descriptions and explanations.

Hume's indictment of the efforts of philosophers to underwrite the claims of scientists had to be taken seriously. His skepticism jeopardized the standing not only of causal explanations, but also of any attempt by scientists to extrapolate from a limited number of observations to law-like generalizations. At a time when the potential of Newton's laws of gravitation and motion seemed limitless, he endangered the representative character of scientific explanations by cutting away at their epistemic foundations.

Challenged by the power of Hume's skepticism, Kant sought a resolution to the emerging rift which threatened to divide philosophy and science. He felt compelled to concur with Hume regarding the influence of our senses and intellectual predispositions on our interpretation of even basic observations. But Kant could not philosophically approbate Hume's skeptical reliance on habit and custom to ground our scientific interpretations of nature. Newton's axioms were simply too powerful to be dismissed as extensions of acculturation. Although we could no longer aspire to the transparent understanding of nature desired by the ancients, Kant felt that we could secure our knowledge of the phenomena and processes in the universe with appeal to categories carved into our intellects. Kant reasoned that the mind contained certain categories, a basic framework of concepts, which filtered and shaped experience. Observations were not imprinted on the mind without distortion, as Aristotle had us believe. Instead, the intellect organized and interpreted these observations through pre-structured categories, categories which were fixed prior to experience and which allowed human beings to make sense of what they saw. According to Kant, these a priori intuitions and concepts permitted scientists to ascertain relationships of causality and to make inductive inferences. On Kant's view, therefore, Newton's laws were less a reflection of what really exists in nature than an insight into the workings of the intellect and, by extension, the necessary preconditions for a scientific understanding of the universe.

In order to resolve the tension between philosophy and science, Kant abandoned all hope of the type of realism to which the ancients aspired. Scientists could apprehend nature, but not "as it was in itself." Instead, scientists illuminated the phenomena and processes of the universe only by interpreting their observations through a network of categories set permanently in their intellects. For Kant, all human beings shared the same set of these categories, so scientific claims to knowledge, while not transparently connected to the physical world, were nevertheless tied to a static conceptual framework which facilitated an interpretive understanding of nature, the only type of understanding for which we could hope.

The Collapse of Foundationalism and the Breakdown of Realism: Popper and Rorty

The viability of the Kantian categories hinged on the continued success of Newton's science. For nearly one hundred years after Kant's death Newton's laws of gravity and motion reigned virtually uncontested. Beginning in 1905, however, scientific and philosophical confidence in the veracity of the Newtonian world-view began to wane. Einstein's special and general theories of relativity directly challenged both the underlying assumptions and the predictive capacities of Newton's laws. By 1926, Einstein's theories had bested Newton's laws in repeated empirical tests, helping transform what was previously thought impossible into a reality: after two-hundred and thirty-eight years, scientists were forced to reject Newtonian physics (Pagels 1982).

Popper's Critique of Epistemic Foundationalism

Once scientists transferred their allegiance to Einstein, the Kantian project collapsed. Philosophers were left, once again, with insufficient and unsatisfactory answers to Hume's twin problems of causation and induction. It is in this light, I believe, that we can best understand Popper's philosophy of science. With the demise of the Newtonian world-view serving as his immediate backdrop, Popper declared that any theory, no matter how well accepted by scientists at any particular time, could fail to account for newly acquired observations. Popper put it succinctly: "No number of true test statements would justify the claim that an explanatory universal theory is true" (1972: 7). Because no test, regardless of how rigorous, could secure a theory from future disconfirmation, Popper concluded that the attempts by philosophers to illuminate the uncontroversial foundations of knowledge simply could not succeed. Indeed, Popper judged Hume's skepticism to be right on the mark. However, where Popper subscribed to Hume's skepticism regarding the ability of philosophers to secure the truth of theories of science, he did not share Hume's "irrationalist" resolution of the related problems of causation and induction. In fact, Popper believed there were no solutions, logical or otherwise, to these problems. The best scientists could do, according to Popper, was subject their theories to the most severe tests possible. If their hypothesized explanations of events in nature survived even the harshest attempts at refutation, then scientists were warranted in granting those explanations qualified approbation. To be more precise, Popper insisted that scientists ought to endorse only those theories which have endured the most stringent tests of their accuracy, but their endorsement should not be based on the evidence *for* these theories, but rather on the *absence* of evidence against them. Science proceeds not by proof, not by justified induction, but instead through a series of bold conjectures and rigorous refutations.[4]

But Popper pressed further. He not only accepted Hume's skepticism regarding inductive inferences about causal relationships in nature, but he also drew strength from Kant, arguing that the theories to which scientists subscribe shape their interpretations of experiments and observations. Popper maintained that *all* sensory input, *all* experiences, were influenced by previously formed concepts and intellectual dispositions. Each of our sense organs "incorporate . . . theory-like expectations. Sense organs, such as the eye, are prepared to react to certain selected environmental events—to those events which they 'expect', and only to those events" (Popper 1972: 145). At first glance, the "theory-impregnation" of our senses appears to provide renewed support for the Kantian argument that pre-fixed categories filter what we see. However, as we have shown above, Popper recognized the inherent fallibility of the categorical frameworks we employ, arguing not for their stasis but for their revisability in the wake of damaging evidence. Scientists were not locked into an invariant network of concepts and theories. However, because they were not, they lacked Kant's certitude regarding the inferences and interpretations they made, since the theories, categories, and concepts through which they observed nature could never themselves be proven correct.

It is my contention, then, that the tradition of scientific realism inspired by Aristotle ends conclusively with Popper's critique of epistemic foundationalism. "What has to be given up is the quest for justification, in the sense of the justification of the claim that a theory is true. *All theories are hypotheses*; all *may* be overthrown" (Popper 1972: 29; emphasis preserved). However, if no theory can ever be connected with certitude to the phenomena and processes predominate in nature, and the theoretical filters through which scientists apprehend and interpret observations are invincibly fallible, what are we to make of the gradually increasing predictive powers of the physical sciences, particularly physics? While it is critical to remember that Newton's laws of gravity and motion facilitated a considerable number of predictions, Einstein demonstrated the empirical limits of Newton's laws, showing that future observations can falsify even the most heuristically potent of scientific theories. Predictive power, as we have seen, does not guarantee the truth of a theory. Despite their inability to secure the truth of explanations in the sciences, predictions still play a crucial role in Popper's falsificationism. On Popper's view, in order for scientists to have warrant to accept a theory, the theory has to pass the most difficult tests possible. If the theory fails to make the appropriate predictions under test conditions, then grounds emerge upon which scientists ought to consider its rejection. The *failure* of a theory to deliver accurate predictions implies, in certain circumstances, its falsification. Although we can never know which theories are true, we can know, over time and after a considerable number of experiments, which theories are false.[5]

Popper's Attempt to Salvage Scientific Realism

Given the aforementioned arguments against even the possibility of providing sufficient justification for theories in science, how can one maintain an adherence to any version of realism? Popper thought it was possible. Sometimes, Popper argued as if, through the process of conjecture and refutation, scientists could more and more closely *approximate* the truth about "what's really out there." Popper wrote: "While we cannot ever have sufficiently good arguments in the empirical sciences for claiming that we have actually reached the truth, we can have strong and reasonably good arguments for claiming that we may have made progress towards the truth" (1972: 58). While inherently elusive, truth still played, for Popper, an important and directive role in science: "our critical discussions of theories are dominated by the idea of finding a true (and powerful) explanatory theory; and we do justify our preferences by an appeal to the idea of truth: truth plays the role of a regulative idea" (1972: 29–30).[6] Popper wanted both to denounce the possibility of knowing when we have reached true explanations of nature and to harbor hope that scientists progress, albeit asymptotically, toward them. The difficulty with this move, however, is that these two views are incompatible.[7] If we renounce the notion that philosophers will ever have in their possession the intellectual tools with which to offer pronouncements on the accuracy of scientific theories, and if we recognize that we will never know for certain that our explanatory conjectures are correct, then how can we say that, as time progresses, scientists are converging, ever so gradually, on the truth about the phenom-

ena and processes of nature?[8] On what possible basis could we make that claim?[9]

Popper endeavored to circumvent *this* problem by introducing *verisimilitude* into his philosophy of science. Rather than calling non-falsified theories true, which he clearly could not do, Popper instead considered these theories as *closer* to the truth, or possessed of greater verisimilitude. Popper wrote: "A theory T1 has less verisimilitude than a theory T2 if and only if (a) their truth contents and falsity contents (or their measures) are comparable, and either (b) the truth content, but not the falsity content, of T1 is smaller than that of T2, or else (c) the truth content of T1 is not greater than that of T2, but its falsity content is greater" (1972: 52). Clearly, in order for Popper to have adopted verisimilitude as a way to judge theories, he must have accepted the basic observation statements of scientists as reasonably unproblematic. How else could he have proposed to ascertain algorithmically the truth-content of theories in terms of the number of corroborated observation statements which they entailed. But if the observations conveyed in these statements are, as Popper elsewhere admitted, theory-laden, and theories are permanently conjectural, then even simple observational reports are not, in the strictest sense, true. They too are fallible. Hence, Popper is still trapped by the logic of his own arguments. The inconsistency latent in his philosophy remains, and realism is left without renewed defense.

Rorty's Critique of Scientific Realism

For at least the last two decades, Richard Rorty (1979; 1988; 1989; 1993) has attempted to demonstrate the impossibility of providing *any* defense for the realism of explanations in the physical sciences. Following Popper, Rorty impugns the philosophical quest for the secured foundations of knowledge and jettisons the affiliated notion that we will ever have in our capacity the means with which to compile true accounts of nature. He differs from Popper, however, in two important respects: (1) the argumentative path he pursues to reach skeptical conclusions regarding foundationalism and the discovery of truth; and (2) the extent to which he pushes the consequences of his epistemic skepticism.

Rorty sees the obsession of philosophers with uncovering the essential, uncontroversial grounds upon which genuine knowledge rests as intimately related with their quest for certainty, for truth. In Rorty's estimation, this quest, which has animated discourse in the West since Plato, has led traditional philosophers to conceive the character of language in the following two ways. First, the quest for truth has persuaded philosophers since Aristotle to consider language as representational, as accurately reproducing nature. The test for the adequacy of a language is the degree to which it corresponds to, or, using Rorty's term, "mirrors" the physical world (1979: 3). Second, the quest for truth has encouraged philosophers to seek the development of a neutral language, one into which scientists would translate competing scientific theories and from which scientists could make assessments of their theories' respective truth content. Such a neutral language, were it to live up to its name, would be both atemporal and complete, implying "that human activity (and inquiry, the search for

knowledge, in particular) takes place within a framework which can be isolated prior to the conclusion of inquiry—a set of presuppositions discoverable apriori" (1979: 8).

Rorty insists that the conceptualization of language as both representational and neutral has ceased profiting philosophy; in fact, it has done damage. Debate on these issues has reached an argumentative impasse, a polemical cul-de-sac in which the defenders of the traditional aims of philosophy are pitted against their ever-widening array of opponents. Rorty sees this impasse, not as an occasion to rehash tired arguments, but as an opportunity to change radically the contours of the debate. They must be changed, Rorty argues, because traditional philosophers demand more from language than it can provide. First, by conceiving language as representational, philosophers have run into the problem of determining how, precisely, the current vocabulary employed by scientists corresponds to nature. In order to resolve this dilemma, philosophers somehow have to transcend the language of science and ascertain the extent to which it captures reality, a daunting task if ever there were one. And second, by demanding a permanent neutral language with which to represent nature traditional philosophers aspire to the impossible: they want to unearth the foundations of inquiry before its closure. Philosophers want to know *now* where the future investigation and debate of scientists will lead in order to be able to regulate and make pronouncements regarding the truth of their findings. Seen this way, the desire for a neutral language seems to defeat the very purpose of inquiry. If philosophers knew a way to determine the truth of a theory, the degree to which it mirrors nature, then the empirical investigations on the part of scientists would be, at best, redundant. The scientific enterprise would collapse to mere deduction. Accordingly, Rorty considers the demand for a neutral language ill-wrought: "There is no such thing as the 'language of a unified science.' We have not got a language which will serve as a permanent neutral matrix for formulating all good explanatory hypotheses, and we have not the foggiest notion of how to get one" (1979: 348–349).

On Rorty's view, then, the traditional philosophical paradigm no longer stands up: philosophers cannot demonstrate the degree to which the language of science represents nature, and they cannot fashion a neutral linguistic grid which would render scientific interchange fully commensurate. In order to circumvent the present impasse, therefore, Rorty urges philosophers to adopt a reconfigured understanding of language, one informed by contemporary post-empiricist and pragmatic alternatives. Following the likes of Quine, Kuhn, Sellars, Davidson, Dewey, and the latter Wittgenstein, Rorty depicts language as holistic rather than representative, as contingent and changing rather than atemporal and permanently fixed. Rorty urges philosophers to realize that the words employed by scientists to describe nature do not correspond without mediation to what is out there, but instead cohere only with *other descriptive words*. As Rorty writes, the difference between the traditional view of the language of science as representing nature and his view is the "difference between saying that we are successfully representing according to nature's own conventions of representation and saying that we are successfully representing according to our own"

(1979: 298). In addition, because philosophers cannot defend the representative character of language, they must, according to Rorty, give up the idea that they can uncover a neutral linguistic framework which would render scientific dialogue commensurable; the language of science, like all languages, is inexorably contingent and incomplete.

Rorty's characterization of language severely compromises the argument for the realism of scientific explanations. Traditional philosophers tie the argument for scientific realism to the case for the correspondence of language to nature. Rorty has challenged the philosophical case for correspondence, maintaining that the language of science is neither representative nor neutral but rather holistic and contingent. While the burden rests with traditional philosopher to provide evidence for correspondence, Rorty insists that the limits of language render their undertaking futile. Nature cannot serve, in any unmediated sense, as an extrinsic touchstone against which to assess the relative merits of competing explanations and descriptions of nature. And when defenders of realism point to the capacity of theories in the natural sciences to anticipate observations and experimental results, Rorty pushes them to indicate precisely why this ability argues in their favor. Since corroborated predictions cannot establish the degree to which a theory captures nature, it is not clear, according to Rorty, why they should supply evidence for realism: "What is so special about prediction and control? Why should we think explanations offered for this purpose are the 'best' explanations" (1988: 66)?

Instead, Rorty adopts a pragmatic approach to explanation in the natural sciences. Since scientists lack uninhibited observational access to nature, Rorty insists that the only standards to which scientists can appeal are those *internal to the language that they share*. Maintains Rorty:

> *to say that . . . knowledge can only be judged by the standards of the inquirers of our own day is not to say that [scientific] knowledge is less noble or important, or more cut off from the world than we had thought. It is merely to say that nothing counts as justification unless by reference to what we already accept, and that there is no way to get outside our beliefs and our language so as to find some test other than coherence. (1979: 178)[10]*

Scientific knowledge is not a matter of deep correspondence with the previously occluded workings of nature. Rather, what counts as scientific knowledge is the product of a consensus among the community of scientists, working today, who share a common body of information, similar values, and a strong sense of solidarity in their investigative enterprise (1993: 452–453). Their approbative agreement, at any particular time, simply highlights their contingent and potentially revisable affirmation of select observations or explanations. It implies nothing deeper. Scientists cannot make the leap from their contextual concurrence to the transhistorical correspondence of their descriptions to nature. As Rorty writes, "The fact that Newton's vocabulary lets us predict the world more easily than Aristotle's does not mean that the world speaks Newtonian" (1989: 6). With its linkage to nature severed, science simply cannot claim to be anything more than an historically rooted and unfinished amalgam of descriptions which we in the Western world find convenient and which, in the end, help us to cope.

Toward a Reconfigured Defense of Scientific Realism

If, with Rorty, we link the case for realism to the ability of philosophers to demonstrate the correspondence of scientific descriptions and explanations to the phenomena and processes of nature, then, as we have clearly seen, the argument for realism is finished. But as we have also seen, this concession does not grant as much as it might first appear. For as Rorty himself indicates, the notion that philosophers could have insights about nature in anticipation of empirical inquiry would foreclose the need for science. By his own standards, Rorty demands something from philosophers that he knows perfectly well they cannot produce. But consider: if we grant Rorty's critique of the demand for foundations, for a philosophical revelation of the mechanism by which we can apprehend the truth about nature, does it necessarily follow that we cannot in any way defend scientific realism?

The answer, I think, is no. In a very crucial sense, Rorty misunderstands what realism is, and, accordingly, how appropriately to argue its case. Scientific realism represents a metaphysics, an overarching stand which we adopt or reject with regard to the adequacy of our explanations and, more broadly, to the adequacy of our intellects to the task of understanding our physical environment. Like any metaphysics, it is a position which can neither be proven nor disproven; it can, however, be defended. To this end I will proceed as follows. First, despite Rorty's critique of the representativeness and neutrality of language, I will argue that scientists have informational and empirical resources which enable them to compare and assess competing theories. Then, against the insuperability of theory-laden observations, I will suggest that, under appropriate conditions, scientists can test their theories in ways which are not circular. Granted, all observations are influenced by the theories accepted by the scientific community. But as long as the instruments used to test new theories do not rely on the accuracy of these theories in order to operate, and as long as scientists hostile to the success of these theories assent to the means by which their predictions are evaluated, then the tests employed by scientists render constructive and progressive results. Finally, I will bring these considerations to bear on the question of scientific realism. On the one hand, I shall insist that philosophers were right to reject predictions as the means by which to *verify* the truth of scientific theories. On the other hand, I will argue that, when the aforementioned conditions are met, philosophers cannot, like Rorty, simply dismiss the capacity of select theories in the natural sciences to anticipate with uncanny accuracy novel observations and experimental results, especially at a rate better than random. In the inevitable absence of proof, this capacity strongly supports scientific realism because, as far as I am aware, opposing philosophers are at a loss to furnish *any* persuasive reason why *mere descriptions* should foreshadow future occurrences or observations, particularly with the accuracy that theories in the natural sciences can. In the end, the evidence shows that, while we will never know to what extent, theories in the natural sciences do indeed permit scientists some contact with, and some understanding of, the physical world.

Scientific Realism as a Metaphysics

Let me back up and develop more fully the initial assertion I made above: to sanction the realism of scientific descriptions and explanations is to adopt a *metaphysical*, not an *empirical* position. Adherence to scientific realism resembles faith in the existence of God more than the approbation of, say, a theory of gravity. Although scientists cannot prove the latter, they can marshal data which would encourage its falsification, its rejection by the investigative community. Much like religious belief, however, *realism is neither provable nor disconfirmable.* Philosophers cannot construct an argument or enlist evidence sufficient to justify or falsify a metaphysics. This is not meant to imply that argument either way is pointless; quite the contrary. Once one grants that scientific realism is a matter of metaphysics and not of empiricism, the role philosophy can play on its behalf changes. Philosophers themselves have demonstrated time and time again their inability to illuminate the epistemic foundations which would facilitate the assessment of the truth content of scientific theories. Philosophers cannot ground realism, but they can organize empirical evidence in such a way as to make its case as strong as possible. No less a philosopher than Isaiah Berlin writes:

> *Philosophy ... is not an empirical study: not the critical examination of what exists or has existed or will exist — this is dealt with by commonsense knowledge and belief, and the methods of the natural sciences. Nor is it a kind of formal deduction as mathematics or logic is. Its subject matter is to a large degree not the items of*

experience, but the ways in which they are viewed, the permanent or semi-permanent categories in terms of which experience is conceived and classified. (1978 [1950]: 9).

As I see it, then, the task is not to prove scientific realism: this is beyond the purview of philosophy. Instead, the task is to fashion a coherent and persuasive argument in its favor, one which draws from empirical data where appropriate and simultaneously raises questions that Rorty's critique cannot adequately answer.

Resources for Inter-theoretic Comparison

With our task clarified, we must now confront the following dilemma: if we grant Rorty's characterization of language as holistic and contingent, as opposed to representative and neutral, how can scientists who advance radically divergent theories communicate clearly with one another and, in the process, adjudicate between their rival approaches? At first this may seem a trivial concern. What would inhibit the ability of scientists to intellectually interact? Why should they encounter difficulty assessing the relative merits of theories which say markedly different things about the physical world? We can see precisely how communication and adjudication become problematic when we push the implications of Rorty's characterization of language to their logical conclusions. With all post-empiricist philosophers, Rorty maintains that scientists do not have unmediated access to nature. Language is the medium by which scientists understand and explain the phenomena and processes which predominate in the universe. But since their vocabulary derives

from theories handed down historically, and because, as we have seen, all theories are conjectural, scientists necessarily analyze nature through the filter of conceptual categories which may, in the future, turn out to be misguided. Further, because language does not permit transparent access to the physical world, and because competing explanations are not fully commensurable, scientists do not simply overlay newly accepted theories on a permanently fixed stratum of nature, as philosophers of science previously thought. As Thomas Kuhn, an intellectual hero of Rorty's once wrote: "what occurs during a scientific revolution is not fully reducible to a reinterpretation of individual and stable data" (1970 [1962]: 121). On this view, one shared by Rorty, scientists who press competing yet theoretically and empirically inconsistent claims about nature may at times lack sufficient resources for constructive deliberation. But is this really the case?

Despite the failure of the foundationalist project, their lack of uninhibited access to nature, and the absence of a neutral linguistic framework which would enable them to translate and assess competing theories, I would argue that scientists still possess intellectual and empirical resources with which they can communicate and ultimately evaluate rival—though not fully commensurate—explanations. These resources are of four types. First, as members of linguistic communities of considerable size, scientists share a common catalogue of basic vocabulary words, words which designate colors, shapes, sounds, or accepted appellations of objects or relationships. To be clear, these words do not comprise a neutral observation language. Instead, they represent the fruit of a transgenerational consensus, one which has permitted human beings to interact productively with their environment. Second, as members of professional communities, scientists share similar educational backgrounds. Over the years, scientists have standardized the presentation of information in their survey classes in the physical sciences. These courses lay out the important theories, concepts, and methods progressively and cumulatively in order to provide students with a basic framework with which to address their future research problems. Third, scientists work with a set of instruments which extend the range of their senses and facilitate the accumulation of precise measures of physical phenomena. Certainly, theories have informed the development of these instruments: optical theories permitted inventors to construct telescopes, theories of electromagnetism underwrite the functioning of computers, and so on. Such theories, as we know, are inherently conjectural. Nevertheless, they have, over the course of history, earned the approbation of scientists. While this consensual approbation is not a guarantee of their truth, no post-modern philosopher has put forward plausible arguments against the effectiveness of telescopes, the calculative powers of computers, or the array of other equipment scientists use to refine their collection and processing of data and test for the viability of competing theories. Fourth and finally, scientists ascribe, whether implicitly or explicitly, to an overarching rationality, a logic which does not determine their theory selection, but which does frame the debate within which they adjudicate between competing explanations of physical phenomena. As the philosophers Kuhn and Quine both indicate, a

history of trials and errors, successes and false starts, breakthroughs and loggerheads has sharpened the commitment of scientists to a network of overriding but sometimes competing values, values such as: accuracy, simplicity, scope, fruitfulness, consistency, conservatism, refutability, and modesty.[12] While not serving as ends in themselves, these values do serve as time-tried indices to the predictive and explanatory potential of theories under consideration. Sure, many post-empiricist and post-modern philosophers have challenged the notion that there is such a cross-historical rationality which orients scientific investigations, insisting that such a stance speaks of either a transcendentalism or an essentialism. But, as McMullin indicates, one does not have to adopt either of these philosophically problematic alternatives in order to see that, through the development and maturation of the sciences, certain methods and values have risen to the fore as the building blocks of hypotheses and explanations. Of course, post-empiricist caveats regarding the transition by scientists to new theories or paradigms still hold: a meta-rationality might guide theory development, but it does not guarantee that scientists will apply their various and sometimes competing values in similar fashions, nor does it guarantee that they will immediately reject futile approaches. Nevertheless, as McMullin concludes, "one can understand the abandonment of . . . alternatives in terms of fairly specific reasons, reasons which would have counted . . . then as well as now", reasons which draw heavily from the desire of scientists to provide heuristically potent explanations for observed phenomena (1988: 35).[13]

Constructive Comparisons Despite Theory-Laden Observations

While a basic vocabulary, an educational history, common instrumentation, and a commitment to an overarching rationality all furnish scientists with resources to resolve theoretical disputes, they still do not permit scientists unmediated access to nature. Without this access, can these resources, which allow scientists to communicate in times of crisis, also help them escape the problem of theory-laden observations? Philosophers from Popper through Rorty have shown that the data scientists use to assess competing explanations are themselves shaped by theories, theories which are conjectural and therefore potentially falsifiable. If scientists cannot secure the truth of the theories which "impregnate" their observations, aren't they guilty of continually begging the question, of making unwarranted assumptions about the reliability of their data in order to carry on with their investigations? To a degree, they are. Scientists cannot avoid entirely the fact that they interpret their observations and construct their measures using categories and concepts drawn from generations of theoretical development. However, when the impact of theories on observations is properly understood, an avenue opens up for the constructive testing of theories in the physical sciences, an avenue which does not provide unfiltered access to nature, but which does render the evaluative efforts of scientists constructive rather than circular.

Given the information and training which scientists share, those who propose new and potentially revolutionary explanations of physical phenomena, ones which would imply a radical transformation of the way they view their world, must try to persuade their colleagues *on terms the latter would accept*. That is, scientists who press for the acceptance of novel explanations must marshal evidence that would call the theory with which they are competing into question. But this evidence should be persuasive, not just to the revolutionary scientists, but also to the traditional ones, those holding out hope that the older, more developed theory will eventually prevail. To make this evidence persuasive, revolutionary scientists must perform two tasks. First, they must determine where the theories in question observationally conflict. But second, and more importantly, they must test these rival theories in ways that appeal to information and instrumentation to which both they and their traditional counterparts consent. Consider the initial assessment of Einstein's work. Einstein's general theory of relativity entailed a deep change in the scientific picture of the universe. At the time when Einstein's ideas were still inchoate, the scientific community wholeheartedly endorsed the Newtonian world-view: they depicted the universe as infinite in all directions; they saw time as distinct from space; they took both space and time to be absolute. Einstein instead told of a universe that was finite but unbounded, in which space and time together comprised a four dimensional continuum, and where both space and time were relative to the observer, not absolute. In the article where he initially presented his more general account of relativity, Einstein held that his theory entailed and explained two observations which were susceptible to immediate corroboration: (1) the bending of stellar light moving through the gravitational field of the sun; and (2) the slight shift detected in the orbit of Mercury upon its perihelion (Pagels 1982: 30).[14] Responding to his first suggestion, scientists tested for the bending of light through the sun's gravitational field in 1919, when Arthur Eddington photographed the stars visible at the edges of the sun during a total eclipse. He then compared this photograph with one taken of the same area in space six months later, after the sun had shifted in the horizon. The results of the comparison supported Einstein's theory: the position of the stars altered according to the specifications of Einstein's relativistic equations (Pagels 1982: 33). Taking up his second recommendation, scientists returned to data collected on the shift in the orbit of Mercury by Urbain Le Verrier nearly fifty years earlier. Using Newton's laws of gravity, Le Verrier had tabulated the influence of the other planets in an attempt to account for the orbital deviation of Mercury. He was unsuccessful; there was a one percent discrepancy between his calculations and his astronomical observations. Before Einstein published his theories of relativity, scientists speculated that Le Verrier had overlooked some factor which would have made up the difference, such as orbiting dust particles or perhaps the oblong shape of the sun. Einstein's theory rendered such speculation inconsequential: the "general theory of relativity predicted small differences from Newton's law of gravity and gave a number of 43 seconds of arc per century—precisely the discrepancy Le Verrier had found" (Pagels 1982: 36). [15]

Note several points. First, supporters of Einstein were versed in the language of Newtonian physics, so few if any communicative impediments existed between the rival camps. Second, in each instance, even those scientists who initially rebuffed Einstein's challenge to Newtonian physics could understand the tests and acknowledge their validity. Both the test for the bending of light rays and the test regarding the orbit of Mercury relied on instruments (telescopes, cameras, and simple calculators) which had earned acceptance by all the members of the scientific community, irrespective of their positions regarding the heuristic potential of the theories of relativity. Third, and most importantly, because supporters of Einstein drew from information and instrumentation upon which all scientists agreed, *their tests of the general theory of relativity evaded circularity.* In other words, the theories which influenced the development of telescopes, cameras, and simple calculators, the instruments initially employed by scientists in their evaluation of relativity, did not depend on, nor were they necessarily related to, the explanations proposed by Einstein. Since the theories which informed these tests were conceptually and logically independent of relativity, they served as conservative and constructive indices of its success. The tests were conservative because they challenged relativity in a hostile environment, on terms which were more closely allied to Newton's physics. The tests were constructive because they enabled scientists to avoid begging the question: since the tests were not tied to relativity, scientists avoided committing ahead of time, one way or the other, to the validity of Einstein's theories. As a result, the results contributed to knowledge; they did more than simply reinforce a tautology.[16]

Completing the Defense: Novel Predictions and the Case for Scientific Realism

Remember, Rorty insists on viewing theoretical developments in science pragmatically because scientists have no means to gauge the representativeness of their vocabulary and because they lack a neutral language within which to translate their divergent explanations and observations. On his view, scientists have no deep rationale for shifting their allegiance from one body of theories to another; they find newer ways of looking at nature more interesting or perhaps more convenient, but nature never demands a change. He concludes:

> *We did not decide on the basis of some telescopic observations, or on the basis of anything else, that the earth was not the center of the universe, that macroscopic behavior could be explained on the basis of microstructural motion, and that prediction and control should be the principle aim of scientific theorizing. Rather, after a hundred years of inconclusive muddle, the Europeans found themselves speaking in a way which took these interlocking theses for granted. Cultural change of this magnitude does not result from applying criteria. (1989: 6)*

The argument presented in this paper suggests that Rorty simply misunderstands the way scientists work. Granted, scientists do not have a decision procedure which would direct them conclusively to the appropriate theory. But no post-positivist philosopher, Popper included, claims that they do. In one way or another, all have realized the futility of the quest for absolute truth, and with it the quest for a secure cannon of induction. Now, Popper was guilty of simplifying the task

scientists face; at times, he urged scientists to drop too quickly those theories which met with apparent empirical disconfirmation. Philosophers such as Kuhn and Quine have admonished him for this, arguing convincingly that scientists apply values which guide, but never determine, the selection of theories. In fact, these values often yield contradictory advice. Little by little, though, they help scientists make sense of the world; without these values, scientists would be cast adrift, with no shore to reach, but also without a point of origin, a shared port to call home. In addition, this paper suggests that scientists who disagree profoundly regarding the merits of a set of theories have at their disposal an array of informational and instrumental resources. Scientists share technical instruction, specialized vocabularies, equipment, and ideational commitments, all of which help them navigate crises in communication and challenges to their traditional views of nature. These resources enable science to move ahead because they provide a stringent testing ground for novel theories. In order to convince doubters, scientists who back new, potentially revolutionary theories need to devise tests which appeal to the information and instrumentation endorsed by the full community of investigators, not just those members on the cutting-edge. If these theories pass such scrutiny, not only will cutting-edge scientists have indicated where their predecessors fell short, but they will have also triumphed with the cards stacked against them, under conditions set by scientists hostile to their success. As a methodology, this approach to the adjudication of theories overcomes postmodern concerns by drawing exclusively on those theories and observations which all scientists approbate. Despite the inability of philosophers to isolate an empirical language which is either representative or neutral, scientists can still assess competing theories, bit by bit, using the vocabulary and equipment consensually handed down from the past. In the final analysis, as long as scientists do not assume the truth of the theories under examination, and as long as those theories do not influence the bases for observation and experimentation, their efforts lead to progress.

But this progress does not yet entail the realism of explanations in the physical sciences, the principle focus of this paper. For this, we need to return one last time to the predictive capacities of theories in the physical sciences. Earlier, I argued that as scientists became increasingly confident in their ability to explain and predict phenomena in nature, philosophers challenged the foundations upon which the inquiry of scientists rested. Philosophers have repeatedly told us that successful predictions do not imply the truth of scientific theories. Yet, since the collapse of the foundationalist project, postmodern philosophers have not persuasively accommodated the mounting predictive triumphs of the physical sciences. Some, like Rorty, dismiss the problem, scoffing at the suggestion that predictions represent anything special. But I insist they do, provided they are properly understood.

Successful theories lead to predictions, not just of recurrences in nature, but of novel observations. According to Imre Lakatos, a survey of the history of science and a reconstruction of its crucial debates reveal that scientists persistently opt for those theories which not only explain past observations, but which also anticipate new ones (1972

[1970]: 119; see also Davies 1992: 82).[17] These unexpected observations, novel facts as Lakatos terms them, are "improbable in the light of, or even forbidden by" those theories previously sanctioned by the scientific community (1972 [1970]: 116). Examples abound, particularly in modern science. To begin, consider this from Paul Davies: "Newton's law of gravity . . . gives us an accurate account of planetary motion, but it also explains the ocean tides, the shape of the earth, the motion of spacecraft, and much else. Maxwell's electromagnetic theory went far beyond a description of electricity and magnetism, by explaining the nature of light waves and predicting the existence of radio waves" (1992: 92). Second, remember that Einstein's famous equation linking mass and energy correctly anticipated the yield of nuclear reactions and the destructive potential of atomic weaponry. Third, still considering Einstein, recall that the general theory of relativity entailed three specific predictions: the bending of light, the precise orbit of the planet Mercury, and the depreciation of clock speed in increasingly strong gravitational fields.[18] The second prediction referred to data previously collected; it sought to account for an anomaly in Newton's laws of gravity and motion, nothing more. But the first and the third predictions intimated observations not yet witnessed, or, for that matter, even conceived. Because Newton's world-view did not permit rays of light to bend, or clocks to wind down in gravitational fields, no one thought to search for such observations. It was only after Einstein developed his general theory of relativity that these predicted observations, and attempts at their corroboration, took on significance. The general theory of relativity even rendered a novel prediction which Einstein himself did not appreciate right away. In 1922, a Soviet physicist named Alexander Friedmann realized that the solutions to the relativistic equations required the universe to either expand or contract, depending upon its aggregate mass. Still wedded to the elegance and simplicity of a static universe, a vision which traces its roots all the way back to Parmenedes, Einstein insisted that Friedmann had to be wrong. He even went so far as to insert in his equations a "cosmological constant", a term which permitted the solution he desired: a universe which endured without change. Of course, Einstein later admitted that, by toying with his own equations, he committed the biggest blunder of his life (Pagels 1982: 38; see also Jastrow 1978: 24-25). Still, his humbling experience is enlightening. Einstein had constructed equations that entailed solutions with which he did not agree. Yet, the disputed solutions later earned empirical support. In 1925, Edwin Hubble determined, through simple telescopic and spectrographic observation, that the farther other galaxies were in relation to ours, the faster they moved away from us. When laid out mathematically, this relationship, now known as Hubble's Law, corresponded exactly to the demands of Einstein's relativistic equations, when, of course, they were properly solved (Jastrow 1978: 42–47; see also Ferris 1988: 47).

Finally, we should consider Stephen Brush's discussion of the triumph of the big bang theory over the steady state theory as the accepted account of the origin of the universe. In 1931, Georges Lemaître developed the big bang cosmology. He maintained that "the universe might have begun as an infinitely small pinpoint—a singularity, in mathematical terms—at time zero...when space was infinitely curved and all matter and energy was concentrated into a single quantum" (Ferris 1988: 211). On Lemaître's view, this quantum of matter and energy exploded at the beginning of time, resulting in both the dispersal of the galaxies away from each other and the unabated expansion of the universe (Brush 1993: 569-572; Hawking 1988: 46). Seventeen years later, in 1948, Herman Bondi, Thomas Gold, and Fred Hoyle proposed the steady state cosmology, an approach which countered Lemaître's argument that the universe originated from a primordial point of quantum singularity. According to Hawking, the steady state theory stipulated that "as the galaxies moved away from each other, new galaxies were continually forming in the gaps in between, from new matter that was being continually created" (1988: 47). Despite the failure of its authors to articulate the mechanism by which matter was spontaneously generated, most cosmologists initially leaned toward the steady state theory, primarily because it squared well with the accepted age of the universe (Brush 1993: 573). Based upon Hubble's Law, the big bang theory projected the age of the universe to be around two billion years, an impossible result considering that scientists had determined the oldest rocks found on earth were at least 4.5 billion years old (Ferris 1988: 209; Brush 1993: 572). Now, scientists soon revised the data upon which they rendered their calculation of the age of the universe, so the big bang theory averted immediate rejection. Nevertheless, at least for a while, the theory continued to resist testability. Soon after the publication of the steady state theory, Hans Alpher and Robert Herman defended Lemaître's big bang cosmology, arguing that if the latter were true, trace amounts of background radiation should be left over from the hypothesized primordial explosion (Brush 1993: 571). Unfortunately, the problem for the empiricists lay in distinguishing this radiation from other types of energy which continually bombarded the earth (Brush 1993: 578). As time progressed, additional scientists began to advocate the big bang cosmology and search for the requisite confirmatory evidence. Yet the crucial empirical support came completely by accident. Two researchers for Bell Telephone Laboratories, Arno Penzias and Robert Wilson, were testing a microwave detector, trying to fine-tune it for use as a radio telescope. Despite their best efforts, they encountered problems trying to alleviate the background noise their antenna kept attracting. After exhausting all possible mechanical problems, they stumbled across the work of Bob Dickie and Jim Peebles, two cosmologists who were continuing the research on the expansion of the universe begun by Friedmann, Lemaître, Alpher, and Herman. They, too, argued that sufficiently sensitive equipment should, in principle, be able to detect the radiation left over from the big bang. After investigating further, Penzias and Wilson soon realized the propitiousness of what they thought were instrument failures. Their equipment had not malfunctioned; indeed, far from it. Rather, they had hit upon the elusive background radiation sought by the defenders of the big bang cosmology (Brush 1993: 578-582; Hawking 41–42). To be sure, this evidence did not conclusively falsify the steady state theory, but it damaged it sufficiently to swing most support behind the big bang cosmology.

Now, for the purposes of this argument, bear in mind four points. First, the instrumentation employed by Penzias and Wilson to illuminate the residual background radiation permeating the universe had earned the acceptance and approbation of the entire community of scientists, whether or not they endorsed the big bang or the steady state cosmology. Second, the testing conditions were at least partially hostile to the success of the big bang theory. Until the Penzias-Wilson discovery, the steady state cosmology had nearly as many supporters in the scientific community (Brush 1993: 587). Third, neither Penzias nor Wilson were looking to confirm the big bang theory. Because they were actually trying to eliminate background noise so as to conduct telescopic research, their findings, although accidental, provide independent and disinterested support for the hypothesis that the universe originated in a primordial explosion. Finally, the big bang cosmology anticipated the existence of background radiation *in advance of its empirical discovery*. Even more, as scientists refined the theory, most settled around the estimate of 2– 4° K for the radiation left over from the big bang, roughly the temperature of the "noise" discovered by Penzias and Wilson. [19]

I could highlight other instances, drawn both from Einstein's theories of relativity and other seminal contributions in the physical sciences, but I think the point has been made.[20] Certain explanations of physical phenomena have the ability not only to account for observations previously accumulated, but also to anticipate the discovery of novel ones. These anticipatory predictions do more than point researchers in general observational directions; they indicate with stunning precision what scientists *will* find when they run their tests and analyze their results. Of course, one could rely on the standard post-modern objection and argue that the tests which scientists conduct to confirm theoretically anticipated observations are themselves theory-laden. But we have shown this move to lack the punch some attribute to it. Background information always informs the development of equipment and frames scientific analyses. Provided that the theories under examination are independent of the information upon which researchers base their tests, and provided the entire community of scientists can accede to the methods of data accumulation, the assessment of the ability of these theories to anticipate novel facts escapes contamination; again, the tests are progressive, not circular. And because the tests are progressive, those philosophers who challenge the realism of scientific explanations must answer the following question: if theories in the physical sciences are simple descriptions, mere conceptual impositions on nature, why can some of them foresee novel observations, with impeccable accuracy, at a rate better than random?

Philosophers who condemn realism as undemonstrable insist that theories in the physical sciences serve as useful ways of looking at nature, but they do not exhibit any intimate connection with its phenomena and processes. Given what we have previously established, that scientists can evade circularity and constructively test rival theories, if dissenting philosophers were correct in viewing the efforts of scientists as mere descriptions overlaid on an indifferent and opaque universe, then no scientific theory should ever deliver novel predictions with a frequency greater than random. If scientists force theories on a universe which refuses to yield its secrets, then how could these theories anticipate unforeseen observations with any degree of regularity? Occasionally they might get lucky and hit their mark. But not consistently, and certainly not repeatedly. So, the evidence compels us to reject Rorty's post-modern dismissal of scientific realism. To reiterate, the ability of theories in the natural sciences to anticipate new observation does not prove them true. Philosophers must abandon once and for all this ironically unrealistic demand. But this ability, under the conditions discussed above, does make the case against realism decidedly harder, because anti-realists have yet to explain persuasively why certain theories should possess this power. In the absence of such a rebuttal, the only viable alternative is the acceptance of the qualified correspondence of our theories to nature and, accordingly, of a modified version of scientific realism.

Conclusion

This approach to the question of scientific realism incorporates the best of contemporary and traditional philosophy. With the former, it rejects attempts to secure the truth of theories in the natural sciences. With the latter, however, it still sees realism as a possibility. Under the appropriate conditions, the ability of scientific theories to anticipate novel observations provides the evidence necessary to make the case for realism in spite of the absence of an unassailable epistemology. This ability indicates that explanations in the physical sciences are not mere descriptions forced on nature. To be sure, I do not endorse a return to a variant of verificationism or to a correspondence theory of knowledge. Nevertheless, I think it fair to say that the evidence supports some connection, albeit undefined, between scientific explanations and the phenomena and processes predominate in nature.

By defending the realism of explanations in the physical sciences in the absence of secure foundations for knowledge, this paper accomplishes four important tasks. First, it suggests a way to talk about scientific progress without reference to the proximity of our theories to the truth about nature. It is Kuhn who may have phrased it best: "The developmental process [of science] . . . has been an evolution *from* primitive beginnings—a process whose successive stages are characterized by an increasingly detailed and refined understanding of nature. But nothing that has been or will be said makes it a process of evolution *toward* anything" (1970 [1962]: 170–171). In other words, through conjecture and refutation, we do not come closer to the truth about nature, at least not in any sense which lends itself to definition. Instead, through this process, we come to know the way the world *is not*. This realization is important. Despite the fact that scientists cannot prove their explanations true, and despite the fact that they cannot know how closely these explanations approximate the actual phenomena and processes of nature, their theories are not empty of content. When tested under the conditions stipulated in this paper, theories which deliver corroborated novel predictions convey information about nature; they are not mere conceptual impositions. Future scientists must come to terms with the predictive capacities of these theories because they erect conceptual and empirical hurdles

over which more potent theories must ascend. That is to say, in order to attract the allegiance of future scientists, any successor theory has to, at a minimum, account for the predictions generated by previous explanations, describe where and why these explanations fell short, and foreshadow observations unanticipated by and inconsistent with the demands of its rivals.

Second, it points to a bridge by which the traditions of philosophy and science, divergent for so long, could come closer together. In the concluding chapter of his book, *A Brief History of Time,* Stephen Hawking extends a hand to philosophers, inviting their input regarding the importance of twentieth-century physics. But he expresses concern that philosophers, of late, may have moved too far away from science because of its increased complexity. He writes: "philosophers [have] reduced the scope of their inquiries so much that Wittgenstein, the most famous philosopher of this century, said 'The sole remaining task for philosophy is the analysis of language.' What a comedown from the great tradition of philosophy from Aristotle to Kant" (1988: 174-175). If philosophers continue to reject the realism of science, then they cannot very well incorporate the findings of physicists, of chemists, or of biologists in their analyses and arguments. Philosophy without such empirical roots, however, is vain speculation, nothing more. On the other hand, if philosophers were once again to take realism seriously, even given the aforementioned qualifications, then empirical and conversational horizons will open up.

Third, this paper rejects the notion, implicit in post-modern philosophy, that the human intellect is somehow alien to or divorced from nature. Post-modern philosophers make quite clear their hostility to the ability of scientists to uncover, not impose, order in the universe. This hostility derives, in large measure, from the failure of traditional philosophers to unearth the conceptual mechanism by which scientists, and in fact all empirical investigators, could know the truth about the physical world. But we have shown the degree to which the traditional aspiration was misinformed. With realism defended without appeal to foundations, scientific inquiry is open and potentially limitless. It is not arbitrary, coerced on an occluded universe; instead, science is receptive to and consistent with nature, because the human intellect has emerged and developed from its processes. As Paul Davies and John Gribbin write:

> *In place of clodlike particles of matter in a lumbering Newtonian machine we have an interlocking network of information exchange—a holistic, indeterministic, and open system—vibrant with potentialities and bestowed with infinite richness. The human mind is a by-product of this vast informational process, a by-product with the curious capability of being able to understand, at least in part, the principles upon which the process runs. (1992: 308)*

Fourth, and finally, this paper encourages philosophers to engage, with scientists, the larger questions that plague not just specialists, but all of us. By renouncing realism, post-modern philosophers cut off all possibilities of ever coming to a deep understanding of either nature, or our existence. As Rorty insists, *"what matters is our loyalty to other human beings clinging together against the dark, not our hope of getting things right* (qtd. in Bernstein 1983:

203-204; emphasis added). He urges members of Western societies to renounce "the metaphysical impulse," as it is futile, no longer returning dividends on our intellectual investment. But what Rorty and other post-modern thinkers do not apparently realize is that this impulse is not so easily shaken. In a nation as pluralistic as America, poll after poll indicates that more than ninety percent of all respondents believe in the existence of God, hardly the number one would expect after reading the obituaries of religion in post-modern texts (Armstrong 1993: 398; Goldman 1993: A25). Regardless of background, people continue to seek answers, or at least informed responses, to the most vexing of metaphysical problems. And where philosophy has lately turned a deaf ear to these demands, scientists have tried to fill the gap. As Robert Wright notes, "One hallmark of twentieth century science, as it draws to a close, is how much fertile ground it has provided for bona fide theological speculation: speculation about whether the universe is a product of intelligent design, whether the human experience is part of some unfolding purpose, whether we are in any sense meant to be here" (1992: 40). What I have tried to show is that philosophy does not have to be left out. A defense of realism without foundations should enable philosophers, at long last, to come in from the cold.

Endnotes

1. I wish to acknowledge Jeffrey Anderson, Lief Carter, Matthew Coffey, Jan Goggin, Geoffrey Levey, Jacob Levy, James Morone, Cristina

Munõz-Fazakas, Dana Ott, Douglas Rasmussen, Nancy Rosenblum, Matthew Sineone, Luke Swain, Matthew Woods, and Alan Zuckerman for their careful scrutiny of my arguments and their challenging insights, comments, and criticisms.

2. Admittedly, dichotomizing philosophers into two groups concerning the question of the realism of scientific explanations is something of a simplification. Yet I consider the division appropriate. When all is said and done, the crucial difference between realist and antirealist philosophers is that the former believe, somehow, that scientific explanations permit us a glimpse into the workings of nature, whereas the latter, in the absence of evidence to justify the realist faith in the heuristic potency of scientific theories, choose to abandon all pretense to the correspondence or representativeness of explanations in science. This paper, in part, is an attempt to rethink the dispute between realist and anti-realist philosophers and reconfigure a defense of a modified version of realism given post-modern doubts about previous foundational or epistemological justifications of the efforts of scientists.

3. I do not have at my disposal any specific instances of realist rejoinders to Rorty's anti-foundationalism. But, from other sources, I imagine that the typical criticisms would run something like this: Rorty argues that all languages must be viewed holistically, that we are, in a very real sense, wedded to the standards and the structure of the 'language-game' within which

we operate. In order for Rorty to establish this point, however, doesn't he have to engage in a meta-linguistic assessment of all possible languages, thereby stepping *outside* of the particular language he is using? Or, Rorty argues that our scientific knowledge does not provide us with a deep understanding of the "way things really are", yet Rorty relies quite heavily on the psychology of Freud to establish the importance of idiosyncrasies and "blind-impresses" in the determination of what we desire and how we cope with moral contingency. What privileges Freud? Why isn't Habermas, for example, equally as justified in drawing from Piaget and Kohlberg to conclude that the stages in the moral development of children are invariant across post-conventional cultures? While these criticisms are strong, and in my opinion justified, they do not advance the debate an inch, since they are only persuasive to those scholars who already disagree with Rorty anyway. Hence the more engaging, less antagonistic tact of my paper. However, for further examples of this line of criticism, see: Douglas B. Rasmussen, "Quine and Aristotelian Essentialism" *The New Scholasticism* 58(1984):316–335; James F. Harris, Against Relativism: *A Philosophical Defense of Method* (LaSalle, Illinois: Open Court, 1992); and Alan S. Zuckerman, *Doing Political Science: An Introduction to Political Analysis* (Boulder: Westview Press, 1991), particularly his discussion of the revisionist work of Paul Feyerabend, pp. 166-167.

4. It is important to be precise here. Popper is usually considered the last of the positivists, at least by certain social scientists and post-modern philosophers. Popper has long denied these charges, and rightfully so. True, Popper spent a considerable amount of time and type trying to forge a philosophical framework which would demarcate science from non-science (belief or ideology, as he termed it). Yet, Popper never claimed that he was separating truth from fiction. This distinction is key, because the positivists, who actively sought a principle of verification, did retain faith that they could identify true scientific statements. With Hume, Popper condemned verificationism as logically indefensible. He put it as starkly as possible: "(1) There is no method of discovering a scientific theory; (2) There is no method of ascertaining the truth of a scientific hypothesis, i.e., no method of verificationism; (3) There is no method of ascertaining whether a hypothesis is 'probable', or probably true" (1956). As I will discuss, later philosophy of science demonstrates that, oftentimes, the choice between theories is not as clear-cut as Popper makes it seem; falsificationism is insufficient. Nevertheless, Popper is not a positivist. In fact, as I hope I have shown, he ought to be included as one of the most important figures in the twentieth century rejection of philosophical foundationalism, which is why I find his complete absence from Rorty's critique of epistemology in-

explicable, and frankly inexcusable.

5. This is a generous reading of Popper. Imre Lakatos has levied the definitive attack on Popper's sometimes "naive" version of falsification. That is, Popper can be read to endorse the position that the first empirical disconfirmation obliges the scientist to reject the theory under consideration. Lakatos terms this Popper's naive methodological falsificationism. He argues, though, that there are strands of Popper's philosophy of science which can be reconstructed to form the basis of sophisticated methodological falsificationism, an approach to the assessment of scientific hypotheses which sanctions the rejection of a series of theories (what Lakatos terms a research program) only in the presence of a competing series of theories which can account for the observations in question. I will use Lakatos' argument later in the paper, but it was important to stipulate a qualification a this juncture. Suffice to say that a benign reading of Popper helps me avert a lengthy discussion of the debate between he and Lakatos, a debate which has been detailed in other places many times. It is not necessary to do so here, save for this brief footnote. For Lakatos' critique of Popper, see his "Falsification and the Methodology of Scientific Research Programs," in *Criticism and the Growth of Knowledge* (Cambridge, England: Cambridge University Press, 1972 [1970]), pp. 91–196.

6. Popper adds "powerful" as a qualifier in order to distinguish scientific theo-

ries from mere tautologies, the latter of which are true, but trivially so, implying nothing interesting about the physical world.

7. I am reminded here of a passage from an essay by C.S. Lewis in *Mere Christianity* (New York: MacMillan Publishing Company, 1952). In discussion what he calls the "moral law," Lewis tries to defend its objectivity by analogy. He says that "the reason why your idea of New York can be truer than mine is that New York is a real place, existing quite apart from what either of us thinks" (25). Of course, if we do not know where New York is or what it looks like, to compare ideas of the city might appear to some pointless. Similarly, if we do not know in what truth consists, and we have no means by which to secure truth, then to talk of one scientific theory being truer than another is, if anything, hollow.

8. The questions with which I close this paragraph derive from my reconstruction of a Kuhnian criticism of Popper. For the text of his critique, see Kuhn's "Reflections on My Critics," in *Criticism and the Growth of Knowledge*, edited by Imre Lakatos and Alan Musgrave (Cambridge, England: Cambridge University Press, 1972), particularly page 265.

9. While this paper represents an effort to reconfigure a case for a qualified scientific realism in a post-modern intellectual age, I should at least take one shot at practicing scientists, particularly physicists. As I have indicated, Popper was one of the first philosophers to provide arguments demonstrating why efforts to construct a foundational epistemic grid were misguided. Yet, practitioners of the physical sciences tend still to talk as if they have in their grasp true theories, infallibly accurate accounts about the world in which we live. Obviously, this is a throwback, a remainder from times when it was philosophically popular to consider corroborated scientific conjectures true. It also hints at the gulf separating science and philosophy today, a gulf which results from the mathematical complexity of contemporary science, making it inaccessible to even advanced philosophers, and from the narrowness and parochialism of philosophy as a professional discipline today, which has rendered philosophy virtually irrelevant to the vast majority of people. Nevertheless, it is a damaging throwback, because it leads scientists in futile and dangerous directions. Witness, for example, the debates currently in fashion regarding the quest for a "theory of everything," a final theory in physics which would subsume relativity and quantum mechanics (see, for instance, Steven Weinberg's *Dreams of a Final Theory* (Princeton: Princeton University Press, 1993). If contemporary philosophy, most specifically Popper, is at all correct, then the whole idea of nailing down a "theory of everything" is seriously ill-considered and frankly misinformed. As Popper himself argues, the creative powers of human beings renders the universe at all times both open and incomplete, rendering the finalization of inquiry impossible. "Our

universe," according to Popper, "is partially causal, partially probabilistic, and partly open: it is emergent" (1982: 130).

10. Where I have included in brackets the word "scientific", Rorty actually wrote "human". I made the substitution simply because the focus of this paper is scientific realism, not moral or aesthetic realism.

11. To his credit, Popper makes much the same argument. See his essay entitled "Two Faces of Common Sense" in *Objective Knowledge: An Evolutionary Approach (Oxford: Oxford University Press*, 1972), pp. 38.

12. I have simply combined the observations of Kuhn and Quine here. Kuhn lists accuracy, simplicity, scope, simplicity, and fruitfulness as the values which guide without determining theory choice in the physical sciences. See his essay, "Objectivity, Value Judgment, and Theory Choice," in T*he Essential Tension* (Chicago: University of Chicago Press, 1977), p. 331. Quine cites five virtues which he claims count toward the plausibility of scientific hypotheses. They are: conservatism, generality, simplicity, refutability, modesty. See his and J.S. Ullian's The *Web of Belief* (New York: Random House, 1970), p. 42–53.

13. Despite rhetoric which would imply otherwise, Kuhn, in reality, would agree that scientists on both sides of a revolutionary division share some common ground, some resources with which to debate and persuade one another. Even he writes:

Though they have no direct access to it, the stimuli to which participants in a communication breakdown respond are, under pain of solipsism, the same. So is their general neural apparatus, however different the programming. Furthermore, except in a small, if all important, area of experience, the programming must be the same, for the [scientists] involved share a history (except the immediate past), a language, an everyday world, and most of a scientific one. Given what they share, they can find out much about how they differ. (1972 [1970]: 276-277)

14. Einstein actually proposed a third test for the general theory of relativity: he suggested that clocks should run slower when caught in a gravitational field. So, if scientists were to place one clock in a "normal" gravitational field, and one in a stronger field, the latter should read an earlier time than the former. While this test does not make appeal to either information or instrumentation which the unpersuaded would find dubious, scientists did not yet have the technical capacities to pull it off. They could not generate a gravitational field strong enough to produce markedly divergent readings, nor did they have clocks precise enough to record the time differential accurately. Despite the added technological demands, I do not consider Einstein's third recommendation counter to the analysis laid out in the text. The basic mechanism of clocks did not, nor do they now, depend on Einstein's theories of relativity for their operation. Further, sup-

porters and opponents of Einstein both understood and approved of clocks. Of course, once the technology developed, Einstein was shown to be correct yet again (Pagels 1982: 36–37).

15. Other more sophisticated tests have been performed on the theories of relativity, all of which have been passed. All I am concerned with, however, are the resources which were available to the scientists right when the theory was first introduced, when Newton's laws still reigned pre-eminent. At that time, defenders of the theories of relativity sought tests which would persuade their opponents—tests which appealed to information and instruments endorsed by the full community, not just by the supporters of Einstein.

16. In his book *Doing Political Science* (Boulder: Westview Press, 1991), Alan Zuckerman makes a similar point. Citing Harold Brown, he writes: "Testing would be circular if what we observed were wholly determined by the theories under test . . . Observation always involves an interaction with an independent physical world that plays a crucial role in determining what we can observe in a given set of circumstances, Thus, even the most theory-laden of observations can surprise us" (qtd in Zuckerman 1991:4). Both Brown and Zuckerman should have noted that observations cannot be influenced, or impregnated, with the theory under consideration. The fact that observations are theory-laden does not necessarily render testing circular. Tests are only circular if they presume

the truth of the theory they are designed to assess, and this theory somehow shapes the observations or experiments upon which scientists base their decisions.

17. In fact, for Lakatos, this criterion—that theories anticipate novel facts—is the crucial element which distinguishes scientific from non-scientific explanations, and, ultimately, progressive from degenerative problemshifts.

18. So as not to cause confusion, I mentioned two of these tests previously in the body of the paper; I discussed the third in a footnote.

19. Penzias and Wilson's findings have been verified quite recently. Just last year, the Cosmic Background Explorer satellite sent back data which indicated that the background radiation in the universe conformed to the specifications of the big bang theory. The satellite determined that the background radiation was uniform in all directions, that the frequency distribution of the radiation conformed to Plank's curve, and that the precise estimate of residual tempature of the universe is 2.726° K. For the full discussion, and the other major findings of the Cosmic Background Explorer Satellite, see "Goals Achieved, Satellite Retired," *The New York Times*, 24 December 1993, A14.

20. The list does go on. However, I should highlight one other recent corroboration of a novel prediction. It involves an analysis of gamma-ray explosions deep in space. Researchers demonstrated that the dimmer these bursts of

gamma radiation are, the longer they last. This finding again confirms predictions derived from the general theory of relativity (see John Noble Wilford, "Gamma-Ray Finding Bolsters Einstein Theory, Report Says," The *New York Times*, 16 January 1994, I, p. 21).

Bibliography

Armstrong, Karen. 1993. *A History of God*. New York: Alfred A. Knoph, Inc.

Berlin, Isaiah. 1981 [1950]. *Concepts and Categories: Philosophical Essays*. New York: Penguin Books.

Bernstein, Richard J. 1983. *Beyond Objectivism and Relativism: Science, Hermeneutics, and Praxis*. Philadelphia: University of Pennsylvania Press.

Bronowski, Jacob. 1973. *The Ascent of Man*. Boston: Little, Brown and Company.

Brush, Stephen G. 1993. "Prediction and Theory Evaluation: Cosmic Microwaves and the Revival of the Big Bang." *Perspectives on Science* 1: 565-602.

Camus, Albert. 1991 [1955]. *The Myth of Sisyphus and Other Essays*. Translated by Justin O'Brien. New York: Vintage International.

Davies, Paul. 1992. *The Mind of God: The Scientific Basis for a Rational World*. New York: Simon and Shuster.

Davies, Paul and John Gribbin. 1992. *The Matter Myth: Dramatic Discoveries That Challenge Our Understanding of Physical Reality*. New York: Simon and Schuster.

Ferris, Timothy. 1988. *Coming of Age in the Milky Way*. New York: William Morrow and Company, Inc.

Goldman, Ari L. 17 July 1993. "Religion Notes." *The New York Times*. A25.

Harris, James F. 1992. *Against Relativism: A Philosophical Defense of Method*. LaSalle, Illinois: Open Court.

Hansen, Norwood Russell. 1965 [1958]. *Patterns of Discovery*. London: Cambridge University Press.

Hawking, Stephen. 1988. *A Brief History of Time*. New York: Bantam Books.

Hume, David. 1952 [1748]. "An Enquiry Concerning Human Understanding." in Robert M. Hutchins, ed. *Great Books of the Western World*. Volume 35. Chicago: Encyclopædia Britannica, Inc.

Jastrow, Robert. 1978. *God and the Astronomers*. New York: W.W. Norton and Company.

Klepp, L.S. 2 December 1990. "Richard Rorty Says, Create Thyself—and Don't Look to Philosophy for the Answers." *The New York Times Magazine*. 57: 111–122.

Kuhn, Thomas S. 1970 [1962]. The *Structure of Scientific Revolutions*. Chicago: The University of Chicago Press.

Kuhn, Thomas S. 1972 [1970]. "Reflections on My Critics." in Imre Lakatos and Alan Musgrave, eds. Criticism and the Growth of Knowledge. Cambridge, England: Cambridge University Press.

Kuhn, Thomas S. 1977. The *Essential Tension: Selected Studies in Scientific Tradition and Change*. Chicago: The University of Chicago Press.

Lakatos, Imre. 1972 [1970]. "Falsification and the Methodology of Scientific Research Programmes." in Imre Lakatos and Alan Musgrave, eds. *Criticism and the Growth of Knowledge*. Cambridge, England: Cambridge University Press.

Laudan, Larry. 1990. *Science and Relativism: Some Key Controversies in the Philosophy of Science.* Chicago: The University of Chicago Press.

Lewis, C.S. 1952. *Mere Christianity.* New York: MacMillan Publishing Company.

McMullin, Ernan. 1988. "The Shaping of Scientific Rationality: Construction and Constraint." in Ernan McMullin, ed. *Construction and Constraint.* Notre Dame: University of Notre Dame Press.

Pagels, Heinz R. 1982. *The Cosmic Code.* New York: Bantam Books.

Popper, Karl R. 1966 [1962]. *The Open Society and Its Enemies: The Spell of Plato.* Volume 1. Princeton: Princeton University Press.

Popper, Karl R. 1972. *Objective Knowledge: An Evolutionary Approach.* Oxford: Clarendon Press.

Popper, Karl R. 1982. The Open Universe: An Argument for Indeterminism. London: Routledge & Keegan Paul.

Popper, Karl R. 1983. *Realism and the Aim of Science.* Totowa, New Jersey: Rowman and Littlefield.

Prosch, Harry. 1964. *The Genesis of Twentieth Century Philosophy: The Evolution of Thought from Copernicus to the Present.* New York: Apollo Editions.

Quine, W.V. 1992 [1990]. *Pursuit of Truth.* Cambridge, Massachusetts: Harvard University Press.

Quine, W.V. 1993. "In Praise of Observation Statements." *The Journal of Philosophy.* 90: 107— 116.

Quine, W.V. amd J.S. Ullian. 1970. *The Web of Belief.* New York: Random House.

Randall, Jr. John H. 1960. *Aristotle.* New York: Columbia University Press.

Rasmussen, Douglas B. 1984. "*Quine and Aristotelian Essentialism.*" The New Scholasticism.58:316–335.

Rorty, Richard. 1979. P*hilosophy and the Mirror of Nature.* Princeton: Princeton University Press.

Rorty, Richard. 1988. "Is Natural Science a Natural Kind?" in Ernan McMullin, ed.*Construction and Constraint.* Notre Dame: University of Notre Dame Press.

Rorty, Richard. 1989. *Contingency, Irony, and Solidarity.* Cambridge: Cambridge University Press.

Rorty, Richard. 1993. "Putnam and the Relativist Menace." *The Journal of Philosophy.* 90:443–461.

Smith, Vincent. 1965. S*cience and Philosophy.* Milwaukee: Bruce Publishing Company.

Sullivan, Roger J. 1989. Immanuel *Kant's Moral Theory.* Cambridge, England: Cambridge University Press.

Wilford, John Noble. 16 January 1994. "Gamma-Ray Finding Bolsters Einstein Theory, Report Says." *The New York Times.* I, 21.

Wright, Robert. 28 December 1992."Science, God, and Man." *Time* 140: 38-46.

Zuckerman, Alan S. 1991. *Doing Political Science.* Boulder: Westview Press.

42

Paul Davies
Is There a
Blueprint?

Optimists and Pessimists

Most scientists who work on fundamental problems are deeply awed by the subtlety and beauty of nature. But not all of them arrive at the same interpretation of nature. While some are inspired to believe that there must be a meaning behind existence, others regard the universe as utterly pointless.

Science itself cannot reveal whether there is a meaning to life and the universe, but scientific paradigms can exercise a strong influence on prevailing thought. In this book I have sketched the story of a new, emerging paradigm that promises to radically transform the way we think about the universe and our own place within it. I am convinced that the new paradigm paints a much more optimistic picture for those who seek a meaning to existence. Doubtless there will still be pessimists who will find nothing in the new developments to alter their belief in the pointlessness of the universe, but they must at least acknowledge that the new way of thinking about the world is more cheerful.

The theme I have been presenting is that science has been dominated for several centuries by the Newtonian paradigm which treats the universe as a mechanism, ultimately reducible to the behaviour of individual particles under the control of deterministic forces. According to this view, time is merely a parameter; there is no real change or evolution, only the rearrangement of particles. The laws of thermodynamics reintroduced the notion of flux or change, but the reconciliation of the Newtonian and thermodynamic paradigms led only to the second law, which insists that all change is part of the inexorable decay and degeneration of the cosmos, culminating in a heat death.

The emerging paradigm, by contrast, recognizes that the collective and holistic properties of physical systems can display new and unforeseen modes of behaviour that are not captured by the Newtonian and thermodynamic approaches. There arises the possibility of *self-organization,* in which systems suddenly and spontaneously leap into more elaborate forms. These forms are characterized by greater complexity, by cooperative behaviour and global coherence, by the appearance of spatial patterns and temporal rhythms, and by the general unpredictability of their final forms.

The new states of matter require a new vocabulary, which includes terms like growth and adaptation—concepts more suited to biology then physics or chemistry. There is thus a hint of unification here. Above all, the new paradigm transforms our view of time. Physical systems can display unidirectional change in the direction of *progress* rather than decay. The universe is revealed in a new, more inspiring light, unfolding from its primitive beginnings and progressing step by step to ever more elaborate and complex states.

The Resurgence of Holism

Many non-scientists find both the Newtonian and thermodynamic paradigms profoundly depressing. They use reductionism as a term of abuse. They regard its successes as somehow devaluing nature, and when applied in the life sciences, devaluing themselves. In a recent television debate in which I took part, the audience was invited to express views about science and God. An irate man complained bitterly. 'Scientists claim that when I say to my wife "I love you" that is nothing but one meaningless mound of atoms interacting with another meaningless mound of atoms.' Such despair over the perceived sterility of reductionist thinking has led many people to turn to holism. In this, they have no doubt been greatly encouraged by the recent resurgence of holistic thinking, in sociology, medicine and the physical sciences.

Yet it would be a grave mistake to present reductionism and holism as somehow locked in irreconcilable combat for our allegiance. They are really two complementary rather than conflicting paradigms. There has always been a place for both in properly conducted science, and it is a gross simplification to regard either of them as 'right' or 'wrong'.

Those who would appeal to holism must distinguish between two claims. The first is the statement that as matter and energy reach higher, more complex, states so new qualities *emerge* that can never be embraced by a lower-level description. Often cited are life and consciousness, which are simply meaningless at the level of, say, atoms.

Examples of this sort seem to be, quite simply, incontrovertible facts of existence.

Holism in this form can only be rejected by denying the reality of the higher-level qualities, e.g. by claiming that consciousness does not really exist, or by denying the meaningfulness of higher-level concepts, such as a biological organism. Since I believe that it is the job of science to explain the world as it appears to us, and since this world includes such entities as bacteria, dogs and humans, with their own distinctive properties, it seems to me at best evasive, at worst fraudulent, to claim that these properties are explained by merely defining them away.

More controversial, however, is the claim that these higher-level qualities demand higher-level laws to explain them. We met this claim, for example, in the suggestion that there exist definite *biotonic* laws for organic systems, and in the ideas of dialectical materialism, which holds that each new level in the development of matter brings its own laws that cannot be reduced to those at lower levels. More generally we saw the possibility of three different types of organizing principles: weak, strong and logical.

The existence of logical organizing principles seems to be fairly well established already, for example, in connection with chaotic systems and Feigenbaum's numbers. Weak organizing principles, in the form of the need to specify various boundary conditions and global constraints are accepted at least as a methodological convenience.

Strong organizing principles—additional laws of physics that refer to the cooperative, collective properties of complex systems, and which cannot be derived from the underlying existing physical laws—remain a challenging but speculative idea. Mysteries such as the origin of life and the progressive nature of evolution encourage the feeling that there are additional principles at work which somehow make it 'easier' for systems to discover complex organized states. But the reductionist methodology of most scientific investigations makes it likely that such principles, if they exist, risk being overlooked in current research.

Predestiny

The new paradigm will drastically alter the way we view the evolution of the universe. In the Newtonian paradigm the universe is a clockwork, a slave of deterministic forces trapped irretrievably on a predetermined pathway to an unalterable fate. The thermodynamic paradigm gives us a universe that has to be started in an unusual state of order, and then degenerates. Its fate is equally inevitable, and uniformly bad.

In both the above pictures *creation* is an instantaneous affair. After the initial event nothing fundamentally new ever comes into existence. In the Newtonian universe atoms merely rearrange themselves, while in the thermodynamic picture the history of the universe is one of *loss,* leading towards dreary featurelessness.

The emerging picture of cosmological development is altogether less gloomy. Creation is not instantaneous; it is an ongoing process. The universe has a life history. Instead of sliding into featurelessness, it rises out of featurelessness, growing rather than dying, developing new structures, processes and potentialities all the time, unfolding like a flower.

The flower analogy suggests the idea of a blueprint—a pre-existing plan or project

which the universe is realizing as it develops. This is Aristotle's ancient teleological picture of the cosmos. Is it to be resurrected by the new paradigm of modern physics?

It is important to appreciate that according to the new paradigm determinism is irrelevant: the universe is intrinsically unpredictable. It has, as it were, a certain 'freedom of choice' that is quite alien to the conventional world view. Circumstances constantly arise in which many possible pathways of development are permitted by the bottom-level laws of physics. Thus there arises an element of novelty and creativity, but also of uncertainty.

This may seem like cosmic anarchy. Some people are happy to leave it that way, to let the universe explore its potentialities unhindered. A more satisfactory picture, however, might be to suppose that the 'choices' occur at critical points (mathematicians would call them singularities in the evolution equations) where new principles are free to come into play, encouraging the development of ever more organized and complex states. In this more *canalized* picture, matter and energy have innate self-organizing tendencies that bring into being new structures and systems with unusual efficiency. Again and again we have seen examples of how organized behaviour has emerged unexpectedly and spontaneously from unpromising beginnings. In physics, chemistry, astronomy, geology, biology, computing—indeed, in every branch of science—the same propensity for self-organization is apparent.

The latter philosophy has been called 'predestinist' by the biologist Robert Shapiro, because it assumes that the present form and arrangement of things is an inevitable outcome of the operation of the laws of nature. I suspect he uses the term pejoratively, and I dislike the mystical flavour it conveys. I prefer the word *predisposition.*

Who are the predestinists?

Generally speaking, they are those who are not prepared to accept that certain key features of the world are simply 'accidents' or quirks of nature. Thus, the existence of living organisms does not surprise a predestinist, who believes that the laws of nature are such that matter will inevitably be led along the road of increasing complexity towards life. In the same vein, the existence of intelligence and conscious beings is also regarded as part of a natural progression that is somehow built into the laws. Nor is it a surprise to a predestinist that life arose on Earth such a short period of time (geologically speaking) after our planet became habitable. It would do so on any other suitable planet. The ambitious programme to search for intelligent life in space, so aptly popularized by Carl Sagan, has a strong predestinist flavour.

Predestiny—or predisposition—must not be confused with predeterminism. It is entirely possible that the properties of matter are such that it does indeed have a propensity to self-organize as far as life, given the right conditions. This is not to say, however, that any particular life form is inevitable. In other words, predeterminism (of the old Newtonian sort) held that everything *in detail* was laid down from time immemorial. Predestiny merely says that nature has a predisposition to progress along the general lines it has. It therefore leaves open the essential unknowability of the future, the possibility for real creativity and endless novelty. In particular it leaves room for human free will.

The belief that the universe has a predisposition to throw up certain forms and structures has become very fashionable among cosmologists, who dislike the idea of special initial conditions. There have been many attempts to argue that something close to the existing large-scale structure of the universe is the inevitable consequence of the laws of physics whatever the initial conditions. The inflationary universe scenario is one such attempt. Another is Penrose's suggestion that the initial state of the universe follows from some as-yet unknown physical principle. A third is the attempt by Hawking and co-workers to construct a mathematical prescription that will fix in a 'natural' way the quantum state of the universe.

There is also a strong element of predestiny, or predisposition, in the recent work on the so-called anthropic principle. Here the emphasis lies not with additional laws or organizing principles, but with the constants of physics. As we saw in Chapter 11, the values adopted by these constants are peculiarly felicitous for the eventual emergence of complex structures, and especially living organisms. Again, there is no compulsion. The constants do not *determine* the subsequent structures, but they do *encourage* their appearance.

Predestiny is only a way of thinking about the world. It is not a scientific theory. It received support, however, from those experiments that show how complexity and organization arise, spontaneously and naturally under a wide range of conditions. I hope the review given in this book will have convinced the reader of the unexpectedly rich possibilities for self-organization that are being discovered in recent research.

There is always the hope that a really spectacular discovery will affirm the predestinist line of thinking. If life were discovered elsewhere in the universe, or created in a test tube, it would provide powerful evidence that there are creative forces at work in matter that encourage it to develop life; not vital forces or metaphysical principles, but qualities of self-organization that are not contained in—or at least do not obviously follow from—our existing laws of physics.

What Does It All Mean?

I should like to finish by returning to the point made at the beginning of this chapter. If one accepts predisposition in nature, what does that have to say about meaning and purpose in the universe?

Many people will find in the predestinist position support for a belief that there is indeed a cosmic blueprint, that the present nature of things, including the existence of human beings, and maybe even each particular human being, is part of a preconceived plan designed by an all-powerful deity. The purpose of the plan and the nature of the end state will obviously remain a matter of personal preference.

Others find this idea as unappealing as determinism. A plan that rigidly legislates the detailed course of human and non-human destiny seems to them a pointless charade. If the end state is part of the design, they ask, why bother with the construction phase at all? An all-powerful deity would be able to simply create the finished product at the outset.

A third point of view is that there is no detailed blueprint, only a set of laws with an inbuilt facility for making interesting things happen. The universe is then free to create itself as it goes along. The general pattern of development is 'predestined', but the details are not. Thus, the existence of intelligent life at some stage is inevitable; it is, so to speak, written into the laws of nature. But man as such is far from preordained.

Critics of predisposition dislike the anthropocentrism to which it seems to lead, but the requirement that the universe merely become self-aware at some stage seems a very weak form of anthropocentrism. Yet the knowledge that our presence in the universe represents a *fundamental* rather than an *incidental* feature of existence offers, I believe, a deep and satisfying basis of human dignity.

In this book I have taken the position that the universe can be understood by the application of the scientific method. While emphasizing the shortcomings of a purely reductionist view of nature, I intended that the gaps left by the inadequacies of reductionist thinking should be filled by additional scientific theories that concern the collective and organizational properties of complex systems, and not by appeal to mystical or transcendent principles. No doubt this will disappoint those who take comfort in the failings of science and use any scientific dissent as an opportunity to bolster their own anti-scientific beliefs.

I have been at pains to argue that the organizational principles needed to supplement the laws of physics are likely to be forthcoming as a result of new approaches to research and new ways of looking at complexity in nature. I believe that science is in principle able to explain the existence of complexity and organization at all levels, including human consciousness, though only by embracing the 'higher-level' laws. Such a belief might be regarded as denying a god, or a purpose in this wonderful creative universe we inhabit.

I do not see it that way. The very fact that the universe *is* creative, and that the laws have permitted complex structures to emerge and develop to the point of consciousness—in other words, that the universe has organized its own self-awareness—is for me powerful evidence that there is 'something going on' behind it all. The impression of design is overwhelming. Science may explain all the processes whereby the universe evolves its own destiny, but that still leaves room for there to be a meaning behind existence.

43   Richard Morris
The
Anthropic Principle

The Strange Properties of Water

In 1913, in his book *Fitness of the Environment,* the American physiologist Lawrence J. Henderson noted that if water did not possess certain strange properties, life could not exist on earth. For example, water is practically unique in that it expands, rather than contracts, when it freezes. If it acted in a more normal manner, Henderson pointed out, then the earth would freeze solid and life could not exist.

Because water expands on freezing, ice floats: A less dense substance will rise to the surface of more dense substances. If water contracted instead, as all "normal" substances do, then the coldest water in a lake or ocean would sink to the bottom and freeze. And of course any ice that formed on the surface would sink. As more ice formed during succeeding winters, the buildup would increase until finally all the bodies of water on earth would be frozen solid. Once this happened, the ice would never melt. After all, ice is a very reflective substance. If the oceans were covered with ice, much of the energy coming from the sun would be reflected back into space and the earth would become colder yet. Under such conditions, it would quickly grow far too cold to support life.

Indeed, water has so many anomalous properties that make it an ideal substance to provide a foundation for life that it is almost as though someone had consciously designed water with living organisms in mind. Another example is that water has a high specific heat. The amount of heat energy that is required to raise the temperature of a certain quantity of water by one degree is much greater than it is for most other substances. This means that, as water gains or loses heat, it will change temperature relatively slowly. As a result, the presence of water tends to stabilize the temperature of the environment. If the surface of the earth were not covered by large bodies of water, or if water did not have this property, temperature swings on the surface of the earth would be much greater, perhaps even too great for living organisms to endure.

In addition, water has the ability to dissolve an unusually great number of different substances. This characteristic makes it a superb medium for the various chemical reactions on which life depends. Water also has a high surface tension, which is important for the biochemical reactions that take place in living cells. And water has a high heat of vaporization; that is, a great deal of energy is required to turn a certain quantity of liquid water into vapor. This makes water an effective coolant, which is a property many living organisms make use of, as anyone who has ever worked up some perspiration or seen a dog with its tongue hanging out is aware.

The Skeptic's Reply

A skeptic might reply that perhaps there is really nothing so remarkable about all this. If water didn't have certain special properties, then obviously creatures like human beings could never have evolved. But so what? Scientists don't know what kinds of life might or might not be possible. If water were not the kind of substance it is, then perhaps life forms based on sulfur compounds, or methane, or ammonia might evolve somewhere and they could construct similar arguments about their favorite life-giving substances.

Anyone who made such an objection might have a point. In fact, scientists tend not to make too much of the "magical" properties of water these days. But they do make similar arguments about other apparently accidental and serendipitous properties of the universe. For they are very much

aware that a universe that can give rise to any kind of life is a very improbable thing.

The Improbability of Carbon-Based Life

In order to understand how miraculous it is that life did emerge in our universe, we can begin by showing that the existence of carbon-based life is very improbable. If our universe did not possess certain apparently accidental properties, there would be no such thing as carbon, or, at best it might exist only in very minute quantities. Elements such as oxygen and nitrogen, which are so common in our world and which are constituents of many important organic molecules, would not exist either.

The presence of carbon depends upon the existence of certain energy levels. According to the laws of quantum mechanics, an electron in an atom, or a particle in an atomic nucleus, cannot possess just any arbitrary quantity of energy. The energy of such a system is said to be quantized. This means that such a system can have only certain various definite amounts of energy, but that it cannot have anything in between. One can construct an analogy by imagining a bucket which could be filled a quarter full, or half full, or three-quarters full, or all the way to the top, but which could not hold any other quantities of water, such as one-eighth.

Because of this rule of atomic energy, when a particle leaps from one energy level to another, it is said to undergo a quantum jump (see Figure 1). The absorption or emission of energy has to be a jump because intermediate energy levels are simply not allowed. This, incidentally, is the reason why so many substances emit light of particular wavelengths. Each separate wavelength of light corresponds to a "jump" between two quantum levels.

One consequence of this is the fact that a system will tend not to absorb a packet of energy if that packet does not "fit." It's like that hypothetical bucket of water. Adding a quarter of a bucket would be easy. But anyone trying to add a sixth or a third of a bucket would have difficulties.

The subject of quantum levels, quantum jumps, and the absorption and emission of energy is one that could be discussed endlessly. But it is best if I do not attempt to go into the subject in too much detail. This would only succeed in obscuring what is really a very simple point: The chance that a nuclear reaction will take place depends upon the placement of the energy levels in the nuclei that are involved. A nuclear reaction is a reaction between previously existing nuclei or individual particles that causes a new kind of nucleus to be formed. An example would be the reaction which takes place in our sun which causes hydrogen nuclei to be bound together to make helium. The creation of a carbon nucleus from three helium nuclei is another.

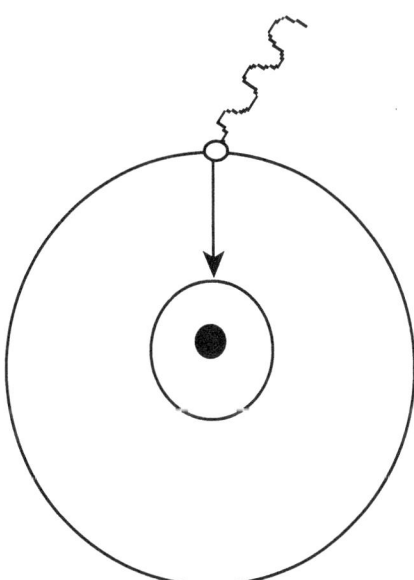

Figure 1. In a quantum jump, an electron in an atom jumps from an outer orbit to one of lower energy, giving off a light wave in the process. Here, the light circle represents an electron and the dark circle the nucleus of the atom. The diagram should not be taken as a literal representation of subatomic reality. The uncertainty principle tells us that the electron's position cannot be pinpointed so exactly as this diagram seems to imply.

If the energy levels happen to be just right, the reactions will take place very readily. If they are not, the reactions will take place only on very rare occasions. This is why some elements are so abundant and some are so rare: The energy levels of the nuclei make it easier to form some than others.

How does all of this relate to the subject of carbon-based life? Well, carbon is an element with a relatively simple structure. Its nucleus contains only six protons and six neutrons. The production of carbon is an intermediate step in the creation of oxygen and other heavier elements. If sufficient quantities of carbon were not created in our universe, these other substances would not be very abundant either.

But the existence of significant quantities of carbon seems to depend upon a fortuitous accident. Carbon and beryllium nuclei just "happen" to have energy levels in precisely the right place so that plenty of carbon is created in the nuclear reactions that take place in stars.

The energy levels in beryllium are important because beryllium, which has a nucleus with four protons and four neutrons, is one of the ingredients from which carbon is made. The process works something like this: Two helium nuclei collide. If they happen to strike one another with just the right energy, a beryllium nucleus is formed. Then, if this nucleus is struck by a third helium nucleus (again with the right energy), a carbon nucleus can be formed. And one must have carbon before oxygen is created. In fact, oxygen nuclei (which have a total of sixteen component particles) are generally created when nuclei of carbon (twelve particles) and helium (four particles) collide.

And how is it that carbon and beryllium have energy levels in just the places that they need to be in order to cause all the familiar elements to be synthesized? No one knows. It seems to be something that happened entirely by chance.

The Inflationary Expansion Again

There are other characteristics of our universe that seem miraculous when we consider that life could not have appeared had these characteristics been the slightest bit different. For example, life would not be possible if the universe had not been expanding at precisely the right rate shortly after the big bang. If the expansion had been slower by a factor of even one part in a million when the universe was just a few seconds old, then, as we have seen in a previous chapter, the expansion would have been halted long before stars and galaxies formed, and the universe would have quickly collapsed in a big crunch. If, on the other hand, the expansion had been at one part in a million faster, the universe would have consisted of nothing but rapidly dispersing hydrogen and helium gas. The expansion of the universe would have caused the gas molecules to fly apart from one another at such a rate that they would never have had a chance to form the vast gas clouds that eventually condensed into stars and galaxies.

At one time, the fact that the expansion of the universe was so finely tuned seemed a great mystery. But today we know—or think we know—how this fine tuning took place. As we discovered in a previous chapter, the inflationary expansion produced a universe that was very nearly flat. And a flat universe is one that is right on the borderline between a too-rapid and a too-slow expansion. Furthermore, cosmologists and theoretical physicists generally tend to believe that the laws of physics support the conclusion that such an expansion was inevitable.

I must emphasize once again, however, that there is no empirical evidence to prove that an inflationary expansion took place in our universe. And of course this raises a whole series of questions: Would it be possible to have a universe in which no inflationary expansion took place? Do such universes exist? If so, should not one consider it an extraordinary coincidence that, in our universe, physical laws have the right character?

Or is it possible that there was no inflationary expansion, and that the expansion rate of our universe was another fortuitous accident?

Di-Protons

Another apparently fortuitous coincidence has to do with the strength of what is called the strong force, the force which binds such particles as neutrons and protons together in nuclei (as you recall, one of the four forces of nature). This strong force is just barely strong enough to bind a proton and a neutron together to make deuterium. But it is not powerful enough to create particles called di-protons, which would consist of two protons bound together. Such particles cannot form because the strong force cannot quite overcome the mutual repulsion of two positively charged protons.

But if the strong force were just a few percentage points stronger, then di-protons could be created, and the results would be

catastrophic. If the creation of di-protons were possible, stars would not burn in the slow and steady manner that they do in our universe. In fact, there would be no such things as stars at all. Concentrations of primordial hydrogen and helium gas would produce nuclear reactions that progressed so rapidly that immense thermonuclear explosions would take place before stars would even form. And, since hydrogen would undergo reactions so readily, such a universe would be nearly 100 percent helium today.

One cannot be absolutely certain that life could not evolve in such a universe. After all, there might be life forms in this universe that are so unlike us that we are unable to imagine what they might be like. But, though one cannot entirely rule out the possibility of life in such a helium-filled universe, it certainly seems improbable.

More definite is the conclusion that no life could exist in a universe in which the masses of the neutron and proton were just slightly different, or in which the strong force was just a little bit weaker. If the strong force were 5 percent weaker than it is, deuterium would not exist, and there would be nothing that could bind a neutron and a proton together. Since the formation of deuterium is one of the steps by which hydrogen is made into helium, a universe with a strong force 5 percent weaker would not contain any stars. The hydrogen gas that it contained might condense under the influence of gravity in the same way that primordial hydrogen and helium did in our. But the nuclear reactions that cause our stars to shine would never begin. At best, such a universe would be filled with brown dwarfs that had been heated by gravitational contraction. They might give off small amounts of heat radiation, but for the most part such a universe would be cold and dark.

The idea that forms of life that are entirely unlike us might evolve in such a universe seems unlikely. Whatever form life takes, after all, depends upon the flow of energy. A very high entropy universe that was filled with brown dwarfs does not look like a very suitable habitat for life of any kind.

A universe in which the ratio of the neutron and proton masses was reversed would be even worse. In our universe, the neutron is about 0.1 percent heavier than the proton. As a result, a neutron that is not bound in a nucleus will spontaneously decay into a proton and an electron. This does not happen because the neutron is a composite particle made up of a proton and an electron. It isn't. The proton and the electron are actually created in the decay process. One particle can become two particles because there is extra mass available.

If the proton were the heavier particle, the neutron would be perfectly stable, and protons would decay into neutrons and positrons when they were found in a free state. In such a universe, space would be filled with neutrons and little else. The positrons that were a product of the proton decay would undergo mutual annihilation with whatever electrons they encountered. Only neutrons would be left. It hardly seems conceivable that such a universe could have life. With only neutrons and nothing else, the complex structures on which life seems to depend could not be created.

The Balance of the Forces

As we have seen, the strength of the strong force must be just right to produce a universe that is suitable for the evolution of life. One can make similar statements about the gravitational, weak, and electromagnetic forces: The other forces of nature. For example, it is the gravitational force which caused primordial clouds of gas to condense into stars. If it were weaker than it is, stars might never have been created at all. A gravitational force that was too strong would produce results that were equally catastrophic, at least from our point of view: The universe might collapse in a big crunch too quickly for life to develop. Or, if it somehow managed to survive for a period of time comparable to that in which ours has existed, it might contain almost nothing but a lot of black holes.

Similarly, if the electromagnetic force, which binds molecules together, was too weak, solids and liquids could not exist, and the universe could contain nothing but gas. If, on the other hand, it was too strong, protons would repel one another too strongly, and complex atomic nuclei could not form.

The balance between the various different forces is important too. In fact, the last example that I gave is really an instance of this. The electrical repulsion between protons must not be so strong as to overcome the effects of the strong force. If it is, nuclei with more than one proton will not be created, and again, none of the reactions that sustain life could happen. But notice that it isn't the absolute strength of the repulsion that is so important; what matters is that it not be stronger than the attraction created by the strong force.

The ratio of the weak and gravitational forces is significant too. Certain nuclear reactions depend on the weak force, and also depend on the rate of expansion of the universe shortly after the big bang. The creation of such substances as helium and deuterium depends on conditions in the early universe. Altering the gravitational force would change the expansion rate, and thus the rate at which these reactions took place.

If the ratio of the weak and gravitational forces had been changed slightly, the universe would have emerged from the big bang either as 100 percent hydrogen or as 100 percent helium. There does not seem to be any special reason why a universe that was initially wholly hydrogen could not support life. On the other hand, it is hard to see how a universe that was 100 percent helium could.

The Dimensionality of Space

Yet another characteristic of our universe that is crucial to its ability to support life is the dimensionality of its space. There seems to be no particular reason why space should have three dimensions. It is quite easy to conceive of universes in which space is quite different. In fact, as we learned in the previous chapter, quantum cosmologists sometimes suggest that the dimensionality of space in our universe was one of the initial conditions, which suggests that it could well have had different characteristics.

We should, in fact, consider ourselves lucky that we live in a universe with three spatial dimensions. If the number were less or greater, life would almost certainly not exist. At least it is difficult to see how life could evolve in a universe with two spatial dimensions. For example, an animal could not possess a digestive tract that ran from one end of it to the other; it would be cut into two pieces. To be sure, attempts have been made to conceive of what life might be like in a two-dimensional world. However, these have something of the character of mathematical games. As far as I know, no one has seriously suggested that two-dimensional life would be possible.

Similarly, a universe that had more than three spatial dimensions would also almost certainly be inimical to life. In such a universe, many of the laws of physics would have a different character than they do in ours (this is also true of a universe with two spatial dimensions). For example, if the dimensionality of space were four or greater, then stable planetary orbits would not be possible. If something resembling a plant did manage to form, it would follow a path that caused it to spiral into its sun.

The Anthropic Principle

The fact that the universe should be so hospitable to life certainly seem a perplexing puzzle, dependent as it is on so many apparently accidental factors. Attempting to solve this puzzle has naturally led to a great deal of speculation, much of which is more philosophical than scientific in character. Nevertheless, scientists rather than philosophers have carried on most of the debate about such questions.

Perhaps there is nothing very surprising about this, since these questions have arisen in the context of cosmological theory rather than that of philosophical debate. So, for better or for worse, some contemporary scientists have been forced to become philosophers. In an attempt to deal with such questions, these scientists have developed what is known as the anthropic principle, which can be expressed both in a "weak" and a "strong" form.

The weak anthropic principle has been stated by the British physicist Brandon Carter as follows: "What we can expect to observe must be restricted by the conditions necessary for our presence as observers." In other words, if the universe did not have certain characteristic properties, we would not be here to see it.

At first, the weak principle sounds almost like a platitude. But when one begins to consider its implications more deeply, it takes on more significance. The use of the weak principle does answer certain questions.

For example, how does it happen that we live in a universe that is about 15 billion years old? One could answer by saying that in a universe that was too young or too old, there would not be any conscious observers. If there is to be intelligent life, it appears that the universe has to be a few billion years old, at least, since it takes time for galaxies and stars, and then life, to evolve. And it is also unlikely that there will be any conscious observers when the universe attains an age of a trillion years. At that time, it will be cold and dark and all but a few dim stars will have died out.

There seems to be nothing very remarkable about the weak anthropic principle. Nevertheless, the idea has had its critics. And, significantly, the principle has been criticized on philosophical rather than scientific grounds. For example, at a symposium which was held at the 1988 meeting of the American Association for the Advancement of Science, the weak anthropic principle was branded as a kind of "cosmic narcissism" by physicist Heinz Pagels. In criticizing it, Pagels drew on certain ideas that had been proposed by the Austrian-British philosopher Karl Popper. He made no attempt to disprove it in the manner that one would try to disprove a scientific theory.

In his 1931 book, *The Logic of Scientific Discovery,* Popper had argued that every scientific hypothesis must be falsifiable. If it is, then it cannot be called "scientific." For example, the statement "God exists" may or may not be true. But true or not, it is not a scientific hypothesis because it is not susceptible to disproof. Einstein's general theory of relativity, on the other hand, is scientific because it makes predictions that can be tested by experiment.

According to Pagels, the weak anthropic principle is not scientific because it cannot be disproved under any conceivable circumstances. I suspect that it is necessary to agree with him on this point. However, even though the weak principle is not really a scientific idea, it does seem capable of answering certain questions that arise within scientific contexts. Not only does it tell us why the universe we see should have a certain approximate age, but it may also tell us why we should find ourselves living on a water-covered planet that revolves around a small-ish, long-lived star, and so on. This may be the only kind of place where life exists. If indeed there is nothing very "scientific" about the weak principle, then perhaps that is only an indication that there are points where the border between science and philosophy becomes somewhat blurred. And perhaps that is not such a bad thing.

The Strong Anthropic Principle

If the weak anthropic principle seems somewhat philosophical, the strong version is positively metaphysical. The strong anthropic principle is an alternative way of interpreting the same phenomenon (the existence of conscious life in the universe), and it has been stated by Carter as follows: "The universe must be such as to admit the creation of observers within it at some stage." In other words, the universe has to be of such a character as to provide an environment in which conscious beings can evolve.

To someone steeped in Western scientific tradition, such an idea had metaphysical or theological overtones which we do not associate with science. It is the kind of idea that was sometimes discussed during the eighteenth and nineteenth centuries, when it was fashionable to see the hand of a Creator in natural phenomena.

I am not claiming that the strong anthropic principle necessarily has religious implications. Nevertheless, it does seem reminiscent of the so-called argument from design. This argument, which was once quite popular and which is still sometimes cited in religious literature, is based on the idea that the existence of God is revealed by the wonders of the natural world. The world, and the life that populated it, could not have come about by accident. Thus its existence could be viewed as a proof of the existence of a deity.

Today, the argument is no longer used by theologians, and many scholars consider that it was demolished by the eighteenth-century German philosopher Immanuel Kant. Nevertheless, one does have to admit that one way of explaining why the universe should be so hospitable to life would be to answer that God designed it that way.

This is not an answer that would appeal to many scientists, however, whether they happened to be religious or not. As a group, scientists are just like everyone else in that some believe one religious creed or another, whereas others are atheists or agnostics. However, even those who believe in a Creator are reluctant to ascribe characteristics of the universe to His conscious design. Even the most devout tend to feel that questions that arise in scientific context should be answered in a scientific context, and that theological considerations should be avoided.

Interpreting the Strong Anthropic Principle

In their book *The Anthropic Cosmological Principle,* scientists John D. Barrow and Frank J. Tipler suggest that, if the strong anthropic principle is true, then there are three different ways of interpreting it.

The first possible interpretation is that the universe was deliberately designed to be hospitable to life. According to Barrow and Tipler, this view is not open either to proof or disproof because it is religious in nature. However, I am not so sure that it has to be. There exist some (admittedly very unlikely) explanations for this interpretation that have nothing to do with religion. For example, scientists of an advanced technological civilization might be able to create universes, and to set the initial conditions so that life is likely to evolve in them. After all, during the period before an inflationary expansion begins, a newly born universe is likely to be nothing but a tiny ball of spacetime that is empty, or nearly empty, of matter. For all we know, our universe may be some graduate student's experiment gone awry.

The second possibility that Barrow and Tipler cite is that observers are necessary to bring the universe into being. In other words, a universe cannot come into existence if it is incapable of producing conscious beings that can observe it. Barrow and Tipler attempt to give this somewhat mystical-sounding view a scientific foundation by relating it to certain recently developed interpretations of quantum mechanics. Here I will have to refer the interested reader to their book. The question of the proper interpretation of quantum mechanics is quite a complex subject, one on which many books have been written. Furthermore, the topic is more philosophical than scientific in nature (when one asks what numerical measurements quantum mechanics predicts, that is science; when one asks what quantum mechanics means, that is philosophy), and I don't have the space to go into such matters here. I will only comment that I personally find speculation about observer-created universes to be metaphysical in the extreme, and I am not sure that relating it to ideas in quantum mechanics makes it any less so.

Infinite Worlds

To my mind, the third possibility cited by Barrow and Tipler is the most straightforward and logical one. I believe that one can interpret the principle to mean that there are a very large number, perhaps an infinite number, of different universes. In such a cases there would be nothing surprising about the fact that conscious life exists in our own. After all, there would also be countless other universes where, because conditions were

not precisely right, life never evolved. In some of these universes, there might never have been an inflationary expansion. Others may never have stopped expanding at an inflationary rate. In some of these universes, stars and galaxies may never have formed. And in others, there might be no elements heavier than hydrogen and helium.

The point is that, if there are really a large (or infinite) number of different universes, all the problems associated with the improbability of a universe hospitable to life disappear. In such a case, our universe would still be a very improbable one. But there would be nothing striking about that because all the other, more likely, kinds of universes would exist too. But of course there would be no one there to see them.

It should be noted, however, that this kind of idea only seems to work if we make the assumption that the laws of nature can vary from one universe to another. For if there were a large number of different universes, and they all had physical laws similar to those which operate in ours, then they would most likely all contain life, and the question of why a universe should be so hospitable to life would remain.

All of this surely sounds like wild speculation. However, it is speculation that can be placed in a real scientific context. After all, scientists are no longer content with discovering what the laws of physics are. They are now also asking why physical laws have the form they do.

There are only two possible answers: One is that there may exist numerous universes and that the laws of physics may not be the same in all of them. The other is that there may be only one set of laws that is logically consistent. They may find that there is some reason why there have to be just four basic forces. There may be some reason why a certain set of subatomic particles exists, whereas others that are theoretically possible don't. They may discover that there is a reason why particles have certain specific masses. It may be that, in any universe, for some logical reason, a neutron *must* have a mass slightly larger than that of a proton, for example. And if this turns out to be the case, the third interpretation of the strong anthropic principle will have been disproved because logic could allow for only one type of universe.

From time to time in this book, I have mentioned superstring theories. Since this is a book on cosmology, not particle physics, I have not attempted to discuss such theories in detail. I should point out, however, that what the superstring theorists are seeking is a "theory of everything," a theory from which all the known laws of physics could be derived. If such a theory is eventually found, it is possible that scientists will discover that the reason that the four fundamental forces have certain characteristic strengths, that certain particles have certain masses, and so on, is that nature had no choice.

On the other hand, it may be discovered that there are many elements in the physical laws that are completely arbitrary. Scientists may find that the strengths of the forces, the masses of the elementary particles, and perhaps even the dimensionality of space may depend entirely fortuitously upon the initial conditions of the universe.

It now appears that whereas the somewhat modest-sounding weak anthropic principle is basically philosophical in nature, the more metaphysical-sounding strong principle can be tested by empirical observation. If a successful superstring theory is ever developed or, alternatively, if the quantum cosmologists ever attain their goals, then we will most likely be able to say whether the third interpretation of the strong principle is true or false.

44 Arthur F. Gianelli
God, Science and Evil

Introduction

Nelson Pike, in the introduction to his book "God and Evil" states the problem of evil thusly:

> *If God is omnipotent, then He could prevent evil if He wanted to. And if God is perfectly good, then He would want to prevent evil if He could. Thus, if God exists and is both omnipotent and perfectly good, then there exists a being who could prevent evil if he wanted to, and who would want to prevent evil if he could. And if this last is true, how can there be so many evils in the world?(1964:1)*

No problem has been more perplexing for the theist than this one. In the prophetic words of Hume, "nothing can shake the solidity of this reasoning, so short, so clear, so decisive."(1959:Part X:69)

Of course the theist can "solve" the problem by sacrificing one or more of God's defining attributes, omniscience, omnipotence or benevolence. But what would be left would no longer be the God of traditional theism, the God of the Judeo, Christian, Islamic tradition. The remaining shell of a god would be of little interest to human beings because he could be of little or no help to us in this world.

Since this solution has never been acceptable to theists they have sought instead solutions to the problem that would preserve God's defining attributes. Such "explanations" of evil that would still allow for the existence of the God of traditional theism have been called theodicies. Traditionally these theodicies have taken two forms: (1) Some have sought to solve the problem of evil by trying to show that there really is no evil in this world and thus there really is no problem. (2) The majority of traditional theodicies have accepted the existence of evil however but have sought to show that evil plays a positive, and perhaps even necessary role, in human life. As might be imagined these traditional theodicies have come under severe criticism in the history of philosophy, and justly so. Not only do they crumble under serious philosophical reflection but they also do great personal harm when used in times of crisis or great suffering. Further, it is not just the atheist who sees the weakness in these theodicies. Most believers intuitively sense that there are problems with them when a tragedy befalls a friend, a family member, or themselves.

It would be a positive development if we could rid theistic discourse of these traditional theodicies once and for all. To that end I wish to add my criticisms because I feel that once we are free of them the outline of a possibly successful theodicy will open up to us. I would then like to develop that outline with the help of very recent work in the sciences.

Restatement of the Problem

To make a discussion of the problem of evil more manageable I would like to use the word "evil" interchangeably with the phrase "human suffering". Now surely there are more evils in the world than human sufferings but such sufferings are the key elements in the problem. Human suffering can be physical, emotional or spiritual (intellectual). When I use the word evil then I am referring primarily to human suffering.

A simple study of the human condition reveals not only that all human beings suffer sometime but that there is a breadth and a depth to suffering that seems to transcend any rational boundary. The breadth of suffering can be seen in the fact that even today the majority of people in the world are living lives of poverty and want. In two of the past twenty years over 25 million people, mostly women and children, died of starvation. The U.N. reports that 42,000 children in the third world die each day of common childhood illnesses.

The depth of suffering can be seen in the unlimited suffering that individual human beings must endure. Some children are born ill and live out their five or six years of life in constant pain. They die at last without ever knowing a day of enjoyment. In fact death seems like a welcome relief. People with AIDS are not immune from cancer. In fact it is almost certain that they will get cancer. A father may have to live out his life alone after an auto accident has killed his wife and three children. The mentally ill may spend forty to fifty years in an institution where the physical and mental torment never ends.

In the context of the breadth and depth

of suffering the problem of evil seems overwhelming. If the God of traditional theism exists why would He have created a universe where this kind of suffering is possible? And why would He let it continue?

The Traditional Theodicies

Before proceeding to an evaluation of the traditional theodicies that try to answer these questions it is important to indicate that the possible existence of an evil force, a devil, operating in the universe does not in any way solve the problem. If there is a devil causing evil such a being is permitted to operate by its omnipotent creator and the problem of evil remains.

As was mentioned traditional theodicies that attempt to solve the problem of human suffering fall into two general categories. Either they attempt to argue that there really is no evil or they argue that evil exists but plays a positive and perhaps even necessary role in human life. Most of those who argue that there is no evil suggest that human beings think there is evil because of their cognitive limitations. God who is infinitely above man sees that everything is good or that the "whole" is good. Of course it is never made clear how we might know that to God everything is good or the "whole" is good. Further, this view contradicts the basic reports of our senses and in so doing renders human existence hopelessly futile and meaningless. It would be hard to reconcile a good God with such an impoverished view of man.

There is however one version of the "no evil" argument that is worth noting. A metaphysics that views evil as non-being has considerable merit. However it would be incumbent upon such a metaphysics to then distinguish between evil and suffering. Evil may be non-being but the suffering it causes is quite real.

The majority of theists accept the reports of our senses that tell us that there is an abundance of evil in the world but they feel that God uses evil for a positive purpose. The more honest of this group, recognizing that they cannot imagine a purpose for the vast amount of gratuitous suffering that they observe, suggest that God has intentionally made the purpose of evil a mystery for us. This again however puts us in a hopeless situation. If evil has a purpose that we are not privy to then it is not at all clear what we are supposed to do with it. Should we try to eliminate all evil or just some evil? If we eliminate all evil would we then also eliminate whatever positive role it plays in human life? And if we should eliminate some evil, but not all, then which evils should we attack, or perhaps, better, *whose* evils should we attack? Human life would become quite confused to say the least.

Most of the theists who accept the existence of evil, suggest that there is a purpose to evil that human beings can know. Evil exists they argue for the sake of good. The purpose of evil is to serve the good. Without evil, it is argued, good would not be possible e.g. without someone in need we could not be charitable. Without evil we would not, by contrast, even know or appreciate the good e.g. hard times help us to enjoy good times. And without evil greater goods would not follow e.g. problems in a family often draw the members of that family closer together.

The problem with this theodicy depends upon how it is nuanced. If the theodicy is used to blur the distinction between good and evil then evil becomes good and we are back to the "no evil" problem. It would become "good" then for earthquakes or disease to occur because they would be occasions for charity. On the other hand if a radical distinction is maintained between good and evil then it follows from this theodicy that a perfectly good God intentionally wills human suffering an obvious contradiction, on the chance that it be an occasion for good. Further since God intentionally wills evil it follows that human efforts to remove it, despite some apparent successes, must ultimately prove futile. Human freedom, if it existed at all, would be severely limited and the meaning of human life would be called into question because we would be literally fighting the will of God if we tried to remove all evil. The theist's position would again be hopeless.

There Is No Necessary Connection Between Evil and Good

Although it is certainly true that evil can be an occasion for good it can also be an occasion for more evil. There is no necessary connection between evil and good in this world.[1] Assigning a positive value to evil, in addition to being an obvious contradiction, also ignores basic human experience. The reports of our senses reveal to us that evil is real and that it has no redeeming value. A positive human response to evil does have significant value but this value doesn't justify the evil.

The reality of evil and its lack of positive value causes the traditional theodicies to fail. *A successful theodicy must accept the reality of evil and its lack of value and also make provision for the perfect goodness of God.* It appears that our analysis of the problem has made a successful theodicy more unlikely. But I believe a deeper look at the analysis, reveals the outline of a theodicy with considerable merit. I would like to now develop that outline.

Preamble to the New Theodicy[2]

A successful theodicy must it seems begin with the following:

1. The reports of our senses are correct. Evil exists, and there is a breadth and a depth to human suffering that can, at times, exceed all rational boundaries.

2. Although this evil can be an "occasion" for good, in itself it has no positive value. Evil is evil, it is never good.

3. A perfectly good God does not use evil for any purpose. A perfectly good God must desire what is best for all His creatures at all times.

But if an all powerful God desires what is best for all His creatures at all times the problem of accounting for the actual existence of evil is certainly not solved. It is however a necessary start for it prevents the contradiction between a perfectly good God and a God who wills evil. The next step is to analyze the idea of creation. The God of traditional theism, as a perfect Being, would not have to create. Creation on His part would be a perfectly free act. If He chose to

---

1. Even when evil is an occasion for good it can in no way be seen as the cause of good.

2. The foundation for this theodicy can found in Bruce Reichenbach's *Evil and a Good God.*

create the God of traditional theism would have two broad options:

1. The creation of a "play toy" reality. This would be a reality in which God would share existence with his creatures and nothing else. The creatures' entire activity, if it had any, would be totally determined by God.

2. The second possibility would be the creation of a significant reality, a reality with which God would share not only existence but also His powers, especially the power to create. Beings with such powers we can call significant beings.

Although neither form of creation would be necessary it would make little sense for a God to create a play toy. But it does make some sense for Him to create significant beings, beings who could become aware of Him and respond to Him by their authentic actions. Let us assume for the sake of our argument that the God of traditional theism made this choice to create significant beings. Since it is impossible for totally isolated beings to be significant, God must also create a "universe" in which they can be significant. Such a "universe" must allow for the meaningful interaction of a plurality of beings.

But what powers must beings possess in order to be significant? One possibility, surely, is that they be rational and free. Rational so that they can know the alternative futures that are possible and how to achieve them. Free so that they can choose from among those futures and actualize their choices.[3] The universe needed to house significant beings must be one then in which a broad range of alternative futures would be possible. In fact if it is only unlimited freedom that is truly meaningful then the range of alternative futures must also be unlimited. In addition to possessing unlimited alternative futures the universe must be also lawlike in it's behavior. Capricious behavior would frustrate rationality. And since the range of alternatives governed by these laws must be unlimited, significant beings must have an unlimited capacity to know in order to be significant.

Statement of the Significant Being Theodicy (SBT)

Since alternative futures would differ in quality a spectrum of such alternatives, ranging from unlimited good on the one extreme to unlimited evil on the other, must exist in a universe in which there are to be significant beings. Thus the character of a significant creation leads us to the first two principles of a new theodicy.

P1. The possibility of (unlimited) evil must exist in order for significant beings to actually exist and

P2. No evil is incorrigible i.e. the possibility of dealing with any evil, by prevention or elimination, must already exist in the universe.

Notice that it is not the actuality of evil that must exist. Actual evil serves no purpose. *But the possibility of evil, as part of an unlimited range of alternatives, must exist in*

---

3. I am using the following operative definitions. Freedom is the ability to choose from among alternative futures and reason would involve the ability to know alternative futures and how to achieve them.

order to allow for the actual existence of significant beings. Notice also that if significant beings possess unlimited reason and unlimited freedom and if the universe is lawlike and admits of unlimited alternative futures then it follows that no evil is incorrigible. Significant beings would not be condemned to suffer and it would not be the case that the God of traditional theism had created a universe where evil *must* occur.

Has Significant Creation Occurred?

So far our discussion has remained within the realm of the theoretical. The question we must address now is the following: Is this universe that we inhabit an example of a significant creation, and are human beings, significant beings? Any evidence to that conclusion would have to be broad and unashamedly inductive but I think such evidence exists and is quite strong. Our scientific study of the universe in the past 400 years has not only revealed an immense and complex reality but as our investigation has intensified there seems to be no evidence that the intelligibility of the universe is being exhausted. Modern science writers like Paul Davies, John Gribbin, Richard Morris and others find no difficulty in using the phrase "unlimited possibilites" when talking about this universe.   Consider the words of Princeton physicist Freeman Dyson as he concludes his suggestively entitled work *Infinite in All Directions:*

> **The hypothesis is that the universe is constructed according to the principle of maximum diversity. The principle of maximum diversity operates both at the physical and at the mental level. It says**

> **that the laws of nature and the initial conditions are such as to make the universe as interesting as possible.(1988:298)**

As rich in possibilities as the universe is now we also know that it is in process. It is not complete. Cosmic evolution cannot be reduced to simply eternal change. There seems to be direction to the process and the best way to define that direction is in terms of powers and possibilities. The Darwinian Centennial Celebration at the University of Chicago in 1954 concluded that evolution was a one way irreversible process in time that generates novelty, diversity and higher levels of organization in all sectors of the universe. The past 40 years have produced nothing to shake that conclusion and a great deal to reinforce it. The most spectacular empirical support has come from two sources, the Principle of Indeterminism in Quantum Physics viewed as a metaphysical principle, and the development of the Anthropic Principle.

The movement from an Uncertainty Principle to a Principle of Indeterminism in Quantum Physics has led to the conclusion that as time passes the universe jumps to higher levels of organization and power. Further, as the universe moves into an open future it enriches itself with possibilities and this process seems to have no limit. The Anthropic Principle on the other hand suggests that the universe is finely tuned in terms of its initial conditions, structure and laws to eventually produce conscious observers, e.g., human beings. In their recent book *The Matter Myth* Davies and Gribbin put the two Principles together and speculate that eventually the universe will be dominated by (human) intelligence. They offer this summation:

*We mention these admittedly speculative ideas to illustrate the profound change in perspective that has accompanied the move toward a postmechanistic paradigm. In place of the clodlike particles of matter in a lumbering Newtonian machine we have an interlocking network of information exchange —a holistic, indeterministic and open system—***vibrant with potentialities and bestowed with infinite richness.*** *The human mind is a by-product of this vast informational process, a by-product with the curious capability of being able to understand, at least in part, the principles on which the process runs. (1993:308–9 Emphasis Mine)*

Although there may be many possible creations in which significant beings could exist the evidence of contemporary science suggests that this universe is one of them. It is reasonable to conclude that the goal of cosmic evolution is the production of significant beings and a universe in which they can be significant. The theist seems justified in saying that, if creation occurred, it was significant.

No Evil Is Incorrigible

Despite the broad empirical evidence that exists to indicate that unlimited alternatives are available to human beings it is still necessary to show that in the here and now evils can be prevented or eliminated. The easiest way to do this is to make an obvious division among evils and then to treat them one at a time. Moral evil is evil freely perpetrated by one human being on another. Natural evils, including accidents, befall human beings because of the normal functioning of nature and usually without any human intention or culpability.

Obviously if moral evils are *freely* per-

petrated upon one human being upon another then no moral evil ever *has* to occur. To suggest that human beings *must* at times behave unjustly or violently is to suggest that they are not really free. The fact that there are people who live lives free of moral evil is inductive evidence that human beings are not compelled to moral evil and is also inductive evidence of real freedom in human beings. Mental illnesses or physical infirmities that lead to human suffering I would classify as examples of natural evil rather than moral evil.

There is also an element of human freedom and culpability in most accidents and natural evils. Automobiles and airplanes, for example, are human artifacts freely invented, freely built, and freely operated. It is not necessary that we operate them recklessly or under the influence of alcohol, drugs, etc. The most famous accident of the past decade was the explosion of the Challenger Space Shuttle accompanied by the deaths of the members of the crew. But surely such an accident could have been avoided. The accident was caused by a failed o-ring in a booster rocket that produced a fuel leak that led to the explosion. The o-ring failed because of the subfreezing temperatures at Cape Kennedy the night before the launch. Several NASA engineers warned of the dangers of a launch under those conditions but NASA officials, under severe economic pressure decided to proceed. The accident did not *have* to occur. Similarly many of our diseases are brought on by what we eat and drink or the environment in which we place our bodies. Our susceptibility to natural disasters often depends upon unwise, imprudent or reckless decisions that we make. The proper exercise of freedom would go a long way in reducing the human suffering caused by accidents and many natural disasters.

Now some will argue that all great human adventures will inevitably involve human suffering and loss of life. Experimental surgery or drugs have to be tested and they often fail or produce unexpected negative results. But *must* such human progress *necessarily* involve human suffering? Perhaps the greatest and most dangerous adventure in human history was the landing of a human being on the moon. Yet that decade-long project was accomplished without the loss of life or even serious injury. The three astronauts who did die during the project were the victims of a fire on the launch pad caused by the fact that one of them forgot to throw an appropriate switch at an appropriate time. Surely this accident did not have to occur and as I mentioned earlier no one was even seriously injured during the missions themselves.

But what of extraordinary natural disasters like earthquakes and tornados that seem to defy human attempts to avoid them? And what about diseases that occur despite heroic efforts at prevention? Surely these evils seem to be beyond the responsibility of human beings. Indeed the sufferings produced by these natural disasters is often beyond the responsibility of human beings. But their prevention or elimination is certainly not beyond the powers of human beings. If earthquakes, tornadoes, hurricanes and diseases all abide by the laws of nature and these laws are knowable then human beings can develop strategies for dealing with them. We have been doing just that for centuries. We are already very close to being able to predict with great accuracy

when, where and with what strength an earthquake will occur. With such information no one would *necessarily* be a victim of such an event. The second time Mount St. Helens erupted there was a 48 hour warning and no one was killed. In like manner the track of hurricanes and other storms can already be predicted with considerable accuracy allowing time for people to take appropriate precautions. Although human suffering still occurs through such natural events it seems clear that such suffering is not necessary.

I have chosen to deal with disease apart from other natural disasters because it seems to be so intimate a part of every human life. Most, if not all, people, feel that degeneration and death are the necessary fate of all biological entities including man. Yet we are also aware of the fact that we have practically eliminated from the face of the earth some of the most insidious diseases like small pox and polio. We are also aware that life spans in certain parts of the world have been doubled in the past century. Some actuarial scientists even predict that people born in the year 2000 may live an average 150 years.

Several things on this matter must be said. First if diseases like AIDS and cancer operate according to the laws of nature and these laws are knowable then we should be able to deal with them. We have already made great progress in learning how to deal with heart disease which may still be our number one killer. Physicians like Dean Ornish not only speak of preventing heart disease but of actually reversing it after it has occurred, and without surgery or drugs. Unfortunately we have not been so successful with AIDS and cancer but the possibility remains.

Secondly physicians like Deepak Chopra suggest that we do not die of old age but rather of diseases we become more susceptible to as we grow older. If we eliminate those diseases or our susceptibility to them we can prolong like indefinitely. Says Chopra in *Ageless Body, Timeless Mind:*

"How many of the following statements do you believe are facts?

- *Aging is natural*
- *Aging is inevitable*
- *Aging is normal*
- *Aging is genetic*
- *Aging is painful*
- *Aging is universal*
- *Aging is fatal*

If you take any or all of these to be statements of fact you are under the influence of beliefs that do not match reality. Each statement contains a little objective truth but each can be refuted, too." (1993:58-59)

Chopra goes on to say that the power to eliminate human suffering due to disease may be within our grasp. It is certainly within the realm of possibility.

A quick review of the litany of evils that plague human beings then reveals that none are incorrigible in principle. What is necessary is that one, the universe be law-like in its behavior (there is plenty of evidence for this) and two, that the human mind be capable of discovering these laws (there seems to be ample evidence for this as well). It is still true, however, that in the present moment we cannot adequately deal with every disease or successfully defend ourselves from every natural disaster. This theodicy if it is to be ultimately successful must answer that charge.

Although I don't consider the response I'm about to give to be complete and I certainly do not consider it to be emotionally comforting I think it takes us in the right direction. Real significance requires that our judgments and choices mean something. We are not born knowing all the laws of nature nor are we born understanding all physical phenomena. If we were we would not be able to exercise freedom in the pursuit of knowledge and thus our significance would be compromised. Instead we must use our power to choose in respect to knowledge and our significance is upheld.

This magnifies our responsibilities however. Just as we may perpetrate moral evils on unborn generations by polluting the atmosphere or by not properly disposing of nuclear waste for example, we may also compromise future generations by our present lack of intellectual and spiritual development. And I want to emphasize that I am not simply speaking of scientific and technological progress here. Evil can be avoided and good enhanced just as significantly by developments in the arts and humanities as well.

This explanation may be intellectually satisfying in the abstract but is of little comfort to those who are suffering in the here and now. The level of moral evil seems to have grown with technological progress and there are still diseases like AIDS and cancer that we cannot effectively deal with. Children, as Camus highlighted for us, still suffer and die despite their innocence. Perhaps we can only expect intellectual satisfaction from a theodicy and not consolation, and perhaps that is the way it should be. Because if we are not consoled maybe we will find it harder to accept unwarranted evil in a universe where actual evil is *not* necessary. Maybe we will fully realize then that the determination of the human condition is ultimately our responsibility. And maybe, just maybe, we will finally say enough to evil once and for all.

Prayer and Miracles

If the God of traditional theism decided to create significant beings, beings with unlimited freedom it follows that He would respect that significance. This leads us to the third principle of the SBT:

P3 God does not enter into the world as an outside agent to compromise significance.

According to this principle the agents in the universe would be natural agents who operate according to the laws of nature. Such agents can be discovered and understood by significant beings. God may also interact with the world but this interaction would have to be understandable by significant beings and not represent a violation of the laws of nature. Further God's interaction could not compromise human freedom.

This third principle of the SBT certainly stands in contradiction to our ordinary understanding of prayer and miracles. Prayers of petition are usually understood as requests of God that He enter into the world and manipulate it in a way favorable to the petitioner. Miracles are usually understood as examples of God entering into the world and producing a result contrary to the result that natural causes would have produced. To exclude God from this kind of participation in the affairs of man seems to make Him distant and perhaps irrelevant.

Contrary to this apparently obvious charge the SBT holds that prayer is indeed meaningful and miracles do indeed occur. If, as has already been indicated, no evil is incorrigible and unlimited alternatives exists for significant beings then the power for all miracles has already been placed in the universe by God. There is no need for Him to re-enter the world to upgrade its capabilities. According to the SBT however it is necessary for significant beings to tap the unlimited power of the universe and actualize its unlimited potential. An indication of how this potential may be tapped lies in the power of the mind to influence the body. Evidence of this power is well established. Profound religious experiences achieved through prayer or a visit to a shrine may indeed allow the mind and spirit of a human person to effect a radically positive change in a physical condition. The fact that we do not understand the mind-body connection very well magnifies the miraculous nature of the effect.

The view that I am expressing here allows us to give meaning and substance to basic theistic notions. Among these notions is the feeling that in God there is always hope. We need never despair, we are never alone. If evil were incorrigible then indeed we would be without hope. But according to the SBT everything is possible and we need never despair. Another basic notion is that God answers all prayers. Usually theists finesse this notion by suggesting that often God's answer is in the negative but for our own good. This leaves us with the problem of trying to figure out, for example, how the death of a young mother of two from breast cancer is in anyone's "best interests." According to the SBT all prayers are answered by God in two ways. First prayer automatically produces a positive metaphysical result by tapping the power that mind and spirit have over matter. Secondly, God responds in an interior way to the person who prays strengthening his character but never compromising his freedom. The Christian notion of grace fits very well here.

I would like to end this section by mentioning two recent attempts to describe the efficacy of prayer and God's role in it by appealing to modern science. The physician Larry Dossey in his book called *Healing Words* (1993:84), describes very serious scientific studies that seem to demonstrate the positive power of prayer. He attempts to account for the *non local* healing effects of prayer by appealing to what is referred to in Quantum Physics as Bell's Theorem. Basically the Irish physicist John Stewart Bell was able to show that if distant objects had once been in contact, a change thereafter in one causes an immediate change in the other, no matter how far apart they are. *Thus* prayer can have a positive effect not only on the person praying but also on the person being prayed for.

The British physicist turned Anglican priest John Polkinghorne (1986:70-77) also sees Quantum Physics as presenting us with the possibility of understanding God's response to prayer. Polkinghorne sees the Principle of Indeterminism as providing a "window" of opportunity for God to maneuver in the universe without compromising human freedom.

I mention these two extraordinary attempts to explain religious notions by an appeal to sophisticated scientific concepts because they are indicative of a trend. Instead of the antagonism between science and religion growing as science becomes more sophisticated the opposite seems to be taking place. Science and religion seem to be gaining in respect for one another and this is leading to a synergistic relationship between them. Such a relationship is a key element in the SBT.

Implications for the Future

Since the SBT suggests that no evil is incorrigible it has extraordinary implications for the future. If we begin to eliminate diseases and protect ourselves from natural disasters we will surely continue to prolong life spans. As that happens the problem of overpopulation will just as surely arise. But given a choice between heart disease, cancer and AIDS on the one hand and overpopulation on the other I would gladly choose the latter. We have discovered in the 20th century that the universe is quite large and with plenty of room for the expansion of the human family. Granted the explorers of the future would literally have to find new worlds but the possibilities are exciting and intriguing.

As evils continue to be prevented or eliminated cultures will also change and change radically. But is any culture that is based upon the actual existence of evil worth preserving? Wouldn't it be wonderful if we did not need a medical profession, or pharmaceutical companies, or a military? Wouldn't a society that needs more artists than policemen be preferable to the society that we have now? And what would be wrong with a society in which animal flesh was not used for food? This by the way is going to happen in the next fifty years, not because human beings will become concerned about the sufferings of animals, although many will, but because human beings will discover that the consumption of animal fat is detrimental to long term health. A cosmic approach to human existence allows us to imagine extraordinary possibilities like this for the future.

Finally it might be worth mentioning that the SBT would stand in opposition to the two possible fates of the universe usually offered by cosmologists because they both represent the actualization of unlimited evil. One possibility is that gravity will recall the galaxies and all life, all civilization will be obliterated in a "big crunch." The other possibility is that gravity will not be able to recall the galaxies and expansion will continue forever. Eventually the energy in the universe would be stretched to the point that significant activity would cease and the universe would effectively be dead. Now the actualization of unlimited evil is possible according to the SBT but it cannot be necessary. There must be a way to avoid these two fates. One possibility is that intelligence will be able to figure out a way of avoiding either fate. Another possibility is that the universe may be finely tuned such that the expansion of the universe will continue forever but continually slow down as well. I think a combination of the two could maintain a universe hospitable to life indefinitely. If this is the case then significance will have its ultimate justification.

Conclusion

In the end the strength of any new theodicy will lie in its ability to respond to the problem of evil as stated at the beginning of this essay and also in its ability to demon-strate its originality. With those points in mind I would like to summarize this essay by listing what I feel are the strengths of the SBT.

1. According to the SBT God does allow evil in the sense that He respects the significant beings that he has created i.e. He respects their freedom. But according to the SBT God never desires that evil actually occur and He has provided significant beings with the powers necessary to effectively deal with any evil. In this way the SBT avoids the obvious contradiction of saying that God is all good and at the same saying that God wills, desires, or causes evil.

2. The SBT, by saying that evil serves no positive purpose, is able to maintain a clear distinction between good an evil. This distinction enables significant beings (human beings) to understand clearly how they should behave in the face of evil. Since no evil is ever of any positive value significant beings should commit themselves to elimination of all evils, from the common cold to cancer, from name calling to genocide. The realization that God does not enter into the world as an outside agent to manipulate it on our behalf only serves to heighten our responsibility for what happens in the world.

3. The God of the SBT is not a distant God. Rather He is a God that responds to His creatures by providing them with the powers and possibilities necessary to accomplish anything in this world. Cosmic evolution is the mecha-

nism for the unfolding of creation. It is continual and never ending. God never ceases to be with us.

Yet candor requires that we also admit that God, in creating truly free beings, took the ultimate risk of being. Real freedom allows us to choose against Him and actualize unlimited evil. If we chose to destroy all life on this planet for example God would not stop us. Will God the perfect Being, suffer if we make that choice? Does He suffer now when we actualize evil? It certainly makes sense to say that a benevolent creator would care about the fate of His creatures. If that means a perfect Being can suffer so be it.

4. The SBT differs from the traditional theodicies in crucial ways. It differs from those theodicies that suggest that there really is no evil in the world by accepting the reports of our senses and the testimony of mankind that says otherwise. Secondly the SBT differs from those theodicies that maintain that evil exists but plays a positive role in human life by showing that there is no empirical evidence to support such a view. Positive *responses* to evil can of course be of enormous value but evil itself is in no way of any positive value.[4]

5. The SBT is different from the "free will defense," as ordinarily understood, in the following way. The SBT suggests that freedom is only meaningful if it is unlimited. Limited freedom is seen as fraudulent. With this in mind the SBT argues that human beings do indeed possess unlimited freedom and that therefore no evil is incorrigible. A free will defense would be incoherent if it allowed that some evil was incorrigible because it would mean that God had created a universe where evil *must* occur. If this were the case freedom would obviously be compromised.

6. Finally, empirical evidence from contemporary science that the universe possesses unlimited richness and that the human person seems to have an unlimited ability to know and understand it also helps to preserve the concept of an omnipotent God. If this universe is the work of a creator it is hard to imagine that it is the creature of an imperfect one. The flight to an imperfect God in the face of evil by some theists was premature and unnecessary. A contemporary teleological argument based upon the SBT would, it seems, have considerable strength.

For as long as gratuitous suffering remains a reality in human life evil will remain a problem for the theist. But I think it is no longer necessary for theists to simply throw up their hands and admit defeat, or steadfastly maintain the truth of contradictory statements, or refuse to acknowledge the obvious reports of our senses. Contemporary science has allowed us to approach a solution to the problem of evil and that is both ironic and fitting. It is ironic because

---

4. I should also add here that actual evil is not necessary in order to know and appreciate the good. A knowledge of alternative futures and a knowledge of the laws would give us the needed contrast. Nor is evil essential to the acquisition of such knowledge.

for the first 300 years of its existence science was seen as antagonistic to belief in the God of traditional theism. It is fitting because, if science is understood in its broad sense as the human effort to know reality, then the search for an understanding of God and the search for an understanding of the universe are joined.

Bibliography

Chopra, Deepak. 1993. *Ageless Body. Timeless Mind.* New York: Harmony Books.

Davies, Paul. 1992. *The Mind of God.* New York: Simon and Schuster.

Davies, Paul and Gribbin, John. 1992. *The Matter Myth.* New York: Simon and Schuster.

Dossey, Larry, M.D. 1993. *Healing Words.* San Francisco: Harper

Dyson, Freeman. 1988 *Infinite in All Directions.* New York: Harper & Row.

Hume, David. (1959) *Dialogues Concerning Natural Religion* ed. by Henry D. Aiken. New York: Hafner Publishing Co.

Jaki, Stanley L. 1989. *Miracles and Physics.* Front Royal, Virginia: Christendom Press.

Morris, Richard 1993. *Cosmic Questions.* New York: John Wiley and Sons, Inc.

Peat, F. David. 1991. *The Philosophers Stone.* New York: Bantam Books.

Penrose, Roger, 1989. *The Emperor's New Mind.* London: Oxford University Press.

Pike, Nelson (1964) "Introduction" in *God and Evil* ed. by Nelson Pike. Englewood Cliffs, NJ: Prentice-Hall, 1964.

Polkinghorne, John 1986 *One World.* Princeton, NJ: Princeton University Press.

Prigogine, Ilya and Stengers, Isabelle Stengers. 1984 *Order Out of Chaos.* New York: Bantam Books.

Reichenbach, Bruce. 1982. *Evil and a Good God.* New York: Fordham University Press.

Smith, George H. 1979. *Atheism: The Case Against God.* Buffalo, NY Prometheus Books.

Swinburne, Richard 1970. *The Concept of Miracle.* London: Macmillan and Co.

Section B

The Challenge
of
Hermeneutics

Language is the house of being.

Martin Heidegger

45 Paul Gaffney
The Hermeneutical Circle: Description and Ultimacy

The End of Philosophy

Philosophers are famous for making implausible remarks; however, of the many strange arguments produced by philosophers in the Western tradition, perhaps strangest of all is the claim, made occasionally in that tradition, that the enterprise of philosophy itself has come to an end.[1] Such an assertion is more than a little odd and, apparently, quite peculiar to the philosophical endeavor, as no other intellectual discipline seems to tempt its practitioners to claim that its work is done. For example, poets, scientists, and theologians do not regularly declare that the fundamental insight, or the final structure, for which they search has been discovered, nor do they seem anxious to do so. They accept, apparently, that there are always more beautiful objects to construct, more occurrences in nature to explain and control, and more mysteries to probe. (We can certainly imagine these intellectuals making some suggestions about finality, but such suggestions would, to the extent that they declare finality, probably evidence prior and independent philosophical convictions.)

The irony of this situation, of course, is lost on no one: philosophers *argue* that their enterprise is completed, usually to a resistant audience. In fact, today one can attend a conference of professional philosophers and join in a lively debate about what it means to say that the end of philosophy is upon us. Aside from the amusing spectacle this gives rise to, the tendency prompts a serious question: What is it about the philosophical enterprise that seems disposed to contemplate its own demise? To what do we attribute this observable fact in the history of ideas? Let us consider the thesis that philosophical arguments are distinguished not because they are difficult or abstract—all serious disciplines can be so characterized—but because they are concerned with *ultimacy*.[2] That is, the philosopher is led by the demands of his discipline to offer some final explanation of the whole of things, and his explanation, as a philosophical argument, succeeds so far as it clarifies fundamental issues. Of course, as Aristotle reminds us,[3] not every intellectual pursuit admits of the same degree of finality and certitude, but the precise determination of the epistemic possibilities in our various pursuits is itself an ultimate issue, and therefore a philosophical question. Philosophy, therefore, makes the limits of its inquiry an explicit issue, and so inevitably confronts the question of its own completion.

---

1. My qualification indicates that I consider the question of the end of philosophy only as it seems to have been a concern of the Western tradition.

2. 'Concern' is a noncommittal term: as we will see, the philosopher can presume neither that there are knowable ultimates, nor the contrary thesis. To establish either thesis is a philosophical argument, and both the positive and negative answer to the question could lead one to conclude that the business of philosophy is done.

3. See *Nicomachean Ethics*, I, 3.

So let us take seriously the question of the end of philosophy. There are two important ways[4] in which the argument has been advanced, and they are related to one another. *First,* philosophers sometime speak of the end of philosophy in the sense of what Bernd Magnus calls a *Vollendung:* a completion, or a culmination. The end of philosophy is upon us because a fundamental and unsurpassable intellectual breakthrough has occurred. The "end of philosophy" here represents the boldest possible assertion concerning the enterprise of philosophy itself, and the particular success achieved by individual human beings.

> *It is the unstated but powerful motivating conviction that a final vocabulary has been achieved, that a given text, discourse, or framework has a privileged attachment to reality, that this particular theory is not still another commentary but is instead the vocabulary in which mute reality would have chosen to describe itself, if it only could have.[5]*

Richard Rorty speaks of these foundational revolts as attempts to "transform philosophy into a science—a discipline in which universally recognized decision-procedures are available for testing philosophical theses."[6] He names Descartes, Kant, Hegel, and Wittgenstein (among others) as examples of thinkers who thought they had succeeded in clearing away forever the false problems that troubled earlier philosophy; in each, there is the conviction that we now have ascertained the ultimate principles or methodology that will allow the human intellect whatever knowledge is within its capacity.

There is still some work to be done, of course, but we can better characterize this (following Thomas Seebohn) as reproductive work, distinguished from the groundbreaking and truly philosophical production work. What remains to be done is *relatively* simple: we must fine-tune our information, seek out its fullest applications, and update our files.

> *History teaches that the productive phases of philosophy are rare and extremely short—two or three generations—and that the phases of reproduction are very long. "Philosophy is at an end" is, seen from here, a judgment which implies that philosophy has exhausted all its possibilities and that philosophical activity in the future is restricted to reproduction and corroborating interpretation.[7]*

---

4. They are important in the sense that they make the end of philosophy a *conceptual* necessity by the implications of their inner logic. These discussions of the end of philosophy are to be distinguished from other senses of philosophy's end as, for example, when the activity of philosophy is politically forbidden, or impossible because of more urgent practical concerns, or simply no longer of interest to people. These contingent senses of the end of philosophy are outlined briefly in B. Magnus, "The End of 'The End of Philosophy'," in *Hermeneutics and Deconstruction,* edited by H.J. Silverman and D. Ihde (Albany: SUNY Press, 1985), pp. 2–10.

5. Magnus, p. 2.

6. R. Rorty, "Metaphilosophical Difficulties of Linguistic Philosophy," *The Linguistic Turn,* ed. R. Rorty (Chicago: University of Chicago Press), pp. 1–40.

7. T. Seebohn, "Three Historical Aphorisms," in *Hermeneutics and Deconstruction,* edited by H.J. Silverman and D. Ihde (Albany: SUNY Press, 1985), pp. 11–23.

One way to understand the philosopher's concern for ultimacy is to say that this kind of success is the implicit ambition of every philosophical system, however grandiose this might sound, simply because it is the nature of the question to which the philosopher addresses himself. If the end has been achieved in this positive sense, we have an unassailable authority, what Magnus calls a sacred text:

> *[I]f a final solution to philosophical questions were achieved, philosophy would become distinguishable from theology primarily with reference to what each took as its sacred text.* **That** *there would have to be such a privileged text or texts—whose meaning and application it would become our job to review—should be obvious.*[8]

Some have characterized the position articulated above as the "God's eye view,"[9] but that label is somewhat misleading. For clearly not all those who would correct the misguided attempts in the history of philosophy do so in a metaphysically ambitious manner. For instance, just to consider some of the names on Rorty's list: Descartes thought that intellectual certitude could be achieved if the mind avoided overambition; it cannot, for example, grasp the purposes of nature. Kant comes to the conclusion that we can never know things in themselves. We must, however, assume that God knows these truths. The preferred term, therefore, is foundationalism.

The fact that foundationalism may be more or less metaphysically ambitious hints at the *second* sense in which we speak of the end of the philosophy. Not only does great achievement effectively end philosophy, but so does lesser expectations. (Of course, to determine the limitations of the human intellect is itself a great philosophical achievement.) That is to say, a philosopher could achieve the end of philosophy by figuring out all the fundamental truths of the universe; alternatively, he may end the practice of philosophy by discovering that there are very few ultimate truths accessible to the human intellect. Taken to its logical extreme, this latter strategy could simply pronounce that there are no philosophical answers to be discovered, that there are in fact no legitimate philosophical issues. To put the point bluntly, the whole enterprise of philosophy, at least as it has traditionally been understood, is bogus. The philosophical ambition of ascertaining the ultimate truths about the world, to discover, as Magnus put it, "the vocabulary in which mute reality would have chosen to describe itself, if it only could have" is not just hopelessly pretentious, but also fundamentally misguided.

What do those who make this argument understand themselves to be doing? Their answers will be different, of course, but they must agree that philosophical truth no longer stands as the ultimate justification of intellectual claims. Rorty suggests that we imagine ourselves as participants in a post-philosophical culture in which the traditional issues of philosophy are now better understood to constitute yet another (and not necessarily superior) genre of literature. Philosophy now accepts itself to be "another voice in the conversation of mankind":

---

8.   Magnus, p. 3.

9.   Magnus attributes this label to Sellars, Rorty, and Putnam (p.2).

[Philosophy] centers on one topic rather than another at some given time not by dialectical necessity but as a result of various things happening elsewhere in the conversation (the New Science, the French Revolution, the modern novel) or of individual men of genius who think of something new (Hegel, Marx, Frege, Freud, Wittgenstein, Heidegger) or perhaps of the resultant of several such factors. Interesting philosophical change (we might say "philosophical progress" but this would be question-begging) occurs not when a new way is found to deal with an old problem but when a new set of problems emerges and the old ones begin to fade away.[10]

On this understanding, the philosopher must content himself to clarify discussions, but he has no proper domain, nor is he capable of ascertaining anything of absolute or eternal value. The value of his discipline, as Magnus puts it, is therapeutic: "There will be no constraints upon philosophical inquiry save conversational ones, shaped by our shared need to cope."[11]

The two senses of the end of philosophy outlined here are related in that each understands itself to be the decisive refutation of the other. The implications of this debate, quite obviously, are profound and far-reaching. If philosophy is simply another voice in the conversation of mankind, one that must abandon any privilege on the basis of truth, the same status would seem, *a fortiori,* to apply to the other disciplines. The character of enterprises such as theology, law, and literature, for example, is now fundamentally and irrecoverably altered. The only thing that can speak in such a world is the voice of politics (which is here understood to operate entirely according to rules of power and persuasion).

It is worth noting that the latter kind of pronouncement, and its resulting all-or-nothing challenge, arrives upon the scene relatively late in the history of philosophy, and demands some explanation. In Marx's *Introduction to the Critique of Hegel's Philosophy of the Right* (1844) there is serious discussion about the end of philosophy, but a more instructive figure to consider to understand the development of this attitude is German philosopher Friedrich Nietzsche (1844–1900). In a series of brilliant writings, but perhaps most pointedly in *Beyond Good and Evil* (1886), Nietzsche develops what has been called a "perspectivist" epistemology. Nietzsche argues, with considerable rhetorical flair, that all serious intellectual achievements are best understood as projections of the human will to power. Philosophers create values, they do not present an accurate world picture that has been discovered from some neutral vantage point. In *Beyond Good and Evil* we are told that

... every great philosophy so far has been [a] personal confession of its author and a kind of involuntary and unconscious memoir; also that the moral (or immoral) intentions in every philosophy constituted the real germ from which the whole plant had grown.[12]

Since one can never escape one's own personal (and limited) perspective, from

---

10.   Richard Rorty, *Philosophy and the Mirror of Nature,* (Princeton University Press, 1979), p. 264. The phrase "voice in the conversation of mankind" Rorty takes from Michael Oakeshott.

11.   Magnus. p. 7.

12.   Friedrich Nietzsche, *Beyond Good and Evil,* trans. by W. Kaufmann (New York: Vintage, 1966), p. 13.

one's own willful grasps at power, it follows that, as he declares in *Human, All Too Human,* that "there are no eternal facts, as there are no absolute truths."[13] The entire program of Nietzsche's perspectivism is captured in his aphoristic refutation of positivism: "there are no facts, there are only interpretations of facts."[14]

The traditional philosopher (i.e., the foundationalist) might instinctively attempt to catch Nietzsche in his own web. He will say that Nietzsche has offered his perspectivism as if it were true, as though it were *the* correct, or at least the best, way to understand what all the noise is about. Thus, goes the argument, Nietzsche's perspectivism self-refutes, just as all the old skeptical rejoinders to philosophical aspiration have been shown to collapse. But Nietzsche has proven to be not so easily dismissed. He would respond that his perspectivism should not be characterized as an epistemology (as was suggested above); furthermore, his views should not be understood as arguments that seek approval from the bar of impartial reason. In fact, the urge to claim possession of absolute truth is a pathological condition that seems to have a hold on professional philosophers, Nietzsche would insist, and *this* is what needs explaining.

The spirit of Nietzsche's philosophy has become formalized in contemporary theories of language, psychology, and epistemology. In fact, one could make a good case for Nietzsche as the single greatest influence on the culture of the twentieth century. Whereas Nietzsche's "arguments" often seem to consist in mere rhetoric, his followers (regardless of how consciously they have identified themselves as such) have undertaken to provide less flippant justifications for the same conclusions. They offer their arguments in earnest, very much in the manner of the traditional philosopher, yet they arrive at the place Nietzsche did: that philosophy truly is at the end, or perhaps better said, we are at the beginning of new era in philosophy, one in which we no longer overestimate the possibilities of our discipline. The Nietzschean premise, which many twentieth century followers accept as an article of faith, is that we are always once-removed from the world that we long to possess intellectually. We have *immediate* access only to our interpretations (not to the interpreted), we should therefore turn our serious attention to the business of interpretation itself. The name we give this effort is *hermeneutics,* which is sometimes calls the "science of interpretation." But since 'science' is a word that carries foundationalist baggage, we do better to understand our new philosophical enterprise to be the rigorous interpretation of interpretations. We turn now to that issue.

---

13. F. Nietzsche, *Human All Too Human,* trans. by H. Zimmern and P.V. Kohn in *The Complete Works of Friedrich Nietzsche,* ed. by O. Levy (New York: Macmillan, 1909-1911).

14. The aphorism has become better known than the accurate wording that is contained in *The Will to Power:* "In opposition to Positivism, which halts at phenomena and says: `There are only *facts* and nothing more,' I would say: No, facts is precisely what is lacking, all that exists consists of interpretation." See F. Nietzsche, *The Will to Power,* trans. by W. Kaufmann and R.J. Holingdale (New York: Vintage Press, 1968), par. 481.

The Hermeneutical Circle

Nietzsche's aphorism, if taken seriously, implies that we are hopelessly trapped within the boundaries of an interpretive context, which context mediates our contact with the "real" world. Since we cannot have an immediate (i.e., a "pure" or theory-innocent) experience of the world, any discussion about that which is beyond our interpretive schemes is impossible. The desire to overleap this contextual limitation reveals, according to Nietzsche, an arrogant longing for a God's eye view.

The resulting dilemma, the fact that all our intellectual efforts to reach the world are now understood to be exercises in frustration because we constantly return to yet another mediating scheme, has come to be known as the "hermeneutical circle." There are a number of ways to understand this term (I will outline two basic senses in this article), but the most immediate picture it conveys may prove the most helpful: we are caught *inside* the circle, the boundaries of which are the interpretative schemes that we possess and constantly reinterpret. (We might understand the Nietzschean impasse as an early articulation of what has come to be known, in the philosophy of language, as the problem of reference.) But the interpretive schemes, which allow us to conceptualize the bare facts of the world, also necessarily prevent our intimacy with it. As Gayle Ormiston and Alan Schrift write:

> If "there are only interpretations . . . of interpretations," then the systematic pursuit of "truth"—"truth" as the object of inquiry—or the search for axiological, epistemological, and metaphysical foundations, will never be brought to completion . . . The search after truth, as it were, is deferred, diverted, caught in a network of contextually bound and generated commentaries.[15]

As this passage implies, the articulation of the truth is a possibility that arises only within a certain kind of conceptual or linguistic context. Even the mere formulation of the question, "Is this true?" begs a host of questions about the presumed structure of the issue. These structures need to be reflected upon, or interpreted, and this is a process of continual self-disclosure that cannot come to an end because each disclosure is itself meaningful only in terms of some other presumed context. Philosophers can continue to pride themselves on their notorious "depth" although we now understand that they are not actually getting anywhere by their digging.

But why should this be so? How have we become convinced that our conceptual and linguistic structures are utterly incapable of reaching the world? We can locate the seed of this problem in the epistemological premises of early modern philosophy. John Locke, for example, was an empiricist who believed that our words "can properly and immediately signify nothing but the ideas that are in the mind of the speaker." The human mind, according to Locke, is originally a blank slate (*tabula rasa*) which records (as ideas) those adventitious impressions made on the senses by

---

15. Gayle L. Ormiston and Alan D. Schrift, "Editors' Introduction," in *The Hermeneutic Tradition* edited by G. Ormiston and A. Schrift (Albany: SUNY press, 1990), p.3.

the objects in the world. Presumably, the ideas *resemble* the actual objects, but what is before the mind is always, by definition, the idea. If we couple this empirical premise with the picture of the Cartesian ego, utterly disengaged from the world, limited to contemplation of the parade of ideas across the mind's stage, we now have all the elements of a hermeneutical circle. We imagine ourselves to be inside the circle, spectating the ideas that sit on the borders of that circle; the world itself is a third thing now once-removed from the mind's direct contemplation. Ian Hacking writes:

> *The Cartesian ego has set the stage. The ego able to contemplate what is within it ponders what lies outside. There are some objects that we can contemplate without being logically committed to the existence of anything other than the ego. These objects are ideas.[16]*

Locke himself never doubts, as does Descartes, that the world is really out there; that its objects are the necessary causes of the ideas in the mind; and that those ideas perfectly replicate the objects of the world in the theater of the mind. But he seems to accept, as do most of the moderns, the paradigm according to which we understand the epistemological problematic, i.e., that the mind "in here" tries to match up with the realities of the world "out there." As we saw above, Locke thought that when we used words properly they signify the ideas in our minds. He goes on to say that men also give to their words two "secret

references," which we must assume are not proper.

> *First, [men] suppose their words to be marks of the ideas in the minds also of other men, with whom they communicate: For else they should talk in vain ... Secondly, because men would not be thought to talk barely of their own imaginations, but of things as they really are; therefore they often suppose their words to stand also for the reality of things.[17]*

Locke evidences some discomfort about language's connection to the world, but he does not seem troubled about the relationship of ideas to the objects in the world. It is George Berkeley who sees clearly the premises and implications of the Lockean paradigm, and the deep epistemological difficulties that are contained therein. Berkeley understands that the "third thing" outside the circle is both ontologically and epistemologically unaccounted for; he believes that its supposition is tantamount to atheism. In *A Treatise Concerning the Principles of Human Knowledge* he declares that "an idea can be like nothing but an idea," by which pronouncement he in effect brings everything *inside* the circle.[18] His own rather severe logic forces him to conclude that "to be is to be perceived" *(esse est percipi),* certainly one of the most challenging positions ever adopted by a philosopher. Berkeley asserts that empiricism necessarily entails immaterialism (there are only active minds and passive ideas, thus eliminating the material "third thing"); fur-

16. Ian Hacking, *Why Does Language Matter to Philosophy?,* (Cambridge University Press, 1975), p. 29.

17. John Locke, *An Essay Concerning Human Understanding,* III, 2,4, edited by Peter Nidditch (Oxford: Clarendon University Press, 1975.) (Italics omitted.)

18. George Berkeley, *A Treatise Concerning the Principles of Human Knowledge,* section 8, (Indianapolis: Bobbs-Merrill, 1957).

thermore, his idealism is dependably realistic because it requires the existence of God, who functions in this worldview as the all-sustaining Absolute Mind.

The difficulties of Berkeley's position are well known, and the path he takes is not followed by all the practitioners of the hermeneutical movement. But he has brought to light a seemingly intractable difficulty for empiricism: if one posits a chasm between mind and the world, nothing can serve adequately to bridge it. No idea is able to "clearly and distinctly" (Descartes' epistemological criterion) convey to the mind the structure of reality on the other side of that chasm (i.e., "outside the circle"). Herein lies the force of Nietzsche's aphorism: the *mediating* ideas are best understood as competing interpretations of that which lies on the other side of the chasm. No interpretation as such can lay claim to an epistemologically privileged status; therefore, prespectivistic differences (which Jacques Derrida emphasizes with the term *différance)* are absolute and insuperable. Ormiston and Schrift summarize:

> *Resemblance and similitude simultaneously betray and employ difference(s). As such, dissimilitude, difference, and dissimulation intrude upon all of our works, judgments and pronouncements.[19]*

The choice, to put it rather simply, seems to be between two alternatives: 1) one can deny that there is a gap, as does Berkeley, and travel the route of idealism; or 2) one can focus attention on the media-tion itself, i.e., on the structure of ideas which inform so far as they resemble the particular objects constituting "reality." In either case, the philosopher now understands himself to be limited to the parameters of his own conceptual world.

The hermeneutical movement, generally speaking, can be understood as a logical outcome of the foregoing dilemma. There is one crucial point to be inserted here: when the early modern philosopher turned his attention to his conceptual world, he understood himself to be contemplating his ideas. For the contemporary philosopher, on the other hand, to contemplate the parameters of one's own conceptual world is to study the language in which and through which propositions are articulable. Ian Hacking has this transition in mind when he calls early modern philosophy (the age of Locke) the "heyday of ideas," and contemporary philosophy the "heyday of meaning." Locke himself had confronted (although does not seem to worry about) the problem that motivates this transition: according to Locke, words *properly* signify the private idea in a speaker's mind. It is only by "secret reference" that they refer to real objects in the world, or that they allow us to communicate with others "in the common acceptation of that language." Beginning with the work of Gottlob Frege (1848–1925), contemporary philosophy has made an issue of the latter secret reference, thus initiating a serious investigation into the nature of meaning.[20] For unlike Locke, the contem-

---

19. Ormiston and Schrift, p. 2.

porary philosopher is less likely to consider private contemplation of ideas to be the epistemological touchstone; avoiding such solipsism (again, the legacy of Descartes) the contemporary philosopher more likely considers communicability (even to oneself in reflection) to be a necessary condition of any knowledge claim. We move away, therefore, from the "picture-theory" of language (i.e., the conviction that the structure of our propositions exactly parallels, and so depicts, that of objective reality) and toward a view according to which words possess meaning through their inclusion in what Ludwig Wittgenstein calls a "language game" (*Sprachspiel*).

To return to the point, the hermeneutical movement should be understood as the attempt by the contemporary philosopher to probe the conceptual schemes according to which and through which the knower has *mediate* access to reality. This enterprise might be called, as it was above, the interpretation of interpretation; perhaps better said, hermeneutics is the critical self-reflection on the ultimate structure of meaning. This implies, in effect, that the fundamental question for the metaphysician, in his attempt to grasp ultimate reality, is the relation of language and being. Increasingly, at least within some circles, this is the way the ultimate questions are posed.

For example, consider the following twentieth-century pronouncements: "Like everything metaphysical, the harmony between thought and reality is to be found in the grammar of the language" (Ludwig Wittgenstein);[21] "Language is not simply one tool which man possesses along with many others; it is only language that makes possible our standing with openness to what is" (Martin Heidegger);[22] and, finally, "Being that can be understood is language" (Hans-Georg Gadamer).[23] Of course, the hermeneutical premise, the conviction that metaphysical speculation is inextricably bound up with the language game in which it participates, may lead thinkers along very different routes, and to quite different conclusions. We shall now briefly consider these possibilities.

Description and Ultimacy

It was promised above that two senses of the hermeneutical circle would be outlined in this paper. Much of the discussion so far has articulated itself in terms of the inside-outside metaphor, which is the first, easily imagined, sense of the hermeneutical circle. According to this sense, the challenge for the metaphysician is to justify the claim that his grasp for the ultimate principles of being and

20. In Frege's view, words can refer to objects in the real world only through their meaning (meaning he calls *Sinn,* distinguished against the reference or *Bedeutung).* See his "On Sense and Nominatum," in *Readings in Philosophical Analysis,* H. Feigl and W. Sellars, eds. (New York: Appleton-Century-Crofts, 1949), pp. 85–102.

21. Ludwig Wittgenstein, *Zettel,* trans, by G.E.M. Anscombe (Berkeley: University of California Press, 1967), section 55.

22. Martin Heidegger, *Erlauterung zu Holderlins Dichtung,* Frankfort, 1944.

23. Hans-Georg Gadamer, *Truth and Method,* trans. by Garrett Barden and John Cumming (New York: Seabury Press, 1977), p. 421.

knowing is not irremediably context-bound. That is, he must demonstrate that somehow he has reached the bare structure of the world, and not simply the inside surface of the perspectivist circle which he inhabits. We can now appreciate the second sense of the circle, which is implied by the first. If the attempt to reach the ultimate facts of being is caught up in the net of interpretation, and if this interpretive net is itself now subject to hermeneutical assessment, there is something necessarily interminable about the hermeneutical study. Michel Foucault observes that an interpretation "always has to interpret itself . . . [it] cannot fail to return to itself."[24] Here the sense is not inside-outside the circle, but rather the circularity of the hermeneutical premise.

It is tempting to assume that the two senses are equivalent. Far from being an automatic inference, however, this question in effect reformulates the fundamental issue for the hermeneutical philosopher. How are the necessary conditions of conceptualization related to the ultimate conditions of being? We can imagine different answers to this question that emerges from the hermeneutical project. The first sense of the circle is clearly perspectivistic; it announces, in effect, the impossibility of philosophical foundationalism. That is to say, to accept the premise of the hermeneutical circle in this sense is to forfeit the possibility of ultimate success, and so announces the end of the philosophical project as originally conceived.

The second sense, however, holds out the possibility of progress in hermeneutical self-reflection. Heidegger, for example, believes that, as he puts it, understanding is a primordial way of being-in-the-world. One cannot avoid the hermeneutical circle, but the circle itself is not vicious, because the progressive disclosure of meaning is of ontological, and not simply of epistemological, significance. We cannot, in this paper, do justice to the deep complexity of the Heideggerian project; suffice to say, however, that the commitment to hermeneutics is not necessarily an abandonment of the traditional metaphysical concerns. For the recognition that any intellectual intimacy with being involves conceptual structure does not preclude the possibility that the intellectual capacity of the human intellect can, paradoxically, transcend that which conditions its operation. Though, at least in one sense, description is necessarily ultimate, it cannot arise *ex nihilo*. That is to say, description must be *about* something. Man exercises his intellectual powers through articulation, but his metaphysical flights seek out that which is thereby articulated. And this is being.

---

24. Michel Foucault, "Neitzsche, Freud, Marx," *Transforming the Hermeneutical Context: From Nietzsche to Nancy,* edited by Gayle L. Ormiston and Alan D. Schrift (Albany: SUNY Press 1990), pp. 59-67.

46

Ludwig Wittgenstein
Language Games and Forms of Life

§2 That [Augustine's] philosophical concept of meaning has its place in a primitive idea of the way language functions. But one can also say that it is the idea of a language more primitive than ours.

Let us imagine a language for which the description given by Augustine is right. The language is meant to serve for communication between a builder A and an assistant B. A is building with buildingstones: there are blocks, pillars, slabs and beams. B has to pass the stones, and that in the order in which A needs them. For this purpose they use a language consisting of the words "block", "pillar", "slab", "beam". A calls them out;— B brings the stone which he has learnt to bring at such-and-such a call.—Conceive this as a complete primitive language.

§3 Augustine, we might say, does describe a system of communication; only not everything that we call language is this system. And one has to say this in many cases where the question arises "Is this an appropriate description or not?" The answer is: "Yes, it is appropriate, but only for this narrowly circumscribed region, not for the whole of what you are claiming to describe."

It is as if someone were to say: "A game consists in moving objects about on a surface according to certain rules . . ."—and we replied: You seem to be thinking of board games, but there are others. You can make your definition correct by expressly restricting it to those games.

§4 Imagine a script in which the letters were used to stand for sounds, and also as signs of emphasis and punctuation. (A script can be conceived as a language for describing sound-patterns.) Now imagine someone interpreting that script as if there were simply a correspondence of letters to sounds and as if the letters had not also completely different functions. Augustine's conception of language is like such an over-simple conception of the script.

§5 If we look at the example in §1, we may perhaps get an inkling how much this general notion of the meaning of the word surrounds the working of language with a haze which makes clear vision impossible. It disperses the fog to study the phenomena of language in primitive kinds of application in which one can command a clear view of the aim and functioning of the words.

A child uses such primitive forms of language when it learns to talk. Here the teaching of language is not explanation, but training.

§6 We could imagine that the language of §2 was the *whole* language of A and B; even the whole language of a tribe. The children are brought up to perform *these* actions, to use *these* words as they do so, and to react in *this* way to the words of others.

An important part of the training will consist in the teacher's pointing to the objects, directing the child's attention to them, and at the same time uttering a word; for instance, the word "slab" as he points to that

---

shape. (I do not want to call this "ostensive definition", because the child cannot as yet *ask* what the name is. I will call it "ostensive teaching of words".—I say that it will form an important part of the training, because it is so with human beings; not because it could not be imagined otherwise.) This ostensive teaching of words can be said to establish an association between the word and the thing. But what does this mean? Well, it may mean various things; but one very likely thinks first of all that a picture of the object comes before the child's mind when it hears the word. But now, if this does happen—is it the purpose of the word?—Yes, it *may* be the purpose.—I can imagine such a use of words (of series of sounds). (Uttering a word is like striking a note on the keyboard of the imagination.) But in the language of §2 it is *not* the purpose of the words to evoke images. (It may, of course, be discovered that that helps to attain the actual purpose.)

But if the ostensive teaching has this effect,—am I to say that it effects an understanding of the word? Don't you understand the call "Slab!" if you act upon it in such-and-such a way?—Doubtless the ostensive teaching helped to bring this about; but only together with a particular training. With different training the same ostensive teaching of these words would have effected a quite different understanding.

"I set the brake up by connecting up rod and lever."—Yes, given the whole of the rest of the mechanism. Only in conjunction with that is it a brake-lever, and separated from its support it is not even a lever; it may be anything, or nothing.

§7 In the practice of the use of language (2) one party calls out the words, the other acts on them. In instruction in the language the following process will occur: the learner *names* the objects; that is, he utters the word when the teacher points to the stone.—And there will be this still simpler exercise: the pupil repeats the words after the teacher—both of these being processes resembling language.

We can also think of the whole process of using words in (2) as one of those games by means of which children learn their native language. I will call these games "language-games" and will sometimes speak of a primitive language as a language-game.

And the processes of naming the stones and repeating words after someone might also be called language-games. Think of much of the use of words in games like ring-a-ring-a-roses.

I shall also call the whole, consisting of language and the actions into which it is woven, the "language-game".

§8 Let us now look at an expansion of language (2). Besides the four words "block", "pillar", etc., let it contain a series of words used as the shopkeeper in (1) used the numerals (it can be the series of letters of the alphabet); further, let there be two words, which may as well be "there" and "this" (because this roughly indicates their purpose), that are used in connexion with a pointing gesture; and finally a number of colour samples. A gives an order like: "d—slab—there". At the same time he shews the assistant a colour sample, and when he says "there" he points to a place on the building site. From the stock of slabs B takes one for each letter of the alphabet up to "d", of the same colour as the sample, and brings them to the place indicated by

A.—On other occasions A gives the order "this—there", at "this" he points to a building stone. And so on.

§9 When a child learns this language, it has to learn the series of 'numerals' a, b, c, . . . by heart. And it has to learn their use.—Will this training include ostensive teaching of the words?—Well, people will, for example, point to slabs and count: "a, b, c slabs".—Something more like the ostensive teaching of the words "block", "pillar", etc. would be the ostensive teaching of numerals that serve not to count but to refer to groups of objects that can be taken in at a glance. Children do learn the use of the first five or six cardinal numerals in this way.

Are "there" and "this" also taught ostensively?—Imagine how one might perhaps teach their use. One will point to places and things—but in this case the pointing occurs in the *use* of the words too and not merely in learning the use.—

§10 Now what do the words of this language *signify*?—What is supposed to shew what they signify, if not the kind of use they have? And we have already described that. So we are asking for the expression "This word signifies *this*" to be made a part of the description. In other words the description ought to take the form: "The word . . . signifies . . ."

Of course, one can reduce the description of the use of the word "slab" to the statement that this word signifies this object. This will be done when, for example, it is merely a matter of removing the mistaken idea that the word "slab" refers to the shape of building-stone that we in fact call a "block"—but the kind of '*referring*' this is, that is to say the use of these words for

the rest, is already known.

Equally one can say that the signs "a", "b", etc. signify numbers; when for example this removes the mistaken idea that "a", "b", "c", play the part actually played in language by "block", "slab", "pillar". And one can also say that "c" means this number and not that one; when for example this serves to explain that the letters are to be used in the order a, b, c, d, etc. and not in the order a, b, d, c.

But assimilating the descriptions of the uses of words in this way cannot make the uses themselves any more like one another. For, as we see they are absolutely unlike.

§11 Think of the tools in a tool-box: there is a hammer, pliers, a saw, a screw-driver, a rule, a glue-pot, glue, nails and screws.—The functions of words are as diverse as the functions of these objects. (And in both cases there are similarities.)

Of course, what confuses us is the uniform appearance of words when we hear them spoken or meet them in script and print. For their *application* is not presented to us so clearly. Especially when we are doing philosophy!

§12 It is like looking into a cabin of a locomotive. We see handles all looking more or less alike. (Naturally, since they are all supposed to be handled.) But one is the handle of a crank which can be moved continuously (it regulates the opening of a valve); another is the handle of a switch, which has only two effective positions, it is either off or on; a third is the handle of a brake-lever, the harder one pulls on it, the harder it brakes; a fourth, the handle of a pump: it has an effect only so long as it is moved to and fro.

§13 When we say: "Every word in

language signifies something" we have so far said *nothing whatever;* unless we have explained exactly *what* distinction we wish to make. (It might be, of course, that we wanted to distinguish the words of language (8) from words 'without meaning' such as occur in Lewis Carroll's poems, or words like "Lilliburlero" in songs.)

§14 Imagine someone's saying: "*All* tools serve to modify something. Thus the hammer modifies the position of the nail, the saw the shape of the board, and so on."— And what is modified by the rule, the glue-pot, the nails?—"Our knowledge of a thing's length, the temperature of the glue, and the solidity of the box."—Would anything be gained by this assimilation of expressions?—

§15 The word "to signify" is perhaps used in the most straight-forward way when the object signified is marked with the sign. Suppose that the tools A uses in building bear certain marks. When A shews his assistant such a mark, he brings the tool that has that mark on it.

It is in this and more or less similar ways that a name means and is given to a thing.— It will often prove useful in philosophy to say to ourselves: naming something is like attaching a label to a thing.

§16 What about the colour samples that A shews to B: are they part of the *language?* Well, it is as you please. They do not belong among the words; yet when I say to someone: "Pronounce the word 'the'", you will count the second "the" as part of the sentence. Yet is has a role just like that of a colour-sample in language-game (8); that is, it is a sample of what the other is meant to say.

It is most natural, and causes least confusion, to reckon the samples among the instruments of the language.

(Remark on the reflexive pronoun "*this* sentence".)

§17 It will be possible to say: In language (8) we have different *kinds of word.* For the functions of the word "slab" and the word "block" are more alike than those of "slab" and "d". But how we group words into kinds will depend on the aim of the classification,—and on our own inclination.

Think of the different points of view from which we can classify tools or chess-men.

§18 Do not be troubled by the fact that languages (2) and (8) consist only of orders. If you want to say that this shews them to be incomplete, ask yourself whether our language is complete;—whether it was so before the symbolism of chemistry and the notation of the infinitesimal calculus were incorporated in it; for these are, so to speak, suburbs of our langauge. (And how many houses or streets does it take before a town begins to be a town?) Our langauge can be seen as an ancient city: a maze of little streets and squares, of old and new houses, and of houses with additions from various periods; and this surrounded by a multitude of new boroughs with straight regular streets and uniform houses.

§19 It is easy to imagine a language consisting only of orders and reports in battle.—Or a language consisting only of questions and expressions for answering yes and no. And innumerable others.—And to imagine a language means to imagine a form of life.

But what about this: is the call "Slab!" in example (2) a sentence or a word?—If a word, surely it has not the same meaning as the like-sounding word of our ordinary language, for in §2 it is a call. But if a sentence, it is surely not the elliptical sentence: "Slab!" of our language,—As far as the first question goes you can call "Slab!" a word and also a sentence; perhaps it could be appropriately called a 'degenerate sentence' (as one speaks of a degenerate hyperbola); in fact it *is* our 'elliptical' sentence.—But that is surely only a shortened form of the sentence "Bring me a slab", and there is no such sentence in example (2).—But why should I not on the contrary have called the sentence "Bring me a slab!" a *lengthening* of a sentence "Slab!"?—Because if you shout "Slab!" you really mean: "Bring me a slab".—Do you say the unshortened sentence to yourself? And why should I translate the call "Slab!" into a different expression in order to say what someone means by it? And if they mean the same thing—why should I not say: "When he says 'Slab!' he means 'Slab!'"? Again, if you can mean "Bring me the slab", why should you not be able to mean "Slab!"?—But when I call "Slab!", then what I want is, *that he should bring me a slab!*—Certainly, but does 'wanting this' consist in thinking in some form or other a different sentence from the one you utter?—

§20 But now it looks as if when someone says "Bring me a slab" he could mean this expression as *one* long word corresponding to the single word "Slab!"—Then can one mean it sometimes as one word and sometimes as four? And how does one usually mean it?—I think we shall be inclined to say: we mean the sentence as *four* words when we use it in contrast with other sentences such as *"Hand* me a slab", "Bring *him* a slab", "Bring *two* slabs", etc.; that is, in contrast with sentences containing the separating words of our command in other

combinations.—But what does using one sentence in contrast with others consist in? Do the others, perhaps, hover before one's mind? *All* of them? And *while* one is saying the one sentence, or before, or afterwards?— No. Even if such an explanation rather tempts us, we need only think for a moment of what actually happens in order to see that we are going astray here. We say that we use the command in contrast with other sentences because *our language* contains the possibility of those other sentences. Someone who did not understand our language, a foreigner, who had fairly often heard someone giving the order: "Bring me a slab!", might believe that this whole series of sounds was one word corresponding perhaps to the word for "building-stone" in his language. If he himself had then given this order perhaps he would have pronounced it differently, and we should say: he pronounces it so oddly because he takes it for a *single* word.—But then, is there not also something different going on in him when he pronounces it,—something corresponding to the fact that he conceives the sentence as a *single* word?—Either the same thing may go on in him, or something different. For what goes on in you when you give such an order? Are you conscious of its consisting of four words *while* you are uttering it? Of course you have a *mastery* of this language—which contains those other sentences as well—but is this having a mastery something that *happens* while you are uttering the sentence?—And I have admitted that the foreigner will probably pronounce a sentence differently if he conceives it differently; but what we call his wrong conception *need* not lie in anything that accompanies the utterance of the command.

The sentence is 'elliptical', not because it leaves out something that we think when we utter it, but because it is shortened—in comparison with a particular paradigm of our grammar.—Of course one might object here: "You grant that the shortened and the unshortened sentence have the same sense.—What is this sense, then? Isn't there a verbal expression for this sense?"—But doesn't the fact that sentences have the same sense consist in their having the same *use?*—(In Russian one says "stone red" instead of "the stone is red"; do they feel the copula to be missing in the sense, or attach it in *thought?*)

§21 Imagine a language-game in which A asks and B reports the number of slabs or blocks in a pile, or the colours and shapes of the building-stones that are stacked in such-and-such a place.—Such a report might run: "Five slabs". Now what is the difference between the report or statement "Five slabs" and the order "Five slabs!"?—Well, it is the part which uttering these words plays in the language-game. No doubt the tone of voice and the look with which they are uttered, and much else besides, will also be different. But we could also imagine the tone's being the same—for an order and a report can be spoken in a *variety* of tones of voice and with various expressions of face—the difference being only in the application. (Of course, we might use the words "statement" and "command" to stand for grammatical forms of sentence and intonations; we do in fact call "Isn't the weather glorious to-day?" a question, although it is used as a statement.) We could imagine a language in which *all* statements had the form and tone of rhetorical questions; or every

command the form of the question "Would you like to . . .?". Perhaps it will then be said: "What he says has the form of a question but is really a command",—that is, has the function of a command in the technique of using the language. (Similarly one says "You will do this: not as a prophecy but as a command. What makes it the one or the other?)

§22 Frege's idea that every assertion contains an assumption, which is the thing that is asserted, really rests on the possibility found in our language of writing every statement in the form: "It is asserted that such-and-such is the case."—But "that such-and-such is the case" is *not* a sentence in our language—so far it is not a *move* in the language-game. And if I write, not "It is asserted that . . . .", but "It is asserted: such-and-such is the case", the words "It is asserted" simply become superfluous.

We might very well also write every statement in the form of a question followed by a "Yes"; for instance" "Is it raining! Yes!" Would this shew that every statement contained a question?

Of course we have the right to use an assertion sign in contrast with a question-mark, for example, or if we want to distinguish an assertion from a fiction or a supposition. It is only a mistake if one thinks that the assertion consists of two actions, entertaining and asserting (assigning the truth-value, or something of the kind), and that in performing these actions we follow the propositional sign roughly as we sing from the musical score. Reading the written sentence loud or soft is indeed comparable with singing from a musical score, but *'meaning'* (thinking) the sentence that is read is not.

Frege's assertion sign marks the *beginning of the sentence*. Thus its function is like that of the full-stop. It distinguishes the whole period from a clause *within* the period. If I hear someone say "it's raining" but do not know whether I have heard the beginning and end of the period, so far this sentence does not serve to tell me anything.

§23 But how many kinds of sentence are there? Say assertion, question, and command?—There are *countless* kinds: countless different kinds of use of what we call "symbols", "words", "sentences". And this multiplicity is not something fixed, given once for all; but new types of language, new language-games as we may say, come into existence, and others become obsolete and get forgotten. (We can get a *rough picture* of this from the changes in mathematics.)

Here the term "language-*game*" is meant to bring into prominence the fact that the *speaking* of language is part of an activity, or of a form of life.

Review the multiplicity of language-games in the following examples, and in others:

Giving orders, and obeying them—
Describing the appearance of an object, or giving its measurements—
Constructing an object from a description (a drawing)—
Reporting an event—
Speculating about an event—

Forming and testing a hypothesis—
Presenting the results of an experiment
in tables and diagrams—
Making up a story; and reading it—
Play-acting—
Singing catches—
Guessing riddles—
Making a joke; telling it—
Solving a problem in practical arithmetic—
Translating from one language into another—
Asking, thanking, cursing, greeting, praying.

—It is interesting to compare the multiplicity of the tools in language and of the ways they are used, the multiplicity of kinds of word and sentence, with what logicians have said about the structure of language. (Including the author of the *Tractatus Logico-Philosophicus.*)

§24 If you do not keep the multiplicity of language-games in view you will perhaps be inclined to ask questions like: "What is a question?"—Is it the statement that I do not know such-and-such, or the statement that I wish the other person would tell me . . . .? Or is it the description of my mental state of uncertainty?—And is the cry "Help!" such a description?

Think how many different kinds of thing are called "description": description of a body's position by means of its co-ordinates; description of a facial expression; description of a sensation of touch; of a mood.

Of course it is possible to substitute the form of statement or description for the usual form of question: "I want to know

---

Imagine a picture representing a boxer in a particular stance. Now, this picture can be used to tell someone how he should stand, should hold himself; or how he should not hold himself; or how a particular man did stand in such-and-such a place; and so on. One might (using the language of chemistry) call this picture a proposition-radical. This will be how Frege thought of the "assumption".

whether . . . ." or "I am in doubt whether . . . ."—but this does not bring the different language-games any closer together.

The significance of such possibilities of transformation, for example of turning all statements into sentences beginning "I think" or "I believe" (and thus, as it were, into descriptions of *my* inner life) will become clearer in another place. (Solipsism.)

§25 It is sometimes said that animals do not talk because they lack the mental capacity. And this means: "they do not think, and that is why they do not talk." But—they simply do not talk. Or to put it better: they do not use language—if we except the most primitive forms of language.—Commanding, questioning, recounting, chatting, are as much a part of our natural history as walking, eating, drinking, playing.

§26 One thinks that learning language consists in giving names to objects. Viz, to human beings, to shapes, to colours, to pains, to moods, to numbers, etc.. To repeat—naming is something like attaching a label to a thing. One cay say that this is preparatory to the use of a word. But *what* is it a preparation *for?*

§27 "We name things and then we can talk about them: can refer to them in talk."—As if what we did next were given with the mere act of naming. As if there were only one thing called "talking about a thing". Whereas in fact we do the most various things with our sentences. Think of exclamations alone, with their completely different functions.

> *Water!*
> *Away!*
> *Ow!*
> *Help!*
> *Fine!*
> *No!*

Are you inclined still to call these words "names of objects"?

In languages (2) and (8) there was no such thing as asking something's name. This, with its correlate, ostensive definition, is, we might say, a language-game on its own. That is really to say: we are brought up, trained, to ask: "What is that called?"—upon which the name is given. And there is also a language-game of inventing a name for something, and hence of saying, "This is . . . ." and then using the new name. (Thus, for example, children give names to their dolls and then talk about them and to them. Think in this connexion how singular is the use of a person's name to *call* him!)

§28 Now one can ostensively define a proper name, the name of a colour, the name of a material, a numeral, the name of a point of the compass and so on. The definition of the number two, "That is called 'two'"—pointing to two nuts—is perfectly exact.—But how can two be defined like that? The person one gives the definition to doesn't know what one wants to call "two"; he will suppose that "two" is the name given to *this* group of nuts!—He *may* suppose this; but perhaps he does not. He might make the opposite mistake; when I want to assign a name to this group of nuts, he might understand it as a numeral. And he might equally well take the name of a person, of which I give an ostensive definition, as that of a colour, of a race, or even of a point of a compass. That is to say: an ostensive definition can be variously interpreted in *every* case.

§29 Perhaps you say; two can only be ostensively defined in *this* way: "This *number* is called 'two'". For the word "number" here shews what place in language, in grammar, we assign to the word. But this means that the word "number" must be explained before the ostensive definition can be understood.—The word "number" in the definition does indeed shew this place; does shew the post at which we station the word. And we can prevent misunderstandings by saying: "This *colour* is called so-and-so", "This *length* is called so-and-so", and so on. That is to say: misunderstandings are sometimes averted in this way. But is there only *one* way of taking the word "colour" or "length"?—Well, they just need defining.—Defining, then, by means of other words! And what about the last definition in this chain? (Do not say: "There isn't a 'last' definition". That is just as if you chose to say: "There isn't a last house in this road; one can always build an additional one".)

Whether the word "number" is necessary in the ostensive definition depends on whether without it the other person takes the definition otherwise than I wish. And that will depend on the circumstances under which it is given, and on the person I give it to.

And how he 'takes' the definition is seen in the use that he makes of the word defined.

§30 So one might say: the ostensive definition explains the use—the meaning— of the word when the overall role of the word in language is clear. Thus if I know that someone means to explain a colour-

word to me the ostensive definition "That is called 'sepia'" will help me to understand the word.—And you can say this, so long as you do not forget that all sorts of problems attach to the words "to know" or "to be clear".

One has already to know (or be able to do) something in order to be capable of asking a thing's name. But what does one have to know?

§31 When one shews someone the king in chess and says: "This is the king", this does not tell him the use of this piece— unless he already knows the rules of the game up to this last point: the shape of the king. You could imagine his having learnt the rules of the game without ever having been shewn an actual piece. The shape of the chessman corresponds here to the sound or shape of a word.

One can also imagine someone's having learnt the game without ever learning or formulating rules. He might have learnt quite simple board-games first, by watching, and have progressed to more and more complicated ones. He too might be given the explanation "This is the king",—if, for instance, he were being shewn chessmen of a shape he was not used to. This explanation again only tells him the use of the piece because, as we might say, the place for it was already prepared. Or even; we shall only say that it tells him the use, if the place is already prepared. And in this case it is so, not because the person to whom we give the

---

Could one define the word "red" by pointing to something that was *not red?* That would be as if one were supposed to explain the word "modest" to someone whose English was weak, and one pointed to an arrogant man and said "That man is *not* modest". That it is ambiguous is no argument against such a method of definition. Any definition can be misunderstood.

But it might well be asked: are we still to call this "definition"?—For, of course, even if it has the same practical consequences, the same *effect* on the learner, it plays a different part in the calculus from what we ordinarily call "ostensive definition" of the word "red".

explanation already knows rules, but because in another sense he is already master of a game.

Consider this further case: I am explaining to someone; and I begin by pointing to a chessman and saying: "This is the king; it can move like this, ... and so on."—In this case we shall say: the words "This is the king" (or "This is called the 'king'") are a definition only if the learner already 'knows what a piece in a game is'. That is, if he has already played other games, or has watched other people playing 'and understood'—*and similar things.* Further, only under these conditions will he be able to ask relevantly in the course of learning the game: "What do you call this?"—that is, this piece in a game.

We may say: only someone who already knows how to do something with it can significantly ask a name.

And we can imagine the person who is asked replying: "Settle the name yourself"—and now the one who asked would have to manage everything for himself.

§32 Someone coming into a strange country will sometimes learn the language of the inhabitants from ostensive definition that they give him; and he will often have to *guess* the meaning of these definitions; and will guess sometimes right, sometimes wrong.

And now, I think, we can say; Augustine describes the learning of human language as if the child came into a strange country and did not understand the language of the country; that is, as if it already had a language, only not this one. Or again: as if the child could already *think,* only not yet speak. And "think" would here mean something like "talk to itself".

§33 Suppose, however, someone were

to object: "It is not true that you must already be master of a language in order to understand an ostensive definition: all you need—of course!—is to know or guess what the person giving the explanation is pointing to. That is, whether for example to the shape of the object, or to its colour, or to its number, and so on."—And what does 'pointing to the shape', 'pointing to the colour' consist in? Point to a piece of paper.—And now a point to its shape—now to its colour—now to its number (that sounds queer).—How did you do it?—You will say that you 'meant' a different thing each time you pointed. And if I ask how that is done, you will say you concentrated your attention on the colour, the shape, etc. But I ask again: how is *that* done?

Suppose someone points to a vase and says "Look at that marvellous blue—the shape isn't the point."—Or: "Look at the marvellous shape—the colour doesn't matter." Without doubt you will do something *different* when you act upon these two invitations. But do you always do the *same* thing when you direct your attention to the colour? Imagine various different cases. To indicate a few:

"Is this blue the same as the blue over there? Do you see any difference?"—
You are mixing paint and you say "It's hard to get the blue of this sky."
"It's turning fine, you can already see blue sky again."
"Look what different effects these two blues have."
"Do you see the blue book over there? Bring it here."
"This blue signal-light means . . . ."
"What's this blue called?—Is it 'indigo'?"

You sometimes attend to the colour by putting your hand up to keep the outline from view; or by not looking at the outline of the thing; sometimes by staring at the object and trying to remember where you saw that colour before.

You attend to the shape, sometimes by tracing it, sometimes by screwing up your eyes as not to see the colour clearly, and in many other ways. I want to say: This is the sort of thing that happens *while* one 'directs one's attention to this or that'. But it isn't these things by themselves that make us say someone is attending to the shape, the colour, and so on. Just as a move in chess doesn't consist simply in moving a piece in such-and-such a way on the board—nor yet in one's thoughts and feelings as one makes the move: but in the circumstances that we call "playing a game of chess", "solving a chess problem", and so on.

§34 But suppose someone said: "I always do the same thing when I attend to the shape: my eye follows the outline and I feel. . . ." And suppose this person to give someone else the ostensive definition "That is called a 'circle'", pointing to a circular object and having all these experiences—cannot his hearer still interpret the definition differently, even though he sees the other's eyes following the outline, and even though he feels what the other feels? That is to say: this 'interpretation' may also consist in how he now makes use of the word; in what he points to, for example, when told: "Point to a circle".—For neither the expression "to intend the definition in such-and-such a way" nor the expression "to interpret the definition in such-and-such a way" stands for a process which accompanies the giving and hearing of the definition.

§35 There are, of course, what can be called "characteristic experiences" of pointing to (e.g.) the shape. For example, following the outline with one's finger or with one's eyes as one points.—But *this* does not happen in all cases in which I 'mean the shape', and no more does any other one characteristic process occur in all these cases.—Besides, even if something of the sort did recur in all cases, it would still depend on the circumstances—that is, on what happened before and after the pointing—whether we should say "He pointed to the shape and not to the colour".

For the words "to point to the shape", "to mean the shape", and so on, are not used in the same way as *these:* "to point to this book (not to that one), "to point to the chair, not to the table", and so on.—Only think how differently we *learn* the use of the words "to point to this thing", "to point to that thing", and on the other hand "to point to the colour, not the shape", "to mean the colour", and so on.

To repeat: in certain cases, especially when one points 'to the shape' or 'to the number' there are characteristic experiences and ways of pointing—'characteristic' because they recur often (not always) when shape or number are 'meant'. But do you also know of an experience characteristic of pointing to a piece in a game *as a piece in a game?* All the same one can say: "I mean that his *piece* is called the 'king', not this particular bit of wood I am pointing to". (Recognizing, wishing, remembering, etc..)

§36 And we do here what we do in a host of similar cases: because we cannot specify any *one* bodily action which we call pointing to the shape (as opposed, for example, to the colour), we say that a *spiritual* [mental, intellectual] activity corresponds to these words.

Where our langauge suggests a body and there is none: there, we should like to say, is a *spirit*.

§37 What is the relation between name and thing named?—Well, what *is* it? Look at language-game (2) or at another one: there you can see the sort of thing this relation consists in. This relation may also consist, among many other things, in the fact that hearing the name calls before our mind the picture of what is named; and it also consists, among other things, in the name's being written on the thing named or being pronounced when that thing is pointed at.

§38 But what, for example, is the word "this" the name of in language-game (8) or the word "that" in the ostensive definition "that is called . . ."?—If you do not want to produce confusion you will do best not to call these words names at all.—Yet, strange to say, the word "this" has been called the only *genuine* name; so that anything else we call a name was one only in an inexact, approximate sense.

This queer conception springs from a tendency to sublime the logic of our language—as one might put it. The proper answer to it is: we call very different things "names"; the word "name" is used to char-

acterize many different kinds of use of a word, related to one another in many different ways;—but the kind of use that "this" has is not among them.

It is quite true that, in giving an ostensive definition for instance, we often point to the object named and say the name. And similarly, in giving an ostensive definition for instance, we say the word "this" while pointing to a thing. And also the word "this" and a name often occupy the same position in a sentence. But it is precisely characteristic of a name that it is defined by means of the demonstrative expression "That is N" (or "That is called 'N'"). But do we also give the definitions: "That is called 'this'", or "This is called 'this'"?

This is connected with the conception of naming as, so to speak, an occult process. Naming appears as a *queer* connexion of a word with an object.—And you really get such a queer connexion when the philosopher tries to bring out *the* relation between name and thing by staring at an object in front of him and repeating a name or even the word "this" innumerable times. For philosophical problems arise when language *goes on holiday.* And *here* we may indeed fancy naming to be some remarkable act of mind, as it were a baptism of an object. And we can also say the word "this" *to* the object, as it were *address* the object as "this"—a queer use of this word, which

---

What is it to *mean* the words "That is blue" at one time as a statement about the object one is pointing to—at another as an explanation of the word "blue"? Well, in the second case one really means "That is called 'blue'".—Then can one at one time mean the word "is" as "is called" and the word "blue" and "'blue'", and another time mean "is" really as "is"?

It is also possible for someone to get an explanation of the words out of what was intended as a piece of information. [Marginal note: Here lurks a crucial superstition.]

Can I say "bububu" and mean "If it doesn't rain I shall go for a walk"?—It is only in a language that I can mean something by something. This shews clearly that the grammar of "to mean" is not like that of the expression "to imagine" and the like.

doubtless only occurs in doing philosophy.

§39 But why does it occur to one to want to make precisely this word into a name, when it evidently is *not* a name?— That is just the reason. For one is tempted to make an objection against what is ordinarily called a name. It can be put like this: *a name ought really to signify a simple.* And for this one might perhaps give the following reasons: The word "Excalibur", say, is a proper name in the ordinary sense. The sword Excalibur consists of parts combined in a particular way. If they are combined differently Excalibur does not exist. But it is clear that the sentence "Excalibur has a sharp blade" makes *sense* whether Excalibur is still whole or is broken up. But if "Excalibur" is the name of an object, this object no longer exists when Excalibur is broken in pieces; and as no object would then correspond to the name it would have no meaning. But then the sentence "Excalibur has a sharp blade" would contain a word that had no meaning, and hence the sentence would be nonsense. But it does make sense; so there must always be something corresponding to the words of which it consists. So the word "Excalibur" must disappear when the sense is analysed and its place be taken by words which name simples. It will be reasonable to call these words the real names.

§40 Let us first discuss *this* point of the argument: that a word has no meaning if nothing corresponds to it.—It is important to note that the word "meaning" is being used illicitly if it is used to signify the thing that 'corresponds' to the word. That is to confound the meaning of the name with the *bearer* of the name. When Mr. N. N. dies one says that the bearer of the name dies,

not that the meaning dies. And it would be nonsensical to say that, for if the name ceased to have meaning it would make no sense to say "Mr. N. N. is dead."

§41 In §15 we introduced proper names into language (8). Now suppose that the tool with the name "N" is broken. Not knowing this, A gives B the sign "N". Has this sign meaning now or not?—What is B to do when he is given it?—We have not settled anything about this. One might ask: what *will* he do? Well, perhaps he will stand there at a loss, or shew A the pieces. Here one *might* say: "N" has become meaningless; and this expression would mean that the sign "N" no longer had a use in our language-game (unless we gave it a new one). "N" might also become meaningless because, for whatever reason, the tool was given another name and the sign "N" no longer used in the language-game.—But we could also imagine a convention whereby B has to shake his head in reply if A gives him the sign belonging to a tool that is broken.—In this way the command "N" might be said to be given a place in the language-game even when the tool no longer exists, and the sign "N" to have meaning even when its bearer ceases to exist.

§42 But has for instance a name which has *never* been used for a tool also got a meaning in that game?—Let us assume that "X" is such a sign and that A gives this sign to B—well, even such signs could be given a place in the language-game, and B might have, say, to answer them too with a shake of the head. (One could imagine this as a sort of joke between them.)

§43 For a *large* class of cases—though not for all—in which we employ the word "meaning" it can be defined thus: the meaning of a word is its use in the langauge.

And the *meaning* of the name is sometimes explained by pointing to its bearer.

§44 We said that the sentence "Excalibur has a sharp blade" made sense even when Excalibur was broken in pieces. Now this is so because in this language-game a name is also used in the absence of its bearer. But we can imagine a language-game with names (that is, with signs which we should certainly include among names) in which they are used only in the presence of the bearer; and so could *always* be replaced by a demonstrative pronoun and the gesture of pointing.

§45 The demonstrative "this" can never be without a bearer. It might be said: "so long as there is a *this,* the word 'this' has a meaning too, whether *this* is simple or complex."—But that does not make the word into a name. On the contrary: for a name is not used with, but only explained by means of, the gesture of pointing.

§46 What lies behind the idea that names really signify simples?—Socrates says in the Theaetetus: "If I make no mistake, I have heard some people say this: there is no definition of the primary elements—so to speak—out of which we and everything else are composed; for everything that exists in its own right can only be *named,* no other determination is possible, neither that it *is* nor that it *is not.* . . . But what exists in its own right has to be . . . named without any other determination. In consequence it is impossible to give an account of any primary element; for it, nothing is possible but the bare name; its

name is all it has. But just as what consists of these primary elements is itself complex, so the names of the elements become descriptive language by being compounded together. For the essence of speech is the composition of names."

Both Russell's 'individuals' and my 'objects' *(Tractatus Logico-Philosophicus)* were such primary elements.

§47 But what are the simple constituent parts of which reality is composed?—What are the simple constituent parts of a chair?—The bits of wood of which it is made? Or the molecules, or the atoms?—"Simple" means: not composite. And here the point is: in what sense 'composite'? It makes no sense at all to speak absolutely of the 'simple parts of a chair'.

47   Hans-Georg Gadamer
The Universality of the Hermeneutical Problem

Why has the problem of language come to occupy the same central position in current philosophical discussions that the concept of thought, or "thought thinking itself," held in philosophy a century and a half ago? By answering this question, I shall try to give an answer indirectly to the central question of the modern age—a question posed for us by the existence of modern science. It is the question of how our natural view of the world—the experience of the world that we have as we simply live out our lives—is related to the unassailable and anonymous authority that confronts us in the pronouncements of science. Since the seventeenth century, the real task of philosophy has been to mediate this new employment of man's cognitive and constructive capacities with the totality of our experience of life. This task has found expression in a variety of ways, including our own generation's attempt to bring the topic of language to the center of philosophical concern. Language is the fundamental mode of operation of our being-in-the-world and the all-embracing form of the constitution of the world. Hence we always have in view the pronouncements of the sciences, which are fixed in nonverbal signs. And our task is to reconnect the objective world of technology, which the sciences place at our disposal and discretion, with those fundamental orders of our being that are neither arbitrary nor manipulable by us, but rather simply demand our respect.

I want to elucidate several phenomena in which the universality of this question becomes evident. I have called the point of view involved in this theme "hermeneutical," a term developed by Heidegger. Heidegger was continuing a perspective stemming originally from Protestant theology and transmitted into our own century by Wilhelm Dilthey.

What is hermeneutics? I would like to start from two experiences of alienation that we encounter in our concrete existence: the experience of alienation of the

aesthetic consciousness and the experience of alienation of the historical consciousness. In both cases what I mean can be stated in a few words. The aesthetic consciousness realizes a possibility that as such we can neither deny nor diminish in its value, namely, that we relate ourselves, either negatively or affirmatively, to the quality of an artistic form. This statement means we are related in such a way that the judgment we make decides in the end regarding the expressive power and validity of what we judge. What we reject has nothing to say to us—or we reject it because it has nothing to say to us. This characterizes our relation to art in the broadest sense of the word, a sense that, as Hegel has shown, includes the entire religious world of the ancient Greeks, whose religion of beauty experienced the divine in concrete works of art that man created in response to the gods. When it loses its original and unquestioned authority, this whole world of experience becomes alienated into an object of aesthetic judgment. At the same time, however, we must admit that the world of artistic tradition—the splendid contemporaneousness that we gain through art with so many human worlds—is more than a mere object of our free acceptance or rejection. Is it not true that when a work of art has seized us it no longer leaves us the freedom to push it away from us once again and to accept or reject it on our own terms? And is it not also true that these artistic creations, which come down through the millennia, were not created for such aesthetic acceptance or rejection? No artist of the religiously vital cultures of the past ever produced his work of art with any other intention than that his creation should be received in terms of what it says and presents and that it should have its place in the world where men live together. The consciousness of art—the aesthetic consciousness—is always secondary to the immediate truth-claim that proceeds from the work of art itself. To this extent, when we judge a work of art on the basis of its aesthetic quality, something that is really much more intimately familiar to us is alienated. This alienation into aesthetic judgment always takes place when we have withdrawn ourselves and are no longer open to the immediate claim of that which grasps us. Thus one point of departure for my reflections in *Truth and Method* was that the aesthetic sovereignty that claims its rights in the experience of art represents an alienation when compared to the authentic experience that confronts us in the form of art itself.

About thirty years ago, this problem cropped up in a particularly distorted form when National Socialist politics of art, as a means to its own ends, tried to criticize formalism by arguing that art is bound to a people. Despite its misuse by the National Socialists, we cannot deny that the idea of art being bound to a people involves a real insight. A genuine artistic creation stands within a particular community, and such a community is always distinguishable from the cultured society that is informed and terrorized by art criticism.

The second mode of the experience of alienation is the historical consciousness— the noble and slowly perfected art of holding ourselves at a critical distance in dealing with witnesses to past life. Ranke's celebrated description of this idea as the extinguishing of the individual provided a popular formula for the ideal of historical

thinking: the historical consciousness has the task of understanding all the witnesses of a past time out of the spirit of time, of extricating them from the preoccupations of our own present life, and of knowing, without moral smugness, the past as a human phenomenon. In his well-known essay, *The Use and Abuse of History,* Neitzsche formulated the contradiction between this historical distancing and the immediate will to shape things that always cleaves to the present. And at the same time he exposed many of the consequences of what he called the "Alexandrian," weakened form of the will, which is found in modern historical science. We might recall his indictment of the weakness of evaluation that has befallen the modern mind because it has become so accustomed to considering things in ever different and changing lights that it is blinded and incapable of arriving at an opinion of its own regarding the objects it studies. It is unable to determine its own position vis-à-vis what confronts it. Neitzsche traces the value-blindness of historical objectivism back to the conflict between the alienated historical world and the life powers of the present.

To be sure, Neitzsche is an ecstatic witness. But our actual experience of the historical consciousness in the last one hundred years has taught us most emphatically that there are serious difficulties involved in its claim to historical objectivity. Even in those masterworks of historical scholarship that seem to be the very consummation of the extinguishing of the individual demanded by Ranke, it is still an unquestioned principle of our scientific experience that we can classify these works with unfailing accuracy in terms of the political tendencies of the time in which they were written. When we read Mommsen's *History of Rome,* we know who alone could have written it, that is, we can identify the political situation in which this historian organized the voices of the past in a meaningful way. We know it too in the case of Treitschke or of Sybel, to choose only a few prominent names from Prussian historiography. This clearly means, first of all, that the whole reality of historical experience does not find expression in the mastery of historical method. No one disputes the fact that controlling the prejudices of our own present to such an extent that we do not misunderstand the witnesses of the past is a valid aim, but obviously such control does not completely fulfill the task of understanding the past and its transmissions. Indeed, it could very well be that only *insignificant* things in historical scholarship permit us to approximate this ideal of totally extinguishing individuality, while the great productive achievements of scholarship always preserve something of the splendid magic of immediately mirroring the present in the past and the past in the present. Historical science, the second experience from which I begin, expresses only one part of our actual experience—our actual encounter with historical tradition—and it knows only an alienated form of this historical tradition.

We can contrast the hermeneutical consciousness with these examples of alienation as a more comprehensive possibility that we must develop. But, in the case of this hermeneutical consciousness also, our initial task must be to overcome the epistemological truncation by which the traditional 'science of hermeneutics' has been absorbed into the idea of modern science. If we consider Schleiermacher's hermeneutics, for instance, we find his view of this discipline peculiarly restricted by the modern idea of science. Schleiermacher's hermeneutics shows him to be a leading voice of historical romanticism. But at the same time, he kept the concern of the Christian theologian clearly in mind, intending his hermeneutics, as a general doctrine of the art of understanding, to be of value in the special work of interpreting Scripture. Schleiermacher defined hermeneutics as the art of avoiding misunderstanding. To exclude by controlled, methodical consideration whatever is alien and leads to misunderstanding—misunderstanding suggested to us by distance in time, change in linguistic usages, or in the meanings of words and modes of thinking—that is certainly far from an absurd description of the hermeneutical endeavor. But the question also arises as to whether the phenomenon of understanding is defined appropriately when we say that to understand is to avoid misunderstanding. Is it not, in fact, the case that every misunderstanding presupposes a 'deep common accord'?

I am trying to call attention here to a common experience. We say, for instance, that understanding and misunderstanding take place between I and thou. But the formulation "I and thou" already betrays an enormous alienation. There is nothing like an "I and thou" at all—there is neither the I nor the thou as isolated, substantial realities. I may say "thou" and I may refer to myself over against a thou, but a common understanding *[Verständigung]* always precedes these situations. We all know that to say "thou" to someone presupposes a deep common accord [*tiefes Einverständnis*]. Something enduring is already present when this word is spoken. When we try to reach agreement on a matter on which we have different opinions, this deeper factor always comes into play, even if we are seldom aware of it. Now the science of hermeneutics would have us believe that the opinion we have to understand is something alien that seeks to lure us into misunderstanding, and our task is to exclude every element through which a misunderstanding can creep in. We accomplish this task by a controlled procedure of historical training, by historical criticism, and by a controllable method of connection with powers of psychological empathy. It seems to me that this description is valid in one respect, but yet it is only a partial description of a comprehensive life-phenomenon that constitutes the 'we' that we all are. Our task, it seems to me, is to transcend the prejudices that underlie the aesthetic consciousness, the historical consciousness, and the hermeneutical consciousness that has been restricted to a technique for avoiding misunderstandings and to overcome the alienations present in them all.

What is it, then, in these three experiences that seemed to us to have been left out, and what makes us so sensitive to the distinctiveness of these experiences? What is the *aesthetic* consciousness when compared to the fullness of what has already addressed us—what we call "classical" in art? Is it not always already determined in this way what will be expressive for us and what we will find significant? Whenever we say with an instinctive, even if perhaps erroneous, certainty (but a certainty that is initially valid for our consciousness) "this

is classical; it will endure," what we are speaking of has already preformed our possibility for aesthetic judgment. There are no purely formal criteria that can claim to judge and sanction the formative level simply on the basis of its artistic virtuosity. Rather, our sensitive-spiritual existence is an aesthetic resonance chamber that resonates with the voices that are constantly reaching us, preceding all explicit aesthetic judgment.

The situation is similar with the historical consciousness. Here, too, we must certainly admit that there are innumerable tasks of historical scholarship that have no relation to our own present and to the depths of its historical consciousness. But it seems to me there can be no doubt that the great horizon of the past, out of which our culture and our present live, influences us in everything we want, hope for, or fear in the future. History is only present to us in light of our futurity. Here we have all learned from Heidegger, for he exhibited precisely the primacy of futurity for our possible recollection and retention, and for the whole of our history.

Heidegger worked out this primacy in his doctrine of the productivity of the hermeneutical circle. I have given the following formulation to this insight: It is not so much our judgments as it is our prejudices that constitute our being. This is a provocative formulation, for I am using it to restore to its rightful place a positive concept of prejudice that was driven out of our linguistic usage by the French and the English Enlightenment. It can be shown that the concept of prejudice did not originally have the meaning we have attached to it. Prejudices are not necessarily unjustified and erroneous, so that they inevitably distort the truth. In fact, the historicity of our existence entails that prejudices, in the literal sense of the word, constitute the initial directedness of our whole ability to experience. Prejudices are biases of our openness to the world. They are simply conditions whereby we experience something—whereby what we encounter says something to us. This formulation certainly does not mean that we are enclosed within a wall of prejudices and only let through the narrow portals those things that can produce a pass saying, "Nothing new will be said here." Instead we welcome just that guest who promises something new to our curiosity. But how do we know the guest whom we admit is one who has something *new* to say to us? Is not our expectation and our readiness to hear the new also necessarily determined by the old that has already taken possession of us? The concept of prejudice is closely connected to the concept of authority, and the above image makes it clear that it is in need of hermeneutical rehabilitation. Like every image, however, this one too is misleading. The nature of the hermeneutical experience is not that something is outside and desired admission. Rather, we are possessed by something and precisely by means of it we are opened up for the new, the different, the true. Plato makes this clear in his beautiful comparison of bodily foods with spiritual nourishment: while we can refuse the former (e.g., on the advice of a physician), we have always taken the latter into ourselves already.

But now the question arises as to how we can legitimate this hermeneutical conditionedness of our being in the face of modern science, which stands or falls with the principle of being unbiased and prejudiceless. We will certainly not accomplish this legitimation by making prescriptions for science and recommending that it toe the line—quite aside from the fact that such pronouncements always have something comical about them. Science will not do us this favor. It will continue along its own path with an inner necessity beyond its control, and it will produce more and more breathtaking knowledge and controlling power. It can be no other way. It is senseless, for instance, to hinder a genetic researcher because such research threatens to breed a superman. Hence the problem cannot appear as one in which our human consciousness ranges itself over against the world of science and presumes to develop a kind of antiscience. Nevertheless, we cannot avoid the question of whether what we are aware of in such apparently harmless examples as the aesthetic consciousness and the historical consciousness does not represent a problem that is also present in modern natural science and our technological attitude toward the world. If modern science enables us to erect a new world of technological purposes that transform everything around us, we are not thereby suggesting that the researcher who gained the knowledge decisive for this state of affairs even considered technical applications. The genuine researcher is motivated by a desire for knowledge and by nothing else. And yet, over against the whole of our civilization that is founded on modern science, we must ask repeatedly if something has not been omitted. If the presuppositions of these possibilities for knowing and making remain half in the dark, cannot the result be that the hand applying this knowledge will be destructive?

The problem is really universal. The hermeneutical question, as I have characterized it, is not restricted to the areas from which I began in my own investigations. My only concern there was to secure a theoretical basis that would enable us to deal with the basic factor of contemporary culture, namely, science and its industrial, technological utilization. Statistics provide us with a useful example of how the hermeneutical dimension encompasses the entire procedure of science. It is an extreme example, but it shows us that science always stands under definite conditions of methodological abstraction and that the successes of modern sciences rest on the fact that other possibilities for questioning are concealed by abstraction. This fact comes out clearly in the case of statistics, for the anticipatory character of the questions statistics answer makes it particularly suitable for propaganda purposes. Indeed, effective propaganda must always try to influence initially the judgment of the person addressed and to restrict his possibilities of judgment. Thus what is established by statistics seems to be a language of facts, but which questions these facts answer and which facts would begin to speak if other questions were asked are hermeneutical questions. Only a hermeneutical inquiry would legitimate the meaning of these facts and thus the consequences that follow from them.

But I am anticipating, and have inadvertently used the phrase, "which answers to which questions fit the facts." This phase is in fact the hermeneutical *Urphänomen:* No assertion is possible that cannot be understood as an answer to a question, and assertions can only be understood in this way. It does not impair the impressive methodology of modern science in the least. Whoever wants to learn a science has to learn to master its methodology. But we also know the methodology as such does not guarantee in any way the productivity of its application. Any experience of life can confirm the fact that there is such a thing as methodological sterility, that is, the application of a method to something not really worth knowing, to something that has not been made a object of investigation on the basis of a genuine question.

The methodological self-consciousness of modern science certainly stands in opposition to this argument. A historian, for example, will say in reply: It is all very nice to talk about the historical tradition in which alone the voices of the past gain their meaning and through which the prejudices that determine the present are inspired. But the situation is completely different in questions of serious historical research. How could one seriously mean, for example, that the clarification of the taxation practices of fifteenth-century cities or of the marital customs of Eskimos somehow first receive their meaning from the consciousness of the present and its anticipations? These are questions of historical knowledge that we take up as tasks quite independently of any relation to the present.

In answering this objection, one can say that the extremity of this point of view would be similar to what we find in certain large industrial research facilities, above all in America and Russia. I mean the so-called random experiment in which one simply covers the material without concern for waste or cost, taking the chance that some day one measurement among the thousands of measurements will finally yield an interesting finding; that is, it will turn out to be the answer to a question from which someone can progress. No doubt modern research in the humanities also works this way to some extent. One thinks, for instance, of the great editions and especially of the ever more perfect indexes. It must remain an open question, of course, whether by such procedures modern historical research increases the chances of actually noticing the interesting fact and thus gaining from it the corresponding enrichment of our knowledge. But even if they do, one might ask: Is this an ideal, that countless research projects (i.e., determinations of the connection of facts) are extracted from a thousand historians, so that the 1001st historian can find something interesting? Of course, I am drawing a caricature of genuine scholarship. But in every caricature there is an element of truth, and this one contains an indirect answer to the question of what it is that really makes the productive scholar. That he has learned the methods? The person who never produces anything new has also done that. It is imagination *[Phantasie]* that is the decisive function of the scholar. Imagination naturally has a hermeneutical function and serves the sense for what is questionable. It serves the ability to expose real, productive questions, something in which, generally speaking, only he who masters all the methods of his science succeeds.

As a student of Plato, I particularly love those scenes in which Socrates gets into a dispute with the Sophist virtuosi and drives them to despair by his questions. Eventu-

ally they can endure his questions no longer and claim for themselves the apparently preferable role of the questioner. And what happens? They can think of nothing at all to ask. Nothing at all occurs to them that is worth while going into and trying to answer.

I draw the following inference from this observation. The real power of hermeneutical consciousness is our ability to see what is questionable. Now if what we have before our eyes is not only the artistic tradition of a people, or historical tradition, or the principle of modern science in its hermeneutical preconditions but rather the whole of our experience, then we have succeeded, I think, in joining the experience of science to our own universal and human experience of life. For we have now reached the fundamental level that we can call (with Johannes Lohmann) the "linguistic constitution of the world." It presents itself as the consciousness that is effected by history *[wirkungsgeschichtliches Bewusstsein]* and that provides an initial schematization for all our possibilities of knowing. I leave out of account the fact that the scholar—even the natural scientist—is perhaps not completely free of custom and society and from all possible factors in his environment. What I mean is that precisely *within* his scientific experience it is not so much the "laws of ironclad inference" (Helmholz) that present fruitful ideas to him, but rather unforeseen constellations that kindle the spark of scientific inspiration (e.g., Newton's falling apple or some other incidental observation).

The consciousness that is effected by history has its fulfillment in what is linguistic. We can learn from the sensitive student of language that language, in its life and occurrence, must not be thought of as merely changing, but rather as something that has a teleology operating within it. This means that the words that are formed, the means of expression that appear in a language in order to say certain things, are not accidentally fixed, since they do not once again fall altogether into disuse. Instead, a definite articulation of the world is built up—a process that works as if guided and one that we can always observe in children who are learning to speak.

We can illustrate this by considering a passage in Aristotle's *Posterior Analytics* that ingeniously describes one definite aspect of language formation.[3] The passage treats what Aristotle calls the *epagoge,* that is, the formation of the universal. How does one arrive at a universal? In philosophy we say: how do we arrive at a general concept, but even words in this sense are obviously general. How does it happen that they are "words," that is, that they have a general meaning? In his first apperception, a sensuously equipped being finds himself in a surging sea of stimuli, and finally one day he begins, as we say, to know something. Clearly we do not mean that he was previously blind. Rather, when we say "to know" [*erkennen*] we mean "to recognize" [*wiedererkennen],* that is, to pick something out [*herauserkennen*] of the stream of images flowing past as being identical.

What is picked out in this fashion is clearly retained. But how? When does a child know its mother for the first time? When it sees her for the first time? No. Then when? How does it take place? Can we really say at all that there is a single event in which a first knowing extricates

the child from the darkness of not knowing? It seems obvious to me that we cannot. Aristotle has described this wonderfully. He says it is the same as when an army is in flight, driven by panic, until at last someone stops and looks around to see whether the foe is still dangerously close behind. We cannot say that the army stops when one soldier has stopped. But then another stops. The army does not stop by virtue of the fact that two soldiers stop. When does it actually stop, then? Suddenly it stands its ground again. Suddenly it obeys the command once again. A subtle pun is involved in Aristotle's description, for in Greek "command" means *arche,* that is, *principium.* When is the principle present as a principle? Through what capacity? This question is in fact the question of the occurrence of the universal.

If I have not misunderstood Johannes Lohmann's exposition, precisely this same teleology operates constantly in the life of language. When Lohmann speaks of linguistic tendencies as the real agents of history in which specific forms expand, he knows of course that it occurs in these forms of realization, of "coming to a stand" [*Zum-Stehen-Kommen*], as the beautiful German word says. What is manifest here, I contend, is the real mode of operation of our whole human experience of the world. Learning to speak is surely a phase of special productivity, and in the course of time we have all transformed the genius of the three-year-old into a poor and meager talent. But in the utilization of the linguistic interpretation of the world that finally comes about, something of the productivity of our beginnings remains alive. We are all acquainted with this, for instance, in the attempt to translate, in practical life or in literature or whatever; that is, we are familiar with the strange, uncomfortable, and tortuous feeling we have as long as we do not have the right word. When we have found the right expression (it need not always be one word), when we are certain that we have it, then it "stands," then something has come to a "stand." Once again we have a halt in the midst of the rush of the foreign language, whose endless variation makes us lose our orientation. What I am describing is the mode of the whole human experience of the world. I call this experience hermeneutical, for the process we are describing is repeated continually throughout our familiar experience. There is always a world already interpreted, already organized in its basic relations, into which experience steps as something new, upsetting what has led our expectations and undergoing reorganization itself in the upheaval. Misunderstanding and strangeness are not the first factors, so that avoiding misunderstanding can be regarded as the specific task of hermeneutics. Just the reverse is the case. Only the support of familiar and common understanding makes possible the venture into the alien, the lifting up of something out of the alien, and thus the broadening and enrichment of our own experience of the world.

This discussion shows how the claim to universality that is appropriate to the hermeneutical dimension is to be understood. Understanding is language-bound. But this assertion does not lead us into any kind of linguistic relativism. It is indeed true that we live within a language, but language is not a system of signals that we send off with the aid of a telegraphic key when we enter the office or transmission station. That is not speaking, for it does not have the infinity of the act that is linguistically creative and world experiencing. While we live wholly within a language, the fact that we do so does not constitute linguistic relativism because there is absolutely no captivity within a language—not even within our native language. We all experience this when we learn a foreign language, especially on journeys insofar as we master the foreign language to some extent. To master the foreign language means precisely that when we engage in speaking it in the foreign land, we do not constantly consult inwardly our own world and its vocabulary. The better we know the language, the less such a side glance at our native language is perceptible, and only because we never know foreign languages well enough do we always have something of this feeling. But it is nevertheless already speaking, even if perhaps a stammering speaking, for stammering is the obstruction of a desire to speak and is thus opened into the infinite realm of possible expression. Any language in which we live is infinite in this sense, and it is completely mistaken to infer that reason is fragmented because there are various languages. Just the opposite is the case. Precisely through our finitude, the particularity of our being, which is evident even in the variety of languages, the infinite dialogue is opened in the direction of the truth that we are.

If this is correct, then the relation of our modern industrial world, founded by science, which we described at the outset, is mirrored above all on the level of language. We live in an epoch in which an increasing leveling of all life-forms is taking place—

that is the rationally necessary requirement for maintaining life on our planet. The food problem of mankind, for example, can only be overcome by the surrender of the lavish wastefulness that has covered the earth. Unavoidably, the mechanical, industrial world is expanding within the life of the individual as a sort of sphere of technical perfection. When we hear modern lovers talking to each other, we often wonder if they are communicating with words or with advertising labels and technical terms from the sign language of the modern industrial world. It is inevitable that the leveled life-forms of the industrial age also affect language, and in fact the impoverishment of the vocabulary of language is making enormous progress, thus bringing about an approximation of language to a technical sign-system. Leveling tendencies of this kind are irresistible. Yet in spite of them the simultaneous building up of our own world in language still persists whenever we want to say something to each other. The result is the actual relationship of men to each other. Each one is at first a kind of linguistic circle, and these linguistic circles come into contact with each other, merging more and more. Language occurs once again, in vocabulary and grammar as always, and never without the inner infinity of the dialogue that is in progress between every speaker and his partner. That is the fundamental dimension of hermeneutics. Genuine speaking, which has something to say and hence does not give prearranged signals, but rather seeks words through which one reaches the other person, is the universal human task—but it is a special task for the theologian, to whom is commissioned the saying-further [*Weitersagen*] of a message that stands written.

Translated by David E. Linge

Notes

*Hans-Georg Gadamer, "Die Universalität des hermeneutischen Problems" in *Kleine Schriften I: Philosophie. Hermeneutik* (Tübingen: J. C. B. Mohr [Paul Siebeck], 1976), pp. 101-112.—ED.

Cf. *Truth and Method,* translated by Garrett Barden and John Cumming (New York: The Seabury Press, 1977), p. 245.—TRANS.

Cf. Johannes Lohmann, *Philosophie and Sprachwissenschaft* (Berlin: Duncker and Humbolt, 1963).

Aristotle, *Posterior Analytics,* 100a 11–13.

48 Thomas S. Kuhn
The Priority of Paradigms

Introduction: A Role for History

History, if viewed as a repository for more than anecdote or chronology, could produce a decisive transformation in the image of science by which we are now possessed. That image has previously been drawn, even by scientists themselves, mainly from the study of finished scientific achievements as these are recorded in the classics and, more recently, in the textbooks from which each new scientific generation learns to practice its trade. Inevitably, however, the aim of such books is persuasive and pedagogic; a concept of science drawn from them is no more likely to fit the enterprise that produced them than an image of a national culture drawn from a tourist brochure or a language text. This essay attempts to show that we have been misled by them in fundamental ways. Its aim is a sketch of the quite different concept of science that can emerge from the historical record of the research activity itself.

Even from history, however, that new concept will not be forthcoming if historical data continue to be sought and scrutinized mainly to answer questions posed by the unhistorical stereotype drawn from science texts. Those texts have, for example, often seemed to imply that the content of science is uniquely exemplified by the observations, laws, and theories described in their pages.

Almost as regularly, the same books have been read as saying that scientific methods are simply the ones illustrated by the manipulative techniques used in gathering textbook data, together with the logical operations employed when relating those data to the textbook's theoretical generalizations. The result has been a concept of science with profound implications about its nature and development.

If science is the constellation of facts, theories, and methods collected in current texts, then scientists are the men who, successfully or not, have striven to contribute one or another element to that particular constellation. Scientific development becomes the piecemeal process by which these items have been added, singly and in combination, to the ever growing stockpile that constitutes scientific technique and knowledge. And history of science becomes the discipline that chronicles both these successive increments and the obstacles that have inhibited their accumulation. Concerned with scientific development, the historian then appears to have two main tasks. On the one hand, he must determine by what man and at what point in time each contemporary scientific fact, law, and theory was discovered or invented. On the other, he must describe and explain the congeries of error, myth, and superstition that have inhibited the more rapid accumulation of the constituents of the modern science text. Much research has been directed to these ends, and some still is.

In recent years, however, a few historians of science have been finding it more and more difficult to fulfil the functions that the

---

concept of development-by-accumulation assigns to them. As chroniclers of an incremental process, they discover that additional research makes it harder, not easier, to answer questions like: When was oxygen discovered? Who first conceived of energy conservation? Increasingly, a few of them suspect that these are simply the wrong sorts of questions to ask. Perhaps science does not develop by the accumulation of individual discoveries and inventions. Simultaneously, these same historians confront growing difficulties in distinguishing the "scientific" component of past observation and belief from what their predecessors had readily labeled "error" and "superstition." The more carefully they study, say, Aristotelian dynamics, phlogistic chemistry, or caloric thermodynamics, the more certain they feel that those once current views of nature were, as a whole, neither less scientific nor more the product of human idiosyncrasy than those current today. If these out-of-date beliefs are to be called myths, then myths can be produced by the same sorts of methods and held for the same sorts of reasons that now lead to scientific knowledge. If, on the other hand, they are to be called science, then science has included bodies of belief quite incompatible with the ones we hold today. Given these alternatives, the historian must choose the latter. Out-of-date theories are not in principle unscientific because they have been discarded. That choice, however, makes it difficult to see scientific development as a process of accretion. The same historical research that displays the difficulties in isolating individual inventions and discoveries gives ground for profound doubts about the cumulative process through which these individual contributions to science were thought to have been compounded.

The result of all these doubts and difficulties is a historiographic revolution in the study of science, though one that is still in its early stages. Gradually, and often without entirely realizing they are doing so, historians of science have begun to ask new sorts of questions and to trace different, and often less than cumulative, developmental lines for the sciences. Rather than seeking the permanent contributions of an older science to our present vantage, they attempt to display the historical integrity of that science in its own time. They ask, for example, not about the relation of Galileo's views to those of modern science, but rather about the relationship between his views and those of his group, i.e., his teachers, contemporaries, and immediate successors in the sciences. Furthermore, they insist upon studying the opinions of that group and other similar ones from the viewpoint—usually very different from that of modern science—that gives those opinions the maximum internal coherence and the closest possible fit to nature. Seen through the works that result, works perhaps best exemplified in the writings of Alexandre Koyré, science does not seem altogether the same enterprise as the one discussed by writers in the older historiographic tradition. By implication, at least, these historical studies suggest the possibility of a new image of science. This essay aims to delineate that image by making explicit some of the new historiography's implications.

What aspects of science will emerge to prominence in the course of this effort? First, at least in order of presentation, is the insufficiency of methodological directives, by themselves, to dictate a unique substantive conclusion to many sorts of scientific questions. Instructed to examine electrical or chemical phenomena, the man who is ignorant of these fields but who knows what it is to be scientific may legitimately reach any one of a number of incompatible conclusions. Among those legitimate possibilities, the particular conclusions he does arrive at are probably determined by his prior experience in other fields, by the accidents of his investigation, and by his own individual makeup. What beliefs about the stars, for example, does he bring to the study of chemistry or electricity? Which of the many conceivable experiments relevant to the new field does he elect to perform first? And what aspects of the complex phenomenon that then results strike him as particularly relevant to an elucidation of the nature of chemical change or of electrical affinity? For the individual, at least, and sometimes for the scientific community as well, answers to questions like these are often essential determinants of scientific development. We shall note, for example, in Section II that the early developmental stages of most sciences have been characterized by continual competition between a number of distinct views of nature, each partially derived from, and all roughly compatible with, the dictates of scientific observation and method. What differentiated these various schools was not one or another failure of method—they were all "scientific"—but what we shall come to call their incommensurable ways of seeing the world and of practicing science in it. Observation and experience can and must drastically restrict the range of admissible scientific belief, else there would be no science. But they cannot alone determine a particular body of such belief. An apparently arbitrary element, compounded of personal and historical accident, is always a formative ingredient of the beliefs espoused by a given scientific community at a given time.

That element of arbitrariness does not, however, indicate that any scientific group could practice its trade without some set of received beliefs. Nor does it make less consequential the particular constellation to which the group, at a given time, is in fact committed. Effective research scarcely begins before a scientific community thinks it has acquired firm answers to questions like the following: What are the fundamental entities of which the universe is composed? How do these interact with each other and with the senses? What questions may legitimately be asked about such entities and what techniques employed in seeking solutions? At least in the mature sciences, answers (or full substitutes for answers) to questions like these are firmly embedded in the educational initiation that prepares and licenses the student for professional practice. Because that education is both rigorous and rigid, these answers comes to exert a deep hold on the scientific mind. That they can do so does much to account both for the peculiar efficiency of the normal research activity and for the direction in which it proceeds at any given time. When examining normal science in Sections III, IV, and V, we shall want finally to describe that research as a strenuous and devoted attempt to force nature into the conceptual boxes supplied by professional education. Simultaneously, we shall wonder whether research could proceed without such boxes, whatever the element of arbitrariness in their historic origins and, occasionally, in their subsequent development.

Yet that element of arbitrariness is present, and it too has an important effect on scientific development, one which will be examined in detail in Sections VI, VII, and VIII. Normal science, the activity in which most scientists inevitably spend almost all their time, is predicated on the assumption that the scientific community knows what the world is like. Much of the success of the enterprise derives from the community's willingness to defend that assumption, if necessary at considerable cost. Normal science, for example, often suppresses fundamental novelties because they are necessarily subversive of its basic commitments. Nevertheless, so long as those commitments retain an element of the arbitrary, the very nature of normal research ensures that novelty shall not be suppressed for very long. Sometimes a normal problem, one that ought to be solvable by known rules and procedures, resists the reiterated onslaught of the ablest members of the group within whose competence it falls. On other occasions a piece of equipment designed and constructed for the purpose of normal research fails to perform in the anticipated manner, revealing an anomaly that cannot, despite repeated effort, be aligned with professional expectation. In these and other ways besides, normal science repeatedly goes astray. And when it does—when, that is, the profession can no longer evade anomalies that subvert the existing tradition of scientific practice—then begin the extraordinary investigations that lead the profession at least to a new set of commitments, a new basis for the practice of science. The extraordinary episodes in which that shift of professional commitments occurs are the ones known in this essay as scientific revolutions. They are the tradition-shattering complements to the tradition-bound activity of normal science.

The most obvious examples of scientific revolutions are those famous episodes in scientific development that have often been labeled revolutions before. Therefore, in Sections IX and X, where the nature of scientific revolutions is first directly scrutinized, we shall deal repeatedly with the major turning points in scientific development associated with the names of Copernicus, Newton, Lavoisier, and Einstein. More clearly than most other episodes in the history of at least the physical sciences, these display what all scientific revolutions are about. Each of them necessitated the community's rejection of one time-honored scientific theory in favor of another incompatible with it. Each produced a consequent shift in the problems available for scientific scrutiny and in the standards by which the profession determined what should count as an admissible problem or as a legitimate problem-solution. And each transformed the scientific imagination in ways that we shall ultimately need to describe as a transformation of the world within which scientific work was done. Such changes, together with the controversies that almost always accompany them, are the defining characteristics of scientific revolution.

These characteristics emerge with particular clarity from a study of, say, the Newtonian or the chemical revolution. It is, however, a fundamental thesis of this essay that they can also be retrieved from the study of many other episodes that were not so obviously revolutionary. For the far smaller professional group affected by them, Maxwell's equations were as revolutionary as Einstein's, and they were resisted accordingly. The invention of other new theories regularly, and appropriately, evokes the same response from some of the specialists on whose area of special competence they impinge. For these men the new theory implies a change in the rules governing the prior practice of normal science. Inevitably, therefore, it reflects upon much scientific work they have already successfully completed. That is why a new theory, however special its range of applications, is seldom or never just an increment to what is already known. Its assimilation requires the reconstruction of prior theory and the re-evaluation of prior fact, an intrinsically revolutionary process that is seldom completed by a single man and never overnight. No wonder historians have had difficulty in dating precisely this extended process that their vocabulary impels them to view as an isolated event.

Nor are new inventions of theory the only scientific events that have revolutionary impact upon the specialists in whose domain they occur. The commitments that govern normal science specify not only what sorts of entities the universe does contain, but also, by implication, those that it does not. It follows, though the point will require extended discussion, that a discovery like that of oxygen or X-rays does not simply add one more item to the population of the scientist's world. Ultimately it has that effect, but not until the professional community has re-evaluated traditional ex-

perimental procedures, altered its conception of entities with which it has long been familiar, and, in the process, shifted the network of theory through which it deals with the world. Scientific fact and theory are not categorically separable, except perhaps within a single tradition of normal-scientific practice. That is why the unexpected discovery is not simply factual in its import and why the scientist's world is qualitatively transformed as well as quantitatively enriched by fundamental novelties of either fact or theory.

The Route to Normal Science

In this essay, 'normal science' means research firmly based upon one or more past scientific achievements, achievements that some particular scientific community acknowledges for a time as supplying the foundation for its further practice. Today such achievements are recounted, though seldom in their original form, by science textbooks, elementary and advanced. These textbooks expound the body of accepted theory, illustrate many or all of its successful applications, and compare these applications with exemplary observations and experiments. Before such books became popular early in the nineteenth century (and until even more recently in the newly matured sciences), many of the famous classics of science fulfilled a similar function. Aristotle's *Physica,* Ptolemy's *Almagest,* Newton's *Principia* and *Opticks,* Franklin's *Electricity,* Lavoisier's *Chemistry,* and Lyell's *Geology*—these and many other works served for a time implicitly to define the legitimate problems and methods of a research field for succeeding generations of practitioners. They were able to do so because they shared two essential characteristics. Their achievement was sufficiently unprecedented to attract an enduring group of adherents away from competing modes of scientific activity. Simultaneously, it was sufficiently open-ended to leave all sorts of problems for the redefined group of practitioners to resolve.

Achievements that share these two characteristics I shall henceforth refer to as 'paradigms,' a term that relates closely to 'normal science.' By choosing it, I mean to suggest that some accepted examples of actual scientific practice—examples which include law, theory, application, and instrumentation together—provide models from which spring particular coherent traditions of scientific research. These are the traditions which the historian describes under such rubrics as 'Ptolemaic astronomy' (or 'Copernican'), 'Aristotelian dynamics' (or 'Newtonian'), 'corpuscular optics' (or 'wave optics'), and so on. The study of paradigms, including many that are far more specialized than those named illustratively above, is what mainly prepares the student for membership in the particular scientific community with which he will later practice. Because he there joins men who learned the bases of their field from the same concrete models, his subsequent practice will seldom evoke overt disagreement over fundamentals. Men whose research is based on shared paradigms are committed to the same rules and standards for scientific practice. That commitment and the apparent consensus it produces are prerequisites for normal science, i.e., for the genesis and continuation of a particular research tradition.

Because in this essay the concept of a paradigm will often substitute for a variety of familiar notions, more will need to be said about the reasons for its introduction. Why is the concrete scientific achievement, as a locus of professional commitment, prior to the various concepts, laws, theories, and points of view that may be abstracted from it? In what sense is the shared paradigm a fundamental unit for the student of scientific development, a unit that cannot be fully reduced to logically atomic components which might function in its stead? When we encounter them in Section V, answers to these questions and to others like them will prove basic to an understanding both of normal science and of the associated concept of paradigms. That more abstract discussion will depend, however, upon a previous exposure to examples of normal science or of paradigms in operation. In particular, both these related concepts will be clarified by noting that there can be a sort of scientific research without paradigms, or at least without any so unequivocal and so binding as the ones named above. Acquisition of a paradigm and of the more esoteric type of research it permits is a sign of maturity in the development of any given scientific field.

If the historian traces the scientific knowledge of any selected group of related phenomena backward in time, he is likely to encounter some minor variant of a pattern here illustrated from the history of physical optics. Today's physics textbooks tell the student that light is photons, i.e., quantum-mechanical entities that exhibit some characteristics of waves and some of particles. Research proceeds accordingly, or rather according to the more elaborate and mathematical characterization from which this usual verbalization is derived. The characterization of light is, however, scarcely half a century old. Before it was developed by Planck, Einstein, and others early in this century, physics texts taught that light was transverse wave motion, a conception rooted in a paradigm that derived ultimately from the optical writings of Young and Fresnel in the early nineteenth century. Nor was the wave theory the first to be embraced by almost all practitioners of optical science. During the eighteenth century the paradigm for this field was provided by Newton's *Opticks,* which taught that light was material corpuscles. At that time physicists sought evidence, as the early wave theorists had not, of the pressure exerted by light particles impinging on solid bodies.

These transformations of the paradigms of physical optics are scientific revolutions, and the successive transition from one paradigm to another via revolution is the usual developmental pattern of mature science. It is not, however, the pattern characteristic of the period before Newton's work, and that is the contrast that concerns us here. No period between remote antiquity and the end of the seventeenth century exhibited a single generally accepted view about the nature of light. Instead there were a number of competing schools and subschools, most of them espousing one variant or another of Epicurean, Aristotelian, or Platonic theory. One group took light to be particles emanating from material bodies; for another it was a modification of the medium that intervened between the body and the eye; still another explained light in terms of an interaction of the medium with an emanation from the eye; and there were other combinations and modifications besides. Each of the corresponding schools derived strength from its relation to some particular metaphysic, and each emphasized, as paradigmatic observations, the particular cluster of optical phenomena that its own theory could do most to explain. Other observations were dealt with by *ad hoc* elaborations, or they remained as outstanding problems for further research.

The Nature of Normal Science

What then is the nature of the more professional and esoteric research that a group's reception of a single paradigm permits? If the paradigm represents work that has been done once and for all, what further problems does it leave the united group to resolve? Those questions will seem even more urgent if we now note one respect in which the terms used so far may be misleading. In its established usage, a paradigm is an accepted model or pattern, and that aspect of its meaning has enabled me, lacking a better word, to appropriate 'paradigm' here. But it will shortly be clear that the sense of 'model' and 'pattern' that permits the appropriation is not quite the one usual in defining 'paradigm.' In grammar, for example, *'amo, amas, amat'* is a paradigm because it displays the pattern to be used in conjugating a large number of other Latin verbs, e.g., in producing *'laudo, laudas, laudat.'* In this standard application, the paradigm functions by permitting the replication of examples any one of which could in principle serve to replace it. In a science, on the other hand, a paradigm is rarely an object for replication. Instead, like an accepted judicial decision in the common law, it is an object for further articulation and specification under new or more stringent conditions.

To see how this can be so, we must recognize how very limited in both scope and precision a paradigm can be at the time of its first appearance. Paradigms gain their status because they are more successful than their competitors in solving a few problems that the group of practitioners has come to recognize as acute. To be more successful is not, however, to be either completely successful with a single problem or notably successful with any large number. The success of a paradigm— whether Aristotle's analysis of motion, Ptolemy's computations of planetary position, Lavoisier's application of the balance, or Maxwell's mathematization of the electromagnetic field—is at the start largely a promise of success discoverable in selected and still incomplete examples. Normal science consists in the actualization of that promise, an actualization achieved by extending the knowledge of those facts that the paradigm displays as particularly revealing, by increasing the extent of the match between those facts and the paradigm's predictions, and by further articulation of the paradigm itself.

Few people who are not actually practitioners of a mature science realize how much mop-up work of this sort of a paradigm leaves to be done or quite how fascinating such work can prove in the execution. And these points need to be understood. Mopping-up operations are what engage most scientists throughout their careers. They constitute what I am here calling normal science. Closely examined, whether historically or in the contemporary laboratory, that enterprise seems an attempt to force nature into the preformed and relatively inflexible box that the paradigm supplies. No part of the aim of normal science is to call forth new sorts of phenomena; indeed those that will not fit the box are often not seen at all. Nor do scientists normally aim to invent new theories, and they are often intolerant of those invented by others. Instead, normal-scientific research is directed to the articulation of those phenomena and theories that the paradigm already supplies.

Perhaps these are defects. The area investigated by normal science are, of course, minuscule; the enterprise now under discussion has drastically restricted vision. But those restrictions, born from confidence in a paradigm, turn out to be essential to the development of science. By focusing attention upon a small range of relatively esoteric problems, the paradigm forces scientists to investigate some part of nature in a detail and depth that would otherwise be unimaginable. And normal science possesses a built-in mechanism that ensures the relaxation of the restrictions that bound research whenever the paradigm from which they derive ceases to function effectively. At that point scientists begin to behave differently, and the nature of their research problems changes. In the interim, however, during the period when the paradigm is successful, the profession will have solved problems that its members could scarcely have imagined and would never have undertaken without commitment to the paradigm. And at least part of that achievement always proves to be permanent.

The Priority of Paradigms

To discover the relation between rules, paradigms, and normal science, consider first how the historian isolates the particular loci of commitment that have just been described as accepted rules. Close historical investigation of a given specialty at a given time discloses a set of recurrent and quasi-standard illustrations of various theories in their conceptual, observational, and instrumental applications. These are the community's paradigms, revealed in its textbooks, lectures, and laboratory exercises. By studying them and by practicing with them, the members of the corresponding community learn their trade. The historian, of course, will discover in addition a penumbral area occupied by achievements whose status is still in doubt, but the core of solved problems and techniques will usually be clear. Despite occasional ambiguities, the paradigms of a mature scientific community can be determined with relative ease.

The determination of shared paradigms is not, however, the determination of shared rules. That demands a second step and one of a somewhat different kind. When undertaking it, the historian must compare the community's paradigms with each other and with its current research reports. In doing so, his object is to discover what isolable elements, explicit or implicit, the members of that community may have *abstracted* from their more global paradigms and deployed as rules in their research. Anyone who has attempted to describe or analyze the evolution of a particular scientific tradition will necessarily have sought accepted principles and rules of this sort.

Almost certainly, as the preceding section indicates, he will have met with at least partial success. But, if his experience has been at all like my own, he will have found the search for rules both more difficult and less satisfying than the search for paradigms. Some of the generalizations he employs to describe the community's shared beliefs will present no problems. Others, however, including some of those used as illustrations above, will seem a shade too strong. Phrased in just that way, or in any other way he can imagine, they would almost certainly have been rejected by some members of the group he studies. Nevertheless, if the coherence of the research tradition is to be understood in terms of rules, some specification of common ground in the corresponding area is needed. As a result, the search for a body of rules competent to constitute a given normal research tradition becomes a source of continual and deep frustration.

Recognizing that frustration, however, makes it possible to diagnose its source. Scientists can agree that a Newton, Lavoisier, Maxwell, or Einstein has produced an apparently permanent solution to a group of outstanding problems and still disagree, sometimes without being aware of it, about the particular abstract characteristics that make those solutions permanent. They can, that is, agree in their *identification* of a paradigm without agreeing on, or even attempting to produce, a full *interpretation* or *rationalization* of it. Lack of a standard interpretation or of an agreed reduction to rules will not prevent a paradigm from guiding research. Normal science can be determined in part by the direct inspection of paradigms, a process that is often aided by but does not depend upon the formulation of rules and assumptions. Indeed, the existence of a paradigm need not even imply that any full set of rules exists.

Inevitably, the first effect of those statements is to raise problems. In the absence of a competent body of rules, what restricts the scientist to a particular normal-scientific tradition? What can the phrase 'direct inspection of paradigms' mean? Partial answers to questions like these were developed by the late Ludwig Wittgenstein, though in a very different context. Because that context is both more elementary and more familiar, it will help to consider his form of the argument first. What need we know, Wittgenstein asked, in order that we apply terms like 'chair,' or 'leaf,' or 'game' unequivocally and without provoking argument?[1]

That question is very old and has generally been answered by saying that we must know, consciously or intuitively, what a chair, or leaf, or game *is*. We must, that is, grasp some set of attributes that all games and that only games have in common. Wittgenstein, however, concluded that, given the way we use language and the sort of world to which we apply it, there need be no such set of characteristics. Though a discussion of *some* of the attributes shared by a *number* of games or chairs or leaves often helps us learn how to employ the corresponding term, there is no set of characteristics that is simultaneously applicable to all members of the class and to them alone. Instead, confronted with a previously unobserved activity, we apply the term 'game' because what we are seeing bears a close

"family resemblance" to a number of the activities that we have previously learned to call by that name. For Wittgenstein, in short, games, and chairs, and leaves are natural families, each constituted by a network of overlapping and crisscross resemblances. The existence of such a network sufficiently accounts for our success in identifying the corresponding object or activity. Only if the families we named overlapped and merged gradually into one another—only, that is, if there were no *natural* families—would our success in identifying and naming provide evidence for a set of common characteristics corresponding to each of the class names we employ.

Something of the same sort may very well hold for the various research problems and techniques that arise within a single normal-scientific tradition. What these have in common is not that they satisfy some explicit or even some fully discoverable set of rules and assumptions that gives the tradition its character and its hold upon the scientific mind. Instead, they may relate by resemblance and by modeling to one or another part of the scientific corpus which the community in question already recognizes as among its established achievements. Scientists work from models acquired through education and through subsequent exposure to the literature often without quite knowing or needing to know what characteristics have given these models the status of community paradigms. And because they do so, they need no full set of rules. The coherence displayed by the research tradition in which they participate may not imply even the

---

1   Ludwig Wittgenstien, *Philosophical Investigations,* trans.G. E. M. Anscombe (New York, 1953), pp. 31-36. Wittgenstein, however, says almost nothing about the sort of world necessary to support the naming procedure he outlines. Part of the point that follows cannot therefore be attributed to him.

existence of an underlying body of rules and assumptions that additional historical or philosophical investigation might uncover. That scientists do not usually ask or debate what makes a particular problem or solution legitimate tempts us to suppose that, at least intuitively, they know the answer. But it may only indicate that neither the question nor the answer is felt to be relevant to their research. Paradigms may be prior to, more binding, and more complete than any set of rules for research that could be unequivocally abstracted from them.

So far this point has been entirely theoretical: paradigms *could* determine normal science without the intervention of discoverable rules. Let me now try to increase both its clarity and urgency by indicating some of the reasons for believing that paradigms actually do operate in this manner. The first, which has already been discussed quite fully, is the severe difficulty of discovering the rules that have guided particular normal-scientific traditions. That difficulty is very nearly the same as the one the philosopher encounters when he tries to say what all games have in common. The second, to which the first is really a corollary, is rooted in the nature of scientific education. Scientists, it should already be clear, never learn concepts, laws, and theories in the abstract and by themselves. Instead, these intellectual tools are from the start encountered in a historically and pedagogically prior unit that displays them with and through their applications. A new theory is always announced together with applications to some concrete range of natural phenomena; without them it would not be even a candidate for acceptance. After it has been accepted, those same applications or others accompany the theory

into the textbooks from which the future practitioner will learn his trade. They are not there merely as embroidery or even as documentation. On the contrary, the process of learning a theory depends upon the study of applications, including practice problem-solving both with a pencil and paper and with instruments in the laboratory. If, for example, the student of Newtonian dynamics ever discovers the meaning of terms like 'force,' 'mass,' 'space,' and 'time,' he does so less from the incomplete though sometimes helpful definitions in his text than by observing and participating in the application of these concepts to problem-solution.

That process of learning by finger exercise or by doing continues throughout the process of professional initiation. As the student proceeds from his freshman course to and through his doctoral dissertation, the problems assigned to him become more complex and less completely precedented. But they continue to be closely modeled on previous achievements as are the problems that normally occupy him during his subsequent independent scientific career. One is at liberty to suppose that somewhere along the way the scientist has intuitively abstracted rules of the game for himself, but there is little reason to believe it. Though many scientists talk easily and well about the particular individual hypotheses that underlie a concrete piece of current research, they are little better than laymen at characterizing the established bases of their field, its legitimate problems and methods. If they have learned such abstractions at all, they show it mainly through their ability to do successful research. That ability can, however, be understood without recourse to hypothetical rules of the game.

These consequences of scientific education have a converse that provides a third reason to suppose that paradigms guide research by direct modeling as well as through abstracted rules. Normal science can proceed without rules only so long as the relevant scientific community accepts without question the particular problem-solutions already achieved. Rules should therefore become important and the characteristic unconcern about them should vanish whenever paradigms or models are felt to be insecure. That is, moreover, exactly what does occur. The pre-paradigm period, in particular, is regularly marked by frequent and deep debates over legitimate methods, problems, and standards of solution, though these serve rather to define schools than to produce agreement. We have already noted a few of these debates in optics and electricity, and they played an even larger role in the development of seventeenth-century chemistry and of early nineteenth-century geology. Furthermore, debates like these do not vanish once and for all with the appearance of a paradigm. Though almost non-existent during periods of normal science, they recur regularly just before and during scientific revolutions, the periods when paradigms are first under attack and then subject to change. The transition from Newtonian to quantum mechanics evoked many debates about both the nature and the standards of physics, some of which still continue. There are people alive today who can remember the similar arguments engendered by Maxwell's electromagnetic theory and by statistical mechanics. And earlier still, the assimilation of Galileo's and Newton's mechanics gave rise to a particularly famous series of debates with Aristotelians, Cartesians, and Leibnizians about the standards legitimate to science. When scientists disagree about whether the fundamental problems of their field have been solved, the search for rules gains a function that it does not ordinarily possess. While paradigms remain secure, however, they can function without agreement over rationalization or without any attempted rationalization at all.

A fourth reason for granting paradigms a status prior to that of shared rules and assumptions can conclude this section. The introduction of this essay suggested that there can be small revolutions as well as large ones, that some revolutions affect only the members of a professional subspecialty, and that for such groups even the discovery of a new and unexpected phenomenon may be revolutionary. The next section will introduce selected revolutions of that sort, and it is still far from clear how they can exist. If normal science is so rigid and if scientific communities are so close-knit as the preceding discussion has implied, how can a change of paradigm ever affect only a small subgroup? What has been said so far may have seemed to imply that normal science is a single monolithic and unified enterprise that must stand or fall with any one of its paradigms as well as with all of them together. But science is obviously seldom or never like that. Often, viewing all fields together, it seems instead a rather ramshackle structure with little coherence among its various parts. Nothing said to this point should, however, conflict with that very familiar observation. On the contrary, substituting paradigms for rules should make the diversity of scientific fields and specialties easier to understand. Explicit rules, when they exist, are usually common to a very broad scientific group, but paradigms need not be. The practitioners of widely separated fields, say astronomy and taxonomic botany, are educated by exposure to quite different achievements described in very different books. And even men who, being in the same or in closely related fields, begin by studying many of the same books and achievements may acquire rather different paradigms in the course of professional specialization.

Consider, for a single example, the quite large and diverse community constituted by all physical scientists. Each member of that group today is taught the laws of, say, quantum mechanics, and most of them employ these laws at some point in their research or teaching. But they do not all learn the same applications of these laws, and they are not therefore all affected in the same ways by changes in quantum-mechanical practice. On the road to professional specialization, a few physical scientists encounter only the basic principles of quantum mechanics. Others study in detail the paradigm applications of these principles to chemistry, still others to the physics of the solid state, and so on. What quantum mechanics means to each of them depends upon what courses he has had, what texts he has read, and which journals he studies. It follows that, though a change in quantum-mechanical law will be revolutionary for all of these groups, a change that reflects only on one or another of the paradigm applications of quantum mechanics need be revolutionary only for the members of a particular professional subspecialty. For the rest of the profession and for those who practice other physical sciences, that change need not be revolutionary at all. In short, though quantum mechanics (or Newtonian dynamics, or electromagnetic theory) is a paradigm for many scientific groups, it is not the same paradigm for them all. Therefore, it can simultaneously determine several traditions of normal science that overlap without being coextensive. A revolution produced within one of these traditions will not necessarily extend to the others as well.

One brief illustration of specialization's effect may give this whole series of points additional force. An investigator who hoped to learn something about what scientists took the atomic theory to be asked a distinguished physicist and an eminent chemist whether a single atom of helium was or was not a molecule. Both answered without hesitation, but their answers were not the same. For the chemist the atom of helium was a molecule because it behaved like one with respect to the kinetic theory of gases. For the physicist, on the other hand, the helium atom was not a molecule because it displayed no molecular spectrum. Presumably both men were talking of the same particle, but they were viewing it through their own research training and practice. Their experience in problem-solving told them what a molecule must be. Undoubtedly their experiences had had much in common, but they did not, in this case, tell the two specialists the same thing. As we proceed we shall discover how consequential paradigm differences of this sort can occasionally be.

49 Richard Rorty
Commensuration and Conversation

I have argued (in chapter three) that the desire for a theory of knowledge is a desire for constraint—a desire to find "foundations" to which one might cling, frameworks beyond which one must not stray, objects which impose themselves, representations which cannot be gainsaid. When I described the recent reaction against the quest for foundations as "epistemological behaviorism" (in chapter four) I was not suggesting that Quine and Sellars enable us to have a new, better, "behavioristic" sort of epistemology. Rather, they show us how things look when we give up the desire for confrontation and constraint. The demise of foundational epistemology, however, is often felt to leave a vacuum which needs to be filled. In chapters five and six I criticized various attempts to fill it. In this chapter I shall be talking about hermeneutics, so I want to make clear at the outset that I am *not* putting hermeneutics forward as a "successor subject" to epistemology, as an activity which fills the cultural vacancy once filled by epistemologically centered philosophy. In the interpretation I shall be offering, "hermeneutics" is not the name for a discipline, nor for a method of achieving the sort of results which epistemology failed to achieve, nor for a program of research. On the contrary, hermeneutics is an expression of hope that the cultural space left by the demise of epistemology will not be filled—that our culture should become one in which the demand for constraint and confrontation is no longer felt. The notion that there is a permanent neutral framework whose "structure" philosophy can display is the notion that the objects to be confronted by the mind, or the rules which constrain inquiry, are common to all discourse, or at least to every discourse on a given topic. Thus epistemology proceeds on the assumption that all contributions to a given discourse are commensurable. Hermeneutics is largely a struggle against this assumption.

By "commensurable" I mean able to be brought under a set of rules which will tell us how rational agreement can be reached on what would settle the issue on every point where statements seem to conflict.[1] These rules tell us how to construct an ideal situation, in which all residual disagreements will be seen to be "noncognitive" or merely verbal, or else merely temporary—capable of being resolved by doing something further. What matters is that there should be agreement about what would have to be done if a resolution *were* to be achieved. In the meantime, the interlocutors can agree to differ—being satisfied of each other's ratio-

1. Note that this sense of "commensurable" is not the same as "assigning the same meaning to terms." This sense—which is the one often used in discussing Kuhn—does not seem to me a useful one, given the fragility of the notion of "sameness of meaning." To say that parties to a controversy "use terms in different ways" seems to me an unenlightening way of describing the fact that they cannot find a way of agreeing on what would settle the issue. See chapter six, section 3, on this point.

nality the while. The dominating notion of epistemology is that to be rational, to be fully human, to do what we ought, we need to be able to find agreement with other human beings. To construct an epistemology is to find the maximum amount of common ground with others. The assumption that an epistemology can be constructed is the assumption that such common ground exists. Sometimes this common ground has been imagined to lie outside us—for example, in the realm of Being as opposed to that of Becoming, in the Forms which both guide inquiry and are its goal. Sometimes it has been imagined to lie within us, as in the seventeenth century's notion that by understanding our own minds we should be able to understand the right method for finding truth. Within analytic philosophy, it has often been imagined to lie in language, which was supposed to supply the universal scheme for all possible content. To suggest that there is *no* such common ground seems to endanger rationality. To question the need for commensuration seems the first step toward a return to a war of all against all. Thus, for example, a common reaction to Kuhn or Feyerabend is that they are advocating the use of force rather than persuasion.

The holistic, antifoundationalist, pragmatist treatments of knowledge and meaning which we find in Dewey, Wittgenstein, Quine, Sellars, and Davidson are almost equally offensive to many philosophers, precisely because they abandon the quest for commensuration and thus are "relativist." If we deny that there are foundations to serve as common ground for adjudicating knowledge-claims, the notion of the philosopher as guardian of rationality seems endangered. More generally, if we say that there is no

such thing as epistemology and that no surrogate can be found for it in, for example, empirical psychology or the philosophy of language, we may be seen as saying that there is no such thing as rational agreement and disagreement. Holistic theories seem to license everyone to construct his own little whole—his own little paradigm, his own little practice, his own little language-game—and then crawl into it.

I think that the view that epistemology, or some suitable successor-discipline, is necessary to culture confuses two roles which the philosopher might play. The first is that of the informed dilettante, the polypragmatic, Socratic intermediary between various discourses. In his salon, so to speak, hermetic thinkers are charmed out of their self-enclosed practices. Disagreements between disciplines and discourses are compromised or transcended in the course of the conversation. The second role is that of the cultural overseer who knows everyone's common ground—the Platonic philosopher-king who knows what everybody else is really doing whether *they* know it or not, because he knows about the ultimate context (the Forms, the Mind, Language) within which they are doing it. The first role is appropriate to hermeneutics, the second to epistemology. Hermeneutics sees the relations between the various discourses as those of strands in a possible conversation, a conversation which presupposes no disciplinary matrix which unites the speakers, but where the hope of agreement is never lost so long as the conversation lasts. This hope is not a hope for the discovery of antecedently existing common ground, but *simply* hope for agreement, or, at least, exciting and fruitful disagreement. Epistemology sees the hope of agreement as a token of the existence of common ground which, perhaps unbeknown to the speakers, unites them in a common rationality. For hermeneutics, to be rational is to be willing to refrain from epistemology—from thinking that there is a special set of terms in which all contributions to the conversation should be put—and to be willing to pick up the jargon of the interlocutor rather than translating it into one's own. For epistemology, to be rational is to find the proper set of terms into which all the contributions should be translated if agreement is to become possible. For epistemology, conversation is implicit inquiry. For hermeneutics, inquiry is routine conversation. Epistemology views the participants as united in what Oakeshott calls an *universitas*—a group united by mutual interests in achieving a common end. Hermeneutics views them as united in what he calls a *societas*—persons whose paths through life have fallen together, united by civility rather than by a common goal, much less by a common ground.[2]

My use of the terms *epistemology* and *hermeneutics* to stand for these ideal opposites may seem forced. I shall try to justify it by noting some of the connections between holism and the "hermeneutic circle." The notion of knowledge as accurate representation lends itself naturally to the notion that certain sorts of representations, certain expressions, certain processes are "basic," "privileged," and "foundational." The criticisms of this notion which I have canvassed in previous chapters are backed up with holistic arguments of the form: We will not be able to isolate basic elements except on the basis of a prior knowledge of the whole fabric within which these elements occur. Thus we will not be able to substitute the notion of "accurate representation" (element-by-element) for that of successful accomplishment of a practice. Our choice of elements will be dictated by our understanding of the practice, rather than the practice's being "legitimated" by a "rational reconstruction" out of elements. This holist line of argument says that we shall never be able to avoid the "hermeneutic circle"—the fact that we cannot understand the parts of a strange culture, practice, theory, language, or whatever, unless we know something about how the whole thing works, whereas we cannot get a grasp on how the whole works until we have some understanding of its parts. This notion of interpretation suggests that coming to understand is more like getting acquainted with a person than like following a demonstration. In both cases we play back and forth between guesses about how to characterize particular statements or other events, and guesses about the point of the whole situation, until gradually we feel at ease with what was hitherto strange. The notion of culture as a conversation rather than as a structure erected upon foundations fits well with this hermeneutical notion of knowledge, since getting into a conversation with strangers is, like acquiring a new virtue or skill by imitating models, a matter of φρόνησις rather than ἐπιστήμη.

The usual way of treating the relation between hermeneutics and epistemology is to suggest that they should divide up culture between them—with epistemology taking care of the serious and important "cognitive" part (the part in which we meet our

---

2.   Cf. "On the Character of a Modern European State" in Michael Oakeshott, *On Human Conduct* (*Oxford, 1975*).

obligations to rationality) and hermeneutics charged with everything else. The ideas behind such a division is that knowledge in the strict sense—$\epsilon\pi\iota\sigma\tau\eta\mu\eta$—must have a $\lambda\acute{o}\gamma o\varsigma$ and that a $\lambda\acute{o}\gamma o\varsigma$ can only be given by the discovery of a method of commensuration. The idea of commensurability is built into the notion of "genuine cognition," so that what is "only a matter of taste" or "of opinion" need not fall within epistemology's charge, and conversely, what epistemology cannot render commensurable is stigmatized as merely "subjective."

The pragmatic approach to knowledge suggested by epistemological behaviorism will construe the line between discourses which can be rendered commensurable and those which cannot as merely that between "normal" and "abnormal" discourse—a distinction which generalizes Kuhn's distinction between "normal" and "revolutionary" science. "Normal" science is the practice of solving problems against the background of a consensus about what counts as a good explanation of the phenomena and about what it would take for a problem to be solved. "Revolutionary" science is the introduction of a new "paradigm" of explanation, and thus of a new set of problems. Normal science is as close as real life comes to the epistemologist's notion of what it is to be rational. Everybody agrees on how to evaluate everything everybody else says. More generally, normal discourse is that which is conducted within an agreed-upon set of conventions about what counts as a relevant contribution, what counts as answering a question, what counts as having a good argument for that answer or a good criticism of it. Abnormal discourse is what happens when someone joins in the discourse who is

ignorant of these conventions or who sets them aside. $E\pi\iota\sigma\tau\eta\mu\eta$ is the product of normal discourse—the sort of statement which can be agreed to be true by all participants whom the other participants count as "rational." The product of abnormal discourse can be anything from nonsense to intellectual revolution, and there is no discipline which describes it, any more than there is a discipline devoted to the study of the unpredictable, or of "creativity." But hermeneutics is the study of an abnormal discourse from the point of view of some normal discourse—the attempt to make some sense of what is going on at a stage where we are still too unsure about it to describe it, and thereby to begin an epistemological account of it. The fact that hermeneutics inevitably takes some norm for granted makes it, so far forth, "Whiggish." But insofar as it proceeds nonreductively and in the hope of picking up a new angle on things, it can transcend its own Whiggishness.

From this point of view, then, the line between the respective domains of epistemology and hermeneutics is not a matter of the difference between the "sciences of nature" and the "sciences of man," nor between fact and value, nor the theoretical and the practical, nor "objective knowledge" and something squishier and more dubious. The difference is purely one of familiarity. We will be epistemological where we understand perfectly well what is happening but want to codify it in order to extend, or strengthen, or teach, or "ground" it. We must be hermeneutical where we do not understand what is happening but are honest enough to admit it, rather than being *blatantly* "Whiggish" about it. This means that we can get epistemological commensuration only where we already have agreed-upon practices of inquiry (or, more generally, of discourse)—as easily in "academic" art, "scholastic" philosophy, or "parliamentary" politics as in "normal" science. We can get it not because we have discovered something about "the nature of human knowledge" but simply because when a practice has continued long enough the conventions which make it possible—and which permit a consensus on how to divide it into parts—are relatively easy to isolate. Nelson Goodman has said of inductive and deductive inference that we discover its rules by discovering what inferences we habitually accept[3]; so it is with epistemology generally. There is no difficulty getting commensura-

tion in theology or morals or literary criticism when these areas of culture are "normal." At certain periods, it has been as easy to determine which critics have a "just perception" of the value of a poem as it is to determine which experimenters are capable of making accurate observations and precise measurements. At other periods—for example, the transitions between the "archaeological strata" which Foucault discerns in the recent intellectual history of Europe—it may be as difficult to know which scientists are actually offering reasonable explanations as it is to know which painters are destined for immortality.

3.   T.S. Kuhn, *The Essential Tension* (Chicago, 1977), pxii.

Section C

The Challenge
of
Metaphysics
After Pragmatism

There is something repugnant in the temper of the grand philosophers, the system builders, the wholesale thinkers. They sound like gods and yet are only men . . . Their errors are fabulous. But then so is their vision.

Paul Weiss

50 Charles Sanders Peirce
Some Consequences of Four Incapacities

Descartes is the father of modern philosophy, and the spirit of Cartesianism—that which principally distinguishes it from the scholasticism which it displaced—may be compendiously stated as follows:

1. It teaches that philosophy must begin with universal doubt; whereas scholasticism had never questioned fundamentals.

2. It teaches that the ultimate test of certainty is to be found in the individual consciousness; whereas scholasticism had rested on the testimony of sages and of the Catholic Church.

3. The multiform argumentation of the middle ages is replaced by a single thread of inference depending often upon inconspicuous premisses.

4. Scholasticism had its mysteries of faith, but undertook to explain all created things. But there are many facts which Cartesianism not only does not explain, but renders absolutely inexplicable, unless to say that "God makes them so" is to be regarded as an explanation.

In some, or all of these respects, most modern philosophers have been, in effect, Cartesians. Now without wishing to return to scholasticism, it seems to me that modern science and modern logic require us to stand upon a very different platform from this.

1. We cannot begin with complete doubt. We must begin with all the prejudices which we actually have when we enter upon the study of philosophy. These prejudices are not to be dispelled by a maxim, for they are things which it does not occur to us *can* be questioned. Hence this initial skepticism will be a mere self-deception, and not real doubt; and no one who follows the Cartesian method will ever be satisfied until he has formally recovered all those beliefs which in form he has given up. It is, therefore, as useless a preliminary as going to the North Pole would be in order to get to Constantinople by coming down regularly upon a meridian. A person may, it is true, in the course of his studies, find reason to doubt what he began by believing; but in that case he doubts because he has a positive reason for it, and not on account of the Cartesian maxim. Let us not pretend to doubt in philosophy what we do not doubt in our hearts.

2. The same formalism appears in the Cartesian criterion, which amounts to this: "Whatever I am clearly convinced of, is true." If I were really convinced, I should have done with reasoning, and should require no test of certainty. But thus to make single individuals absolute judges of truth is most pernicious. The result is that metaphysicians will all agree that metaphysics has reached a pitch of certainty far beyond that of the physical sciences;—only they can agree upon nothing else. In sciences in which

Reprinted by permission of the publishers from *The Collected Papers of Charles Sanders Peirce,* Vols. I and V, edited by Charles Hartshorne and Paul Weiss, Cambridge, Mass: The Belnap Press of Harvard University Press, Copyright© 1931, 1932, 1934, 1935, 1959, 1960 by the President and Fellows of Harvard College.

men come to agreement, when a theory has been broached, it is considered to be on probation until this agreement is reached. After it is reached, the question of certainty becomes an idle one, because there is no one left who doubts it. We individually cannot reasonably hope to attain the ultimate philosophy which we pursue; we can only seek it, therefore, for the *community* of philosophers. Hence, if disciplined and candid minds carefully examine a theory and refuse to accept it, this ought to create doubts in the mind of the author of the theory himself.

3.   Philosophy ought to imitate the successful sciences in its methods, so far as to proceed only from tangible premises which can be subjected to careful scrutiny, and to trust rather to the multitude and variety of its arguments than to the conclusiveness of any one. Its reasoning should not form a chain which is no stronger than its weakest link, but a cable whose fibres may be ever so slender, provided they are sufficiently numerous and intimately connected.

4.   Every unidealistic philosophy supposes some absolutely inexplicable, unanalyzable ultimate; in short, something resulting from mediation itself not susceptible of mediation. Now that anything *is* thus inexplicable can only be known by reasoning from signs. But the only justification of an inference from signs is that the conclusion explains the fact. To suppose the fact absolutely inexplicable, is not to explain it, and hence this supposition is never allowable.

In the last number of this journal will be found a piece entitled "Questions concerning certain Faculties claimed for Man," which has been written in this spirit of opposition to Cartesianism. That criticism of certain fac-

ulties resulted in four denials, which for convenience may here be repeated:

1.   We have no power of Introspection, but all knowledge of the internal world is derived by hypothetical reasoning from our knowledge of external facts.

2.   We have no power of Intuition, but every cognition is determined logically by previous cognitions.

3.   We have no power of thinking without signs.

4.   We have no conception of the absolutely incognizable.

These propositions cannot be regarded as certain; and, in order to bring them to a further test, it is now proposed to trace them out to their consequences. We may first consider the first alone; then trace the consequences of the first and second; and see what else will result from assuming the third also; and, finally, add the fourth to our hypothetical premises.

In accepting the first proposition, we must put aside all prejudices derived from a philosophy which bases our knowledge of the external world on our self-consciousness. We can admit no statement concerning what passes within us except as a hypothesis necessary to explain what takes place in what we commonly call the external world. Moreover when we have upon such grounds assumed one faculty or mode of action of the mind, we cannot, of course, adopt any other hypothesis for the purpose of explaining any fact which can be explained by our first supposition, but must carry the latter as far as it will go. In other words, we must, as far as we can do so without additional hypotheses, reduce all kinds of mental action to one general type.

The class of modifications of consciousness with which we must commence our inquiry must be one whose existence is indubitable, and whose laws are best known, and, therefore (since this knowledge comes from the outside), which most closely follows external facts; that is, it must be some kind of cognition. Here we may hypothetically admit the second proposition of the former paper, according to which there is no absolutely first cognition of any object, but cognition arises by a continuous process. We must begin, then, with a *process* of cognition, and with that process whose laws are best understood and most closely follow external facts. This is no other than the process of valid inference, which proceeds from its premiss, A, to its conclusion, B, only if, as a matter of fact, such a proposition as B is always or usually true when such a proposition as A is true. It is a consequence, then , of the first two principles whose results we are to trace out, that we must, as far as we can, without any other supposition than that the mind reasons, reduce all mental action to the formula of valid reasoning.

But does the mind in fact go through the syllogistic process? It is certainly very doubtful whether a conclusion—as something existing in the mind independently, like an image—suddenly displaces two premisses existing in the mind in a similar way. But it is a matter of constant experience, that if a man is made to believe in the premisses, in the sense that he will act from them and will say that they are true, under favourable conditions he will also be ready to act from the conclusion and to say that that is true. Something, therefore, takes place within the organism which is equivalent to the syllogistic process.

At any moment we are in possession of certain information, that is, of cognitions which have been logically derived by induction and hypothesis from previous cognitions which are less general, less distinct, and of which we have a less lively consciousness. These in their turn have been derived from others still less general, less distinct, and less vivid; and so on back to the ideal first, which is quite singular, and quite out of consciousness. This ideal first is the particular thing-in-itself. It does not exist *as such.* That is, there is no thing which is in-itself in the sense of not being relative to the mind, though things which are relative to the mind doubtless are, apart from that relation. The cognitions which thus reach us by this infinite series of inductions and hypotheses (which though infinite *a parte ante logice,* is yet as one continuous process not without a beginning *in time*) are of two kinds, the true and the untrue, or cognitions whose objects are *real* and those whose objects are *unreal.* And what do we mean by the real? It is a conception which we must first have had when we discovered that there was an unreal, an illusion; that is, when we first corrected ourselves. Now the distinction for which alone this fact logically called, was between an *ens* relative to private inward determinations, to the negations belonging to idiosyncrasy, and an *ens* such as would stand in the long run. The real, then, is that which, sooner or later, information and reasoning would finally result in, and which is therefore independent of the vagaries of me and you. Thus, the very origin of the conception of reality shows that this conception essentially involves the notion of a COMMUNITY, without definite limits, and capable of a definite increase of knowledge. And so those two series of cognitions—the real and the unreal—consist of those which, at a time sufficiently future, the community will always continue to reaffirm; and of those which, under the same conditions, will ever after be denied. Now, a proposition whose falsity can never be discovered, and the error of which therefore is absolutely incognizable, contains, upon our principle, absolutely no error. Consequently, that which is thought in these cognitions is the real, as it really is. There is nothing, then, to prevent our knowing outward things as they really are, and it is most likely that we do thus know them in numberless cases, although we can never be absolutely certain of doing so in any special case.

But it follows that since no cognition of ours is absolutely determinate, generals must have a real existence. Now this scholastic realism is usually set down as a belief in metaphysical fictions. But, in fact, a realist is simply one who knows no more recondite reality than that which is represented in a true representation. Since, therefore, the word "man" is true of something, that which "man" means is real. The nominalist must admit that man is truly applicable to something; but he believes that there is beneath this a thing in itself, an incognizable reality. His is the metaphysical figment. Modern nominalists are mostly superficial men, who do not know, as the more thorough Roscellinus and Ockham did, that a reality which has no representation is one which has no relation and no quality. The great argument for nominalism is that there is no man unless there is some particular man. That, however, does

not affect the realism of Scotus; and although there is no man of whom all further determination can be denied, yet there is a man, abstraction being made of all further determination. There is a real difference between man irrespective of what the other determinations may be, and man with this or that particular series of determinations, although undoubtedly this difference is only relative to the mind and not *in re*. Such is the position of Scotus. Ockham's great objection is, there can be no real distinction which is not *in re,* in the thing-in-itself; but this begs the question, for it is itself based only on the notion that reality is something independent of representative relation.

Such being the nature of reality in general, in what does the reality of mind consist? We have seen that the content of consciousness, the entire phenomenal manifestation of mind, is a sign resulting from inference. Upon our principle, therefore, that the absolutely incognizable does not exist, so that the phenomenal manifestation of a substance is the substance, we must conclude that the mind is a sign developing according to the laws of inference. What distinguishes a man from a word? There is a distinction doubtless. The material qualities, the forces which constitute the pure denotative application, and the meaning of the human sign, are all exceedingly complicated in comparison with those of the word. But these differences are only relative. What other is there? It may be said that man is conscious, while a word is not. But consciousness is a very vague term. It may mean that emotion which accompanies the reflection that we have animal life. This is a consciousness which is dimmed when animal life is at its ebb in old age, or sleep, but which is not dimmed when the spiritual life is at its ebb; which is the more lively the better *animal* a man is, but which is not so, the better *man* he is. We do not attribute this sensation to words, because we have reason to believe that it is dependent upon the possession of an animal body. But this consciousness, being a mere sensation, is only a part of the *material quality* of the man-sign. Again, consciousness is sometimes used to signify the *I think,* or unity in thought; but the unity is nothing but consistency, or the recognition of it. Consistency belongs to every sign, so far as it is a sign; and therefore every sign, since it signifies primarily that it is a sign, signifies its own consistency. The man-sign acquires information, and comes to mean more than he did before. But so do words. Does not electricity mean more now than it did in the days of Franklin? Man makes the word, and the word means nothing which the man has not made it mean, and that only to some man. But since man can think only by means of words or other external symbols, these might turn round and say: "You mean nothing which we have not taught you, and then only so far as you address some word as the interpretant of your thought." In fact, therefore, men and words reciprocally educate each other; each increase of a man's information involves and is involved by, a corresponding increase of a word's information.

Without fatiguing the reader by stretching this parallelism too far, it is sufficient to say that there is no element whatever of man's consciousness which has not something corresponding to it in the word; and the reason is obvious. It is that the word or

sign which man uses *is* the man himself. For, as the fact that every thought is a sign, taken in conjunction with the fact that life is a train of thought, proves that man is a sign; so, that every thought is an *external* sign, proves that man is an external sign. That is to say, the man and the external sign are identical, in the same sense in which the words *homo* and *man* are identical. Thus my language is the sum total of myself; for the man is the thought.

It is hard for man to understand this, because he persists in identifying himself with his will, his power over the animal organism, with brute force. Now the organism is only an instrument of thought. But the identity of a man consists in the *consistency* of what he does and thinks, and consistency is the intellectual character of a thing; that is, is its expressing something.

Finally, as what anything really is, is what it may finally come to be known to be in the ideal state of complete information, so that reality depends on the ultimate decision of the community; so thought is what it is, only by virtue of its addressing a future thought which is in its value as thought identical with it, though more developed. In this way, the existence of thought now, depends on what is to be hereafter; so that it has only a potential existence, dependent on the future thought of the community.

The individual man, since his separate existence is manifested only by ignorance and error, so far as he is anything apart from his fellows, and from what he and they are to be, is only a negation. This is man,

. . . proud man.
Most ignorant of what he's most assured,
His glassy essence.

51

Charles Sanders Peirce
How to Make our Ideas Clear

The principles set forth in the first part of this essay lead, at once, to a method of reaching a clearness of thought of higher grade than the "distinctness" of the logicians. It was there noticed that the action of thought is excited by the irritation of doubt, and ceases when belief is attained; so that the production of belief is the sole function of thought. All these words, however, are too strong for my purpose. It is as if I had described the phenomena as they appear under a mental microscope. Doubt and Belief, as the words are commonly employed, relate to religious or other grave discussions. But here I use them to designate the starting of any question, no matter how small or how great, and the resolution of it. If, for instance, in a horse-car, I pull out my purse and find a five-cent nickel and five coppers, I decide, while my hand is going to the purse, in which way I will pay my fare. To call such a question Doubt, and my decision Belief, is certainly to use words very disproportionate to the occasion. To speak of such a doubt as causing an irritation which needs to be appeased, suggests a temper which is uncomfortable to the verge of insanity. Yet, look-

ing at the matter minutely, it must be admitted that, if there is the least hesitation as to whether I shall pay the five coppers or the nickel (as there will be sure to be, unless I act from some previously contracted habit in the matter), though irritation is too strong a word, yet I am excited to such small mental activity as may be necessary to deciding how I shall act. Most frequently doubts arise from some indecision, however momentary, in our action. Sometimes it is not so. I have, for example, to wait in a railway-station, and to pass the time I read the advertisements on the walls. I compare the advantages of different trains and different routes which I never expect to take, merely fancying myself to be in a state of hesitancy, because I am bored with having nothing to trouble me. Feigned hesitancy, whether feigned for mere amusement or with a lofty purpose, plays a great part in the production of scientific inquiry. However the doubt may originate, it stimulates the mind to an activity which may be slight or energetic, calm or turbulent. Images pass rapidly through consciousness, one incessantly melting into another, until at last, when all is over—it may be in a fraction of a second, in an hour, or after long years—we find ourselves decided as to how we should act under such circumstances as those which occasioned our hesitation. In other words, we have attained belief.

And what, then, is belief? It is the demi-cadence which closes a musical phrase in the symphony of our intellectual life. We have seen that it has just three properties: First, it is something that we are aware of; second, it appeases the irritation of doubt; and, third, it involves the establishment in our nature of a rule of action, or, say for short, a *habit*. As it appeases the irritation of doubt, which is the motive for thinking, thought relaxes, and comes to rest for a moment when belief is reached. But, since belief is a rule for action, the application of which involves further doubt and further thought, at the same time that it is a stopping-place, it is also a new starting-place for thought. That is why I have permitted myself to call it thought at rest, although thought is essentially an action. The *final* upshot of thinking is the exercise of volition, and of this thought no longer forms a part; but belief is only a stadium of mental action, an effect upon our nature due to thought, which will influence future thinking.

The essence of belief is the establishment of a habit; and different beliefs are distinguished by the different modes of action to which they give rise. If beliefs do not differ in this respect, if they appease the same doubt by producing the same rule of action, then no mere differences in the manner of consciousness of them can make them different beliefs, any more than playing a tune in different keys is playing different tunes.

It appears, then, that the rule for attaining the third grade of clearness of apprehension is as follows: Consider what effects, that might conceivably have practical bearings, we conceive the object of our conception to have. Then, our conception of these effects is the whole of our conception of the object.

Let us illustrate this rule by some examples; and, to begin with the simplest one possible, let us ask what we mean by calling a thing *hard*. Evidently that it will not be scratched by many other substances. The whole conception of this quality, as of every other, lies in its conceived effects. There is

absolutely no difference between a hard thing and a soft thing so long as they are not brought to the test. Suppose, then, that a diamond could be crystallized in the midst of a cushion of soft cotton, and should remain there until it was finally burned up. Would it be false to say that that diamond was soft? This seems a foolish question, and would be so, in fact, except in the realm of logic. There such questions are often of the greatest utility as serving to bring logical principles into sharper relief than real discussions ever could. In studying logic we must not put them aside with hasty answers, but must consider them with attentive care, in order to make out the principles involved. We may, in the present case, modify our question, and ask what prevents us from saying that all hard bodies remain perfectly soft until they are touched, when their hardness increases with the pressure until they are scratched. Reflection will show that the reply is this: there would be no *falsity* in such modes of speech. They would involve a modification of our present usage of speech with regard to the words hard and soft, but not of their meanings. For they represent no fact to be different from what it is; only they involve arrangements of facts which would be exceedingly maladroit. This leads us to remark that the question of what would occur under circumstances which do not actually arise is not a question of fact, but only of the most perspicuous arrangement of them. For example, the question of free-will and fate in its simplest form, stripped of verbiage, is something like this: I have done something of which I am ashamed; could I, by an effort of the will, have resisted the temptation, and done otherwise? The philosophical reply is, that this is not a question of fact, but only of the arrangement of facts. Arranging them so as to exhibit what is particularly pertinent to my question—namely, that I ought to blame myself for having done wrong—it is perfectly true to say that, if I had willed to do otherwise than I did, I should have done otherwise. On the other hand, arranging the facts so as to exhibit another important consideration, it is equally true that, when a temptation has once been allowed to work, it will, if it has a certain force, produce its effect, let me struggle how I may. There is no objection to a contradiction in what would result from a false supposition. The *reductio ad absurdum* consists in showing that contradictory results would follow from a hypothesis which is consequently judged to be false. Many questions are involved in the free-will discussion, and I am far from desiring to say that both sides are equally right. On the contrary, I am of the opinion that one side denies important facts, and that the other does not. But what I do say is, that the above single question was the origin of the whole doubt; that, had it not been for this question, the controversy would never have arisen; and that this question is perfectly solved in the manner which I have indicated.

52 Charles Sanders Peirce
The Scientific Attitude and Fallibilism

All positive reasoning is of the nature of judging the proportion of something in a whole collection by the proportion found in a sample. Accordingly, there are three things to which we can never hope to attain by reasoning, namely, absolute certainty, absolute exactitude, absolute universality. We cannot be absolutely certain that our conclusions are even approximately true; for the sample may be utterly unlike the unsampled part of the collection. We cannot pretend to be even probably exact; because the sample consists of but a finite number of instances and only admits special values of the proportion sought. Finally, even if we could ascertain with absolute certainty and exactness that the ratio of sinful men to all men was as 1 to 1; still among the infinite generations of men there would be room for any finite number of sinless men without violating the proportion. The case is the same with a seven-legged calf.

Now if exactitude, certitude, and universality are not to be attained by reasoning, there is certainly no other means by which they can be reached.

53 Alfred North Whitehead The Century of Genius

The previous chapters were devoted to the antecedent conditions which prepared the soil for the scientific outburst of the seventeenth century. They traced the various elements of thought and instinctive belief, from their first efflorescence in the classical civilization of the ancient world, through the transformations which they underwent in the Middle Ages, up to the historical revolt of the sixteenth century. Three main factors arrested attention—the rise of mathematics, the instinctive belief in a detailed order of nature, and the unbridled rationalism of the thought of the later Middle Ages. By this rationalism I mean the belief that the avenue to truth was predominantly through a metaphysical analysis of the nature of things, which would thereby determine how things acted and functioned. The historical revolt was the definite abandonment of this method in favour of the study of the empirical facts of antecedents and consequences. In religion, it meant the appeal to the origins of Christianity; and in science it meant the appeal to experiment and the inductive method of reasoning.

A brief, and sufficiently accurate, description of the intellectual life of the European races during the succceeding two centuries and a quarter up to our own times is that they have been living upon the accumulated capital of ideas provided for them by the genius of the seventeenth century. The men of this epoch inherited a ferment of ideas attendant upon the historical revolt of the sixteenth century, and they bequeathed formed systems of thought touching every aspect of human life. It is the one century which consistently, and throughout the whole range of human activities, provided intellectual genius adequate for the greatness of its occasions. The crowded stage of this hundred years is indicated by the coincidences which mark its literary annals. At its dawn Bacon's *Advancement of Learning* and Cervantes' *Don Quixote* were published in the same year (1605), as though the epoch would introduce itself with a forward and a backward glance. The first quarto edition of *Hamlet* appeared in the preceding year, and a slightly variant edition in the same year. Finally Shakespeare and Cervantes died on the same day, April 23, 1616. In the spring of this same year Harvey is believed to have first expounded his theory of the circulation of the blood in a course of lectures before the College of Physicians in London. Newton was born in the year that Galileo died (1642), exactly one hundred years after the publication of Copernicus' *De Revolutionibus*. One year earlier Descartes published his *Meditationes* and two years later his *Principia Philosophiae*. There simply was not time for the century to space out nicely its notable events concerning men of genius.

I cannot now enter upon a chronicle of the various stages of intellectual advance included within this epoch. It is too large a topic for one lecture, and would obscure the ideas which it is my purpose to develop. A mere rough catalogue of some names will be sufficient, names of men who published to the world important work within these limits of time: Francis Bacon, Harvey, Kepler, Galileo, Descartes, Pascal, Huyghens, Boyle, Newton, Locke, Spinoza, Leibniz. I have limited the list to the sacred number of twelve, a number much too small to be properly representative. For example, there is only one Italian there, whereas Italy could have filled the list from its own ranks. Again Harvey is the only biologist, and also there are too many Englishmen. This latter defect is partly due to the fact that the lecturer is English, and that he is lecturing to an audience which, equally with him, owns this English century. If he had been Dutch, there would have been too many Dutchmen; if Italian, too many Italians; and if French, too many Frenchmen. The unhappy Thirty Years' War was devastating Germany; but every other country looks back to this century as an epoch which witnessed some culmination of its genius. Certainly this was a great period of English thought; as at a later time Voltaire impressed upon France.

The omission of physiologists, other than Harvey, also requires explanation. There were, of course, great advances in biology within the century, chiefly associated with Italy and the University of Padua. But my purpose is to trace the philosophic outlook, derived from science and presupposed by science, and to estimate some of its effects on the general climate of each age. Now the scientific philosophy of this age was dominated by physics; so as to be the most obvious rendering, in terms of general ideas, of the state of physical knowledge of that age and of the two succeeding centuries. As a matter of fact, these concepts are very unsuited to biology; and set for it an insoluble problem of matter and life and organism, with which biologists are now wrestling. But the science of living organisms is only now coming to a growth adequate to impress its conceptions upon philosophy. The last half century before the present time has witnessed unsuccessful attempts to impress biological notions upon the materialism of the seventeenth century. However this success be estimated, it is certain that the root ideas of the seventeenth century were derived from the school of thought which produced Galileo, Huyghens and Newton, and not from the physiologists of Padua. One unsolved problem of thought, so far as it derives from this period, is to be formulated thus: Given configurations of matter with locomotion in space as assigned by physical laws, to account for living organisms.

My discussion of the epoch will be best introduced by a quotation from Francis Bacon, which forms the opinion of Section (or 'Century') IX of his *Natural History,* I mean his *Silva Silvarum.* We are told in the contemporary memoir by his chaplain, Dr. Rawley, that this work was composed in the last five years of his life, so it must be dated between 1620 and 1626. The quotation runs thus:

'It is certain that all bodies whatsoever, though they have no sense, yet they have perception; for when one body is applied to another, there is a kind of election to embrace that which is agreeable, and to exclude or expel that which is ingrate; and whether the body be alterant or altered, evermore a perception precedeth operation; for else all bodies would be like one to another. And sometimes this perception, in some kind of bodies, is far more subtile than sense; so that sense is but a dull thing in comparison of it:

we see a weatherglass will find the least difference of the weather in heat or cold, when we find it not. And this perception is sometimes at a distance, as well as upon the touch; as when the loadstone draweth iron; or flame naphtha of Babylon, a great distance off. It is therefore a subject of a very noble enquiry, to enquire of the more subtle perceptions; for it is another key to open nature, as well as the sense; and sometimes better. And besides, it is a principal means of natural divination; for that which in these perceptions appeareth early, in the great effects cometh long after.'

There are a great many points of interest about this quotation, some of which will emerge into importance in succeeding lectures. In the first place, note the careful way in which Bacon discriminates between *perception,* or *taking account of,* on the one hand, and *sense,* or *cognitive experience,* on the other hand. In this respect Bacon is outside the physical line of thought which finally dominated the century. Later on, people thought of passive matter which was operated on externally by forces. I believe Bacon's line of thought to have expressed a more fundamental truth than do the materialistic concepts which were then being shaped as adequate for physics. We are now so used to the materialistic way of looking at things, which has been rooted in our literature by the genius of the seventeenth century, that it is with some difficulty that we understand the possibility of another mode of approach to the problems of nature.

In the particular instance of the quotation which I have just made, the whole passage and the context in which it is embedded, are permeated through and through by the experimental method, that is to say, by

attention to 'irreducible and stubborn facts', and by the 'inductive method of eliciting general laws.' Another unsolved problem which has been bequeathed to us by the seventeenth century is the rational justification of this method of Induction. The explicit realisation of the antithesis between the deductive rationalism of the scholastics and the inductive observational methods of the moderns must chiefly be ascribed to Bacon; though, of course, it was implicit in the mind of Galileo and of all the men of science of those times. But Bacon was one of the earliest of the whole group, and also had the most direct apprehension of the full extent of the intellectual revolution which was in progress. Perhaps the man who most completely anticipated both Bacon and the whole modern point of view was the artist Leonardo Da Vinci, who lived almost exactly a century before Bacon. Leonardo also illustrated the theory which I was advancing in my last lecture, that the rise of naturalistic art was an important ingredient in the formation of our scientific mentality. Indeed, Leonardo was more completely a man of science than was Bacon. The practice of naturalistic art is more akin to the practice of physics, chemistry and biology than is the practice of law. We all remember the saying of Bacon's contemporary, Harvey, the discoverer of the circulation of the blood, that Bacon 'wrote of science like a Lord Chancellor.' But at the beginning of the modern period Da Vinci and Bacon stand together as illustrating the various strains which have combined to form the modern world, namely, legal mentality and the patient observational habits of the naturalistic artists.

In the passage which I have quoted from Bacon's writings there is no explicit mention of the method of inductive reasoning. It is unnecessary for me to prove to you by any quotations that the enforcement of the importance of this method, and of the importance, to the welfare of mankind, of the secrets of nature to be thus discovered, was one of the main themes to which Bacon devoted himself in his writings. Induction has proved to be a somewhat more complex process than Bacon anticipated. He had in his mind the belief that with a sufficient care in the collection of instances the general law would stand out of itself. We know now, and probably Harvey knew then, that this is a very inadequate account of the processes which issue in scientific generalisations. But when you have made all the requisite deductions, Bacon remains as one of the great builders who constructed the mind of the modern world.

The special difficulties raised by induction emerged in the eighteenth century, as a result of Hume's criticism. But Bacon was one of the prophets of the historical revolt, which deserted the method of unrelieved rationalism, and rushed into the other extreme of basing all fruitful knowledge upon inference from particular occasions in the past to particular occasions in the future. I do not wish to throw any doubt upon the validity of induction, when it has been properly guarded. My point is, that the very baffling task of applying reason to elicit the general characteristics of the immediate occasion, as set before us in direct cognition, is a necessary preliminary, if we are to justify induction; unless indeed we are content to base it upon our vague instinct that of course it is all right. Either there is something about the immediate occasion which affords knowledge of the past and the future, or we are

reduced to utter scepticism as to memory and induction. It is impossible to over-emphasize the point that the key to the process of induction, as used either in science or in our ordinary life, is to be found in the right understanding of the immediate occasion of knowledge in its full concreteness. It is in respect to our grasp of the character of these occasions in their concreteness that the modern developments of physiology and of psychology are of critical importance. I shall illustrate this point in my subsequent lectures. We find ourselves amid insoluble difficulties when we substitute for this concrete occasion a mere abstract in which we only consider material objects in a flux of configurations in time and space. It is quite obvious that such objects can tell us only that they are where they are.

Accordingly, we must recur to the method of the school-divinity as explained by the Italian medievalists whom I quoted in the first lecture. We must observe the immediate occasion, and *use reason* to elicit a general description of its nature. Induction presupposes metaphysics. In other words, it rests upon an antecedent rationalism. You cannot have a rational justification for your appeal to history till your metaphysics has assured you that there *is* a history to appeal to; and likewise your conjectures as to the future presupposes some basis of knowledge that there *is* a future already subjected to some determinations. The difficulty is to make sense of either of these ideas. But unless you have done so, you have made nonsense of induction.

You will observe that I do not hold Induction to be in its essence the derivation of general laws. It is the divination of some characteristics of a particular future from the known characteristics of a particular past. The wider assumption of general laws holding for all cognisable occasions appears a very unsafe addendum to attach to this limited knowledge. All we can ask of the present occasion is that it shall determine a particular community of occasions, which are in some respects mutually qualified by reason of their inclusion within that same community. That community of occasions considered in physical science is the set of happenings which fit on to each other—as we say—in a common space-time, so that we can trace the transitions from one to the other. Accordingly, we refer to *the* common space-time indicated in our immediate occasion of knowledge. Inductive reasoning proceeds from the particular occasion to the particular community of occasions, and from the particular community to relations between particular occasions within that community. Until we have taken into account other scientific concepts, it is impossible to carry the discussion of induction further than this preliminary conclusion.

The third point to notice about this quotation from Bacon is the purely qualitative character of the statements made in it. In this respect Bacon completely missed the tonality which lay behind the success of seventeenth century science. Science was becoming, and has remained, primarily quantitative. Search for measurable elements among your phenomena, and then search for relations between these measures of physical quantities. Bacon ignores this rule of science. For example, in the quotation given he speaks of action at a distance; but he is thinking qualitatively and not quantitatively. We cannot ask that he should anticipate his younger contemporary Galileo, or his dis-

tant successor Newton. But he gives no hint that there should be a search for quantities. Perhaps he was misled by the current logical doctrines which had come down from Aristotle. For, in effect, these doctrines said to the physicist *classify* when they should have said *measure*.

By the end of the century physics had been founded on a satisfactory basis of measurement. The final and adequate exposition was given by Newton. The common measurable element of *mass* was discerned as characterising all bodies in different amounts. Bodies which are apparently identical in substance, shape, and size have very approximately the same mass: the closer the identity, the nearer the equality. The force acting on a body, whether by touch or by action at a distance, was (in effect) defined as being equal to the mass of the body multiplied by the rate of change of the body's velocity, so far as this rate of change is produced by that force. In this way the force is discerned by its effect on the motion of the body. The question now arises whether this conception of the magnitude of a force leads to the discovery of simple quantitative laws involving the alternative determination of forces by circumstances of the configuration of substances and of their physical characters. The Newtonian conception has been brilliantly successful in surviving this test throughout the whole modern period. Its first triumph was the law of gravitation. Its cumulative triumph has been the whole development of dynamical astronomy, of engineering, and of physics.

This subject of the formation of the three laws of motion and of the law of gravitation deserves critical attention. The whole development of thought occupied exactly two generations. It commenced with Galileo and ended with Newton's *Principia;* and Newton was born in the year that Galileo died. Also the lives of Descartes and Huyghens fall within the period occupied by these great terminal figures. The issue of the combined labours of these four men has some right to be considered as the greatest single intellectual success which mankind has achieved. In estimating its size, we must consider the completeness of its range. It constructs for us a vision of the material universe, and it enables us to calculate the minutest detail of a particular occurrence. Galileo took the first step in hitting on the right line of thought. He noted that the critical point to attend to was not the motion of bodies but the changes of their motions. Galileo's discovery is formularised by Newton in his first law of motion:—'Every body continues in its state of rest, or of uniform motion in a straight line, except so far as it may be compelled by force to change that state.'

This formula contains the repudiation of a belief which had blocked the progress of physics for two thousand years. It also deals with a fundamental concept which is essential to scientific theory; I mean, the concept of an ideally isolated system. This conception embodies a fundamental character of things, without which science, or indeed any knowledge on the part of finite intellects, would be impossible. The 'isolated' system is not a solipsist system, apart from which there would be nonentity. It is isolated as within the universe. This means that there are truths respecting this system which require reference only to the remainder of things by way of a uniform systematic scheme of relationships. Thus the conception of an

isolated system is not the conception of substantial independence from the remainder of things, but of freedom from casual contingent dependence upon detailed items within the rest of the universe. Further, this freedom from casual dependence is required only in respect to certain abstract characteristics which attach to the isolated system, and not in respect to the system in its full concreteness.

The first law of motion asks what is to be said of a dynamically isolated system so far as concerns its motion as a whole, abstracting from its orientation and its internal arrangement of parts. Aristotle said that you must conceive such a system to be at rest. Galileo added that the state of rest is only a particular case, and that the general statement is 'either in a state of rest, or of uniform motion in a straight line.' Accordingly, an Aristotelian would conceive the forces arising from the reaction of alien bodies as being quantitatively measurable in terms of the velocity they sustain, and as directively determined by the direction of that velocity; while the Galilean would direct attention to the magnitude of the acceleration and to its direction. This difference is illustrated by contrasting Kepler and Newton. They both speculated as to the forces sustaining the planets in their orbits. Kepler looked for tangential forces pushing the planets along, whereas Newton looked for radial forces diverting the directions of the planets' motions.

Instead of dwelling upon the mistake which Aristotle made, it is more profitable to emphasise the justification which he had for it, if we consider the obvious facts of our experience. All the motions which enter into our normal everyday experience cease unless they are evidently sustained from the outside. Apparently, therefore, the sound empiricist must devote his attention to this question of the sustenance of motion. We here hit upon one of the dangers of unimaginative empiricism. The seventeenth century exhibits another example of this same danger; and, of all people in the world, Newton fell into it. Huyghens had produced the wave theory of light. But this theory failed to account for the most obvious facts about light as in our ordinary experience, namely, that shadows cast by obstructing objects are defined by rectilinear rays.

Accordingly, Newton rejected this theory and adopted the corpuscular theory which completely explained shadows. Since then both theories have had their periods of triumph. At the present moment the scientific world is seeking for a combination of the two. These examples illustrate the danger of refusing to entertain an idea because of its failure to explain one of the most obvious facts in the subject matter in question. If you have had your attention directed to the novelties in thought in your own lifetime, you will have observed that almost all really new ideas have a certain aspect of foolishness when they are first produced.

Returning to the laws of motion, it is noticeable that no reason was produced in the seventeenth century for the Galilean as distinct from the Aristotelian position. It was an ultimate fact. When in the course of these lectures we come to the modern period, we shall see that the theory of relativity throws complete light on this question; but only by rearranging our whole ideas as to space and time.

It remained for Newton to direct attention to *mass* as a physical quantity inherent in the nature of a material body. Mass remained permanent during all changes of motion. But the proof of the permanence of mass amid chemical transformations had to wait for Lavoisier, a century later. Newton's next task was to find some estimate of the magnitude of the alien force in terms of the mass of the body and of its acceleration. He here had a stroke of luck. For, from the point of view of a mathematician, the simplest possible law, namely the product of the two, proved to be the successful one. Again the modern relativity theory modifies this extreme simplicity. But luckily for science the delicate experiments of the physicists of today were not then known, or even possible. Accordingly, the world was given the two centuries which it required in order to digest Newton's laws of motion.

Having regard to this triumph, can we wonder that scientists placed their ultimate principles upon a materialistic basis, and thereafter ceased to worry about philosophy? We shall grasp the course of thought, if we understand exactly what this basis is, and what difficulties it finally involves. When you are criticising the philosophy of an epoch, do not chiefly direct your attention to those intellectual positions which its exponents feel it necessary explicitly to defend. There will be some fundamental assumptions which adherents of all the variant systems within the epoch unconsciously presuppose. Such assumptions appear so obvious that people do not know what they are assuming because no other way of putting things has ever occurred to them. With these assumptions a certain limited number of types of philosophic systems are possible, and this group of systems constitutes the philosophy of the epoch.

One such assumption underlies the whole philosophy of nature during the modern period. It is embodied in the conception which is supposed to express the most concrete aspect of nature. The Ionian philosophers asked, What is nature made of? The answer is couched in terms of stuff, or matter, or material—the particular name chosen is indifferent—which has the property of simple location in space and time, or, if you adopt the more modern ideas, in space-time. What I mean by matter, or material, is anything which has this property of *simple location.* By simple location I mean one major characteristic which refers equally both to space and to time, and other minor characteristics which are diverse as between space and time.

The characteristic common both to space and time is that material can be said to be *here* in space and *here* in time, or *here* in space-time, in a perfectly definite sense which does not require for its explanation any reference to other regions of space-time. Curiously enough this character of simple location holds whether we look on a region of space-time as determined absolutely or relatively. For if a region is merely a way of indicating a certain set of relations to other entities, then this characteristic, which I call simple location, is that material can be said to have just these relations of position to the other entities without requiring for its explanation any reference to other regions constituted by analogous relations of position to the same entities. In fact, as soon as you have settled, however you do settle, what you mean by a definite place in space-time, you can adequately state the relation of a particular material body to space-time by saying that it is just there, in that place; and, so far

as simple location is concerned, there is nothing more to be said on the subject.

There are, however, some subordinate explanations to be made which bring in the minor characteristics which I have already mentioned. First, as regards time, if material has existed during any period, it has equally been in existence during any portion of that period. In other words, dividing the time does not divide the material. Secondly, in respect to space, dividing the volume does divide the material. Accordingly, if material exists throughout a volume, there will be less of that material distributed through any definite half of that volume. It is from this property that there arises our notion of density at a point of space. Anyone who talks about density is not assimilating time and space to the extent that some extremists of the modern school of relativists very rashly desire. For the division of time functions, in respect to material, quite differently from the division of space.

Furthermore, this fact that the material is indifferent to the division of time leads to the conclusion that the lapse of time is an accident, rather than of the essence, of the material. The material is fully itself in any sub-period however short. Thus the transition of time has nothing to do with the character of the material. The material is equally itself at an instant of time. Here an instant of time is conceived as in itself without transition, since the temporal transition is the succession of instants.

The answer, therefore, which the seventeenth century gave to the ancient question of the Ionian thinkers, 'What is the world made of?' was that the world is a succession of instantaneous configurations of matter—or of material, if you wish to include stuff more subtle than ordinary matter, the ether for example.

We cannot wonder that science rested content with this assumption as to the fundamental elements of nature. The great forces of nature, such as gravitation, were entirely determined by the configurations of masses. Thus the configurations determined their own changes, so that the circle of scientific thought was completely closed. This is the famous mechanistic theory of nature, which has reigned supreme ever since the seventeenth century. It is the orthodox creed of physical science. Furthermore, the creed justified itself by the pragmatic test. It worked. Physicists took no more interest in philosophy. They emphasised the anti-rationalism of the Historical Revolt. But the difficulties of this theory of materialistic mechanism very soon became apparent. The history of thought in the eighteenth and nineteenth centuries is governed by the fact that the world had got hold of a general idea which it could neither live with nor live without.

This simple location of instantaneous material configurations is what Bergson has protested against, so far as it concerns time and so far as it is taken to be the fundamental fact of concrete nature. He calls it a distortion of nature due to the intellectual 'spatialisation' of things. I agree with Bergson in his protest: but I do not agree that such distortion is a vice necessary to the intellectual apprehension of nature. I shall in subsequent lectures endeavour to show that this spatalytion is the expression of more concrete facts under the guise of very abstract logical constructions. There is an error; but it is merely the accidental error of mistaking the abstract for the concrete. It is

an example of what I will call the 'Fallacy of Misplaced Concreteness.' This fallacy is the occasion of great confusion in philosophy. It is not necessary for the intellect to fall into the trap, though in this example there has been a very general tendency to do so.

It is at once evident that the concept of simple location is going to make great difficulties for induction. For, if in the location of configurations of matter throughout a stretch of time there is no inherent reference to any other times, past or future, it immediately follows that nature within any period does not refer to nature at any other period. Accordingly, induction is not based on anything which can be observed as inherent in nature. Thus we cannot look to nature for the justification of our belief in any law such as the law of gravitation. In other words, the order of nature cannot be justified by the mere observation of nature. For there is nothing in the present fact which inherently refers either to the past or to the future. It looks, therefore, as though memory, as well as induction, would fail to find any justification within nature itself.

I have been anticipating the course of future thought, and have been repeating Hume's argument. This train of thought follows so immediately from the consideration of simple location, that we cannot wait for the eighteenth century before considering it. The only wonder is that the world did in fact wait for Hume before noting the difficulty. Also it illustrates the anti-rationalism of the scientific public that, when Hume did appear, it was only the religious implications of his philosophy which attracted attention. This was because the clergy were in principle rationalists, whereas the men of science were content with a simple faith in the order of nature. Hume himself remarks, no doubt scoffingly, 'Our holy religion is founded on faith.' This attitude satisfied the Royal Society but not the Church. It also satisfied Hume and has satisfied subsequent empiricists.

There is another presupposition of thought which must be put beside the theory of simple location. I mean the two correlative categories of Substance and Quality. There is, however, this difference. There were different theories as to the adequate description of the status of space. But whatever its status, no one had any doubt but that the connection with space enjoyed by entities, which are said to be in space, is that of simple location. We may put this shortly by saying that it was tacitly assumed that space is the locus of simple location. Whatever is in space is *simpliciter* in some definite portion of space. But in respect to substance and quality the leading minds of the seventeenth century were definitely perplexed; though, with their usual genius, they at once constructed a theory which was adequate for their immediate purposes.

Of course, substance and quality, as well as simple location, are the most natural ideas for the human mind. It is the way in which we think of things, and without these ways of thinking we could not get our ideas straight for daily use. There is no doubt about this. The only question is, How concretely are we thinking when we consider nature under these conceptions? My point will be, that we are presenting ourselves with simplified editions of immediate matters of fact. When we examine the primary elements of these simplified editions, we shall find that they are in truth only to be justified as being elaborate logical construc-

tions of a high degree of abstraction. Of course, as a point of individual psychology, we get at the ideas by the rough and ready method of suppressing what appear to be irrelevent details. But when we attempt to justify this suppression of irrelevance, we find that, though there are entities left corresponding to the entities we talk about, yet these entities are of a high degree of abstraction.

Thus I hold that substance and quality afford another instance of the fallacy of misplaced concreteness. Let us consider how the notions of substance and quality arise. We observe an object as an entity with certain characteristics. Furthermore, each individual entity is apprehended through its characteristics. For example, we observe a body; there is something about it which we note. Perhaps, it is hard, and blue, and round, and noisy. We observe something which possesses these qualities: apart from these qualities we do not observe anything at all. Accordingly, the entity is the substratum, or substance, of which we predicate qualities. Some of the qualities are essential, so that apart from them the entity would not be itself; while other qualities are accidental and changeable. In respect to material bodies, the qualities of having a quantitative mass, and of simple location somewhere, were held by John Locke at the close of the seventeenth century to be essential qualities. Of course, the location was changeable, and the unchangeability of mass was merely an experimental fact except for some extremists.

So far, so good. But when we pass to blueness and noisiness a new situation has to be faced. In the first place, the body may not be always blue, or noisy. We have already allowed for this by our theory of accidental qualities, which for the moment we may accept as adequate. But in the second place, the seventeenth century exposed a real difficulty. The great physicists elaborated transmission theories of light and sound, based upon their materialistic views of nature. There were two hypotheses as to light: either it was transmitted by the vibratory waves of a materialistic ether, or—according to Newton—it was transmitted by the motion of incredibly small corpuscles of some subtle matter. We all know how that the wave theory of Huyghens held the field during the nineteenth century, and at present physicists are endeavouring to explain some obscure circumstances attending radiation by a combination of both theories. But whatever theory you choose, there is no light or colour as a fact in external nature. There is merely motion of material. Again, when the light enters your eyes and falls on the retina, there is merely motion of material. Then your nerves are affected and your brain is affected, and again this is merely motion of material. The same line of argument holds for sound, substituting waves in the air for waves in the ether, and ears for eyes.

We then ask in what sense are blueness and noisiness qualities of the body. By analogous reasoning, we also ask in what sense is its scent a quality of the rose.

Galileo considered this question, and at once pointed out that, apart from eyes, ears, or noses, there would be no colours, sounds, or smells. Descartes and Locke elaborated a theory of primary and secondary qualities. For example, Descartes in his 'Sixth Meditation' says: 'And indeed, as I perceive different sorts of colours, sounds, odours, tastes, heat, hardness, etc., I safely conclude that there are in the bodies from which the diverse perceptions of the senses proceed, certain varieties corresponding to them, although, perhaps, not in reality like them; . . .'

Also in his *Principles of Philosophy,* he says: 'That by our senses we know nothing of external objects beyond their figure (or situation), magnitude, and motion.'

Locke, writing with a knowledge of Newtonian dynamics, places mass among the primary qualities of bodies. In short, he elaborates a theory of primary and secondary qualities in accordance with the state of physical science at the close of the seventeenth century. The primary qualities are the essential qualities of substances whose spatio-temporal relationships constitute nature. The orderliness of these relationships constitutes the order of nature. The occurrences of nature are in some way apprehended by minds, which are associated with living bodies. Primarily, the mental apprehension is aroused by the occurrences in certain parts of the correlated body, the occurrences in the brain, for instance. But the mind in apprehending also experiences sensations which, properly speaking, are qualities of the mind alone. These sensations are projected by the mind so as to clothe appropriate bodies in external nature. Thus the bodies are perceived as with qualities which in reality do not belong to them, qualities which in fact are purely the offspring of the mind. Thus nature gets credit which should in truth be reserved for ourselves: the rose for its scent: the nightingale for his song: and the sun for his radiance. The poets are entirely mistaken. They should address their lyrics to themselves, and should turn them into odes of self-congratulation on the excellency of the human mind. Nature is a dull affair, soundless, scentless, colourless; merely the hurrying of material, endlessly, meaninglessly.

However you disguise it, this is the practical outcome of the characteristic scientific philosophy which closed the seventeenth century.

In the first place, we must note its astounding efficiency as a system of concepts for the organisation of scientific research. In this respect, it is fully worthy of the genius of the century which produced it. It has held its own as the guiding principle of scientific studies ever since. It is still reigning. Every university in the world organises itself in accordance with it. No alternative system of organising the pursuit of scientific truth has been suggested. It is not only reigning, but it is without a rival.

And yet—it is quite unbelievable. This conception of the universe is surely framed in terms of high abstractions, and the paradox only arises because we have mistaken our abstraction for concrete realities.

No picture, however generalised, of the achievements of scientific thought in this century can omit the advance in mathematics. Here as elsewhere the genius of the epoch made itself evident. Three great Frenchmen, Descartes, Desargues, Pascal, initiated the modern period in geometry. Another Frenchman, Fermat, laid the foundations of modern analysis, and all but perfected the methods of the differential calculus. Newton and Leibniz, between them, actually did create the differential calculus as a practical method of mathematical reasoning. When the century ended, mathematics as an instrument for application to physical problems was well established in something of its modern proficiency. Modern pure mathematics, if we except geometry, was in its infancy, and had given no signs of the astonishing growth it was to make in the nineteenth century. But the mathematical physicist had appeared, bringing with him the type of mind which was to rule the scientific world in the next century. It was to be the age of 'Victorious Analysis.'

The seventeenth century had finally produced a scheme of scientific thought framed by mathematicians, for the use of mathematicians. The great characteristic of the mathematical mind is its capacity for dealing with abstractions; and for eliciting from them clear-cut demonstrative trains of reasoning, entirely satisfactory so long as it is those abstractions which you want to think about. The enormous success of the scientific abstractions, yielding on the one hand *matter* with its *simple location* in space and time, on the other hand *mind,* perceiving, suffering, reasoning, but not interfering, has foisted onto philosophy the task of accepting them as the most concrete rendering of fact.

Thereby, modern philosophy has been ruined. It has oscillated in a complex manner between three extremes. There are the dualists, who accept matter and mind as on an equal basis, and the two varieties of monists, those who put mind inside matter, and those who put matter inside mind. But this juggling with abstractions can never overcome the inherent confusion introduced by the ascription of *misplaced concreteness* to the scientific scheme of the seventeenth century.

54

Alfred North Whitehead Speculative Philosophy

Section I

This course of lectures is designed as an essay in Speculative Philosophy. Its first task must be to define 'speculative philosophy,' and to defend it as a method productive of important knowledge.

Speculative Philosophy is the endeavour to frame a coherent, logical, necessary system of general ideas in terms of which every element of our experience can be interpreted. By this notion of 'interpretation' I mean that everything of which we are conscious, as enjoyed, perceived, willed, or thought shall have the character of a particular instance of the general scheme. Thus the philosophical scheme should be coherent, logical, and in respect to its interpretation, applicable and adequate. Here 'applicable' means that some items of experience are thus interpretable, and 'adequate' means that there are no items incapable of such interpretation.

'Coherence,' as here employed, means that the fundamental ideas, in terms of which the scheme is developed, presuppose each other so that in isolation they are meaningless. This requirement does not mean that they are definable in terms of each other; it means that what is indefinable in one such notion cannot be abstracted from its relevance to the other notions. It is the ideal of speculative philosophy that its fundamental notions shall not seem capable of abstraction from each other. In other words, it is presupposed that no entity can be conceived in complete abstraction from the system of the universe, and that it is the business of speculative philosophy to exhibit this truth. This character is its coherence.

The term 'logical' has its ordinary meaning, including 'logical' consistency, or lack of contradiction, the definition of constructs in logical terms, the exemplification of general logical notions in specific instances, and the principles of inference. It will be observed that logical notions must themselves find their places in the scheme of philosophic notions.

It will also be noticed that this ideal of speculative philosophy has its rational side and its empirical side. The rational side is expressed by the terms 'coherent' and 'logical.' The empirical side is expressed by the terms 'applicable' and 'adequate.' But the two sides are bound together by clearing away an ambiguity which remains in the previous explanation of the term 'adequate.' The adequacy of the scheme over every item does not mean adequacy over such items as happen to have been considered. It means that the texture of observed experience, as illustrating the philosophic scheme, is such that all related experience must exhibit the same texture. Thus the philosophic scheme should be 'necessary,' in the sense of bearing in itself its own warrant of universality throughout all experience, provided that we confine ourselves to that which communicates with immediate matter of fact. But what does not so communicate is unknowable, and the unknowable is unknown;[1] and so this universality defined by 'communication' can suffice.

This doctrine of necessity in universality means that there is an essence to the universe which forbids relationships beyond itself, as a violation of its rationality. Speculative philosophy seeks that essence.

Section II

Philosophers can never hope finally to formulate these metaphysical first principles. Weakness of insight and deficiencies of language stand in the way inexorably. Words and phrases must be stretched towards a generality foreign to their ordinary usage; and however such elements of language be stabilized as technicalities, they remain metaphors mutely appealing for an imaginative leap.

There is no first principle which is in itself unknowable, not to be captured by a flash of insight. But, putting aside the difficulties of language, deficiency in imaginative penetration forbids progress in any form other than that of an asymptotic approach to a scheme of principles, only definable in terms of the ideal which they should satisfy.

The difficulty has its seat in the empirical side of philosophy. Our datum is the actual world, including ourselves; and this actual world spreads itself for observation in the guise of the topic of our immediate experience. The elucidation of immediate experience is the sole justification for any thought; and the starting-point for thought is the analytic observation of components of this experience. But we are not conscious of any clear-cut complete analysis of immediate experience, in terms of the various details which comprise its definiteness. We habitually observe by the method of difference. Sometimes we see an elephant, and sometimes we do not. The result is that an elephant, when present, is noticed. Facility of observation depends on the fact that the object observed is important when present, and sometimes is absent.

The metaphysical first principles can never fail of exemplification. We can never catch the actual world taking a holiday from their sway. Thus, for the discovery of metaphysics, the method of pinning down thought to the strict systematization of detailed discrimination, already effected by antecedent observation, breaks down. This collapse of the method of rigid empiricism is not confined to metaphysics. It occurs whenever we seek the larger generalities. In natural science this rigid method is the Baconian method of induction, a method which, if consistently pursued, would have left science where it found it. What Bacon omitted was the play of a free imagination, controlled by the requirements of coherence and logic. The true method of discovery is like the flight of an aeroplane. It starts from the ground of particular observation; it makes a flight in the thin air of imaginative generalization; and it again lands for renewed observation rendered acute by rational interpretation. The reason for the success of this method of imaginative rationalization is that, when the method of difference fails, factors which are

---

1. This doctrine is a paradox. Indulging in a species of false modesty, 'cautious' philosophers undertake its definition.

constantly present may yet be observed under the influence of imaginative thought. Such thought supplies the differences which the direct observation lacks. It can even play with inconsistency; and can thus throw light on the consistent, and persistent, elements in experience by comparison with what in imagination is inconsistent with them. The negative judgment is the peak of mentality. But the conditions for the success of imaginative construction must be rigidly adhered to. In the first place, this construction must have its origin in the generalization of particular factors discerned in particular topics of human interest; for example, in physics, or in physiology, or in psychology, or in aesthetics, or in ethical beliefs, or in sociology, or in languages conceived as storehouses of human experience. In this way the prime requisite, that anyhow there shall be some important application, is secured. The success of the imaginative experiment is always to be tested by the applicability of its results beyond the restricted locus from which it originated. In default of such extended application, a generalization started from physics, for example, remains merely an alternative expression of notions applicable to physics. The partially successful philosophic generalization will, if derived from physics, find applications in fields of experience beyond physics. It will enlighten observation in those remote fields, so that general principles can be discerned as in process of illustration, which in the absence of the imaginative generalization are obscured by their persistent exemplification.

Thus the first requisite is to proceed by the method of generalization so that certainly there is some application; and the test of some success is application beyond the immediate origin. In other words, some synoptic vision has been gained.

In this description of philosophic method, the term 'philosophic generalization' has meant 'the utilization of specific notions, applying to a restricted group of facts, for the divination of the generic notions which apply to all facts.'

In its use of this method natural science has shown a curious mixture of rationalism and irrationalism. Its prevalent tone of thought has been ardently rationalistic within its own borders, and dogmatically irrational beyond those borders. In practice such an attitude tends to become a dogmatic denial that there are any factors in the world not fully expressible in terms of its own primary notions devoid of further generalization. Such a denial is the self-denial of thought.

The second condition for the success of imaginative construction is unflinching pursuit of the two rationalistic ideals, coherence and logical perfection.

Logical perfection does not here require any detailed explanation. An example of its importance is afforded by the role of mathematics in the restricted field of natural science. The history of mathematics exhibits the generalization of special notions observed in particular instances. In any branches of mathematics, the notions presuppose each other. It is a remarkable characteristic of the history of thought that branches of mathematics, developed under the pure imaginative impulse, thus controlled, finally receive their important application. Time may be wanted. Conic sections had to wait for eighteen hundred years. In more recent years, the theory of probability, the theory of tensors, the theory of matrices are cases in point.

The requirement of coherence is the

great preservative of rationalistic sanity. But the validity of its criticism is not always admitted. If we consider philosophical controversies, we shall find that disputants tend to require coherence from their adversaries, and to grant dispensations to themselves. It has been remarked that a system of philosophy is never refuted; it is only abandoned. The reason is that logical contradictions, except as temporary slips of the mind—plentiful, though temporary—are the most gratuitous of errors; and usually they are trivial. Thus, after criticism, systems do not exhibit mere illogicalities. They suffer from inadequacy and incoherence. Failure to include some obvious elements of experience in the scope of the system is met by boldly denying the facts. Also while a philosophical system retains any charm of novelty, it enjoys a plenary indulgence for its failures in coherence. But after a system has acquired orthodoxy, and is taught with authority, it receives a sharper criticism. Its denials and its incoherences are found intolerable, and a reaction sets in.

Incoherence is the arbitrary disconnection of first principles. In modern philosophy Descartes' two kinds of substance, corporeal and mental, illustrate incoherence. There is, in Descartes' philosophy, no reason why there should not be a one-substance world, only corporeal, or a one-substance world, only mental. According to Descartes, a substantial individual 'requires nothing but itself in order to exist.' Thus this system makes a virtue of its incoherence. But, on the other hand, the facts seem connected, while Descartes' system does not; for example, in the treatment of the body-mind problem. The Cartesian system obviously says something that is true. But its notions are too

abstract to penetrate into the nature of things.

The attraction of Spinoza's philosophy lies in its modification of Descartes' position into greater coherence. He starts with one substance, *causa sui,* and considers its essential attributes and its individualized modes, i.e., the *'affectiones substantiae.'* The gap in the system is the arbitrary introduction of the 'modes.' And yet, a multiplicity of modes is a fixed requisite, if the scheme is to retain any direct relevance to the many occasions in the experienced world.

The philosophy of organism is closely allied to Spinoza's scheme of thought. But it differs by the abandonment of the subject-predicate forms of thought, so far as concerns the presupposition that this form is a direct embodiment of the most ultimate characterization of fact. The result is that the 'substance-quality' concept is avoided; and that morphological description is replaced by description of dynamic process. Also Spinoza's 'modes' now become the sheer actualities; so that, though analysis of them increases our understanding, it does not lead us to the discovery of any higher grade of reality. The coherence, which the system seeks to preserve, is the discovery that the process, or concrescence, of any one actual entity involves the other actual entities among its components. In this way the obvious solidarity of the world receives its explanation.

In all philosophic theory there is an ultimate which is actual in virtue of its accidents. It is only then capable of characterization through its accidental embodiments, and apart from these accidents is devoid of actuality. In the philosophy of organism this ultimate is termed 'creativity'; and God is its primordial, non-temporal accident. In monistic philosophies, Spinoza's or absolute idealism, this ultimate is God, who is also equivalently termed 'The Absolute.' In such monistic schemes, the ultimate is illegitimately allowed a final, 'eminent' reality, beyond that ascribed to any of its accidents. In this general position the philosophy of organism seems to approximate more to some strains of Indian, or Chinese, thought, than to western Asiatic, or European, thought. One side makes process ultimate; the other side makes fact ultimate.

Section III

In its turn every philosophy will suffer a deposition. But the bundle of philosophic systems expresses a variety of general truths about the universe, awaiting coordination and assignment of their various spheres of validity. Such progress in coordination is provided by the advance of philosophy; and in this sense philosophy has advanced from Plato onwards. According to this account of the achievement of rationalism, the chief error in philosophy is overstatement. The aim at generalization is sound, but the estimate of success is exaggerated. There are two main forms of such overstatement. One form is what I have termed, elsewhere, the 'fallacy of *misplaced concreteness*'. This fallacy consists in neglecting the degree of abstraction involved when an actual entity is considered merely so far as it exemplifies certain categories of thought. There are aspects of actualities which are simply ignored so long as we restrict thought to these categories. Thus the success of a philosophy is to be measured by its comparative avoidance of this fallacy, when thought is restricted within its categories.

The other form of overstatement consists in a false estimate of logical procedure in respect to certainty, and in respect to premises. Philosophy has been haunted by the unfortunate notion that its method is dogmatically to indicate premises which are severally clear, distinct, and certain; and to erect upon these premises a deductive system of thought.

But the accurate expression of the final generalities is the goal of discussion and not its origin. Philosophy has been misled by the example of mathematics; and even in mathematics the statement of the ultimate logical principles is beset with difficulties, as yet insuperable. The verification of a rationalistic scheme is to be sought in its general success, and not in the peculiar certainty, or initial clarity, of its first principles. In this connection the misuse of the *ex absurdo* argument has to be noted; much philosophical reasoning is vitiated by it. The only logical conclusion to be drawn, when a contradiction issues from a train of reasoning, is that at least one of the premises involved in the inference is false. It is rashly assumed without further question that the peccant premise can at once be located. In mathematics this assumption is often justified, and philosophers have been thereby misled. But in the absence of a well-defined categorical scheme of entities, issuing in a satisfactory metaphysical system, every premise in a philosophical argument is under suspicion.

Philosophy will not regain its proper status until the gradual elaboration of categorical schemes, definitely stated at each stage of progress, is recognized as its proper objective. There may be rival schemes, inconsistent among themselves; each with its own merits and its own failures. It will then be the purpose of research to conciliate the differences. Metaphysical categories are not dogmatic statements of the obvious, they are tentative formulations of the ultimate generalities.

If we consider any scheme of philosophic categories as one complex assertion, and apply to it the logician's alternative, true or false, the answer must be that the scheme is false. The same answer must be given to a like question respecting the existing formulated principles of any science.

The scheme is true with unformulated qualifications, exceptions, limitations, and new interpretations in terms of more general notions. We do not yet know how to recast the scheme into a logical truth. But the scheme is a matrix from which true propositions applicable to particular circumstances can be derived. We can at present only trust our trained instincts as to the discrimination of the circumstances in respect to which the scheme is valid.

The use of such a matrix is to argue from it boldly and with rigid logic. The scheme should therefore be stated with the utmost precision and definiteness, to allow of such argumentation. The conclusion of the argument should then be confronted with circumstances to which it should apply.

The primary advantage thus gained is that experience is not interrogated with the benumbing repression of common sense. The observation acquires an enhanced penetration by reason of the expectation evoked by the conclusion of the argument. The outcome from this procedure takes one of three forms: (i) the conclusion may agree with the observed facts; (ii) the conclusion may exhibit general agreement, with disagreement in detail; (iii) the conclusion may be in complete disagreement with the facts.

In the first case, the facts are known with more adequacy and the applicability of the system to the world has been elucidated. In the second case, criticisms of the observation of the facts and of the details of the scheme are both required. The history of thought shows that false interpretations of observed facts enter into the records of their observation. Thus both theory, and received notions as to fact, are in doubt. In the third case, a fundamental reorganization of theory is required either by way of limiting it to some special province, or by way of entire abandonment of its main categories of thought.

After the initial basis of a rational life, with a civilized language, has been laid, all productive thought has proceeded either by the poetic insight of artists, or by the imaginative elaboration of schemes of thought capable of utilization as logical premises. In some measure or other, progress is always a transcendence of what is obvious.

Rationalism never shakes off its status of an *experimental adventure*. The combined influences of mathematics and religion, which have so greatly contributed to the rise of philosophy, have also had the unfortunate effect of yoking it with static dogmatism. Rationalism is an adventure in the clarification of thought, progressive and never final. But it is an adventure in which even partial success has importance.

Section IV

The field of a special science is confined to one genus of facts, in the sense that no statements are made respecting facts which lie outside that genus. The very circumstance that a science has naturally arisen concerning a set of facts secures that facts of that type have definite relations among themselves which are very obvious to all mankind. The common obviousness of things arises when their explicit apprehension carries immediate importance for purposes of survival, or of enjoyment—that is to say, for purposes of 'being' and of 'well-being.' Elements in human experience, singled out in this way, are those elements concerning which language is copious and, within its limits, precise. The special sciences, therefore, deal with topics which lie open to easy inspection and are readily expressed by words.

The study of philosophy is a voyage towards the larger generalities. For this reason in the infancy of science, when the main stress lay in the discovery of the most general ideas usefully applicable to the subject matter in question, philosophy was not sharply distinguished from science. To this day, a new science with any substantial novelty in its notions is considered to be in some way peculiarly philosophical. In their later stages, apart from occasional disturbances, most sciences accept without question the general notions in terms of which they develop. The main stress is laid on the adjustment and the direct verification of more special statements. In such periods scientists repudiate philosophy; Newton justly satisfied with his physical principles, disclaimed metaphysics.

The fate of Newtonian physics warns us that there is a development in scientific first principles, and that their original forms can only be saved by interpretations of meaning and limitations of their field of application—interpretations and limitations unsuspected during the first period of successful employment. One chapter in the history of culture is concerned with the growth of generalities. In such a chapter it is seen that the older generalities, like the older hills, are worn down and diminished in height, surpassed by younger rivals.

Thus one aim of philosophy is to challenge the half-truths constituting the scientific first principles. The systematization of knowledge cannot be conducted in watertight compartments. All general truths condition each other; and the limits of their application cannot be adequately defined apart from their correlation by yet wider generalities. The criticism of principles must chiefly take the form of determining the proper meanings to be assigned to the fundamental notions of the various sciences, when these notions are considered in respect to their status relatively to each other. The determination of this status requires a generality transcending any special subject matter.

If we may trust the Pythagorean tradition, the rise of European philosophy was largely promoted by the development of mathematics into a science of abstract generality. But in its subsequent development the method of philosophy has also been vitiated by the example of mathematics. The primary method of mathematics is deduction; the primary method of philosophy is descriptive generalization. Under the influence of mathematics, deduction has been foisted onto philosophy as its standard method, instead of taking its true place as an essential auxiliary mode of verification whereby to test the scope of generalities.

This misapprehension of philosophic method has veiled the very considerable success of philosophy in providing generic notions which add lucidity to our apprehension of the facts of experience. The depositions of Plato, Aristotle, Thomas Aquinas, Descartes, Spinoza, Leibniz, Locke, Berkeley, Hume, Kant, Hegel, merely mean that ideas which these men introduced into the philosophic tradition must be construed with limitations, adaptations, and inversions, either unknown to them, or even explicitly repudiated by them. A new idea introduces a new alternative, and we are not less indebted to a thinker when we adopt the alternative which he discarded. Philosophy never reverts to its old position after the shock of a great philosopher.

Section V

Every science must devise its own instruments. The tool required for philosophy is language. Thus philosophy redesigns language in the same way that, in a physical science, pre-existing appliances are redesigned. It is exactly at this point that the appeal to facts is a difficult operation. This appeal is not solely to the expression of the facts in current verbal statements. The adequacy of such sentences is the main question at issue. It is true that the general agreement of mankind as to experienced facts is best expressed in language. But the language of literature breaks down precisely at the task of expressing in explicit form the larger generalities—the very generalities which metaphysics seeks to express.

The point is that every proposition refers to a universe exhibiting some general systematic metaphysical character. Apart from this background, the separate entities which go to form the proposition, and the proposition as a whole, are without determinate character. Nothing has been defined, because every definite entity requires a systematic universe to supply its requisite status. Thus every proposition proposing a fact must, in its complete analysis, propose the general character of the universe required for that fact. There are no self-sustained facts, floating in nonentity. This doctrine, of the impossibility of tearing a proposition from its systematic context in the actual world, is a direct consequence of the fourth and the twentieth of the fundamental categoreal explanations which we shall be engaged in expanding and illustrating. A proposition can embody partial truth because it only demands a certain type of systematic environment, which is presupposed in its meaning. It does not refer to the universe in all its detail.

One practical aim of metaphysics is the accurate analysis of propositions; not merely of metaphysical propositions, but of quite ordinary propositions such as 'There is beef for dinner today,' and 'Socrates is mortal.' The one genus of facts which constitutes the field of some special science requires some common metaphysical presupposition respecting the universe. It is merely credulous to accept verbal phrases as adequate statements of propositions. The distinction between verbal phrases and complete propositions is one of the reasons why the logicians' rigid alternative, 'true or false,' is so largely irrelevant for the pursuit of knowledge.

The excessive trust in linguistic phrases has been the well-known reason vitiating so much of the philosophy and physics among the Greeks and among the medieval thinkers who continued the Greek traditions. For example John Stuart Mill writes:

> *They (the Greeks) had great difficulty in distinguishing between things which their language confounded, or in putting mentally together things which it distinguished; and could hardly combine the objects in nature into any classes but those which were made for them by the popular phrases of their own country; or at least could not help fancying those classes to be natural, and all others arbitrary and artificial. Accordingly, scientific investigation among the Greek schools of speculation and their followers in the Middle Ages, was little more than a mere sifting and analyzing of the notions attached to common language. They thought that by determining the meaning of words they could become acquainted with facts.*

Mill then proceeds to quote from Whewell a paragraph illustrating the same weakness of Greek thought.

But neither Mill, nor Whewell, tracks this difficulty about language down to its sources. They both presuppose that language does enunciate well-defined propositions. This is quite untrue. Language is thoroughly indeterminate, by reason of the fact that every occurrence presupposes some systematic type of environment.

For example, the word 'Socrates,' referring to the philosopher, in one sentence may stand for an entity presupposing a more closely defined background than the word 'Socrates,' with the same reference, in another sentence. The word 'mortal' affords an analogous possibility. A precise language must await a completed metaphysical knowledge.

The technical language of philosophy represents attempts of various schools of thought to obtain explicit expression of general ideas presupposed by the facts of experience. It follows that any novelty in metaphysical doctrines exhibits some measure of disagreement with statements of the facts to be found in current philosophical literature. The extent of disagreement measures the extent of metaphysical divergence. It is, therefore, no valid criticism on one metaphysical school to point out that its doctrines do not follow from the verbal expression of the facts accepted by another school. The whole contention is that the doctrines in question supply a closer approach to fully expressed propositions.

The truth itself is nothing else than how the composite natures of the organic actualities of the world obtain adequate representation in the divine nature. Such representations compose the 'consequent nature' of God, which evolves in its relationship to the evolving world without derogation to the eternal completion of its primordial conceptual nature. In this way the 'ontological principle' is maintained—since there can be no determinate truth, correlating impartially the partial experiences of many actual entities, apart from one actual entity to which it can be referred. The reaction of the temporal world on the nature of God is considered subsequently in Part V: it is there termed 'the consequent nature of God.'

Whatever is found in 'practice' must lie within the scope of the metaphysical description. When the description fails to include the 'practice,' the metaphysics is inadequate and requires revision. There can be no appeal to practice to supplement metaphysics, so long as we remain contented with our metaphysical doctrines. Metaphysics is nothing but the description of the generalities which apply to all the details of practice.

No metaphysical system can hope entirely to satisfy these pragmatic tests. At the best such a system will remain only an approximation to the general truths which are sought. In particular, there are no precisely stated axiomatic certainties from which to start. There is not even the language in which to frame them. The only possible procedure is to start from verbal expressions which, when taken by themselves with the current meaning of their words, are ill-defined and ambiguous. These are not premises to be immediately reasoned from apart from elucidation by further discussion; they are endeavours to state general principles which will be exemplified in the subsequent description of the facts of experience. This subsequent elaboration should elucidate the meanings to be assigned to the words and phrases employed. Such meanings are incapable of accurate apprehension apart from a correspondingly accurate apprehension of the metaphysical background which the universe provides for them. But no language can be anything but elliptical, requiring a leap of the imagination to understand its meaning in its relevance to immediate experience. The position of metaphysics in the development of culture cannot be understood without remembering that no verbal statement is the adequate expression of a proposition.

An old established metaphysical system gains a false air of adequate precision from the fact that its words and phrases have passed into current literature. Thus propositions expressed in its language are more easily correlated to our flitting intuitions into metaphysical truth. When we trust these verbal statements and argue as though they adequately analysed meaning, we are led into difficulties which take the shape of negations of what in practice is presupposed. But when they are proposed as first principles they assume an unmerited air of sober obviousness. Their defect is that the true propositions which they do express lose their fundamental character when subjected to adequate expression. For example consider the type of propositions such as 'The grass is green,' and 'The whale is big.' This subject-predicate form of statement seems so simple, leading straight to a metaphysical first principle; and yet in these examples it conceals such complex, diverse meanings.

It has been an objection to speculative philosophy that it is over-ambitious. Rationalism, it is admitted, is the method by which advance is made within the limits of particular sciences. It is, however, held that this limited success must not encourage attempts to frame ambitious schemes expressive of the general nature of things.

One alleged justification of this criticism is ill-success: European thought is represented as littered with metaphysical systems, abandoned and unreconciled.

Such an assertion tacitly fastens upon philosophy the old dogmatic test. The same criterion would fasten ill-success upon science. We no more retain the physics of the seventeenth century than we do the Cartesian philosophy of that century. Yet within limits, both systems express important truths. Also we are beginning to understand the wider categories which define their limits of correct application. Of course, in that century, dogmatic views held sway; so that the validity both of the physical notions, and of the Cartesian notions, was misconceived. Mankind never quite knows what it is after. When we survey the history of thought, and likewise the history of practice, we find that one idea after another is tried out, its limitations defined, and its core of truth elicited. In application to the instinct for the intellectual adventures demanded by particular epochs, there is much truth in Augustine's rhetorical phrase, *Securus judicat orbis terrarum.* At the very least, men do what they can in the way of systematization, and in the event achieve something. The proper test is not that of finality, but of progress.

But the main objection, dating from the sixteenth century and receiving final expression from Francis Bacon, is the uselessness of philosophic speculation. The position taken by this objection is that we ought to describe detailed matter of fact, and elicit the laws with a generality strictly limited to the systematization of these described details. General interpretation, it is held, has no bearing upon this procedure; and thus any system of general interpretation, be it true or false, remains intrinsically barren. Unfortunately for this objection, there are no brute, self-contained matters of fact, capable of being understood apart from interpretation as an element in a system. Whenever we attempt to express the matter of immediate experience, we find that its understanding leads us beyond itself, to its contemporaries, to its past, to its future, and to the universals in terms of which its definiteness is exhibited. But such universals, by their very character of universality, embody the potentiality of other facts with variant types of definiteness. Thus the understanding of the immediate brute act requires its metaphysical interpretation as an item in a world with

some systematic relation to it. When thought comes upon the scene, it finds the interpretations as matters of practice. Philosophy does not initiate interpretations. Its search for a rationalistic scheme is the search for more adequate criticism, and for more adequate justification, of the interpretations which we perforce employ. Our habitual experience is a complex of failure and success in the enterprise of interpretation. If we desire a record of uninterpreted experience, we must ask a stone to record its autobiography. Every scientific memoir in its record of the 'facts' is shot through and through with interpretation. The methodology of rational interpretation is the product of the fitful vagueness of consciousness. Elements which shine with immediate distinctness, in some circumstances, retire into penumbral shadow in other circumstances, and into black darkness on other occasions. And yet all occasions proclaim themselves as actualities within the flux of a solid world, demanding a unity of interpretation.

Philosophy is the self-correction by consciousness of its own initial excess of subjectivity. Each actual occasion contributes to the circumstances of its origin additional formative elements deepening its own peculiar individuality. Consciousness is only the last and greatest of such elements by which the selective character of the individual obscures the external totality from which it originates and which it embodies. An actual individual, of such higher grade, has truck with the totality of things by reason of its sheer actuality; but it has attained its individual depth of being by a selective emphasis limited to its own purposes. The task of philosophy is to recover the totality obscured by the selection. It replaces in rational experience what has been submerged in the higher sensitive experience and has been sunk yet deeper by the initial operations of consciousness itself. The selectiveness of individual experience is moral so far as it conforms to the balance of importance disclosed in the rational vision; and conversely the conversion of the intellectual insight into an emotional force corrects the sensitive experience in the direction of morality. The correction is in proportion to the rationality of the insight.

Morality of outlook is inseparably conjoined with generality of outlook. The antithesis between the general good and the individual interest can be abolished only when the individual is such that its interest is the general good, thus exemplifying the loss of the minor intensities in order to find them again with finer composition in a wider sweep of interest.

Philosophy frees itself from the taint of ineffectiveness by its close relations with religion and with science, natural and sociological. It attains its chief importance by fusing the two, namely, religion and science, into one rational scheme of thought. Religion should connect the rational generality of philosophy with the emotions and purposes springing out of existence in a particular society, in a particular epoch, and conditioned by particular antecedents. Religion is the translation of general ideas into particular thoughts, particular emotions, and particular purposes; it is directed to the end of stretching individual interest beyond its self-defeating particularity. Philosophy finds religion, and modifies it; and conversely religion is among the data of experience which philosophy must weave into his own scheme. Religion is an ultimate craving to infuse into

the insistent particularity of emotion that non-temporal generality which primarily belongs to conceptual thought alone. In the higher organisms the differences of tempo between the mere emotions and the conceptual experiences produce a life-tedium, unless this supreme fusion has been effected. The two sides of the organism require a reconciliation in which emotional experiences illustrate a conceptual justification, and conceptual experiences find an emotional illustration.

This demand for an intellectual justification of brute experience has also been the motive power in the advance of European science. In this sense scientific interest is only a variant form of religious interest. Any survey of the scientific devotion to 'truth,' as an ideal, will confirm this statement. There is, however, a grave divergence between science and religion in respect to the phases of individual experience with which they are concerned. Religion is centered upon the harmony of rational thought with the sensitive reaction to the percepta from which experience originates. Science is concerned with the harmony of rational thought with the percepta themselves. When science deals with emotions, the emotions in question are percepta and not immediate passions—other people's emotion and not our own; at least our own in recollection, and not in immediacy. Religion deals with the formation of the experiencing subject; whereas science deals with the objects, which are the data forming the primary phase in this experience. The subject originates from, and amid, given conditions; science conciliates thought with this primary matter of fact; and religion conciliates the thought involved in the process with the sensitive reaction involved in that same process. The process is nothing else than the experiencing subject itself. In this explanation it is presumed that an experiencing subject is one occasion of sensitive reaction to an actual world. Science finds religious experiences among its percepta; and religion finds scientific concepts among the conceptual experiences to be fused with particular sensitive reactions.

The conclusion of this discussion is, first, the assertion of the old doctrine that breadth of thought reacting with intensity of sensitive experience stands out as an ultimate claim of existence; secondly, the assertion that empirically the development of self-justifying thoughts has been achieved by the complex process of generalizing from particular topics, of imaginatively schematizing the generalizations, and finally by renewed comparison of the imagined scheme with the direct experience to which it should apply.

There is no justification for checking generalization at any particular stage. Each phase of generalization exhibits its own peculiar simplicities which stand out just at that stage, and at no other stage. There are simplicities connected with the motion of a bar of steel which are obscured if we refuse to abstract from the individual molecules; and there are certain simplicities concerning the behaviours of men which are obscured if we refuse to abstract from the individual pecularities of particular specimens. In the same way, there are certain general truths, about the actual things in the common world of activity, which will be obscured when attention is confined to some particular detailed mode of considering them. These general truths, involved in the meaning of every particular notion respecting the actions of things, are the subject-matter for speculative philosophy.

Philosophy destroys its usefulness when it indulges in brilliant feats of *explaining away*. It is then trespassing with the wrong equipment upon the field of particular sciences. Its ultimate appeal is to the general consciousness of what in practice we experience. Whatever thread of presupposition characterizes social expression throughout the various epochs of rational society must find its place in philosophic theory. Speculative boldness must be balanced by complete humility before logic, and before fact. It is a disease of philosophy when it is neither bold nor humble, but merely a reflection of the temperamental presuppositions of exceptional personalities.

Analogously, we do not trust any recasting of scientific theory depending upon a single performance of an aberrant experiment, unrepeated. The ultimate test is always widespread, recurrent experience; and the more general the rationalistic scheme, the more important is this final appeal.

The useful function of philosophy is to promote the most general systematization of civilized thought. There is a constant reaction between specialism and common sense. It is the part of the special sciences to modify common sense. Philosophy is the welding of imagination and common sense into a restraint upon specialists, and also into an enlargement of their imaginations. By providing the generic notions philosophy should make it easier to conceive the infinite variety of specific instances which rest unrealized in the womb of nature.

55

William James
What Pragmatism Means

Some years ago, being with a camping party in the mountains, I returned from a solitary ramble to find every one engaged in a ferocious metaphysical dispute. The *corpus* of the dispute was a squirrel—a live squirrel supposed to be clinging to one side of a tree-trunk; while over against the tree's opposite side a human being was imagined to stand. This human witness tries to get sight of the squirrel by moving rapidly round the tree, but no matter how fast he goes, the squirrel moves as fast in the opposite direction, and always keeps the tree between himself and the man, so that never a glimpse of him is caught. The resultant metaphysical problem now is this: *Does the man go round the squirrel or not?* He goes round the tree, sure enough, and the squirrel is on the tree; but does he go round the squirrel? In the unlimited leisure of the wilderness, discussion had been worn threadbare. Every one had taken sides, and was obstinate; and the numbers on both sides were even. Each side, when I appeared, therefore appealed to me to make it a majority. Mindful of the scholastic adage that whenever you meet a contradiction you must make a distinction, I immediately sought and found one, as follows: "Which party is right," I said, "depends on what you *practically mean* by 'going round' the squirrel. If you mean passing from the north of him to the east, then to the south, then to the west, and then to the north of him

again, obviously the man does go round him, for he occupies these successive positions. But if on the contrary you mean being first in front of him, then on the right of him, then behind him, then on his left, and finally in front again, it is quite as obvious that the man fails to go round him, for by the compensating movements the squirrel makes, he keeps his belly turned towards the man all the time, and his back turned away. Make the distinction, and there is no occasion for any further dispute. You are both right and both wrong according as you conceive the verb 'to go round' in one practical fashion or the other."

Although one or two of the hotter disputants called my speech a shuffling evasion, saying they wanted no quibbling or scholastic hair-splitting, but meant just plain honest English "round," the majority seemed to think that the distinction had assuaged the dispute.

I tell this trivial anecdote because it is a peculiarly simple example of what I wish now to speak of as *the pragmatic method.* The pragmatic method is primarily a method of settling metaphysical disputes that otherwise might be interminable. Is the world one or many?—fated or free?—material or spiritual?—here are notions either of which may or may not hold good of the world; and disputes over such notions are unending. The pragmatic method in such cases is to try to interpret each notion by tracing its respective practical consequences. What difference would it practically make to any one if this notion rather than that notion were true? If no practical difference whatever can be traced, then the alternatives mean practically the same thing, and all dispute is idle. *Whenever a dispute is serious, we ought to be able to show some practical difference that must follow from one side or the other's being right.*

A glance at the history of the idea will show you still better what pragmatism means. The term is derived from the same Greek word πράγμα, meaning action, from which our words "practice" and "practical" come. It was first introduced into philosophy by Mr. Charles Peirce in 1878. In an article entitled "How to Make Our Ideas Clear,' in the *Popular Science Monthly* for January of that year Mr. Peirce, after pointing out that our beliefs are really rules for action, said that, to develop a thought's meaning, we need only determine what conduct it is fitted to produce: that conduct is for us its sole significance. And the tangible fact at the root of all our thought-distinctions, however subtle, is that there is no one of them so fine as to consist in anything but a possible difference of practice. To attain perfect clearness in our thoughts of an object, then, we need only consider what conceivable effects of a practical kind the object may involve— what sensations we are to expect from it, and what reactions we must prepare. Our conception of *these effects, whether immediate or remote, is then for us the whole of our conception of the object, so far as that conception has positive significance at all.*

This is the principle of Peirce, the principle of pragmatism. It lay entirely unnoticed by any one for twenty years, until I, in an address before Professor Howison's Philosophical Union at the University of California, brought it forward again and made a special application of it to religion.

By that date (1898) the times seemed ripe for its reception. The word "pragmatism" spread, and at present it fairly spots the pages of the philosophic journals. On all hands we find the "pragmatic movement" spoken of, sometimes with respect, sometimes with contumely, seldom with clear understanding. It is evident that the term applies itself conveniently to a number of tendencies that hitherto have lacked a collective name, and that it has "come to stay."

To take in the importance of Peirce's principle, one must get accustomed to applying it to concrete cases. I found a few years ago that Ostwald, the illustrious Leipzig chemist, had been making perfectly distinct use of the *principle of pragmatism* in his lectures on the philosophy of science, though he had not called it by that name.

"All realities influence our practice," he wrote me, "and that influence is their meaning for us. I am accustomed to put questions to my classes in this way: In what respects would the world be different if this alternative or that were true? If I can find nothing that would become different, than the alternative has no sense."

That is, the rival views mean practically the same thing, and meaning, other than practical, there is for us none. Ostwald in a published lecture gives this example of what he means. Chemists have long wrangled over the inner constitution of certain bodies called "tautomerous." Their properties seemed equally consistent with the notion that an instable hydrogen atom oscillates inside of them, or that they are instable mixture of two bodies. Controversy raged, but never was decided. "It would never have begun," says Ostwald, "if the combatants had asked themselves what particular experimental fact could have been made different by one or the other view being correct. For it would then have appeared that no difference of fact could possibly ensue; and the quarrel was as unreal as if, theorizing in primitive times about the raising of dough by yeast, one party should have invoked a 'brownie,' while another insisted on an 'elf' as the true cause of the phenomenon."

It is astonishing to see how many philosophical disputes collapse into insignificance the moment you subject them to this simple test of tracing a concrete consequence. There can *be* no difference anywhere that doesn't *make* a difference elsewhere—no difference in abstract truth that doesn't express itself in a difference in concrete fact and in conduct consequent upon that fact, imposed on somebody, somehow, somewhere, and somewhen. The whole function of philosophy ought to be to find out what definite difference it will make to you and me, at definite instants in life, if this world-formula or that world-formula be the true one.

There is absolutely nothing new in the pragmatic method. Socrates was an adept at it. Aristotle used it methodically. Locke, Berkeley, and Hume made momentous contributions to truth by its means. Shadworth Hodgson keeps insisting that realities are only what they are "known as." But these forerunners of pragmatism used it in fragments: they were preluders only. Not until in our times has it generalized itself, become conscious of a universal mission, pretended to a conquering destiny. I believe in that destiny, and I hope I may end by inspiring you with my belief.

Pragmatism represents a perfectly familiar attitude in philosophy, the empiricist attitude, but it represents it, as it seems to me, both in a more radical and in a less objectionable form than it has ever yet assumed. A pragmatist turns his back resolutely and once for all upon a lot of inveterate habits dear to professional philosophers. He turns away from abstraction and insufficiency, from verbal solutions, from bad *a priori* reasons, from fixed principles, closed systems, and pretended absolutes and origins. He turns towards concreteness and adequacy, towards facts, towards action and towards power. That means the empiricist temper regnant and the rationalist temper sincerely given up. It means the open air and possibilities of nature, as against dogma, artificiality, and the pretence of finality in truth.

At the same time it does not stand for any special results. It is a method only. But the general triumph of that method would mean an enormous change in what I called in my last lecture the "temperament" of philosophy. Teachers of the ultra-rationalistic type would be frozen out, much as the courtier type is frozen out in republics, as the ultramontane type of priest is frozen out in protestant lands. Science and metaphysics would come much nearer together, would in fact work absolutely hand in hand.

Metaphysics has usually followed a very primitive kind of quest. You know how men have always hankered after unlawful magic, and you know what a great part in magic *words* have always played. If you have his name, or the formula of incantation that binds him, you can control the spirit, genie, afrite, or whatever the power may be. Solomon knew the names of all the spirits, and having their names, he held them subject to his will. So the universe has always appeared to the natural mind as a kind of enigma, of which the key must be sought in the shape of some illuminating or power-bringing word or name. That word names the universe's *principle,* and to possess it is after a fashion to possess the universe itself. "God," "Matter," "Reason," "the Absolute," "Energy," are so many solving names. You can rest when you have them. You are at the end of your metaphysical quest.

But if you follow the pragmatic method, you cannot look on any such word as closing your quest. You must bring out of each word its practical cash-value, set it at work within the stream of your experience. It appears less as a solution, then, than as a program for more work, and more particularly as an indication of the ways in which existing realities may be *changed.*

Theories thus become instruments, not answers to enigmas, in which we can rest. We don't lie back upon them, we move forward, and, on occasion, make nature over again by their aid. Pragmatism unstiffens all our theories, limbers them up and sets each one at work. Being nothing essentially new, it harmonizes with many ancient philosophic tendencies. It agrees with nominalism, for instance, in always appealing to particulars; with utilitarianism in emphasizing practical aspects; with positivism in its disdain for verbal solutions; useless questions and metaphysical abstractions.

All these, you see, are *anti-intellectualist* tendencies. Against rationalism as a pretension and a method pragmatism is fully armed and militant. But, at the outset, at least, it stands for no particular results. It has no dogmas, and no doctrines save its method. As the young Italian pragmatist Papini has well said, it lies in the midst of our theories, like a corridor in a hotel. Innumerable chambers open out of it. In one you may find a man

writing an atheistic volume; in the next some one on his knees praying for faith and strength; in a third a chemist investigating a body's properties. In a fourth a system of idealistic metaphysics is being excogitated; in a fifth the impossibility of metaphysics is being shown. But they all own the corridor, and all must pass through it if they want a practicable way of getting into or out of their respective rooms.

No particular results then, so far, but only an attitude of orientation, is what the pragmatic method means. *The attitude of looking away from first things, principles, "categories," supposed necessities; and of looking towards last things, fruits, consequences, facts.*

So much for the pragmatic method! You may say that I have been praising it rather than explaining it to you, but I shall presently explain it abundantly enough by showing how it works on some familiar problems. Meanwhile the word pragmatism has come to be used in a still wider sense, as meaning also a certain *theory of truth.* I mean to give a whole lecture to the statement of that theory, after first paving the way, so I can be very brief now. But brevity is hard to follow, so I ask for your redoubled attention for a quarter of an hour. If much remains obscure, I hope to make it clearer in the later lectures.

One of the most successfully cultivated branches of philosophy in our time is what is called *inductive logic*, the study of the conditions under which our sciences have evolved. Writers on this subject have begun to show a singular unanimity as to what the laws of nature and elements of fact mean, when formulated by mathematicians, physicists and chemists. When the first mathematical, logical, and natural uniformities, the first *laws,* were discovered, men were so carried away by the clearness, beauty and simplification that resulted, that they believed themselves to have deciphered authentically the eternal thoughts of the Almighty. His mind also thundered and reverberated in syllogisms. He also thought in conic sections, squares and roots and ratios, and geometrized like Euclid. He made Kepler's laws for the planets to follow; he made velocity increase proportionally to the time in falling bodies; he made the law of the sines for light to obey when refracted; he established the classes, orders, families and genera of plants and animals, and fixed the distances between them. He thought the archetypes of all things, and devised their variations; and when we rediscover any one of these his wondrous institutions, we seize his mind in its very literal intention.

But as the sciences have developed further, the notion has gained ground that most, perhaps all, of our laws are only approximations. The laws themselves, moreover, have grown so numerous that there is no counting them; and so many rival formulations are proposed in all the branches of science that investigators have become accustomed to the notion that no theory is absolutely a transcript of reality, but that any one of them may from some point of view be useful. Their great use is to summarize old facts and to lead to new ones. They are only a man-made language, a conceptual shorthand, as some one calls them, in which we write our reports of nature; and languages, as is well known, tolerate much choice of expression and many dialects.

Thus human arbitrariness has driven divine necessity from *scientific logic.* If I mention the names of Sigwart, Mach, Ostwald, Pearson, Milhaud, Poincaré, Duhem, Ruyssen, those of you who are students will easily identify the tendency I speak of, and will think of additional names.

Riding now on the front of this wave of scientific logic Messrs. Schiller and Dewey appear with their pragmatistic account of what truth everywhere signifies. Everywhere, these teachers say, *"truth"* in our idea and beliefs means the same thing that it means in science. It means, they say, nothing but this, that ideas (which themselves are but parts of our experience) become true just in so far as they help us to get into satisfactory relation with other parts of our experience, to summarize them and get about among them by conceptual short-cuts instead of following the interminable succession of particular phenomena. Any idea upon which we can ride, so to speak; any idea that will carry us prosperously from any one part of our experience to any other part, linking things satisfactorily, working securely, simplifying, saving labor; is true for just so much, true in so far forth, true *instrumentally.*

56 William James
The Dilemma
of Determinism

What does determinism profess? It professes that those parts of the universe already laid down absolutely appoint and decree what the other parts shall be. The future has no ambiguous possibilities hidden in its womb: the part we call the present is compatible with only one totality. Any other future complement than the one fixed from eternity is impossible. The whole is in each and every part, and welds it with the rest into an absolute unity, an iron block, in which there can be no equivocation or shadow of turning.

With earth's first clay they did the last man knead,
And there of the last harvest sowed the seed.
And the first morning of creation wrote What the last dawn of reckoning shall read.

Indeterminism, on the contrary, says that the parts have a certain amount of loose play on one another, so that the laying down of one of them does not necessarily determine what the others shall be. It admits that possibilities may be in excess of actualities, and that things not yet revealed to our knowledge may really in themselves be ambiguous. Of two alternative futures which we conceive, both may now be really possible; and the one become impossible only at the very moment when the other excludes it by becoming real itself. Indeterminism thus denies the world to be one unbending unit of fact.

It says there is a certain ultimate pluralism in it; and, so saying, it corroborates our ordinary unsophisticated view of things. To that view, actualities seem to float in a wider sea of possibilities from out of which they are chosen; and, *somewhere,* indeterminism says, such possibilities exist, and form a part of truth.

Determinisim, on the contrary, says they exist *nowhere,* and that necessity on the one hand and impossibility on the other are the sole categories of the real. Possibilities that fail to get realized are, for determinism, pure illusions: they never were possibilities at all. There is nothing inchoate, it says, about this universe of ours, all that was or is or shall be actual in it having been from eternity virtually there. The cloud of alternatives our minds escort this mass of actuality withal is a cloud of sheer deceptions, to which "impossibilities" is the only name that rightfully belongs.

The issue, it will be seen, is a perfectly sharp one, which no eulogistic terminology can smear over or wipe out. The truth *must* lie with one side or the other, and its lying with one side makes the other false.

The question relates solely to the existence of possibilities, in the strict sense of the term, as things that may, but need not, be. Both sides admit that a volition, for instance, has occurred. The indeterminists say another volition might have occurred in its place: the determinists swear that nothing could possibly have occurred in its place. Now, can science be called in to tell us which of these two point-blank contradicters of each other is right? Science professes to draw no conclusions but such as are based on matters of fact, things that have actually happened; but how can any amount of assurance that something actually happened give us the least grain of information as to whether another thing might or might not have happened in this place? Only facts can be proved by other facts. With things that are possibilities and not facts, facts have no concern. If we have no other evidence than the evidence of existing facts, the possibility-question must remain a mystery never to be cleared up.

And the truth is that facts practically have hardly anything to do with making us either determinists or indeterminists. Sure enough, we make a flourish of quoting facts this way or that; and if we are determinists, we talk about the infallibility with which we can predict one another's conduct; while if we are indeterminists, we lay great stress on the fact that it is just because we cannot foretell one another's conduct, either in war or statecraft or in any of the great and small intrigues and businesses of men, *that life is so intensely anxious and hazardous a game.* But who does not see the wretched insufficiency of this so-called objective testimony on both sides? What fills up the gaps in our minds is something not objective, not external. What divides us into *possibility* men and *anti-possibility* men is different faiths or postulates—postulates of rationality. To this man the world seems more rational with possibilities in it—to that man more rational with possibilities excluded; and talk as we

will about having to yield to evidence, what makes us monists or pluralists, determinists or indeterminists, is at bottom always some sentiment like this.

57 John Dewey
Changed Conceptions of the Ideal and the Real

It has been noted that human experience is made human through the existence of associations and recollections, which are strained through the mesh of imagination so as to suit the demands of the emotions. A life that is humanly interesting is, short of the results of discipline, a life in which the tedium of vacant leisure is filled with images that excite and satisfy. It is in this sense that poetry preceded prose in human experience, religion antedated science, and ornamental and decorative art while it could not take the place of utility early reached a development out of proportion to the practical arts. In order to give contentment and delight, in order to feed present emotion and give the stream of conscious life intensity and color, the suggestions which spring from past experiences are worked over so as to smooth out their unpleasantness and enhance their enjoyableness. Some psychologists claim that there is what they call a natural tendency to obliviscence of the disagreeable—that men turn from the unpleasant in thought and recollection as they do from the obnoxious in action. Every serious-minded person knows that a large part of the effort required in moral discipline consists in the courage needed to acknowledge the unpleasant consequences of one's past and present acts. We squirm, dodge, evade, disguise, cover up, find excuses and palliations—anything to render the mental scene less uncongenial. In short, the tendency of spontaneous suggestion is to idealize experience, to give it in consciousness qualities which it does not have in actuality. Time and memory are true artists; they remould reality nearer to the heart's desire.

As imagination becomes freer and less controlled by concrete actualities, the idealizing tendency takes further flights unrestrained by the rein of the prosaic world. The things most emphasized in imagination as it reshapes experience are things which are absent in reality. In the degree in which life is placid and easy, imagination is sluggish and bovine. In the degree in which life in uneasy and troubled, fancy is stirred to frame pictures of a contrary state of things. By reading the characteristic features of any man's castles in the air you can make a shrewd guess as to his underlying desires which are frustrated. What is difficulty and disappointment in real life becomes conspicuous achievement and triumph in revery; what is negative in fact will be positive in the image drawn by fancy; what is vexation in conduct will be com-

pensated for in high relief in idealizing imagination.

These considerations apply beyond mere personal psychology. They are decisive for one of the most marked traits of classic philosophy:—its conception of an ultimate supreme Reality which is essentially ideal in nature. Historians have more than once drawn an instructive parallel between the developed Olympian Pantheon of Greek religion and the Ideal Realm of Platonic philosophy. The gods, whatever their origin and original traits, become idealized projections of the selected and matured achievements which the Greeks admired among their mortal selves. The gods were like mortals, but mortals living only the lives which men would wish to live, with power intensified, beauty perfected, and wisdom ripened. When Aristotle criticized the theory of Ideas of his master, Plato, by saying that the ideas were after all only things of sense eternalized, he pointed out in effect the parallelism of philosophy with religion and art to which allusion has just been made. And save for matters of merely technical import, is it not possible to say of Aristotle's Forms just what he said of Plato's Ideas? What are they, these Forms and Essences which so profoundly influenced for centuries the course of science and theology, save the objects of ordinary experience with their blemishes removed, their imperfections eliminated, their lacks rounded out, their suggestions and hints fulfilled? What are they in short but the objects of familiar life divinized because reshaped by the idealizing imagination to meet the demands of desire in just those respects in which actual experience is disappointing?

That Plato, and Aristotle in somewhat different fashion, and Plotinus and Marcus Aurelius and Saint Thomas Aquinas, and Spinoza and Hegel all taught that Ultimate Reality is either perfectly Ideal and Rational in nature, or else has absolute ideality and rationality as its necessary attribute, are facts well known to the student of philosophy. They need no exposition here. But it is worth pointing out that these great systematic philosophies defined perfect Ideality in conceptions that express the opposite of those things which make life unsatisfactory and troublesome. What is the chief source of the complaint of poet and moralist with the goods, the values and satisfactions of experience? Rarely is the complaint that such things do not exist; it is that although existing they are momentary, transient, fleeting. They do not stay; at worst they come only to annoy and tease with their hurried and disappearing taste of what might be; at best they come only to inspire and instruct with a passing hint of truer reality. This commonplace of the poet and moralist as to the impermanence not only of sensuous enjoyment, but of fame and civic achievements was profoundly reflected upon by philosophers, especially by Plato and Aristotle. The results of their thinking have been wrought into the very fabric of western ideas. Time, change, movement are signs that what the Greeks called Non-Being somehow infect true Being. The phraseology is now strange, but many a modern who ridicules the conception of Non-Being repeats the same thought under the name of the Finite or Imperfect.

Wherever there is change, there is instability, and instability is proof of something the matter, of absence, deficiency, incompleteness. These are the ideas common to the connection between change, becoming and perishing, and Non-Being, finitude and imperfection. Hence complete and true Reality must be changeless, unalterable, so full of Being that it always and forever maintains itself in fixed rest and repose. As Bradley, the most dialectically ingenious Absolutist of our own day, expresses the doctrine "Nothing that is perfectly real moves." And while Plato took, comparatively speaking, a pessimistic view of change as mere lapse and Aristotle a complacent view of it as tendency to realization, yet Aristotle doubted no more than Plato that the fully realized reality, the divine and ultimate, is changeless. Though it is called Activity or Energy, the Activity knew no change, the energy did nothing. It was the activity of an army forever marking time and never going anywhere.

From this contrast of the permanent with the transient arise other features which mark off the Ultimate Reality from the imperfect realities of practical life. Where there is change, there is of necessity numerical plurality, multiplicity, and from variety comes opposition, strife. Change is alteration, or "othering" and this means diversity. Diversity means division, and division means two sides and their conflict. The world which is transient *must* be a world of discord, for in lacking stability it lacks the government of unity. Did unity completely rule, these would remain an unchanging totality. What alters has parts and partialities which, not recognizing the rule of unity, assert themselves independently and make life a scene of contention and discord. Ultimate and true Being on the other hand, since it is changeless is Total, All-Comprehensive and One. Since it is One, it knows only harmony, and therefore enjoys complete and eternal Good. It is Perfection.

Degrees of knowledge and truth correspond with degrees of reality point by point. The higher and more complete the Reality the truer and more important the knowledge that refers to it. Since the world of becoming, of origins and perishings, is deficient in true Being, it cannot be known in the best sense. To know it means to neglect its flux and alteration and discover some permanent form which limits the processes that alter in time. The acorn undergoes a series of changes; these are knowable only in reference to the fixed form of the oak which is the same in the entire oak species in spite of the numerical diversity of trees. Moreover, this form limits the flux of growth at both ends, the acorn coming from the oak as well as passing into it. Where such unifying and limiting eternal forms cannot be detected, there is mere aimless variation and fluctuation, and knowledge is out of the question. On the other hand, as objects are approached in which there is no movement at all, knowledge becomes really demonstrative, certain, perfect—truth pure and unalloyed. The heavens can be more truly known than the earth, God the unmoved mover than the heavens.

From this fact follows the superiority of contemplative to practical knowledge, of pure theoretical speculation to experimentation, and to any kind of knowing that depends upon changes in things or that induces change in them. Pure knowing is pure beholding, viewing, noting. It is complete in itself. It looks for nothing beyond itself; it lacks nothing and hence has no aim or purpose. It is most emphatically its own excuse for being. Indeed, pure contemplative knowing is so much the most truly self-enclosed

and self-sufficient thing in the universe that it is the highest and indeed the only attribute that can be ascribed to God, the Highest Being in the scale of Being. Man himself is divine in the rare moments when he attains to purely self-sufficient theoretical insight.

In contrast with such knowing, the so-called knowing of the artisan is base. He has to bring about changes in things, in wood and stone, and this fact is of itself evidence that his material is deficient in being. What condemns his knowledge even more is the fact that it is not disinterestedly for its own sake. It has reference to results to be attained, food, clothing, shelter, etc. It is concerned with things that perish, the body and its needs. It thus has an ulterior aim, and one which itself testifies to imperfection. For want, desire, affection of every sort, indicate lack. Where there is need and desire—as in the case of all practical knowledge and activity—there is incompleteness and insufficiency. While civic or political and moral knowledge rank higher than do the conceptions of the artisan, yet intrinsically considered they are a low and untrue type. Moral and political action is practical; that is, it implies needs and effort to satisfy them. It has an end beyond itself. Moreover, the very fact of association shows lack of self-sufficiency; it shows dependence upon others. Pure knowing is alone solitary, and capable of being carried on in complete, self-sufficing independence.

In short, the measure of the worth of knowledge according to Aristotle, whose views are here summarized, is the degree in which it is purely contemplative. The highest degree is attained in knowing ultimate Ideal Being, pure Mind. This is Ideal, the Form of Forms, because it has no lacks, no needs, and experiences no change or variety. It has no desires because in it all desires are consummated. Since it is perfect Being, it is perfect Mind and perfect Bliss;—the acme of rationality and ideality. One point more and the argument is completed. The kind of knowing that concerns itself with this ultimate reality (which is also ultimate ideality) is philosophy. Philosophy is therefore the last and highest term in pure contemplation. Whatever may be said for any other kind of knowledge, philosophy is self-enclosed. It has nothing to do beyond itself; it has no aim or purpose or function—except to be philosophy—that is, pure, self-sufficing beholding of ultimate reality. There is of course such a thing as philosophic *study* which falls short of this perfection. Where there is learning, there is change and becoming. But the function of study and learning of philosophy is, as Plato put it, to convert the eye of the soul from dwelling contentedly upon the images of things, upon the inferior realities that are born and that decay, and to lead it to the intuition of supernal and eternal Being. Thus the mind of the knower is transformed. It becomes assimilated to what it knows.

Through a variety of channels, especially Neo-Platonism and St. Augustine, these ideas found their way into Christian theology; and great scholastic thinkers taught that the end of man is to know True Being, that knowledge is contemplative, that True Being is pure Immaterial Mind, and to know it is Bliss and Salvation. While this knowledge cannot be achieved in this stage of life nor without supernatural aid, yet so far as it is accomplished it assimilates the human mind to the divine essence and so constitutes salvation. Through this taking over of the conception of knowledge as Contemplative into the dominant religion of Europe, multitudes were affected who were totally innocent of theoretical philosophy. There was bequeathed to generations of thinkers as an unquestioned axiom the idea that knowledge is intrinsically a mere beholding or viewing of reality—the spectator conception of knowledge. So deeply engrained was this idea that it prevailed for centuries after the actual progress of science had demonstrated that knowledge is power to transform the world, and centuries after the practice of effective knowledge had adopted the method of experimentation.

Let us turn abruptly from this conception of the measure of true knowledge and the nature of true philosophy to the existing practice of knowledge. Nowadays if a man, say a physicist or chemist, wants to know something, the last thing he does is merely to contemplate. He does not look in however earnest and prolonged way upon the object expecting that thereby he will detect its fixed and characteristic form. He does not expect any amount of such aloof scrutiny to reveal to him any secrets. He proceeds to *do* something, to bring some energy to bear upon the substance to see how it reacts; he places it under unusual conditions in order to induce some change. While the astronomer cannot change the remote stars, even he no longer merely gazes. If he cannot change the stars themselves, he can at least by lens and prism change their light as it reaches the earth; he can lay traps for discovering changes which would otherwise escape notice. Instead of taking an antagonistic attitude toward change and denying it to the stars because of their divinity and perfection, he is on constant and alert watch to find some change through which he can form an inference as to the formation of stars and systems of stars.

Change in short is no longer looked upon as a fall from grace, as a lapse from reality or a sign of imperfection of Being. Modern science no longer tries to find some fixed form or essence behind each process of change. Rather, the experimental method tries to break down apparent fixities and to induce changes. The form that remains unchanged to sense, the form of seed or tree, is regarded not as the key to knowledge of the thing, but as a wall, an obstruction to be broken down. Consequently the scientific man experiments with this and that agency applied to this and that condition until something begins to happen; until there is, as we say, something doing. He assumes that there is change going on all the time, that there is movement within each thing in seeming repose; and that since the process is veiled from perception the way to know it is to bring the thing into novel circumstances until change becomes evident. In short, the thing which is to be accepted and paid heed to is not what is originally given but that which emerges after the thing has been set under a great variety of circumstances in order to see how it behaves.

Now this marks a much more general change in the human attitude than perhaps appears at first sight. It signifies nothing less than that the world or any part of it as it presents itself at a given time is accepted or acquiesced in only as *material* for change. It is accepted precisely as the carpenter, say, accepts things as he finds them. If he took them as things to be observed and noted for their own sake, he never would be a carpenter. He would observe, describe, record the structures, forms and changes which things exhibit to him, and leave the matter there. If

perchance some of the changes going on should present him with a shelter, so much the better. But what makes the carpenter a *builder* is the fact that he notes things not just as objects in themselves, but with reference to what he wants to do to them and with them; to the end he has in mind. Fitness to effect certain special changes that he wishes to see accomplished is what concerns him in the wood and stones and iron which he observes. His attention is directed to the changes they undergo and the changes they make other things undergo so that he may select that combination of changes which will yield him his desired result. It is only by these processes of active manipulation of things in order to realize his purpose that he discovers what the properties of things are. If he foregoes his own purpose and in the name of a meek and humble subscription to things as they "really are" refuses to bend things as they "are" to his own purpose, he not only never achieves his purpose but he never learns what the things themselves are. They *are* what they can do and what can be done with them,—things that can be found by deliberate trying.

The outcome of this idea of the right way to know is a profound modification in man's attitude toward the natural world. Under differing social conditions, the older or classic conception sometimes bred resignation and submission; sometimes contempt and desire to escape; sometimes, notably in the case of the Greeks, a keen esthetic curiosity which showed itself in acute noting of all the traits of given objects. In fact, the whole conception of knowledge as beholding and noting is fundamentally an idea connected with esthetic enjoyment and appreciation where the environment is beautiful and life is serene, and with esthetic repulsion and depreciation where life is troubled, nature morose and hard. But in the degree in which the active conception of knowledge prevails, and the environment is regarded as something that has to be changed in order to be truly known, men are imbued with courage, with what may almost be termed an aggressive attitude toward nature. The latter becomes plastic, something to be subjected to human uses. The moral disposition toward change is deeply modified. This loses its pathos, it ceases to be haunted with melancholy through suggesting only decay and loss. Change becomes significant of new possibilities and ends to be attained; it become prophetic of a better future. Change is associated with progress rather than with lapse and fall. Since changes are going on anyway, the great thing is to learn enough about them so that we be able to lay hold of them and turn them in the direction of our desires. Conditions and events are neither to be fled from nor passively acquiesced in; they are to be utilized and directed. They are either obstacles to our ends or else means for their accomplishment. In a profound sense knowing ceases to be contemplative and becomes practical.

Unfortunately men, educated men, cultivated men in particular, are still so dominated by the older conception of an aloof and self-sufficing reason and knowledge that they refuse to perceive the import of this doctrine. They think they are sustaining the cause of impartial, thorough-going and disinterested reflection when they maintain the traditional philosophy of intellectualism—that is, of knowing as something self-sufficing and self-enclosed. But in truth, historic intellectualism, the spectator view of knowledge, is a purely compensatory doctrine which men of an intellectual turn have built up to console themselves for the actual and social impotency of the calling of thought to which they are devoted. Forbidden by conditions and held back by lack of courage from making their knowledge a factor in the determination of the course of events, they have sought a refuge of complacency in the notion that knowing is something too sublime to be contaminated by contact with things of change and practice. They have transformed knowing into a morally irresponsible estheticism. The true import of the doctrine of the operative or practical character of knowing, of intelligence, is objective. It means that the structures and objects which science and philosophy set up in contrast to the things and events of concrete daily experience do not constitute a realm apart in which rational contemplation may rest satisfied; it means that they represent the selected obstacles, material means and ideal methods of giving direction to that change which is bound to occur anyway.

This change of human disposition toward the world does not mean that man ceases to have ideals, or ceases to be primarily a creature of the imagination. But it does signify a radical change in the character and function of the ideal realm which man shapes for himself. In the classic philosophy, the ideal world is essentially a haven in which man finds rest from the storms of life; it is an asylum in which he takes refuge from the troubles of existence with the calm assurance that it alone is supremely real. When the belief that knowledge is active and operative takes hold of men, the ideal realm is no longer something aloof and separate; it is rather that collection of imagined possibilities that stimulates men to new efforts and realizations. It still remains true that the troubles which men undergo are the forces that lead them to project pictures of a better state of things. But the picture of the better is shaped so that it may become an instrumentality of action, while in the classic view the Idea belongs ready-made in a noumenal world. Hence, it is only an object of personal aspiration and consolation, while to the modern, an idea is a suggestion of something to be done or of a way of doing.

An illustration will, perhaps, make the difference clear. Distance is an obstacle, a source of trouble. It separates friends and prevents intercourse. It isolates, and makes contact and mutual understanding difficult. This state of affairs provokes discontent and restlessness; it excites the imagination to construct pictures of a state of things where human intercourse is not injuriously affected by space. Now there are two ways out. One way is to pass from a mere dream of some heavenly realm in which distance is abolished and by some magic all friends are in perpetual transparent communication, to pass, I say, from some idle castle-building to philosophic reflection. Space, distance, it will then be argued, is merely phenomenal; or, in a more modern version, subjective. It is not, metaphysically speaking, real. Hence the obstruction and trouble it gives is not after all "real" in the metaphysical sense of reality. Pure minds, pure spirits, do not live in a space world; for them distance is not. Their relationships in the true world are not in any way affected by special considerations. Their intercommunication is direct, fluent, unobstructed.

Does the illustration involve a caricature of ways of philosophizing with which we are all familiar? But if it is not an absurd caricature, does it not suggest that much of what philosophies have taught about the ideal and noumenal or superiorly real world, is after all, only casting a dream into an elaborate dialectic form through the use of a speciously scientific terminology? Practically, the difficulty, the trouble, remains. Practically, however it may be "metaphysically," space is still real:—it acts in a definite objectionable way. Again, man dreams of some better state of things. From troublesome fact he takes refuge in fantasy. But this time, the refuge does not remain a permanent and remote asylum.

The idea becomes a standpoint from which to examine existing occurrences and to see if there is not among them something which gives a hint of how communication at a distance can be effected, something to be utilized as a medium of speech at long range. The suggestion or fancy though still ideal is treated as a possibility capable of realization *in* the concrete natural world, not as a superior reality apart from that world. As such, it becomes a platform from which to scrutinize natural events. Observed from the point of view of this possibility, things disclose properties hitherto undetected. In the light of these ascertainments, the idea of some agency for speech at a distance becomes less vague and floating: it takes on positive form. This action and reaction goes on. The possibility or idea is employed as a method for observing actual existence; and in the light of what is discovered the possibility takes on concrete existence. It becomes less of a mere idea, a fancy, a wished-for possibility, and more of an actual fact. Invention proceeds, and at last we have the telegraph, the telephone, first through wires, and then with no artificial medium. The concrete environment is transformed in the desired direction; it is idealized in fact and not merely in fancy. The ideal is realized through its own use as a tool or method of inspection, experimentation, selection and combination of concrete natural operations.

Let us pause to take stock of results. The division of the world into two kinds of Beings, one superior, accessible only to reason and ideal in nature, the other inferior, material, changeable, empirical, accessible to sense-observation, turns inevitably into the idea that knowledge is contemplative in nature. It assumes a contrast between theory and practice which was all to the disadvantage of the latter. But in the actual course of the development of science, a tremendous change has come about. When the practice of knowledge ceased to be dialectical and became experimental, knowing became preoccupied with changes and the test of knowledge became the ability to bring about certain changes. Knowing, for the experimental sciences, means a certain kind of intelligently conducted doing; it ceases to be contemplative and becomes in a true sense practical. Now this implies that philosophy, unless it is to undergo a complete break with the authorized spirit of science, must also alter its nature. It must assume a practical nature; it must become operative and experimental. And we have pointed out what an enormous change this transformation of philosophy entails in the two conceptions which have played the greatest role in historic philosophizing—the conceptions of the "real" and "ideal" respectively. The former ceases to be something ready-made and final; it becomes that which has to be accepted as the material of change, as the obstructions and the means of certain specific desired changes. The ideal and rational also ceased to be a separate ready-made world incapable in being used as a lever to transform the actual empirical world, a mere asylum from empirical deficiencies. They represent intelligently thought-out possibilities *of* the existent world which may be used as methods for making over and improving it.

Philosophically speaking, this is the great difference involved in the change from knowledge and philosophy as contemplative to operative. The change does not mean the lowering in dignity of philosophy from a lofty plane to one of gross utilitarianism. It signifies that the prime function of philosophy is that of rationalizing the *possibilities* of experience, especially collective human experience. The scope of this change may be realized by considering how far we are from accomplishing it. In spite of inventions which enable men to use the energies of nature for their purposes, we are still far from habitually treating knowledge as the method of active control of nature and of experience. We tend to think of it after the model of a spectator viewing a finished picture rather than after that of the artist producing the painting. Thus there arise all the questions of epistemology with which the technical student of philosophy is so familiar, and which have made modern philosophy in especial so remote from the understanding of the everyday person and from the results and processes of science. For these questions all spring from the assumption of a merely beholding mind on one side and a foreign and remote object to be viewed and noted on the other. They ask how a mind and world, subject and object, so separate and independent can by any possibility come into such relationship to each other as to make true knowledge possible. If knowing were habitually conceived of as active and operative, after the analogy of experiment guided by hypothesis, or of invention guided by the imagination of some possibility, it is not too much to say that the first effect would be to emancipate philosophy from all the epistemological puzzles which now perplex it. For these all arise from a conception of the relation of mind and world, subject and object, in knowing, which assumes that to know is to seize upon what is already in existence.

Modern philosophic thought has been so preoccupied with these puzzles of epistemology and the disputes between realist and idealist, between phenomenalist and absolutist, that many students are at a loss to know what would be left for philosophy if there were removed both the metaphysical task of distinguishing between the noumenal and phenomenal worlds and the epistemological task of telling how a separate subject can know an independent object. But would not the elimination of these traditional problems permit philosophy to devote itself to a more fruitful and more needed task? Would it not encourage philosophy to face the great social and moral defects and troubles from which humanity suffers, to concentrate its attention upon clearing up the causes and exact nature of these evils and upon developing a clear idea of better social possibilities; in short upon projecting an idea or ideal which, instead of expressing the notion of another world or some far-away unrealizable goal, would be used as a method of understanding and rectifying specific social ills?

This is a vague statement. But note in the first place that such a conception of the proper province of philosophy where it is released from vain metaphysics and idle epistemology is in line with the origin of philosophy sketched in the first hour. And in the second place, note how contemporary society, the world over, is in need of more general and fundamental enlightenment and guidance than it now possesses. I have tried to show that a radical change of the conception of knowledge from contemplative to active is the inevitable result of the way in which inquiry and invention are now conducted. But in claiming this, it must also be conceded, or rather asserted, that so far the change has influenced for the most part only the more technical side of human life. The sciences have created new industrial arts. Man's physical command of natural energies has been indefinitely multiplied. There is control of the sources of material wealth and prosperity. What would once have been miracles are now daily performed with steam and coal and electricity and air, and with the human body. But there are few persons optimistic enough to declare that any similar command of the forces which control man's social and moral welfare has been achieved.

Where is the moral progress that corresponds to our economic accomplishments? The latter is the direct fruit of the revolution that has been wrought in physical science. But where is there a corresponding human science and art? Not only has the improvement in the method of knowing remained so far mainly limited to technical and economic matters, but this progress has brought with it serious new moral disturbances. I need only cite the late war, the problem of capital and labor, the relation of economic classes, the fact that while the new science has achieved wonders in medicine and surgery, it has also produced and spread occasions for diseases and weaknesses. These considerations indicate to us how undeveloped are our politics, how crude and primitive our education, how passive and inert our morals. The causes remain which brought philosophy into existence as an attempt to find an intelligent substitute for blind custom and blind impulse as guides to life and conduct. The attempt has not been successfully accomplished. Is there not reason for believing that the release of philosophy from its burden of sterile metaphysics and sterile epistemology instead of depriving philosophy of problems and subject-matter would open a way to questions of the most perplexing and the most significant sort?

Let me specify one problem quite directly suggested by certain points in this lecture. It has been pointed out that the really fruitful application of the contemplative idea was not in science but in the esthetic field. It is difficult to imagine any high development of the fine arts except where there is curious and loving interest in forms and motions of the world quite irrespective of any use to which they may be put. And it is not too much to say that every people that has attained a high esthetic development has been a people in which the contemplative attitude has flourished—as the Greek, the Hindoo, the medieval Christian. On the other hand, the scientific attitude that has actually proved itself in scientific progress is, as has been pointed out, a practical attitude. It takes forms as disguises for hidden processes. Its interest in change is in what it leads to, what can be done with it, to what use it can be put. While it has brought nature under control, there is something hard and aggressive in its

attitude toward nature unfavorable to the esthetic enjoyment of the world. Surely there is not more significant question before the world than this question of the possibility and method of reconciliation of the attitudes of practical science and contemplative esthetic appreciation. Without the former, man will be the sport and victim of natural forces which he cannot use or control. Without the latter, mankind might become a race of economic monsters, restlessly driving hard bargains with nature and with one another, bored with leisure or capable of putting it to use only in ostentatious display and extravagant dissipation.

Like other moral questions, this matter is social and even political. The western peoples advanced earlier on the path of experimental science and its applications in control of nature than the oriental. It is not, I suppose wholly fanciful, to believe that the latter have embodied in their habits of life more of the contemplative, esthetic and speculatively religious temper, and the former more of the scientific, industrial and practical. This difference and others which have grown up around it is one barrier to easy mutual understanding, and one source of misunderstanding. The philosophy which, then, makes a serious effort to comprehend these respective attitudes in their relation and due balance, could hardly fail to promote the capacity of peoples to profit by one another's experience and to co-operate more effectually with one another in the tasks of fruitful culture.

Indeed, it is incredible that the question of the relation of the "real" and the "ideal" should ever have been thought to be a problem belonging distinctively to philosophy. The very fact that this most serious of all human issues has been taken possession of by philosophy is only another proof of the disasters that follow in the wake of regarding knowledge and intellect as something self-sufficient. Never have the "real" and the "ideal" been so clamorous, so self-assertive, as at the present time. And never in the history of the world have they been so far apart. The world war was carried on for purely ideal ends:—for humanity, justice and equal liberty for strong and weak alike. And it was carried on by realistic means of applied science, by high explosives, and bombing airplanes and blockading marvels of mechanism that reduced the world well nigh to ruin, so that the serious-minded are concerned for the perpetuity of those choice values we call civilization. The peace settlement is loudly proclaimed in the name of the ideals that stir man's deepest emotions, but with the most realistic attention to details of economic advantage distributed in proportion to physical power to create future disturbances.

It is not surprising that some men are brought to regard all idealism as a mere smoke-screen behind which the search for material profit may be more effectually carried on, and are converted to the materialistic interpretation of history. "Reality" is then conceived as physical force and as sensations of power, profit and enjoyment; any politics that takes account of other factors, save as elements of clever propaganda and for control of those human beings who have not become realistically enlightened, is based on illusions. But others are equally sure that the real lesson of the war is that humanity took its first great wrong step when it entered upon a cultivation of physical science and an application of the fruits of science to the improvement of the instruments of life—industry and commerce. They will sigh for the return of the day when, while the great mass died as they were born in animal fashion, the few elect devoted themselves not to science and the material decencies and comforts of existence but to "ideal" things, the things of the spirit.

Yet the most obvious conclusion would seem to be the impotency and the harmfulness of any and every ideal that is proclaimed wholesale and in the abstract, that is, as something in itself apart from the detailed concrete existences whose moving possibilities it embodies. The true moral would seem to lie in enforcing the tragedy of that idealism which believes in a spiritual world which exists in and by itself, and the tragic need for the most realistic study of forces and consequences, a study conducted in a more scientifically accurate and complete manner than that of the professed *Realpolitik*. For it is not truly realistic or scientific to take short views, to sacrifice the future to immediate pressure, to ignore facts and forces that are disagreeable and to magnify the enduring quality of whatever falls in with immediate desire. It is false that the evils of the situation arise from absence of ideals; they spring from wrong ideals. And these wrong ideals have in turn their foundation in the absence in social matters of that methodic, systematic, impartial, critical, searching inquiry into "real" and operative conditions which we call science and which has brought man in the technical realm to the command of physical energies.

Philosophy, let it be repeated, cannot "solve" the problem of the relation of the ideal and the real. That is the standing problem of life. But it can at least lighten the burden of humanity in dealing with the problem of emancipating mankind from the errors which philosophy has itself fostered—the existence of conditions which are real apart from their movement into something new and different, and the existence of ideals, spirit and reason independent of the possibilities of the material and physical. For as long as humanity is committed to this radically false bias, it will walk forward with blinded eyes and bound limbs. And philosophy can effect, if it will, something more than this negative task. It can make it easier for mankind to take the right steps in action by making it clear that a sympathetic and integral intelligence brought to bear upon the observation and understanding of concrete social events and forces, can form ideals, that is aims, which shall not be either illusions or mere emotional compensations.

58 Paul Weiss Philosophical Method

Each philosophy, worthy of the name, has caught the scheme of things entire, but because the product of a man, finite and bewildered, it is somewhat out of focus. It cannot, unfortunately, be profitably patched up from within, for since in philosophy, method and result, the structure of the system and the meaning of its parts are inseparable, nothing less than a reexamination of the whole enterprise is necessary in order to

make a correction significant and intelligible. The history of philosophy is a series of finite, unique achievements, each having the form of a novel scheme, begun from a new perspective. The main endeavor of each is to correct the bias of its predecessors, without sacrificing their insights. It is, in fact, vain to hope to write a philosophy; philosophies are always rewritten.

The philosopher is not concerned with discovering more empirical facts than those he already naively knows, but in providing a systematic account of the entire universe. It is not his object to determine whether bodies move at this rate or that, but what movement is and why bodies move at all. He cares not a whit whether the infant cries for pleasure or from pain, but what it is to be a creature that cries and does as babies do; he does not ask what the antecedents and relations between particular things may be, but what it means to be a thing, to have antecedents and be related; he is not concerned with what mortals fear, but how it is that something which is not, nevertheless has power enough to disturb their even tenor. These are questions any man can pose, though few do ask them. No acuteness of observation, no refinement of instrument, no study of the special sciences can accelerate their resolution. They can be resolved only within the embrace of a speculative, coherent system, through the progressive analysis and elaboration of what everybody already knows.

One must begin at the point where one actually begins. This is an identical proposition, and like all identical propositions, taken at their psychological value, is simply a formula for concentrating attention. It means that it is basic and obvious, not recondite and derivative data which are to provide the system with its guide, its touchstone and excuse. A heavy book, a crying child, a shooting star, these alone yield almost stuff enough to build a philosophy. Such objects, and any others which may be equally familiar and obvious to both sage and simpleton, hold every question and answer in solution. But such objects are available for theoretical purposes only so far as they are known, remembered, expected, supposed, etc., and they can be apprehended in these ways only if someone exists to apprehend them. One who inquires into the nature of the real must thus presuppose that there are valid ways of knowing what he unquestionably knows. But, on the other hand, one who seeks to know what knowing is, must presuppose that knowing is a real act of a real being in a real universe. A theory of reality, an ontology, depends for its possibility on the validity of some form of knowledge, while a theory of knowledge, an epistemology, depends for its possibility on the fact that there are realities to be known. A system which begins with one must assume what is validated in the other; but then it must begin afresh with that other, developing, clarifying and correcting it, to achieve a rounded system of two independently developed parts, which at once support and presuppose one another.

A philosophy consisting only of epistemology is myopic, unable to distinguish between the existent and the nonexistent, and incapable of determining whether it characterized the activities of impossible, possible or actual beings in our or in an entirely different world. On the other hand, a philosophy consisting only of ontology is unconscious, unable to know whether what it said was significant or meaningless, necessary or gratuitous. If we begin with the former, we must eventually move to the latter to certify the existence of those realities which had originally been acknowledged with surety though understood but vaguely. And if we begin with the latter, we must eventually move to the former to certify the validity of those principles which had been originally acknowledged without question and uncritically used. A theory of knowledge assumes realities whose nature is made manifest, not there, but in ontology, while the basic assumptions of that ontology are themselves justified only in the theory of knowledge; an ontology begins with criteria which can be evaluated only in an epistemology, whose necessary assumptions require validation from the ontology. As ontology and epistemology necessarily find their justification in one another, a comprehensive philosophic discourse necessarily commits a *petitio principii*, assuming in one branch what it dissects in the other. Ideally, all philosophic procedure is circular. That is its check against dogmatism and sterility. It avoids the capriciousness involved in beginning with empty or arbitrary propositions, precisely because it is so structuralized that the assumptions which it makes ultimately achieve their derivation. The ontology assumed in epistemology, and conversely, is fragmentary, elusive, naive; the results of a true ontology and epistemology are compatible with one another, richer, clearer and also systematically validated. An epistemology following on an adequate ontology and an ontology following on an adequate epistemology yield a system which is not so prone to end in contradiction or confusion, or in those unbridgeable dualisms of unknowable worlds and unactualizable acts of knowing which decree a philosopher's demise. If the initial assumptions of one are incompatible with the conclusions of the other, they must both be rectified until they finally coalesce. We can measure the growth of our understanding of philosophic truth by the amount we progressively shorten the gap which there originally was between the ends of our philosophic circle.

A philosophy must be systematic, developed within the pattern of confining principles. But though the ideals of consistency, precision and clarity are most readily approached in a system modelled on that of mathematics, philosophy cannot avail itself of mathematics as a guide. Mathematical systems, as is well known, start by using certain "undefined" and thus, in some sense, ultimate material, from which everything else is derived by definition and deduction. The mathematician does not claim that any thing in his system is objectively ultimate or that what he does not define has some private virtue denied to the others; nor does he care about explaining the nature of things, but only in developing the consequences of that which he originally assumed. The primitive ideas which the mathematician employs have only a systemic ultimacy—the ultimacy of not being defined in that particular system. In another system, which he could have just as readily adopted, these ultimates could have been derived from a different set, themselves derivatives in the first system. If one uses the notion of a point without defining it, and in terms of this and other undefined notions constructs a definition of a line, in another system of equal validity the procedure could be reversed and the line taken as an ultimate in terms of which the point was defined. No one of a set of such equally well integrated systems is superior in content, importance or truth to any other. The ultimates of mathematics are relative to the system chosen; they are the unanalyzed not the uanalyzable, the unquestioned not the indubitable, systemically simple they may nevertheless actually be complex. The philosopher tempted to imitate the pattern of systems of mathematics must then acknowledge that his supposed ultimates were arbitrarily accepted and were possible derivatives from other supposed ultimates just as justifiably or unjustifiably chosen. Could any philosopher succeed in so mimicking mathematics, he would have succeeded in mathematicizing philosophy out of existence.

59
Paul Weiss
A Vision
of the Whole

This is a book in philosophy. As a philosophic work should, it attempts to articulate a vision of the whole of things. This means that it must run counter to the temper not only of critics of philosophy but of many contemporary philosophers as well. Every one of us, in these last decades, has often heard the complaint that the world of knowledge has grown enormously and that it is now too big for anyone to envisage. Too many of us have too quickly said that it is futile to hope that the meaning of the whole, or even of man's place within it, can be grasped by anyone. A man must be content, it has been supposed, to master limited branches of knowledge, to try to learn exactly what is the case here or there; he should give up the attempt to say something more. No one seemed to have a real fear that such self-restraint might turn him into a partial man. Encyclopedias and staff conferences, surveys and texts, it was felt, could bring him and all the rest together and in harmony. Co-operation, interchange, and communication would produce well-made parts, and interrelate them, to give a clearer, more lasting, a better articulated account of whatever fraction of the totality of things was available for knowledge. As a consequence, many today are somewhat content to be community thinkers, union men, who know how to work together.

It seems safe to say that the intellectual advances made in recent years over a wide range of disciplines are in good part traceable to the fact that we have specialized together. But it is equally safe to say that these achievements depended in part on our refusal to use our rational powers to the full. A world of experts, each concerned with asserting only what he himself really knows, is a world of men who must accept without cavil what the other experts offer to them as data, method, and outcome—or it is a world of separated items, cut off from all else. Such experts practice what none is willing to preach. On the one side they accept nothing

but what they can themselves certify, and on the other they embrace with equal confidence that which they confessedly could not possibly certify.

He who simply accepts whatever others affirm unwarrantedly supposes that those others are right in result, method, and value. He does not really know whether or not their frames are wide enough, their methods sound enough, their values rich enough for the world in which we all live. By putting the actual failure or inadequacy of other disciplines outside the reach of real questioning he denies himself the opportunity of knowing whether or not they are really sound, and whether or not they will ever betray him. To know how reliable other disciplines are, he must know something more than what they report of themselves.

It is fairly safe to say that the successes of our modern ways of thought depend in good part on the chance that the methods and outcomes of our different specialized inquiries happen for the time to fit together. When parts are dealt with in independence of one another, discords almost inevitably arise among them. Even now different disciplines are sometimes found to conflict. The realms of specialized knowledge are not yet integrated. There are methods and results in almost every vigorous science which no one has made cohere with the rest. Nor has anyone ever related the achievements and methods of all the sciences to one another, or brought the natural sciences into harmony with history, law, and anthropology. And what has been discerned by the poets, the mystics, the philosophers is still far from being united with what has been learned elsewhere.

But, it will perhaps be said, this is as it

should be. Every living enterprise is incomplete; its problems are its nerve ends, its growth tips. It would be foolhardy to force the different disciplines into harmony now, to try to get rid of the gaps in and between them at once. The critical powers, it can justly be urged, should not be suspended, nor should they be allowed to destroy the tolerance on which co-operative inquiry depends. We should be patient. The occasional breaks and discords in and between the different disciplines will soon and surely must eventually be overcome. Knowledge is accumulative and grows in cohesiveness as it grows in magnitude. Ignorance, and ignorance alone, is what keeps honest inquiring men apart.

There is force in this reply. We have a right to expect, as we progress in our mastery of the world and of ourselves, that what we know will form a more solid block than it now does. Yet, what might at the end of an inquiry have the status of knowledge in that inquiry may not have had that status when outside it or when it is made part of a different inquiry. There are certainties in some disciplines and only probabilities in others; some prefer local truths while others specialize in cosmic ones. Their different claims must be assigned different weights; account must be taken of their different methods and ranges. What we call knowledge in physics is not exactly what we call knowledge in history or philosophy or perhaps even biology. The items in one discipline are obtained along a different route and must meet criteria and be certified in ways not relevant to the items in other disciplines. It makes no difference whether or not we take one of the disciplines as the model for the others, or whether or not we look outside them all for

some standard in terms of which we can determine what is and what is not knowledge. In either case we are forced to evaluate and perhaps modify or qualify the claims which each, even at the end of its road, takes to be reliable and true. Some, and perhaps even all of a given discipline's certified truths might have to be altered if they are to be brought into accord with the certified truths of other inquiries. Unless we can somehow stand outside all disciplines, unless we can somehow use common principles, categories, values, we cannot hope to adjudicate authoritatively the claims which each discipline makes even within its own framework; we can therefore have no surety that its results will ever form part of a single harmonious body of knowledge.

No one of course knows everything. No one even knows one limited field exhaustively. Yet if we did not somehow grasp the nature of all there is, we would not be able to have specialties, nor could we deal adequately with their different claims and contributions. Only if we know what it is to be a man can we engage in co-ordinate investigations into his nature; only if we know what it is to be a man can we estimate the rival contentions of doctors, biologists, psychologists, anthropologists, and the rest. Only if we know what it is to be, to inquire, to understand, can we recognize that we are all dealing with different phases of the same subject, and can know how to bring together the different results that were obtained along different routes of investigation. Before, while, and after we specialize, we have and must have a grasp of the whole, vague, blurred, and even incoherent though this may be. To ignore that whole is to ignore our roots, to misunderstand our aims, to lose our basic tests. It is to forget that we engaged in limited inquiries in order to understand what is real from many independent and, we hoped, convergent sides. It is to adopt the prejudice that only the limited and piecemeal is significant and intelligible, and that without any guidance each bit will inevitably form one seamless unity with all the rest. It is to be so impatient to get down to work that no time is left to ask what it is that is being sought, and why. If we are to engage in limited enterprises, if we are to know what they diversely seek and express, if we are to understand what contribution they can make to the enterprise of life and learning, we must somehow take account of all there is and can be known. Whether we wish it or not, we must, we do think cosmically. Our choice is only to do it uncritically, precipitately moving to the body of some limited enterprise and vainly trying to remain there always, or critically, by taking some thought of where we start and ought to end, and in a sense always are.

No matter how much this last observation be softened, it can, I fear, never be entirely freed from the smell of paradox and dogmatism, presumption and foolhardiness—and of decayed and discarded systems of the past. There is something repugnant in the temper of the grand philosophers, the system builders, the wholesale thinkers. They sound like gods and yet are only men. Even the best of them contradict themselves and one another, omit much that should have been included, and at crucial points are most unclear and unreliable. Their errors are fabulous. But then so is their vision. They leave us with no alternative but to try for ourselves to understand the real world in a way they could not. And this is possible, for they

taught us through their achievements and by their failures something of what we ought to say and what we ought to avoid. And we also have at our disposal, as they unfortunately did not, such excellent guides and instruments as the history of later thought, modern science, modern poetry, modern music, modern painting, recent analysis, and symbolic logic.

There are today, I think, signs of a renewed interest in fundamental questions on the part of many thinkers. There is a new spirit just beginning to stir, transforming the world of ideas. Occupied primarily in getting a firm grip on reality, it has so far ignored the question of how to judge and adjudicate the various specialized inquiries. These must eventually look to it, and it to them. But first it must come to clearer and more systematic expression. What now seems likely is that a re-examination of fundamentals will force us to entertain a view of ourselves and of the world which is quite different from that entertained in the past.

We must become at once more bold and humble, more catholic and cautious, freer and more disciplined than before. For too long a time prejudice has been allowed to narrow our perspectives; for too long a time impatience has made us receptive to ideals and values not adequate to our full being and the world. We need a new viable systematic philosophy which is alert to the basic questions raised by the various sciences, by metaphysics and theology, by history and the arts, if we are to remain intellectually abreast of the world in which we live.

60

Paul Weiss
The Modes of Being

One had, I became convinced, to distinguish and assume in turn the perspectives of four distinct realities—Actuality, Ideality, Existence, and God. All four, one had to affirm, are final, irreducible modes of being with their own integrity and careers. The universe they together exhaust requires for its understanding a system in which each is recognized to be as basic, as explanatory, and as incomplete as the others.

It is the task of this work to lay bare the nature of these four beings and to grasp something of the way they affect one another. Before engaging in it, it is desirable, I think, to know why it is necessary for any one—not only the author—to consider these four. It may be worth while too to have some preliminary idea of their diverse natures and roles.

Actualities are finite beings in space and time. To complete themselves they strive to realize relevant, essential objectives which in different ways, they specify out of a single common future Good. Since man is the only Actuality who can focus on the Good in its full universal form, only he can seek to realize that Good in himself and in others. He cannot, as an individual, do full justice to that Good. That can be done only through the conjoint effort of all that there is. A man can hope to do all he ought only if he can accept as his own all the work done, on behalf of the Good, by all the rest. We would, with this observation, reach an end to our system were it not that we had presupposed Existence as an energizing field in which Actualities act. This terminates in the Good, and endows the divine with a temporal dignity. We also presupposed God as a unity in which all Actualities and the Good can be together, and in which Existence finds the unitary essence it needs in order to be intelligible. Both Existence and God are of course also presupposed by the Good; these sustain it in different but necessary ways.

And we ought to make a beginning with Good—or rather with the Ideal, which is the Good when this has been freed from an exclusive reference to realizing Actualities. It has a nature of its own, as is evident from the fact that it is striven for. Indeed it has power enough to attract a man and to make him concerned with its fulfillment. The Good is a correlate of Actualities, a possibility which acts to master Actualities by turning them into types, meanings, representatives of itself. From the standpoint of the Good all that ought to be done is done if whatever there be is idealized, turned into an instance of the Good. This action of the Good on Actualities is the reciprocal of action by those Actualities on it. And, like those Actualities, the Good presupposes material to work upon. Just as Actuality presupposes the Good, the Good presupposes Actuality, and both of them presuppose Existence and God as regions in which they can be together.

The Good is incomplete, indeterminate. It needs completeness, and achieves this only so far as it is fractionated into more determinate and limited forms of itself. It demands not specific activities by Actualities but the provision of opportunities so that it can transform those Actualities from what is external to it into what is subordinate. By offering the Actualities attractive objectives, desirable goals, commanding choices, obligating goods, restraining laws, and finally a luring destiny, it turns the Actualities into purposive, preferring, choosing, willing kinds of beings, into citizens of a state, and finally into beings who could fulfill themselves while enabling all other Actualities to be similarly idealized.

From the perspective of the Good men are required to adopt roles, to become public and representative beings. So far as they achieve this status the Good becomes determinate, not by virtue of the introduction of alien material, but by the Good's adoption of what for it are nothing more than diverse, fragmentary, and harmonious parts of itself. Man's task from the standpoint of the Good is the making of this fractionalization easy, complete, and concordant, just as it is the task of the Good, from the standpoint of man, to be receptive of his efforts to make it concrete. The Good ennobles, universalizes Actualities when and as they sustain it, just as Actualities enrich the Good, make it concrete when and as it lures and guides them.

Actualities and the Ideal, even when made one by mastery or fractionization have an integrity of their own, continue to enjoy an independent status. An examination of them separately and in relation to one another enables us to encompass much of what is—but not all. God and Existence are also essential realities, inescapable dimensions of the universe, illuminating what is left dark by the joint use of the perspectives of Actuality and Ideality.

God is that being who, among other things, makes a unity of what otherwise would be a detached set of occurrences. He sees to it that the Ideal is realized, and that Actualities are perfected. This means that men should recognize that they inevitably submit themselves and their acts to God, as the being who alone can make them adequate to the demands of the Ideal. Since men, their acts, and their aspirations are part of a realm of Existence, where alone they can be vital and present, no account of God can be complete which forgets that Existence is his counterweight, the locus of the data he supports and interrelates.

Existence is a restless force at once ingredient in and overflowing the borders of Actualities, connecting each with every other and coming to a focus in the Ideal. Actuality and Ideality are consequently subject to a single cosmic flux. But any study which begins with Existence should be supplemented with accounts where God, the Ideal, and the Actual are recognized to have independent natures and functions. Without them there would be no unified world of values, no focused and uniting futures, and no distinct loci of action.

Actuality, the Ideal, Existence, and God are data for one another. Each has a role to play in relation to the others, and requires the others to assume a role for it. In addition, all merge with and qualify one another. They can have these different functions only because each has an irreducible, final being of its own, outside of which and over against which the others are. Each stands out against the rest as possessing a distinctive career and a characteristic way of dealing with the others. Actualities strive to be completely adjusted to all there is; the Ideal strives to encompass everything; Existence is engaged in a perpetual effort to separate itself off from all else; God strives to make unity present everywhere. Each helps and restrains the others, making it possible for them to attain a greater success than they otherwise could, and preventing them from ever achieving perfect success. No one of them can ever advance beyond the stage where it is but one of a number of beings. Being is diversely and exhaustively exhibited in four interlocked, irreducible modes.

This swift survey through which I have just gone will arouse rather than quiet a number of persistent questions and doubts: Is there a real need to acknowledge as many as four fundamental, irreducible realities? Are just the items here isolated *the* modes of being? Is there not a need to acknowledge five or six or perhaps even a greater number, as basic and as essential as any of these? The work as a whole, and particularly the last chapters offer answers to these questions. But it may help now to remark that no one can avoid acknowledging something Actual, for that is what each one of us is and what each one of us daily confronts. But Actuality can be made intelligible, we will find, only if account is taken of the other three modes as well. Each of these three in turn demands the acknowledgment of Actuality and two other modes. Each mode requires at least three others. We cannot acknowledge any less than four modes without making something in the nature or function of the universe unnecessarily mysterious or unintelligible. But there is no need to acknowledge more than four until and unless there are difficulties which cannot be resolved except by taking this further step. One ought not to multiply entities beyond necessity.

Each mode stands apart from the rest, and is also a component in them. Each offers evidence regarding the nature and reality of the others. But so long as we remain with any one of them, those others will seem to be nothing more than attenuations of it, imagined or fanciful objects, or the termini of hazardous inferences. One must get over to where those others are. Nothing less than an adequate grasp of the other modes in their own terms will enable us to have the data in terms of which an initially accepted mode can be fully understood. There are many ways in which this result can be achieved. Dialectic is a primary way, but there is also sympathy and imagination, direct encounter and a use of abstractions. All will be acknowledged in their appropriate places.

Each mode of being needs the others to enable it to be itself. The universe is an interlocked whole of four modes of being, no one of which can be unless the others also are effective in it, and effective apart from it. The names that have here been assigned to them may occasionally prove misleading, for while the ideas are somewhat new the language is rather old. Some of the functions of the modes have perhaps even been misconstrued, for not all parts of the cosmos come equally well into the focus of one endeavor. In view of the manner in which the view gradually unfolded, and in the light of our western tradition's emphasis on things and men and its readiness to look with suspicion at anything which is not directly known, there may be an undue stress here on Actuality. The greatest obstacle in the way of understanding what is here intended is, more likely than not, the author's and perhaps the reader's tendency to minimize the reality or the function of the Ideal, Existence, or God. Completeness and impartiality require that all four modes be dealt with as equally basic, equally real, equally indispensable.

61 Paul Weiss
Limits of Pargmatism

Peirce's pragmatic principle which affirmed that the meaning of a concept was to be found in the conceived practical effects of that concept ("Consider what effects, that might conceivably have practical bearings, we conceive the object of our conception to have. Then, our conception of these effects is the whole of our conception of the object.") spawned a whole family of doctrines. In essence all of them attempt to give meaning to something by subjecting it to the demands of some alien domain. What that domain does not allow to be distinguished is said to be in fact without distinct meaning, and whatever that domain does distinguish is said in fact to possess a distinct meaning. These doctrines evidently offer a kind of reductionism, asking that items in one domain be evaluated in terms of another. According to James the evaluation is to be framed in terms of particular acts or sensations or beliefs; for Dewey society or democracy provides the measure; for Peirce it is the community of scientific inquirers occupied with observable phenomena.

These doctrines make at least three limitative suppositions: (1) they suppose that some special part of experience offers the final test of the meaning or legitimacy of concepts. Peirce, James, and Dewey differ primarily as to just what part of experience one is to use as a test; (2) they suppose that only concepts are to be tested, overlooking the fact that what practice distinguishes theory (say, logic or mathematics) might justifiably identify, and what practice identifies theory might justifiably distinguish, so that it would be legitimate to give a kind of "pragmatic" reduction for practice, coordinate with that which these men give for theory; and (3) they suppose that the reduction they provide makes the initial distinctions vanish. This supposition, too, is mistaken. The fact that a distinction is not useful in some domain merely points up the difference between that domain and one where it is useful. From the standpoint of a geometry there may be no difference between the line a–b and the line b–a, but for geography there is such a difference. For a religious man much that science, practice, ethics fail to distinguish should be distinguished, and much that they distinguish should not be distinguished.

62 Paul Weiss
Speculative Dialectic

At every moment we presuppose much. We presuppose a body of funded knowledge, for we come into a world which has been partly understood and evaluated by those who educate us. We presuppose good sense, without which we could not live in the world or with our fellows. We presuppose principles by means of which we organize what we encounter, and without which we would have little more than a sad heterogeneity of separate bits of knowledge. And we presuppose an objective world, a world of substantial beings, values, existence, and eternity, which give body to and explain the world we directly encounter.

The historically minded thinker and the conservative philosopher tend to acknowledge only the funded knowledge we all have. They offer a healthy antidote to those who would speculate in a vacuum. But since our funded knowledge is not necessarily reliable, coherent, satisfactory, as the cataclysmic turns in the history of thought make evident, these thinkers evidently have a philosophy which more likely than not cannot outlast the epoch in which they live. A dominant school of English philosophers, on the other hand, tends to devote a major portion of its energies to the isolation of the presupposed common sense from which men often take their theoretic flights. Philosophy, it clearly sees, is no deduction of a universe, no mere play of fancy, but the grasp of what men of good judgment and sound sense know to be the case. But no man is merely a man of good sense; what we uncritically accept is a mixture of the sound

and the foolish, of the superficial and the bed rock. Epistemologists concentrate instead on the principles which justify the acceptance of this or that as true, reliable, or real. But if we attempt, as many students of language, semantics, and logic do, to ignore what is the case apart from our epistemology, we will end with a theory of knowledge which has nothing to do with men in fact, and the world they are supposed to know. Finally, there are ontologically oriented thinkers who concentrate on the nature of being; since they do not ask themselves how they might determine which of their assertions are valid, reliable, unbiased, true, they have no way of knowing whether what they claim is fancy or fact, a mere coherent fiction or a report of what is the case. Nothing less than a critical examination of all these presuppositions, with a consequent speculative systematic interrelating of the results, will protect one from a precipitate dogmatism, and permit of an acknowledgment of the purified accumulated wisdom of the race, of the good sense of the day, of sound criteria for acceptable knowledge, and of the being of ourselves and of what we know.

There are many and even conflicting statements of the nature of dialectic. But we come somewhat close to what all have in mind when we observe that dialectic is the recognition and the provision of that which would complete a given datum. Marx was inclined to think of dialectic as a work of nature; Aristotle was inclined to think of it as the work of the intellect; Plato and Hegel were inclined to think of it as both at once. A philosophic system, being the work of the mind, would tend to support Aristotle's interpretation, but only with the additional proviso that what dialectic brings about answers to the nature of what indeed is the case. Dialectic is a method enabling men to understand what in fact lies outside them. It need not, though, be supposed that the universe is dialectical or that dialectic is merely an agency for obtaining probable results. When we generalize from the material of daily life we get to the modes of being as terminal points; dialectic is our way of moving to those beings as in fact substantial, necessary correlates, completing one another.

63 Kevin Kennedy
Prospects for Systematic Metaphysics

Systematic metaphysics can be described as the attempt to develop an interrelated set of categories which answer, insofar as this is possible, our root question about the nature of reality: What is the meaning of it all? This question defines us as human beings; no other animal is so perplexed. Yet most people are content to leave the question alone or be satisfied with a religious, cultural or mythological answer which they only vaguely comprehend. The question is then evaded until it is forced upon us by tragic circumstances or ennui.

It seems wiser, though, to wrestle with this question at our leisure, thereby preparing ourselves for its unwelcome appearances. Immediately, we see that a multitude of questions are involved: Are some things merely appearances? Do they depend on other kinds of things which are more fundamentally real? What is the nature of knowledge? Is reality essentially one or many? Is the nature of the universe such that it has a purpose? Was it created? Even beginning to understand these questions and the possible answers will require some struggle. We should waste no time and get right to work.

On the other hand, even a brief introduction to the history of Western metaphysics demonstrates that the "science" of metaphysics has taken a consistent battering from the time of Hume on. Questions have been raised about the evidence it works from, the categories it uses, the hidden motives which drive its conclusions and even the universe it proposes to discern. Why would anyone be interested in pursuing this discipline when it has been so widely rejected? In spite of the importance of the questions metaphysics raises, it does not seem to be able to ever answer them definitively. I would like to explain here why I think there are reasons to continue, making use of both the insights and the failures of the past.

One response to the criticisms of metaphysics is to point out that they have not, in fact, been devastating. If the critics misunderstood what they were criticizing, then their criticisms would be ineffective. This, it seems, may have been the case in a number of places. For instance, the British empiricists misinterpret Aristotle's concept of substance as meaning *sub stare* or something unknowable underlying the phenomenal reality. They then conclude that it is a useless idea. However, since this is not what Aristotle meant, the criticism of metaphysical reasoning based on it is beside the point.

On the other hand, a more interesting possibility is that they have in some sense been right! Such critics may have been correct in pointing out the weakness of some metaphysical account. Or they have undermined that particular approach to metaphysical problems. Perhaps they have suggested, even against their own intentions, an alternative metaphysical scheme.

I do not wish to save metaphysics through a detection of misinterpretations. While they are often the basis of a critique, this kind of response is usually the strategy of someone trying to defend a great system of the past. Such scholarship is important, but an emphasis on it alone obscures the fact that systems come to be understood in wooden and unimaginative ways which block the accommodation of new insights. Whether the system "itself" (whatever that means) is refuted by its cramped development is another question. However, reinterpreting or patching up a system implies that the preservation of its key insights can only be accomplished through the retention of the entire system. Rather than this, what may be more important in metaphysical reasoning is producing the best possible system at this time.

To use an analogy, systematic philosophical reflection is like having several junked cars in your driveway. Some of them may still drive, others may have been gutted already. Nearly all of them, though, will still have usable parts in them. What we generally want to do is take the one which is in the best working condition and use the others to supply parts for it. Similarly, in systematic philosophical reflection we find ourselves pillaging systems of the past for insights that can help strengthen our own way of looking at things. We have the same problem here that we have in the automotive situation in that some parts will be incompatible with some other cars. For example, parts from a Japanese car may not be usable in an American car and vice versa. Systematic philosophy has the further problem that in a well developed system the parts come to be organically, not merely mechanically, connected. Therefore, the compatibility between parts cannot be merely an external relation but in some sense must be an internal one also. This is comparable perhaps to needing to file down parts or jerry rigging connections but even to a greater extent. Some thinkers, those who tout the incommensurability of alternative conceptual schemes, would regard this piecing together as impossible. If it were, however, we could never learn anything from the past by retaining its insights in our present view of things. We must be aware of the difficulty, however, and how such piecing together may leave fault lines that endanger the unity of the system.

What have we learned from the refutations of past systems that we could use to make our system "go"? Here are some general ideas that I believe are warranted by a reading of the Western tradition:

1. Monism, and the rationalist disparagement of the physical world, particularly in Parmenides' version, is hopeless. If true it cannot be stated; it takes three words to claim that "Being is One." Nor is the doctrine of any use unless interpreted as having some significance for the daily life it dispar-

ages. On the other hand, Parmenides' poetic ascent to the ultimate reality haunts not only the history of philosophy but also systematic philosophers today who wish to comprehend all there is and root their reflections in what "is and in no way is not." The desire must not drive us to an all-consuming monism.

2. If we want to defend an account of some kind of ultimate or unchanging reality, like Plato's Forms, we must avoid dualism and the absurdity of the infinite regress of the Third Man. As Aristotle pointed out, the distance is too great between what Plato offers as an answer and the world which raises the question.

3. The existence of God can be rationally understood from reflection on the existence, order and goodness of the world. However, this is not a presuppositionless or purely deductive proof. It is a rational explanation of the world as created by a Supreme Being. Someone who does not accept it merely leaves certain questions unanswered. What anyone, believer or not may gain from this is twofold. First, the most fundamental realities can only be understood by a reflection on what we already believe and then later make intelligible. In this way, pragmatists are seen as having something in common with Anselm's *credo ut intelligam*. Second, religion as well as art and science are fundamental ways of understanding the world which philosophy must encompass.

4. We should not assume that we know

either essences, innate ideas or even sense impressions with absolute certainty. In fact, the attempt to found scientific or metaphysical knowledge on absolute certitudes usually leads to disaster. Rather, we ought to understand all our intellectual disciplines as ongoing, culturally embedded, surrounded by presuppositions and fallible.

5. There is no more an absolute limit for metaphysical speculation than there is an indubitable criterion for its success. Hence, metaphysical skepticism can be just as dogmatic, and just as little justified, as speculation.

6. There are good moral reasons for caution in metaphysics as a cultural practice, viz., the development of tolerance, as well as for boldness, viz., inspiration for a noble and courageous life.

7. There is nothing left but for an educated person to articulate as best they can their metaphysical system, or as James says, "our more or less dumb sense of what life honestly and deeply means."

This hopeful interpretation of the prospects of systematic metaphysics takes much from Charles S. Peirce. Not only is his fallibilism worth retaining but also his attempt to articulate a version of what he called "scholastic realism" and a semiotic of an evolving universe. Should we be concerned to have a certain or intuitive knowledge if the universe is evolving, that is, the laws and natures which are the relatively stable aspects of it are themselves changing?

Possibly, yet somehow this part of the inheritance of Western metaphysics, based as it is on a dichotomy between the Changeless and the Changing, the formal and the material, seems to have lost its explanatory power. What if, Peirce wonders, the changing but relatively stable intelligible aspects are like words or signs? That is, they are capable of change, through interpretation and development, yet they are still quintessentially intellectual? Then we could know them whenever we have a hypothesis which more or less corresponds to them. The hypothesis is sign-like and so is the reality. The scientific hypothesis can and does develop and change, as does the reality. However, what happens to certitude in this picture? Certitude seems to be a function of a direct grasp of an unchanging reality through a timeless medium. Thus, in Ancient and Medieval epistemology, *nous* or the agent intellect is joined through a kind of illumination with its object, and both are outside of time and matter. However, on the thesis that knowledge takes place through the interpretation of signs, the passage of time is an essential factor. This passage from one sign to another also allows for the possibility of error at any point. In this view, however, truth is a function of outcome not genesis. It is not some sign's immediate connection with its object that makes it true, but its fruitful interpretation, consequences or predictions. Do not these in turn require immediate evidence so that we can judge their "fruitfulness"? No, only what we for the moment are willing to take for evidence, which need not be immediate or deductive certitude.

Given that in scientific inquiry one formulates a hypothesis and then seeks to confirm or falsify it, this picture would be commensurable with the progress of science. However, is metaphysical enquiry to be modeled on the practice of science? Peirce sounds this way at times and at others he explicitly makes the claim. If that is the case, then there will be many issues about which it would seem that we cannot make warrantable, because testable, claims.

Paul Weiss makes a strong argument against this kind of limitation of speculative inquiry. The chief characteristic of philosophy is not its greater certitude compared to other enquiries but its unwillingness to leave any set of assumptions or presuppositions permanently beyond question. Many forms of inquiry depend for their progress on some key assumptions which it would be pointless to question from the perspective of their research. It is not clear that this is true for philosophy. Even such fundamental notions as the law of non-contradiction can be questioned as to their ultimate status, basis and interpretation. Is it a law of the mind, or of reality or both? Yet, at some point a wise philosopher will make the judgement that nothing of significance is to be gained through the obsessive questioning of some fundamental assumption. That judgement, however, is just that; a conclusion based on a certain amount of reasoning.

If metaphysical inquiry is modeled on the practice of science it has the clear-cut drawback of hobbling it as a cultural tool. If philosophy can say nothing about art, religion, custom, politics, etc., except that they make scientifically unwarranted, undecidable or false claims, then its use is greatly compromised. Perhaps philosophy has no right to this role of cultural critic. After all, on what does it base its claim to this role, surely not its certitude, which

Richard Rorty mocks? No, the claim is based not on certitude but comprehensiveness.

The philosopher may first note that such cultural criticism takes place anyway, often with an inadequate grasp of its own presuppositions. To bring these into play is precisely the role of the philosophical critic. But where does the philosophical critic stand when doing this? On the not so firm ground of a well-rounded view, a view whose credentials are its capacity to answer the questions that are put to it about its presuppositions and assumptions in a way that its competitors fail to do.

Nor does philosophy need to claim that it somehow steps outside of its culture and time. Philosophy, like every other intellectual endeavor, begins from within some human situation which is marked by limited practices and traditions. Philosophy need not attempt, as once was done, to escape from this situation into a presuppositionless one, either through universal doubt or the employment of an artificial language. Rather, as Weiss points out, we must begin where we are. This, as H.G. Gadamer and Alasdair MacIntyre have noted, is inside some tradition where certain things are taken for granted. In fact, the most traditional parts of our intellectual vision are those which it would not even occur to us to doubt. This is not a problem for us intellectually, if we take pragmatism seriously. Pragmatism can be interpreted as bequeathing to us the insight that we need not answer all conceivable doubts in the search for certitude. It is also true that we may go beyond pragmatism by allowing voluntary and theoretical doubts to prompt speculation at our leisure.

A philosophical system usually seizes on a particular problem and develops a solution to that problem. Then, since it intends to be systematic, it develops the consequences of the solution it offers to see if they imply any unacceptable consequences. In this way it works first analytically, isolating and discovering the problem; then creatively, proposing what would serve as an answer to the problem if it were true; then deductively, reasoning to what follows necessarily from the proposed solution.

Most solutions to problems, even intellectual ones, are relatively ad hoc; they neither can nor are meant to be extendable to all other issues. Consequently, such solutions do not achieve the level of a philosophical explanation. In other words, it can only be considered true within very limited boundaries. For example, the working hypothesis of empirical psychology must be that human actions and thought can be explained within a causal nexus. While this provides a paradigm for research, it seems self-contradictory at the level of philosophical anthropology. If ultimately true, then the very assumption of the hypothesis and arguments offered for and against its acceptance by human beings would all be in some sense predetermined. One might answer that this hypothesis about causal systems at the level of complexity of intelligent organic systems does not say they are rigidly determined. Hence, the reductio ad absurdum argument, the appeal to the seeming absurdity of seeing ourselves as, even now, functioning in a predetermined way, is a failure. However, while this objection is possibly quite correct it also seems true that at a certain level the causal explanation becomes less and less *causal*. Rather, what is isolated in the explanation are more like preconditions which allow the organism to "choose" or act in some sense freely—and this is precisely what the science, by definition, cannot discover. How the organism then will act will require explanations that increasingly make reference to its goals or, in our case, conception of the good. Socrates' remark about Anaxagorous in the *Phaedo* is still instructive: reference to "bones and sinews" are an inadequate form of explanation of why Socrates remains sitting in prison. In principle, then, if we speak of the human brain as the cause of our actions, something is being left out.

However, I also wish to state here that the appropriate response to the limitation of scientific hypotheses is not to postulate some entity, faculty, power, etc., known only to philosophers, which magically explains what is inaccessible to the specialized science. The problems with this response are:

1. The history of philosophy (like the history of science) is littered with examples of such explanations which are humiliated by an empirical discovery, e.g., Aristotle's account of the motion of the heavenly bodies. What is interesting in such cases is the defeat as well as the recovery of such doctrines; the properly philosophical character of the doctrine is revealed by it refutation as a scientific hypothesis and once clearly understood in this way it may retain much of its original value. For example, Aristotle's theory fails as a representation of the celestial order but succeeds as a teleological interpretation of the universe.

2. Such explanations often fail to provide independent evidence for their claims. In Molieres' example, they explain the soporific effect of opium by its "dormitive power"; that is, they merely give the phenomenon requiring explanation a name and then consider the name the explanation.

3. Such explanations notoriously block the road of inquiry. They become the "official" answer which serves as a peg where there is made to hang an entire series of moral, political and even theological beliefs. When someone then challenges the purported explanation they are immediately suspected of intentionally or unintentionally attempting to undermine these vital beliefs. The hypothesis of the immateriality of the soul is just such a thesis. While it may be false in some crucial ways (like the soul is not of a entirely different order of being than material things) what hangs on it (free will, knowledge of fundamental truths, immortality) might be true though not at all explained by the theory.

Notice that in what I have said here nothing is charged against properly philosophical explanations. What is being asserted is that philosophers must be careful to distinguish the explanatory value of their explanations from that of the scientific theorist. This is admittedly very difficult for any philosopher and for pre-scientific philosophers could only occur through commentary much later.

If a so-called "properly philosophical" explanation must avoid these pitfalls, what is it that it must do? A philosophical explanation should be one that provides a perspective on the whole of reality and knowledge. Of course, an expression like "the whole" is easier to utter than to define; in fact, it cannot be defined, except abstractly. We could not explain and describe the whole of things without speaking infinitely and this would defeat our purpose which is limited—to see how the whole is but as finite humans. Abstractly, then, we can isolate certain continuities, distinctions and fundamentals. That is, we seek samenesses and differences of such fundamental sorts that we cannot discover any more primary. These then are developed into the conceptual tools of a systematic outlook which enables us to address ourselves to new questions as they come up. Such a system reduces the infinite complexity and plurality of the world to an organic system of fundamental ideas and connectives which enable us to see the world as organic and coherent. If the system is too tight it leaves out too much—there are realities we must by its terms call irrational or inexplicable. If it is too loose it leaves parts disconnected, floating about without any acceptable or understandable connections; an outcome this sort of view often accepts. We can see these polarities if we compare G.W.F. Hegel and William James, interpreting each of them unsympathetically. Hegel forces everything into an arbitrary set of ideas, the march of Absolute Reason through human history, which was later scorned as the "bloodless dance of categories." James lets the universe dissipate into the so-called "pluralistic universe" which has no final unity or necessary wholeness. This reduces philosophy to a kind of rootless commentary on this and that, nothing being ultimate: Rorty celebrates this development as the longed for "end of philosophy".

There are obviously two extremes to be avoided. A metaphysical system, then, can be overbearing and inattentive to what does not fit easily into its chosen scheme of categories. Or, it can be a non-system, opting for "piecemeal" rather than "wholesale" philosophy based on its perhaps self-contradictory assertion that the whole of reality is not a whole.

Exactly how should the system be gauged? How systematic and how unsystematic should it be? Exactly speaking, it ought not be *exactly* gauged, for it is meant to be responsive to all there is. It therefore must be particularly careful that it does not seek to address everything it comes across with one, rigid, technical langauge. A systematic metaphysics will need to use metaphoric language, images, analogy and even poetic insights. If, however, it goes too far in this direction, it runs the risk of not being entirely systematic. Balancing these is necessarily a question of judgment or what Aristotle would call *phronesis.* A judgment that is neither arbitrary nor deductively certain—a judgment such as the experienced person makes about what is appropriate in a given situation. This is similar to the way a judge's decision is not a mathematical or formally deductive result. In philosophy, the power of correct judgement is developed through philosophical education, but never guaranteed. That is why familiarity with the crucial problems in the Western tradition and the systematic responses to them is of use: it inculcates in us, hopefully, the habit of making philosophical judgments.

Besides the necessity of developing a particular kind of philosophical judgment, we also need a metaphysical scheme that is adapted to our rather recent discovery that a number of perspectives are essential to understanding the complexity of the world.

From the development of relativity theory and the uncertainty principle in physics to the social reality of multiculturalism, any number of disciplines have encountered the plurality of equally legitimate perspectives. This is the fundamental problem addressed by Paul Weiss and the germ of his entire philosophy: how can one grasp the whole in a pluralistic universe? This is, in a sense, what has been known as the problem of the One and the Many. Both of these fundamental ideas describe ways the world is and they do so in dynamic, dialectical relation with one another. Overemphasize the One and Parmenidean monism or Hegelian rationalism results. Overemphasize the Many and irreducible pluralism and irrationality result. Plato is still right in seeing that these are in tension with one another, while he may or may not be right in thinking that they themselves are fundamental entities, "the One" and "the Many," separate from the material world.

For Weiss, the whole of reality is a set of interlocked fundamental ways of being, punctuated by radical individuals. The fundamental ways of being, known as modes, finalities or ultimates, are "Ones" holding many individuals together according to some specific manner of being. The individuals or actualities are a "Many". For instance, the fact that everything seems to be capable, at least in principle, of being understood rationally and subject to logical laws is a result of the action of a mode of being known as the Ideal. It constrains individual realities to be part of the same rational order. The individual realities, on the other hand, resist this imposition, making their *complete* comprehension in rational terms impossible. We also experience, particularly through art,

that not just individuals but all of reality seems to escape the bounds of rationality. We see this in the rhythm and vibrancy of music, dance, etc. For Weiss, this is evidence of a fundamental mode of being known as Existence.

Since there are indefinitely many individuals and as many as five modes, the possible interactions resulting in particular derivative ways of being are quite numerous. However, some kinds of interactions are of particular philosophical significance because they make sense of different ways of looking at things, whether in different disciplines like physics and biology or from the perspective of different societies.

With such a system we have a way of understanding the border skirmishes of the various disciplines as well as a perspective on their characteristic claims. More importantly, and distinctively in the thought of Paul Weiss, we have a unified view of a pluralistic universe. That is, we can have a perspective on the whole of things without that perspective being the only true one. Rather, the whole of things is made intelligible as we move through it by means of a number of its fundamental dimensions. While Weiss once estimated the number of these fundamental moves as 256—four modes interacting yields 4 x 4 x 4 x 4 possibilities — the point is that we can save the integrity of a considerable number of approaches to reality while not allowing the universe to dissipate. Unlike Hegel, these many possibilities do not ultimately have to resolve themselves into an Absolute Idea. This approach, which I call "dialectical pluralism," has not been adequately tried before. It promises to shed light on a vastly complicated but unified cosmos and provide a philosophical point of view which can accommodate multiculturalism, alternative conceptual schemes, difference and the Other, without being undone by that accommodation.

Where are we then? A general reflection on the history of Western metaphysics leaves us with the following convictions:

1. Systematic philosophy or metaphysics is not only possible but a desirable pursuit.

2. It makes use of the insights of the past insofar as these can be made to grow together organically into a system and help us now articulate a view of the Whole.

3. The system does not achieve certitude at the beginning, end or in the middle. Rather, it justifies itself through its comprehensive character, i.e., its ability to make more intelligible than other ways of looking at things do, and its capacity to situate a meaningful life.

4. There is nothing necessarily beyond the capacity of systematic philosophy to render intelligible, whether it be Being itself or God. We certainly wish to reach these as the fundamental ground if possible, recognizing as we try the problems of monism, dualism and dogmatism.

5. Systematic philosophy is not to ignore religious, scientific, or artistic truth; nor should the role of philosophy be confused with them.

6. Systematic philosophy seems, according to the light of our contemporary situation, to need to encompass plurality without dissipation. Dialectical pluralism seeks to discern the lines of connection of a set of interactions of a plurality of fundamental ways of being. Such a conceptual scheme promises a greater capacity for appreciating and understanding the vast array of approaches to reality encountered in a multicultural world where a number of seemingly incommensurable paradigms are operating.